THE STOIC TRADITION
FROM ANTIQUITY
TO THE EARLY MIDDLE AGES-I

STUDIES IN THE HISTORY
OF
CHRISTIAN THOUGHT

EDITED BY

HEIKO A. OBERMAN, Tübingen

IN COOPERATION WITH
HENRY CHADWICK, Cambridge
JAROSLAV PELIKAN, New Haven, Conn.
BRIAN TIERNEY, Ithaca, N.Y.
E. DAVID WILLIS, Princeton, N.J.

VOLUME XXXIV

MARCIA L. COLISH

THE STOIC TRADITION
FROM ANTIQUITY
TO THE EARLY MIDDLE AGES-I

LEIDEN
E. J. BRILL
1985

THE STOIC TRADITION
FROM ANTIQUITY
TO THE EARLY MIDDLE AGES

I. *Stoicism in Classical Latin Literature*

BY

MARCIA L. COLISH

LEIDEN
E. J. BRILL
1985

ISBN 90 04 07267 5

To Gérard Verbeke

CONTENTS

PREFACE

This book has been long in the making. In the course of its preparation I have accumulated many debts, which it is my pleasure to acknowledge here. My research was funded primarily by a Younger Scholar Fellowship from the National Endowment for the Humanities in 1968–69, a Research Status appointment from Oberlin College in the same year, and a Fellowship from the Institute for Research in the Humanities at the University of Wisconsin in 1974–75. The liberal financial support provided by these institutions was enriched by the hospitality of the American Academy in Rome, The Institute at Wisconsin, and the Warburg and Classical Institutes at the University of London, which offered congenial and stimulating environments in which to work in 1968–69, 1974–75, and the spring of 1975 respectively.

I would also like to acknowledge my thanks to several publishers for their courtesy in allowing me to quote or to use material on which they hold the copyrights. These include the Folio Society, Ltd., of London, for permission to quote from K. R. Mackenzie's translation of Vergil's *Georgics*, published by the Folio Society for its members in 1969, the *American Journal of Jurisprudence*, for permission to draw upon parts of my article, "The Roman Law of Persons and Roman History: A Case for an Interdisciplinary Approach," published in volume 19 (1974), 112–27, and *Res Publica Litterarum*, for permission to use material that appeared in my article "The Stoic Hypothetical Syllogisms and Their Transmission in the Latin West through the Early Middle Ages," which appeared in volume 2 (1979), 19–26.

Individual colleagues, no less than institutions, have played an important part in my work, for their combination of scholarly guidance, warm encouragement, and stringent correction. The late Roland H. Bainton, William J. Courtenay, Francis C. Oakley, and Jaroslav J. Pelikan gave generously and repeatedly of their professional support and their critical insights as the project took shape and developed. A particular vote of thanks is due to James J. Helm and Charles T. Murphy. It was their learning and patience that, quite literally, made possible the research on which a significant part of this book is based. Fanny J. Le-Moine, Friedrich Solmsen, and Paul C. Plass did yeoman service, reading chapters of the manuscript in an earlier incarnation and then going over the entire manuscript with a fine-tooth comb in its semifinal state. What clarity and precision have resulted owe much to them; although the sins of commission and omission that remain must of course be charged to my own account. The one person to whom this book owes its greatest single debt is unquestionably Gérard Verbeke. It was he who encouraged me to take the plunge initially. His own scholarship in the field, his many kindnesses, and his continuing personal support have been an inspiration to me. It is thus with a lively sense of gratitude and with my deepest respect that I dedicate the present volume to him.

A technical note on orthography and punctuation needs to be made in closing. Largely in order to reduce the cost of setting the type, as well as to dispel the irritation of readers who do not know Greek, I have Romanized the spelling of Greek words where they occur in the text, the footnotes, and the bibliography. Also, for the sake of uniformity, in Latin quotations I have rendered "u" as "v" where it plays that role and I have capitalized the words standing at the beginnings of sentences.

M. L. C.
Oberlin, Ohio

LIST OF ABBREVIATIONS

AGP	*Archiv für Geschichte der Philosophie*
AJP	*American Journal of Philology*
Budé	Collection des Universités de France, publiée sous le patronage de l'Association Guillaume Budé
CB	*Classical Bulletin*
CJ	*Classical Journal*
CP	*Classical Philology*
CQ	*Classical Quarterly*
CW	*Classical World*
HSCP	*Harvard Studies in Classical Philology*
JHI	*Journal of the History of Ideas*
JRS	*Journal of Roman Studies*
LAC	*L'Antiquité classique*
LEC	*Les Études classiques*
Loeb	Loeb Classical Library
REA	*Revue des études anciennes*
REL	*Revue des études latines*
RFC	*Rivista di filologica classica*
RM	*Rheinisches Museum für Philologie*
RSC	*Rivista di studi classici*
RTP	*Revue de théologie et de philosophie*
SDHI	*Studia et documenta historiae et iuris*
TAPA	*Transactions and Proceedings of the American Philological Association*
WS	*Wiener Studien*
ZSS	*Zeitschrift der Savigny-Stiftung für Rechtsgeschichte*, romanistische Abteilung

INTRODUCTION

The decision to write this book arose from the fact that the influence of Stoicism on the Latin mind of antiquity and the early Middle Ages has never been given the attention it deserves. The significance of Greek philosophy in this era and in this linguistic milieu has been approached most typically from the vantage points afforded by the Platonic and Aristotelian traditions. The view from these twin peaks, to be sure, is capable of taking in a great deal of the landscape. Still, the panorama remains incomplete unless the Hellenistic schools of Greek philosophy are situated comprehensibly in relation to the larger intellectual landmarks. Among these schools Stoicism certainly asserts a lively claim to scholarly regard, since it commanded an allegiance from the Latin world of antiquity and the Middle Ages far wider and deeper than that of any of its Hellenistic contemporaries and competitors.

Extended studies of the Stoic tradition in the classical and post-classical era have hitherto tended to focus on the impact of Stoicism on the Greek Christian writers, on the history of individual Stoic themes, and on the Stoic elements in the thought of individual Latin authors. The span of time covered by this book has also received cursory treatment in broad surveys of Stoicism across the ages. A good deal of important and useful information has been brought to light by researches of these kinds and we will have frequent occasion to refer to it. At the same time, there has been no full-length study of the Latin tradition of Stoicism from antiquity to the early Middle Ages that has been sufficiently detailed and sufficiently synthetic. The emphasis in previous studies of this subject, furthermore, has more often been placed on the detection of isolated Stoic ideas in ancient or medieval thinkers and on the effort to infer or to demonstrate their lines of filiation than it has on the situation of those Stoic ideas in the mentality of the authors who used them.

Neither the procedures involved in *Quellenforschung* nor a strictly textual and philological methodology is adequate to this task. To begin with, there is an irrefragable problem that attends the study of the Stoic tradition as it passes from Greece to Rome and from Rome to the Middle Ages. The ancient and middle Stoics who formulated the school's basic doctrines wrote in Greek and their teachings are preserved only in very fragmentary form. The works of the Roman Stoics are far better preserved but they are also far less important from a speculative standpoint. Even so, Seneca is the only one of the Roman Stoics who wrote in Latin. The Latin Stoic tradition is thus, perforce, an indirect tradition. Methods of the sort that might be applied to some other ancient philosophical

school, based on the analysis of textual parallels and the resurrection of
the manuscript tradition from the earliest days of the school, are literally
impossible in dealing with the Stoa. Nor can one limit one's horizons to
the purely philosophical authors or to the doxographers. For they, too,
wrote in Greek and not in Latin. More importantly, they are not the
only or necessarily the most significant sources of Stoicism. The chief
Latin authors who absorbed Stoicism in Rome and who transmitted it
to the Middle Ages were belleslettrists and men who contributed to a
number of technical and pedagogical disciplines. Their point of view is
rarely doxographical and is often lacking in philosophical rigor. They
are just as likely to use Stoic ideas in ways that are not overt and not
acknowledged as they are to attribute their references to Stoicism expressly. A preclusive concern with identifying explicit *testimonia* can lead
to the neglect of these inadvertent debts to Stoicism, which are often vital
signs of an author's attitude toward the Stoa and of the ways that he
could transmit its doctrines to the post-classical era. Moreover, a preclusive concern with finding and analyzing textual parallels can lead to the
dismembering of the texts under analysis, removing them from the contexts in which their authors placed them. Such a procedure obscures
rather than illuminating the way that the Stoic material is functioning
in a particular work and in its author's overall orientation.

The study of selected Stoic themes, while it has the merit of directing
the reader's attention to the continuities and transformations which certain Stoic *topoi* undergo over the centuries, may have a similar tendency
to abstract Stoic ideas from the minds which expressed them and to abstract those minds from the historical personalities of which they formed
a part. In its extreme forms this type of analysis can lead to the sort of
Ideengeschichte which divorces thought from the human beings who produce it, ignoring their lives, their historical circumstances, their professional identities, their intellectual proclivities, their education and associations, the genres in which they wrote, their personal concerns and
convictions, and the ways that these considerations condition their attitude toward the Stoic themes that they choose to treat and the manner
in which they treat them. The human environment out of which the
ideas emerge can be neglected only at the risk of elevating those ideas to
the status of autonomous realities.

It is the desire to avoid the limitations of these approaches that has
suggested the mode of analysis and organization followed in this book.
The material in most of the chapters is presented topically according to
several genres of Latin literature, with the writers who contributed to
each genre or professional discipline treated individually in turn. On the
whole, the genres are presented in order of their declining importance in

the history of the Stoic tradition. The topical organization reflects the fact that certain literary genres and professional treatises tended to attract their own clusters of Stoic themes and to instill their own norms and traditions in the minds of the men who produced them. Yet, not all epic poets or teachers of the liberal arts, for example, adopted the same attitude toward Stoicism. Individual differences of opinion from author to author also count for a great deal. Thus, within each chapter each thinker is treated as an individual in the effort to discern how he personally comes to grips with the Stoicism on which he draws. Each author is provided with a brief biography, in order to anchor him in time, since the topical approach results in frequent shifts in chronology from chapter to chapter, and because his concrete historical situation often sheds light on his treatment of Stoic ideas and other related matters.

There a few exceptions to this rule. Chapter 1 serves as a general introduction to the book by providing a summary of what is presently known about the philosophy of Stoicism itself. This chapter is designed to lay a foundation and to provide a reference point for the chapters which follow. No effort has been made to develop an original interpretation of Stoicism. It has been necessary on occasion to take a stand on points where no scholarly consensus exists, but we have relegated the controversial literature and the historiographical orientation to the notes rather than encumbering the text with them. Here it must be stressed that it is not our intention in Chapter 1 to enter the lists on these controversies or to seek a settlement of the many technical problems connected with them. It is true that the Stoics borrowed many ideas from other philosophical schools. But our concern is neither to locate them unassailably in the history of Greek philosophy nor to determine whether their thought is philosophically tenable, whether they succeeded in refuting their ancient critics, or whether their ideas conform to the standards of twentieth-century philosophical analysis. Rather our principal goal in Chapter 1 is to summarize the ideas that are typically and distinctively Stoic, whatever their merits or derivation, so that their incidence and use later on can be appreciated.

In this same connection, attention has been devoted in Chapter 1 not only to the recognizable constants in Stoic thought but also to the changes it underwent up through the age of the Roman Stoics. This historical conspectus shows both organic developments and shifts in emphasis as well as adaptations on the part of individual Stoics that led them to diverge from the school's basic teachings. Such modifications are most noticeable among the Roman Stoics, none of whom was a professional philosopher or the head of the Stoa as a formal school and all of whom drew on Stoicism very selectively, giving the aspects of it that they used their own personal stamp rather than trying to present a balanced survey of Stoic doctrine. This fact has raised the question of which authors to include in Chapter 1. At some points it is difficult to discriminate between a Roman Stoic who wrote in Latin and a Latin author who was influenced by Stoicism. In particular, how should Seneca and Cicero be treated, from this perspective? We have decided to include Seneca in the introductory chapter and to devote a separate chapter to Cicero. This decision is not a judgment on the comparative importance of these two authors in the development of our theme. Rather, the choice was made on the basis of how each of them viewed himself and how each of them was understood in his own time. Seneca decidedly saw himself, and was seen by antiquity, as an exponent of Stoicism. On the other hand, the same simply cannot be said of Cicero.

Cicero is another exception to the overall approach taken to the presentation of the material in this book, in that an entire chapter, Chapter 2, is devoted to him. Cicero is the only figure discussed so extensively. He receives more consideration than any other author discussed in this study because of the magnitude and complexity of his position as a critic, exponent, and transmitter of Stoicism. There is a profusion of Ciceronian works that require analysis. They are grouped topically in Chapter 2 because the divisions of philosophy into which they fall affect decisively Cicero's point of view toward Stoicism within them. Chapter 6, finally, departs from the rule in that no biographical information is supplied for any of the jurists whose ideas are discussed there. Lack of biographical data and the peculiarities attaching to the form in which the jurists' works are preserved in Justinian's redaction account for this omission. On the other hand, the jurists as a whole manifest the most distinct corporate ethos and guild mentality of any of the professional groups included in this study. It seemed plausible, therefore, to substitute a brief general history of the development of Roman jurisprudence as a discipline for the individual biography in their case.

This book has a double objective. It cuts across the boundaries of philosophy, literature, and law in order to assess the Stoicizing inclinations of many Roman authors in a wide range of fields whose position as Stoicizers has sometimes been overestimated or underestimated. To a large extent this situation stems from the fact that the majority of these authors are belleslettrists who have been studied primarily by classical philologists. Tastes and literary theories within this discipline have shifted over time. In some periods the modern commentators have been preoccupied with the influence of Greek philosophy on Latin literature and have sought evidences of Stoicism so zealously that they have exaggerated the Stoic content of certain literary works. Some philologists have been inadequately informed about Stoicism itself, which has led them to make imprecise or unsubstantiated inferences about its presence in the authors. The philologists, also, have been inclined to neglect literary works which may be excellent examples of Stoicism in Latin literature but which are aesthetically uninteresting. On their part, historians of philosophy who have addressed themselves to the Stoic tradition have been inclined to ignore works of an essentially literary, pedagogical, or jurisprudential nature, showing little sensitivity to the fact that such works may have a philosophical content that merits serious attention. Scholars in both of these fields have been far too casual in dealing with the jurisprudential materials and have thereby perpetuated misapprehensions concerning the place of Stoicism in Roman law long after such views have been discarded by the specialists in the history of Roman jurisprudence. It is hoped that the positive contributions of these several disciplines can be united harmoniously within the embrace of intellectual history and that the influence of Stoicism in Roman thought can be placed on a more accurate footing, whether this involves the inflation or deflation of the Stoic reputation of a number of authors and groups.

The second objective of this book is to orient the classical Latin writers to their medieval posterity. In appropriating Stoicism in their own works, they also became the channels of its transmission to the Latin west in the post-classical era. For this reason, attention is paid to the posthumous reputation of the authors and to their later accessibility. Both the range and type of their literary popularity and the history of their manuscript traditions in antiquity and the early Middle Ages will therefore be discussed. This book, it should also be noted, is the first volume of a projected two-volume study. The second volume will trace the Stoic tradition from antiquity to the early Middle Ages in the Christian Latin authors from the second to the sixth century. Many of these Christian writers depended heavily on the classical authors treated in this book both as sources of information and as literary models, absorbing their attitudes and reflecting them naturally as a consequence of their own education in the liberal arts. Although it can be read in its own terms as a free-standing piece of work, the present book thus also points ahead to the next stage of the indirect transmission of Stoicism to the medieval west through the agency of the Latin Christian authors of the apologetic and patristic age. From the perspective of the medieval future, then, no less than from the perspective of Roman culture in relation to its Greek past, the authors studied in this book need to be understood as the portals through which the philosophy of Stoicism entered the Latin-speaking world.

CHAPTER ONE

STOICISM IN ANTIQUITY

I. Historical Introduction

The history of Stoicism in antiquity can be traced from 301 B.C., when the school opened in Athens, until A.D. 263, when the last reference to Stoicism as an organized school occurs in Porphyry's biography of Plotinus. The school was called "Stoic" because its founder, Zeno of Cittium, taught at a stoa or covered colonnade in the agora of Athens. Stoicism was brought to Rome in the second century B.C. After that time, although the Stoic philosophy was perpetuated by professed adherents and teachers, it often becomes impossible to detect the head of the school, or even if the school had an acknowledged head. The dissemination of Stoic ideas by tutors or by informal contact becomes much more common at that point; and, indeed, Stoicism attained widespread influence among educated Romans from the first century B.C. onward. The last major representative of Stoicism, Marcus Aurelius, died in A.D. 180. Although the school as such is known to have survived the next century, it numbered no important adherents after Marcus Aurelius. After the third century evidence of organized instruction ceases, although the philosophy of Stoicism continued to be taught informally.

Stoicism may be divided into three historical periods: the ancient Stoa, the middle Stoa, and the Roman Stoa. Most of the proponents of Stoicism in these three periods maintained the basic teachings of the school, but they show differing emphases and sometimes disagreed with each other. A great many efforts have been made to explain the emergence of Stoicism as a function of the historical circumstances of the fourth century B.C., particularly the collapse of the Greek *polis* and the rise of the Macedonian empire. Such efforts have often reflected the tendency to regard post-Aristotelian philosophy as a symptom of cultural decline. This interpretation has been reversed decisively in recent scholarship, in line with a more positive re-evaluation of the Hellenistic era.[1] The earliest

---

[1] Some authors, in attempting to explain the emergence of Stoicism, have seen it as an instance of "Semitism" or "orientalism" impinging on Greek culture in its decline. See Émile Bréhier, *The Hellenistic and Roman Age (The History of Philosophy, 2)*, trans. Wade Baskin (Chicago, 1965), pp. 36, 37; R. D. Hicks, *Stoic and Epicurean* (New York, 1910), p. 21; Max Pohlenz, *Die Stoa: Geschichte einer geistigen Bewegung*, 2nd ed., 2 vols. (Göttingen, 1955-59), *1*, 22, 31, 66, 107-108; "Stoa und Semitismus," *Neue Jahrbücher für Wissenschaft*

Stoic, Zeno of Cittium, lived in an age when, in addition to the Platonic and Aristotelian schools, whose current exponents do not seem to have shared the genius of their founders, there flourished a number of newer philosophical schools such as the Cynic, the Epicurean, and the Skeptic. Contemporary philosophy also showed a considerable interest in reviving the teachings of the pre-Socratics. Stoicism can be regarded as a reaction against or as a response to all of these movements. As is frequently true in such cases, it borrowed a fair amount from them, even those which it criticized.

---

und Jugendbildung, *2* (1926), 257–69; Georges Rodier, *Études de philosophie grecque* (Paris, 1926), p. 220. Others see it as an ethics of individualism and an escapist cosmopolitanism in reaction to the collapse of the *polis*; see, for example, W. W. Capes, *Stoicism* (London, 1888), p. 27; Gilbert Murray, *Stoic, Christian, and Humanist* (London, 1940), pp. 92–94.

It is now much more typical for scholars to reject these views and to see Stoicism as fully within the Greek tradition, addressing itself to issues already raised in Greek philosophy before the Hellenistic age. See, for example, E. Vernon Arnold, *Roman Stoicism: Being Lectures on the History of the Stoic Philosophy with Special Reference to Its Development within the Roman Empire* (New York, 1958 [repr. of 1911 ed.]), pp. 29–77; Donald R. Dudley, *A History of Cynicism from Diogenes to the 6th Century A.D.* (London, 1937), pp. 97–99, 100–03, 118–19, 187–98, 199; Ludwig Edelstein, *The Meaning of Stoicism*, Martin Classical Lectures, 21 (Cambridge, Mass., 1966), pp. 22–23; A. M.-J. Festugière, *Liberté et civilisation chez les grecs* (Paris, 1947), pp. 51–54, 58–65; *La révélation d'Hermès Trismégiste*, 2ᵐᵉ éd. (Paris, 1949), *2*, xii–xiv, 266 n. 1; Josiah B. Gould, *The Philosophy of Chrysippus* (Albany, 1970), pp. 18–27, who adds that attention should be paid to contemporary medical writers, pp. 39–40, a point developed in detail by Friedrich Solmsen, "The Vital Heat, the Inborn Pneuma, and the Aether," *Journal of Hellenic Studies*, 77 (1957), 119–23 and Gérard Verbeke, *L'Évolution de la doctrine du pneuma du Stoïcisme à S. Augustin*, Bibliothèque de l'Institut supérieur de philosophie de l'Université de Louvain (Paris, 1945), pp. 6–7, 11–15, 175–219; Charles Huit, "Les origines grecques du stoïcisme," *Séances et travaux de l'Académie des sciences morales et politiques*, n.s. *151*:1 (1899), 462–504; A. A. Long, *Hellenistic Philosophy: Stoics, Epicureans, Sceptics* (London, 1974), pp. 1–4, 10–13; J. M. Rist, *Stoic Philosophy* (Cambridge, 1969), passim, and for the Cynics, pp. 63–73, 78–79; F. H. Sandbach, *The Stoics* (London, 1975), pp. 23–25.

The most important general studies of Stoicism are Arnold, *Roman Stoicism;* Paul Barth, *Die Stoa* (Stuttgart, 1903), and 6th ed. (Stuttgart, 1946), which is not invariably superior to the earlier ed.; Bréhier, *Hellenistic and Roman Age*, ch. 2–5; Edelstein, *Meaning of Stoicism*; Long, *Hellenistic Philosophy*, pp. 107–235; Pohlenz, *Die Stoa*; Rist, *Stoic Philosophy*; Sandbach, *The Stoics*; Eduard Zeller, *The Stoics, Epicureans and Sceptics*, trans. Oswald J. Reichel, rev. ed. (New York, 1962), pp. 19–403; and the brief but excellent Gérard Verbeke, "Le Stoïcisme, une philosophie sans frontières," *Aufstieg und Niedergang der römischen Welt: Geschichte und Kultur Roms im Spiegel der neueren Forschung*, ed. Hildegard Temporini (Berlin, 1973), *1*, part 4, 3–42.

Of lesser importance but also useful are Marcel Bazin, "La significance du Stoïcisme," *Académie royale de Belgique, Bulletin de la classe des lettres et des sciences morales et politiques*, 5ᵉ sér., *35* (1949), 94–105; Edwyn Bevan, *Stoics and Sceptics* (New York, 1959 [repr. of 1913 ed.]); André Bridoux, *Le Stoïcisme et son influence* (Paris, 1966), weak on influence; Johnny Christensen, *An Essay on the Unity of Stoic Philosophy* (Copenhagen, 1962), who underrates the differences among Stoics in the interests of his thesis; P. Merlan, "Greek Philosophy from Plato to Plotinus," *The Cambridge History of Later Greek and Early Medieval Philosophy*, ed. A. H. Armstrong (Cambridge, 1967), pp. 14–132; Michel Spanneut, *Permanence du Stoïcisme de Zénon à Malraux* (Gembloux, 1973), pp. 20–100.

The founder of Stoicism, Zeno of Cittium (333/32-262 B.C.),[2] arrived in Athens unexpectedly, as the result of a shipwreck while on a business trip in 312/11. He began his philosophical studies under the Cynic Crates of Thebes, and then moved on to study at other schools. Zeno strenuously opposed the dualism between matter and spirit as he perceived it in both Platonism and Aristotelianism. Over against this split he proposed a philosophy in which matter and spirit are identical. He also opposed the hedonistic ethical criterion of the Epicureans as well as the atomic physics which they had revived, because of the scope it gave to chance and accident in the world of nature. Against the Epicureans he propounded a moral system based on the criterion of reason, not pleasure. But, like the Epicureans, he himself revived a pre-Socratic physics, going back to the cyclical cosmology of Heraclitus. Zeno rejected utterly the Skeptic claim that man cannot possess certain knowledge. He argued instead that the senses and the reason do make certain knowledge possible. He agreed with Plato and Aristotle that virtue is a correlative of knowledge and he supported the Cynic view that the goods prized by the unenlightened are *adiaphora*, matters of indifference. However, he challenged the exclusively personal ethics of the Cynics and Epicureans alike by insisting on the social dimensions of the duties of the sage, while at the same time challenging Plato and Aristotle by rooting his social ethics not in one particular *polis* but in a *cosmopolis* transcending all local institutions. Zeno achieved a great measure of fame during his own lifetime. The Athenians deposited the keys to the city walls with him and honored him with a golden crown and a bronze statue, later setting up a tomb for him in the Ceramicus at public expense. His native city of Cittium also erected a statue in his honor. Zeno was invited by King Antigonus Gonatas to come to his court and advise him, a commission which the philosopher declined, remaining in Athens to teach until his death.

The teachings of the other two principal leaders of the ancient Stoa, Cleanthes of Assos (342-232 B.C.) and Chrysippus of Soli (277-ca. 204

---

[2] In addition to the works cited in note 1, see K. von Fritz, "Zenon von Kition," *Paulys Realencyclopädie der classischen Altertumswissenschaft,* 2nd ed. (München, 1972), *19*, cols. 83-121; Andreas Graeser, *Zenon von Kition: Positionen und Probleme* (Berlin, 1975); H. A. K. Hunt, *A Physical Interpretation of the Universe: The Doctrine of Zeno the Stoic* (Melbourne, 1976); Amand Jagu, *Zénon de Cittium: Son Rôle dans l'établissement de la morale stoïcienne* (Paris, 1946); and Robert Philippson, "Das 'Erste Naturgemässe'," *Philologus, 87* (1932), 445-66 on Zeno's ethical doctrine and its sources. Other good expositions of Zeno's philosophy are U. Döring, "Zeno, der Gründer der Stoa," *Preussische Jahrbücher, 107* (1902), 213-42 and Max Pohlenz, "Zenon und Chrysippe," *Nachrichten der Gesellschaft der Wissenschaft zu Göttingen,* philologisch-historische Klasse, Fachgruppe 1, Altertumswissenschaft, n.F. 2:9 (1938), 173-210. An interesting study of Zeno's use of figures of speech to illustrate his philosophical doctrines is Leonhard Stroux, *Vergleich und Metapher in der Lehre des Zenon von Kition* (Berlin, 1965).

B.C.), at once begin to show the shifts in emphasis which started to occur in the philosophy of Stoicism after Zeno, as a consequence of the intellectual environment and the personal inclinations of its exponents. Cleanthes,[3] who began his life as a professional athlete and who earned the fees for his philosophical instruction by manual labor as a water-carrier, arrived in Athens in around 280 B.C. He took over the leadership of the Stoic school upon Zeno's death in 262 B.C. The most characteristic feature of Cleanthes' interpretation of Stoicism is the theological cast which he gave to it. Cleanthes perceived and addressed himself to the world system elaborated by his predecessor with profound religious feeling.

The third, and after Zeno, the greatest figure in the ancient Stoa was Chrysippus,[4] who succeeded Cleanthes as the head of the school in 232 B.C. Chrysippus was extremely prolific, writing voluminously on all aspects of the Stoic philosophy. His chief objective was to refine, elaborate, and defend Stoicism in the face of attacks on the part of rival schools. The Skeptics seem to have been the most energetic opponents of the Stoics at this time, criticizing particularly their theory of knowledge and the paradoxes in which they were fond of expressing many of their favorite precepts. In responding to these criticisms, Chrysippus contributed heavily to the development of Stoic logic and epistemology.

The middle Stoa, whose two chief exponents are Panaetius of Rhodes (185/80-110/00 B.C.) and Posidonius of Apamea (140/30-59/40 B.C.), shows a considerable development in the doctrines of the school. Both Panaetius and Posidonius were familiar with a wide range of current thought, scientific as well as philosophical, and did not hesitate to draw upon non-Stoic sources in elaboration of their ideas. Panaetius[5] was the first to introduce Stoicism to Rome. While studying in Greece with the then leaders of the school, he met Scipio Africanus, who was himself a student in Athens. After completing his education, Panaetius went to Rome in about 146 B.C., where he became a leading member of the circle of important thinkers, writers, and statesmen which the Scipios assembled

---

[3] The only modern general study of Cleanthes is Gérard Verbeke, *Kleanthes van Assos*, Verhandelingen van de Koninklijke Vlaamse Academie voor Wetenschappen, Letteren en Schone Kunsten van België, Klasse der Letteren, *11*:9 (Brussel, 1949).

[4] The best general studies of Chrysippus are Émile Bréhier, *Chrysippe et l'ancien Stoïcisme*, nouv. éd. (Paris, 1951) and Gould, *Philos. of Chrysippus*.

[5] Important studies are Rist, *Stoic Philos.*, pp. 173-98; Basile N. Tatakis, *Panétius de Rhodes, le fondateur du moyen stoïcisme: Sa vie et son oeuvre* (Paris, 1931); and most important, Modestus Van Straaten, *Panétius: Sa vie, ses écrits et sa doctrine avec une édition des fragments* (Amsterdam, 1946), which has served as the basis for the most recent work. Also useful is Louis Meylan, "Panétius et la pénétration du stoïcisme à Rome au dernier siècle de la République," *RTP*, n.s. *17* (1929), 172-201.

around themselves. Panaetius remained in Rome for fifteen years, during which time his connections with the Scipionic circle enabled him to disseminate Stoicism to a prominent and influential group of Romans of the late Republican era.[6] In 129 B.C. Panaetius returned to Athens to head the Stoic school, a position which he retained until his death. Panaetius rejected some of the cosmological and psychological doctrines of the ancient Stoa but his main concern, whether as a result of his own inclinations or as a response to the Roman environment to which he made his addresses, was ethics. He is responsible for significant refinements in the philosophy of Stoicism in this area. Panaetius made the ideal of virtue less rigid and more accessible by admitting a carefully thought out range of proximate goods and by elaborating the principles of ethical casuistry to permit the application of general moral principles to particular cases, persons, and circumstances.

Posidonius,[7] the second great leader of the middle Stoa, is one of the

---

[6] The most detailed study of the introduction of Stoicism to Rome is Ruth Martin Brown, *A Study of the Scipionic Circle*, Iowa Studies in Classical Philology, *1* (Scottsdale, Pa., 1934), pp. 3-84. Pierre Boyancé, "Le Stoïcisme à Rome," *Actes du VIIe congrès de l'Association Guillaume Budé*, Aix-en-Provence, 1-6 avril 1963 (Paris, 1964), pp. 218-55 gives an excellent summary of recent scholarship on the subject. Also useful are Karlhans Abel, "Die kulturelle Mission des Panaitios," *Antike und Abendland*, *17*:2 (1971), 119-43; R. Chevallier, "Le milieu stoïcienne à Rome au 1er siècle après Jésus-Christ ou l'âge héroïque du stoïcisme romain," *Bulletin de l'Association Guillaume Budé*, suppl. *Lettres d'humanité*, *19* (1960), 543-62; M. L. Clarke, *The Roman Mind: Studies in the History of Thought from Cicero to Marcus Aurelius* (Cambridge, Mass., 1956), pp. 32-151; Samuel Dill, *Roman Society from Nero to Marcus Aurelius* (New York, 1956), pp. 289-440; Ilsetraut Hadot, "Tradition stoïcienne et idées politiques au temps des Gracques," *REL*, *48* (1970), 133-79; Clarence W. Mendell, *Our Seneca* (New Haven, 1941), pp. 52-53. A. E. Astin, *Scipio Aemilianus* (Oxford, 1967), pp. 294-306 warns that one should not assume that all contemporary philhellenes and literati belonged to the Scipionic circle or that all of Scipio's political allies took part in it or that Panaetius served as Scipio's *éminence grise*, but confirms the importance of the circle for disseminating Panaetius' influence. However, J. E. G. Zetzel, "Cicero and the Scipionic Circle," *HSCP, 76* (1972), 173-79 thinks that the circle is largely a figment of Cicero's literary imagination.

[7] Scholarly perspectives on Posidonius have shifted significantly in recent decades, moving away from the four dominant approaches characteristic of the late nineteenth and early twentieth centuries—*Quellenforschung*, Posidonius as an eclectic whose philosophy has no discernible connective tissue, Posidonius as the founder of Neoplatonism, and the hyper-imaginative reconstruction of Posidonius based on an intuitive feeling for the "inner form" of his philosophy but bearing only a tenuous connection with the sources. A critique of the faulty methodology involved in the latter approach was first made by J. F. Dobson, "The Posidonius Myth," *CQ, 12* (1918), 179-95. The most important recent study of Posidonius is Marie Laffranque, *Poseidonius d'Apamée: Essai de mise au point* (Paris, 1964), who gives a good survey of the previous literature in ch. 1. Other good bibliographical guides are Laffranque, "Poseidonius d'Apamée, philosophe héllenistique," *Actes du VIIe congrès de l'Assoc. Guillaume Budé*, pp. 296-98; Giancarlo Mazzoli, "Genesi e valore del motivo escatologico in Seneca: Contributo alla questione posidoniana," *Rendiconti dell'Istituto Lombardo, Accademia di scienze e lettere*, classe di lettere e scienze morali e storiche, *101* (Milano, 1967), 203-10. Other good treatments of Posidonius are Ludwig

most interesting and influential philosophers of his age and is easily the most controversial figure in the history of Stoicism. He studied under Panaetius in Athens around 125-114 B.C. and then established himself in Rhodes, where he became a leading citizen. He was elected to various public offices, serving as an ambassador to Rome in 86 B.C. A number of eminent Romans were personally acquainted with Posidonius; Cicero studied with him in Rhodes in 78-77 B.C. and Pompey visited him twice, in 67/66 and 63/62 B.C. Posidonius' mastery of contemporary thought extended into an astonishing variety of fields. It is not known whether he followed other schools of philosophy formally after studying with Panaetius or whether he was an autodidact. In any case, one of his principal sources of information was his own observation, acquired during his extensive travels throughout the Mediterranean world, probably undertaken after 105 B.C. In addition to the standard subdivisions of philosophy treated by the Stoics, physics, logic, and ethics, Posidonius studied mathematics, geography, history, and ethnography. Natural science was his overriding interest, and he was both learned and original in this field. Posidonius incorporated non-Stoic teachings into his philosophy and on many points his views do not square with the orthodoxies of the ancient Stoa. The goal of his work, however, appears to have been the refurbishment of Stoicism in the context of the most up-to-date thought available and in the light of his own empirical observations. Nor does he shrink from using doctrines of other schools which would make Stoicism easier to defend.

The third and final stage of ancient Stoicism is the Roman Stoa. While dependent on the ancient and middle Stoa for the content of their philosophy, the Roman Stoics mark an important shift from their predecessors in two ways. In the first place, none of the Roman Stoics was an official head of the school. While some of them set forth their doctrines for pedagogical purposes, none felt called upon to engage in formal polemics with other schools. Each of the Roman Stoics reflects his own personal tastes and attitudes and feels free to pick and choose among Stoic and other ideas, to a much more marked degree than is true of the ancient or middle Stoics. Secondly, the Roman Stoics show a virtually preclusive interest in ethics. Ethics had certainly been a central concern in prior Stoic teaching, but, except for Aristo, a pupil of Zeno, the school hitherto had insisted on the importance of physics and logic as well. Disinclined to study physics and logic, the Roman Stoics showed little speculative interest in ethics itself. With the middle Stoics, they shared

Edelstein, "The Philosophical System of Posidonius," *AJP*, 57 (1936), 286-325; Arthur Darby Nock, "Posidonius," *JRS*, 49 (1959), 1-15; Rist, *Stoic Philos.*, pp. 201-18.

a taste for the application of ethical principles to specific cases and situations, being even more concrete and practical in their orientation. They show a good deal of perceptiveness in using Stoic ethics to meet their own personal needs and those of their immediate audience.

The earliest of the Roman Stoics and the only one who wrote in the Latin language was Seneca (4 B.C.–A.D. 65).[8] Born of a wealthy and em-

---

[8] The basic older biography of Seneca is René Waltz, *Vie de Sénèque* (Paris, 1909). It has been superceded recently by Miriam T. Griffin, *Seneca: A Philosopher in Politics* (Oxford, 1976) and Pierre Grimal, *Sénèque: Sa vie, son oeuvre, avec un exposé de sa philosophie* (Paris, 1957). Two excellent brief biographies are John Ferguson, "Seneca the Man," in *Neronians and Flavians: Silver Latin I*, ed. D. R. Dudley (London, 1972), pp. 1-23 and Miriam T. Griffin, " 'Imago vitae suae'," in *Seneca*, ed. C. D. N. Costa (London, 1974), pp. 1-38. See also Ernst Bickel, "Seneca und Seneca-Mythus," *Das Altertum, 5* (1959), 90-100. There is also an unsuccessful recent attempt to diagnose Seneca as an overprotected child by M. Rozelaar, "Seneca: A New Approach to His Personality," *Lampas, 7* (1974), 33-42.

The best general study of Seneca's thought is Pierre Aubenque and Jean-Marie André, *Sénèque* (Paris, 1964). Other good general studies include Wilhelm Ganss, *Das Bild des Weisen bei Seneca* (Schaan, 1952); Mario Gentile, *I fondamenti metafisici della morale di Seneca* (Milano, 1932); Marie Laffranque, "Sénèque et le moyen stoïcisme," *Actas del Congreso internacional de filosofía en conmemoractión de Séneca, en el XIX centenario de su meurte* (Madrid, 1966), pp. 185-95; Italo Lana, *Lucio Anneo Seneca* (Torino, 1955); Winfried Trillitzsch, *Senecas Beweisführung*, Deutsche Akademie der Wissenschaft zu Berlin, Schriften der Sektion für Altertumswissenschaft, 37 (Berlin 1962). On Seneca's sources see Pierre Grimal, "Nature et limites de l'éclecticisme philosophique chez Sénèque," *LEC, 38* (1970), 3-17; "Sénèque et la pensée grecque," *Bull. de l'Assoc. Guillaume Budé*, 4ᵐᵉ sér., *3* (1966), 317-30.

Recent scholarship has paid increasing attention to Seneca's plays as a source for his philosophy. A few scholars see the philosophical themes in the plays as commonplaces and as poorly integrated with their plots and characters, as, for example, Léon Herrmann, *La Théatre de Sénèque* (Paris, 1924), pp. 482-518; Mendell, *Our Seneca*, pp. 153-68. The prevailing view sees Seneca's plays reflecting his philosophy in a more integral way, as in Theodor Birt, "Was hat Seneca mit seinen Tragödies gewollt?" *Neue Jahrbücher für das klassische Altertum, 27* (1911), 336-64, who also thinks that the plays were written to be performed, a view no longer held; Aurèle Cattin, "L'âme humaine et la vie future dans les textes lyriques des tragédies de Sénèque," *Latomus, 15* (1956), 359-65, 544-50; J.-M. Croisille, "Lieux communes, *sententiae* et intentions philosophiques dans la Phèdre de Sénèque," *REL, 42* (1964), 276-301; F. Egermann, "Seneca als Dichterphilosoph," *Neue Jahrbücher für Antike und deutsche Bildung, 3* (1940), 18-36; Francesco Giancotti, *Saggio sulle tragedie di Seneca* (Roma, 1953); C. J. Heringon, "Senecan Tragedy," *Arion, 5* (1966), 422-71; Christine M. King, "Seneca's *Hercules Oetaeus*: A Stoic Interpretation of the Greek Myth," *Greece & Rome*, ser. 2:*18* (1971), 215-22; Eckard Lefèvre, "Quid ratio possit? Senecas Phaedra als stoisches Drame," *WS*, n.F. *3* (1969), 131-60; A. D. Leeman, "Schicksal und Selbstverschuldung in Senecas Agamemnon," *Hermes, 94* (1966), 482-96; "Seneca's *Phaedra* as a Stoic Tragedy," *Miscellanea Tragica in Honorem J. C. Kamerbeek*, ed. J. M. Bremer, S. L. Radt, and G. J. Ruijgh (Amsterdam, 1976), pp. 199-212; Berthe M. Marti, "The Prototypes of Seneca's Tragedies," *CP, 42* (1947), 1-17; "Seneca's Tragedies: A New Interpretation," *TAPA, 76* (1945), 216-45, which proposes a specific sequence in which the author thinks the plays were intended to be read, a view that has proved controversial; Norman T. Pratt, Jr., "The Stoic Base of Senecan Drama," *TAPA, 79* (1948), 1-11; Otto Regenbogen, "Schmerz und Tod in den Tragödien Senecas," *Vorträge der Bibliothek Warburg, 1927-28* (Leipzig, 1930), pp. 167-218; Robert Benson Steele, "Seneca the Philosopher," *Sewanee Review, 30* (1922), 79-94.

inent family in Córdoba, distinguished in both letters and politics, Seneca
was educated in Rome. He followed the *cursus honorum* as well as cultivating literature and philosophy. As a politician, Seneca was unfortunate
enough to serve under three of the worst emperors in Roman history,
Caligula, Claudius, and Nero. His career suffered numerous vicissitudes
as a result of the whims of members of the imperial court. During Claudius' reign, the empress Messalina accused him of an intrigue with Julia
Livilla, the sister of Nero, which led to Seneca's banishment to Corsica
for eight years. At that point, Agrippina, Claudius' current wife, secured
his return, and he was made tutor to her son Nero in A.D. 49. Seneca was
a leading statesman during Nero's reign, a mixed blessing, as he was to
discover. While he acquired a great deal of wealth, honor, and power
under Nero, he was also ordered to help plot the assassination of the
dowager empress Agrippina, his former benefactress, and then to justify
Nero's matricide before the senate in A.D. 59. Seneca retired from public
life in A.D. 62 and remained in retirement until his death. In A.D. 65 he
was ordered by Nero to commit suicide, having been suspected of com-
plicity in a plot against the government led by Piso.[9] The particular themes
on which Seneca focuses reveal two facets of his mind—his astuteness as
a psychologist and his desire to extract from philosophy a balm for the
wounds which life had inflicted upon himself and upon the group of
friends and relatives to whom he addressed his works. Seneca shows a
great deal of sensitivity in his analysis of the vices and virtues and the
dynamics of the soul. He is preoccupied with the questions of friendship,
beneficence, clemency, and the right use of wealth. His concern with
topics such as the relative merits of the contemplative life and the active
life, the issue of whether withdrawal from public life can be justified when
the ruler under whom one serves makes it impossible to serve with honor,
and his repeated discussion of the conditions under which suicide may
be justified are clearly not speculative in origin, but spring from the grim
and practical necessities of Seneca's own life.

Seneca had an extensive reputation as a statesman, a man of letters,
and a philosopher in later antiquity and the Middle Ages. Since he alone
of the ancient Stoics wrote in the Latin language, his works provided his
ancient and medieval successors with direct access to his professed, if

---

[9] Dill, *Roman Society*, pp. 39-40 and Ramsay MacMullen, *Enemies of the Roman Order:
Treason, Unrest, and Alienation in the Empire* (Cambridge, Mass., 1966), pp. 1-94 think that
the Stoics did form a political opposition. On the other hand, Gaston Boissier, *L'Opposition
sous les Césars*, 6me éd. (Paris 1909), pp. 97-105; Clarke, *The Roman Mind*, p. 52; and Italo
Lana, *L. Anneo Seneca e la posizione degli intelletuali romani di fronte al principato* (Torino,
1964), think that, while Stoics may have criticized the emperors on moral grounds, their
philosophy rules out revolt.

somewhat eclectic, Stoic views. Seneca's writings fall into six categories both from the standpoint of genre and from the standpoint of their survival in the post-classical period,[10] or seven categories if we include the forgeries, plagiarisms, and spurious works attributed to him. Approximately twenty of Seneca's works on a range of subjects have not survived at all, although they are mentioned by ancient authors. Scholars have achieved little consensus on the dating and sequence of those that remain. There are ten treatises on ethical subjects written in dialogue form and dedicated to members of Seneca's immediate circle of friends and relatives: the *De ira, De providentia, De constantia sapientis, Ad Marciam de consolatione, De beata vita, De otio, De tranquillitate animi, De brevitate vitae, Ad Polybium de consolatione,* and *Ad Helviam de consolatione.* Seneca also wrote two moral essays that are not dialogues, the *De clementia* dedicated to Nero in A.D. 55 or 56 and the *De beneficiis.* His *Quaestiones naturales,* a summary of selected lore in the field of natural philosophy, probably dates from his years in retirement. 124 of his *Epistulae morales* survive. They were written to Seneca's friend Lucilius but partake of the philosophical genre of the letter of ethical counsel rather than being a private correspondence destined for the addressee alone. Seneca also wrote nine or ten tragedies based heavily on the plays of Sophocles and Euripides: the *Hercules, Hercules Oetaeus, Troades, Phoenissae, Oedipus, Medea, Phaedra, Agamemnon,* and *Thyestes.* The authorship of the tenth tragedy, the *Octavia,* has been debated. Finally, Seneca contributed to the Latin tradition of Menippean satire in his comedy, the *Apocolocyntosis* or *Ludus de morte Claudii,* written soon after the death of the emperor Claudius in A.D. 54.

While the works just mentioned constitute no mean corpus of authentic writings, late classical or early medieval authors swelled the list of titles

---

[10] For the survival of Seneca's works in general see Paul Faider, *Études sur Sénèque* (Gand, 1921), pp. 109-27; Max Manitius, *Philologisches aus alten Bibliothekskatalogen (bis 1300) zusammengestellt,* Erganzungsheft, *RM,* n.F. *47* (1892), 44-48. For the traditions of particular works and groups of works see L. D. Reynolds, "The Medieval Tradition of Seneca's *Dialogues,*" *CQ,* n.s. *18* (1968), 355-73; *The Medieval Tradition of Seneca's Letters* (London, 1965); J.-M. Déchanet, "Seneca Noster: Des lettres à Lucilius a la Lettre aux Frères de Mont-Dieu," *Mélanges Joseph de Ghellinck, S. J.* (Gembloux, 1951), *2,* 753-66; Otto Foerster, *Handschriftliche Untersuchungen zu Senecas Epistulae morales und Naturales quaestiones* (Stuttgart, 1936); Clotilde Picard-Parra, "Une utilisation des *Quaestiones naturales* de Sénèque au milieu du XIIᵉ siècle," *Revue du moyen âge latin, 5* (1949), 115-26; Giorgio Brugnoli, "La tradizione manoscritta di Seneca tragico alla luce della testimonianze medioevali," *Atti della Accademia nazionale dei Lincei,* classe di scienze morali, storiche e filologiche, *354,* ser. 8, *8*:3 (Roma, 1957), 199-287; Ezio Franceschini, *Studi e note di filologia latina medievale* (Milano, 1938), pp. 1-105, 177-97; idem, ed., *Il Commento di Nicola Trevet al Tieste di Seneca* (Milano, 1938); Vincenzo Ussani, "Per il testo delle tragedie di Seneca," *Atti della Accademia nazionale dei Lincei,* classe di scienze morali, storiche e filologiche, *356,* ser. 8, *8*:7 (Roma, 1959), 489-552; Marcia L. Colish, "Seneca's *Apocolocyntosis* as a Possible Source for Erasmus' *Julius Exclusus,*" *Renaissance Quarterly, 39* (1976), 362-63.

believed in the Middle Ages to have issued from Seneca's pen. The first and most curious of these spurious works is the forged fourth-century correspondence between Seneca and St. Paul.[11] It was first mentioned by St. Jerome and St. Augustine, both of whom refer to it laconically and without evaluating its authenticity. None the less, the idea that Paul had won the ancient philosopher to the Christian faith crops up periodically starting from about the seventh century and it had gained some currency at the point when Erasmus demonstrated that the letters were a forgery. Some authorities on this subject believe that the myth of Seneca's conversion played a major role is assuring his influence in the Middle Ages while others argue with equal persuasiveness against this thesis.[12] The author of the forgery has not been identified. This is also the case with the *Proverbiae Senecae* and the *Liber de moribus* pseudonomously attributed to Seneca. Neither do scholars know when these spurious works were composed, although the *Liber de moribus* was first cited in the sixth century and the earliest manuscript of the *Proverbiae* comes from the ninth century. The most widely copied and cited plagiarist of Seneca has, however, been known for centuries. He is Martin, the sixth-century archbishop of Braga, who wrote a *De ira* based on Seneca's dialogue by the same title and the *Formula vitae honestae*, a pseudo-Senecan pastiche to which he attached the philosopher's name. Under this title and later under the title *De quattuor virtutibus cardinalibus* this work was frequently reproduced and circulated in the Middle Ages. Over 600 manuscript copies survive. It was translated into several vernacular tongues and was subjected to numerous commentaries both in prose and in verse. It continued to be used as a school text well into the Renaissance even though Petrarch succeeded in attributing it correctly to Martin in the fourteenth century. Apart from the unacknowledged pilfering of Seneca's works to which these spurious and pseudonomous treatises attest, Seneca's sententious-

---

[11] The most recent review of the history and criticism of this legend is Laura Bocciolini Palagi, *Il carteggio apocrifo di Seneca e San Paolo* (Firenze, 1978), pp. 7-47. On the spurious works see also Claude W. Barlow, ed., *Epistolae Senecae ad Paulum et Pauli ad Senecam 'quae vocantur'*, Papers and Monographs of the American Academy in Rome, *10* (Horn, 1938), pp. 3-4, 7, 110-12; idem, ed., *Martini Episcopi Bracarensis Opera omnia*, Papers and Monographs of the American Academy in Rome, *12* (New Haven, 1950), pp. 7, 204-08; E. Bickel, "Die Schrift des Martinus von Bracara formula vitae honestae," *RM*, n.F. *6* (1905), 505-51; N. G. Round, "The Mediaeval Reputation of the *Proverbiae Senecae*: A Partial Survey Based on Recorded MSS.," *Proceedings of the Royal Irish Academy, 72*, C, 5 (1972), 103-51.

[12] The strongest proponents of this view are Barlow, *Epistolae Senecae ad Paulum*, p. 93 and Winfried Trillitzsch, *Seneca im literarischen Urteil der Antike: Darstellung und Sammlung der Zeugnisse*, 2 vols. (Amsterdam, 1971), *1*, 170-85. The major opponents are Arnaldo Momigliano, "Note sulla leggenda del cristianesimo di Seneca," *Rivista storica italiana, 62* (1950), 325-38 and Reynolds, *Tradition of Seneca's Letters*, pp. 82-89.

ness, his gravity, and his aphoristic style made him a natural favorite for inclusion in medieval *florilegia*.

Seneca's popularity in the Middle Ages reflects a decided shift in attitude in comparison with his reputation among late classical readers. From his own day until the end of the classical era Seneca was known and cited repeatedly; but it can scarcely be said that he was held in universal esteem. Some ancient authors praised him as a learned and virtuous man while others castigated him as a hypocrite who had failed to live up to the ideals he professed. Later classical writers treated Seneca less as a philosopher than as a prose stylist and as a statesman. In both of these respects he received a generally bad press. Late Latin poets referred to his tragedies and to some of his other works and the grammarians cited him occasionally to illustrate points of usage and style. But the main figures responsible for Seneca's ancient reputation were Quintilian and the archaists of the second century A.D., who objected to his prose style for its failure to correspond with Ciceronian canons, and the historians, who either dissociated themselves pointedly from his political activities or who charged him with abusing his official position to extend his own wealth and power.

It was the Christian apologists and Church Fathers, starting in the second century, who gave Seneca a new and more positive appreciation. These authors were less concerned with his biography and his literary style than with his moral philosophy, which they found strikingly compatible with Christian ethics at some points. They concentrated their attention on his ethical works, borrowing heavily from them and occasionally mentioning him by name as a sage.[13] This apologetic and patristic revaluation of Seneca's reputation proved decisive for the Middle Ages. Seneca's influence reached new heights during the Carolingian renaissance and attained its medieval apogée in the twelfth century, extending itself into the spheres of philosophy, theology, and Latin and vernacular literature. In the twelfth century Seneca became the most popular Latin prose author after Cicero, an eminence that stimulated interest in his spurious works no less than his authentic works and which multiplied the citations of Seneca in the *florilegia*.[14]

---

[13] The fullest treatment is found in Trillitzsch, *Seneca im literarischen Urteil der Antike*, *1*, 33–210, 251–65, with the *testimonia* given in *2*, 331–93. See also Faider, *Études sur Sénèque*, pp. 15–107.

[14] On Seneca's reputation and influence in the Middle Ages see Claude W. Barlow, "Seneca in the Middle Ages," *Classical Weekly*, 34 (1940–41), 257–58; Rudolf Brummer, "Auf den Spuren des Philosophen Seneca in der romanischen Literaturen des Mittelalters und des Frühhumanismus," *Romanica: Festschrift Prof. Dr. Fritz Neubert*, ed. Rudolf Brummer (Berlin, 1948), pp. 58–84; Faider, *Études sur Sénèque*, pp. 135–49; Richard Mott Gummere, "Seneca the Philosopher in the Middle Ages and the Early Renaissance," *TAPA*,

To a large extent the medieval veneration of Seneca as a moral authority helps to explain the differing post-classical fortunes enjoyed by the
different categories of works in his *oeuvre*. There are over fifty manuscripts
of his *Quaestiones naturales*, but they date at the earliest to the twelfth
century, when their fortunes were joined with those of Pliny's *Natural
History*. Medieval interest in this Senecan work had to wait until the
twelfth-century revival of scientific thought. The manuscript tradition of
Seneca's tragedies exists in two versions, one beginning in the eleventh
century and the other, which includes the *Octavia*, beginning only in the
fourteenth century. It was not until the thirteenth century that medieval
readers devoted any sustained attention to the tragedies. The renewal of
interest in these works began with the commentaries of Nicholas Trevet
and Albertino Mussato, from which point it flowed immediately into the
revival of classical drama that marked the Italian Renaissance. The earliest manuscripts of Seneca's *Apocolocyntosis* go back to the Carolingian era
and the work appears to have been known by Vincent of Beauvais in the
thirteenth century; but it exercised no literary influence until the time of
Erasmus.

On the other hand, Seneca's expressly ethical works enjoyed a much
more fruitful posterity in both the early and the high Middle Ages. His
dialogues are the most mutilated and the least well preserved of his moral
treatises, with the earliest manuscripts dating from the eleventh century,
although they are well represented in manuscripts from the thirteenth
century onward. The oldest manuscript of the *De beneficiis* and *De clementia*, however, goes back to the eighth century. Of all his moral works
Seneca's *Epistulae morales* have the richest manuscript tradition and possessed the most extensive medieval influence. Two separate traditions of
the letters have come down to us, the first covering letters 1–88 and the
second covering letters 89–124. These two manuscript traditions were not
united until the tenth century. The first of them is the better represented.
It goes back to the ninth century and the manuscripts deriving from the
period before the twelfth century are the most numerous and the best.
The second tradition is less widespread but in this case too the fullest and
best manuscripts derive from the Carolingian era.

The peak periods of Senecan influence correspond exactly with the
periods when the involvement of medieval readers with classical litera-

---

41 (1910), xxxviii–xl; Luigi Manicardi, "Di un antico volgarizzamento inedito delle 'Ep-
istole morali' di Seneca (23.7.05)," *Zeitschrift für romanische Philologie*, 30 (1906), 53–70;
Klaus-Dieter Nothdurft, *Studien zum Einfluss Senecas auf die Philosophie und Theologie des
zwölften Jahrhunderts* (Leiden, 1963); Reynolds, *Tradition of Seneca's Letters*, ch. 6, 9; G. M.
Ross, "Seneca's Philosophical Influence," in *Seneca*, ed. Costa, pp. 116–42; Anne Marie
Marthe Smit, *Contribution à l'étude de la connaissance de l'antiquité au moyen âge* (Leiden, 1934).

ture and with speculative thought was the most intense: the patristic era, the Carolingian renaissance, and the renaissance of the twelfth century, with the momentum gathering and spreading from that point unabated into the Italian Renaissance. The provenance of Seneca manuscripts and the incidence of his works in medieval library catalogues likewise provide a faithful reflection of the major currents of medieval thought and of the great medieval centers of learning. Certain concerns of a more particularized nature also played their part in the transmission and reputation of Seneca in the Middle Ages. The Cistercians in the twelfth and thirteenth centuries, for example, reveal a marked taste for his *Epistulae morales* because of their relevance to the ethos of friendship which this order had a special corporate interest in developing. And ethics, indeed, was the label that the Middle Ages attached to Seneca. From the time of Tertullian's *Seneca saepe noster* to the time of Dante's *Seneca morale*, it was above all as a moral philosopher and as an ancient *exemplum virtutis* that Seneca was read and prized by his wide and devoted medieval following.

A somewhat younger contemporary of Seneca was Musonius Rufus (before A.D. 30–end of the first century).[15] Little is known of his status or education, but he was publicly regarded as a Stoic philosopher and he identified himself with Nero's political victims, being banished after the Pisonian plot. He returned to Rome following Nero's death. In A.D. 71 Vespasian exempted him from the general banishment of philosophers which had been ordered, although Musonius was later exiled for unknown reasons. He was recalled under the emperor Titus. During the intermittent periods when he was in Rome, Musonius taught philosophy, numbering Epictetus among his pupils. Musonius revived the stringent ethics of the ancient Stoa. Two topics which he elaborated more fully than other members of the school are sexual equality and the dignity of manual labor. He also taught the duty of acquiescence in the face of a tyrant, a doctrine which makes his political activities or at least his political reputation difficult to understand.

Epictetus (ca. A.D. 50–130),[16] the pupil of Musonius and one of the

---

[15] See Cora E. Lutz, "Musonius Rufus, 'The Roman Socrates'," *Yale Classical Studies, 10* (1947), 3–147, which includes an edition and translation of the extant fragments. Other important studies are Martin Percival Charlesworth, *Five Men: Character Studies from the Roman Empire*, Martin Classical Lectures, 6 (Cambridge, Mass., 1936), pp. 33–61; Charles Favez, "Un féministe romain: Musonius Rufus," *Bulletin de la société des Études de Lettres de Lausanne, 8* (1933), 1–8; A. C. van Geytenbeek, *Musonius Rufus and Greek Diatribe*, rev. ed., trans. B. L. Hijmans (Assen, 1962); Renato Laurenti, "Musonio e Epitteto," *Sophia, 34* (1966), 317–35; intro. to his ed. and trans. of Musonius Rufus, *Le diatribe e i frammenti minori* (Roma, 1967), pp. 5–37.

[16] The best study of Epictetus is Joseph Moreau, *Épictète, ou le secret de la liberté* (Paris, 1964). Other good full-length treatments are Adolf Bonhöffer, *Epiktet und die Stoa: Untersuchungen zur stoischen Philosophie* (Stuttgart, 1890); *Die Ethik des stoikers Epiktet* (Stuttgart,

starkest and most arresting exponents of Stoic ethics, was a Greek slave living in Rome who was manumitted during the reign of Nero. Epictetus was a cripple owing to the sadistic brutality of one of his masters, who deliberately broke both of his legs. While still a slave, Epictetus was permitted to study with Musonius. After suffering exile along with other philosophers during the reign of Domitian, he established a school at Nicopolis. His works survive in the form in which they were taken down by his disciple, Flavius Arrianus. Epictetus is a rigorist with a comparatively ascetic morality. He refuses to make the kinds of ethical accommodations which the middle Stoa and Seneca had made. A dominant theme in Epictetus' thought is moral freedom. Moral liberty, for Epictetus, is the only thing of true value; and it lies within the power of each man to achieve it through the exercise of his reason and will. Epictetus places a heavier accent on the will than is true of other Stoics in his efforts to limit the sphere of ethical relevance to those things within the subjective control of the individual.

The last of the major Roman Stoics is Marcus Aurelius (A.D. 121-180).[17] A member of the Antonine house, Marcus was emperor of Rome

1894). Useful shorter studies include Ernest Bosshard, "Épictète," *RTP*, n.s. *17* (1929), 201-16; Phillip DeLacy, "The Logical Structure of the Ethics of Epictetus," *CP,38* (1943), 112-25; Paul Geigenmüller, "Stellung und Pflichten des Menschen im Kosmos nach Epiktet," *Neue Jahrbücher für Wissenschaft und Jugendbildung*, 5 (1929), 529-42; B. L. Hijmans, *Askesis: Notes on Epictetus' Educational System* (Assen, 1959); "A Note on *Physis* in Epictetus," *Mnemosyne*, 4th ser., *20* (1967), 279-84; Renato Laurenti, "Il 'filosofo ideale' secondo Epitteto," *Giornale di metafisica*, *17* (1962), 501-13; R. J. Ryle, "Epictetus," *Proceedings of the Aristotelian Society*, *2*:3 (1894), 123-32; P. Zarella, "La cocezione del 'discepolo' in Epitteto," *Aevum*, *40* (1966), 211-29. On Epictetus' relation to his sources see Amand Jagu, *Épictète et Platon: Essai sur les relations du Stoïcisme et du Platonisme à propos de la morale des Entretiens* (Paris, 1946); Laurenti, "Musonio e Epitteto," *Sophia*, *34* (1966), 317-35. On the redaction of Epictetus' works see Ermengildo Bolla, *Arriano di Nicomedia: Saggio storico-filologico* (Torino, 1890), pp. 45-53.

[17] For the biography of Marcus Aurelius see Anthony Birley, *Marcus Aurelius* (London, 1966). Aspects of his health and its possible relation to his thought have been treated by Thomas W. Africa, "The Opium Addiction of Marcus Aurelius," *JHI*, *22* (1961), 97-102; Robert Dailly and Henri van Effenterre, "Le cas Marc-Aurèle: Essai de psychomatique historique," *REA*, *56* (1954), 347-65; J. E. G. Whitehorne, "Was Marcus Aurelius a Hypochondriac?" *Latomus*, *36* (1977), 413-21; and Edward Charles Witke, "Marcus Aurelius and Mandragora," *CP*, *60* (1965), 23-24. Efforts to show that Marcus' public policies reflect his Stoicism have been made with debatable success by Ph. Lotmar, "Marc Aurels Erlass über die Freilassungsauflage," *ZSS, 33* (1912), 304-82 and P. Noyen, "Marcus Aurelius, the Greatest Practician of Stoicism,"*LAC*, *24* (1955), 372-83.

Useful espositions of Marcus' thought include André Bonnard, "Marc-Aurèle," *RTP*, n.s. *17* (1929), 217-36; André Cresson, *Marc-Aurèle: Sa vie, son oeuvre avec un exposé de sa philosophie* (Paris, 1939), esp. pp. 19-67; Pierre Hadot, "La physique comme exercice spirituel ou pessimisme et optimisme chez Marc Aurèle," *RTP*, sér. 3:22 (1972), 225-39; Walter Siegfried, "Stoische Haltung, nach Mark Aurel," *Hermeneia: Festschrift Otto Regenbogen zum 60. Geburtstag am 14. Februar 1951 dargebracht von Schülern und Freunden* (Heidelberg, 1952), pp. 144-63.

from 161 to 180. In addition to the normal cares of administration and the inevitable court intrigues, his reign was made extremely burdensome to him by the ghastly necessities of war. Marcus spent a great many years of his reign defending the Empire against a variety of aggressors on different frontiers, and died on the battlefield. During the last year of his reign a serious plague broke out in Rome. Marcus' personal life was debilitated by perpetual ill health from his youth onward and recurrently saddened by the death in infancy of eight of his twelve children. A central theme in his philosophy is the tension between his yearning for philosophical repose and his sense of his duty to serve society, a tension raised to the level of maximum intensity by his responsibilities as emperor. A second dominant theme in Marcus' philosophy is death—its omnipresence, its inevitability, and the need to resign oneself to it. Marcus Aurelius is easily the most eclectic of the Stoic philosophers and certainly the most personal. His philosophy was designed to serve as a mode of self-consolation and examination of conscience, and was written in the form of a journal not intended for other readers.

II. The Teachings of the Stoics

The brief historical outline given above illustrates one of the problems in dealing with Stoic philosophy in summary form: the doctrine grew, changed and was channelled in certain directions, widening or shrinking in scope at the hands of its different exponents across a span of six centuries. There are points on which not all Stoics agree. For the purposes of this exposition, however, it will be best to concentrate on those teachings which are generally held by the Stoics, indicating only briefly the significant divergences. A second difficulty in studying the teachings of the Stoics, far more intractable, is the problem of the sources.[18] The only

---

[18] The basic collection of fragments of the ancient Stoa is Hans F. A. von Arnim, *Stoicorum veterum fragmenta*, 4 vols. (Leipzig, 1903-24). An abridged version may be found in C. J. de Vogel, *Greek Philosophy: A Collection of Texts with Notes and Explanations* (Leiden, 1959), *3*, 44-183. Among the most important ancient witnesses are Diogenes Laertius, *Lives of Eminent Philosophers, 2*, trans. R. D. Hicks, Loeb (London, 1925); Sextus Empiricus, *Against the Logicians*, ed. and trans. R. G. Bury, Loeb (Cambridge, Mass., 1935); *Against the Physicists. Against the Ethicists*, ed. and trans. R. G. Bury, Loeb (Cambridge, Mass., 1936); *Against the Professors*, ed. and trans. R. G. Bury, Loeb (Cambridge, Mass., 1949); *Outlines of Pyrrhonism*, ed. and trans. R. G. Bury, Loeb (London, 1933); and Plutarch, *On the Contradictions of the Stoics. On Common Notions against the Stoics*, trans. Émile Bréhier in *Les Stoïciens*, ed. and trans. É. Bréhier and P.-M. Schuhl (Paris, 1962).

Fragments of members of the ancient Stoa have been translated by Rosario Anastasi, trans., *I frammenti degli stoici antichi*, Pubblicazioni dell'Istituto universitario di magistero di Catania, testi e documenti, 8 (Padova, 1962), *3*; G. Blin and M. Keim, trans., "Chrysippe: De la partie hégémonique de l'âme," *Mesures*, 5:2 (1939), 163-74; Michael Balkwill, trans., Cleanthes' *Hymn to Zeus*, in *The Oxford Book of Greek Verse in Translation*, ed.

Stoics whose works we possess in anything resembling completeness are
the Roman Stoics. Yet, they are the least speculative members of the
school, having virtually nothing to say on logic or physics. The principal
creators of Stoic philosophy, the ancient and middle Stoics, are known
only through fragments. The fragments have been collected and edited.
Still, some of the fullest ancient witnesses to the Stoics' teachings are
authors who are either pedestrian compilers or critics of the Stoics, who
may well have distorted their ideas for polemical purposes and who usually relate them out of context. Even making allowances for this difficulty,
the fragments do not permit as full a reconstruction of Stoic thought as
one would like to have. There are many works written by the Stoics,
mentioned in the ancient texts, of which no trace has survived. The evidence that does remain is sometimes contradictory. There are lacunae in
the sources which make it impossible to know what the Stoics might have
actually thought on certain subjects. Some scholars have sought to overcome this problem by inferring, or even by inventing answers to questions
for which there is no textual evidence. It is more straightforward to admit
that there are unavoidable gaps in our knowledge of Stoicism, and to
indicate them where they occur.

A) Physics

1. *Cosmology*

The Stoics, like other ancient philosophical schools, divide philosophy

C. M. Bowra and T. F. Higham (Oxford, 1938); Gordon H. Clark, trans., *Selections from
Hellenistic Philosophy* (New York, 1940); Nicola Festa, ed. and trans., *I frammenti degli stoici
antichi*, 2 vols. (Bari, 1932-35); James Adam, trans., Cleanthes' *Hymn to Zeus*, in *The Greek
Poets*, ed. Moses Hadas (New York, 1953) and in *The Stoic and Epicurean Philosophers*, ed.
Whitney J. Oates (New York, 1940); Max Pohlenz, trans., *Stoa und Stoiker: Die Grunder.
Panaitios. Posidonius* (Zürich, 1950); Jason L. Saunders, ed. and trans., *Greek and Roman
Philosophy after Aristotle* (New York, 1966).
    The basic collections of fragments of the middle Stoics are Modestus Van Straaten,
ed., *Panaetii Rhodii fragmenta*, 3rd ed. (Leiden, 1962) and Posidonius, *The Fragments*, ed.
L. Edelstein and I. G. Kidd (Cambridge, 1972), *1*. Some fragments of Panaetius and
Posidonius are translated in Pohlenz, *Stoa und Stoiker* and Saunders, *Greek and Roman Phi-
losophy*.
    The works of the Roman Stoics have all been published with translations accompany-
ing the basic editions of the texts: Seneca, *Ad Lucilium epistulae morales*, trans. Richard M.
Gummere, Loeb (London, 1925-34); *Apocolocyntosis*, trans. W. H. D. Rouse, Loeb (London, 1913); *Moral Essays*, trans. John W. Basore, Loeb (London, 1928-35); *Naturales
quaestiones*, trans. Thomas H. Corcoran, Loeb (Cambridge, Mass., 1971); *Tragedies*, trans.
Frank Justus Miller, Loeb (London, 1929-38); see also the index to Seneca's ideas by
Anna Lydia Motto, *Seneca Sourcebook: Guide to the Thought of Lucius Annaeus Seneca* (Amsterdam, 1970); Lutz, "Musonius Rufus," *Yale Classical Studies*, *10* (1947), 3-147; Epictetus, *The Discourses as Reported by Arrian, the Manual, and Fragments*, trans. W. A. Oldfather,
Loeb (London, 1926); Marcus Aurelius Antoninus, *The Communings with Himself together
with His Speeches and Sayings*, ed. and trans. C. R. Haines, Loeb (London, 1930).

into three branches, physics, logic, and ethics. They do not always agree on the proper order in which these subjects should be studied, some beginning with logic and others with physics. They all agree, however, that ethics is the most important part of philosophy, and that physics and logic should be studied not merely for their own intrinsic interest but for the light which they shed on ethics.[19] The Stoics employ a metaphor to illustrate the relations among physics, logic, and ethics: Philosophy is a walled garden in which logic is the wall, physics is the tree, and ethics is the fruit. One could actually begin an exposition of Stoic philosophy with any one of its three branches, since there are key ideas and organic interconnections which bind them all together. We will begin with physics and then treat ethics and logic in turn.

The main objective of Stoic physics is to overcome the dualism between mind and matter taught by other Greek philosophical schools.[20] The Stoics achieve this goal by identifying mind and matter with each other and with God. They therefore propose a totally unitary reality, a monism in which God is mind, God is matter, and God is the universe.[21] One may speak of mind or of matter, but this is merely a façon de parler. For the Stoics, everything that acts is a body.[22] There is a continuum between mind and body. They are completely translatable into each other; they are simply two ways of viewing the content within the continuum. In Stoic physics, matter is not "dead" matter in the Cartesian sense; it is dynamic, charged with vital force. Mind is not something external to matter, an abstract ideal quality, a principle of rest toward which an imperfect material world aspires; it is rather an active principle, the creative force permeating the universe and holding it together.[23] God is called by several names in Stoic physics—the *logos*,[24] the rational structure

---

[19] *SVF, 3*, 68, 282.

[20] The basic work is S. Sambursky, *Physics of the Stoics* (New York, 1959). Sambursky also supplies a summary of his larger work and a report on recent scholarship in "Le dynamisme stoïcien et le monde physique," *Actes du VIIe congrès de l'Assoc. Guillaume Budé*, pp. 278-84. Also worth consulting is John J. I. Döllinger, *The Gentile and the Jew in the Courts of the Temple of Christ: An Introduction to thr History of Christianity*, trans. N. Darnell (London, 1862), *1*, 348-51. A good recent general treatment is Bethia S. Currie, "God and Matter in Early Stoic Physics," (New School for Social Research Ph.D. diss., 1971).

[21] *SVF, 1*, 85, 87, 102, 153-54, 159-62, 299-328, 526. An excellent analysis of this point is provided by Robert B. Todd, "Monism and Immanence: The Foundations of Stoic Physics," in *The Stoics*, ed. John M. Rist (Berkeley, 1978), pp. 137-60.

[22] *SVF, 1*, 89-90; *2*, 341, 346a, 358-59, 467, 665, 797, 848; *3*, 84.

[23] This point has been well developed by Edelstein, *Meaning of Stoicism*, pp. 30-33.

[24] The best studies of the idea of the *logos* in Greek thought and the Stoic use of it are Anathon Aall, *Der Logos: Geschichte seiner Entwicklung in der griechischen Philosophie und der christlichen Litteratur* (Leipzig, 1896), *1*, 7-167; Max Heinze, *Die Lehre vom Logos in der griechischen Philosophie* (Oldenburg, 1872), pp. xii, 9-172. See also James Adam, *The Vitality of Platonism and Other Essays*, ed. Adela Marion Adam (Cambridge, 1911), pp. 77-103;

of the universe; *pneuma*,[25] the fiery breath of life, the creative fire; or *tonos*, the vital tension holding each thing together within itself and making the whole universe cohere.[26] The entire universe, or God, constitutes one living organism, at the same time sentient, rational, and material, existing in and of itself. The universe is its own creative force and its own source of growth, change, and activity. God, or the universe, is not only its own cause; it is the one cause and explanation of all things.[27]

In explaining how the universe is organized, the Stoics draw upon ideas taken from their predecessors and contemporaries and combine them with insights of their own.[28] From Heraclitus they appropriate the notion of a cyclical cosmology in which the world repeatedly undergoes an *ekpyrosis* and a *diakosmesis*, a conflagration and then a reconstitution or recreation of itself.[29] All things, therefore, change, although the process itself is eternal; and there is an economy of matter and energy within the system. In the *diakosmesis* part of the cycle, God, the creative fire, generates air, which generates water, which generates earth.[30] Then God, the creative fire, the active principle, acts upon the other elements, which are passive in relation to fire, arranging them in the mixtures which make up the individual beings in the natural order.[31] The fact that the Stoics

---

Émile Bréhier, *Études de philosophie antique* (Paris, 1955), pp. 163-65; Wilhelm Kelber, *Die Logoslehre von Heraklit bis Origines* (Stuttgart, 1958) pp. 44-88.

[25] The basic authority on this subject is Verbeke, *L'Évolution de la doctrine du pneuma*. On the cosmic aspects of the *pneuma* see also Joseph Moreau, *L'Âme du monde de Platon aux Stoïciens* (Paris, 1939), esp. pp. 158-86; Gerald H. Rendall, "Immanence, Stoic and Christian," *Harvard Theological Review, 14* (1921), 1-14. On *tonos* see Timothy M. Murphy, "Early Stoic Teleology," (Harvard University Ph.D. diss., 1970), pp. 106-114.

[26] *SVF, 1,* 99, 563; *2,* 407, 439, 442, 444, 447-50, 453, 863.

[27] *SVF, 1,* 89; *2,* 341, 346a, 1021.

[28] Two good general expositions of Stoic cosmology are Émile Bréhier, "La cosmologie Stoïcienne à la fin du paganisme," *Revue de l'histoire des religions, 64* (1911), 1-20 and G.-L. Duprat, "La Doctrine stoïcienne du monde, du destin, et de la providence d'après Chrysippe," *AGP, 23,* n.F. 16 (1910), 472-511. On the Greek backgrounds of Stoic cosmology see J. Baudry, *Le problème de l'origine et de l'eternité du monde dans la philosophie grecque de Platon à l'ère chrétienne* (Paris, 1931), esp. pp. 230-95, who errs, however, in regarding the Stoics as dualists; Charles Mugler, *Deux thèmes de la cosmologie grecque: Devenir cyclique et pluralité des mondes* (Paris, 1953), pp. 13-84. The debate over the sources of Stoic physics and cosmology still continues. Reacting against the view of Stoic physics as a throwback to pre-Socratic thought and stressing the debts of the Stoics to contemporary scientific writers is David E. Hahm, *The Origins of Stoic Cosmology* (Columbus, 1977). This view is supported by Michael Lapidge, "*Archai* and *Stoicheia*: A Problem in Stoic Cosmology," *Phronesis, 18* (1973), 240-78; "Stoic Cosmology," in *The Stoics,* ed. Rist, pp. 161-85. Todd, "Monism and Immanence," ibid., p. 138 emphasizes the eclecticism of the Stoics and their departures from Platonic and Aristotelian physics; A. A. Long, "Heraclitus and Stoicism," *Philosophia, 5-6* (1975-76), 133-56 reasserts the importance of the Heraclitean contribution.

[29] *SVF, 1,* 98, 102, 107, 109, 497; *2,* 310, 413a, 413b, 418, 421, 432, 498, 510-11, 558, 591, 593, 598, 606-07, 620, 625-26, 944.

[30] *SVF, 1,* 102, 171, 495; *2,* 405-06, 413, 1027.

[31] *SVF, 1,* 85, 102-04, 496; *2,* 411, 413, 418, 421, 432, 483, 555.

see the elements as generated out of fire in a particular sequence does not imply for them a chain of being in which some elements are metaphysically less real than others. For all the elements can change into other elements and do so. The elements, for all the Stoics except Posidonius,[32] are also capable of mutual interpenetration, or *krasis*, so that two units of matter may permeate each other, each retaining its own character, while both occupy the same space at the same time.[33] This is a process which may occur at any point during the cosmic cycle. The universe is made up of an eternally changing sequence of concrete individual events, of individual things in process. But change, for the Stoics, is not a sign of the imperfection of nature in comparison with God. The universe changes continually, and so does God; for God is the universe. In the Stoics' view, process is a sign of vitality, not a sign of incompletely realized being. At all points in the cosmic cycle, the *logos* is equally present in the universe; and the universe enjoys an equal plenitude and perfection at all times.[34]

In the *ekpyrosis* phase of the cycle, the elements are reabsorbed into fire, moving in a pattern inverse to that of the *diakosmesis*: earth becomes water; water becomes air; air becomes fire. The universe is consumed by the divine fire, a conflagration which the Stoics do not see as a destruction but as a recreation. The *ekpyrosis* requires the existence of space outside the universe, since, as the Stoics note, heat causes matter to expand. While internally the universe is a plenum, and local motion is accomplished by one unit of infinitely divisible matter impinging upon another, the universe as a whole is surrounded by the void.[35] The Stoics are among the few ancient philosophers who felt really comfortable with the idea of infinite space. The Stoics posit the existence of the void because it is necessary for the cosmic conflagration. Predictably, Panaetius,[36] and probably Posidonius,[37] the only Stoics who reject the idea of a cyclical cosmology, also reject the idea of the void which is correlative to it.

The void exists, for the Stoics, but of course it is immaterial. The void is a member of a group of entities which the Stoics call "incorporeals," a group which also includes space, time, and meanings (*lekta*).[38] The

---

[32] Edelstein-Kidd, frag. F96.

[33] *SVF*, 2, 463–81, 485, 486–87; Robert B. Todd, ed., *Alexander of Aphrodisias on Stoic Physics: A Study of the De mixtione with Preliminary Essays, Text, Translation and Commentary* (Leiden, 1976).

[34] *SVF*, 2, 584.

[35] *SVF*, 1, 94–97; 2, 522–24, 534–46.

[36] Van Straaten, frags. 64–69.

[37] Edelstein-Kidd, frags. F97a, F97b.

[38] A good study is Émile Bréhier, "La théorie des incorporels dans l'ancien stoïcisme," *AGP*, 22, n.F. 15 (1909), 114–25. On particular incorporeals see Victor Goldschmidt, *Le*

incorporeals are somewhat anomolous, an anomaly which the Stoics recognize and try to circumvent by saying that, unlike material beings, they do not exist, but merely subsist.[39] The nature of the void is self-defining. Its function, as noted above, is to provide room for the expansion of the universe during the cosmic conflagration. *Lekta,* or meanings, are defined as the intellectual intentions behind men's thoughts and words.[40] They are distinguished from thoughts and words themselves, which are material, and from the external realities which thoughts and words represent, which are likewise material. *Lekta* have a purely intramental existence. They play an important role in Stoic logic, where we will meet them again in more detail below. Space and time, for the Stoics, are purely neutral qualities which are defined by the bodies which exist and act within them. Space is conceivable only in terms of the exterior dimensions of bodies; they define it, not vice versa. Time is defined as the interval of movement. Only present time actually subsists, although our language permits us in the present to speak of past and future time.[41] Time is simply a way of registering what bodies do, but in no sense does it cause anything to happen. The point that the Stoics seem to be making in their doctrine of the incorporeals is that bodies themselves possess their own inner rationale for their existence, extension, and activity. It is their inner *tonos* which accounts for their operations, not the presence of abstract, ideal, or quantifiable entities lying outside of them.

Following the traditional cosmology of their era, the Stoics hold that the cosmos is arranged in a geocentric order, with the sun, the planets, and the stars revolving around the earth in fixed spherical orbits, the whole universe being symmetrical and spherical in shape.[42] Their doctrines of *tonos* and *pneuma,* however, give a dynamic force to this theory. At the outside edge of the cosmos, just before the beginning of the void, lies a band of *aether,* a rarefied combination of fire and air. Some of the *aether* condenses to form the heavenly bodies. What keeps the heavenly bodies in their orbits and prevents them from flying off into the void is the cosmic *tonos* or *pneuma,* an effluvium emanating from the center of the earth, which nourishes the stars and planets and which exerts upon them a power analogous to the functions of gravity and centripetal force, al-

---

système stoïcien et l'idée de temps, 2me éd. (Paris, 1969); A. A. Long, "Language and Thought in Stoicism," in *Problems in Stoicism,* ed. A. A. Long (London, 1971), pp. 90-104.

[39] *SVF, 1,* 93-95; *2,* 331, 501-02, 511, 514.

[40] *SVF, 1,* 488; *2,* 132, 166, 168, 170, 181, 183, 335. See also Andreas Graeser, "A propos *huparchein* bei den Stoikern," *Archiv für Begriffsgeschichte, 15* (1971), 299-305.

[41] *SVF, 2,* 509, 511, 517. On this point see A. C. Lloyd, "Activity and Description in Aristotle and the Stoa," Dawes-Hicks Lecture on Philosophy, 1970, *Proceedings of the British Academy,* 61 (1971), 8-16.

[42] *SVF, 1,* 99; *2,* 547, 558, 582-83.

though this power is always to be understood in a vitalistic sense. The model for cosmology in the Stoa is clearly a biological one.

Just as the universe as a whole has *tonos, pneuma,* and *logos* holding it together, so each individual thing in the universe has its own *tonos, pneuma,* and *logos,* regulating its physical and metaphysical metabolism, so to speak, keeping it within its own skin, and accounting for its vital functions. All things are thus related to the cosmic *pneuma* and to each other, since *tonos* and *pneuma* are the same whether operating on a cosmic level or on the level of the individual being. This force operates differently, however, in different kinds of creatures. Inorganic nature is vivified by *hexis,* organic nature by *physis,* and man by *psyche.* Between *psyche,* on the one hand, and *hexis* and *physis* on the other, the Stoics draw a sharp distinction, which is qualitative and not merely quantitative. *Psyche* alone is rational, being a fragment of the divine *logos.* According to the Stoics, animals have no rational faculty whatsoever.[43] They are radically distinct from man, and there is no basis for any kind of moral community between the two.[44]

2. *Psychology*

Man's *logos* is described by the Stoics as his *hegemonikon,* or ruling principle. It is consubstantial with the divine *logos.* Just as the divine *logos* permeates and orders the whole universe, so the human *logos* or *pneuma* permeates man's entire being and accounts for all of his activities.[45] The psychology of the ancient Stoa, like the physics of which it is an aspect, is monistic.[46] It is based on the doctrine of the *pneuma.* The *pneuma* in man, as in the universe, is a warm breath, a combination of the elements of air and fire. Most of the Stoics teach that it arises as an effluvium from the blood. Some of them make its physiological seat the heart; others locate it in the brain.[47] This concern with the physical seat of the human *pneuma* parallels the Stoics' tendency to locate the cosmic *pneuma* preem-

---

[43] *SVF,* 2, 725; 3, 219-20, 337-39, 367-76.

[44] An excellent study of this point which contrasts the Stoic view incisively with that of Aristotelianism is C. O. Brink, "*Oikeiosis* and *oikeiotes*: Theophrastus and Zeno on Nature in Moral Theology," *Phronesis, 1* (1956), 123-45.

[45] *SVF, 1,* 134-43, 216-23, 518-26; *2,* 773-89, 823-49; *3,* 544-656.

[46] The basic work is still Ludwig Stein, *Die Psychologie der Stoa,* Berliner Studien für classische Philologie und Archaeologie, 2 (Berlin, 1886), *1.* See also Adolf Bonhöffer, "Zur stoischen Psychologie," *Philologus, 54* (1895), 403-29; Guido Mancini, *L'etica stoica da Zenone a Crisippo* (Padova, 1940), pp. 80-89; Robert Philippson, "Zur Psychologie der Stoa," *RM,* n.F. *86* (1937), 140-79; Karl Schindler, *Die stoische Lehre von den Seelenteilen und Seelenvermögen inbesondere bei Panaitios und Poseidonios und ihre Verwendung bei Cicero* (München, 1934); André-Jean Voelke, "L'Unité de l'âme humaine dans l'ancien stoïcisme," *Studia Philosophica, 25* (1965), 154-81.

[47] *SVF, 2,* 836a, 837-39, 842.

inently in one place or another, be it the sun, the center of the earth, or the circumference of the cosmos. The human *pneuma* directs all the activities of mind and body through the faculties of the soul. The ancient Stoics numbered eight parts or faculties of the soul: the five senses, speech, procreation, and the *hegemonikon* or directive *logos*.[48] It is important to note that a mind-body split is inconceivable in this psychology, since one and the same force directs the physical senses and the cognitive and intellectual processes. Strictly speaking, there are no irrational faculties in man. The Stoics admit the existence of instincts, such as the instinct for self-preservation. But neither instinctual nor sensuous behavior is explained as arising from the body, as distinct from the *logos*. Instincts are pre-conscious drives which are on a continuum with conscious rational behavior, and which are transformed into rational behavior when the individual leaves his childhood and enters the age of reason. The senses are controlled by the *hegemonikon*, the same force that controls intellection. The goal of this psychological monism, outside of the fact that it promotes a harmonious analogy between the human microcosm and the cosmic macrocosm, is twofold. In the first place, it enables the Stoics to obliterate the question of whether sensation or reason is the criterion of true knowledge. Secondly, it enables them to argue that an ethics in which reason rules all human behavior is a descriptive ethics as well as a normative one. The implications of the psychology of the ancient Stoa for epistemology and ethics will be explored more fully below.

Considering the centrality of psychological monism to the Stoic system of ethics, it may be surprising to learn that this doctrine was rejected by members of the middle Stoa and by some of the Roman Stoics as well. Panaetius reduces the parts of the soul to six in number, eliminating speech and reproduction. He also holds that the soul has irrational faculties and that the functions of nutrition, growth, and procreation pertain to them.[49] Posidonius also divides the soul into rational and irrational faculties, further subdividing the irrational faculty into two parts, the concupiscible, which seeks pleasure, and the irascible, which seeks power.[50] The influence of Platonic and Aristotelian psychology on the teaching of the middle Stoics is clearly at work. The question remains as to why the middle Stoics admitted the distinction between rational and irrational faculties in man, which Zeno had labored to combat. If we reject the hypothesis that Panaetius and Posidonius were incoherent ec-

---

[48] *SVF*, 2, 836; Diogenes Laertius, *Lives* 7.110, 7.157; Graeser, *Zenon*, p. 68.

[49] Van Straaten, frags. 85-89. See also Van Straaten, "Notes on Panaetius' Theory of the Constitution of Man," *Images of Man in Ancient and Medieval Thought: Studia Gerardo Verbeke* (Leuven, 1976), pp. 93-109.

[50] Edelstein-Kidd, frags. F31-35, F142, F145-46, F148, F152, F157.

lectics, two possibilities remain, which have been suggested with a certain amount of plausibility by recent scholarship on the middle Stoa.[51] One is the idea that they taught the existence of irrational faculties in man simply because this was a conclusion which squared with their own personal observation. The second is that they adopted psychological dualism as a means of defending certain ethical doctrines of the Stoa, wishing in particular to account more convincingly for the origin of the passions than the ancient Stoics had been able to do and to elaborate a more gradualistic approach to the development of virtue. It is certainly true that the ethical strategy of the middle Stoics undergoes a major shift in relation to that of their predecessors. It is also true that their ethical objective remains consistent with that of the ancient Stoa—the submission of all human activities to reason. The ethics of the middle Stoics will be treated in more detail below. If the current interpretation of their philosophy is correct, one may conclude that they are willing to adopt heterodox psychological means to achieve orthodox ethical ends. Seneca and Marcus Aurelius are even more inconsistent. While they refer repeatedly to the all-pervading *logos,* they speak at the same time of the corporality of the soul[52] and its trifold faculties, two of which are irrational;[53] and they describe the body as a fetter or a corpse in which the soul is constrained to reside.[54] But they are as likely to adhere to an ethics flowing from orthodox monism as they are to side with the middle Stoa on ethics; they do not, in effect, show any pressing desire to correlate their ethics systematically with their psychology.[55]

If the nature of the soul was a debated question among the adherents of Stoicism, so also was the question of the soul's posthumous survival.[56] The cyclical cosmology of the Stoa suggested two major possibilities for the fate of the soul after death, each of which was symbolized in classical

---

[51] Edelstein, *Meaning of Stoicism,* pp. 60–70; "The Philos. System of Posidonius," *AJP,* 57 (1936), 213–14; Josiah B. Gould, "Reason in Seneca," *Journal of the History of Philosophy, 3* (1965), 13–25; I. G. Kidd, "Posidonius on Emotion," in *Problems in Stoicism,* ed. Long, pp. 200–14; Laffranque, *Poseidonius,* pp. 64–65, 106, 515–18; B. L. Hijmans, "Posidonius' Ethics," *Acta Classica, 2* (1959), 27–42; Rist, *Stoic Philos.,* pp. 173–98, 201–18; Tatakis, *Panétius,* passim; Van Straaten, *Panétius,* pp. 41–43, 48–52; Eduard Zeller, *Outlines of the History of Greek Philosophy,* 13th ed., ed. Wilhelm Nestle, trans. L. R. Palmer (New York, 1931), p. 249.

[52] Seneca, *Ep.* 106.3–5.

[53] Seneca, *Ep.* 92.1, 92.8; Marcus Aurelius, 3.16, 7.55, 7.57, 12.3, 12.30.

[54] Seneca, *Ep.* 24.17, 65.16, 65.21, 70.17, 79.12, 88.34, 92.13, 92.33–34, 102.26–27, 120.14, 120.16; *Ad Helviam* 11.7; *Ad Marciam* 23.2; *De beneficiis* 3.20.1; Marcus Aurelius, 4.41. See also Epictetus, *Discourses* 1.1.9.

[55] On this whole topic see Verbeke, *L'Évolution de la doctrine du pneuma,* pp. 149–50, 165–71; Hartmut Erbse, "Die Vorstellung von der Seele bei Marc Aurel," *Festschrift für Friedrich Zucker zum 70. Geburtstag* (Berlin, 1954), pp. 127–52.

[56] *SVF, 1,* 134a, 136, 146–47; *2,* 773a, 908; Diogenes Laertius, *Lives* 7.156–57.

antiquity by a myth: the myth of the Phoenix and the myth of Hercules.[57] In the first case, the soul survives after the body's death until the next *ekpyrosis*, at which time it is reabsorbed into the divine fire and its constituent elements are redistributed in the next *diakosmesis*. According to this view, the soul is immortal only in the sense of the eternity of the cosmic process and the economy of matter. The members of the ancient Stoa adhere to this doctrine. Since they reject the idea of the *ekpyrosis* and *diakosmesis*, Panaetius[58] and Posidonius[59] hold that the soul as well as the body return to their constituent elements immediately after death, a view which Epictetus[60] shares although he does not abandon the cyclical cosmology of the ancient Stoa.

The second posthumous alternative, symbolized by the myth of Hercules, is that the great man who perfects his virtue is rewarded by apotheosis. Raised to the level of the gods, he enjoys a celestial immortality. After passing through the fire which liberates his divine soul, he dwells amid the stars with the blessed. This view bears distinct traces of Hellen-

---

[57] On Stoic eschatology see Pierre Benoît, "Les idées de Sénèque sur l'au-delà," *Revue des sciences philosophiques et théologiques*, *32* (1948), 38-51; Cattin, "L'âme humaine," *Latomus*, *15* (1956), 359-65, 544-50; Franz Cumont, *After Life in Roman Paganism* (New Haven, 1922), pp. 77, 82, 98, 103-104, 113-14, 161, 196, 205; *Lux Perpetua* (Paris, 1949), pp. 114-23, 140, 151, 161, 164-70, 201, 235, 304; E. R. Dodds, *Pagan and Christian in an Age of Anxiety: Some Aspects of Religious Experience from Marcus Aurelius to Constantine*, Wiles Lectures, Queen's University, Belfast, 1963 (Cambridge, 1965), pp. 7-11, 131; Döllinger, *Gentile and Jew*, p. 351; René Hoven, *Stoïcisme et stoïciens face au problème de l'au-delà*, Bibliothèque de la Faculté de philosophie et lettres de l'Université de Liège, 197 (Paris, 1971); Roger Miller Jones, "Posidonius and the Flight of the Mind through the Universe," *CP*, *21* (1926), 97-113; Anna Lydia Motto, "Seneca on Death and Immortality," *CJ*, *50* (1955), 187-89; Carlo Pascal, *Le credenze d'oltretomba nelle opere letterarie dell'antichità classica* (Catania, 1912), *1*, 6, 159, 163-64; *2*, 140, 157-58; Erwin Rohde, *Psyche: The Cult of Souls and Belief in Immortality among the Greeks*, 8th ed., trans. W. B. Hillis (London, 1950), pp. 367-504; Paul Schubert, *Die Eschatologie des Poseidonios*, Veröffentlichungen des Forschungsinstitut für vergleichende Religionsgeschichte an der Universität Leipzig, 2:4 (Leipzig, 1927); Verbeke, *L'Évolution de la doctrine du pneuma*, pp. 27-31, 129-30, 150-51.
On the connection between the Stoics' cyclical cosmology, the myth of the Phoenix, and the apotheosis of Hercules by fire, see Mircea Eliade, *The Myth of the Eternal Return*, trans. Willard R. Trask, Bollingen Series, 46 (New York, 1954), pp. 88, 123-24, 131-32; Carl-Martin Edsman, *Ignis Divinus: Le feu comme moyen de rajeunissement et d'immortalité. Contes, légendes, mythes et rites*, Skrifter utgivna av Vetenskaps-Societeten i Lund, 34 (Lund, 1949), pp. 178-203, 233-45; G. Karl Galinsky, *The Herakles Theme: The Adaptations of the Hero in Literature from Homer to the Twentieth Century* (Oxford, 1972), pp. 5, 104, 127-28, 129, 167-84; Jean Hubaux and Maxime Leroy, *Le Mythe du Phénix dans les littératures grecque et latine*, Bibliothèque de la Faculté de philosophie et lettres de l'Université de Liège, 82 (Liège, 1939), passim and esp. pp. 213-52; Gerhart B. Ladner, *The Idea of Reform: Its Impact on Christian Thought and Action in the Age of the Fathers* (Cambridge, Mass., 1959), p. 21 n. 21; R. Van den Broek, *The Myth of the Phoenix according to Classical and Early Christian Traditions*, trans. I. Seeger (Leiden, 1972), pp. 102, 182, 338-39.
[58] Van Straaten, frags. 83-84.
[59] Edelstein-Kidd, frag. F108.
[60] Epictetus, *Disc.* 2.1, 2.17-19, 4.7, 4.15.

istic religion and it is certainly true that the cult of Hercules was not limited to the Stoics. Nevertheless, in revering him as an ideal sage and hero, the Stoics attach particular traits to him. They internalize Hercules' fortitude in overcoming obstacles to signify man's moral triumph over self and the resignation of the wise man in the face of external events. For some Stoics adhering to the cyclical cosmology, Hercules' apotheosis by fire was suggestive of a macrocosmic-microcosmic link between the absorption of the universe into the divine fire and the divinization of the individual. Following this line of thought, Posidonius, Seneca, and Marcus Aurelius teach that the souls of virtuous men enjoy a celestial immortality. The inconsistencies concerning the nature of the soul found in the thought of the latter two figures are paralleled by an even greater inconsistency in the realm of eschatology. Seneca and Marcus Aurelius sometimes argue for the extinction of consciousness along with the death of the body. At other times they argue for various kinds of psychic survival after death, ranging from a postlude only until the next conflagration to a blissful eternity in the company of the deity. Seneca even adds as other possibilities metempsychosis and a purificatory interim between death and the soul's reception into its celestial abode. Both Seneca and Marcus Aurelius quite frankly confess their uncertainly about the truth of the alternatives which they present. The main point that each of them wishes to make is that, regardless of the ultimate destiny of the soul, death is nothing to be feared.[61]

3. *Natural Law,* Logoi Spermatikoi, *Divination, Theodicy, Free Will*

Whatever his views on the future of the soul may be, the Stoic faces death without fear for the same reason that he faces life with an attitude of philosophical optimism. Since the entire universe is governed by the divine *logos,* since, indeed, the universe is identical with the divine *logos,* then the universe, by definition, must be reasonable. The *logos* organizes all things according to the rational laws of nature, in which all events are bound by strict rules of cause and effect. Chance and accident have no place in the Stoic system.[62] The causal nexus in the universe is identified

---

[61] See the references in Motto, *Seneca Sourcebook,* pp. 61-62; Marcus Aurelius, 3.3; also 2.2, 2.17, 5.13, 11.19, 12.5, 12.14.

[62] The most useful general treatments are Walther Eckstein, *Das antike Naturrecht in sozialphilosophischer Beleuchtung* (Wien, 1926), pp. 49-91 for pre-Stoic views and pp. 99-112 on the Stoics; Victor Ehrenberg, "Anfänge des griechischen Naturrechts," *AGP, 35,* n.F. 28 (1928), 119-43; Robert M. Grant, *Miracle and Natural Law in Graeco-Roman and Early Christian Thought* (Amsterdam, 1952), passim and esp. pp. 21-23; Gérard Verbeke, "Aux origines de la notion de 'loi naturelle'," *La filosofia della natura nel medioevo,* Atti del 3° congresso internazionale di filosofia medioevale, Passo della Mendola (Trento), 31 agosto-5 settembre 1964 (Milano, 1966), pp. 164-73. Of more limited usefulness are Raghu-

with both fate and providence;[63] fate, in turn, is rationalized and identified with the good will of the deity.[64]

There are several important corollaries which flow from this key Stoic principle. In the first place, the Stoics note that apparently inexplicable changes occur in nature, which the normal chain of causal relations makes it difficult or impossible to predict. Since the *logos* rules all things, there can be no recourse to chance or accident as a way out of this dilemma. The solution adopted by the Stoics is the doctrine of the *logoi spermatikoi*, the seminal reasons or seeds of the *logos*.[65] These *logoi* contain within themselves the germs of everything they are to become. They account for normal, unexceptional growth and development, as in the case of the human embryo which contains its soul as a seminal reason, to blossom forth as reason itself once the child is born. They also account for exceptional events. In this case, the *logoi spermatikoi* are understood as individual seeds planted by the divine *logos* with a delayed reaction or time bomb effect, triggered to go off at some later date according to a divinely ordained schedule.

The Stoics draw a second corollary from the doctrine of a universal

---

veer Singh, "Heraklitos and the Law of Nature," *JHI, 24* (1963), 457–72, who exaggerates the extent to which the full-blown Stoic view can be found in Heraclitus; Gerald Watson, "The Natural Law and Stoicism," in *Problems in Stoicism*, ed. Long, pp. 217–36, who omits Heraclitus from his survey of pre-Stoic views and who attributes the Stoic theory more to Cicero than to the Stoics themselves; Glenn R. Morrow, "Plato and the Law of Nature," *Essays in Political Theory Presented to George H. Sabine*, ed. Milton R. Konvitz and Arthur E. Murphy (Ithaca, 1948), pp. 17–44, who gives a good exposition of the Stoic view but who sees Plato as its major source. On Aristotle's position in itself and/or compared with that of the Stoics see James Luther Adams, "The Law of Nature in Greco-Roman Thought," *Journal of Religion*, 25 (1945), 107–11; Rudolf Hirzel, *Agraphos nomos*, Abhandlungen der königl. sächsischen Gesellschaft der Wissenschaft, philologisch-historische Klasse, *20*:1 (Leipzig, 1900), 3–4, 7–14, 16–19, 20–98; Joachim Ritter, '*Naturrecht*' *bei Aristoteles: Zum Problem einer Erneuerung des Naturrechts* (Stuttgart, 1961), pp. 14–18; Max Salomon, *Der Begriff der Gerechtigkeit bei Aristoteles nebst einem Anhang über den Begriff des Tauschgeschäftes* (Leiden, 1937), pp. 48–68.

[63] *SVF, 1*, 160, 162a, 162b, 172–77, 548–51; *2*, 580, 913, 916–17, 921, 926, 935, 937, 944, 975, 1106–26. See also Myrto Dragona-Monachou, *The Stoic Arguments for the Existence and Providence of the Gods* (Athens, 1976); G.-L. Duprat, "La Doctrine stöcienne du monde, du destin, et de la providence d'après Chrysippe," *AGP, 23*, n.F. 16 (1910), 472–551.

[64] L. Guillermit and J. Vuillemin, *Le sens du destin* (Neuchâtel, 1948) pp. 35–60 give a good survey of pre-Stoic views of fate in classical literature and philosophy as well as a clear exposition of the Stoic position. Three other good treatments of this topic are Josiah B. Gould, "The Stoic Conception of Fate," *JHI, 35* (1974), 17–32; William Chase Greene, *Moira: Fate, Good, and Evil in Greek Thought* (Cambridge, Mass., 1944), pp. 337–54; Margaret E. Reesor, "Fate and Possibility in Early Stoic Philosophy," *Phoenix, 19* (1965), 285–97; "Necessity and Fate in Stoic Philosophy," in *The Stoics*, ed. Rist, pp. 198–202; Charlotte Stough, "Stoic Determinism and Moral Responsibility," ibid., pp. 203–31.

[65] *SVF, 1*, 87, 101–03, 110–11; *2*, 580, 717. On this point see Hans Meyer, *Geschichte der Lehre von den Keimkräften von der Stoa bis zum Ausgang der Patristik nach den Quellen dargestellt* (Bonn, 1914), pp. 7–26.

law of rational causation. If all things in nature are mutually connected by rational relationships,[66] one should be able to predict what is going to occur in one sector of the universe on the basis of what happens in another sector. In particular, the correspondence between the human microcosm and the universal macrocosm suggested to the Stoics that events in the heavens or phenomena on earth are signs and portents of developments in human affairs. On this basis, the Stoics admit the practice of divination and the study of astrology,[67] thus finding a rationale for accepting these popular religious practices of their time.[68] Posidonius adds the refinement that divination is made possible not only because of the objective correspondences between different parts of the universe but also on the basis of the seer's subjective receptivity. The seer must have a soul in a state of abstraction, which may occur involuntarily during sleep, or which may be induced artificially by concentration, music, and certain kinds of natural surroundings.[69] Two of the Stoics, Epictetus and Panaetius, reject divination, the former on the grounds that it is unnecessary in the light of man's possession of reason, which enables him to judge what to do without recourse to external pointers of any kind,[70] and the latter because he opposes all manifestations of popular religion, holding that the philosopher should have no traffic with it.[71]

Seneca, too, has some harsh words on the futility of sacrifices and other pagan cultic practices which he labels superstitious, insisting that true worship lies rather in self-examination, uprightness, modesty, the acceptance of the universe, and the imitation of God's beneficence.[72] While the Stoics in general wholeheartedly support Seneca's elevated conception of the religious life, Cleanthes adding prayer and the offering of hymns of praise, most Stoics none the less perceive no discrepancy between a philosophical attitude and a stance of accommodation toward popular religion. In addition to the philosophical support which they lend to the practice of divination, the Stoics also achieve a *modus vivendi* with popular religion by allegorizing its divinities and myths. In this the Stoics are by no means alone. There was a lengthy tradition of allegorical exegesis of Homer and Hesiod, developed first by Greek grammarians who aimed at finding a more profound interpretation than that derived from the literal sense of the text. Allegoresis of Greek religion was also

---

[66] *SVF, 1,* 110-11; *2,* 475, 534, 546, 633-45, 912.

[67] *SVF, 1,* 174; *2,* 912, 939, 1189-92.

[68] On divination see A. Bouché-Leclercq, *Histoire de la divination dans l'antiquité* (Bruxelles, 1963 [repr. of Paris, 1897 ed.]), *1,* 31-53 on pre-Stoic views and 58-64 on the Stoics.

[69] Verbeke, *L'Évolution de la doctrine du pneuma,* pp. 126-28.

[70] Epictetus, *Disc.* 2.7.

[71] Van Straaten, frags. 68, 70-71, 73-74.

[72] *Ep.* 95.47-50, 115.5; *De benef.* 1.6.3, 4.25.1.

adopted by believers and philosophers alike. The believers used it against the attacks of rationalizing critics to demonstrate that their faith had a valuable content despite its mythic form. Alternatively, the philosophers used it as a universal solvent with which to dispose of the gods' unedifying behavior so that they could be seen as personifications of philosophical principles. In this way the philosopher could have the best of both worlds; he could find a way of accepting the gods and myths without having to believe in them literally, and he could attach the authority of Homer to his own particular teaching, an advantage well appreciated when those teachings proved controversial. With this aim in mind, the allegorizing philosophers could defend the myths as a first step toward philosophy for the uninstructed. The Stoics' particular aim in their allegoresis was to adjust their conception of a unitary deity and a monist physics to a polytheistic religion. They do this by interpreting the gods and apotheosized heroes as manifestations of the one central God. Also typical of the Stoics' treatment of myth is their use of etymology as an exegetical technique. Despite attacks by proponents of rival outlooks who objected either to the impiety, the superstition, or the specific doctrinal conclusions involved in Stoic allegoresis, it gained many adherents in classical antiquity and served as a bridge between the austerity of the ethics of the Stoics and the spiritual conventions of their milieu.[73] One convention which the Stoics refused to adhere to, however, was the automatic deification of current or recently deceased rulers, a point enlarged on with refreshing wit by Seneca in his *Apocolocyntosis,* in which the emperor Claudius, far from being apotheosized, is pumpkinified, or shown to have been a pumpkin-head all along.

A third important consequence of the Stoic doctrine that all things are ordered by a rational and benevolent God is the need to deal with the problem of evil. Theodicy is a prominent feature of the thought of all the Stoics, but Epictetus' theodicy is the most detailed. The conclusion that the world order is intrinsically rational and good follows, he argues, from the harmoniousness and usefulness of the cosmos and all its parts, and from the adaptive order which it reflects.[74] The Stoics do not resort to the idea that evil is non-being as a corollary of their identification of God and the universe with the good. They admit the existence of evil, but seek to rationalize it. Starting from the premise that the world order is intrinsically good, they argue that good and evil are antithetical. But a

---

[73] The standard authority on this subject is Jean Pépin, *Mythe et allegorie: Les origines grecques et les contestations judéo-chrétiennes* (Paris, 1958), pp. 85-167. See also Rudolf Pfeiffer, *History of Classical Scholarship from the Beginnings to the End of the Hellenistic Age* (Oxford, 1968), pp. 237-44.

[74] Epictetus, *Disc.* 1.6.

thesis presupposes its antithesis. Therefore, evil exists. Evil, however, does not exist in nature; it exists only in man. Since the world is good, nothing that happens in the natural order is evil. Some events may appear to be evil to a mind insufficiently enlightened or to a mind guilty of an erroneous judgment. But all things in nature work for good, and all things will be seen to be good if viewed correctly from the perspective of the whole. Real evil, as contrasted with apparent evil, lies solely in the moral and intellectual order of the human mind. There is no evil in God or in the world itself. All evil stems from human ignorance, error, and vice, and is entirely a consequence of man's free will.

This brings us to the fourth and last corollary of the Stoic physical system. The idea that nothing escapes the causal nexus uniting all events in the universe raises the question of human free will. Given the determinism of the Stoics' world order and its identification with divine providence, in what sense can man be free? It should be noted that free will is an absolute necessity to the Stoic philosophy.[75] Not only is it the sole source of evil, but it is essential if the ethics of the Stoics is to work at all. It might well be argued that no deterministic philosophy has solved this problem satisfactorily. The Stoics are no exception. Their physics forces them to limit free will while their ethics forces them to exalt it. The Stoics attempt to rationalize this dilemma by drawing a distinction between necessity and possibility.[76] Necessity involves a thing's given nature as well as those events that have already taken place, neither of which can be altered in any way. Man has no choice in matters controlled by necessity. However, within the limits of a thing's given nature and history there exists a realm of possibility. Thus, the present and the future admit of some open alternatives, which are contingent on man's choice. The Stoics, following Chrysippus, illustrate this argument with one of their most famous metaphors: A cylinder is at rest. If it is set in motion it will move necessarily in a circular manner, in obedience to its given shape. But whether it is set in motion or not lies within the realm of possibility. So, the Stoics conclude, man is determined by his given nature, but he is free to act in terms of it. Whether this reasoning is convincing or not is a moot point. But the goal of the Stoic doctrine of determinism and free will is to save the divine *logos* as the ruler of the universe while at the same time saving the human *logos*. For the human *logos* is a fragment of the divine *logos*. Unless it possesses the capacity to act autonomously, not only ethics but ultimately physics itself is rendered meaningless.

---

[75] See the excellent recent study by André-Jean Voelke, *L'Idée de volunté dans le stoïcisme* (Paris, 1973).

[76] *SVF*, 2, 956–60, 974, 979, 991, 997, 1000, 1003.

B) Ethics

For the Stoics, ethics is integrally and organically related to physics.[77] The *logos* in man plays the same directive role which the divine *logos* plays in the universe. The Stoics define virtue, the *summum bonum*, as life in accordance with nature, or life in accordance with reason, which is the same thing. Like many other schools of Greek philosophy, Stoicism proposes an ethics of *eudaimonia*. Man, the Stoics hold, is so constructed that he naturally craves the good. Man naturally seeks to be in harmony with nature. Through his possession of the *logos*, man naturally possesses the power to achieve this harmony, the state of virtue. The Stoics see no gap whatever between the ethical fulfillment of the individual, the ethical fulfillment of the entire human race, and the rational law of nature. One of their distinctive contributions is the integration of the universal law of nature with ethics by making it the goal and norm of virtue just as it is the ruling principle of the cosmos. This principle is central to Stoic ethics. Virtually all the ethical teaching of the school flow from it.

1. *Slavery, Sexual Equality*

In the first place, it is inconceivable for the Stoics that there could be any conflict between the good of the individual, the good of the group,

---

[77] Two good general studies are Hans Reiner, "Die ethische Weisheit der Stoiker heute," *Gymnasium, 70* (1969), 330-51, which includes a survey of the literature of the subject, mostly in German, and Geneviève Rodis-Lewis, *La morale stoïcienne* (Paris, 1970). Studies exploring the sources of Stoic ethics include A. A. Long, "Aristotle's Legacy to Stoic Ethics," University of London, Institute of Classical Studies, *Bulletin, 15* (1968), 72-85, who acknowledges the tenuousness of the evidence; Otto Rieth, *Grundbegriffe der stoischen Ethik: Eine traditionsgeschichtliche Untersuchung* (Berlin, 1933); Bohdan Wiśniewski, "Sur les origines du *homologoumenos tê phusei zên* des stoïciens," *Classica et Mediaevalia, 22* (1961), 106-16.

Important topics in Stoic ethics are dealt with by Ernst Grumach, *Physis und Agathon in der alten Stoa* (Berlin, 1932), pp. 1-43; G. B. Kerferd, "The Search for Personal Identity in Stoic Thought," *Bulletin of the John Rylands Library, 55* (1972), 177-96; A. A. Long, "The Stoic Concept of Evil," *Philosophical Quarterly, 18* (1968), 329-43; Helen F. North, *Sophrosyne: Self-Knowledge and Self-Restraint in Greek Literature*, Cornell Studies in Classical Philology, 35 (Ithaca, 1966), pp. 213-31; and, on *oikeiosis*, Nicholas P. White, "The Basis of Stoic Ethics," *HSCP, 83* (1979), 143-78. On the ethics of the middle and Roman Stoa see Arthur Bodson, *La morale sociale des derniers stoïciens: Sénèque, Épictète et Marc Aurèle*, Bibliothèque de la Faculté de philosophie et lettres de l'Université de Liège, 156 (Paris, 1967); Julio Campos, "La educación de la consciencia en Séneca," *Actas del congreso ... en conmemoración de Séneca* (Madrid, 1966), pp. 109-20; I. G. Kidd, "The Relation of Stoic Intermediaries to the *Summum Bonum*, with Reference to Change in the Stoa,"*CQ, 49* (1955), 181-94; Ulrich Knoche, *Magnitudo animi: Untersuchungen zur Entstehung und Entwicklung eines römisches Wertgedanke, Philologus*, Supplementband 27:3 (Leipzig, 1935), 45-86; Rudolf Rieke, *Homo, Humanus, Humanitas: Zur Humanität in der lateinischen Literatur des ersten nachchristlichen Jahrhunderts* (München, 1967), pp. 89-137; Gérard Verbeke, "Ethische paideia in het latere Stoïcisme en het vroege Christendom," *Tijdschrift voor filosofie, 27* (1965), 3-53.

and the good of the universe, for the same *logos* permeates and rules them all. From this premise the Stoics work out a number of distinctive ideas in the field of social and political theory.[78] The *logos* of each man is the *logos* of every man. In their common possession of reason, a fragment of the divine *logos*, all men by nature are equal.[79] On this basis, the Stoics argue that slavery and sexual inequality are contrary to the law of nature. The Stoics' critique of slavery is consistent throughout the history of the school. Some Stoics who owned slaves manumitted them. At the same time, the Stoics do not expressly demand the abolition of slavery as a social institution, contenting themselves with exhortations on the duty to recognize the moral dignity of slaves and to treat them humanely.[80]

The principle of sexual equality is emphasized more by some Stoics than by others. An important model for the Stoics in this area was the ethics of Cynicism. The Cynics argued that men and women should

---

[78] The most important work is Margaret E. Reesor, *The Political Theory of the Old and Middle Stoa* (New York, 1951), pp. 9-60. Also excellent are H. C. Baldry, *The Unity of Mankind in Greek Thought* (Cambridge, 1965), pp. 152-94; "Zeno's Ideal State," *Journal of Hellenic Studies*, 79 (1959), 3-15, although he argues unconvincingly that Zeno's theory was intended as a programmatic reform; Anton-Hermann Chroust, "The Ideal Polity of the Early Stoics: Zeno's Republic," *Review of Politics*, 27 (1965), 173-83; Francis Edward Devine, "Stoicism on the Best Regime," *JHI*, 31 (1970), 323-36; Nicola Festa, *La "Repubblica" di Zenone* (Roma, 1928); John Ferguson, *Utopias of the Classical World* (London, 1975), ch. 13; Manfred Fuhrmann, "Die Alleinherrschaft und das Problem der Gerechtigkeit (Seneca: De clementia)," *Gymnasium*, 70 (1963), 481-514; Maria Józefowicz, "Les Idées politiques dans la morale stoïcienne de Marc-Aurèle," *Eos*, 59 (1971), 341-51; Fritz-Joachim von Rintelin, "Lucius Annaeus Seneca über die 'Einheit des Menschengeschechtes'," *Zeitschrift für philosophische Forschung*, 19 (1965), 563-76; G. R. Stanton, "The Cosmopolitan Ideas of Epictetus and Marcus Aurelius," *Phronesis*, 13 (1968), 183-95. D. Babut, "Les Stoïciens et l'amour," *Revue des études grecques*, 76 (1963), 55-63 argues correctly against opposing scholars that the Stoics tolerated homosexuality as one of the *adiaphora*, not necessarily because they wished to attack traditional matrimony. B.-L. Hijmans, "Sénèque et les arts libéraux, un chapitre dans l'histoire du déclin de l'ancien stoïcisme," *Actes du VIIe congrès de l'Assoc. Guillaume Budé*, pp. 258-60 correctly interprets Seneca's criticism of the liberal arts as a return to ancient Stoic thought. His analysis is supported by Giancarlo Mazzoli, *Seneca e la poesia*, Pubblicazioni della Facoltà di lettere e filosofia dell'Università di Pavia, Istituto di letteratura latina (Milano, 1970), pp. 9-18. For the views of other Stoics on this point see G. Pire, *Stoïcisme et pédagogie de Zénon à Marc-Aurèle, de Sénèque à Montaigne et à J.-J. Rousseau* (Liège, 1958), pp. 19-161.

Scholars have debated the relation between the Stoic idea of the cosmopolis and Hellenistic thought. J. Bidez, "La Cité du monde et la cité du soleil chez les Stoïciens," *Bulletins de l'Académie royale de Belgique*, classe des lettres, 5e sér., *18*:7-9 (Paris, 1932), 244-91 thinks that the Stoic theory was influenced by Persian and Chaldean astrology. W. W. Tarn, *Alexander the Great and the Unity of Mankind*, Proceedings of the British Academy, 19 (London, 1933), pp. 3-26 thinks that the idea originated with Alexander who drew on Isocrates and the theory of Hellenistic kingship; Tarn is supported by Adams, "Law of Nature," *Journal of Religion*, 25 (1945), 109. Festugière, *La révélation d'Hermès Trismégiste*, 2, 176, 188-89, 195, 264-66 restores the credit to Zeno.

[79] *SVF*, 3, 215, 314, 317, 319, 333, 339.

[80] *SVF*, 3, 351.

wear the same kind of clothing and receive the same kind of education. They also taught that marriage should be seen as a moral companionship between equals and not merely as a biological and economic necessity, views which they put into practice in their own personal lives as well as in their teaching. The Stoics adopted the Cynic position and linked it to their own theory of human nature.[81] In this way they gave their sexual egalitarianism a much more solid philosophical foundation. None the less, although he was influenced by Cynic ethics, Zeno adheres to the Platonic doctrine of the community of wives,[82] despite its obvious incompatibility with the moral equality of the sexes. Chrysippus drops Zeno's sexual communism and it does not reappear in the teachings of the Stoa after his time. The Stoics' general tendency to internalize the virtues, making them human and not merely masculine possibilities, coupled with Panaetius' elaboration of rules for the application of ethical principles to all kinds of people, strengthened the case for sexual equality. But it is the Roman Stoa which presents the best developed teaching on this subject, both in theory and in practice. Seneca and Musonius Rufus develop such themes as the equal capacity for virtue and the equal moral obligations which nature gives to men and women, arguing that the sexes share an equal need for philosophical education and attacking any notion of a double standard.[83] Seneca couples the theory with a practical concern for the moral cultivation of women, addressing consolation and spiritual direction to a number of women in his circle of friends and relations.

2. *The Cosmopolis, the Active and the Contemplative Life, Friendship*

The idea that all men share in the common possession of reason also means, for the Stoics, that all men by nature have moral obligations to each other. All men form a natural moral community of rational beings. In ideal terms this community is a cosmopolis transcending all existing social and political configurations.[84] In practical terms, this doctrine gives Stoic ethics an inescapable social dimension. On the social and political level, according to the Stoics, natural law entails duties, not

---

[81] *SVF*, *1*, 257; *3*, 253; Clement of Alexandria, *Stromateis* 4.8, ed. D. Nicolai le Nourry in *Patrologia graeca*, 8, ed. J. P. Migne (Paris, 1857).

[82] *SVF*, *1*, 269.

[83] Seneca, *Ep.* 94.26; *De benef.* 2.18.1; *Ad Marciam* 16.1–2; Lutz, "Musonius Rufus," no. 3–4, 12, pp. 38–48, 84–88. Good discussions are provided by Edelstein, *Meaning of Stoicism*, pp. 73–75; Favez, "Un féministe romain," *Bull. de la soc. des Études de Lettres de Lausanne, 8* (1933), 1–8; A. L. Motto, "Seneca on Women's Liberation," *CW, 65* (January, 1962), 155–57. C. E. Manning, "Seneca and the Stoics on the Equality of the Sexes," *Mnemosyne*, ser. 4:*26* (1973), 170–77 argues unconvincingly that Seneca held women to be morally inferior to men.

[84] *SVF*, *1*, 262–63; *3*, 323, 333, 340, 342, 369.

rights. The failure of the spotted reality to correspond with the ideal cosmopolis is never used by any Stoic as a justification for civil disobedience or revolution. Nor is social reform a particularly burning issue for members of the school. The fact that society is far from perfect does not obliterate the duty of the sage to serve it.[85] In contrast to Aristotelianism, which sees participation in civic life as a means to the actualization of virtue, Stoicism sees service to society as a duty incumbent upon the sage, whose wisdom and virtue are already perfectly realized.

In the ideal cosmopolis there are few institutions.[86] They are not needed, for in this state men function in terms of their natural reason. Therefore, the cosmopolis has no need of law courts, the coinage of money, schools, temples, or gymnasia. To the extent that any leadership is necessary it is supplied by the sages, at least for those Stoics who do not assume that all citizens of the cosmopolis are sages *ipso facto*. Natural reason enables the dwellers in the cosmopolis to throw off the shackles of conventions which have no basis in reason. Sexual needs may therefore be met in whatever manner pleases the individual, including prostitution, incest, masturbation, and homosexuality. Adultery is the only sexual practice at which the Stoics draw the line.[87] Musonius Rufus is the only member of the school who dissents from its sexual latitudinarianism. The only sexual acts which Musonius regards as virtuous are those engaged in by spouses for the purpose of procreation.[88] Cannibalism is admitted by some ancient Stoics as a perfectly reasonable and sanitary way of disposing of the dead.[89] Chrysippus even holds it permissible to urinate in rivers and public fountains,[90] although he can scarcely justify this practice on hygienic grounds. In addition to advancing the idea of a cosmopolis with relatively unconventional morés, most Stoics also adhere to a theory of the Golden Age,[91] whose outlines are quite similar to those of the ideal cosmopolis. From the extant evidence, however, it is not clear whether they see an integral connection between these two doctrines.

The mutual natural obligations which constitute the ideal cosmopolis are also incumbent on the Stoic in this imperfect world. The sage has a natural duty to serve his fellow man, a duty which may be performed by

---

[85] *SVF*, 3, 611, 616, 628.

[86] *SVF*, 1, 146, 262, 264-68.

[87] On sexual ethics in general see *SVF*, 1, 249-51, 254-56, 285; 3, 745, 753, 755; Diogenes Laertius, *Lives* 7.118; Sextus Empiricus, *Against the Ethicists* 3.190-192; on adultery see *SVF*, 3, 729.

[88] Lutz, "Musonius Rufus," no. 12, p.86.

[89] *SVF*, 1, 254, 256; 3, 685, 744, 747, 753; Sextus Empiricus, *Against the Ethicists* 3.192-194.

[90] *SVF*, 3, 754.

[91] Sextus Empiricus, *Against the Physicists* 1.28.

participating in civic affairs or by withdrawal into the contemplative life, or by a combination or alternation of both of these styles of life.[92] The ancient Stoics place more emphasis on the sage's commitment to the active life. The sage should engage in politics, they argue, irrespective of the form of government under which he lives. The Stoics do not consistently advocate the superiority of one form of government over another. Some prefer a republic, some a monarchy, and others a mixed government.[93] The main importance attaching to the constitution of a given state in which a sage may happen to dwell is that it provides parameters which indicate the type of public service in which he should engage. Individual Stoics, as is known from their biographies, acted as public officials in polities ranging from republics to tyrannies. Indeed, they served as counsellors to kings more frequently and successfully than did members of any other ancient school of philosophy.[94]

The sage may also fulfill his obligations to his fellow man by leading a life of retirement and philosophical contemplation. He also serves who contemplates, for the contemplative shares the fruits of his insights with others, instructing, exhorting, consoling, and guiding his fellows. The Stoic who places the heaviest emphasis on the contemplative life is Seneca. He shares the orthodox position urging participation in public affairs, but he has little to say about public service and does not discuss it at length. On the other hand, he devotes a great deal of attention to the virtues of retirement. Seneca restates the orthodox view of the choice between the active and contemplative life as basically a matter of indifference, agreeing that both are conducive to virtue and to the service of others. But he takes pains to underline the attractions of the contemplative life, noting, among its more traditional assets, that it enables the sage to remove himself from the company of vicious men, especially those in authority,[95] a position which no doubt reflects the tensions of his own personal career as well as his opinion of what constitutes good advice to the individuals to whom he addresses his works. The dominant note in Marcus Aurelius' treatment of this theme, on the other hand, is the overriding duty to serve society. Even though the exercise of this commitment to public service may be a living martyrdom, Marcus describes the man who would flee from it as a criminal.[96]

---

[92] This point has been well treated by R.-A. Gauthier, *Magnanimité: L'Idéal de la grandeur dans la philosophie païenne et dans la théologie chrétienne* (Paris, 1951), pp. 129-30; Alberto Grilli, *Il problema della vita contemplativa nel mondo greco-romano* (Roma, 1953), pp. 89-164.

[93] *SVF, 1,* 269; *3,* 700, 728.

[94] Dudley, *Cynicism,* p. 69.

[95] Seneca, *Ep.* 19-20, 22.11-12, 68.1-2, 73.1-16; *De otio* 1.4-4.2, 6.1-5; *De brevitate vitae* 14.3-20.5.

[96] Marcus Aurelius, 4.29; also 3.5, 6.2, 6.7, 7.5, 9.12, 9.16, 9.23, 9.31, 11.4, 11.21, 12.20.

Whichever career the sage chooses, the Stoics insist on his obligation to marry, to raise a family, and to work. Marriage and family life, they argue, are in no sense impediments to the cultivation of virtue. Marriage and the family are natural states, and hence good. All Stoics agree on this point, but Musonius Rufus gives it the most extensive treatment. The moral community shared by two spouses in a companionship of equals is enhanced by the presence of children. Musonius adds the thought that family life, especially in a large family, is a school for virtue.[97] Work, likewise, receives a strongly positive valuation as a social virtue. Rather than seeing physical labor as degrading, as a necessary evil which distracts the individual from the quest of virtue, the Stoics regard it as dignified, natural, and compatible with virtue. Work is a means of serving others as well as a means of exercising one's own ethical integrity.[98] Their own Cleanthes the water-carrier serves as the Stoics' model for the moral perfection of the workman-philosopher. Conceivably, the positive value which they place on manual labor is one of the reasons why the Stoics appealed to Hercules as an ideal hero. The Roman Stoics regard farming and animal husbandry as the most appropriate kinds of work, and praise great men such as Scipio Africanus and Quinctius Cincinnatus who did not hesitate to labor on their own lands.[99]

A final index of the sage's capacity for social virtue is his capacity for friendship. Friendship represents a particularly distilled form of the rational communion among men which the anthropology of the Stoa makes available in general. For the Stoics, true friendship is a relationship between the wise, wisdom and virtue being prerequisites for it.[100] Friends enjoy a perfect meeting of minds, sharing the same values and goals and enriching each other's lives in a completely unexploitative way. Friendship is a freely chosen state reflecting a delight in rational companionship; it is not a means of gratifying or expressing man's instinctual needs. Of all the Stoics, Seneca develops the theme of friendship in most detail; and he exemplifies his teaching in his epistolary relationship with his correspondent Lucilius. Seneca modifies the orthodox doctrine somewhat by departing from the idea that friends must be fully perfected sages. While agreeing that friendship is a good *per se* rather than a means to an end, he thinks that friends should help each other as teachers, counselors, and guides in virtue.[101]

---

[97] Lutz, "Musonius Rufus," no. 13-15, pp. 88-96.
[98] This point has been discussed sensitively by Edelstein, *Meaning of Stoicism*, pp. 75-80.
[99] Lutz, "Musonius Rufus," no. 11, pp. 80-84; Seneca, *Ep.* 86.5; *De brev. vit.* 17.6.
[100] *SVF, 3,* 631.
[101] For Seneca on friendship see Wolfgang Brinckmann, *Der Begriff der Freundschaft in*

3. *Vice and Virtue, the Passions,* Apatheia

Conformity to the rational law of nature entails a moral relationship with other men, for the Stoics. It likewise entails the harmonizing of the self with the outside world of nature. All events in nature are good, and man must use his reason to acknowledge this fact and to adjust himself to it.[102] No evil stems from nature. Evil has one cause only, human vice. Vice in turn springs from the passions—pleasure, pain, fear, and desire—which divert man away from the good.[103] In order to avoid evil it is therefore necessary to achieve a state of *apatheia,* in which the *logos* frees man from the power of the passions.[104] Stoic *apatheia* is not a state of *anaesthesia* in which the subject feels nothing at all. The Stoics hold that some emotions, such as benevolence, mercy, sympathy, and the sober joys of friendship, are good, because they are rational passions,[105] consistent with the duties and relationships which flow from the *logos.*[106] They aim at substituting these *eupatheia,* or good emotions, for the morally negative passions.

One of the major cruxes in Stoic philosophy, and a topic on which there is considerable change from the ancient to the middle Stoa, is this question of the passions. In the monistic psychology of the ancient Stoa, there is no explanation for the existence of the passions, since all the faculties of the soul are permeated by the rational *pneuma*. The passions, thus, are not merely sub-natural but anti-natural. Ontologically they should have no status at all. Yet they clearly exist. The ancient Stoics argue that the passions arise from false judgments, in which the intellect errs in perceiving the nature and value of its objects.[107] Pleasure and

---

Senecas Briefen (Köln, 1963); U. Knoche, "Der Gedanke der Freundschaft in Senecas Briefen an Lucilius," *Commentationes in honorem Edwin Linkomies sexagenarii A.D. MCMLIV editae,* Arctos: Acta philologica fennica, n.s. 1 (Helsinki, 1954), pp.83-96; Marcos F. Manzanedo, "La amistad humana, vista por Séneca," *Estudios sobre Séneca: Ponencias y comunicaciones,* Octava semana española di filosofía (Madrid, 1966), pp. 200-17; Rudolf Schottlaender, "Epikureisches bei Seneca: Ein ringen um den Sinn von Freude und Freundschaft," *Philologus, 99* (1955), 133-48.

[102] *SVF, 1,* 155, 179-81, 186-89, 202, 552, 555; *3,* 4-9, 12-16, 38-67, 44, 124-26, 140, 180-81, 188-89, 197-244.

[103] *SVF, 1,* 211; *2,* 378, 381, 386, 391, 412, 444; *3,* 412.

[104] *SVF, 1,* 422, 434, 499; *3,* 144, 201, 448. Good discussions of this point are provided by A. C. Lloyd, "Emotion and Decision in Stoic Psychology," in *The Stoics,* ed. Rist, pp. 233-46; John M. Rist, "The Stoic Concept of Detachment," ibid., pp. 259-72.

[105] *SVF, 3,* 431-32, 499.

[106] Edelstein, *Meaning of Stoicism,* pp. 3-4; Richard P. Haynes, "The Theory of Pleasure of the Old Stoa," *AJP, 83* (1962), 412-19; Nicholas P. White, "Two Notes on Stoic Terminology," *AJP, 99* (1978), 115-19.

[107] *SVF, 1,* 202, 206-09; *2,* 115; *3,* 61, 202a, 412; Diogenes Laertius, *Lives* 7.92-93. See also A. A. Long, "The Early Stoic Concept of Moral Choice," *Images of Man in Ancient and Medieval Thought,* pp. 77-92.

pain arise from false judgments about man's experience in the present; fear and desire arise from false judgments about what to expect in the future. This argument raises a further question: Why is it that man makes false judgments? The reply of the ancient Stoics is that a man makes false judgments because he is influenced by the bad example of the unenlightened people around him.[108] This answer merely pushes the question one step further back: What causes the people giving bad example to make the erroneous judgments which they make? To this question the ancient Stoics have no answer, so there is no point in pressing them for one. What is perhaps most striking about the ancient Stoic treatment of the origin of the passions is not its adequacy but its drive to assimilate the origins of vice to the human intellect. Since the passions arise entirely from intellectual error, they are within the jurisdiction of reason, for reason possesses the capacity to make correct judgments about moral values and thus to substitute virtue for vice. The *logos* can do this if it so chooses. By a single massive act of will it can alter its moral stance. Stoic ethics is as much an ethics of will as it is an ethics of reason.

If indeed the *logos*, which has the capacity to identify and to reject false judgments, wills to do so, a correct level of *tonos* will be established within the individual. The negative passions will lose their power and virtue will result. This idea has two important implications in Stoic ethics. In the first place, it means that virtue is essentially a consistent orientation or state of being on the part of the mind and will, created by a healthy *tonos*. Vice likewise is a consistent state of being created by a flabby or poorly functioning *tonos*, which allows the passions to betray the mind into error. Virtue and vice, for the Stoa, are not a collection of deeds; they are states of being reflecting fixed intentionalities.[109] On the basis of this view the Stoics achieve a radical internalizing of ethics. Although virtue ought to express itself in outward acts, ethics deals primarily with inner motivations, motivations which lie fully within man's conscious control.

The necessary connection between act and intentionality is reflected in the way the Stoics view the virtues. They adhere to the four traditional cardinal virtues, prudence, courage, temperance, and justice, but conceive of them in a distinctive way.[110] For the Stoics, the preeminent virtue is prudence (*phronesis*). Stoic *phronesis* unites the manner of virtue with the matter of virtue; it is a synthesis between practical and specu-

---

[108] *SVF, 3*, 228.

[109] *SVF, 1*, 249, 254–56, *3*, 3, 16, 44, 75, 504, 517, 744–46.

[110] *SVF, 1*, 200–01; *3*, 262–94. On this point see Helen F. North, "Canons and Hierarchies of the Cardinal Virtues in Greek and Latin Literature," *The Classical Tradition: Literary and Historical Studies in Honor of Harry Caplan*, ed. Luitpold Wallach (Ithaca, 1966), pp. 174–78.

lative wisdom.[111] Courage is the correct judgment as to what must be endured. Temperance is the correct judgment in the choice of things. Justice is the correct judgment in the use of things. All the virtues are thus consequences of man's inner intellectual judgments.

This point leads the Stoics to an important conclusion. What is ethically relevant is what man can control. Through his *logos* man can control his subjective attitudes toward things. What lies outside man's control is ethically irrelevant. Thus, all things fall into one of three categories: the good, defined as virtue, and sufficient unto itself; the evil, defined as vice and all things conducive to it; and the *adiaphora*, or everything else.[112] The *adiaphora* are morally neutral, since they lie outside man's rational control. Loosely speaking, the *adiaphora* include the vicissitudes of life—wealth or poverty, sickness or health, life or death, etc. Some of the *adiaphora* may be preferable to others; health, for instance, is preferable to illness. But strictly speaking, the sage maintains an attitude of equanimity in the face of the presence or absence of things indifferent. His happiness is not dependent on them, but on virtue alone. Stoic *apatheia* is thus another way of describing the consistent state of being which enables man to be virtuous. *Apatheia* is not virtue but is a necessary precondition for it. It does not denote a state of passivity but the detachment from things evil and indifferent which gives the sage the moral liberty to judge and to act rightly.

There is a second important corollary of the Stoic definition of virtue as a correct state of the *tonos* in man or as a consistent inner disposition. Since vice and virtue result from consistent states of being, all vices are equally vicious and all virtues are equally virtuous.[113] There are no grades of either vice or virtue. The sage possesses all virtues; the fool possesses all vices.[114] To possess one vice or one virtue is to possess them all, for vice and virtue are not a congeries of individual acts but expressions of unified, consciously determined states of being. Thus both vice and virtue are all-or-nothing propositions. For the ancient Stoa there is scarcely any possibility of a gradual change from folly to wisdom or vice versa.[115] The moral life is not a question of piecemeal effort or habituation to the good. If the fool sees the light and chooses to shed his vicious orientation, he can experience an instant conversion to wisdom. Since

---

[111] A good discussion of this point is P. Aubenque, "La 'phronésis' chez les stoïciens," *Actes du VIIe congrès de l'Assoc. Guillaume Budé*, pp. 291–92.

[112] *SVF, 1,* 191–96, 230–32, 239, 559–62; *3,* 71, 117–58, 491–423.

[113] *SVF, 1,* 224–25; *3,* 524–43.

[114] *SVF, 1,* 216, 226–29; *3,* 544–688. For various paradoxes concerning the sage see *SVF, 1,* 122, 220–21, 223a; *3,* 613, 615, 618–23.

[115] Some possibility of moral progress is suggested by Zeno, *SVF, 1,* 234; *3,* 530–43.

the fool's *logos* is not in harmony with nature, nothing he does is good; since the sage's *logos* is in conformity with nature, everything he does will be good automatically. A great many of the paradoxes regarding the sage which the ancient Stoics put forth and which their enemies delighted in attacking spring from this line of reasoning. Given the psychology of the ancient Stoa its position is consistent. It carries to new heights the Socratic identification of virtue with knowledge and the Greek tendency to internalize ethics which had been going on for some time. Concurrently, however, ancient Stoic ethics leaves unresolved the problem of the origin of the passions; and some of its conclusions are hard to defend, especially if taken out of context.

The alterations which the middle Stoa imposes on the ethics of the ancient Stoa may be seen as attempts to deal with these problems, and to soften the rigor of the orthodox position in some respects. The psychology adopted by Panaetius and Posidonius enables them to find an origin for the passions in man's irrational faculties. While their psychology aims at being descriptive, their ethics remains normative. While man possesses irrational faculties by nature, they argue, reason alone remains his moral ego and the sole criterion of virtue. Panaetius and Posidonius differ significantly in the way that they relate their psychological dualism to ethical monism. Following Plato, Panaetius holds that the irrational faculties may produce energies that may be channeled in a virtuous direction under the guidance of reason. He identifies four basic appetites in man which reason may correlate with the four cardinal virtues. The first of the appetites is the desire for truth, which may be related to the virtue of prudence. Greatness of soul or magnanimity is the second drive. Its correlative virtue is courage, which has two directions, inward and outward. Courage may move the soul toward the performance of noble deeds. The third drive is the desire for self-preservation and independence. Its companion virtue is justice, which teaches it how to adjust itself to the needs of others and to the general good. Finally, there is the desire for order, measure, and decorum, an aesthetic as well as a psychological drive, which may be ordered by reason to the virtue of temperance.[116]

On the other hand, while he agrees that the passions arise from the irrational faculties of the soul, Posidonius thinks that they are incapable of leading to virtue in any way. The passions must be put down rigorously and definitively. While Panaetius advocates the rationalizing of the subrational, Posidonius develops a non-rational battle plan for uprooting the

---

[116] Van Straaten, frags. 87-89; noted by Tatakis, *Panétius*, pp. 216-24; discussed in greater detail by Anne Glibert-Thirry, "La théorie stoïcienne de la passion chez Chrysippe et son évolution chez Posidonius," *Revue philosophique de Louvain*, 75 (1977), 423-35; Van Straaten, *Panétius*, pp. 138-202.

passions. Since the passions are irrational by nature, he argues, they cannot be affected by the application of rational means of control. They can be dealt with only by non-rational means. Indeed, one of the reasons why Posidonius concerns himself with the study of geography is that he believes in the influence of climatic and environmental factors on those parts of the human personality controlled by the irrational faculties. Posidonius' strategy for allaying the passions is to inflame them in the belief that they possess only a limited amount of energy and that they can be forced in this way to burn themselves out. The passions are to be manipulated and exhausted by such devices as music, poetry, and the imagination.[117] This programme is rational only in its objectives, in the sense that the reason plans and administers it in order to eliminate the obstacles cast up in its own path by the passions.

Although Panaetius and Posidonius differ in the way in which they deal with the passions, they arrive at a similar conclusion, which is at variance with the ancient Stoic doctrine of instant conversion from folly to wisdom. Since they have abandoned a monistic psychology, the middle Stoics do not need to adhere to the idea of a *tonos* which is either entirely healthy or entirely dysfunctional. It therefore becomes possible for them to move systematically to an ethics in which gradual progress toward virtue can take place.[118] For Panaetius, training in virtue consists of the reorientation and disciplining of the irrational faculties by the reason, while for Posidonius the passions are to be cornered in their own lair and destroyed by the artful use of irrational stimuli. In line with his gradualistic approach, there is a significant shift in Panaetius' handling of the *adiaphora*. While agreeing with the ancient Stoa that all things are either good, bad, or indifferent, the things indifferent being divisible into the more and the less preferable, he adds that the preferables may be conductive to virtue. The preferables are certainly not good in and of themselves, and it may be necessary to abandon them if they conflict at any time with the demands of virtue. But ordinarily they can be regarded as lesser goods and employed to move man step by step to the *summum bonum*.

---

[117] Edelstein-Kidd, frags. F163-68; good discussions in Edelstein, *Meaning of Stoicism*, pp. 60-70; "Posidonius," *AJP, 57* (1936), 213-14, 296, 301, 305-16; B.-L. Hijmans, "Posidonius' Ethics," *Acta Classica, 2* (1959), 27-42; Kidd, "Posidonius on Emotions," in *Problems in Stoicism*, ed. Long, pp. 200-14; Laffranque, *Poseidonios*, pp. 160, 370-438. 466-94; Gerhard Nebel, "Zur Ethik des Poseidonios," *Hermes*, 74 (1939), 34-57.

[118] Rist, *Stoic Philos.*, pp. 95-96. Ernst Bickel, *"Metaschematizesthai:* Ein übersehener Grundbegriff des Poseidonios," *RM*, n.F. *100* (1957), 98-99 cites a text in which Posidonius is reported to have adhered to the ancient Stoic doctrine of the instantaneous transformation from folly to wisdom, but does not show how he integrates this idea with the progressive conception of virtue more typical of his ethics.

Equally striking is Panaetius' handling of the duties. Panaetius' interest in casuistry is perhaps one of the major reasons why the Stoicism he introduced into Rome was so well received there, for he shows a relative disinclination to speculate on the nature of the good, devoting his main attention to analyzing its application in practice. Although this taste marks a shift in emphasis from the ancient Stoa, Panaetius' casuistry is consistent with the teachings of his predecessors.[119] In Panaetius' teaching, a physics consisting of individual events rather than of abstract essences is paralleled by an ethics dealing with concrete rules for individual cases. Panaetius works out four criteria to be borne in mind in deciding on an ethical course of action. The individual must first take account of his participation in human nature in general, with its attendant general duties. But these obligations may be fulfilled in a variety of ways. In determining how to fulfill them, the individual must consider, secondly, his own personal gifts and limitations. Thirdly, he must bear in mind the social rank into which he was born, with its own particular opportunities and responsibilities. Finally, he must consider what he can make of himself by the exercise of his free will.[120] In this doctrine Panaetius particularizes the ancient Stoic distinction between necessity and possibility in the moral sphere by delineating the areas in the moral life in which the individual must work in terms of givens and those in which he may exercise choice. While Panaetius perpetuates the ancient Stoic conviction that there can be no intrinsic conflict between human nature as such and the nature and needs of the individual, he also personalizes Stoic ethics markedly and makes it more broadly accessible. For Panaetius, any conscientious person can achieve virtue. The same goal may be attained by different persons in different ways under different circumstances.

The Roman Stoics draw on the ethics of both the ancient and the middle Stoa, although they do not as a rule feel the need to correlate their ethical teachings systematically with their psychology. Nor are they always consistent. Epictetus adheres most rigorously to the ancient Stoa, stressing that virtue and vice stem entirely from the individual's judgment

---

[119] There is some evidence of causistry in the ancient Stoa; see *SVF, 3*, 685-742. The ancient Stoic background to Panaetius' teaching on the duties and the changes this doctrine underwent in response to Skeptic criticism have been studied by A. A. Long, "Carneades and the Stoic Telos," *Phronesis, 12* (1967), 59-90; Gerhard Nebel, "Der Begriff des *Kathêkon* in der alten Stoa," *Hermes, 70* (1935), 439-60; Damianos Tsekourakis, *Studies in the Terminology of Early Stoic Ethics, Hermes* Einzelschriften, *32* (Wiesbaden, 1974), ch. 1; White, "Two Notes on Stoic Terminology," *AJP, 99* (1978), 111-15; W. Wiersma, *Telos und Kathêkon in der alten Stoa*," *Mnemosyne*, ser. 3:5 (1937), 219-28. An old but still useful study of Panaetius' casuistry is Raymond Thamin, *Un problème morale dans l'antiquité: Étude sur la casuistique stoïcienne* (Paris, 1884).

[120] Van Straaten, frags. 96-99.

and will. The main thrust of his teaching is the idea that correct moral judgments and the correct desires which flow from them can free man from slavery to error and vice. In arguing for this orthodox position, Epictetus underlines the doctrine that the only things which are ethically relevant are the things within our control, to the point of denying the division of the *adiaphora* into things more and less preferable. There is one salient exception to this rule in Epictetus' teaching on the *adiaphora*. He holds that suffering, far from being indifferent, is a good, for it aids in the development of the moral character, a point which Seneca shares with him.[121] Outside of this, however, Epictetus treats all the *adiaphora* as equally indifferent and as equally irrelevant to the acquisition of moral freedom. In his faithfulness to the ancient Stoa, Epictetus departs from his teacher, Musonius Rufus, who agrees with Panaetius that virtue can be taught progressively and that it is necessary to take into account the personal endowments of an individual in determining the vocation through which he should seek to achieve it. On the other hand, Musonius shares with his pupil the Cynicizing tone of the ancient Stoics in demanding a style of life simple to the point of asceticism. One index of this rigorist orientation in the Stoa is the attitude which an individual Stoic takes toward matters tonsorial, his policy on hair being a guide to where a Stoic stands in the asceticism-moderation spectrum. In Epictetus and Musonius the Cynicizing strain can be seen in their assertion that cosmetic practices such as cutting the hair and shaving the beard are contrary to nature and should therefore be shunned.[122]

For Stoics such as Seneca, who adopts a more moderate ethical stance, unwillingness to resort to a barber is criticized, along with any other bizarre form of personal appearance. As Seneca points out, with both wit and acuity, the slob may be just as much of a poseur as the fop. An unconventional presentation of self may mask a perverted desire for self-display. Such behavior, furthermore, is not reasonable for a philosopher, since it may alienate his audience. Deliberate bad grooming on the part of the sage is thus neither a sign of virtue nor a sign of common sense.[123] Seneca tends to adhere to the middle Stoa rather than to the ancient Stoa on ethics. He rejects the doctrine of an instant conversion from folly to wisdom in preference for a progressive mode of ethical development. He reiterates Panaetius' idea that persons, times, and circumstances should be taken into account in applying ethical precepts to concrete cases, both by stating this principle expressly and by exemplifying it in

---

[121] Epictetus, *Disc.* 1.2.24; *Manual* 50-51; Seneca, *Ep.* 13.1-3, 110.3; *Ad Helviam* 2.3; *Ad Marciam* 5.5; *De providentia* 1.6, 2.4-12, 4.1-5, 4.11.

[122] Lutz, "Musonius Rufus," no. 21, p. 128; Epictetus, *Disc.* 1.16, 3.1.

[123] Seneca, *Ep.* 5.1-3.

the advice he gives to different members of his circle. Seneca is inconsistent on the passions. He frequently asserts that they must be uprooted
entirely and that the sage has nothing to do with them. At other times
he disagrees with this view, advocating with Panaetius that the passions
should be moderated and reoriented by the reason and not suppressed
completely. Elsewhere, however, he supports the Posidonian doctrine of
the manipulation of the passions by non-rational means. While Seneca
thus wavers between one theory of the passions and another, he is extremely subtle in his analysis of their dynamics. He is also the only Stoic
sensitive to the tension between the intellectual understanding of the good
and the will's commitment to pursue it.[124]

Seneca is orthodox on the *adiaphora,* but he achieves a striking refinement of Stoic doctrine with respect to two of them, wealth and death.
While he agrees that wealth is neither good nor bad in itself, he argues
repeatedly that wealth may be justified as a means of exercising the virtue
of beneficence and charity toward others. The inability to tolerate riches
even when they are being used for morally constructive ends, he says, is
a sign of weakness of character.[125] Of even greater concern to Seneca is
death. Since it is a matter of indifference, death is not an evil. But Seneca
sometimes describes it as a good, calling it, without much originality, a
haven of refuge and a harbor in a stormy sea. In some circumstances,
according to Seneca, death may be preferable to life, if life means the loss
of liberty, chastity, or good conscience. Should death be preferable to
life, every man has the right to commit suicide.[126] Suicide, says Seneca,
is the road to moral freedom in circumstances of this sort. He adduces
various great heroes as examples of virtuous men who have liberated
themselves in this fashion. Seneca goes into considerable detail in outlining the conditions under which suicide may be justified. Appropriate
justifications include destitution, the infirmity of old age, incurable disease, insanity, and the tyranny of a despot from which there is no escape.
He is not entirely consistent, however, for elsewhere he argues that a king
should be obeyed even if he is unjust; and he devotes a good deal of
attention to the positive features of old age, with its freedom from the
distractions of youth and its leisure for philosophical reflection. Suicide,
according to Seneca, is not morally acceptable if it is committed to escape
boredom, to allay the fear of death by embracing it, to gratify a craving

---

[124] *Ep.* 21.1.

[125] *Ep.* 5.6.

[126] An excellent study of suicide in Seneca is Nicole Tadic-Gilloteaux, "Sénèque face
au suicide," *LAC, 32* (1963), 541-51. On suicide in the ancient Stoa see *SVF, 1,* 196; *3,*
687, 757. On the whole question of death in the Stoa see Ernst Benz, *Das Todesproblem
in der stoischen Philosophie* (Stuttgart, 1929).

for death, to terminate a curable illness, or if it means the abandonment of friends or relatives who need one. This analysis of suicide suggests a principle which Seneca elsewhere elaborates expressly—the importance of examining one's conscience and avoiding self-delusion in the moral choices one makes.[127]

Seneca's sensitivity to moral ambiguity is one of his major contributions to Stoic ethics. He also signalizes a shift in tone which is developed more strongly in the thought of Marcus Aurelius. For Seneca there is a basic sadness to life. Life is likely to be bitter on the tongue; at least, this is a plausible expectation. Where Epictetus counsels detachment for the sake of moral liberty, Seneca counsels detachment in order to avoid disappointment. Marcus Aurelius shares Seneca's preoccupation with death, although he is disinclined to discuss suicide. Marcus comes to grips with death in a much more cosmic perspective. For Marcus, the cyclical alternations of the cosmos do not inspire optimism or a sense of the perpetual renewal of all things. Rather, they suggest an inevitable state of flux in which everything that one holds dear will be taken away. Transience is the basic character of reality for Marcus. Yet, the universal order is rational, necessary, and good. In the light of this fact, the only acceptable moral stance is resignation. As transience is to the cosmos, so death is to the individual. Death is the only one of the *adiaphora* which Marcus examines in detail. It is a central topic in his philosophy. According to Marcus, the chief task of philosophy and the chief virtue that one can acquire is to unshackle oneself from the fear of death.[128] Philosophy teaches man to acquire this virtue by expounding the inexorable law of the universe and by steeling man to accept it as the law of his own being. He who judges this law falsely will succumb to grief or fear or anger in the face of the inevitable. Like the man who shirks his social duties he is described not merely as a fool but as a criminal.[129] For Marcus Aurelius the tranquillity of the sage comes not so much from allaying or reorienting the passions as from silencing the intellectual doubts which might lead to pessimism, despair, and inactivity. These are the temptations which he seeks to combat within himself in his journal.

C) Logic

Logic in the Stoic philosophy deals broadly with the way men think and speak about the world. The Stoics' theory of knowledge, their formal

---

[127] Seneca, *De ira* 3.36.1-2; *De clementia* 1.1.1.
[128] Marcus Aurelius, 2.17, 3.7, 3.16.
[129] Ibid. 10.25.

dialectic, and their theories of language, grammar, rhetoric, and poetics show an intimate relationship to their physics and ethics. The *logos* of thought and speech is a cognate of the *logos* as the rational principle of the universe and of the human *logos* which enables man to make the correct judgments on which his ethical life depends.

1. Theory of Knowledge

This correlation is very clearly visible in the Stoic theory of cognition.[130] The views of the Stoics on this subject reached their fullest form with Chrysippus and do not appear to have been altered significantly after his time. The Stoic theory of knowledge reflects a firm confidence in the idea that true and certain knowledge about the real world may be possessed by man. This conviction is predicated on the unitary conception of human psychology taught by the ancient Stoa, in which all of man's faculties are activated by the ruling *pneuma*, the rational *logos*. The Stoics hold that man acquires all his knowledge by means of the senses. There are no innate ideas. There are several stages in the cognitive process. First, the senses gather their data. In so doing, they are not passive receptacles of the data impressed on them from outside. According to the Stoics, a current of *pneuma* flows from the *hegemonikon* to the sense organ. Leaving the body through the sense organ, the *pneuma* interacts with the air between the sense organ and its object. Then it returns to the subject by way of the sense organ and deposits a sensory image, or *phantasia*, in his mind.[131] The Stoics thus envisage the process of sensation as a basically tactile interaction between the *pneuma* and the sense object and the air in between them. The *pneuma* forms a material bridge on which sensory information travels into the mind of the subject. This doctrine reflects the Stoic principle that the universe is a plenum, and that change as well as motion occur through the physical impact of one body upon another.

Once the *phantasia* has been deposited in the mind, it must be evaluated by the subject, who now proceeds to judge both its correctness and its moral value.[132] The act of judgment, or *synkatathesis*, is performed by the *hegemonikon*. *Synkatathesis* is a free and conscious act, whereas sense per-

---

[130] The most important studies are Antoinette Virieux-Reymond, *La logique et l'épistémologie des Stoïciens* (Chambéry, 1949); Gerald Watson, *The Stoic Theory of Knowledge* (Belfast, 1966). See also Stein, *Die Psychologie der Stoa*, 2, 89–387; Adolfo Levi, "Sulla psicologia gnoseologica degli Stoici," *Athenaeum*, n.s. 3 (1925), 186–98, 253–64.

[131] *SVF*, 1, 53–73; 2, 52–71, 84, 91, 141, 850, 858, 862, 871–72. On this point see Robert B. Todd, "Synentasis and the Stoic Theory of Perception," *Grazer Beiträge*, 2 (1974), 251–61.

[132] *SVF*, 1, 60–61, 63, 66, 68c, 69, 73d; 2, 53, 54a, 55–56, 59–60, 63, 74, 78, 90, 105, 107; Diogenes Laertius, *Lives* 7.52–54.

ception is an automatic function of the sense organs. If the *hegemonikon* judges that the *phantasia* is correct and when it has assigned the *phantasia* its proper moral value, the *phantasia* becomes a *phantasia kataleptike*, or an apprehensive presentation held with certainty. The *hegemonikon* makes its judgment as a free act of will; it does not simply register the intellegibility of the *phantasia* and its congruity with its object. When the process of transforming a *phantasia* into a *phantasia kataleptike* has been completed, the mind possesses the knowledge so obtained with both subjective and objective certainty.

It should be noted at this point that there is absolutely no subject-object problem in the Stoic theory of knowledge, for the same reason that there is no mind-matter distinction in Stoic physics. The world, for the Stoics, is intrinsically intelligible, and man's mind is fully adequate to it. The world is permeated by the *pneuma*; the same *pneuma* permeates and directs the act of human cognition at all stages of the process, functioning as the *hegemonikon*, the faculty responsible for the *synkatathesis*, just as it permeates and directs the activities of the sense organs. There is a division of labor but there is no basic ontological distinction between the senses and the reason. The senses, the reason, and the universe outside the subject are all aspects of the *logos*, which is mind and matter at the same time. A good deal of debate took place in antiquity on the question of where the criterion of truth lay in the Stoic theory of knowledge. Individual Stoics do not always locate it at the same point in the cognitive process. The Skeptics in particular capitalized on these discrepancies as much as they could. The inconsistency, however, is only apparent. Given the fact that one and the same *pneuma* directs the entire process of cognition, the problem is essentially a false one.[133] It appears to be real only when the Stoic theory of knowledge is divorced from Stoic physics and from Stoic ethics. The aim of the Stoic theory of knowledge is to preserve for the human *logos* the freedom, the power, and the responsibility to judge the data it receives and to accept or reject an idea as good or bad, correct or incorrect, on the basis of reason. Thus, despite the empirical foundation of their epistemology, the Stoics substitute reason for the Epicurean pleasure-pain criterion. And they are empiricists. Even the common notions, or *ennoia*, which all men share, are arrived at by each in-

---

[133] Bréhier, *Chrysippe*, pp. 80-107; *Hellenistic and Roman Age*, pp. 38 ff.; Goldschmidt, *Le système stoïcien*, pp. 112-15; Virieux-Reymond, *La logique et l'épistémol. des Stoïciens*, pp. 61-63. Cf. on the other hand Barth, *Die Stoa* (1903), pp. 65-71; Mario Mignucci, "Il problema del criterio di verità presso gli stoici antichi," in *Posizione e criterio del discorso filosofico*, ed. Carlo Giacon (Bologna, 1967), pp. 145-69. F. H. Sandbach, "Phantasia Kataléptikê," in *Problems in Stoicism*, ed. Long, p. 18 argues unconvincingly that the criterion is "a kind of intuition."

dividual through his own processing of sense data; they are not innate.[134] The fact that all men should spontaneously arrive at the same idea of the good, and other common notions, is perfectly consistent with the Stoic principle that the human mind is energized by the *logos*, which is ontologically the same in all men.

2. *Dialectic, the Categories*

In moving from the theory of knowledge to the other topics which the Stoics include within the third branch of their philosophy, it must be noted that they draw a sharp distinction between logic and language. All the remaining topics can be grouped either on one side of this distinction or the other. The Stoics define language as utterance. Language is sound. It is corporeal, material, and sensible.[135] Hence, language is part of the world of real being. Words, real beings themselves, are natural signs of natural objects. Logic, on the other hand, falls within the category of the incorporeals. Logical statements are *lekta*.[136] They have meaning, but since they are not corporeal, they do not have full being. They exist only intramentally. The *lekta* include predicates, arguments, syllogisms, and fallacies. They are not natural signs of natural objects.

This classification of logical statements as *lekta* has important implications for the way in which the Stoics handle dialectic, or logic as a formal branch of philosophical investigation.[137] Their logic is proposi-

---

[134] *SVF, 2,* 83, 473, 1009; *3,* 69, 218. Useful discussions can be found in Bréhier, *Chrysippe*, p. 67; Maryanne Cline Horowitz, "The Stoic Synthesis of the Idea of Natural Law in Man: Four Themes," *JHI, 35* (1974), 5-10; Arnold Reymond, "La logique stoïcienne," *RTP,* n.s. *17* (1929), 164; F. H. Sandbach, "*Ennoia* and *Prolepsis* in the Stoic Theory of Knowledge," *CQ, 24* (1930), 44-51; Ruth Schian, *Untersuchungen über das 'argumentum e consensu omnium'* (Hildesheim, 1973), pp. 133-66; Robert B. Todd, "The Stoic Common Notions: A Reexamination and Reinterpretation," *Symbolae Osloenses, 18* (1973), 47-76; Watson, *Stoic Theory of Knowledge*, pp. 22 ff.

[135] *SVF, 1,* 74; *2,* 140-41, 144a.

[136] See the references cited in note 35 above; Diogenes Laertius, *Lives* 7.63-81.

[137] The traditional view of Stoic logic, treating it as beneath consideration because of its departures from Aristotelian logic, is stated clearly by Carl Prantl, *Geschichte der Logik im Abendlande* (Leipzig, 1927), *1,* 401-96. It has been superseded by a positive reinterpretation of Stoic logic, marked by two trends. One understands Stoic logic and its differences from Aristotelian logic in the light of its connections with the rest of the Stoic system. The most important studies in this area are Urs Egli, *Zur stoischen Dialektik* (Basel, 1967), pp. 93-104; Michael Frede, *Die stoische Logik*, Abhandlungen der Akademie der Wissenschaften in Göttingen, philosophisch-historische Klasse, *3*:88 (Göttingen, 1974); and Virieux-Reymond, *La logique et l'épistémol. des Stoïciens.* See also Bréhier, *Hellenistic and Roman Age*, pp. 41 ff.; V. Brochard, *Études de philosophie ancienne et de philosophie moderne*, nouv. éd. (Paris, 1926), pp. 220-51; Carlo Diano, *Forma ed evento: Principii per una interpretazione del mondo greco* (Venezia, 1952), pp. 9-20; Edelstein, *Meaning of Stoicism*, pp. 27-29; Goldschmidt, *Le système stoïcien*, pp. 82-83; Josiah B. Gould, "Chrysippus: On the Criteria for the Truth of a Conditional Proposition," *Phronesis, 12* (1967), 152-61; *Chrysippus*, pp. 66-88; Charles H. Kahn, "Stoic Logic and Stoic LOGOS," *AGP, 51* (1969), 158-72;

tional. The variables in Stoic syllogisms are propositions, in contrast to the variables in Aristotelian syllogisms, which tend to be terms and classes. The Stoics are sensitive to the grammatical precision of their logical propositions; they elaborate a more precise way of expressing negation than had been used hitherto, prefixing a negative word to the entire proposition and not just to the verb. Thus, instead of saying "It is not day," they say "Not: it is day." While less idiomatic, this is a more unambiguous way of specifying what is being negated, similar to the usage "Not-p" in modern symbolic logic. Indeed, the technical ingenuity of Stoic logic is considerable, resulting in a number of ideas which had been neglected in Aristotle's logic.

Since *lekta* are not natural signs of natural objects, the Stoic preference in logic is for hypothetical syllogisms.[138] Unlike the categorical, deductive, or inductive syllogisms used by Aristotle, the hypothetical syllogism does not begin with an axiomatic statement about a general class of beings, nor does it conclude with a statement about the fixed, essential nature of things. For the Stoics, such a procedure would have been in conflict with a propositional logic whose aim is to demonstrate the logical tenability of the conclusions of one's premises, not their empirical or ontological verifiability. At the same time, and although they are *lekta*, the Stoics' hypothetical syllogisms are compatible with the physics which they espoused, for their syllogisms deal with the changing relations between concrete individual events rather than with a changeless structure

---

Lorenzo Pozzi, "Il nesso di implicazione nella logica stoica," *Atti del convegno di storia della logica,* Parma, 8-10 ottobre 1972 (Padova, 1974), pp. 177-87; Giulio Preti, "Sulla dottrina del *semeîon* nella logica stoica," *Rivista critica di storia della filosofia, 2* (1956), 5-14; Reymond, "La logique stoïcienne," *RTP,* n.s. *17* (1929), 161-71; Carlo Augusto Viano, "La dialettica stoica," *Rivista di filosofia, 49* (1958), 179-227; Antoinette Virieux-Reymond, "Le 'sunemménon' stoïcien et la notion de la loi scientifique," *Studia Philosophica, 9* (1949), 162-69.

The second group consists of scholars primarily interested in modern logic, who have rediscovered Stoic logic because of the affinities they perceive between it and the school of Carnap and Frege. The essay which began this movement is Jan Lukasiewicz, "Zur Geschichte der Aussagenlogik," *Erkenntnis, 5* (1935), 111-31. The most important technical treatment of Stoic logic within this or any other perspective is Benson Mates, *Stoic Logic* (Berkeley, 1953). See also Nimio de Anquin, "Sobre la lógica de los Estoicos," *Sapientia, 11* (1956), 166-72; Oskar Becker, *Zwei Untersuchungen zur antiken Logik* (Wiesbaden, 1957); I. M. Bocheński, *Ancient Formal Logic* (Amsterdam, 1951), pp. 77-102; William Kneale and Martha Kneale, *The Development of Logic* (Oxford, 1962), pp. 113-76; Leo Lugarini, "L'orrizonte linguistico del sapere in Aristotele e la sua trasformazione stoica," *Il Pensiero, 8* (1963), 327-51; Jürgen Mau, "Stoische Logik: Ihre Stellung gegenüber der aristotelische Syllogistik und dem modernen Aussagekalkül," *Hermes, 85* (1957), 147-58; Mario Mignucci, *Il significato della logica stoica,* 2ª ed. (Bologna, 1967); Jan Mueller, "An Introduction to Stoic Logic," in *The Stoics,* ed. Rist, pp. 1-26.

[138] *SVF, 2,* 182, 207-08, 213, 215, 241-42, 245.

of fixed essences.[139] The five main types of syllogisms used by the Stoics may be schematized as follows:

Conditional: "If it is light, it is day."
Conjunctive: "It is light and it is day."
Disjunctive: "Either it is light or it is day."
Causal: "It is light because it is day."
Likely: "It is more likely that it is day than that it is night."

In all cases both the initial premises and whatever conclusions may follow from them refer to transient events. Having demonstrated a proposition by means of these syllogisms, one has still not claimed to have said anything about an enduring natural phenomenon. This is a perfectly reasonable choice for the Stoics given both their physics of dynamic events and their conception of the *lekta*.

In addition to developing the hypothetical syllogism, Stoic logic also elaborated categories, which likewise stand in contrast to Aristotelian thought. The Stoics teach that there are four categories: substance, quality, disposition, and relative disposition.[140] Rather than being horizontal, signifying aspects of an enduring substance which are accidental and which can be shorn from it without destroying its essence, the Stoic categories are vertical. They move from lesser to greater levels of concreteness. None is accidental; all must be present in a given reality if that reality is to be grasped in all its individuality. Substance denotes the materiality of a thing and is possessed by everything except the incorporeals. Quality denotes the way in which matter is organized to form an individual being. Disposition includes times, places, actions, size, and color. It describes the particular situation and attributes of the individual. All the features covered by the category of disposition, including color,[141] are regarded by the Stoics as inherent in the individual. This

---

[139] For the parallels in physics see *SVF*, 2, 13, 114, 395-97. Good analyses of this point can be found in Jacques Brunschwig, "Le modèle conjonctif," *Les Stoïciens et leur logique,* Actes du Colloque de Chantilly, 18-22 septembre 1976 (Paris, 1978), pp. 61-65; Edelstein, *Meaning of Stoicism,* pp. 27-29; Michael Frede, "Stoic vs. Aristotelian Syllogistic," *AGP, 56* (1974), 1-32; Goldschmidt, *Le système stoïcien,* pp. 82-83; Gould, "Chrysippus," *Phronesis, 12* (1967), 152-61; *Chrysippus,* pp. 66-88; A. A. Long, "Dialectic and the Stoic Sage," in *The Stoics,* ed. Rist, pp. 101-24; Virieux-Reymond, "Le 'sunemménon' stoïcien," *Studia Philosophica, 9* (1949), 162-69. William H. Hay, "Stoic Use of Logic," *AGP, 51* (1969), 145-57 argues unconvincingly that the Stoic syllogisms also reflect an interest in abstract subjects and universal conclusions.

[140] *SVF*, 2, 368-75. On the other hand, Andreas Graeser, "The Stoic Categories," *Les stoïciens et leur logique,* pp. 199-221; "The Stoic Theory of Meaning," in *The Stoics,* ed. Rist, p. 78 sees the categories as linguistic expressions signifying syntactical classifications.

[141] *SVF, 1,* 91.

view harmonizes with the doctrine in Stoic physics that bodies create their own extension and their own time and space, so to speak, through their *tonos* and activity. Relative disposition denotes the way that an individual thing is related to other phenomena. None of the four Stoic categories can be removed from an individual being without that being ceasing to be itself. At each level of specificity the categories refer to something integral to the individual being's reality. The categories mirror the physics of concrete individual events taught by the Stoa. Although officially classified under logic, the Stoic categories are really pertinent to physics since they are modes of expressing reality.[142]

3. Language, Grammar, Literary Theory

When we turn to language, however, we are truly in the realm of natural reality. Language is sound; it is material and corporeal; and it has a direct and natural correlation with the physical realities which it signifies.[143] The Stoics distinguish between the inarticulate cries of animals and the articulate human voice.[144] Only the latter is considered to be language. Human utterance may be written or unwritten. If it is written it employs an alphabet of twenty-four letters. If the words made up of the alphabet make sense, they are called *logos*, or language, the expressive side of the rational *logos* in man, which corresponds to the *logos* of nature. Other topics which the Stoics include under this heading, outside of the letters of the alphabet and words, are etymology and onomatopoeia; they are among those thinkers in antiquity who hold that, since there is a natural correspondence between words and things, the derivations and sounds of words provide insight into the nature of the things they signify. The Stoics also include within the category of language the study of grammar, syntax, music, rhetoric, diction, and poetic meter, as well as incorrect uses of language such as barbarism, solecism, and colloquialism.

---

[142] Bochénski, *Ancient Formal Logic*, p. 87; Bréhier, *Chrysippe*, pp. 132-33; Phillip De-Lacy, "The Stoic Categories as Methodological Principles," *TAPA, 76* (1945), 246-63; Goldschmidt, *Le système stoïcien*, p. 23; Samburksy, *Physics of the Stoics*, p. 18; Sandbach, *The Stoics*, pp. 93-94. On the other hand, A. C. Lloyd, "Grammar and Metaphysics in the Stoa," in *Problems in Stoicism*, ed. Long, p. 65 and Rist, *Stoic Philos.*, pp. 152-60 argue that the categories should be regarded entirely as *lekta*.

[143] A good general study is Karl Barwick, *Probleme der stoischen Sprachlehre und Rhetorik*, Abhandlungen der sächsischen Akademie der Wissenschaft zu Leipzig, philologisch-historische Klasse, *49*:3 (Berlin, 1957). Concise summaries with a good recent bibliography can be found in Lucio Melazzo, "La teoria del segno linguistico negli Stoici," *Lingua e stile, 10* (1975), 199-230; Gérard Verbeke, "La philosophie du signe chez les Stoïciens," *Les stoïciens et leur logique*, pp. 401-24; "Philosophie et séméiologie chez les Stoïciens," *Études philosophiques offerts au Dr. Ibrahim Madkour* (Gebo, 1974), pp. 15-38.

[144] *SVF, 1,* 74; *2,* 140-41, 144a.

The Stoics are concerned with grammar because they see language as a natural process.[145] The structure of language, for them, is not conventional.[146] The Stoics take a firm stand on this question, which was debated in antiquity. They were among the earliest thinkers to formulate grammar and the parts of speech in the Greek language. The ancient Stoics begin by defining four parts of speech: the noun, both proper and appellative; the verb, which may have active, passive, neuter, and reflexive-causative moods, which may be personal or impersonal, transitive or intransitive, and past, present, future, imperfect, perfect, or pluperfect; the article, which includes pronouns and demonstratives; and the conjunction, which includes prepositions and particles. Antipater of Tarsus, a pupil of Chrysippus, adds on the participle and possibly the adverb. For the same reason that they dislike making axiomatic statements in logic, the Stoics reject a grammar in which the relations between words and the structural changes which they undergo in different grammatical contexts can be reduced to a set of rules and patterns. They carried on a lengthy debate with grammarians of the school of Alexandria, who were rule-oriented and who saw the relations between words and grammatical structures as governed by analogy, a fixed method of conjugating and declining words according to strict formal parallels among different parts of speech. The Stoics, on the other hand, see grammar as paralleling nature. Since the natural order is always in a state of change, they therefore prefer to explain the relationships between words and grammatical structures as resemblances in which variety and anomaly are to be expected. The Stoic position on grammar also influences the way that Stoic pedagogues deal with the liberal arts. They tend to subsume the other arts of the trivium under grammar, since all the arts use words, and they correlate the trivium closely with the quadrivium, since the verbal *logos* corresponds with the *logos* of the physical world.

The Stoics' theory of language as a natural sign carries over into their

---

[145] The basic work still remains Rudolphus Schmidt, *Stoicorum grammatica* (Halle, 1839). More recent studies include Lloyd, "Grammar and Metaphysics," in *Problems in Stoicism*, ed. Long, pp. 58-71; Pfeiffer, *Hist. of Classical Scholarship*, pp. 244-46; Pire, *Stoïcisme et pédagogie*, pp. 47-50; Max Pohlenz, "Die Begründung der abendländischen Sprachlehre durch die Stoa," *Kleine Schriften*, ed. Heinrich Dörrie (Hildesheim, 1965) *1*, 39-86; R. H. Robins, *Ancient and Medieval Grammatical Theory in Europe with Particular Reference to Modern Linguistic Doctrine* (London, 1951), pp. 25-36; John Edwin Sandys, *A History of Classical Scholarship from the Sixth Century B.C. to the End of the Middle Ages* (Cambridge, 1903), *1*, 144-58. Also of interest, although the author's chief concern is to show the sense in which Stoic grammar is comparable with the list of topics discussed by later grammarians, is Michael Frede, "Principles of Stoic Grammar," in *The Stoics*, ed. Rist, pp. 27-75.
[146] Diogenes Laertius, *Lives* 7.57-58.

theory of literary style, both rhetorical and poetic.[147] In this area the Roman Stoics take the lead. The Stoics place a high value on literature as a medium for philosophical expression. They make extensive use of ancient rhetorical forms such as the diatribe and the *consolatio*.[148] They are the most favorably disposed of all ancient schools of philosophy toward poetry, as can be seen not only by their treatment of Homer as a philosopher and their frequent quotations from the poets in their arguments, but also in their use of the poetic medium themselves.[149] Literature is important to the Stoics because of the parallelism or identity which they see between language and reality and because of the ethical imperatives of their philosophy. Literature, they argue, should be permeated by the *logos* so that words will not be used unnaturally. Words should communicate truth and goodness to the hearer. For the Stoics, the function of literature is preeminently didactic. In contrast to Cicero's idea that literature should delight and persuade as well as teach, the Stoics emphasize the teaching function preclusively. Literature, they hold, should appeal above all to the reason.

These ideas about the nature and function of literature set up certain prescriptions for both the content and the style of literary works, whether prose or poetry.[150] A work of literature, for the Stoics, must be mimetic. It must conform to nature and to truth, or else it distorts the natural function of language. If literature fails to communicate truth, it will also fail to be of moral and intellectual utility to the audience. In both prose and poetry, a work's mimetic quality must be visible in terms of the verisimilitude of the characters, actions, passions, and situations it sets

---

[147] The basic work on this topic is Charles Newton Smiley, *Latinitas and Hellenismos: The Influence of the Stoic Theory of Style as Shown by the Writings of Dionysius, Quintilian, Pliny the Younger, Tacitus, Fronto, Aulus Gellius, and Sextus Empiricus*, Bulletin of the University of Wisconsin, 143, Philology and Literature Series, 3:3 (Madison, 1906), pp. 205-72; "Seneca and the Stoic Theory of Literary Style," *Classical Studies in Honor of Charles Forster Smith*, University of Wisconsin Studies in Language and Literature, 3 (Madison, 1919), pp. 50-61. See also George Converse Fiske, "The Plain Style in the Scipionic Circle," ibid., pp. 65-67; Frank Ivan Merchant, "Seneca the Philosopher and His Theory of Style," *AJP*, 26 (1905), 44-59. The best study of Stoic poetics is Phillip DeLacy, "Stoic Views of Poetry," *AJP*, 69 (1948), 241-71. The most recent general treatment is P. Costil, "L'Esthétique stoïcienne," *Actes du 1er congrès de la fédération internationale des Associations d'études classiques*, Paris, 28 août-2 septembre 1950 (Paris, 1951), pp. 360-64.

[148] Johannes Geffken, *Kynika und Verwandtes* (Heidelberg, 1909), pp. 1-53 treats the Cynic-Stoic use of the diatribe; André Oltramare, *Les origines de la diatribe romain* (Lausanne, 1926) gives a history of its use by various philosophical schools and the fullest analysis of its forms and themes as well as a detailed treatment of Seneca's use of diatribe, pp. 252-92. See also Geytenbeek, *Musonius Rufus and Greek Diatribe*. The best study of the *consolatio* as used by philosophical writers is Rudolf Kassel, *Untersuchungen zur griechischen und römischen Konsolations-literatur* (München, 1958), who treats the Stoics pp. 17-29.

[149] DeLacy, "Stoic Views of Poetry," *AJP*, 69 (1948), 241.

[150] Diogenes Laertius, *Lives* 7.59.

forth as well as in the objective truth and moral correctness of its message as a whole. By the same token, the style of a literary work must conform to nature and to truth. At the same time, it must serve the needs of its didactic function. This means, for the Stoics, a preference for the *verba antiqua* of the older authors, which had been used before arbitrary neologisms crept into the language; they regard the vocabulary of the ancients as closer to nature than that of more recent writers. In the realm of rhetoric the Stoics elaborate five basic canons of style: purity of language; clarity and distinctness; conciseness, even tending toward paratactic constructions; the avoidance of inaccuracy, colloquialism, barbarism, and solecism; and appropriateness of style. Appropriateness of style means its appropriateness to the subject matter, in the light of which the speaker should select his figures and should decide whether to employ the high, middle, or low style. In contrast to Aristotelian rhetoric, the Stoics do not think that the ethos of the audience needs to be taken into account in selecting the level of style to be used by the orator, since in all cases the speaker is addressing himself to the *logos* of his hearers, and the *logos* is the same in all men.

The poetic theory of the Stoics shares the intellectualistic slant of their literary theory in general, while at the same time recognizing the differences between poetic and rhetorical diction. According to the Stoics, poetry manifests the mimetic character which all literature should possess not only in its overall content but in the delineation of its characters and situations. Poetic mimesis can also be achieved through the onomatopoeia of individual words and through figures of speech, which the Stoics permit much more extensively in poetry than they do in prose. The Stoics elaborate a theory of eight types of ambiguity to account for figurative diction in poetry. Among the sorts of figures which they treat are *catachresis*, or the application of the name of one thing to something else; *metalepsis*, or the use of a synonym in a non-synonymous way to supply a middle term in a transition; *emphasis*, where an inferior is used to suggest a superior; and *aenigma*, or unclear allegory. In all cases there must be a mimetic basis for the poetic figures selected.

The prevailing notion in Stoic literary theory is a direct appeal to the intellect of the audience. Their rhetoric tends to avoid diffuseness and coloristic embellishment in favor of lucidity, simplicity, and straightforwardness. Their poetics recognizes the power of aesthetic appeals to the imagination as an amplification of the prosaic human voice, making it capable of expressing a divine theme and enhancing its capacity for intellectual and moral instruction. In a way it is one of those paradoxes of history that the Roman Stoics, who are not particularly interested in broad speculation or in the physical and logical correlatives of ethics, should have been the ones to give the most eloquent literary expression to a theory of style in which the *logos* of physics and the *logos* of ethics are so integrally related with the *logos* of language. And it is a paradox vital to the transmission of Stoicism to the medieval west, for the literature of the Romans served as a crucial link in the perpetuation of Stoic ideas in the Latin language.

CHAPTER TWO

CICERO

Cicero holds a special place in the history of the Stoic tradition, a place second only to that occupied by the middle and Roman Stoics themselves. His importance as a late Republican statesman, as a historical source for the political life of the first century B.C., and as an authoritative exponent of classical Latin oratory and rhetorical theory have long been recognized. However, Cicero's contributions as a philosophical thinker have attracted sustained scholarly interest only in the modern era.[1] In our study of the Stoic tradition it is Cicero's philosophical work that will command our primary attention. But his position as a philosophical thinker can by no means be detached from the other aspects of his mentality or from the vicissitudes of his political career and his personal life.

I. LIFE AND WRITINGS

We are fortunate in possessing, largely from Cicero himself, more biographical and autobiographical information about him than is available for any other single figure in ancient history.[2] Cicero (106-43 B.C.) was born in Arpinum of an equestrian family and was the first of its members to aspire to high political office. He received his early education in Rome, studying literature with the poet Archias and the rhetorician Molo and philosophy with Phaedrus the Epicurean, Philo of Larissa of the New Academy, and Diodotus the Stoic. The last named teacher became a close friend of Cicero and a member of his household, remaining there until his death in 59 B.C. In preparation for a career as an advocate,

---

[1] A. E. Douglas, *Cicero*, Greece & Rome: New Surveys in the Classics, 2 (Oxford, 1968), provides an excellent survey of the critical literature on Cicero and its shifts in historiographical perspective. Also useful are S. E. Smethurst, "Cicero's Rhetorical and Philosophical Works: A Bibliographical Survey," *CW*, *51* (1957), 1-4, 24; *58* (1964), 36-45; *61* (1967), 125-33 and Olof Gigon, "Cicero und die griechische Philosophie," *Aufstieg und Niedergang der römischen Welt, 1*, part. 4, 260-61.

[2] The leading biographer of Cicero is Matthias Gelzer, *Cicero: Ein biographischer Versuch* (Wiesbaden, 1969). Other good studies include D. R. Shackleton Bailey, *Cicero* (London, 1971); J. P. V. D. Balsdon, "Cicero the Man," in *Cicero*, ed. T. A. Dorey (London, 1965), pp. 171-214; H. H. Scullard, "The Political Career of a 'Novus Homo'," ibid., pp. 1-25; David Stockton, *Cicero: A Political Biography* (Oxford, 1971). Cicero has not escaped the attentions of the pyscho-historians, as in the case of Paul Briot, "Cicéron: Approches d'une psychanalyse," *Latomus, 28* (1969), 1040-49, who diagnoses his subject as the victim of an Oedipus complex.

Cicero then studied law with the jurisconsults Quintus Mucius Scaevola and his nephew of the same name.

Cicero entered public life as an advocate in 81 B.C. and rapidly gained distinction at the bar thanks to his oratorical talent. Endowed with neither noble birth nor a well established place in the social and political world of late Republican Rome, he neither inherited nor acquired an entrenched *clientela* whose wealth and influence he could rely on for support, although he did establish some connections with senatorial families through his first wife Terentia. The patronage which Cicero received in the early stages of his career came largely from prominent families whose members he defended successfully in court. This type of backing, coupled with Cicero's own abilities, was sufficient to promote his advancement, but it proved too weak in terms of kinship or interest to protect him against powerful enemies in times of adversity.

During the years 79–77 B.C. Cicero interrupted his legal practice, leaving Rome because his recent and spirited defense of the controversial Sextus Roscius made it prudent to absent himself from the capital for a time. He made use of this opportunity to further his education in philosophy and rhetoric. In Athens he became the pupil of Antiochus of Ascalon of the Old Academy; then, travelling to Rhodes, he studied with Posidonius and with his earlier teacher Molo, later pursuing additional rhetorical studies in a number of eastern Mediterranean centers with Xenocles, Dionysius, and Menippus.

On his return to Rome in 77 B.C. Cicero began an aggressive and successful quest for political preferment, quickly scaling the ladder of the *cursus honorum* from the quaestorship in 75 B.C. to its highest rung, the office of consul, in 63 B.C. The most famous event of Cicero's consulship was his suppression of the conspiracy of Catiline, a resolute act which brought him considerable public acclaim but which also paved the way to his political downfall. Having detected the revolt planned by the Catilinarians, Cicero averted it by arresting the plotters and putting them to death. In so doing he forestalled a violent coup d'état and protected the authority of the senate, currently under assault at the hands of would-be dictators. Not the least among those seeking to subvert the Republican constitution were Julius Caesar and his associates. In suppressing the Catilinarian conspiracy Cicero preserved the Republican order and won the thanks of its supporters; but in so doing he provided Caesar and his party with a legal basis for attacking him and avenging themselves against a leader who had persistently refused to favor their cause. The Caesarians charged Cicero with a violation of lawful procedure in his ordering of Catiline's execution without a trial. On these grounds they secured Cicero's conviction of malfeasance in office and his exile. On his return from this exile, which had lasted from 58 to 57 B.C., Cicero labored to wean Pompey away from his association with Caesar and Crassus. His efforts were in vain and would probably have led to a second exile had not Cicero retracted his opposition to the triumvirs in 56 B.C.

Despite this recantation, Cicero found himself excluded from high office and from a position of influence at the capital after 56 B.C. He continued to function as an advocate and was elected to the ceremonial office of augur in 53 or 52 B.C.[3] Between 52 and 50 B.C. he served as proconsul of Cilicia, a governorship entailing considerable responsibility but one which placed him in a province on the easternmost frontier of the empire in Asia Minor. During his proconsulship Cicero took advantage of his location by continuing his philosophical studies and by widening his intellectual horizons. In 51 B.C. he returned to Greece where he visited the brother of Antiochus in Athens and met Cratippus the Peripatetic at Mytilene. When Cicero returned to Rome at the end of his proconsulate in 49 B.C. he found Italy in a state of civil war, with the triumvirate torn apart by a struggle for primacy among its members. He wavered on whom to support and eventually backed Pompey. In 48 B.C. Pompey was defeated by Caesar at the battle of Pharsalus and Cicero found it prudent to withdraw to his villa at Brundisium. A year later Caesar granted him a full pardon for having sided with the loser, enabling him to return to Rome in 47 B.C. Here Cicero was treated with outward respect by the dictator and his partisans but was given no opportunity to participate in the government; in any event, Caesar's domination of the senate and the courts tended to restrict the scope of Cicero's habitual spheres of political activity. In 46 B.C. Cicero withdrew from Rome once again, moving after brief stays to one after another of his country villas. Events in his private life preoccupied him during this period. He divorced Terentia and took a second wife, Publilia, in 47/46 B.C. and suffered the death of his beloved daughter Tullia in 45 B.C.

When Caesar was assassinated in 44 B.C. Cicero made his last attempt to resurrect his political career and to urge the current leaders to restore the Republic. Events swiftly showed that he had misjudged the realities of the contemporary situation. The heirs to Caesar's power, the second triumvirate of Mark Antony, Octavius, and Lepidus, reacted to his criticisms and proposals with hostility and ordered his death in 43 B.C. Cicero's efforts to avert the final collapse of the Republic, whether by forthright action, prevarication, procrastination, or precept, died with him.

---

[3] The date traditionally assigned is 53 B.C. but Jerzy Linderski, "The Aedileship of Favonius, Curio the Younger, and Cicero's Election to the Augurate," *HSCP, 76* (1972), 190–200 argues for the year 52 B.C.

The same Ciceronian writings that allow us to chart the dramatic ups and downs of the author's public and private life also supply us with a wealth of information about his intellectual interests and philosophical compositions, or at least about the light in which Cicero wanted them to be read and understood. In his private correspondence Cicero often discusses his reading, his literary projects, and his aims as a writer. He usually introduces his philosophical works with prefaces explaining their scope and purpose. Especially noteworthy in this connection is the *De divinatione*, the preface to whose second book provides a resumé listing most of the treatises that Cicero had written up to that point along with an agenda of his future works, as well as a general rationale for his literary activity. The fact that Cicero chose to write different kinds of works at different times is closely related to the events and circumstances of his life. His orations, the largest single subdivision of his *oeuvre*, recording his activities as an advocate, prosecutor, and senatorial politician, span his entire career. Aside from these orations, both forensic and deliberative, and his letters, which begin in 68 B.C., Cicero's works prior to 56 B.C. reflect the mentality of a student and a young man producing school exercises or summaries of information pertinent to his budding career. During his teens Cicero wrote a poem on Marius and translated Aratus' *Phaenomena* and Xenophon's *Oeconomica*. In about 86 B.C. he put together a brief rhetorical handbook, *De inventione*, and in 60 B.C. translated another work of Aratus, the *Prognostica*. A striking shift in subject matter can be seen in the works that Cicero wrote after 56 B.C. It is at this stage of his career that he composed his *magna opera* of mature rhetorical theory, the *De oratore* of 55 B.C., the *De partitione oratoria*, *Brutus*, and *De optimo genere oratorum* of 46 B.C., and the *Topica* of 44 B.C. It is also from the period after 56 B.C. that Cicero's philosophical works can be dated: the *De republica* of 54-51 B.C., the *De legibus* of 52 B.C. and after,[4] the *Paradoxa Stoicorum* and probably the now fragmentary *Hortensius* of 46 B.C., and the *De finibus*, *Tusculanarum disputationum*, the lost *Consolatio* and *De gloria*, the *Academica*, a translation of Plato's *Timaeus*, the *De natura deorum*, *De senectute*, *De divinatione*, *De fato*, *De amicitia*, and *De officiis*, all of 45 and 44 B.C. The *Philippics*, written against Antony in 44 B.C., of which fourteen sur-

---

[4] The dating of the *De legibus* is a matter of some controversy. The most thorough review of the literature on this question is Peter Lebrecht Schmidt, *Die Abfassungszeit von Ciceros Schrift über die Gesetze*, Collana di studi ciceroniani, 4 (Roma, 1969), pp. 15-23, 26, 49, 75, 292. See also Joseph Busuttil, "Cicero: De Legibus Book I, An Introduction, a Translation and a Commentary," (University of London Ph.D. diss., 1964), pp. 16-25; L. P. Kentner, *M. Tullius Cicero De legibus: A Commentary on Book I*, trans. Margie L. Leenheer-Braid (Amsterdam, 1972), pp. 1-5; Georges de Plinval, intro. to his ed. and trans. of Marcus Tullius Cicero, *Traité des lois*, Budé (Paris, 1959), p. viii and n. 3.

vive, are the only major orations written by Cicero during this final period.

II. The Critical Background

It is only in modern times that scholars have devoted systematic attention to this host of philosophical writings; but their assessments of Cicero's importance as a philosopher have undergone a number of drastic transformations.[5] Having enjoyed high repute as a philosophical thinker in the seventeenth and eighteenth centuries, Cicero was abruptly demoted in the middle of the nineteenth century to the status of a dabbler, a compiler, a peevish and slovenly hack. This cataclysmic shift in interpretation can be attributed principally to Theodor Mommsen,[6] whose authority in all fields of Roman studies was so massive that it succeeded in dominating Cicero criticism effortlessly for many decades. The first wave of anti-Mommsen revisionism swept forward in the late nineteenth century with the *Quellenforscher* in the vanguard.[7] These scholars turned on its head the very syncretism which Mommsen had seen as an index of Cicero's intellectual shortcomings, reappraising it as his main positive contribution in that it provided a means of reconstructing the doctrines of a wide range of later Greek philosophical schools about which little or nothing can be known apart from what Cicero reports about them. Many of the *Quellenforscher*, however, had a tendency to slide insensibly from a study of Cicero as the source for other people's ideas to conclusions about the philosophical complexion of Cicero's own ideas as compared with his presumed sources, even in the absence of independent *testimonia* of the doctrines whose authentic understanding by Cicero this exercise was designed to test. The next major upheaval in interpretation linked a growing exasperation with the tautological methodology of the *Quellenforscher* with a pervasive loss of faith in the assumption that Roman writers are *ipso facto* the inferiors of the Greeks and worthy of study from the sole perspective of their success in keeping Greek ideas in circulation. This second wave of revisionism, which has enlisted a growing number of

---

[5] Aside from the historiographical information provided by Douglas, *Cicero* on this topic, useful recent surveys of the changing currents of opinion can be found in Karl Büchner, "Cicero, Grunzüge seines Wesens," in *Cicero*, Studien zur römischen Literatur, 2 (Wiesbaden, 1962), pp. 1-24 and Woldemar Görler, *Untersuchungen zu Ciceros Philosophie*, Bibliothek der klassischen Altertumswissenschaft, n.F. 2:50 (Heidelberg, 1974), pp. 1-19.

[6] Theodor Mommsen, *The History of Rome*, new ed., trans. William Purdie Dickson (London, 1913), 5, 504-05, 508-10.

[7] Among the classic exponents of *Quellenforschung* as applied to Cicero one may cite Rudolf Hirzel, *Untersuchungen zu Ciceros philosophischen Schriften*, 3 vols. (Leipzig, 1877-83); C. Thiacourt, *Essai sur les traités philosophiques de Cicéron et leurs sources grecques* (Paris, 1885).

twentieth-century Cicero scholars in its ranks, has rejected *Quellenforschung* as the most profitable or interesting approach to Cicero's thought.[8] Cicero has, consequently, reemerged in the twentieth century as a philo-'sophical personality worthy of consideration in his own right, whether as a critical interpreter of one or more of the Hellenistic schools of philosophy or as the creator of a specific philosophical program of his own. While the most recent commentators have reached no consensus on Cicero's overall merits, goals, and allegiances as a philosophical writer, they have none the less produced a striking revaluation of his place in intellectual history, to the point where one contemporary scholar has been able to state with no fear of contradiction that Cicero's philosophical writings "exercised an inestimable influence on Western civilization, and constitute the most important body of his works from the historical point of view. ... and helped to shape the Western way of life."[9]

While Cicero and Stoicism is the theme of the present inquiry, it will rapidly become evident why we need to consider the broader question of Cicero and philosophy in order to understand and assess the place of Stoicism in his thought. The abandonment of a disparaging or purely doxographical approach to Cicero has still left contemporary scholars in a state of some disagreement as to how his philosophical ideas and intentions may best be comprehended. There are a number of methodological problems in this connection that need to be addressed. One of the thorniest is whether Cicero's frequent statements about his philosophical sources, concerns, and intentions can always be taken at face value. On the one hand, his letters and prefaces contain a good deal of material on this subject and it seems absurd to ignore the information that he takes such pains to supply about the books he was reading or sought to obtain while composing particular works,[10] about his long-term interest in phi-

---

[8] A clear statement of the methodological objections to *Quellenforschung*, although it is not entirely free from it, can be found in Flaviana Moscarini, *Cicerone e l'etica stoica nel III libro del 'De finibus'*, Pubblicazioni della scuola di filosofia della R. Università di Roma, 2 (Roma, 1930), pp. 7-8. Typical examples of the more recent and more fully developed critique of *Quellenforschung* can be noted in Pierre Boyancé, *Études sur l'humanisme cicéronien*, Collection Latomus, 121 (Bruxelles, 1970), pp. 201-04; Martin van den Bruwaene, *La théologie de Cicéron* (Louvain, 1937), pp. xiv-xvi; Douglas, *Cicero*, pp. 28-29; Michel Ruch, "Un exemple du syncrétisme philosophique de Cicéron: *Academica posteriora*, ¶21," *REL*, 48 (1970), 205-28. The older view of Cicero as a "mere transmitter" has also retained some influential adherents; see, for example, Ulrich Knoche, "Cicero: Ein Mittler griechischer Geisteskultur," *Hermes*, 87 (1959), 57-74.

[9] A. D. Leeman, *Orationis Ratio: The Stylistic Theories and Practice of the Roman Orators, Historians and Philosophers* (Amsterdam, 1963), *1*, 211.

[10] Marcus Tullius Cicero, *Ad Atticum* 22.2, 23.4, 26.1, 30.3, 36.3, 305.2, 309.2, 313, 420.4, ed. and trans. D. R. Shackleton Bailey (Cambridge, 1965-68); *Ad familiares* 7.20.3, 9.25.1, trans. W. Glynn Williams, Loeb (Cambridge, Mass., 1958-60). References to these works will be made to the editions cited.

losophy,[11] about the authorities he says he has relied on,[12] about his aims in specific works and his directions on how to read them.[13] On the other hand, it would be ingenuous to accept these assertions uncritically. Despite his stated reliance on certain authorities, the works in which Cicero says he depends on them often reveal his omission of apposite points made by these same authorities and his use of sources derived from alternative philosophical traditions, which he neglects to credit. It would be even more naive to accept Cicero's stated intentions on faith. Most of his philosophical works contain a hidden agenda of one kind or another, whether personal or political or both. These features of Cicero's works have been noticed by many commentators and have led some of them to stress the propagandistic or self-serving character of his philosophical *oeuvre* as its main source of consistency.[14] Other commentators, however, remain convinced of Cicero's basic sincerity and genuine public spirit.[15] At the bottom of this controversy lies the temptation to abstract the overlapping motivations that Cicero may have had from the context of a complicated mentality in the effort to reduce that mentality to a pure, and manageable, type.

Another difficult problem in the interpretation of Cicero's thought is his frequent inconsistency and inaccuracy in reporting philosophical ideas. It is certainly true that he expresses different opinions about the same subjects in different works, sometimes supporting a particular philo-

---

[11] *Ad fam.* 4.4.4; *De natura deorum* 1.3.6, livre premier, ed. and trans. M. van den Bruwaene, Collection Latomus, 107 (Bruxelles, 1970); *Tusculanarum disputationum* 5.2.5-6, trans. J. E. King, 2nd ed., Loeb (Cambridge, Mass., 1960). References to the latter work and to the first book of the *De nat. deor.* will be made to the editions cited.

[12] *Ad Att.* 89.3, 420.4; *Ad fam.* 1.9.23; 7.19.1; *De inventione* 2.2.4-5, 2.2.6-10, trans. H. M. Hubbell, Loeb (Cambridge, Mass., 1960); *De officiis* 1.2.6, ed. and trans. Maurice Testard, Budé (Paris, 1965-70); *De partitione oratoria* 40.139, trans. H. Rackham, Loeb (Cambridge, Mass., 1960); *De senectute* 1.3, trans. William Armistead Falconer, Loeb (London, 1959); *Topica* 1.1.1-5, trans. H. M. Hubbell, Loeb (Cambridge, Mass., 1960); *Tusc. disp.* 2.3.9. References to these works will be made to the editions cited.

[13] *Ad fam.* 9.8.1; *De amicitia* 1.4-5, trans. William Armistead Falconer, Loeb (London, 1959); *De divinatione* 2.1.1-4, 2.2.4-7, idem; *De fato* 1.1, 1.2-2.4, ed. and trans. Karl Bayer (München, 1963); *De finibus bonorum et malorum* 1.1.1-1.4.12, trans. H. Rackham, Loeb (Cambridge, Mass., 1961); *De nat. deor.* 1.3.6-1.4.9, 1.5.10; *De off.* 1.1.2; *Tusc. disp.* 1.1.1-1.4.8. References will be made to the editions cited. A detailed study of Cicero's prefaces in this connection has been made by Michel Ruch, *Le préambule dans les oeuvres philosophiques de Cicéron: Essai sur la genèse et l'art du dialogue,* Publications de la Faculté des lettres de l'Université de Strasbourg, 136 (Paris, 1958).

[14] Stanley J. Adamczyk, "Political Propaganda in Cicero's Essays, 47-44 B.C.," (Fordham University Ph.D. diss., 1961); Antonius Selem, intro. to his ed. of *De finibus* (Roma, 1962), pp. viii-ix.

[15] Bailey, *Cicero,* pp. x-xi; Boyancé, *Études,* pp. 205-21; Tenney Frank, "Cicero," *Proceedings of the British Academy,* 1932 (London, 1932), pp. 126-27; Jürgen Graff, *Ciceros Selbstauffassung* (Heidelberg, 1963), pp. 46-54; James S. Ried, intro. to his ed. of *Academica* (Heidelberg, 1966 [repr. of London, 1885 ed.]), p. 24.

sophical school in one work and attacking it in another. Since philosophical study was a life-long avocation for Cicero, it would seem unreasonable to charge him with the superficiality of an enthusiastic but misinformed latecomer to this discipline. Since his philosophical works were
all written within a rather short span of years, his discrepancies cannot
be accounted for in terms of the progressive development of his thought.
The older, or Mommsenesque, tendency was to attribute Cicero's inconsistencies to his own intellectual mediocrity and to a hasty and hence
slapdash method of philosophical composition. In reappraising Cicero as
a highly intelligent and broadly educated man, the revisionists have had
to find alternative explanations for his internal contradictions. One view
that has been advanced with some cogency is that Cicero must be understood as an example of Hellenistic philosophy, a tradition represented by
his teachers and by many of the authors he cites, and a tradition marked
by eclecticism and the tendency to blur the distinctive positions of the
earlier Greek schools. Cicero thus reflects the lack of clarity and precision
characteristic of the Hellenistic age.[16] Another interpretation which by
no means excludes the one just mentioned stresses the fact that Cicero
was first and foremost a professional rhetorician, sensitive to the principle
that different kinds of arguments should be advanced in different works
depending on the objective at issue. Thus, he sometimes advocates one
position and at other times another; his discrepancies, reversals, and
omissions are a calculated rhetorical strategy.[17] Still another group of
scholars argues that Cicero's use of philosophical ideas is not inaccurate
or confused at all, but simply selective. Cicero, they urge, was not interested in developing a consistent philosophical system but sought rather
to find solutions to a number of particular problems, which were not
always connected organically in his mind. One must not, therefore, judge
him according to standards alien to his own conception of the philosophical enterprise.[18]

---

[16] Frank, "Cicero," pp. 126-27; Gelzer, *Cicero*, p. 294 n. 282; Georg Luck, *Der Akademiker Antiochos* (Bern, 1953); Annemarie Lueder, *Die philosophische Persönlichkeit des Antiochos von Askalon* (Göttingen, 1940); Philip Merlan, "Greek Philosophy from Plato to
Plotinus," *Cambridge History of Later Greek and Early Medieval Philosophy*, ed. A. H. Armstrong (Cambridge, 1967), pp. 53-56; Alain Michel, "La philosophie de Cicéron avant
54," *REA*, 67 (1965), 327; Max Pohlenz, intro. to *Tusc. disp.*, ed. Otto Heines (Stuttgart,
1957 [repr. of 5th ed., 1912]), p. 11.

[17] Görler, *Untersuchungen*, pp. 27-184; Harold Guite, "Cicero's Attitude toward the
Greeks," *Greece & Rome*, 2nd ser., 9 (1962), 142-59; Ruch, *Le préambule*, pp. 185-321.

[18] G. B. Kerferd, "Cicero and Stoic Ethics," *Cicero and Virgil: Studies in Honour of Harold
Hunt*, ed. John R. C. Martyn (Amsterdam, 1972), pp. 60-74; J. T. Muckle, "The Influence of Cicero in the Formation of Christian Culture," *Transactions of the Royal Society of
Canada*, ser. 3:42, sect. 2 (1948), 107-25; Spanneut, *Permanence du Stoïcisme*, pp. 112-19. A
tour de force along the same lines is provided by Augusto Traversa, *L'Antica e media Stoà*

The accuracy with which Cicero, or his immediate authorities, may have used their sources is linked to the question of Cicero's motivation on another level of debate. Some scholars believe that Cicero is perfectly straightforward in works where he assumes a doxographical stance; he is merely summarizing the views of a series of philosophical schools.[19] Other scholars assert, with equal confidence, that Cicero makes use of the doxographical method as a literary device for expressing either his own personal eclecticism or his unwillingness to commit himself.[20] Yet another approach stresses the importance of accepting Cicero's doxographical reports literally as the only way to avoid the circular reasoning of the *Quellenforscher*. In cases where there are no independent *testimonia* that enable us to determine how accurately Cicero is adhering to his presumed sources, it is urged, his relationship to his sources can be tested by comparing the opinions he states elsewhere with the passages in which he reports the *doxa* of the schools.[21]

The very paucity of independent witnesses to many of the Hellenistic philosophies in question raises serious doubts about the possibility of discovering so confidently the degree to which Cicero's thought is original or unoriginal, the degree to which he milked one source rather than another for an idea available in more than one place, the degree to which his grasp of his sources is accurate or inaccurate, and the degree to which those omissions or misconstructions that can be tested by recourse to external witnesses result from obtuseness and confusion on the part of Cicero or his immediate authorities or from some calculated strategy on his part. These difficulties notwithstanding, scholars have not hesitated to classify Cicero in relation to one ancient philosophical school or another, or to interpret him as a thinker with some clear-cut personal position.

Scholars in quest of Cicero's intellectual allegiances have tended to focus primarily on his relationship to the Platonic and Stoic traditions. Only a few commentators have emphasized the exhaustiveness or directness of his access to Stoicism.[22] Much more typical is the view that

---

dalle opere filosofiche di Cicerone (Torino, 1957), whose book is a compendium of fragments taken from Cicero's works showing how much Stoic doctrine can be reconstructed thereby.

[19] John Ferguson, "Cicero's Contribution to Philosophy," *Studies in Cicero*, Collana di studi ciceroniani, 2 (Roma, 1962), pp.104-11; "The Religion of Cicero," ibid., pp. 83-96.

[20] Alain Michel, "Doxographie et histoire de la philosophie chez Cicéron (Lucullus, 128 sqq.)," *Studien zur Geschichte und Philosophie des Altertums*, ed. J. Harmatta (Amsterdam, 1968), pp. 113-20.

[21] Bruwaene, *La théologie de Cicéron*, pp. vii-ix.

[22] See the references cited in note 18, above all Traversa.

he probably obtained the relatively few Stoic ideas he possessed from non-Stoic sources.[23] Far more attention has been paid to Cicero's attitude toward the Academy. In his own time this school was split into two branches, the Old and New Academy.[24] The New Academy had arisen under the tutelage of the skeptics Arcesilas and Carneades. In Cicero's day it was represented by his master Philo of Larissa. The New Academy argued that there is no infallible criterion of truth. Some conclusions can be established as probable and these probabilities are adequate foundations for action. The New Academics were much less interested in constructing a philosophy on the basis of such probabilities than they were in challenging the claims to certitude advanced by other philosophical schools. The Academic skeptics regarded themselves as faithful followers of Plato. They found a warrant for skepticism in Socrates' method of questioning and in the openended style of Plato's dialogues, seeing in them a rejection of dogmatism, a willingness to suspend judgment, and a model for the critical testing of any and all opinions. In this way the New Academy sought to convert Platonism from a constructive philosophy with a positive metaphysics, physics, epistemology, and ethics into a critical philosophy concerned only with epistemology.

The Old Academy, represented in Cicero's day by his teacher Antiochus of Ascalon, rejected the skepticism of the New Academy as incompatible with Platonism, seeking instead to revive the Platonic doctrine of ideas as a basis for cognitive certitude. In its own way, however, the Old Academy diverged just as far from the mind of Plato as the New. Antiochus argued that the Peripatetic, Epicurean, and Stoic schools were all basically in agreement with each other and with Platonism. He believed that the debates among these schools were merely debates over terminology and not over real doctrinal substance. Their conflict could be ended, he thought, if the fundamental similarities among the schools were demonstrated. Antiochus' faith in the unanimity of these opposing schools led him to ignore or to underestimate their many divergences from each other and from Platonism, out of the conviction that he could find a common denominator among them. Where the Old Academy sought to harmonize all philosophies by reducing them to Platonism, the New Academy sought to analyze and refute all philosophies by subjecting

---

[23] Karl Büchner, "Cicero und Panaitios," in *Resultate römischen Lebens in römischen Schriftwerken*, Studien zur römischen Literatur, 6 (Wiesbaden, 1967), pp. 83-92.

[24] On this topic see John Dillon, *The Middle Platonists, 80 B.C. to A.D. 220* (Ithaca, 1977), pp. 52-106; Luck, *Antiochos*; Lueder, *Antiochos*; Richard McKeon, "Introduction to the Philosophy of Cicero," in M. T. Cicero, *Brutus. On the Nature of the Gods. On Divination. On Duties*, trans. Hubert M. Poteat (Chicago, 1950), pp. 25-30; Merlan, "Plato to Plotinus," *Cambridge Hist. of Later Greek and Early Medieval Philos.*, pp. 53-56.

them to Socratic dialectic. The Old Academy charged the New with defecting from Platonism by refusing to deal constructively with the problems of positive philosophy; the New Academy charged the Old with having reverted to Stoicism and not to Platonism. In this internecine feud, both sides reveal a shaky grasp of the essential features of Plato's thought and both sides appear to have misappropriated or falsified the history of philosophy and the teachings of the other schools with which they were concerned.

A large number of scholars regard Cicero as an Academic of one kind or another. The Old Academy has received few votes.[25] One commentator interprets Cicero's philosophical studies as an effort to test the claims of the two Academies by comparing them directly with Plato, the conclusion being that he adhered to the New Academy because he judged it to be more authentically Platonic.[26] Another position which has gained wider support sees Cicero as attracted to the New Academy because of its doctrine of probability. As a rhetorician, Cicero was accustomed to a mode of argument that traded in probabilities rather than certainties. Thus, the idea that probabilities afforded sufficient grounds for action squared with his professional and literary presuppositions.[27] One variant on this theme sees Cicero as attracted to Academic probabilism because it could be yoked more easily than dogmatism with the *mos maiorum* of the Romans.[28] Another group of scholars in this camp emphasizes the skepticism rather than the probabilism of the New Academy as the basis of its appeal for Cicero, noting at the same time that he felt free to apply Academic skepticism with a good deal of flexibility. Skepticism, for Cicero, did not denote an unwavering critical stance flowing from the premise that the truth cannot be known with certitude. Rather, Cicero adopted skepticism as a method in order to acknowledge the difficulty of distinguishing truth from error, as an act of intellectual humility. Thus, Cicero's appropriation of skepticism did not necessarily entail a rejection of all the positions attacked by the New Academy. He feels just as free to criticize the New Academy as to criticize its alternatives, or to adopt

---

[25] The major and almost only strong supporters of this view are Balsdon, "Cicero," in *Cicero*, ed. Dorey, p. 203; H. A. K. Hunt, *The Humanism of Cicero* (Melbourne, 1954).

[26] Walter Burkert, "Cicero als Platoniker und Skeptiker: Zum Platonsverständnis der 'Neuen Akademie'," *Gymnasium*, 72 (1965), 175-200.

[27] McKeon, intro. to *Brutus*, trans. Poteat, pp. 25-30; Pohlenz, intro, to *Tusc. disp.*, ed. Heines, pp. 12-13; Reid, intro. to his ed. of *Academica*, pp. 10-24; Wilhelm Süss, *Cicero: Ein Einführung in seine philosophischen Schriften (mit Ausschluss der staatsphilosophischen Werke)*, Akademie der Wissenschaften und der Literatur in Mainz, Abhandlungen der geistes- und sozialwissenschaftlichen Klasse, 1965, 5 (Wiesbaden, 1966), pp. 13, 20; Thiacourt, *Essai*, pp. 338-42.

[28] Graff, *Ciceros Selbstauffassung*, pp. 54-58.

dogmatic positions if he finds them convincing, or to withhold his assent in cases where he finds no position persuasive.[29]

This last-mentioned interpretation provides a good basis for correlating Cicero's frequently noted eclecticism with a strong if elastic commitment to one dominant philosophical orientation. Most commentators, however, see no grounds for identifying him primarily with any one school and are content to describe him as an eclectic *tout court*. Cicero was an eclectic, they argue, for the simple reason that he believed that some philosophers provided better answers in some areas and other philosophers provided better answers in other areas. He felt no discomfort at being a skeptic in the field of epistemology and a Stoic in the field of ethics. He simply picked and chose among the schools with little or no concern for the connections that might obtain between one branch of philosophy and another.[30] But in making his own those principles that he found useful in various areas Cicero was not merely reporting or mechanically transmitting the ideas of the Greeks. He evaluated them, criticized them, and reexpressed them in ways that would be comprehensible and appealing to his Roman audience.

It is in this process of interpreting and reformulating the philosophy of the Greeks that Cicero's chief contribution as a philosophical thinker is seen to lie by many commentators. Cicero was the first Roman to propound a reasoned defense of philosophy to a community lacking an indigenous tradition of speculative thought. In this sense his self-justifications in the prefaces of his philosophical works are more than just an attempt to come to terms with his own unlooked-for *otium*.[31] In the novel act of writing philosophical works in Latin Cicero was moved to formulate a philosophical vocabulary in the Latin language and to adapt and develop Latin literary genres for the exposition of philosophical ideas.[32] Still other commentators have located Cicero's most original

---

[29] The best statement of this interpretation is found in Bruce Fairgray Harris, "Cicero as an Academic: A Study of *De Natura Deorum*," *University of Auckland Bulletin, 58,* Classics ser., 2 (1961), 3–37. See also Karl Büchner, *Cicero: Bestand und Wandel seiner geistigen Welt* (Heidelberg, 1964), p. 381; A. E. Douglas, "Cicero the Philosopher," in *Cicero*, ed. Dorey, pp. 135–50; Gelzer, *Cicero*, pp. 294–313, 335–41, 343–54, 357–63; R. G. Tanner, "Cicero on Conscience and Morality," in *Cicero and Virgil*, ed. Martyn, pp. 87–112.

[30] Bailey, *Cicero*, pp. x–xi; Robert Seymour Conway, "The Originality of Cicero," in *Makers of Europe: Being the James Henry Morgan Lectures in Dickinson College for 1930* (Cambridge, Mass., 1931), pp. 22–45; Frank O. Copley, intro. to his trans. of *On Old Age and On Friendship* (Ann Arbor, 1967), pp. xiii–xv; Ferguson, "Cicero's Contribution to Philosophy," *Studies in Cicero*, pp. 104–11; Virginia Guazzoni Foà, "Il metodo di Cicerone nell' indagine filosofica," *Rivista di filosofia neo-scolastica, 48* (1956), 293–315; Reid, intro. to his ed. of *Academica*, pp. 10–28; Süss, *Cicero*, pp. 5–6; Traversa, *L'Antica e media Stoà*, pp. iv, ix–x.

[31] Reid, intro. to his ed. of *Academica*, pp. 24–25.

[32] J. C. Davies, "The Originality of Cicero's Philosophical Works," *Latomus, 30* (1971),

achievement in his synthesis of philosophy and literature, particularly the prose forms of rhetoric and history. For Cicero history serves as an empirical test for the ethical claims of the different philosophical schools. While history supplies *exempla virtutis,* philosophy in turn provides norms for judging the choices that men must make in their own historical environment. This integration of the abstractions of the philosophers with the concreteness of history is what made Cicero's philosophical ideas relevant to his Roman audience.[33] The use of historical examples is itself a rhetorical technique. Philosophers before Cicero's time had devoted some attention to rhetorical theory, but he was the first professional rhetorician to unite philosophical speculation with rhetorical theory and practice. In addition to using philosophical principles in his rhetoric and rhetorical strategies in his philosophical works, Cicero reoriented the treatment of these two disciplines by observing that philosophy and rhetoric have a common subject matter which can be treated by a common methodology. Cicero thus recasts philosophical topics of all kinds as rhetorical *controversiae* and *suasoriae.* He is the first and most important exponent in the Latin language of the idea that philosophy must be presented in an eloquent and pleasing style if it is to accomplish its didactic objectives.[34]

The most enthusiastic wing of the revisionist movement is represented by a number of scholars who seek to portray Cicero as the proponent of some sort of systematic philosophical program of his own. In contrast to other critical perspectives, this approach has the merit of dealing with Cicero's philosophical works as a whole. At the same time, none of the delineations of a Ciceronian master plan that has been put forth to date is completely satisfactory. All omit some of his works from the proposed system or leave other unanswered questions.

The simplest and most inadequate of these interpretations is the one offered by Patrick A. Sullivan, who argues that Cicero wished to reproduce a complete curriculum of the topics traditionally dealt with by philosophers, following the threefold division of the subject into logic, ethics, and physics.[35] However, Sullivan ignores a number of Cicero's works, even though they are clearly a part of ethics, and he fails to explain why

---

105-19. See also Gigon, "Cicero," *Aufstieg und Niedergang der römischen Welt, 1,* part 4, 226-61; Selem, intro. to his ed. of *De fin.,* pp. viii-ix; Thiacourt, *Essai,* pp. 334-38.

[33] G. W. R. Ardley, "Cicero on Philosophy and History," *Prudentia, 1* (1969), 28-41.

[34] Michael J. Buckley, "Philosophical Method in Cicero," *Journal of the History of Philosophy, 8* (1970), 143-54; Alain Michel, *Rhétorique et philosophie chez Cicéron: Essai sur les fondements philosophiques de l'art de persuader* (Paris, 1960); "Rhétorique et philosophie dans les *Tusculanes," REL, 39* (1961), 158-71.

[35] Patrick A. Sullivan, "The Plan of Cicero's Philosophical Corpus" (Fordham University Ph.D. diss., 1951).

Cicero did not write anything dealing expressly with physics or dialectic.

In contrast, Margaret Young Henry sees the main theme of Cicero's system as the desire to find solutions to philosophical problems which he felt had been left hanging by the contemporary schools, particularly the Stoic and Academic. The most pressing of these problems was the tension between skepticism and dogmatism. Henry argues that Cicero was basically an affirmative thinker who found in the doctrine of probability a middle position between Academic skepticism and Stoic dogmatism.[36] Outside of the fact that she blurs the distinctions between the Old and New Academies and uses key terms according to anachronistic definitions, Henry's thesis is incapable of dealing with works where Cicero holds the ideas he espouses on either axiomatic, traditional, or intuitive grounds.

A much more elaborate analysis of Cicero as a philosophical system-builder is the interpretation presented by H. A. K. Hunt.[37] According to Hunt, Cicero took the philosophy of Antiochus as his point of departure, accepting Antiochus' definitions of the problems that philosophers ought to treat and the order in which they should be treated. But, in following that order, from epistemology to cosmology to theology to ethics, Cicero criticizes many of Antiochus' teachings and substitutes Academic skepticism and middle Stoic ethics. One of the merits of Hunt's work is that he recognizes the fact that Cicero was aware of the differences between the ancient and middle Stoa, that he sometimes acknowledges these differences and sometimes does not, and that he was willing and able to test Antiochus' conception of Stoicism by comparing it with the original product. At the same time there are serious weaknesses in Hunt's interpretation. He fails to explain why Cicero wrote the *De republica* and *De legibus*, both of which can be viewed as a subdivision of ethics and both of which contain a significant element of cosmology, before he had addressed himself to these stages of his alleged philosophical program. He ignores Cicero's rhetorical theory completely. He also omits from his consideration three of Cicero's ethical works, the *De gloria*, the *De senectute*, and the *De amicitia*, on the mystifying grounds that they are "works of philosophical sentiment not essential to the development of his argument."[38] Finally, he seeks to explain Cicero's translation of the *Timaeus* as a prelude to his treatises on cosmology,[39] but he does not clarify why

---

[36] Margaret Young Henry, *Relation of Dogmatism and Scepticism in the Philosophical Treatises of Cicero* (Geneva, N.Y., 1925).

[37] Hunt, *Humanism of Cicero*, passim and summary pp. 188-205.

[38] Ibid., p. 1.

[39] Ibid., pp. 128-31.

Cicero felt no need to produce analogous translations as introductions to the other segments of his philosophical thought.

An alternative point of view is visible in the studies of Wilhelm Süss, Luigi Alfonsi, Otto Plasberg, and Klaus Bringmann, all of whom shift their focus to a biographical explanation in which the interrelations between Cicero's public and private concerns provide the reason for the timing, sequence, and subject matter of his philosophical works. Süss sees the year 45 B.C. as the relevant point of departure. Although Cicero had written philosophical works before this time to fill his leisure and as a substitute for political action, his main motivation was to speculate on ethical questions that were of deep personal concern to him. It was the death of Tullia which caused these private ethical concerns to surface. An index of Cicero's exclusively personal approach to moral philosophy, according to Süss, can be seen in the contrast between works like the *Tusculanarum disputationum* and the Platonic dialogues on which Cicero modeled them. Where Plato gives his dialogues a civic setting, Cicero sets his dialogues in private houses outside the city limits.[40] Süss' preclusive stress on the private ethical dimension has the vice of omitting all of Cicero's rhetorical and political theory, despite its connection with ethics, and the *Paradoxa Stoicorum*, which does deal expressly with ethics but which was written before Tullia's death. Most importantly, Süss underestimates the importance of civic virtue to Cicero, a topic in which he was interested to the point of obsessiveness. Süss is incapable of ignoring the fact that there are political and propagandistic elements in a number of Cicero's ethical works,[41] but he does not succeed in incorporating this fact comprehensibly into his interpretation.

Alfonsi sees two main periods in Cicero's philosophical activity, the 50s B.C. when he wrote the *De republica* and *De legibus* and the years from 46 to 44 B.C. when he had to substitute writing for action and when he was preoccupied by private sorrows.[42] Like Süss, he omits Cicero's rhetorical theory, making no effort to correlate it with either his public or private concerns. However, in contrast to Süss, he sees the *De officiis* as a return to Cicero's earlier civic orientation. But he fails to explain why Cicero should have reverted to a public perspective at the end of his life.

Plasberg agrees that Cicero's philosophical career can be divided into two periods, before and after 46 B.C. The reason for this division, however, is not merely or mainly the death of Tullia but the political circum-

---

[40] Süss, *Cicero*, p. 68.

[41] Ibid., pp. 135-36, 141, 143-61.

[42] Luigi Alfonsi, "Cicerone filosofo (linee per lo studio del suo 'iter' speculativo)," *Marco Tullio Cicerone*, Scritti commemorativi pubblicati nel bimillenario della morte, Roma, Istituto di studi romani, Centro di studi ciceroniani (Firenze, 1961), pp. 177-85.

stances of the time and Cicero's conception of the degree to which he could recover a leading role in public affairs.[43] Cicero's political career was in fact over in 56 B.C., but he did not internalize this fact until his falling out with Caesar ten years later. Cicero wrote the *De republica* and *De legibus* before 46 B.C. because he still regarded himself as an influential statesman whose views on law and politics would be taken seriously. His works of mature rhetorical theory, which stress the connection between wisdom, eloquence, and public service, were undertaken in the first period for similar reasons.[44] It was only after Cicero's political hopes had been shattered irretrievably that he turned away from topics directly connected with public life and concerned himself instead with private ethics. Plasberg's interpretation has two conspicuous merits. First, he deals cogently with Cicero's rhetorical and political theory and relates it comprehensibly with the rest of his thought. Second, he recognizes the point that it was not so much events themselves as events as Cicero understood them which inspired his perceptions or misconceptions about himself, his times, and the range of the possible. The main weakness of Plasberg's study is that he gives extremely short shrift to the works written after 46 B.C., making it difficult for him to prove that they are indeed as exclusively private in focus as he claims.

Bringmann, whose study of Cicero's philosophical works in general is the most recent, rectifies this weakness to a considerable extent, while developing and correcting the overall line of argument laid down by Plasberg. Bringmann agrees that Cicero's philosophical writings are best explained in relation to the political situation, at least as he evaluated it, as well as to his personal circumstances. He also agrees that Cicero's rhetorical theory cannot be divorced from the rest of his thought. In Bringmann's estimation, however, it is just as great a mistake to divorce public from private concerns in the writings of Cicero's last years. According to Bringmann, Cicero was working for the same goals in all of his philosophical writings. But he shifted his strategy at different moments, depending on the circumstances and his estimate of how he could be most effective. Without ignoring Cicero's interest in philosophy as personal consolation, Bringmann sees a consistent and twofold motivation behind all of Cicero's philosophical works. First, he wanted to educate his contemporaries in civic virtue while at the same time forging a connection between civic virtue and the Republican constitution. Second, he wanted to vindicate his own political cause by exposing the

---

[43] Otto Plasberg, *Cicero in seinen Werken und Briefen,* ed. Wilhelm Ax, Das Erbe der Alten, *11* (Leipzig, 1926), pp. 8-9.

[44] Ibid., pp. 39-41, 107-41.

vices of his enemies and by demonstrating his own intellectual and moral qualifications for active public service. By one means or another, all of Cicero's philosophical works, at whatever time they were written, address themselves to these same themes.[45]

So far as it goes, Bringmann's interpretation is quite persuasive. He has the merit of bringing together many more works and many more facets of Cicero's personality than is true of virtually any other commentator. He offers many illuminating insights into particular Ciceronian works and succeeds in resolving a number of controversial points, notably Cicero on *otium*, effectively disposing of a lengthy and unenlightening argument on that topic.[46] Bringmann presents a view of Cicero in which his unwavering sense of duty, his need to justify himself, his relish for debate, his eclectic tastes, his backing and filling, his illusions concerning

---

[45] Klaus Bringmann, *Untersuchungen zum späten Cicero* (Göttingen, 1971).

[46] Much of the debate on this issue stems from the fact that scholars have tended to assess Cicero's idea of *otium* from the perspective of one work or set of works, or at one point in his life. There are two major positions which connect the idea of *otium* with Cicero's period of active statesmanship or with the period in which he made his peace with Caesar. For E. Rémy, "Dignitas cum otio," *Le Musée Belge, 32* (1928), 113-27, *otium* was Cicero's synonym for peace, and *dignitas* meant the duties of the ruling class. His combination of these terms in one motto means his voluntary acceptance of the established order and is a formula enabling him to accomodate himself to Caesar's coup d'état without loss of face. C. Wirszubski, "Cicero's *cum dignitate otium*: A Reconsideration," *JRS, 44* (1954), 1-13 agrees that *otium* on one level means peace, but argues that it is the quiescence enjoined on those opposing the senatorial class by Cicero as a member of the ruling elite, and it also signifies the leisure enabling aristocrats to engage in public life or the temporary respite from their public duties. This position is also supported by Büchner, "Cicero, Grundzüge seines Wesens," *Cicero*, p. 7; Ferguson, *Utopias of the Classical World*, p. 158; and Manfred Fuhrmann, "Cum dignitate otium: Politisches Programm und Staatstheorie bei Cicero," *Gymnasium, 67* (1960), 483-99.

On the other hand stands the theory that *otium* signifies the contemplative life, an existence for which Cicero had to develop a positive rationale once he was forced into retirement. The term thus has a personal moral meaning for him and is not merely a propaganda slogan. The chief exponent of this view is Pierre Boyancé, "Cum dignitate otium," *REA, 43* (1941), 172-91; "Cicéron et la vie contemplative," *Latomus, 26* (1967), 3-26, who is also concerned with the philosophical sources for the notion, which he traces to Platonism and Aristotelianism. In the same vein are the positions of Dieter Perlich, "Otium oder accedere ad rem publicam: Das Problem der politischen Betätigung bei Cicero," *Der altsprachliche Unterricht, 13*:1 (1970), 5-16 and Ruch, *Le préambule*, pp. 83-85, who argue that Cicero always viewed the contemplative life as a second-best choice, Ruch adding the opinion that he thought it was incapable of affording *dignitas*. Ettore Lepore, *Il princeps ciceroniano e gli ideali politici della tarda repubblica* (Napoli, 1954), pp. 144-55 sees the philosophical source for *otium* as Aristotelianism and sees Cicero as striving to find a mean between the active and the contemplative life. However, Marianne Kretchmar, *Otium, Studia litterarum, Philosophie und Bios Theoretikos im Leben und Denken Ciceros* (Würzburg, 1938) and E. de Saint-Denis, "La théorie cicéronienne de la participation aux affaires publiques," *Revue de philologie, 12* (1938), 193-215 have surveyed what Cicero says about *otium* throughout his career and have arrived at the conclusion that he reinterprets this topic in the light of his circumstances, choosing different philosophical positions on it at different times.

his own importance and the possibilities of his times can all be accommodated without the need to depict him as a mediocrity, a hypocrite, or a schizophrenic. The main limitation of Bringmann's study, as he has conceived it, is that he begins with the year 47 B.C. because he thinks that it opened the final stage of Cicero's life as a political outsider. This decision leads him to deal much too superficially with the *De republica* and *De oratore*, despite their importance. He also inexplicably omits the *De senectute,* which likewise meshes perfectly with his thesis. Still, the positive merits of Bringmann's interpretation outweigh the defects. His Cicero emerges as less of a doctrinaire and more of a would-be tactician than the Ciceros presented to the reader's view by the other commentators who have treated him as the formulator of a philosophical master plan.

There is still another very important side to the question of Cicero's philosophical thought which is immediately pertinent to the issue of Cicero's Stoicism but which has remained unexplored, even by Bringmann. Cicero's attitude toward philosophy in general, and toward Stoicism in particular, is conditioned not only by his political standpoint and his rhetorical style but also by the specific branch of philosophy which he happens to be dealing with in a given work. He takes a sharply differing stance toward philosophy, and toward particular schools of philosophy, depending on the subject matter. In some areas of his thought he is highly enthusiastic about Stoicism and draws on it heavily. In other areas he attacks Stoic principles forcefully. In still other areas he expressly reformulates them. In yet other areas he manifests only a low level of interest in Stoic ideas and mingles them indiscriminately with doctrines drawn from other schools. Sometimes he presents the Stoic ideas at his command accurately, straightforwardly, and in their full strength. Sometimes he does not. This too is a function not of intellectual sloppiness so much as of the particular branch of philosophy with which he is concerned. Cicero without question makes a great deal of Stoicism available to his readers, whether overtly or not. His unacknowledged references to Stoic doctrines, from the standpoint of intellectual transmission, are just as important as his express opinions on the Stoa.

Because the philosophical subject matter is of such critical importance in specifying Cicero's attitude toward Stoicism we will follow a topical approach in our own analysis. No effort will be made to stir the turbid waters of *Quellenforschung*; the analysis will focus on the Stoic ideas as they appear in the contexts where they appear without any attempt to speculate on their provenance. Given the large number of Ciceronian works which must be discussed and given Cicero's propensity for repeating himself and reworking his arguments from one treatise to another, a certain amount of overlapping in the coverage of the material will be unavoidable. We will examine Cicero's handling of Stoicism under the headings of rhetorical theory, political theory, epistemology, theology and cosmology, and ethics. This is roughly the order in which he wrote most of his philosophical works; but the emphasis will be topical rather than chronological. We will conclude by summarizing the Stoic content of Cicero's thought according to the categories of physics, logic, and ethics into which the Stoics themselves divided their philosophy.

III. RHETORICAL THEORY

Cicero's rhetorical treatises contain a good many references to Stoicism. On the whole, his attitude toward Stoicism in this segment of his thought is negative. A few commentators have ignored[47] or exaggerated[48] the importance of the Stoic material in these works. The dominant view, which the evidence supports, sees Cicero the oratorical theorist as referring to Stoicism, when he refers to it, within the context of a primarily Aristotelian conception of rhetoric. Cicero stands squarely within the anti-sophistic tradition stretching back to the time of Plato. He borrows certain themes from the Stoics; but his rhetorical theory and the criteria he advocates for its practice reflect his adherance to the Peripatetic tradition.[49]

On the surface, Cicero's rhetorical theory appears to be more Stoic in sympathy than it actually is. He stresses a point also emphasized by the Stoics in his repeated assertion that oratory cannot be separated from wisdom and virtue. The orator must be well versed in philosophy, cosmo-

---

[47] Benedetto Riposati, *Studi sui 'Topica' di Cicerone* (Milano, 1947), pp. 5-6.

[48] Pasquale Giuffrida, "La dottrina stoica della *phone* e l'*Orator* di Cicerone," *Scritti vari pubblicati della Facoltà di magistrato dell' Università di Torino, 1* (1950), 115-28; McKeon, intro. to *Brutus*, trans. Poteat, pp. 34, 37; Hans Kurt Schulte, *Orator: Untersuchungen über das ciceronianische Bildungsideal* (Frankfurt am Main, 1935), pp. 32-34.

[49] The most important statements are by Michel, *Rhétorique et philosophie*, pp. 235-331, 341-44, 362-841; Friedrich Solmsen, "Aristotle and Cicero on the Orator's Playing upon the Feelings," *CP, 33* (1938), 390-404; "The Aristotelian Tradition in Ancient Rhetoric," *AJP, 62* (1941), 173-74, 176, 178-82. There is a nice general appreciation by E. Gilson, "Eloquence et sagesse selon Cicéron," *Phoenix, 7* (1953), 1-19. See also Bringmann, *Untersuchungen*, pp. 41-59; Olof Gigon, "Cicero und Aristoteles," *Hermes, 87* (1959), 143-62; Graff, *Ciceros Selbstauffassung*, pp. 69-76; W. Leonard Grant, "Cicero on the Moral Character of the Orator," *CJ, 38* (1943), 472-78; Wilhelm Kroll, "Cicero und die Rhetorik," *Neue Jahrbücher für das klassische Altertum, 11* (1903), 681-89; Leeman, *Orationis Ratio, 1*, 121, 204-05; Edward H. Madden, "The Enthymeme: Crossroads of Logic, Rhetoric, and Metaphysics," *Philosophical Review, 61* (1952), 368-73; James J. Murphy, *Rhetoric in the Middle Ages: A History of Rhetorical Theory from Saint Augustine to the Renaissance* (Berkeley, 1974), pp. 8-22; Pasquale Giuffrida, *Ricerche sull'ecletticismo ciceroniano*, ed. Felicità Portalupi (Torino, 1963), pp. 31-33; Gabriel Nuchelmans, "Philologia et son mariage avec Mercure jusqu'à la fin du XIIᵉ siècle," *Latomus, 16* (1957), 85.

logy, and logic. In the latter field Chrysippus walks hand in hand with
Aristotle as an authority.[50] The orator must also be educated in law, in
history, and in a wide range of disciplines both theoretical and practical.[51] For Cicero, as for the Stoics, the orator's aim is to instruct his
hearers in the good[52] and he must be a virtuous man himself, who communicates the ethical values he professes by his personal example. Cicero
links the morality of the speaker with a specific set of political attitudes.
He charges the Gracchi with sophistry because he thinks that the reforms
they promoted failed to serve the public good; their eloquence is thus
castigated as self-serving demagoguery.[53] On the other hand, he chooses
Republican statesmen of the party he admires as the speakers in the
Brutus and the *De oratore*[54] and praises the virtues of a number of other
Republican worthies, such as Rutilius and Tubero, whose moral excellence he describes in specifically Stoic terms, adverting to their self-sufficiency and their ethical rigorism in the same breath as their bold and
steadfast patriotism.[55] This Stoicizing of the virtue he esteems in orators
and public men is reinforced by Cicero's assertion of the Stoic principle
that all the virtues are equal and on a par: *Sunt omnes virtutes aequales et
pares*. Among them, none the less, oratory is one of the supreme virtues
because it embraces all knowledge and it is ordained to the end of public
service.[56] In the *De oratore* Scaevola cites Panaetius as an authority on
rhetoric[57] while another speaker in the same work, Crassus, praises the
Stoics as the only philosophical school to define eloquence as a virtue and
as a form of wisdom.[58]

Yet Cicero by no means subscribes to the Stoic conception of the sage
as the only truly good orator; nor does he support the Stoic stylistic norms
of brevity, restraint, minimal decoration, and the exclusive appeal to the
intellect of the audience. Crassus in the *De oratore*, notwithstanding his
appreciation of the Stoics' evaluation of rhetoric, dismisses them abruptly

---

[50] *Orator* 32.15, trans. H. M. Hubbell, Loeb (Cambridge, Mass, 1962). Citations will
be made to this edition.

[51] *Brutus* 6.23, trans. G. L. Hendrickson, Loeb (Cambridge, Mass., 1962); *Orator*
4.14-5.19, 33.118-34.122; *De oratore* 1.11.48-1.16.73, 2.2.5-7, trans. E. W. Sutton and H.
Rackham, (Cambridge, Mass., 1959-60). Citations will be made to these editions.

[52] *De inventione* 1.1.1, 1.3.4-5.

[53] Graff, *Ciceros Selbstauffassung*, pp. 47-55, 78-79.

[54] In *De oratore* 1.1.1, Cicero makes a point of explaining this as well as simply doing
it. On the *Brutus* in this connection, see Matthias Gelzer, "Cicero's 'Brutus' als politische
Kundgebung," *Philologus*, *93* (1938), 128-31.

[55] *Brutus* 29.114-115, 31.117.

[56] *De oratore* 3.14.54-3.16.62; the quotation occurs at 3.14.55.

[57] *De or.* 1.17.74.

[58] *De or.* 3.17.65. Elsewhere he also praises the Stoics' honesty in saying what they
mean plainly and straightforwardly in contrast to hypocrites who use hyperrefined eu-
phemisms, *Ad fam.* 9.22.4-5.

as useless guides to the art of oratory. First, he says, the Stoics teach that everyone who is not a sage is a fool, a doctrine which could not be stated before a mixed audience without giving offense. Second, the Stoics have their own technical definitions of certain ethical terms, which, if adopted, would make a speaker unintelligible to most people. Third, Crassus objects to the aridity of the Stoics' literary style.[59] This last point is one that Cicero returns to repeatedly. Antoninus, another speaker in the same dialogue, also berates the Stoics for their dry, cramped, and charmless style, adding that their lack of fluency gives the lie to their theory that the wise man automatically possesses eloquence. He and Scaevola agree that it is the Stoics' excessive preoccupation with dialectical hairsplitting that prevents them from expressing themselves in a pleasing style, Crassus adding that Chrysippus cannot be thought of as a great philosopher, despite his reputation as a dialectician, owing to his lack of eloquence.[60]

In the *Brutus* the same personages whom the interlocutors praise for their Stoic virtue and Republican patriotism are also criticized for their shortcomings as orators. Rutilius, a pupil of Panaetius, was keen and systematic in his reasoning but severe and meager in his style, and unskilled at winning over a general audience; Tubero's oratory was flawed by a rough and harsh manner of speaking; Spurius Mummius, another disciple of the Stoics, spoke with objectionable conciseness. These failings all derive from the Stoics' taste for disputation, which may have made them acute but which did not make them eloquent. The virtues unquestionably possessed by these men can in no sense be equated with oratorical skill. Indeed, Cato the younger is the only exemplar of Stoic virtue and Republican heroism whom Cicero is willing to describe as eloquent, but he is an exception who proves the rule.[61] Cicero finds the same faults, *ieiunitas* and *siccitas*, meagerness and aridity, in the Stoic orators as he finds in the Attic style of rhetoric,[62] which, like the floridity of the *Asiatici*, is a style he criticizes frequently. This parallel suggests that his broadside against Stoic rhetoric may have been motivated at least in part by his desire to use it as a weapon in his ongoing literary feud with the Atticists.

The didactic and ethical emphasis in Cicero's rhetorical theory, which seems to harmonize with Stoicism at first glance, is thus only a superficial similarity which breaks down on closer inspection. Cicero unmistakably

---

[59] *De or.* 3.18.65-66. See also *Ad fam.* 15.19.1.

[60] *De or.* 1.10.43, 1.11.50, 1.18.83, 2.28.157-159.

[61] *Brutus* 25.94, 29.113-31.121. Noted by Leeman, *Orationis Ratio, 1,* 204-05. Another example of Cicero's praise of Cato in a rhetorical context is *Pro Murena* 35.74-36.76, trans. Louis E. Lord, Loeb (Cambridge, Mass., 1959), although this praise is ironic since he treats Cato as a caricature of Stoic rigidity, 29.60-31.66.

[62] *Brutus* 82.285. Noted by Michel, *Rhétorique et philosophie*, pp. 436-42.

opposes the Stoic view that the sole objective of rhetoric is to communicate truth and that it should direct itself exclusively to the intellect of the audience. Instead, he states repeatedly that rhetoric has the triple objective of teaching, delighting, and persuading its audience and that it ought to appeal to the emotions as well as to the intellect. In describing the orator's threefold goal, he also emphasizes the point that the goal of persuasion is the most critical of the three:

> Optimus enim orator qui dicendo animos audientium et docet et delectat et permovet. Docere debitum est, delectare honorarium, permovere necessarium.[63]

> The supreme orator, then, is the one whose speech instructs, delights, and moves the minds of his audience. The orator is duty bound to instruct; giving pleasure is a free gift to the audience; to move them is indispensable.

In advising the orator on how to do this Cicero does not hesitate to recommend that he suppress part of the truth or that he twist the truth to his advantage, reporting only those facts that support his case and advancing only those themes that will be acceptable to his audience.[64] The important thing is to win the case.

The orator, furthermore, must know the passions and how to arouse them. Cicero provides detailed instructions on how to do this.[65] The passions in question are the classic Stoic quartet: *Motus autem animi incitatio aut ad voluptatem aut ad molestiam aut ad metum aut ad cupiditatem* ("the passions of the soul are a stimulus either to pleasure or pain or fear or desire.")[66] Rather than controlling and quelling the passions by an appeal to reason, however, Cicero advises the orator to stimulate and manipulate them. Indeed, while he calls logic and rhetoric the twin handmaidens of wisdom, it is for this reason that he exalts rhetoric above logic, for rhetoric is better adapted to speak to the emotions and thus it can more readily teach and persuade the majority of men.[67] In this connection Cicero uses a Stoic metaphor to illustrate the basically non-Stoic position he is advocating. He refers to Zeno's comparison between logic as a closed fist and rhetoric as an open palm;[68] but, for Cicero the comparison sug-

---

[63] *De optimo genere oratorum* 1.3.4, trans. H. M. Hubbell, Loeb (Cambridge, Mass., 1960). The same idea is also found ibid., 5.16; *Brutus* 49.185, 53.197-198; *Orator* 21.69; *De or.* 2.27.115-116, 2.28.121.

[64] *De inventione* 1.2.29-30; *De part. or.* 25.89-91.

[65] *Brutus* 23.89; *Orator* 37.128-38.133; *De or.* 1.12.53, 1.13.60, 2.42.178-179, 2.43.182-197, 2.50.204-2.70.289, 2.77.311-313, 2.89.324, 3.30.118; *De part. or.* 3.9, 3.10-5.15 and passim. See also Grant, "Cicero on Moral Character," *CJ, 38* (1943), 472-78.

[66] *De part. or.* 3.9.

[67] *De part. or.* 23.79.

[68] *Orator* 32.113.

gests the superiority of fair address over rigor as a means of engaging the audience's good will and assent.

The stylistic correlative of Cicero's theory is developed in his analysis of the three kinds of style, the plain, the middle, and the high, which are adapted respectively to proof, pleasure, and persuasion. They must also be geared to the ethos of the audience and to the particular occasion. Cicero lists an array of figures of speech and provides a copious assortment of strategies for rhetorical embellishment. The orator's *sapientia* consists in his ability to select and apply the proper *colores rhetorici*. Cicero invokes the norm of decorum in discussing this topic, but it is a norm clearly related in his mind to an aesthetic of decoration rather than to one of sober intellectualism.[69] He expressly rejects the Stoics' preclusive adherence to the plain style, their preference for the *verba antiqua,* their distaste for coloristic devices, and their insistence on unadorned didacticism.[70] Instead, his concern with the need to know and to manipulate the emotions and his sensitivity to the ethos of the audience point to his Aristotelian proclivities as a rhetorical theorist. At the same time, his elevation of rhetoric above logic can be seen as a criticism of the Aristotelian no less than of the Stoic tradition. Cicero sounds a theme here that he orchestrates over and over again in his other philosophical works, a theme which is his most fundamental justification for reformulating philosophical ideas in attractive literary modes. He wishes to stress the principle that truth and goodness, important as they are, will remain inaccessible to most people unless they are made appealing by the art of rhetoric. It is not merely a question of wisdom and virtue informing the orator; more importantly, wisdom and virtue are dependent on eloquence as the means by which they may win men's minds and hearts.

In working out his rhetorical principles, then, Cicero indicates that he is familiar with Stoic rhetorical theory and that he finds it seriously wanting. He rejects it in favor of an anti-sophistic rhetoric framed in Aristotelian terms. This preference is one he also states expressly by referring to Peripatetic works as oratorical authorities.[71] At the same time, one can find passages in Cicero's rhetorical works where his treatment of Stoic principles is dubious and where he ignores the differences between the Stoic and Aristotelian doctrines at issue. In the *Topica,* for instance, he defines the term *notionum* or common notion, using the Stoic terms *ennoia* and *prolepsis.* But, in contrast to the Stoics, who rooted common notions

---

[69] *Orator* 8.24-27, 21.69, 21.70-74, 35.234-36.125; *De or.* 3.55.210-212.

[70] *Orator* 24.81, 26.91-28.96; *De or.* 3.10.37, 3.21.91, 3.25.96-3.27.108, 3.37.149-3.61.227; *De part. or.* 6.19-6.22. Also noted by Bringmann, *Untersuchungen,* pp. 56-58.

[71] *Ad fam.* 1.9.23, 7.19.1; *De inventione* 2.2.4-10; *Topica* 1.1.1-5.

in sense data, Cicero says that they derive from innate ideas.[72] Elsewhere in the same work he uses Stoic logical formulae without appearing to realize that they are Stoic and not Aristotelian. At the beginning of the *Topica* Cicero states that systematic treatments of argumentation can be divided into two parts, one, called topics, concerned with the *inventio* of arguments and the other, called dialectic, concerned with weighing their validity. Aristotle, he notes, was the founder of both topics and dialectic. The Stoics devoted their attention only to dialectic, neglecting topics despite the superior utility of topics to the orator. Thus, he concludes, the Aristotelians have more to offer than the Stoics to the subject of the present book.[73] But, despite this assertion, in his actual discussion of the *topos* that especially concerns logicians, that dealing with consequents, antecedents, and contradictions, Cicero proceeds to list four of the five Stoic hypothetical syllogisms, the conditional, causal, disjunctive, and conjunctive, along with three alternate or negative versions of the first, the third, and the fourth of these forms. His presentation of these syllogisms may be schematized in the following way:

If A, then B; but A, therefore B.
If not-A, then not-B; but B, therefore A.
Not (A and not-B); but A, therefore B.
Either A or B; but A, therefore not-B.
Either A or B; but not-A, therefore B.
Not (A and B); but A, therefore not-B.
Not (A and B); but not-A, therefore B.[74]

Cicero, however, does not attribute these hypothetical syllogisms to the Stoics. Indeed, he sets the whole discussion in the context of an analysis of the Aristotelian enthymeme, or rhetorical syllogism, as if Aristotle himself had used hypotheticals to illustrate his treatment of the enthymeme. Likewise, in the *De inventione*, he offers the Stoic conditional syllogisim, "If it is light, it is day," as an example of the Aristotelian enthymeme,[75] crediting to the Aristotelians a doctrine that is properly Stoic. Cicero's conflation of the Stoic hypothetical syllogism with the Aristotelian enthymeme may be seen either as a reflection of post-Aristotelian eclecticism within the Peripatetic school, as an act of misinformed or partisan doxography on Cicero's part, or as an inspired association of two doc-

---

[72] *Topica* 7.31. Also noted by Michel, *Rhétorique et philosophie*, pp. 191-93.
[73] *Topica* 2.6-7.
[74] *Topica* 12.53-13.55. The Stoic derivation of the syllogisms outlined in this passage has also been noted by Gelzer, *Cicero*, p. 343; Hubbell, intro. to his trans. of *Topica*, pp. 422-23; Michel, *Rhétorique et philosophie*, pp. 181-83.
[75] *De inventione* 1.46.86.

trines which in fact work quite well together. In any case, his handling of this subject bears out his tendency to appropriate Stoicism, whether acknowledged or not, within the framework of Aristotelian rhetoric.

There are two other areas related to the use of Stoicism in Cicero's rhetorical works that deserve consideration, largely because the positions he takes on them in this context differ markedly from the way he handles them elsewhere in his philosophical *oeuvre*. One of these areas is ethics. Cicero analyzes virtue in general and in particular in two of his rhetorical works, using definitions that are partly Stoic and partly non-Stoic and which have some other interesting peculiarities. In the *De inventione*, Stoicism and Aristotelianism share the honors in Cicero's definition of virtue in general as *animi habitus naturae modo atque rationis consentaneus* ("a habit of mind in harmony with reason and the order of nature,")[76] a formula which acknowledges both the Stoic norm of conformity with reason and nature and the Aristotelian principle of *habitus*. Moving next to the four cardinal virtues, Cicero gives a definition of wisdom that is purely Stoic: *Prudentia est rerum bonarum et malarum neutrarumque scientia* ("Wisdom is the knowledge of what is good, what is bad, and what is neither good nor bad,") a formula reflecting the practical rather than speculative directionality of Stoic *prudentia* and one that gives full weight to the concept of the *adiaphora*. His definition of temperance also has a Stoic coloration: *Temperantia est rationis in libidinem atque in alios non rectos impetus animi firma et moderata dominatio* ("Temperance is a firm and moderate control exercised by reason over lust and other improper impulses of the mind.") Here Cicero gives a nod in the direction of the Aristotelian principle of moderation but his stress is on the rational control of passions which are seen as arising from the mind and not from any infrarational faculties in man, a distinctively Stoic idea. In handling courage and justice, however, Cicero departs abruptly from Stoicism. He defines courage as a purely external virtue revealing no trace of the Stoic stress on inner intentionality and no whisper of the casuistic amplifications which the middle Stoics had applied to it: *Fortitudo est considerata periculorum susceptio et laborum perpessio* ("Courage is the undertaking of dangerous deeds and the endurance of hardships.") In his definition of justice, finally, Cicero invokes the Aristotelian idea of *habitus* and attaches the term *dignitas* to the traditional *suum cuique* formula, a procedure which associates justice with a specifically upper-class Roman set of social and

---

[76] For the definitions which follow, *De inv.* 2.53.159-2.55.164. I have altered Hubbell's translation slightly. An alternative definition of the cardinal virtues in Cicero's rhetorical works can be found in *De part. or.* 22.75-78, where he treats wisdom alone as consisting in knowledge and all the other virtues as consisting in action, an approach that is even less Stoic.

political prerogatives: *Iustitia est habitus animi communi utilitate conservata suam quique tribuens dignitatem* ("Justice is a habit of mind which accords to every man his proper dignity while preserving the common advantage.")

Equally interesting in this definition of justice is Cicero's use of the term *utilitas* rather than some more idealistic term like *salus* or *bonum*. This usage bears directly on the distinction between the *honestum* and the *utile* which he draws in the *De inventione*. The *honestum*, he says, is what is sought wholly or partly for its own sake; the *utile* is sought only with reference to some other end. Virtues fall into the category of the *honestum* while advantages, such as glory, rank, power, influence, and friendship, fall into the category of the *utile*.[77] According to this formulation, virtue actually participates in both the *honestum* and the *utile*, since it can be seen both as a means to some other end as well as an end in itself. Another noteworthy feature of this discussion is Cicero's inclusion of friendship within the class of the *utile*. The reader should not be surprised at this, he takes pains to point out, even though such a definition does not exhaust the meanings of friendship, since the author is analyzing ethical principles from the perspective of their use in debates on public issues. In this context, he notes, it is proper to associate friendship with the political benefits that can be derived from it, for this is the most apposite use of the term as a *topos* in political oratory.[78]

In a similar vein, Cicero analyzes the distinction between the *honestum* and the *utile* in the *De partitione oratoria*, considering this topic from the standpoint of the class of cases in which the orator seeks to promote or to prevent some particular course of action on the grounds that it is good, feasible, useful, or the reverse. From this angle of vision, goods may be divided into those that are necessary, such as life, freedom, and self-respect, and those that are not necessary. The second class can be divided into goods that are desirable *per se* on account of their intrinsic worth, their *honestum*, and goods that are desirable because of the advantages they confer. Certain goods in the latter category, such as honor and glory, also possess some sort of moral value while others, such as beauty, wealth, and rank, have no particular moral value.[79] In the *De inventione* Cicero includes a measure of *utilitas* in his definition of the *honestum*, both in general and in his treatment of justice; in the *De partitione oratoria* he ascribes a measure of *honestum* to goods which he has defined as means to other ends. At the same time, in the *De partitione oratoria*, he defines as

---

[77] *De inv.* 2.53.159–2.56.168.
[78] *De inv.* 2.56.167–168.
[79] *De part. or.* 24.83–87.

necessary some goods which might be regarded as extrinsic while label-
ling as not necessary the only goods that possess intrinsic value.

On the surface Cicero's approach to ethics in these rhetorical works
seems to lack any kind of logical or terminological consistency. There is,
however, a rationale for his procedure. He stresses throughout his discussion of virtue in the *De inventione* and the *De partitione oratoria* that an
orator, when he counsels any course of action, has to propose it as a good.
As an orator he is not concerned with arriving at a definition of the good
that could be defended consistently in the abstract. Rather, he is concerned with persuading his hearers to do what he wants. Thus, insofar
as the orator needs to face the task of reconciling the *honestum* with the
utile, he must keep in the forefront of his mind what his audience believes
about these principles. His speech ought to conform not so much to the
truth as to the ethos of his audience. In addressing a cultivated audience
he may flatter their conception of themselves by appealing to the higher
values. Uneducated audiences, on the other hand, can best be moved by
an appeal to profit or pleasure; but at the same time the orator can
enlarge this kind of audience in their own estimation by treating these
inferior values as endowed with moral worth and not just with utility.[80]
The criterion throughout this discussion, and the framework within
which ethical principles are assessed, is the rhetorical aim of persuasion.
He speaks as a professional orator to other orators. From this standpoint
Cicero holds that the blurring of ethical categories which he distinguishes
more sharply or which he defines differently elsewhere is not only permissible but desirable.

There is an exact parallel to this treatment of ethics in the analysis of
law which Cicero provides in his rhetorical works. Cicero is perfectly
familiar with the Roman legal distinction between jurisprudence and
advocacy. While the role of the jurisconsult is to state what the law is,
the role of the advocate is to argue cases on behalf of his clients. An
advocate himself, who seeks in his rhetorical works to communicate the
fine points of the art to others in the same profession, Cicero asserts that
advocacy is more important than jurisprudence.[81] As an advocate, he
states, an orator must be well acquainted with the law, for he must be
able to use it as a weapon in his rhetorical armory. He must know how
to exploit its gaps, conflicts, and ambiguities; he must be aware of the
juridical tradition attaching to particular legal rules so that he can cite
cases where they have been interpreted in the way he wants to

---

[80] *De part. or.* 25.89-26.94.
[81] *Orator* 41.141-142. For a more extensive discussion of this distinction in Roman legal
practice see below, ch. 6, part II.

interpret them; he must be able to construe the law strictly or loosely; he must know how to set the presumed intention of the legislator over against the letter of the law. The law, in other words, marks the boundaries of the realm in which the advocate exercises his profession; but it is at the same time a malleable entity that can be twisted to meet his immediate needs.[82]

It is within this forensic context that Cicero introduces the important Stoic theme of natural law. Strictly speaking, he treats it as a rhetorical *topos* under the heading of *inventio*. The theory of natural law provides the orator with arguments that permit him to amplify the civil law and to compare it with non-juridical principles. A strategy of argument based on natural law is particularly helpful when the speaker wants to persuade his hearers that a given act, although illegal, is none the less right.[83] Cicero is fully aware of the fact that the civil law is the only law that binds in Rome and that the Roman civil law does not depend on any standard other than itself for its own legitimation. Thus, he acknowledges, the rights flowing from natural law have no normative bearing on the civil law.[84] Cicero is also aware of the fact that Roman jurisprudence draws no distinction between *ius* in its denotation as law and *ius* in its denotation as right; a *ius*, for the jurisconsults, is deemed right in virtue of the fact that it is what the law enjoins. Still, he notes, the orator may invoke natural law as an ethical principle, in which connection Cicero uses the terms *aequum*[85] and *ius*,[86] as a means of appealing to the moral sentiments of the court in cases where the civil law, applied literally, would disadvantage his cause.

In addition to handling the theory of natural law in this highly pragmatic way, Cicero defines it quite narrowly in his rhetorical works, providing it with a sense that is not particularly Stoic either in its source or in its substance. Natural law, he says, is implanted in man as *quaedam innata vis* ("some innate force.")[87] As for its substance, natural law can be contrasted with human law whether customary or statutory. Natural

---

[82] *De part. or.* 37.131-39.138; *Topica* 25.95-96. This point has been well developed by Alan Watson, *Law in the Making in the Later Roman Republic* (Oxford, 1974), pp. 3-5, 169-72.

[83] *De inventione* 2.22.65-68; *De part. or.* 37.129; *Topica* 23.89.

[84] *De inventione* 2.22.67. Noted by Watson, *Law in the Making*, pp. 177-78; Giorgio Jossa, " 'L'utilitas rei publicae' nel pensiero di Cicerone," *Studi romani, 12* (1964), 285-86.

[85] *Topica* 23.89. This point has not been grasped by Georges Ciulei, *L'Équité chez Cicéron* (Amsterdam, 1972), pp. 14-19, 25-31, 33-61.

[86] *De part. or.* 37.129. This point has been noted by Jacques Michel, "Sur les origines du 'jus gentium'," *Revue internationale des droits de l'antiquité*, 3ᵉ sér., *3* (1956), 339.

[87] *De inventione* 2.22.66. My own translation is given. Cicero provides a virtually identical definition, ibid., 2.54.161.

law includes the right to private property, the right to revenge, and those obligations pertaining to religion. Human law embraces decisions, covenants, and rules controlling private and public rights. Human law, according to Cicero, may derive to some slight degree from natural law. But what sanctions human law is not such modest connections with natural law as it may have but long-standing usage in the case of custom and formal institution in the case of statute.[88]

Cicero's overall treatment of law, in theory and practice, in his rhetorical works reflects clearly his subordination of this topic to the needs or persuasion and to the legal institutions actually governing the Roman courts. Although he brings up an important Stoic theme in discussing natural law he in no sense defines or uses it in a Stoic manner. Far from functioning as a metaphysical or moral absolute capable of validating or limiting the civil law in force, natural law functions here as a source of moralistic commonplaces which have no actual juristic weight but which may add a veneer of coloristic plausibility to an otherwise weak case. Cicero's advice for the use of natural law theory, like his advice for the use of law in general and like his handling of Stoicism throughout his rhetorical works indicates clearly that the standard to which he is referring the discussion is not one of truth or goodness but one of literary preference and rhetorical utility.

IV. POLITICAL THEORY

We can get a vivid sense of how Cicero puts his rhetorical principles into practice as we move from his oratorical to his political theory. Cicero treats a number of the same ethical and legal issues in the *De republica* and *De legibus* as he does in his rhetorical works, but he handles them in a strikingly different way. The *De republica* and *De legibus* are overtly modeled on Plato's *Republic* and *Laws*. Cicero's political views in these works are nuanced at strategic points by Aristotelianism and are illustrated copiously from Roman institutions and Roman history. Yet, it is in his *ex professo* political and legal theory that Cicero's dependence on Stoicism is the heaviest and it is in this same field that his creative application and elaboration of Stoic doctrine is most plainly visible.

Despite its fragmentary state, Cicero's *De republica* had received an inordinate amount of commentary, largely, one suspects, because modern scholars have been impelled to evaluate his political views in the light of their own constitutional preferences.[89] The work has also provided much

---

[88] *De inv.* 2.2.65–68, 2.54.161–162; *De part. or.* 37.129–130; *Topica* 23.89–90.
[89] There are several excellent surveys of the literature on the *De republica*. For the period before 1954 see Richard Heinze, "Ciceros 'Staat' als politische Tendenzschrift,"

grist for the mills of the *Quellenforscher*.[90] There is a minority opinion on the *De republica* which treats Cicero as a bantamweight in the field of political theory, dismissing the work as an effusion of nostalgia and as a merely literary exercise.[91] Most scholars, however, regard it as an important theoretical statement. It is in the *De republica*, several writers have noted, that Cicero first develops the doctrine of philosophical *otium* as a worthy means of public service, an idea harking back to the Stoic theory of the sage and his proper vocation.[92] Some scholars view the work as an effort on Cicero's part to synthesize the political theory of a number of Greek philosophical schools and to apply the resulting amalgam to Roman history.[93] A more typical approach has been to treat the *De republica* as a work of political propaganda in which Cicero justifies a specific constitution or the leadership of a particular individual or group. Some commentators in this category see Cicero as an advocate of Augustus,[94] some as a defender of Pompey,[95] on the grounds that the strong

in *Vom Geist des Römertums: Ausgewählte Aufsätze*, 3rd ed., ed. Erich Burck (Stuttgart, 1960), pp. 141-48; Lepore, *Il princeps ciceroniano*, pp. 9-19. More recent analyses include Adamczyk, "Political Propaganda," pp. 20-23; Gelzer, *Cicero*, p. 213 n. 445; and Peter L. Schmidt, "Cicero 'De republica': Die Forschung der letzten fünf Dezennien," *Aufstieg und Niedergang der römischen Welt, 1*, part 4, 262-333.

[90] The leading contestants in this field, who have battled to a draw for forty years on Cicero's sources for the *De republica*, are Boyancé, *Études sur l'humanisme cicéronien*, pp. 186-96, 276-93 and Bruwaene, *La théologie de Cicéron*, pp. 237-41. See also Büchner, "Cicero und Panaitios," in *Resultate römischen Lebens in römischen Schriftwerken*, p. 84; R. G. G. Coleman, "The Dream of Scipio," *Proceedings of the Cambridge Philological Society, 190*, n.s. 10 (1964), 1-14; Georg Luck, "Studia divina in vita humana: On Cicero's 'Dream of Scipio' and Its Place in Graeco-Roman Philosophy," *Harvard Theological Review, 19* (1956), 307-18; André Piganiol, "Sur la source du Songe de Scipion," *Comptes rendus de l'Académie des inscriptions et belles lettres de Paris*, 1957 (Paris, 1957), pp. 88-93; E. K. Rand, "The Humanism of Cicero," *Proceedings of the American Philosophical Society, 71* (1932), 213-14; George Holland Sabine and Stanley Barney Smith, intro. to their trans. of Cicero, *On the Commonwealth* (Columbus, 1929), pp. 40, 46-56; Niels Wilsing, *Aufbau und Quellen von Ciceros Schrift 'De re publica'* (Leipzig, 1929).

[91] Stockton, *Cicero*, pp. 304, 343-45.

[92] Alberto Grilli, *I proemi del De re publica di Cicerone* (Brescia, 1971), pp. 18-25; Georg Pfligersdorfer, *Politik und Musse: Zum Proömium und Einleitungsgespräch von Ciceros De re publica* (München, 1969), passim and especially pp. 27-28, 40.

[93] Franz Hampl, " 'Stoische Staatsethik' und frühes Rom," *Historische Zeitschrift, 184* (1957), 249-71; W. W. How, "Cicero's Ideal in His *De republica*," *JRS, 20* (1930), 24-42; McKeon, intro. to *Brutus*, trans. Poteat, pp. 52-54; Viktor Pöschl, *Römische Staat und griechisches Staatsdenken bei Cicero: Untersuchungen zu Ciceros Schrift De re publica*, Neue deutsche Forschung, 104, Abteilung klassische Philologie, 5 (Berlin, 1936), pp. 7-9 and passim.

[94] The most influential proponent of this view is R. Reitzenstein, "Die Idee des Principats bei Cicero und Augustus," *Nachrichten von der königlichen Gesellschaft der Wissenschaften zu Göttingen*, philologisch-historische Klasse, 1917 (Berlin, 1918), pp. 399-436; "Zu Ciceros De re publica," *Hermes, 59* (1924), 356-62. See also E. Ciaceri, "Il trattato di Cicerone De re publica e le teorie di Polibio sulla costituzione romana," *Rendiconti della reale Accademia dei Lincei*, classe di scienze morali, storiche, e filologiche, ser. 5:27 (1918), 311-15; Maximilian Schäfer, "Des Panaitios *aner archikos* bei Cicero: Ein Interpretationsbeitrag zu Ciceros Schrift De republica," *Gymnasium, 67* (1960), 500-16.

[95] Eduard Meyer, *Caesars Monarchie und das Principat des Pompejus: Innere Geschichte Roms von 66 bis 44 v. Chr.*, 3rd ed. (Stuttgart, 1922), p. 189.

rule of one man is the only way to protect the citizens' legal rights. Others have argued that Cicero is advocating the rule of an entire social class, the *optimates*, rather than any one individual; he seeks to defend the aristocratic constitution of the Republic not to rationalize a shift away from it.[96] A compromise between these two positions urges that Cicero is promoting the leadership of aristocratic statesman who are indeed powerful individual rulers but who operate strictly within the legitimate framework of the Republican constitution.[97]

The thesis that Cicero's aim was to justify a specific constitutional form, whether autocratic or oligarchic, fails to pay sufficient attention to the fact that he is deeply concerned with the problem of tyranny while, at the same time, he offers no explanation in institutional terms for the collapse of the Roman Republic, despite the fact that he portrays it as the ideal constitution. There is unquestionably a strong element of propaganda in the *De republica*. Cicero's use of Republican heroes of an earlier generation as the interlocutors in the dialogue, his express identification of the Roman Republic of the second century B.C. with the ideal mixed polity praised by Aristotle and associated with the Republic more recently by Polybius, and his apotheosis of Scipio at the end of the work clearly bespeak his desire to uphold the Republic of the recent past as the model state and its virtuous leaders as the model statesman. At the same time, Cicero is all too painfully aware of the fact that the Republican constitution, for all its alleged conformity with the Polybian ideal, failed to protect the polity from its own leaders' lust for power. This circumstance has led a number of scholars to emphasize correctly that the *De republica* is not merely an exercise in self-consolation, nostalgia, or Republican propaganda. Embracing yet surpassing these concerns, the work is also a quest for an understanding of the dynamics of political life. Cicero ends his inquiry by positing a principle that outdistances a constitutional definition of the ideal polity. For Cicero liberty and tyranny, justice and the common good, are ultimately not pure political categories that can be brought into being and perpetuated by constitutional forms alone. They are, rather, moral categories, descriptions of the ethos of the rulers and citizens who make up the political community. The ethical attitude of its public men is the animating spirit that vivifies and regulates the state. This animating spirit is the real foundation and criterion of political life, transcending constitutional structures. Lacking

---

[96] The leading proponent of this view is Heinze, "Ciceros 'Staat' als politische Tendenzschrift," *Vom Geist des Römertums*, pp. 148–59, whose thesis has been refined and amplified by Lepore, *Il princeps ciceroniano*, passim. See also Ferguson, *Utopias*, p. 160.

[97] Alain Michel, *Histoire des doctrines politiques à Rome* (Paris, 1971), pp. 40–41; Gelzer, *Cicero*, pp. 213–24.

public men with the proper moral character, no state, however closely it approximates the ideal of the mixed polity, can function in good health and survive intact.[98]

Cicero's political theory thus goes well beyond the kind of analysis derived from the Platonic and Aristotelian traditions. In his stress on the animating ethos that transcends governmental forms Cicero takes a principle from Stoicism and develops it more concretely in connection with politics than the Stoics before him had done. This aspect of Cicero's political thought is evident above all in his delineation of the ideal statesman and in his analysis of law, both in the *De republica* and the *De legibus*. Cicero's ideal statesman is a Stoic sage whose governance of the *polis* is a specific application of the proper ordering of the physical and moral universe by the divine and human *logos*. The liberty and harmony which the ruler pledges himself to promote can neither be understood nor attained except by a man who has achieved the moral liberty and inner harmony which stem from Stoic *apatheia* and autarchy. The statesman is fit to rule others because he has brought his own being under the control of his *hegemonikon*. The ruler's relationship to the state parallels the control of the human *logos* over man's other faculties just as it parallels the function of the divine *logos* ruling the natural universe. This is a case, however, where the parallel lines converge, for in each instance the ruling principle is the same immanent vital force energizing and ordering the phenomena which it regulates from within, not from above.[99] Just as Cicero applies the same Stoic principles that govern ethics and cosmology to his analysis of rulership, so he applies the same criteria to his analysis of law in the *De republica* and the *De legibus*. His Stoicizing of politics and law in these works is the most impressive feature of his political theory, despite his numerous borrowings from other traditions.

Having begun the *De republica* with a Stoic defense of political philosophy as a worthy occupation for a statesman in retirement, both by insisting on the political wisdom which he himself possesses[100] and by populating his dialogue with Republican statesman who carry on their discussion during a public holiday,[101] Cicero proceeds to outline in Book

---

[98] Karl Büchner, "Die beste Verfassung," in *Cicero*, Studien sur römischen Literatur, 2, pp. 25-115; "Der Tyrann und sein Gegenbild in Ciceros 'Staat'," ibid., pp. 139-45; Heinze, "Ciceros 'Staat'," *Vom Geist des Römertums*, pp. 156-59; How, "Cicero's Ideal," *JRS, 20* (1930), 24-42; Jossa, " 'L'utilitas rei publicae'," *Studi romani, 12* (1964), 270; S. E. Smethurst, "Politics and Morality in Cicero," *Phoenix, 9* (1955), 116-21.

[99] This theme has been developed most fully by Lepore, *Il princeps ciceroniano*, pp. 66-70. See also Alice Dermience, "La notion de 'libertas' dans les oeuvres de Cicéron," *LEC, 25* (1957), 161-62.

[100] *De republica* 1.1.1-1.8.3, ed. Petrus Krarup (Firenze, 1967).

[101] *De rep.* 1.9.14.

1 the three traditional types of government in their good and bad forms, noting their assets and drawbacks and tracing their cyclical alternations from monarchy to ochlocracy and back again. He praises mixed government as the most stable form. In Book 2 he gives a historical survey of the Roman state as an illustration in real life of the theory expounded in Book 1. He finds that the combination of monarchy, aristocracy, and democracy achieved by the late Republican constitution corresponds with the ideal of mixed government. In Book 3 he provides a theory of law. Book 4, which comes down to us in very fragmentary form, treats educational and cultural institutions from the standpoint of their intellectual, physical, and moral effects on the citizens. In Book 5 Cicero discusses the qualifications and functions of the ideal statesman, a topic continued in Book 6, which concludes with the dream of Scipio. Throughout the work, Cicero mentions a number of philosophers by name, sometimes as authorities and sometimes in order to criticize them. The criteria he invokes to judge them are the same whatever school they represent. Be he Plato, Aristotle, Chrysippus, Panaetius, or Carneades,[102] a philosopher is criticized when his speculation is deemed too abstract to be relevant, when it is destructive rather than constructive, or when it cannot be verified empirically by reference to Roman history. The Greek thinkers held to be best versed in politics are Panaetius and Polybius, for their theories square best with the history of the Roman Republic.[103] This, at any rate, is the criterion that Cicero puts forth in principle. However, in elaborating his specific views on rulership and law, he does not adhere to this criterion in practice. In actuality, he judges the theories of the philosophers not so much in the light of their congruence with the historical institutions of Rome as in the light of their congruence with Stoic ethics and cosmology.

In dealing with the ruler and his relationship to the state, Cicero makes an explicit application of two distinctively Stoic principles: the connaturality of the soul of the upright man with the divine *logos* and the doctrine that an inner virtuous intention is the essence of the moral life. Although he scarcely hides his preference for an aristocratic republic, he is also interested in developing a definition of the statesman that can apply to rulership in any kind of polity. The ideal statesman, or *rector rerum publicarum*,[104] is the protector of the common weal. It is his virtue, manifested above all in his commitment to the common good, that authorizes him to rule in whatever kind of constitution, not his ascribed

---

[102] *De rep.* 1.10.15, 1.17.26–1.20.33, 2.11.21–22, 2.29.51, 2.30.52, 3.5.9, 3.8.12.
[103] *De rep.* 1.21.34.
[104] *De rep.* 5.4.6.

status or the external delegation of power to him.[105] Scipio Aemilianus, who develops this line of reasoning in the dialogue, argues that virtuous rulers are most likely to emerge in aristocratic polities where they must win the assent of an electorate. But the existence of an artistocratic constitution is, in itself, no guarantee that morally worthy statesman will present themselves as candidates or that they will appeal to the voters.

If the ideal statesman's qualification for office is his own virtue, his function once in office is to seek the good of the community he rules. For Cicero this task involves not only his promotion of the material well-being and glory of the community but also the cultivation of its moral perfection.[106] Cicero places the community's material needs and its desire for grandeur on the same plane as the aspiration toward virtue for its own sake. In the political context, the *utile* is just as much an end as the *honestum*. The difference between Cicero's handling of the *honestum-utile* issue in his political philosophy and in his rhetorical works can be illustrated by his analysis of friendship in the *De republica*, which he expresses in the relations among the interlocutors in the dialogue in general and in the character of Scipio in particular. Here Cicero introduces for the first time the Stoic theme of friendship as a relationship between sages, arising from free choice and their recognition of each other as virtuous men joined in a common commitment to public service. At the same time, by reconstructing the Scipionic circle as the setting of the dialogue, he reminds the reader that the bond uniting his cast of characters is one that also entails partisanship, patron-client relationships, and the other associations and practical advantages connoted by friendship in its more strictly political incarnation.[107] As with the duties of the statesman, so the nature of friendship in the *De republica* partakes of both the lower and the higher goods, inclining less exclusively to the *utile* here than in Cicero's rhetorical works.

The dream of Scipio at the end of the *De republica* develops to its most explicit level Cicero's correlation between statesmanship and Stoic ethics and cosmology. Scipio Africanus appears in a dream to his descendant, the Scipio Aemilianus of the dialogue, prophesying his future exploits as a protector of Rome and firing his zeal for public service by describing the posthumous rewards in store for the virtuous statesman. The soul of the statesman-sage is connatural with God, Scipio learns. Having ruled human life in the same way that God governs the universe, the virtuous statesman will escape the recurrent conflagrations of the cosmos and the

---

[105] *De rep.* 1.34.51-53.

[106] *De rep.* 5.6.8, 6.1.1.

[107] This point has been well developed by Karl Büchner, "Der Laelius Ciceros," *Cicero, Studien zur römischen Literatur*, 2, pp. 84-94.

need for spiritual purgation after death. Instead, he will enjoy an eternal happy life in the realm of the stars and the divine intelligences.[108] The eschatology and psychology expounded in the dream of Scipio were held widely among the Hellenistic philosophers, including some of the Stoics. It can scarcely be said that Cicero is presenting a uniquely Stoic teaching. However, he succeeds in imbuing this common doctrine with a Stoic aura. Scipio Africanus, the apotheosized statesman, was known for his connection with Panaetius, having founded the Scipionic circle through which Panaetius' ideas were first disseminated to the Romans. Scipio was also esteemed as a model of Stoic virtue, above all in his abstention from the full exercise of power over the vanquished which he earned by right as a victorious general. In describing the topography of the heavens, Scipio associates a generally accepted theory with the distinctive Stoic theme of cosmic conflagrations. Just as Cicero's quest for the dynamics of political life takes him beyond the external constitutional formulations of Plato and Aristotle into the realm of the immanent Stoic *logos*, so his analysis of the ideal statesman takes him beyond the Hellenistic commonplaces, the allusions to the vision of Er in Plato's *Republic*, and the traditional Roman *exempla virtutis* into a firmament where these elements revolve around an axis of Stoic doctrine. The dream of Scipio evokes the apotheosis of Hercules the Stoic saint as the model and context in whose terms Cicero's ideal of statesmanship must finally be understood.[109]

Cicero's Stoicizing of the statesman in the *De republica* is carried over into his analysis of the law by which the ruler guides the polity. Cicero's theory of law is developed in both the *De republica* and the *De legibus*. There are some shifts in emphasis in his treatment of the subject in these two works. But in both cases he expands the Stoic doctrine of natural law and applies it to political life by arguing that the natural law is the standard against which the civil law should be measured. Cicero provides a conception of natural law in these works which differs sharply from his approach to the same subject in his rhetorical theory. As an orator he treats natural law as an extra-legal *topos* which may be invoked for its emotional appeal when an advocate's case is weak on legal grounds. On the other hand, as a political philosopher he treats natural law as a

---

[108] *De rep.* 6.3.3-6.26.29.

[109] C. Atzert, *Die Apotheose der Virtus Romana in Ciceros Schrift "De republica": Ein Beitrag zur Würdigung Ciceros*, 2nd ed. (Breslau, 1933), pp. 9-10, 16-17; Enrico Berti, *Il "De re publica" di Cicerone e il pensiero politico classico*, Pubblicazioni della scuola di perfezionamento in filosofia dell'Università di Padova, 1 (Padova, 1963), pp. 21-26 and Karl Büchner, *Somnium Scipionis: Quellen, Gestalt, Sinn, Hermes* Einzelschriften, 36 (Wiesbaden, 1976), 47-95, although they depreciate the Stoic content; Gelzer, *Cicero*, pp. 213-24; Festugière, *La Révélation d'Hermès Trismègiste*, 2, 437. Galinsky, *The Herakles Theme*, p. 162, has noted the association between Scipio and Hercules.

supra-legal sanction to which the law in force ought to conform. In elaborating this legal theory in his political works Cicero develops the Stoic doctrine of natural law well beyond the point to which the Stoics themselves had taken it. He translates the Stoic idea of natural law as an ethical and cosmic principle into a legal principle to be used as the norm of the legitimacy of the civil law of a given historical community.[110] This is an important and creative accomplishment and one destined to be extremely influential in post-classical legal and political thought.

Cicero gives a thoroughly Stoic definition of law in Book 3 of the *De republica*:

> Est quidem vera lex recta ratio naturae congruens, diffusa in omnis, constans, sempiterna, quae vocet ad officium iubendo, vetando a fraude deterreat; quae tamen neque probos frustra iubet aut vetat nec improbos iubendo aut vetando monet. Huic legi nec obrogari fas est, neque derogare aliquid ex hac licet, neque tota abrogare potest, nec vero aut per senatum aut per

---

[110] A number of scholars have noted the fact that, while there is a good deal of information about the Roman civil law of his day in Cicero's rhetorical and political writings, his approach differs from that of the jurisconsults, and that he, not they, is the source for the application of Stoic natural law theory to Roman legal and political thought. The best general study of this subject is Michel Villey, "Rückkehr zur Rechtsphilosophie," in *Das neue Cicerobild*, ed. Karl Büchner, Wege der Forschung, 27 (Darmstadt, 1971), pp. 259-303. See also Vincenzo Arangio-Ruiz, "Cicerone giurista," in *Marco Tullio Cicerone*, pp. 191-207; Baldry, *The Unity of Mankind*, pp. 194-203; Karl Büchner, "Römische Konstanten und De legibus," *Werkanalysen*, Studien zur römischen Literatur, 8 (Wiesbaden, 1970), pp. 21-39; Clarke, *The Roman Mind*, pp. 49-50; Enrico Cocchia, "Cicerone oratore e giureconsulto," *Atti della Reale accademia di archeologia, lettere e belli arti di Napoli*, n.s. 9 (1926), 442-59; Frank, "Cicero," *Proceedings of the British Academy*, 1932, pp. 120-23; Armand Gasquy, *Cicéron jurisconsulte* (Paris, 1887), pp. 18-46, 64-290; Valentin-Al. Georgesco, " 'Nihil hoc ad ius, ad Ciceronem!' Note sur les relations de M. T. Cicéron avec la *iurisprudentia* et la profession de *iuris consultus*," *Mélanges de philologie, de littérature, et d'histoire anciennes offerts à J. Marozeau* (Paris, 1948), pp. 192-206, who provides a useful review of the literature on this question up to his time; Richard Harder, "Zu Ciceros Rechtsphilosophie (De legibus I)," *Kleine Schriften*, ed. Walter Marg (München, 1960), pp. 196-400; Horowitz, "Stoic Synthesis of the Ideal of Natural Law," *JHI*, 35 (1974), 4-5; Ulrich Knoche, "Ciceros Verbindung der Lehre vom Naturrecht mit dem römischen Recht und Gesetz: Ein Beitrag zu der Frage, philosophische Begründung und politische Wirklichkeit in Ciceros Staatsbild," in *Cicero: Ein Mensch seiner Zeit*, ed. Gerhard Radke (Berlin, 1968), pp. 40-60; Th. Mayer-Maly, "Gemeinwohl und Naturrecht bei Cicero," *Völkerrecht und rechtliches Weltbild: Festschrift für Alfred Verdross*, ed. K. Zemanek et al. (Wien, 1960), pp. 200-02; A. Michel, *Rhétorique et philosophie*, pp. 443-536; J. Michel, "Les origines du 'jus gentium'," *R. internat. des droits de l'antiquité*, 3ᵉ sér., 3 (1956), 313-48; Jacques-Henri Michel, "Le droit romain dans le *Pro Murena* et l'oeuvre de Servius Sulpicius Rufus," *Ciceroniana: Hommages à Kazimierz Kumaniecki*, ed. Alain Michel et Raoul Verdière (Leiden, 1975), pp. 181-95; Olis Robleda, "Estudio jurídico sobre el 'Pro Caecina' de Cicerón," *Humanidades*, 1 (1949), 55-81; "La 'aequitas' en Cicerón," ibid., 2 (1950), 31-57; "Filosofía jurídica de Cicerón," *Studi in onore di Biondo Biondi* (Milano, 1965), 2, 467-82; Watson, "The Natural Law and Stoicism," in *Problems in Stoicism*, ed. Long, pp. 224-32. For alternative views see below, ch. 6, part I, pp. 341 and 345, nn. 1 and 14.

populum solvi hac lege possumus, neque est quaerendus explanator aut interpretes Sextus Aelius, nec erit alia lex Romae alia Athenis, alia nunc alia post hac, sed et omnis gentes et omni tempore una lex et sempiterna et inmutabilis continebit, unusque erit communis quasi magister et imperator omnium deus: ille legis huius inventor, disceptator, lator; cui qui non parebit, ipse se fugiet ac naturam hominis aspernatus hoc ipso luet maximas poenas, etiamsi cetera supplicia quae putantur effugerit.[111]

There is a certain true law, right reason in accordance with nature, diffused everywhere, unchanging and eternal, which exhorts us to duty by its commands and deters us from crime by its prohibitions. It neither commands nor constrains upright men in vain, nor does it move the wicked either by exhortation or by prohibition. It is neither right to abrogate this law nor permissible to restrict it in any way; nor can it be entirely annulled. We cannot be exempted from this law either by the senate or the people; nor need we seek any Sextus Aelius to expound or interpret it. And neither will this law be different in Rome and in Athens, nor different now and in the future. But one, eternal, and unchanging law will be kept by all people and at all times. And there will be, as it were, one common teacher and ruler over all, God, who is the author, initiator, and judge of this law. Whosoever seeks to disobey it flees from himself and rejects the nature of man. And on this account he will suffer the severest punishment, even if he otherwise escapes what are regarded as punishments.

In this passage we see expressed for the first time in the Latin language the Stoic conception of a universal and eternal law of nature, identified with God and right reason and superimposed on the laws and institutions of Rome, treated as the norm of their legitimacy. The connection between this legal theory and Stoic cosmology is evident in Cicero's equation of the supreme law with the deity. Its connection with Stoic ethics is equally apparent in its equation with the faculty of reason. Since it is identical with right reason, the natural law is predictably ignored by the fool while the sage makes it the law of his own being. Cicero extends this physical and ethical theory to encompass the civil law. The state, he asserts, cannot abrogate the natural law, which overrides the authority of the civil law if that civil law fails to conform to it.

This argument represents a truly seminal expansion of Stoicism into the sphere of political theory; but it is not lacking in paradoxical aspects in Cicero's thought. In his rhetorical works he acknowledges the fact that the natural law has no actual binding force in Roman jurisprudence. In the De republica he proposes a Stoic criterion of natural law against which the institutions of Rome may be measured and limited, even though he

---

[111] De rep. 3.22.33. The translation is mine. See also Filippo Cancelli, "Sull'origine del diritto secondo un motivo ricorrente in scrittori ellenistichoromani, e Cicerone 'De re publica 5.3," SDHI, 37 (1971), 331-37.

discards a number of philosophical positions elsewhere in the work because they fail to correspond with those same Roman historical institutions. In the *De legibus* the paradox remains, but with a new twist. In this work Cicero claims that the institutions of the Roman Republic can be identified with the Stoic natural law. But, in making the Republic the embodiment of the ideal law he invests with universality a set of institutions unique to one people and he ascribes eternity to a historical phenomenon which was already on its deathbed when he began the *De legibus*.

The *De legibus* preserves the dialogue form used by Cicero in the *De republica* although, following the model of Plato's *Laws*, he sets the work in a later period than the *De republica* and uses interlocutors who are his own contemporaries, including himself, his brother Quintus, and his friend Atticus. In the *De legibus* he repeats and develops much further the Stoic conception of natural law already articulated in the *De republica*. After an initial book elaborating on natural law in theory Cicero goes on to describe the legal institutions that would be consistent both with the natural law in principle and with the ideal republic that he had outlined in the *De republica*. His intention is to set forth religious law, public law, and private law, but the books devoted to the latter topic have not survived. The *De legibus*, like the *De republica*, serves as a vehicle for Cicero's political partisanship and personal ambition as well as a means of strengthening the conceptual bonds he forges between Stoic ethics and cosmology and political theory.[112] In this case, however, the incongruities between the theories advanced and the institutions defended as their incarnation on earth make the propagandistic element much more apparent.

In Book I of the *De legibus*, following an introductory statement reiterating his justification of philosophical *otium* in the service of society[113] and his clear distinction between the task of the jurisconsult and that of

---

[112] The *De legibus* is one work of Cicero on which there is a refreshing degree of consensus, although there is still some doubt about his sources. The most recent general studies are by Ada Hentschke, "Zur historischen und literarischen Bedeutung von Ciceros Schrift, 'De legibus'," *Philologus*, *115* (1971), 118-30 and Elizabeth Rawson, "The Interpretation of Cicero's 'De legibus'," *Aufstieg und Niedergang der römischen Welt*, *1*, part 4, 334-56, who provide a good review of the literature. See also Busuttil, "Cicero: De legibus," pp. 34-38, 86-89, 115-16; Philipp Finger, "Die drei Grundlagen des Rechts im I. Buch von Ciceros Schrift De legibus," *RM*, n.F. *81* (1932), 155-77, 243-62; Harder, "Zu Ciceros Rechtsphilosophie," *Kleine Schriften*, pp. 196-400; Kenter, *De legibus*, pp. 75-77, 81-88, 95, 97-102, 122-23, 129-30, 146, 172; Clinton Walker Keyes, intro. to his trans. of *De leg.*, Loeb (Cambridge, Mass., 1959), pp. 291-93; Plinval, intro. to his ed. of *De leg.*, pp. xxiii-lviii; Schmidt, *Die Abfassungszeit von Ciceros Schrift über die Gesetze*, pp. 145-52, 171-79.

[113] *De leg.* 1.3.8-1.4.14.

the legal theorist,[114] Cicero once again offers a thoroughly Stoic definition of law:

Lex est ratio summa, insita in natura, quae iubet ea quae facienda sunt, prohibetque contraria. Eadem ratio, cum est in hominibus mente confirmata et *per*fecta, lex est. ... Quod sit ita recta dicitur, ut mihi quidem plerumque videri solet, a lege ducundum est iuris exordium. Ea est enim naturae vis, ea mens ratioque prudentis, ea iuris atque iniuriae regula. ... Constituendi vero iuris ab illa summa lege capiamus exordium, quae, saeclis *communis* omnibus, ante nata est quam scripta lex ulla aut quam omnino civitas constituta.[115]

Law is supreme reason, ingrafted in nature, which ordains what ought to be done and prohibits the opposite. This reason, when established and brought to its full development in the human mind, is law. ... Now if this is correct, as it seems to me to be in general, then the origin of justice follows from law. For it is a force of nature, the mind and reason of the prudent man, the norm of right and wrong. ... Indeed, in defining justice let us make our point of departure this supreme law, which, common throughout all ages, was born before any written law existed and before any state was founded.

Cicero goes on to refine this conception of nature and reason rather than legislative will as the foundation of law in an even more specifically Stoic sense. Noting that men, unlike the animals, are endowed with reason, he argues that all men possess a common nature which unites them with each other and with the gods:

Solum est enim ex tot animantium generibus atque naturis particeps rationis et cogitationis, cum cetera sint omnia expertia. ... Est igitur, quoniam nihil est ratione melius, eaque *est* in homine et in deo, prima homini cum deo ratione societas. Inter quos autem ratio, inter eosdem etiam recta ratio [et] communis est: quae cum sit lex, lege quoque consociati homines cum dis putandi sumus. Inter quos porro est communio legis, inter eos communio iuris est. Quibus autem haec sunt inter eos communia, et civitas eiusdem habendi sunt ... ut iam universus *sit* hic mundus una civitas communis deorum atque hominum existimanda.[116]

---

[114] *De leg.* 1.4.14, 1.5.16-17.

[115] *De leg.* 1.6.18-19. The translation is mine. For other passages where Cicero identifies nature as the source of law see 1.6.20, 1.7.23-1.9.27, 1.10.28, 1.11.31, 1.13.35-36, 1.14.40. He also defines law as right reason applied to command and prohibition in 1.12.33. The words Italicized in the passage quoted follow Plinval's emendations.

[116] *De leg.* 1.7.22-23. The translation is mine. It is in this context that Cicero quotes Terence's famous line on nothing human as alien, 1.12.33. On the Stoic distinction between men and animals in Cicero, see Vittorio d'Agostino, "Il contrapposto fra l'uomo e gli animali nelle opere di Cicerone," *RSC, 12* (1964), 150-59. On the moral equality of men, transcending the limits of nationality, class, sex, and occupation, see also *Hortensius,* frags. 53, 89, ed. Albertus Grilli (Milano, 1962).

> For he [man] alone among so many kinds of living beings shares in reason
> and intelligence, which the others lack entirely. ... It is on this account, since
> nothing is better than reason and since it exists both in man and God, that
> reason is the primary bond between man and God. Those who share reason
> also share right reason as a common possession. And since right reason is
> law, we must hold that men and gods are bound together by the law. Now
> those who have law in common have justice in common. Those who share
> these things are therefore members of the same commonwealth. ... Thus the
> whole universe must be regarded as one commonwealth in which gods and
> men share equal membership.

Law, for Cicero, is clearly a universal principle springing from nature
and reason; but it cannot be argued that he regards justice as grounded
in universal consensus any more than he regards it as grounded in will.
Cicero in fact attacks the idea that everything found in the laws of nations
(*in populorum institutis aut legibus*) is *ipso facto* just. All men, to be sure,
possess reason, which enables them to judge correctly and to act virtu-
ously. At the same time, men are also capable of error and vice. Vice, he
repeats, arises from the four Stoic passions, *molestiae, laetitiae, cupiditates,
timores* ("pains, pleasures, desires, and fears.")[117] Capitulation to these
passions, whether in ethics or politics, alienates man from his nature and
makes it impossible for him to function justly. The laws of nations may
have been imposed by tyrants or other rulers who lack the constitutional
right to enact them. The legislators, even if they hold office legitimately,
may be fools, capable only of enacting laws that are vicious. It is not the
legitimacy of the legislators' title or the fact that they represent the will
of the community but the conformity of their laws with nature, reason,
and virtue that endows the statutes of any nation with justice. The fact
that many or all nations may agree on a particular legal principle is
likewise no guarantee that it is just. Here, as in the *De republica,* Cicero
emphasizes the idea that it is inner virtue that is the norm of justice,
rather than political structures or popular consent. Law, like statesmanship, must be assessed in terms of its conformity with nature. This is a
criterion which all men have the capacity to invoke, but, because their
minds may be perverted by temptations and false judgments, they may
not choose to do so.[118]

Having laid down the Stoic theory of natural law in clear and uncompromising terms, Cicero then proceeds to outline the religious and public
law through which this ideal law would govern the ideal republic. In
moving from the abstract theory to its concrete applications he also moves
from lucidity to ambiguity. The principles which he has so rigorously

---

[117] *De leg.* 1.11.31.
[118] *De leg.* 1.15.42–1.17.47.

laid down in the first book of the *De legibus* end by being subordinated
to other, less ideal and less overtly stated, criteria. Cicero's scheme of
organization in the next two books is the same. In each, he begins with
the assertion that the natural law is the principle governing the particular
code of law to be discussed. Then, in his own persona as a speaker in the
dialogue, he devotes the rest of the book to a commentary on this code
of law. This, at any rate, is what he appears to be doing in Books 2 and 3
of *De legibus*. In actuality, what he does is to set forth the religious and
public law of the late Roman Republic essentially as it stands, with only
a few minor modifications, thus assimilating the natural law to the institutions currently in force. Far from providing a method by which the
laws of Rome or any other state might be evaluated for their correspondence with reason and nature, his strategy is to invoke natural law as the
justification for the institutions and policies that he personally favors.

In Book 2 Cicero intends to discuss religious law; thus, he approaches
natural law from the standpoint of the mind of God and what God has
ordained in the sphere of religion, rather than considering it from the
standpoint of human reason.[119] The religious law that Cicero proceeds
to lay down as a manifestation of the mind of God is a summary of the
existing cult practices of Rome, which, he argues, should be observed
because they conform with reason and nature. In virtually every case,
however, his real argument is that the rituals in question are grounded
in tradition, convention, and social utility.[120] The only religious practice
for which he attempts to supply a rational defense is divination, a topic
worth singling out because it has distinct Stoic associations and because
the position Cicero takes on it in the *De legibus* is somewhat onesided in
comparison with what he says about it elsewhere. The plausibility of
divination, he says, follows from the belief that the gods exist, that they
concern themselves with men, and that they have the power to manifest
signs of future events to men. He adds that history also testifies to the
claim that divination works in practice.[121] As a rational argument this
is a rather feeble one. Apart from introducing evidence from historical
events whose interpretation begs the question, it depends on a prior demonstration of the existence and nature of the gods which Cicero fails to
supply. The special attention that Cicero gives to divination in this work
may perhaps be explained by the fact that the only public post he held
while he was writing the *De legibus* was that of augur. He may have
wished, accordingly, to underscore the importance of this office.

---

[119] *De leg.* 2.4.8-10, 2.5.11-13, 2.7.16.
[120] This point is visible throughout but is stated expressly at *De leg.* 2.11.26.
[121] *De leg.* 2.13.32-33.

Book 3 follows a similar pattern and exudes a similar aroma of personal interest. Just as Cicero tries to show in Book 2 how the natural law is made operative in the religious institutions of Rome, so in Book 3 he tries to show how it is made operative in the magistracy, according to the form taken by the government of the late Republican period. He begins be stating that the magistrates rule the people in the same way that the natural law rules the magistrates. In relation to the people, the magistrates are the embodiment and expression of the supreme law. It is in this sense that Cicero produces the eminently quotable line, *magistratum leges esse loquentem, legem autem mutum magistratum* ("the magistrate is the law speaking and the law is a silent magistrate.")[122] This formula evokes the widely held late classical notion of the ruler as *lex animata*. Cicero, however, gives this Hellenistic commonplace a Stoic coloration. Rather than identifying the *lex animata* idea with kingship and using it as a justification for the notion that the ruler is *legibus solutus*, he argues that this principle can be applied to rulers in any kind of polity, where it serves to remind them that they must govern in accordance with a higher law.[123] After this sturdy defense of natural law as the norm of constitutional law, Cicero lays down a code of public law which corresponds with the constitution of the late Republic except for a few small alterations. Here, as in the case of the religious law, he makes no serious effort to show that the public law he advocates is a demonstrable manifestation of natural law. For instance, although he argues in Book 1 that all men are equal by nature through their common possession of reason, he makes no attempt to apply this principle to politics. He defends an aristocratic polity laden with aristocratic privilege. He also makes a point of criticizing the Gracchi for instituting the office of tribune of the people, which he thinks extended too much power to the plebeians.[124]

The element of partisanship and self-advertisement percolates up through the surface argument of the *De legibus* at a number of other points as well. Under the guise of sketching a constitution in conformity with natural law Cicero provides an extended commentary on the rights and wrongs of the recent political history of Rome, using Book 3 as a vehicle for his justification of oligarchy and for the opinion that the sorry state of present-day Rome is a result of the unscrupulous behavior of the leaders whom he opposes.[125] A similar personal note can be detected in

---

[122] *De leg.* 3.1.2-3.
[123] *De leg.* 3.1.2-3.3.25. An excellent analysis of this point is provided by Lester K. Born, "Animate Law in the Republic and the Laws of Cicero," *Transactions of the American Philosophical Association, 64* (1933), 128-37.
[124] *De leg.* 3.8.19-3.11.26.
[125] *De leg.* 3.10.23-3.11.26, 3.13.30-3.14.32.

Cicero's defense of traditional religion in Book 2, and not merely in his stress on the importance of augury. He makes a point of observing that when he was exiled his enemies violated the religious law with respect to the Cicero family. They desecrated the family gods by building a temple to another deity on the site dedicated to the family's household shrines. A friend who tried to intervene was prevented from halting this sacrilege. Cicero thus presents himself as a defender of religion and of familial religious rights in contrast to his impious enemies.[126] In still broader terms, his attempt to show that the constitutional and religious forms which he favors are a manifestation of the law of nature is an attempt to argue that only a person, like himself, who understands the law of nature, is qualified to govern. The entire *De legibus* is designed to prove that Cicero is indeed such a man, but that corrupt opponents have unjustly prevented him from taking his proper place in public life.[127] The argument in the *De legibus* is controlled not only by what Cicero thinks is needful for the Rome of his day but also by what is useful to himself. Neither the Stoic principles nor the historical realities which he acknowledges can override this stress on public and personal utility. Thus, on one level, he validates historical institutions by their conformity with Stoic natural law. On another level he uses natural law as an extrinsic support for the institutions of Rome as they recently have been. On the most basic level of the argument he weighs both history and theory in the balance of partisan interest and personal grievance.

A similar illustration of the way in which Cicero shifts the grounds of his argument, although it is handled with less dexterity, can be seen in his overt estimate of the different schools of philosophy in the *De legibus*. At one point he refers to the rule that he had proposed in the *De republica*, namely that philosophical theories will be deemed relevant to the extent that they can be related concretely to the historical institutions of Rome. On these grounds Cicero praises Theophrastus, Diogenes the Stoic, and Panaetius and rejects all the other philosophers as too abstract and impractical.[128] Likewise, he finds the Epicureans and New Academics wanting for their failure to agree with his definition of natural law. The self-indulgence and lack of civic spirit of the former and the destructive criticism of the latter are to blame, characteristics that make these schools useless guides to political life.[129] However, at another point Cicero invokes the criterion of the *honestum* as a means of judging both political life and the theories of the schools, seeming to forget that he elsewhere

---

[126] *De leg.* 2.16.41–2.17.42.
[127] *De leg.* 1.4.14–1.6.18, 1.22.58–1.24.63.
[128] *De leg.* 3.5.13–3.7.16.
[129] *De leg.* 1.13.37.

evaluates the schools on the basis of their *utilitas*. The *honestum* in politics is the virtue of justice, which, like friendship, should be sought for its own sake; it would be perverted if any shadow of calculation or expediency entered into it.[130] The philosophical schools which agree in defining the *honestum* as the good and those which regard it as the criterion of political life are the same schools, he says, that support his definition of law. These schools, the Peripatetic, Old Academic, and Stoic, may thus be viewed as reliable authorities in the field of political theory.

Cicero adds that the three schools just mentioned profess the same moral philosophy, although they express it in different terms. This conclusion, however, does not square with the evidence he cites concerning their ethical teachings. Zeno, he notes, taught that the *honestum* is the only good and distinguished it clearly from the *adiaphora*, some of which he regarded as more preferable than others, but none of which he regarded as goods. This doctrine, Cicero observes, has been generally accepted by the other Stoics with the exception of Aristo, who admitted no gradations among the *adiaphora*. For their part, the Old Academics teach that all things that are in accordance with nature and helpful to life can be called goods. Cicero equates this view with Zeno's. He either ignores or glosses over the fact that the range and type of goods properly so called is much wider for the Old Academy than it is for the Stoa, blurring the distinction between a hierarchy of goods ranging from the *utile* to the *honestum* which are different species of the same genus and a gradation of preferables which, taken as a whole, are morally neutral and not goods.[131] In assessing the Stoic element in Cicero's *De legibus*, then, his lack of clarity regarding the Stoics' doctrine of the good and his tendency to shift the operative criterion of his argument from the rational and natural to the historical and practical and from there to the partisan and personal has to be taken into account and set side by side with his wholesale appropriation of the Stoic doctrine of natural law and his energetic expansion of its horizons to include political and legal theory.

V. Epistemology

The chief work in which Cicero deals with epistemological questions is the *Academica*. This dialogue was written in two parts, named traditionally after the two original speakers, Catulus and Lucullus, statesmen of the early first century B.C., generals, and supporters of Sulla. Cicero emphasizes by his choice of these speakers that public service is united

---

[130] *De leg.* 1.12.34, 1.14.41, 1.18.48–1.20.52.
[131] *De leg.* 1.13.37–39, 1.20.52–1.21.55.

with an interest in philosophy in men of a superior type.[132] After completing the *Academica* Cicero decided to dedicate it to Varro. He therefore revised the work and substituted two new speakers, himself and Varro, for Catulus and Lucullus. In all other respects the conception of the work remained the same: the Cicero/Catulus character argues for the New Academy while the Varro/Lucullus character defends the Old Academy. Cicero evidently conceived of this dialogue in both redactions as an internal debate between the two branches of the Academic school.[133] Only a portion of the *Academica* has come down to us, the second half of the Catulus-Lucullus version and about a quarter of the first part of the Cicero-Varro version, along with a few fragments. The *Academica* as we have it touches lightly on ethics and physics. The bulk of the work is devoted to skepticism versus dogmatism, the epistemological issue that split the Academics. Despite the intra-Academic character of the work, Stoicism occupies an important place in the *Academica*; indeed, it functions as a doctrinal shibboleth for the rival Platonic positions. The Old Academic speakers view Stoicism as an elaboration and refinement of Platonism, consistent with the teachings of Antiochus, whom they regard as a faithful exponent of Plato's philosophy.[134] The New Academic speakers take advantage of this argument. By attacking Stoicism they seek to attack Antiochus as a confused thinker and as a traitor to the Platonic heritage which, in their view, entails skepticism.[135] Both the fragmentary nature of the *Academica* and the possibility that Cicero may have wished to flatter Varro by putting the better arguments in his mouth make it difficult to state with confidence whether Cicero associates himself with either of the positions advanced, even though he speaks as an advocate of the New Academy in the second redaction. Notwithstanding the polemical context in which the material is set forth, the *Academica* presents some noteworthy information concerning Stoic epistemology, along with a few points bearing on Stoic ethics and physics.

The richest source of Stoic epistemology in the *Academica* is Varro's speech in Book 1. Varro explains that Zeno made some significant departures from his predecessors both in the content of his epistemology and in his terminology. Zeno's theory of knowledge, he observes, involves three stages. In the first stage, sensation, the mind receives *quadam quasi impulsione oblata extrinsecus* ("a sort of impact offered from outside.") Next comes the intellectual judgment of the sensible presentation, *quam esse volt in nobis positam et voluntarium* ("which he [Zeno] makes out to reside in us

---

[132] *Academica* 2.2.5-7, trans. H. Rackham, Loeb (London, 1961).
[133] *Ad fam.* 9.8.1.
[134] *Acad.* 1.12.43, 2.5.13-2.6.16.
[135] *Acad.* 2.22.69-71.

and to be a voluntary act.") Some of these presentations are also judged
to be kataleptic (*comprendibile*) and are grasped by the mind as knowledge
possessed with certainty, a point which Zeno illustrates by comparing the
open palm, the semi-closed fist, and the tightly clenched fist with the
three stages of knowledge.[136] Varro concludes by noting that Zeno's chief
innovation in the field of epistemology and the main difficulty which his
critics have found with it are one and the same, his simultaneous location
of the criterion of certitude in two processes, sensation and the voluntary
assent of the reason.

In Varro's words Cicero provides a clear and perceptive summary of
the Stoic position, so far as it goes. However, he neglects the role of the
pneuma in Stoic epistemology. He omits the point that the Stoics understood sensation as the interaction between the *pneuma* flowing from the
sense organ with the *pneuma* emitted by the sensed object, not as a passive
reception of data imprinted on the senses from outside. Nor is Cicero
sensitive to the fact that what appears to be a double criterion of certitude
in Stoic epistemology is actually a function of the unitary *pneuma* or *hegemonikon*, directing the processes of intellection and sensation alike. Cicero repeats Varro's summary of Stoic epistemology in Book 2 of the
Academica in the speech of Lucullus. Here, however, he seems to forget
the teaching expounded in Book 1, for in defending the principle of cognitive certitude as put forth by the Stoics, Lucullus rests his case on empirical certitude alone. His efforts to refute the traditional arguments for
the fallibility of the senses are tepid and inconclusive.[137] Lucullus thus
weakens the position stated by Varro; but Varro's speech does communicate much of the distinctive content of Stoic epistemology.

Catulus' defense of the New Academy offers much less information on
the Stoic theory of knowledge than does the Old Academic side of the
debate. Catulus does contribute one important point in the sphere of
logic, although his handling of this point reflects his own or Cicero's
misappropriation of it. Catulus seeks to attack Antiochus by attacking
the Stoics and the dogmatists in general, whom he treats as empiricists.
Thus, according to his strategy, if he can show that the senses are fallible
he will be able to destroy the dogmatists' criterion of certitude. This is
the line of argument he takes without pausing to establish whether all
the dogmatists in question actually did maintain an empirical criterion.
Catulus further asserts that the dogmatists' philosophy is not consistent
with their presumed empirical criterion, for they claim certitude for their
speculations in fields such as cosmology, metaphysics, and psychology,

---

[136] *Acad.* 1.11.40–42. The fist metaphor is repeated at 2.47.145.
[137] *Acad.* 2.6.17, 2.7.19–22.

where the evidence cannot be subjected to empirical tests.[138] In a second line of attack, Catulus argues that dogmatism must be wrong because not all the dogmatists agree with each other. He faults Antiochus in particular for his belief that the major schools agree, a view which, he notes, fails to recognize their basic differences, such as the unique doctrines professed by Zeno.[139] Catulus' third and last major argument emphasizes that, if the senses convey no certitude, neither can dialectic be regarded as a criterion of extramental realities. He illustrates this point by citing two of the Stoic syllogisms, "If it is light, it is day" and "It is either light or it is not," which he attributes to Chrysippus and Antiochus, noting that these syllogisms in no way establish any necessary conclusions about the real world.[140] Given the fact that Catulus' argument is directed against the Stoics his tactics at this point are rather peculiar. He asserts as true the Stoic conception of logic as a purely formal art, a set of rules governing thought which do not authorize the thinker to make positive inferences about the world outside the mind. This is, indeed, a distinctive feature of Stoic logic. However, Catulus appears to believe that he can dispose of ancient logic as such by invoking this principle against it. Even stranger, he invokes it against the Stoics, using it as a weapon against a position which they did not profess. This curious discrepancy goes undetected by Catulus' vis-à-vis in the dialogue, despite the comparative cogency with which the Old Academic spokesman, in the persona of Varro, reports the Stoic theory of knowledge.

It is not easy to determine whether it is the author's ignorance, his selective omission, his rhetorical gamesmanship, or a desire to make one or more of the interlocutors appear misinformed or dull-witted that lies behind Cicero's treatment of Stoic epistemology in the *Academica*. On balance the Old Academics emerge with a fuller and more accurate exposition of it. On the other hand, the honors are divided somewhat more evenly in the passages where Cicero adverts to Stoic ethics and physics, although both sets of interlocutors are responsible for omissions and misapprehensions in these areas. Catulus deals with Stoic ethics as a specific instance of the general premise that the dogmatists must all be wrong because they do not all agree. He argues at one point by contrasting one Stoic with another but mainly by contrasting Stoicism with Platonism, as a means of criticizing Antiochus' equation of these two different positions. In his first foray Catulus observes that Zeno propounded three ethical categories: the good, or virtue; the evil, or everything contrary to

---

[138] *Acad.* 2.25.79–2.28.90, 2.39.122–127.
[139] *Acad.* 2.35.112–2.38.121, 2.42.129–2.47.146.
[140] *Acad.* 2.28.91, 2.30.95–98.

virtue; and the *adiaphora*.[141] One may note that at this point Cicero treats
Aristo's opinion as indicative of a serious division within the Stoa, although he interprets it elsewhere as the one and only departure from a
position that the other Stoics support unanimously. In comparing the
Stoics as a group with the other schools, Catulus notes that a number of
different philosophers use the formula "life in accordance with nature"
as a definition of virtue but that they do not all define "nature" in the
same way. Some schools regard physical goods as natural but Zeno limits
nature to rational goods, applying the term *honestum* to this type of good
alone. The Stoics also depart from the other schools, especially the Old
Academy, in their doctrine that all sins are equal and that the sage possesses all the perfections.[142] These arguments, all designed to underline
ways in which Stoic ethics diverges from Platonic ethics, yield clear descriptions of a number of Stoic principles, although Catulus is not necessarily advocating them.

On the other hand, in defending Antiochus' view that the Stoics are
saying the same thing as the Platonists, but for their differing and inaccessible terminology,[143] Varro gets entangled in the Stoic doctrines he
tries to expound. Zeno, he says, defined happiness as consisting in virtue
alone, seeing virtue or reason as the only good, a position, Varro notes,
that is at variance with the Platonic notion of a hierarchy of goods. This
is a strange argument for one who seeks to equate Stoicism and Platonism. Varro goes on to say that Zeno posited two ethical categories, the
good and the preferables, the preferables being graded by their relative
conformity with nature. Here Varro ignores the category of the evil in
Stoic ethics, although he simultaneously observes that Zeno placed *officium*, or the observance of the preferables, in between virtuous action and
vice. While he is inconsistent on these two points, he does acknowledge
that Zeno saw virtue as perfected by reason, not by habit. However, on
a related topic, Varro like Catulus errs by asserting that Stoic virtue
entails the complete suppression of the emotions. Both speakers ignore
the Stoic conception of *eupatheia*.[144] Finally, although the overall aim of
his argument with respect to Stoicism is to show that it is congruent with
Platonism, Varro pinpoints areas in his brief remarks on Stoic physics
where these two schools diverge sharply. He points out that Zeno rejected
the idea of quintessence, that he held the mind to be material, composed
mainly of fire, and that he taught that everything which acts must have

---

[141] *Acad.* 2.42.130.
[142] *Acad.* 2.42.131, 2.43.132–2.44.137.
[143] *Acad.* 1.2.7.
[144] *Acad.* 1.10.35–39, 2.44.135.

a body, thereby decreeing that incorporeals are incapable of action.[145] These points are stated accurately, but it is impossible to see how they support Varro's ostensible defense of Antiochus. Given the style and structure of the *Academica*, at least in the form in which it has survived, one is tempted to suggest that Cicero wanted to show that each branch of the Academic school was capable of coming to a correct understanding of Stoicism at some points but that each branch was capable of misappropriating Stoic doctrines at points where it was impeded by its own particular blind spots. In any case, despite the gaps in the text and despite the Platonic setting in which Stoicism is addressed in the work, the *Academica* manages to transmit a substantial amount of Stoic epistemology, along with some important if misapplied points in Stoic logic, a few accurate if disconnected points in Stoic physics, and an unclear and inconsistent picture of Stoic ethics.

VI. Theology and Cosmology

Cicero's *De natura deorum, De divinatione,* and *De fato* contain a good deal of information about Stoic cosmology and theology. This material is sometimes presented in a positive light and sometimes subjected to heavy criticism. The ambiguities in his treatment both of Stoicism and of religion in general in these works have inspired considerable debate on the part of Cicero scholars. The Stoics' lack of unanimity on theology and eschatology was as well known to Cicero as it is to the modern authors who have wrestled with the sources of his theological ideas, leading to controversies among the *Quellenforscher* in this field that have been unusually acrimonious and protracted.[146] Equally troublesome are the perceived discrepancies between the religious views Cicero states in his theological works and those he expresses elsewhere. Here, for instance, certain religious practices, such as divination, which he advocates in the

---

[145] *Acad.* 1.11.39-40.

[146] An excellent review of the *Quellenforschung* literature on the *De natura deorum* up through 1958 is provided by A. J. Kleywegt, *Ciceros Arbeitsweise im zweiten und dritten Buch der Schrift De natura deorum* (Groningen, 1961), pp. 2-9. His own views on sources are presented pp. 128, 223-30. The major contestants in the debate have been Bruwaene, *La théologie de Cicéron,* pp. 84-121, 134-38, 185-205; and the preface to his ed. of the first book of *De nat. deor.,* pp. 10-11, 22-32; and Boyancé, *Études sur l'humanisme cicéronien,* pp. 300-34. More recently see also Olof Gigon, "Posidonia-Ciceroniana-Lactantiana," *Romanitas et Christianitas: Studia J. H. Waszink,* ed. W. den Boer et al. (Amsterdam, 1973), pp. 145-80. On the *Quellenforschung* issue in the *De divinatione* see Falconer, intro. to his trans. of *De div.,* pp. 216-19; on the *De fato* see Amand, *Fatalisme et liberté,* pp. 73-74, 78-80; Albert Yon, intro. to his ed. and trans. of *Traité du destin,* Budé (Paris, 1933), pp. xiii-l; Bayer in the commentary in his ed. of *De fato,* pp. 112-13 concludes that there is insufficient evidence on which to identify Cicero's sources in this work with certainty.

De legibus as reasonable and conformable with natural law, are derided
as superstitious. Some scholars have dealt with this dilemma by concluding that Cicero was simply inconsistent or even hypocritical in the sphere
of religion, ignobly avoiding the responsibility of reconciling his adherence to the traditional rites with his philosophical objections to them.[147]
One author interprets this disparity as the consequence of a conversion
experience, in which Cicero lost his faith as a result of his philosophical
speculations.[148] Another commentator argues that Cicero's critique of
divination does not really bespeak any basic opposition to the practice,
which he continues to justify on the grounds of social utility.[149] Still
another scholar suggests that the positions Cicero takes in the *De legibus*
and in his theological works represent different stages or types of religious
awareness, the ritualistic type being suitable for uneducated people and
the philosophical type being adapted to the enlightened.[150] Ingenious as
it is, however, this last view requires a demonstration of the premise that
Cicero wrote the *De legibus* and his theological dialogues for two different
audiences.

In contrast, several scholars have offered a more plausible solution,
which takes account of the rhetorical element in Cicero's theological writings while at the same time locating the issue of religion within the personal and political context that is never far from his thought. While Cicero does not hide his own values in his theological dialogues, these
scholars point out, he is also using these works as a means of setting forth
the theology of a number of competing philosophical schools. He considers the arguments which the schools have advanced to establish or to
refute three theses: that the gods exist, that they control the lives of men,
and that they manifest signs of future events. Cicero expresses the positions of the schools through the speeches of several different interlocutors
whose presentation of the ideas they are attacking or defending is often
inaccurate, rambling, marked by the omission of important points, or
otherwise poorly argued. This feature of the dialogues is a deliberate
gambit on Cicero's part, designed to expose the weaknesses in the ways
that the philosophers have dealt with theological questions. Cicero, in
other words, is not displaying his own ignorance in these works. Nor is

---

[147] Pierre Defourny, "Les fondements de la religion d'après Cicéron," *LEC*, 22 (1954),
241-53, 366-78; Ferguson, "The Religion of Cicero," *Studies in Cicero*, pp. 89-94; Jürgen
Kroymann, "Cicero und die römische Religion," *Ciceroniana: Hommages à K. Kumaniecki*,
ed. Michel et Verdière, pp. 116-28.

[148] Falconer, intro. to his trans. of *De div.*, pp. 215-16.

[149] Silvia Jannacone, "Divinazione e culto ufficiale nel pensiero di Cicerone," *Latomus*,
14 (1955), 116-19.

[150] Jean-Marie André, "La philosophie religieuse de Cicéron," *Ciceroniana*, ed. Michel
et Verdière, pp. 11-21.

he trying to advance the claims of any one school. Nor is he trying to inspire agnosticism or irreligion. Rather, he is seeking to detach his own theological convictions from a forced philosophical association with other ideas that he does not believe in or which he thinks cannot be proved. Many of the principles that Cicero espouses in the field of theology are doctrines professed by some or all of the Stoics. At the same time, many of the principles and arguments from which he seeks to unhinge them are also Stoic. Cicero's overall approach in his theological works thus reflects a very independent attitude toward Stoicism. Those aspects of Stoic theology which he attacks are attacked because he thinks that they cannot be defended successfully. Those aspects of Stoic theology which he supports are usually consistent with the views on human nature, the nature of the deity, and the traditional religious practices that he defends elsewhere in his *oeuvre*.[151]

The *De natura deorum* is one of those works in which a hidden agenda lies behind the veil of apparently objective doxography. Here and elsewhere Cicero tells us that his aim in this work is simply to present the arguments of the major philosophical schools, not to advance his own opinion, so that the reader can evaluate the available theories and decide among them for himself.[152] However, within the dialogue there are a number of clues pointing to the fact that a different set of priorities is involved. Cicero tells us that he is writing the *De natura deorum* to fill his leisure, to console himself for the death of his daughter, and to present Greek ideas fluently and attractively in Latin.[153] At the same time he makes it clear that the inquiry is not purely a literary, personal, or theoretical one. The nature of the gods must be investigated, he notes, because theology has an immediate impact on civic behavior and social ethics, affecting one's sense of honor and loyalty to oaths and informing one's attitude toward temples and shrines, rituals, sacrifices, and religious duties. Cicero speaks here not only as a pious and public-spirited citizen but also as an augur who presides over the interpretation of the auspices, which he depicts as vital to the formation of public policy.[154]

The same connection between theology, eloquence, and ethics is rein-

---

[151] Bringmann, *Untersuchungen*, pp. 171-81; R. J. Goar, *Cicero and the State Religion* (Amsterdam, 1972), pp. 35-109, 114-26; Harris, "Cicero as an Academic," *Univ. of Auckland Bulletin, 58*, Classics ser. 2 (1961), 12-26, 30-37; Ursula Heibges, "Cicero, A Hypocrite in Religion?" *AJP, 90* (1969), 304-12; McKeon, intro. to *Brutus*, trans. Poteat, pp. 41-42; Giampaolo Vallot, "La cosmologia stoica nella polemica di Velleio (Cic. *De nat. deor.* I 18-24)," *Atti dell'Istituto veneto di scienze, lettere ed arti*, classe di scienze morali e lettere, *121* (1962-63), 1-15.
[152] *De nat. deor.* 1.5.10; *De fato.* 1.1
[153] *De nat. doer.* 1.3.6-1.4.9.
[154] *De nat. deor.* 1.6.13-14.

forced by Cicero's choice of interlocutors in the *De natura deorum* and in the setting of the work. In some of his dialogues he uses Republican worthies and in others he chooses his own contemporaries as speakers. In the *De natura deorum* he combines these two strategies by selecting three men who are several decades older than he is but whose lives overlapped his own, including himself also as a character in the dialogue. Balbus speaks for the Stoics. Alone among the interlocutors, his career apart from his philosophical interests is not known. Velleius, who speaks for the Epicureans, was a senator. The spokesman for the Old Academy, Cotta, in whose house the dialogue is set, served, like Cicero, as an orator, a senator, a consul, and a proconsul.[155] The conversation in the *De natura deorum* takes place during the same state holiday that provides the occasion for the *De republica*. In both cases Cicero wishes to imply that philosophical discussion is a worthy and necessary activity for orators and statesmen and that it is a characteristic occupation of those men who represent the political and ethical values that he associates with the Republic and that he professes himself. The parallels just noted between the *De republica* and the *De natura deorum* confer on the more recent interlocutors in the latter work and on Cicero himself the status of Republican *exempla virtutis* possessed by the speakers in the *De republica*, as well as attaching to the theological considerations which follow the same high tone of civic relevance and urgency.

Given the fact that the three other interlocutors clearly stand for Stoicism, Epicureanism, and the Old Academy,[156] there is a strong implication, which Cicero does nothing to dispel, that he himself intends to represent the New Academy. He does, in fact, pay that school a number of compliments. He states that the New Academics are prudent to withhold their consent to theories about the gods, since doctrines in this area are numerous and confusing; he credits them with the technique of arguing for and against all the schools which he follows in this work; and he asserts that opinions based on probabilities afford sufficient certitude for the wise man in the sphere of religion.[157] Yet at the same time Cicero firmly rejects the skeptic principle that theological truths cannot be known with certainty. To be sure, he argues, the truth is difficult to distinguish from falsehood, but it is not impossible to discover.[158] Thus,

---

[155] *De nat. deor.* 1.6.15, 2.1.1, trans. H. Rackham, Loeb (London, 1961), whose ed. of Books 2 and 3 will be cited. For further details on the interlocutors, see Rackham's intro., pp. xiv–xv.

[156] *De nat. deor.* 1.6.15–16.

[157] *De nat. deor.* 1.1.1, 1.5.11–12.

[158] *De nat. deor.* 1.5.11–12. The fact that Cicero has a positive ontological and epistemological basis for his theology has been noted by Virginia Guazzoni Foà, *I fondamenti filosofici della teologia ciceroniana*, Pubblicazioni dell'Istituto di filosofia, Facoltà di magistero dell'Università di Genova, 13 (Milano, 1970), pp. 41-45, 49-76, 110-15.

to the extent that Cicero identifies himself with the New Academy it is an identification that comes to a full stop short of their central premise of Academic skepticism. Nor does Cicero assign to himself any speech remotely as long as those he provides for Balbus, Velleius, or Cotta. It is not Cicero, the exponent of the New Academic technique of assessing all the schools, who acts as the critic of the Old Academic, Epicurean, and Stoic positions expressed by the other speakers. Instead, after his opening remarks, he recedes abruptly from view as a character in the dialogue and assigns to Cotta the role of criticizing both Stoicism and Epicureanism.

Stoicism in the *De natura deorum* is presented in three different ways. In its most overt form it is expounded by Balbus as the Stoic spokesman. It is also set forth critically by Velleius, who, in arguing for Epicureanism, devotes much of his time to Stoicism as the major position he feels he needs to refute. Stoicism is also presented in a positive light, both openly and not so openly, by Cotta, in the course of his critique of Epicureanism. It may seem strange that Cicero does not allow Balbus to defend his own territory against Velleius' attack. One possible reason is the view, stated by Cotta as a disciple of Antiochus, that the Stoics and Platonists are in substantial agreement, diverging only in their terminology. If this is the case, an Old Academic would be perfectly well equipped to criticize Epicureanism in the light of Stoic principles. But Balbus takes forceful exception to Cotta's assertion, pointing out that there are fundamental differences of opinion among the Stoics, Peripatetics, and Platonists. As an example he notes that the Stoics distinguish clearly between the *honestum* and the *utile* in kind, and not just in degree as do the other two schools.[159] In this exchange of views Cicero once again reveals the fact that he is aware of the basic differences between Stoicism and Platonism and, with this, the fact that the Old Academics have confused rather than clarified their relationship. Although Cotta is not assigned a speech in which he gives a positive exposition of Old Academic theology which the other interlocutors can then criticize from their own particular standpoints, Cicero in this way encourages the reader to raise questions about Antiochus' position on theology and on Stoicism in the light of its consistency with his own claims and on the basis of its ability to defend itself and those theological values that Cicero thinks merit credence.

Velleius' attack on Stoic theology in Book 1 of the *De natura deorum* lists a significant number of points which convey that doctrine correctly. At the same time the plausibility of his presentation is cast in doubt by his ascription to Epicureanism of positions which that school did not advo-

---

[159] *De nat. deor.* 1.7.16.

cate and by the flabby way in which he marshals his argument against the Stoics. He begins by observing that Zeno held God to be a living being, a material nature composed of aether, and that he defined God as reason, immanent in the cosmos, which can be equated with the law of nature that ordains what is just and forbids the opposite. Zeno taught, moreover, that the various gods of the pantheon are simply allegorical names referring to this central and all-pervading deity. Velleius adds that the Stoics after Zeno sometimes made other points about God. Aristo stated that God lacks sense perception; Cleanthes sometimes identified God with the world and at other times he asserted that the stars are divine. Persaeus said that the heroes can be apotheosized. Chrysippus applied the concept of divinity likewise to those human beings who have attained immortality, but extended it also to reason, the soul or mind pervading the universe, to fate or necessity, to aether and the other elements, and to the eternal law, as well as to the unitary deity which the gods of the pantheon represent allegorically. The point of this argument, insofar as there is one, seems to be the idea that these descriptions and definitions of God put forth by various Stoics are somehow inconsistent or mutually exclusive.[160] However, Velleius makes no effort to show that this is actually the case. Indeed, a few paragraphs further on, he reveals his understanding of the fact that the Stoic conception of God as the chief cause of all events, the idea of God as providence, which logically undergirds the Stoic defense of divination, is itself a logical corollary of the Stoic doctrine of God as the active principle pervading the universe. Velleius attempts no serious refutation of this conception of God or of the logical inferences that the Stoics draw from it. All he does is to assert rather flippantly that the Stoic God is too overworked and too much of a busybody and that divination is unnecessary and superstitious. He proposes an alternative conception of God, a deity who is perfectly at rest and who spends his time contemplating his own wisdom.[161] Velleius then concludes by observing that the existence of the gods can be proved by *consensus omnium*,[162] a Stoic argument which he annexes to Epicureanism without taking account of the fact that it is disproved by the rest of the case he has been trying to build, which is designed to show a lack of consensus among the Stoics themselves as well as a discrepancy between the Stoics' conception of God and the one that he puts forth.

This weakness provides Cotta with an opening in his critique of Velleius' argument. In his response to Velleius Cotta sometimes draws on

---

[160] *De nat. deor.* 1.14.36–1.14.41.
[161] *De nat. deor.* 1.20.52–53, 1.20.55–56.
[162] *De nat. deor.* 1.16.43–45.

Stoicism expressly and sometimes uses it without acknowledging it. He occasionally omits one or more key points in the Stoic doctrine involved. A propos of the *consensus omnium* argument, for instance, the Stoics sometimes appealed to it but they also acknowledged the principle that many people adhere to falsehoods through their own folly or the influence of convention or bad example. Cicero himself adverts to this Stoic argument in the *De legibus*. Cotta, however, does not exploit the Stoic rationale against Velleius as energetically as he might. His argument against *consensus omnium* here is based purely on empirical or common sense reasoning. In real life, he points out, some people believe in the gods and others do not. Thus, no consensus actually exists. Further, the *consensus omnium* argument presupposes that those people whose opinions we are not acquainted with correspond with those of people whom we know.[163]

In addressing himself to the substance of Velleius' Epicurean theology, Cotta upholds Stoicism over Velleius' conception of God, arguing that the Stoic position is much more logically defensible. The Epicurean God, he notes, is accorded the attribute of supreme goodness but is denied the attribute of benevolence, which is a logical corollary of goodness. The Stoics, who base God's care for mankind on God's desire to communicate his goodness to other rational beings, thus have a far more coherent conception of God. This conclusion can be reinforced, he adds, by arguing analogically from human goodness to the divine nature. God can be compared with the sages who enjoy friendship with each other as a function of their rational and benevolent nature. If men possess this capacity for friendship it must be an attribute of God *a fortiori*, for, needing nothing at all himself, God is that much better equipped to express his selfless beneficence by concerning himself with the well-being of man.[164] Cotta also invokes the Stoic disjunctive syllogism to disprove the Epicurean contention that nothing occurs in the universe of necessity. In a disjunctive proposition, he notes, either one of the two alternatives must be true. If one of the alternatives is true, it is true necessarily. Hence necessity exists; and hence it cannot be claimed that there is no necessity in the universe.[165] What Cotta is doing here is to use a Stoic principle in an unStoic manner. The facile leap which he makes from logical to ontological necessity is a performance that no Stoic would assay given the strictly formal character of logic as the Stoics taught it.

If a great deal of Stoic theology is presented in the defense and critique

---

[163] *De nat. deor.* 1.22.62-1.23.64. On this point compare the analysis of Guazzoni Foà, *I fondamenti*, pp. 26-27, 30-35; McKeon, intro. to *Brutus*, trans. Poteat, pp. 41-42; Schian, *Untersuchungen über das 'argumentum e consensu omnium'*, pp. 154-63, 166-67.

[164] *De nat. deor.* 1.43.121-122.

[165] *De nat. deor.* 1.25.69-70.

of Epicureanism in the *De natura deorum,* some of it accurately and some of it not so accurately, the same can certainly be said for Books 2 and 3, where Stoic theology is expressly expounded and attacked at still greater length.[166] Balbus' speech in Book 2, in fact, is the most extensive presentation of Stoic theology and cosmology found anywhere in Cicero's writings. Yet, a number of non-Stoic arguments are permitted to intrude and the logical solidity of Balbus' defense leaves much to be desired. He begins well enough, by subdividing his subject into four logically interrelated parts: the proof of the gods' existence, the nature of the gods, the gods' governance of the universe, and the gods' concern for human affairs. However, in his handling of these topics Balbus does not always adhere to the logical order he lays down. He also applies to the Stoics an Aristotelianized conception of the universe which does not mesh at all with their own cosmology.

Of the series of proofs which Balbus presents for the existence of the gods, only one is uniquely Stoic. It is based on the conception of *vis caloris* as a cosmic force.[167] All beings, he asserts, contain heat, so there must be a fiery first cause that permeates the natural order, preserves it, and holds it together. All nature contains such a force within it. In intelligent beings this force is called reason, the *hegemonikon* or ruling principle. In the cosmos as a whole this force is the divine *logos* which can be identified with heat, the vital creative and sustaining power in the world. Having developed this one solidly Stoic argument, however, Balbus at once assimilates it to Aristotelian metaphysics. The universe, he says, can be envisioned as a chain of being containing vegetable, animal, and rational beings, beginning with man and culminating with the deity who is absolute reason. God can be distinguished from the lower beings in that he alone is perfectly realized while all other beings exist in a state of becoming as they strive to actualize their potentialities and to attain their ends. This position certainly weakens the force of the *vis caloris* argument and compromises the Stoicism of Balbus' defense. It will be remembered that, at the beginning of Book 1, this same speaker had entered an incisive objection to Cotta's obfuscation of the Stoics' teachings on the *honestum* as compared to the teachings of the Platonists and Aristotelians. Here,

---

[166] A detailed summary of the anti-Stoic arguments in these books is provided by Ludwig Krumme, *Die Kritik der stoischen Theologie in Ciceros Schrift De natura deorum* (Düsseldorf, 1941).

[167] *De nat. deor.* 2.9.23–2.12.32. A good analysis of this argument can be found in Friedrich Solmsen, "Cleanthes or Posidonius? The Basis of Stoic Physics," *Mededelingen der koninklijke nederlandse Akademie van Wetenschappen,* afd. Letterkunde Nieuwse Reeks, *24:9* (Amsterdam, 1961), pp. 265–69. See also Endre von Ivánka, "Die stoische Anthropologie in der lateinischen Literatur," *Anzeiger der österreiche Akademie der Wissenschaften,* philosophisch-historische Klasse, *87* (1950), 178–92.

however, he shows himself equally capable of blurring the distinction between Stoicism and Aristotelianism in the field of metaphysics.

Balbus makes relatively few points in the second subdivision of his topic, the nature of the gods. He is mainly concerned with showing that the deity is spherical in shape, the sphere being the perfect figure, that God is creative, artistic, and benevolent toward man, and that the gods may be thought of as apotheosized heroes or as personifications of natural forces, although without the anthropomorphic or superstitious approach to the pantheon typical of popular religion.[168] The main emphasis of his speech is on the defense of the Stoic doctrines of providence and divination. His argument for providence recapitulates some of the points made by Cotta against Velleius in Book 1, the theme stressed being the beauty, order, and coherence of the world and of human nature as a sign of God's rational and beneficent governance of the universe.[169] Balbus also makes a number of specifically Stoic points in this context which are not articulated elsewhere in the *De natura deorum*. Speaking of the harmonious interrelations among the parts of the cosmos, he states that there is a centripetal force binding the universe together, which he calls *vinculum*;[170] this is none other than the Stoic *tonos*. In illustrating the interdependence of the parts of the universe he cites as an example the idea that the stars are nourished by exhalations from the earth.[171] He also outlines as an aspect of providence the Stoic theory of cosmic conflagration, adding that Panaetius disagrees with the other Stoics in denying it.[172] This section of the dialogue thus supplies significant information about Stoic physics, reported accurately. The final section of Balbus' speech extends the conception of providence in general to the specific level of the gods' particular concern for man, seen in their ordering of the universe for man's needs, their patronage of certain individuals, and their providing of signs of future events which men may interpret through divination.[173] The position which Balbus takes on providence and divination is consistently Stoic and amplifies without significantly adding to the Stoic defense of these doctrines which Cotta makes against Velleius in the first book.

As he begins his review of Balbus' arguments in Book 3, Cotta strikes a chord which may be regarded as Cicero's real theme in the *De natura deorum*. He announces that he believes in the traditional religion of Rome

---

[168] *De nat. deor.* 2.16.45–2.28.72.
[169] *De nat. deor.* 2.29.73–2.61.153.
[170] *De nat. deor.* 2.45.115.
[171] *De nat. deor.* 2.46.118.
[172] *De nat. deor.* 2.46.118–119.
[173] *De nat. deor.* 2.61.154–2.66.167.

and that the foundation of this belief, which he finds perfectly satisfactory, is the authority of the ancients. This faith stands firm regardless of the theological arguments put forth by the philosophers.[174] Faith based on authority, thus, is sufficient. And such a faith is intellectually respectable, considering the confusion that philosophical discussion on the subject spreads in its wake. The travesties that Cicero has been perpetrating on the teachings of the schools through his interlocutors thus emerge as a deliberate tactic for reinforcing the plausibility of the point of view articulated by Cotta. Cotta, as we have already seen, is not exempt himself from philosophical errors, confusions, and inconsistencies. In Book 3 he both levels this charge against Balbus and compounds the same mistake by misapplying a Stoic ethical doctrine against Balbus' Stoic theology.

Cotta's attack on Balbus' proofs of God's existence and nature does not ignore the genuinely weak points in his vis-à-vis' presentation. He criticizes Balbus' use of the *consensus omnium* argument, but here offers reasons different from those he had cited against Velleius' use of it, reasons which are also interesting in themselves. If the existence of the gods were self-evident, he states, it would be neither necessary nor expedient to invoke consensus as a proof. The very act of raising the issue may arouse doubts in the believer's mind that might never have been stimulated otherwise. Thus, the argument from *consensus omnium* should be eschewed lest it scandalize the faithful. This objection may seem peculiar unless we keep in mind the principle which Cotta states at the beginning of Book 3, that philosophy does not supply the sufficient reason for religious belief and practice. More interesting from the standpoint of the Stoic tradition is a second objection which Cotta makes to the argument from consensus, now developed on the basis of a fully Stoic analysis of the sort that Cicero expounds in the *De legibus*: truth is conformity with reason and not with the opinions of most people, who can be expected to be fools.[175] Cotta also makes a pointed attack on Balbus' confusion between Stoic and Aristotelian metaphysics, noting that the one system entails an immanent God identified with nature and the other entails a conception of nature independent of direct divine causation once it has been set in motion.[176]

Cotta is clearly willing to criticize Balbus' confusions and inconsistencies in handling Stoic doctrine when it comes to the proof of the gods' existence. In treating the other three topics on Balbus' agenda, however, he shows himself equally capable of contradicting his own earlier asser-

---

[174] *De nat. deor.* 3.2.5-6.
[175] *De nat. deor.* 3.6.14-15.
[176] *De nat. deor.* 3.8.20-3.14.37.

tions and of misapplying Stoic doctrine in his own way. He argues, for instance, that despite the Stoics' claim that divination is a logical corollary of the benevolent nature of the gods and despite their assertion that they are rationalizing theology by allegorizing the pantheon, what they have actually done has been to reinforce superstition.[177] This, despite his own defense of the logic of divination against Velleius and despite his own profession of faith in traditional religion. Even more interesting is his attack on the notion that one can establish the benevolence of God by arguing analogically from human rationality and goodness, an argument he had supported in Book 1. In human terms, he states, goodness is not a necessary corollary of reason. Criminals, after all, are bad men even though they are rational beings. It is not the faculty of reason alone that makes men good but its virtuous use, which in turn depends on man's exercise of his will, a faculty subject to his own control.[178] Here Cotta seeks to turn the Stoic analysis of free will as an essential ingredient in moral choices, which, so far as he takes it, he reports correctly, against the Stoic doctrine of providence by stressing that man is morally autonomous from God. This argument is actually less Stoic than it appears at first glance, however, for Cotta has omitted a key point: the Stoics' identification of the divine *logos* with the human *logos,* which makes the ruling principle controlling man's moral choices the same as the ruling principle governing the cosmos.

If Cotta at the beginning of Book 3 proclaims the durability of the traditional faith regardless of the lucubrations of the philosophers, Balbus annexes to himself an equal concern with defending the faith as the dialogue draws to its conclusion. Balbus charges Velleius and Cotta, both magistrates with the duty to protect religion, with hypocrisy and impiety in their arguments against Stoicism. He implies at the same time that Stoicism is the philosophy most consistent with piety and that religious beliefs and obligations would remain unshaken even if Stoic theology were successfully refuted. In his own persona, speaking for the first time since the beginning of Book 1, Cicero observes that, while Velleius thought that Cotta had made the best case, he himself awarded the palm to Balbus.[179] It is not clear whether Cicero is praising Balbus' Stoicism or his claim that no philosophical demonstration or refutation has the power to establish or overturn religious faith, the latter position being in substantial agreement with Cotta's appeal to traditional religion. This parting shot, oblique though it may be, still serves to reinforce the thesis set forth throughout the *De natura deorum* by example as well as by precept.

---

[177] *De nat. deor.* 3.15.39–3.35.64.
[178] *De nat. deor.* 3.26.66–3.36.88.
[179] *De nat. deor.* 3.40.94–95.

Cicero reminds the reader of the weakness of all philosophical approaches to religion and suggests a preference for Stoicism at least to the extent that it may supply a positive if extrinsic rationale for religious precepts that he holds on other grounds. Cicero's capacity to handle his philosophical materials with more subtlety than he is sometimes given credit for emerges from the *De natura deorum*, if in an indirect manner. He shows that he is well aware of the differences between what the Stoics taught and the ways in which their ideas had been used and abused by other philosophical schools. This fact is visible in the ways he characterizes the speakers through their arguments and from the inevitable comparisons which arise between the Stoic content of the *De natura deorum* and the Stoicism that appears in his other works.

In the *De divinatione* and *De fato* Cicero expands on a number of topics discussed generally in the *De natura deorum*. Cicero and his brother Quintus are the interlocutors in the *De divinatione*, which they introduce as a companion piece to the *De natura deorum*.[180] Theology, politics, and the personal situation of the interlocutors are associated in a similar way in both works. The *De divinatione* is the place where Cicero expounds his most elaborate rationale for *otium litterarium*.[181] He also emphasizes that a knowledge of religious truth is important for the commonwealth since one otherwise runs the risk of offending the gods either by neglecting their rites or by venerating them superstitiously.[182] Cicero makes it clear that there is a knowable truth in this area and that it lies between the poles of agnosticism and vulgar credulity. While he claims in the *De divinatione* and elsewhere that he is not advocating a positive position in this dialogue but is only citing the views that are most probable,[183] or presenting and refuting a thesis,[184] or offering a variety of arguments so that the reader can make up his own mind,[185] he is actually defending the same principle that he defends in the *De natura deorum*, and by similar means.

Cicero singles out the Stoics for special attention in the *De divinatione*. Theirs is the philosophical defense of divination which Quintus supports and which Cicero attacks. In focusing on the Stoics Cicero acknowledges the fact that other people also believe in divination and that the Stoics are not the only philosophers who have come to its aid. Consensus, he does not fail to reiterate, is no guarantee of truth; and even among the

---

180 *De div.* 1.5.8-1.6.10.
181 *De div.* 1.6.11, 2.1.1-2.2.7.
182 *De div.* 1.4.7.
183 *De div.* 2.72.150.
184 *De div.* 1.4.7.
185 *De fato* 1.1.

Stoics Panaetius dissents from the general view on divination. None the less, Cicero argues that the burden of proof can be placed on the shoulders of the Stoics since they defend divination more exhaustively than any other school.[186]

The central issue in the *De divinatione*, however, is not so much Stoicism in particular as philosophical theology in general, an approach that Cicero has already shown to be unacceptable in the *De natura deorum* and which he wishes to expose yet again by the same sort of *reductio ad absurdum*. The argumentation in the *De divinatione* shows that much can be said in favor of the Stoic position on divination and much can be said against it. More important, it is designed to show that the proponents of both sides of the debate are guilty of logical inconsistency, tunnel vision, and intellectual arrogance. In order to make this point he encumbers both himself and Quintus with speeches that contain many shaky or contradictory arguments.

Quintus' speech adds little to the Stoic material already presented in the *De natura deorum*. Nor does he make very good use of what he presumably could have found in that work, although he says that he has read it. His defense of divination is based on an argument from *consensus omnium*, an argument from historical experience, and an argument from reason.[187] His argument from consensus ignores all the objections leveled against it in the *De natura deorum*. His argument from history begs the question just as much as Cicero's similar sally in the *De legibus*. The only difference is that this time Cicero, the character in the *De divinatione*, unmasks the weaknesses of the argument in his rebuttal of Quintus. Quintus' sturdiest argument is his argument from reason. Here he repeats the Stoic justification developed by Cotta and reiterated by Balbus in the *De natura deorum*, which Cicero had also offered in the *De legibus*: divination follows logically from the existence and beneficence of the gods. Quintus adds only one new element to this position. He observes that God can be equated with fate and with natural law, or the orderly sequence of causes that links all events in the universe together. Since God or fate is the causal principle in the world, everything that occurs is fated to occur by God.[188] Quintus advances this deterministic position as a logical basis for the claim that the future can be predicted. But even here, in the most Stoic portion of his speech, he misconstrues the doctrine at issue by ignoring the fact that the Stoics found a place for contingency within their teaching on fate, a fact of which Cicero was perfectly well aware.[189]

---

[186] *De div.* 1.1.1–1.4.7.
[187] *De div.* 1.6.12–1.48.132.
[188] *De div.* 1.45.125–126.
[189] See for instance *Ad fam.* 9.4.1; *De fato* 9.17–18.

In his rebuttal of Quintus, Cicero the interlocutor tries to show that the Stoic position on divination is self-contradictory and that Quintus has done a deplorable job of defending it. He succeeds in achieving the second goal without very much difficulty, his assumption being that this will persuade the reader that the first objective has also been won. Cicero's own speech, however, is replete with contradictory arguments. Unlike many of the anti-Stoic attacks in the *De natura deorum*, however, none of these arguments draws on any Stoic principles, so they need not detain us. Despite his critique of Quintus Cicero by no means intends to leave the substantive issue of divination in doubt. At the beginning of the dialogue he asserts that both disdain for the rites and superstitious reverence for them be avoided lest the gods be offended and the commonwealth be ill-served through impiety. Elsewhere in the work he takes pains to reiterate the point that soothsaying and augury should be fostered for reasons of social utility.[190] While some philosophers have attacked divination and while it may be impossible to develop a convincing philosophical rationale for it this is no warrant for dispensing with it. The existence of the gods and their right to be worshipped according to certain fixed forms are beliefs sanctioned by tradition and are not dependent on the philosophers' arguments for or against divination. Insofar as there is any philosophical doctrine that promotes religious belief, says Cicero, it is the Stoic doctrine of the beauty, order, and harmony of the cosmos.[191] But this doctrine is in no sense the foundation on which he rests his case. It is, rather, the one he singles out for approval because it is the one most fully consistent with the non-philosophical principles on which he bases his theology.

Of the three dialogues he devotes to theology, Cicero presents the most positive attitude toward Stoicism in the *De fato*. Like the *De divinatione*, this work is introduced as an appendix to the *De natura deorum* and as a dialogue written in the form of thesis and antithesis. It also reflects a similar ethical and political orientation. The two interlocutors are Cicero and his friend Hirtius, a consul-designate and a man who, like Cicero, had been interested in philosophy from his youth. The *De fato* is set chronologically in the period immediately following the assassination of Caesar, when fresh civic strife portends, a situation that both Cicero and Hirtius are anxious to avert. Cicero emphasizes the connection between philosophy and political suasion by remarking on the relevance of speculation on fate to the profession of the interlocutors as orators and public men. Also, in the opening lines of the dialogue Cicero offers a

---

[190] *De div.* 2.12.28.
[191] *De div.* 2.17.41, 2.33.70–2.39.83, 2.72.148.

definition of moral philosophy, thus suggesting that the entire discussion must be viewed in the context of ethics in general. From an ethical standpoint an understanding of fate is of critical importance because it impinges directly on the doctrine of free will.[192] Cicero does not attempt to prove that man has free will on philosophical grounds anywhere in the *De fato*. He simply assumes that man possesses free will as an axiom which he then uses to evaluate the philosophical arguments he considers. The philosophical position which he espouses, because it is consistent with this criterion, is the doctrine of fate taught by Chrysippus.[193]

The *De fato* has come down to us in a fragmentary state. The first part of the dialogue, in which Hirtius argues on behalf of fatalism, has not survived. What remains is the second part, where Cicero attacks fatalism in the name of the more balanced teaching of Chrysippus, a position which permits contingency and freedom in some areas while admitting that man is limited and constrained in other areas. There are a few unusual points which Cicero makes about individual Stoics in this work that are worth pointing out because they do not agree with other ancient sources. He attributes to Chrysippus the idea that climate has a formative effect on character,[194] a view more typically assigned to Posidonius, and he depicts Posidonius as an adherent of an uncompromising fatalism that admits no shadow of contingency,[195] an opinion no one else ascribes to him. Cicero's main concern in the surviving portion of the *De fato* is to defend Chrysippus' doctrine of necessity and possibility as illustrated by the metaphor of the rolling cylinder and to attack the arguments of Chrysippus' critics. It is impossible to know for certain, but his particular choice of critics may be a function of the argument in the lost speech of Hirtius.

Cicero begins with Diodorus the Megarian, who sought to refute Chrysippus with the argument that all true propositions are true necessarily, and that hence nothing true is contingent. Cicero judges that this refutation is logically tenable, but that it is acceptable only if one is willing

---

[192] *De fato* 1.1–2.4.

[193] A good analysis of this point can be found in Pier Luigi Donini, "Crisippo e la nozione del possibile," *Rivista di filologia e di istruzione classica, 101* (1973), 333-51, who, however, is not convincing in his argument that Cicero is reporting Chrysippus' position inaccurately in his "Fato e volontà umana in Crisippo," *Atti della Accademia delle scienze di Torino*, classe di scienze morali, storiche e filologiche, *109:2* (1975), 187-96; Margaret Y. Henry, "Cicero's Treatment of the Free Will Problem" *TAPA, 58* (1927), 32-42. On the other hand, Weische, *Cicero und die neue Akademie*, pp. 28-34 interprets the *De fato* as a skeptic attack on Stoicism. A useful textual analysis is provided by A. J. Kleywegt, "Fate, Free Will, and the Text of Cicero," *Mnemosyne*, ser. 4:*26* (1973), 342-49.

[194] *De fato* 4.7-8.

[195] *De fato* 3.5-4.7. Cf. *Hortensius*, frag. 48, where Cicero attributes the doctrine of complete fatalism to all of the Stoics.

to subscribe to absolute determinism.[196] He is clearly unwilling to do this, which is why he rejects Diodorus' argument even though he admits that it is logically defensible. Next, he notes, the Epicureans attacked Chrysippus because they objected to the idea of an orderly nexus of causes in the universe. But they countered with the theory of atoms swerving fortuitously in the void, which is self-contradictory and impossible to prove.[197] Carneades, however, provided a more serious challenge to Chrysippus. Carneades drew a distinction between external causes and internal, self-motivated causes. He placed free will in the latter category, arguing that freely willed acts do have causes albeit they are not caused by fate. Chrysippus countered with an alternative theory which drew a distinction between simple and complex events. According to Chrysippus, Cicero notes, simple events are fated and will occur regardless of man's will. Complex events, however, entail some active collaboration on man's part, and thus combine fate and free will. In his effort to attack this position, Cicero continues, Carneades fell back on the argument that if all things are caused, they are fated. This argument was a mere debating point on Carneades' part, says Cicero, and a very weak one at that, because in his effort to annihilate Chrysippus' conception of complex events and to reduce him to sheer fatalism Carneades ended by annihilating his own distinction between external and internal causes, consigning himself to fatalism as well. Carneades' attack thus fails, according to Cicero. Carneades' view also has another limitation in comparison with Chrysippus', for it does not acknowledge the difference between cause and circumstance, between remote and efficient causes.[198]

Cicero goes on to discuss this additional advantage of Chrysippus' theory, his distinction between principal and perfect causes and auxiliary and proximate causes, which helps to specify the relationship between fate and free will in complex events. In such a case, fate acts as an auxiliary or proximate cause while the principal and perfect cause is human free will, which lies within man's own power to control. This Chrysippian doctrine recommends itself to Cicero as a weapon against those who claim that any belief in fate necessarily entails unmitigated determinism. Having demolished Chrysippus' critics to his own satisfaction and having underlined the merits of Chrysippus' own position as an offensive and defensive strategy, Cicero concludes that Chrysippus' doctrine of fate is superior to all others. It is capable of showing how some events may be destined from all eternity while others take place through free choice or

---

[196] *De fato* 6.12-9.18.

[197] *De fato* 9.18-19.

[198] *De fato* 11.23-16.38. Elsewhere Cicero takes a less positive attitude toward the Stoic division of causes into direct and indirect; see, for example, *Topica* 15.58-59.

contingency. It refutes the position that Cicero wants to refute. And, it coincides with his own opinion.[199]

There is only one feature of Chrysippus' theory that he thinks merits criticism: his terminology is not as clear as it might be. Here Cicero raises an objection that recalls similar complaints about the Stoics' terminology which he voices elsewhere in his works. He illustrates this problem by adverting again to Chrysippus' definition of fate as the proximate cause and free will as the principal cause in a complex event. This language, Cicero says, is likely to confuse people who attach different meanings to the terms. A sensationalist, for instance, would regard the proximate cause of knowledge and assent as sense data. But in Chrysippus' sense of the term this would mean that the entire cognitive process was fated and that it in no sense entailed the exercise of free will. As Cicero points out, this is by no means what Chrysippus taught in the sphere of epistemology. So, Chrysippus' terminology might easily give rise to misapprehensions about this theory of knowledge no less than about his theory of causation. However, Cicero concludes, if one does pay attention to what Chrysippus means by the terms he uses, his doctrine of fate is fully acceptable.[200]

Cicero is considerably more generous to Chrysippus in the *De fato* than he is to the Stoics or to the other philosophers in the *De natura deorum* and the *De divinatione*. While he faults Chrysippus for his confusing terminology, he still makes it clear that Chrysippus' terms can be understood with a modicum of effort and that when this is done an inquirer will have access to a valid and useful doctrine. The Stoic doctrine of fate itself is one to which Cicero grants far greater approval than he accords to any of the other Stoic theological or cosmological ideas discussed in his other works, except for the theory of natural law as treated in the *De republica* and *De legibus*. At the same time Cicero's emphasis in his handling of the topic of fate in the *De fato* is basically quite similar to his treatment of the philosophical issues with which he deals in his other theological dialogues. In all cases, ethics takes pride of place and supplies the stated or unstated criteria in terms of which the analysis is conducted. In some of Cicero's theological dialogues, social ethics is the main perspective from which he views the issues; in other cases, personal ethics is stressed, although the public and private implications of any ethical attitude are never separated in his thought. In the case of the *De fato*, it is the implications of the doctrine of fate for personal ethics that receive Cicero's primary attention. It is his axiomatic belief in free will within the framework of a causal order, providing the foundations for the kind of moral

---

[199] *De fato* 16.38, 18.41.
[200] *De fato* 10.21, 18.41-19.45.

life that he finds acceptable, that serves as the standard he uses to judge the philosophical arguments concerning fate that he raises for consideration.

Cicero has personal reasons for holding this view on fate and free will just as he has personal reasons for holding the views on the gods and on religious practice that he expresses in the *De natura deorum* and the *De divinatione*. A theory of free will that placed total control of events in the hands of the individual would not have been able to supply Cicero with the consolation he sought or the rationalization he needed to explain his own failures in public life, misfortunes placed in sharp relief by his continuing inability to influence events after Caesar's assassination. On the other hand, a theory of fate advocating total determinism would have had little appeal to a man like Cicero, who seems to have had a constitutional need to commit himself to some form of action he could conceive of as constructive and freely chosen, a man whose hopes no amount of adversity was able to dim, a man seemingly untroubled by the sense of futility and despair to which someone else in his position might easily have succumbed. Cicero finds the Stoic doctrine of fate persuasive because its particular balance between fate and free will resonates harmoniously with his own inner ethical needs. He therefore is less inclined in the *De fato* than in the *De natura deorum* and the *De divinatione* to subject the Stoics to as much criticism as he applies to the other philosophers or to rest his case so explicitly on non-philosophical principles. Yet, even in the case of the *De fato*, as in his other theological and cosmological works, the Stoic position Cicero supports so warmly receives his support less because he is rationally convinced of its truth and of the untenability of competing views than because it corresponds with and substantiates extrinsically a deeply felt ethical value which neither springs from nor is ultimately validated by philosophical reasoning.

VII. Ethics

Of all the philosophical topics to which Cicero turns his attention he devotes the largest number of works to ethics. The association between morality, rhetoric, politics, and personal concerns that recurs throughout the rest of his philosophical writings is also clearly visible in his ethical works. As an ethical thinker Cicero draws very heavily on Stoicism. It can truly be said that, after Seneca, he is the principal Latin source for Stoic ethics.[201] But beyond the simple act of transmission, Cicero is ex-

---

[201] Milton Valenti, *L'Éthique stoïcienne chez Cicéron* (Paris, 1956), p. xiii. This is the best survey of the subject.

pressly concerned with developing a personal attitude toward the ethics of the Stoa. As we have seen, he also feels moved to take a particular stance toward Stoicism in the other subdivisions of his philosophical *oeuvre*. In the case of rhetoric this attitude is largely negative; in this context Stoicism functions as the foil for the largely Aristotelian position which he develops. In the case of political and legal theory, on the other hand, his attitude is both positive and creative, leading to his extension of Stoicism well beyond the boundaries within which it had operated before his time. In the case of theology and cosmology Cicero approves of comparatively few Stoic doctrines and criticizes many others. The chief role that Stoicism plays for him in this sphere is to typify the problems entailed by the philosophical approach to theology, or, at best, to provide extrinsic support for religious or moral values that he holds for other reasons. In the case of ethics Cicero takes still another attitude toward philosophy in general. Ethics provides much more to him than just a speculative means of rationalizing beliefs derived from non-philosophical sources. For Cicero ethics is the one branch of philosophy that not only conveys an understanding of the truths pertaining to its subject matter but also endows the seeker with the capacity to translate principles into practice. Cicero thus accords to ethics much more importance than he assigns to other types of philosophy. For ethics and ethics alone has the power to transform one's life. From this standpoint he assays a number of philosophical schools and finds the Stoics the most impressive. But there are also points at which he finds their doctrine worthy of criticism, both in its substance and in its mode of expression. Cicero thus makes Stoicism his point of departure in ethics but subjects it to significant modifications, emerging with a position of his own that is heavily in-debted to Stoicism although it is by no means identical with it.

Cicero initiates his ethical inquiry in the *Paradoxa Stoicorum* by considering the ancient Stoic paradoxes concerning the sage. Even in this initial work in the series he begins to indicate some of the areas in which he finds this conception unacceptable or subject to revision. He continues the process of substantiating or modifying Stoic ethics in the *De senectute, De amicitia, De finibus,* and *Tusculanarum disputationum.* Finally, in the *De officiis,* he expresses his own reformulated position. To a significant extent Cicero arrives at this ultimate destination by substituting middle Stoicism for the rigors of the ancient Stoa. There are, however, areas in which he departs sharply from middle Stoicism as well. He puts forth the resulting theory in the mode of rhetoric and in the context of his specific conception of political life. Cicero thus retains the same organic connection between these themes and stylistic considerations in his ethical works as he displays in his other philosophical writings.

Cicero's *Paradoxa Stoicorum* is written as a defense of six of the classic Stoic ethical paradoxes: (1) Virtue is the only good, (2) Virtue is sufficient for happiness, (3) All vices and all virtues are equal, (4) All fools are madmen, (5) The sage alone is free, and (6) Only the wise man is rich. Commentators have not failed to notice that Cicero argues on behalf of these paradoxes in the *Paradoxa Stoicorum* although he or interlocutors in some of his dialogues ridicule one or more of them elsewhere. Some scholars explain this discrepancy by dismissing the *Paradoxa Stoicorum* as a mere literary *jeu d'esprit*[202] or as a thesis which Cicero is setting up only to refute in his other writings.[203] Another way to dispose of the problem has been to interpret Cicero's handling of the topic of the Stoic sage in the different rhetorical contexts in which it occurs as a New Academic *reductio ad absurdum* of Stoicism.[204] The *Paradoxa Stoicorum* has also been explained as an effort to console and strengthen a number of contemporary statesmen identified with Stoicism, such as Cato, who, like Cicero, were defenders of the Roman Republic but who, unlike him, still remained active in the political arena.[205] There are, to be sure, some traces of political propaganda in the *Paradoxa Stoicorum*. Cicero does depict himself in the introduction as the author of a literary exercise. At the same time it would be a mistake to view the rhetorical elements in this work as mere intellectual game-playing. Rhetoric, after all, is a serious business for Cicero. The *Paradoxa Stoicorum* provides him with the occasion for effecting a transition from oratorical and political theory to ethical theory but it is also firmly connected in theme and style with works that he produced both before and after it. Cicero's objective in the *Paradoxa Stoicorum* is to reformulate the Stoic paradoxes in a literary mode. He treats them as rhetorical *topoi*, to be defended by diatribe, invective, and satire and supported by forensic arguments and historical *exempla*. He invokes Republican heroes both ancient and recent as models of the sage and he alludes to contemporary enemies or rivals as examples of the fool. At the same time, while his goal on one level is to defend the Stoic paradoxes, and to defend them better than the Stoics themselves are able to do,[206]

---

[202] A. G. Lee, intro. to his ed. of *Paradoxa Stoicorum* (London, 1953), p. xxii; H. Rackham, intro. to his trans. of *Par. Sto.*, Loeb (Cambridge, Mass., 1960), pp. 252-53.

[203] A. Michel, "Cicéron et les paradoxes stoïciens," *Acta antiqua Academiae scientarum Hungaricae, 16* (1968), 223-32.

[204] Jean Molager, intro. to his ed. and trans. of *Par. Sto.*, Budé (Paris, 1971), pp. 39-54.

[205] Kazimierz Kumaniecki, "Ciceros Paradoxa Stoicorum und die römische Wirklichkeit," *Philologus, 101* (1957), 113-34; followed by Molager, intro. to his ed. of *Par. Sto.*, p. 24.

[206] Bringmann, *Untersuchungen*, pp. 60-71; Molager, intro. to his ed. of *Par. Sto.*, pp. 16-24; Rackham, intro. to his trans. of *Par. Sto.*, p. 253.

the strategies he employs for this purpose sometimes subvert the ethical principles at issue. There is thus more going on in the *Paradoxa Stoicorum* than initially meets the eye.

Cicero introduces the *Paradoxa Stoicorum* by referring to Cato, famed as a model of Stoic virtue and elsewhere identified by Cicero as the only Stoic who possesses eloquence. While he may be the best of the Stoic orators, Cato, in Cicero's view, is still guilty of the stylistic vices of that school, which dissociates itself from ornament, refinement, and copious dilation, *sed minutis interrogatiunculis quase punctis quod proposuit efficit* ("but proves its case by means of tiny little interrogatory pin-pricks.")[207] Finding this style of argument both unpersuasive and aesthetically offensive, Cicero sets out to do the Stoics one better by recasting their ethical paradoxes in a more pleasing and convincing form. He has selected the paradoxes concerning the sage, he says, because the doctrine they contain is valid but the Stoics have met with great difficulty in proving it, since the ideas involved run counter to common opinion.[208] The paradoxes thus offer a philosophical challenge in their own right, and one that Cicero thinks a skilled orator like himself is better qualified to meet than the Stoics themselves are.

This rationale is one that Cicero develops consistently in the body of the work. He does not provide philosophical arguments alone in support of the paradoxes. The emphasis, rather, is on rhetorical modes of proof of one kind or another. When he does use philosophical reasoning it is not necessarily Stoic in character. In handling the first paradox Cicero advances only one philosophical argument, which is an authentically Stoic one: man alone among all created beings is endowed with reason, the faculty that distinguishes him from animals and that enables him to pursue the good. Man should therefore define the good in exclusively rational terms and order his moral life in the light of his rational capacities.[209] Cicero also uses a fully Stoic argument in defending the second paradox. Here he rests his case on the doctrine that moral autarchy is the only true source of happiness. Happiness depends on the possession of a good that cannot be lost and this condition applies only to those things that lie within our own control.[210]

---

[207] *Par. Sto.* prooemium 2-3, ed. Molager; trans. Rackham.

[208] *Par. Sto.* prooemium 3-5.

[209] *Par. Sto.* 14.

[210] *Par. Sto.* 17-19. On Stoic moral autarchy see also *Ad fam.* 5.13.1; *Hortensius*, frag. 74. Discussion on this point in the *Hortensius* is provided by Michel Ruch, *L'Hortensius de Cicéron: Histoire et reconstruction,* Collection d'études anciennes, publiée sous le patronage de l'Association Guillaume Budé (Paris, 1958), pp. 143-44; Danuta Turkowska, *L'Hortensius de Cicéron et le Protreptique d'Aristote,* Polska Akademia Nauk, Prace Komisje Filologii Klasycznej, 6 (Wrocław, 1965).

The most elaborate philosophical argument of all is the one that Cicero offers in support of the equality of all vices and all virtues, although in this case he subordinates it to a forensic line of reasoning which has the effect of undermining the Stoic character of his defense. The general definitions of virtue and vice Cicero provides in this instance are thoroughly Stoic. Virtue is a constant conformity with reason; *virtus est consentiens cum ratione et perpetua constantia* while vices are deformities of the mind, *pravitates animi*.[211] All virtues are equal in that each of them is a manifestation of the same fixed inner intention toward the good. Once he has proved the equality of the virtues in this manner, Cicero proceeds to prove the equality of the vices by analogy with the virtues.[212] But, while he stresses inner intentionality as the determinant of moral value and argues for the radical equality of all vices and virtues, he at once proceeds to offer examples illustrating this principle which cause the argument to slide abruptly out of a Stoic frame of reference. Cicero first recapitulates the Stoic argument that a drowning man drowns just the same whether he is under one inch or one foot of water, or that a seduced woman suffers the same assault on her chastity whether she is of high or low social status. Having mentioned an example drawn from the criminal law, he then goes on to define all crimes as equal because they all involve an identical decision to break the law. At the same time, he notes, a given crime may not always bear the same penalty; it depends on the status of the person injured and on his relation to the malefactor. This criterion is perfectly valid, according to Cicero, because some crimes, judged by these external standards, are more heinous than others.[213] So, although he begins by following the Stoa in rooting vice and virtue in the fixed inner intention of the subject and in asserting that the vices and the virtues are therefore equal, he ends by establishing gradations of vice and virtue on the basis of a criterion of value imposed from outside.

Cicero achieves a swift stylistic transition in his handling of the next two paradoxes, which involves a heavy use of rhetorical arguments. He defends the fourth paradox by attacking an unnamed personal enemy, whom he blames for his own exile, castigating him as a fool while simultaneously depicting himself as a sage. His exile was no hardship, Cicero asserts, for he possesses the Stoic virtue of equanimity. His enemy's madness and folly consist *ipso facto* in his failure to appreciate Cicero's wisdom and virtue and his consequent belief that exiling him would make any difference to him.[214] In this argument self-justification usurps the

---

[211] *Par. Sto.* 22.
[212] *Par. Sto.* 21-22.
[213] *Par. Sto.* 20-21, 24-26.
[214] *Par. Sto.* 29-32.

place of a Stoic defense of the paradox in question. The fifth paradox is also framed as an attack on an unidentified person, this time a military leader who, in Cicero's opinion, is unworthy of his command because he cannot govern his passions; thus he is not even a free man. Cicero here defines freedom as the power to live as one wills. Will is the critical element in the equation. Freedom involves the rational control of one's behavior, based on one's free assent to the goodness of one's course of action. The sage alone is free because his will, enlightened by his judgment, freely chooses the good. Everyone else is a slave, regardless of his social status.[215] While Cicero goes on to provide many anecdotal examples of moral slavery, the reasoning on which he rests his case is authentically Stoic.

Cicero also uses anecdotes about frugal worthies in defending the sixth paradox. Here too he subordinates them to an essentially Stoic rationale, which harks back to the argument concerning moral autarchy elaborated in connection with the second paradox. Riches, he says, are an endowment of the mind. Virtue is the only true wealth, because it alone provides enduring contentment despite the vicissitudes of fortune.[216] As a rule for daily life, he adds, we should own only what is sufficient for our needs. People make miscalculations in this area, he notes, because they confuse their reasonable needs with their unreasonable desires, a tendency which leads men in positions of authority to violate the laws they are supposed to enforce, abusing the privileges of public office to satisfy their irrational passions.[217] The chord which Cicero is striking here reminds the reader yet again of the political and personal themes that weave their way through the *Paradoxa Stoicorum*, where the unidentified culprits who have been guilty of malfeasance or opposition to Cicero illustrate the vices just as the defenders of the Republic, including himself, illustrate the virtues. The same kind of association between philosophy, propaganda, and rhetoric which is visible in Cicero's other works can be seen in operation in the *Paradoxa Stoicorum* as well.

Most of the rhetorical arguments which Cicero uses in the *Paradoxa Stoicorum* are supplements to, or substitutes for, a more strictly Stoic defense, except in the case of the third paradox, where he decisively alters the content of the Stoic doctrine of vice and virtue by his rhetorical reformulation of this issue. In the *Paradoxa Stoicorum* Cicero invokes the rhetorical style as an express criticism of the ability of the Stoics to defend their own teachings adequately. On the other hand, in the *De senectute*, *De amicitia*, and *De finibus*, Cicero reverts to the dialogue form and chooses

---

[215] *Par. Sto.* 33-40.
[216] *Par. Sto.* 42-44, 50-52.
[217] *Par. Sto.* 46-47. On self-sufficiency and its antithesis see also *Ad fam.* 7.16.3.

as his interlocutors leading Republican statesmen and orators who had known Stoic connections. However, the positions which they take are not necessarily orthodox from a Stoic point of view. In fact their speeches are the vehicles for a modification of Stoic ethics far more extensive than what Cicero accomplishes in the *Paradoxa Stoicorum*.

Both the *De senectute* and the *De amicitia* are dedicated to Atticus and both purport to express purely private concerns.[218] However, the political and philosophical associations evoked by the interlocutors in these two works indicate that something more complex is at issue. The main speaker in the *De senectute* is Cato the elder, who proposes a highly Stoic rationale for his position at the beginning of the work. At the same time, in the preface Cicero cites as an authority a work on old age by the Peripatetic Aristo of Ceos[219] and the actual doctrine set forth by Cato has little specifically Stoic content. Cato begins by observing that his placid acceptance of old age should cause no wonder, since, for those who possess moral autarchy, contentment is possible at any time of life. No dismay is caused by the necessary changes brought about by aging. Nature imposes these changes and nature is the guide to the moral life; nothing that she decrees can therefore be regarded as an evil, including aging and dying.[220]

But despite this Stoic-sounding introduction, the body of Cato's argument is only quasi-Stoic at best. He notes, for instance, that old age does not deprive him of the pleasures of agriculture, which he regards as the best occupation for the wise man and the statesman. In this connection Cato refers to the example of Cincinnatus at the plow.[221] His argument and his example certainly sound Stoic. At the same time the praise of agriculture can also be seen as a literary device for fleshing out the character of Cato, who wrote a *De agri cultura*. Even more interesting is the fact that Cicero fastens on an aspect of the Cincinnatus story that is generally ignored by other authors who cite him as a moral example. Once in office, Cato notes, Cincinnatus appointed Servilius Ahala as his master of the horse, who in turn arrested Spurius Mummius and put him

---

[218] *De amicitia* 1.2.4, 1.4.5. However, Luigi Alfonsi, "Il pensiero ciceroniano nel *De senectute*," *Studi letterari: Miscellanea in onore di Emilio Sentini* (Palermo, 1956), pp. 1-16 has noted the political dimensions of *De sen.* as well.

[219] *Caton l'Ancien (De la vieillesse)* 1.3, ed. and trans. P. Wuilleumier, Budé (Paris, 1940). Citations will be made to this edition. Most scholars have emphasized the non-Stoic sources of the *De sen.* The most useful review of the literature is Paola Venini, "La vecchiaia nel *De senectute* di Cicerone," *Athenaeum*, *38* (1960), 101-02, who supports the majority opinion. Wuilleumier, intro. to his ed. of *De sen.*, pp. 37-67, places more emphasis on Stoic sources.

[220] *De sen.* 2.4-5, 19.71.

[221] *De sen.* 15.51, 16.56-17.60.

to death for attempting to overthrow the Republic and install a monarchy.[222] If Cincinnatus, and by extension, Ahala, are to be praised as *exempla virtutis,* it follows by implication that Cicero's own summary policy against Catiline should likewise merit approbation. Similarly, although Cato argues that death is not an evil, he by no means treats it as a Stoic *adiaphoron.* The human soul, he says, may be annihilated at the time of death or it may continue to exist in a happy state, in communion with its divine source and the other blessed souls, liberated at long last from its incarceration in a material body. Cato argues for the second possibility which, he notes, was the doctrine taught by Pythagoras, Socrates, and Plato.[223] Some Stoics, of course, also believed in the eternal blessedness of the souls of the wise, but the notion of the body as a fetter or a prison, substantially distinct from a nonmaterial soul, is certainly not Stoic. The Stoic sage of the *De senectute* thus borrows freely from other philosophical traditions and conjoins his arguments with the praise of the Roman Republic and its virtuous statesmen, within whose ranks Cicero enlists himself by implication.

Cicero's alteration of Stoic ethics from within a Stoic context is even more visible in the *De amicitia.* Here too he draws on non-Stoic as well as Stoic ideas[224] and adverts as well to the traditional political conception of friendship,[225] which he himself sometimes advances and sometimes criticizes in the name of Stoic idealism in other works. Cicero sets this dialogue in an especially Stoic environment, the Scipionic circle. He chooses as his interlocutors Laelius, a close friend of Scipio, and his two sons-in-law Quintus Mucius Scaevola and Gaius Fannius, all three of whom were distinguished orators, jurisconsults, or statesmen. The ties between the *De amicitia* and earlier dialogues in which Cicero uses interlocutors of the same generation and type are deliberately emphasized by

---

[222] *De sen.* 16.56.

[223] *De sen.* 19.66–20.74, 21.77–23.84.

[224] Several scholars have noted that ancient authorities such as Diogenes Laertius and Aulus Gellius give a lost work by Theophrastus as Cicero's source. Most commentators, however, argue that the position taken by Cicero cannot be confined to any one source. The most recent study, with an excellent survey of the literature, is Maria Bellincioni, *Struttura e pensiero del Laelius ciceroniano* (Brescia, 1970), esp. pp. 13-31, 91-146, 179-237. See also Karl Büchner, "Der Laelius Ciceros," *Cicero,* Studien zur römischen Literatur, 2, p. 178 n. 7; Bringmann, *Untersuchungen,* pp. 208-09, 268-70; L. Laurand, intro. to his ed. and trans. of *L'Amitié,* Budé (Paris, 1928), p. v n. 2; Falconer, intro. to his trans. of *De amic.,* p. 106.

[225] There is an extensive literature on this subject. See Balsdon, "Cicero the Man," in *Cicero,* ed. Dorey, pp. 188-89; Bringmann, *Untersuchungen,* pp. 214, 220-26, 270-77; Douglas, *Cicero,* pp. 1, 12; Konrad Heldmann, "Ciceros Laelius und die Grenzen der Freundschaft: Zur Interdependenz von Literatur und Politik 44/43 v. Chr.," *Hermes, 104* (1976), 72-103; Piero Pucci, "Politica ed ideologia nel *De amicitia,*" *Maia, 15* (1963), 342-58; Stockton, *Cicero,* pp. 66-67.

Laelius, who refers expressly to the *De republica* and the similarity between his own views and Scipio's.[226] The main stylistic difference between the *De amicitia* and the *De senectute* is that in the *De amicitia* the pros and cons of the Stoic doctrine under review are more out in the open. The speakers accept some aspects of the Stoic theory of friendship and reject others, substituting alternative ideas for the ones to which they object. As a result, they emerge with their own conclusions on friendship, which draw on both the traditional utilitarian view and on the idealistic Stoic view but which cannot be identified entirely with either of these positions.

Laelius proposes a conception of friendship which alters the ancient Stoic conception in two ways. One of these alterations results from his redefinition of a number of key terms in the Stoic formula. The other is less overt and results from the fact that the whole discussion in the *De amicitia* takes place among speakers who are related by marriage, interest, and political partisanship. In Laelius' crispest definition of friendship, he states that *est enim amicitia nihil aliud, nisi omnium divinarum humanarumque rerum cum benevolentia et caritate consensio* ("friendship then is nothing else than agreement in all things divine and human, with good will and affection.")[227] This reference to things human and divine reminds the reader of one of Cicero's earlier definitions of natural law and his use of the terms *benevolentia* and *caritas* evokes the Stoic idea of *eupatheia*, the affections that are virtuous because they are in conformity with reason. Laelius adds two other notes which Stoicize this conception still further. Friendship, he says, springs from man's common humanity, which entails common social obligations of various kinds. Friendship differs from other forms of human association in that it is gratuitous, spontaneous, and freely willed. It is not based on need or calculation but arises out of the intrinsic appeal of the moral excellence of one's friends. Thus, in addressing himself to the question of whether friendship is an end in itself or a means to some other end, Laelius argues that, while friends may indeed provide assistance to each other, true friendship seeks no advantage. In this way he retains most of the force of the Stoic ideal without completely ruling out the benefits that may accrue through the help of one's friends.[228]

However, Laelius goes on to analyze the concepts of nature and virtue in such a way as to effect a decisive departure from the Stoic position on these concepts and the way that they are related to friendship. Those who argue that virtue is the *summum bonum*, he says, are correct. But the notion that the *summum bonum* is the only good he finds too rigid and

---

[226] *De amic.* 4.13-14.
[227] *De amic.* 6.20. See also 4.15.
[228] *De amic.* 5.19-20, 8.26-9.32, 14.48-15.55, 21.79-22.85, 27.100-104.

exclusive. He proposes to substitute a more flexible and less unattainable standard, lest no one be virtuous enough to bear the name of friend. Friendship, he agrees, is conformable to nature and is a relationship possible only for sages. But the abstruse philosophers, by which he means the Stoics, have attached such unrealistic canons of behavior to the conception of virtue that there are many recognized sages, such as Paulus, Cato, Gallus, and Scipio, who would not be able to meet the Stoics' expectations.[229] If the ideal cannot be attained even by its most distinguished exponents, then the ideal needs to be reconceived and equated instead with the type of virtue manifested by the sages mentioned, a type of virtue that is less extreme and that bears a more specific set of political loyalties than Stoicism requires. Laelius goes on to illustrate the point that friends are not necessarily perfect sages. He asks whether one should do wrong for the sake of a friend or whether outbursts of vice weaken a friendship,[230] questions that would never arise if the friends were virtuous men in a Stoic sense. He also stresses the point that loyalty and the absence of hypocrisy are the mainstays of a friendship,[231] which not only takes the discussion out of a recognizably Stoic ambiance but also injects into it a subtle note of criticism levelled against the false friends who did not hesitate to use Cicero when his star was ascendant but who abandoned him in his hour of need. The conclusion that Laelius arrives at in the *De amicitia* is that the Stoic formulation of friendship is acceptable in part, but only if one substitutes a more realistic conception of human nature and of virtue for the uncompromising rationalism of the Stoa. This conclusion is one that Cicero sustains and extends to other moral issues in his remaining ethical works.

The *De finibus* directs the reader's attention to the theme of the *summum bonum* and the relationship of other goods to it. This topic arises in the *De amicitia* and in a number of Cicero's other works but it receives the most detailed treatment in the *De finibus*. In this work Cicero poses as a doxographer, cataloguing the pros and cons of the teachings of the Greek ethicists and recasting them in eloquent Latin form, whether he accepts them or not, on the grounds that this effort is of use to society.[232] The three chief schools reviewed are Epicureanism, Stoicism, and Aristotelianism, although the latter position is put forth under the aegis of the Old Academy. The chief interlocutors are contemporary statesmen, including Cicero. The *De finibus* has been variously interpreted as a critique of

---

[229] *De amic.* 5.17-19, 6.20-21, 13.45.
[230] *De amic.* 10.35-13.45, 21.76.
[231] *De amic.* 18.65-66.
[232] *De finibus* 1.1.1-1.4.12.

Stoicism,[233] as an Academic-Stoic critique of Epicureanism,[234] and as a debate between ancient and middle Stoicism.[235] It is certainly true that Cicero is doing more than reporting other people's opinions concerning the good. He is indeed trying to arrive at some personal resolution of the issue. In this connection his treatment of Stoicism and of himself as a character in the dialogue are by no means straightforward. Cicero appears three times as an important speaker in *De finibus*. In Book 2 he argues against the Epicureanism advocated by Torquatus in Book 1. In Book 4 he criticizes Stoicism as it had been expounded by Cato in Book 3. In Book 5 he argues against the Aristotelian position presented by Piso, criticizing his doctrine from a Stoic standpoint. The claim that he uses the ethics of the middle Stoa to correct the difficulties that he finds with the views of the ancient Stoics is valid up to a point. In the *De finibus* he throws these difficulties into clear relief and he suggests the sorts of arguments which he eventually uses to deal with them, but he does not resolve them completely under the guidance of any one philosophical position.

In contrast to the procedure in his theological works, Cicero does not use Stoicism to any great extent in the *De finibus* as a weapon against Epicureanism, at least not in his own express attack on that school in Book 2. He does invoke Zeno's comparison between rhetoric as an open palm and dialectic as a closed fist, in order to advocate the superiority of rhetoric as a method of philosophical exposition,[236] a point he also makes elsewhere, but he misappropriates the metaphor by describing these two disciplines as subdivisions of the broad category of speech, neglecting the Stoic distinction between rhetoric as a branch of speech and dialectic as the analysis of *lekta*. In a general sense, he says that the Stoics' position on the good is consistent with its first principles, but he extends the same compliment to a number of other schools as well.[237] He acknowledges the fact that among the Stoics Aristo was an exception to the rule in his rejection of any intermediate category between vice and virtue. He also differentiates clearly between the Stoic view, which posits the good, the evil, and the indifferent, and the Aristotelian view, which posits a supreme good that admits of lesser but still valid goods.[238] This last point indicates that Cicero is fully aware of the distinction between a Stoic gradation of the preferables which are still ethically neutral en

---

233 Francesco Giancotti, "Der innere Grundzug von 'De finibus'," in *Das neue Cicerobild*, ed. Büchner, pp. 388–416.

234 Selem, intro. to his ed. of *De fin.*, pp. x–xi.

235 Moscarini, *Cicerone e l'etica stoica nel III libro del 'De finibus'*, pp. 13–23, 28.

236 *De fin.* 2.6.17.

237 *De fin.* 2.11.34–35.

238 *De fin.* 2.12.37–38, 2.13.43, 2.21.68.

bloc and the gradation of goods in the Peripatetic tradition, a theme to which he reverts in considerable detail later in the *De finibus* and also in the *Tusculanarum disputationum*.

The most elaborate exposition of Stoic ethics in the *De finibus* is found in Cato's speech in Book 3. As a dévoté of Stoicism, he is given the task of presenting its position on the good, even though he as well as other interlocutors take the Stoics to task for their over-subtle reasoning, their tortuous and unrelenting style of debate, and their propensity for using terms in unconventional ways.[239] In his presentation Cato adverts exclusively to the ethics of the ancient Stoa, thereby setting forth the doctrine in its most rigid and uncompromising form. In the *De senectute* Cato is given the opportunity to modify the Stoic position in areas where Cicero wishes to alter it but in the *De finibus* this role is assumed instead by Cicero himself.

The main points that Cato makes on behalf of the Stoic doctrine of the good can be grouped under two related headings. The first involves the Stoic conception of nature as entirely rational and the application of this norm as a description of man's constitution and functions. The second involves the principle that the Stoic gradation of the preferables is quite different from the gradation of the good. Cato, in full Stoic form, defines virtue (*honestum*) as the only good and identifies it with life in accordance with reason or nature. The passions of pleasure, pain, fear, and desire (*laetitia, aegritudo, formido, libido*) spring, he agrees, from erroneous intellectual judgments, judgments which depart from the kataleptic presentations to which men assent because of their intrinsic truth and conformity with reason.[240] Reason is the faculty which differentiates men from animals and which binds all men together in bonds of mutual obligation and affection, engendering social life at all levels from the family to the cosmopolis. It is the expression of reason in benevolence that inspires the sages, of whom Cato cites Hercules as a model, to protect the weak, to provide for their descendants, and to perform their various social duties.[241] The sage is perfectly happy and possesses all benefits because he has a fixed inner orientation toward the rational good alone.[242] This love of the good is a widely visible psychological phenomenon, which attests to the presence of the rational faculty in all men.[243] The urge toward the good, Cato continues, manifests itself in different ways at different stages of human development. Infants, who exist in a pre-conscious state, are

---

[239] *De fin.* 2.35.119, 3.1.3, 3.2.5, 3.2.7, 3.12.40, 4.1.2.
[240] *De fin.* 3.3.10-14, 3.5.17-18, 3.10.35.
[241] *De fin.* 3.19.62-3.20.68.
[242] *De fin.* 3.7.26-3.8.29, 3.9.32, 3.22.75.
[243] *De fin.* 3.11.36-39.

motivated through their internal drives to seek their own preservation. As man develops from infancy to adulthood, the conscious application of rational norms supersedes the pre-rational infantile state. Man henceforth makes all his ethical decisions on an exclusively rational basis. For Cato, as for the ancient Stoics, the primary or instinctual natural goods of childhood are acceptable only if seen as transitory values applying exclusively to that stage of the life cycle. Such infantile goods cannot be seen as intermediary or partial goods for adults. Once man attains adult consciousness, he can address himself properly only to the rational good, which is the only good and an end in itself. Values which might have been acceptable in infancy now pass irrevocably into the category of the morally indifferent.[244]

With this foundation solidly laid, Cato goes on to develop the second aspect of his argument, dealing with the relationship between the *adiaphora* and the *summum bonum*. He expands on the point made by Cicero the interlocutor in the second book: the Stoic position, with its doctrine of reason as the sole good and a series of things indifferent, differs drastically from the Peripatetic doctrine of a hierarchy of good which includes bodily advantages along with rational ends. In the Peripatetics' view the lesser goods can contribute to virtue while in the Stoics' view they may be more or less advantageous but they remain ethically expendable. The Stoic *adiaphora* may indeed by treated as more or less preferable, and here Cato lists a number of examples, including suicide. He also lists a number of things that are good in themselves, including philosophy and friendship, observing that the virtues they embody are all equal in contrast to the preferables, which admit of gradations. The preferable, the appropriate (*officium*), is thus not simply one stage or series of stages along a continuum of goods. The good is different in kind, and not just different in degree, from the preferables. Given this fundamental distinction between the conceptions of the good put forth by Stoicism and Aristotelianism, Cato concludes, the Academics who assert that the differences between these two schools are merely terminological are guilty of a serious misconception.[245]

Cato's argument represents the ancient Stoic position accurately and in considerable strength, without misapplications of its principles or serious omissions as is sometimes the case when Cicero portrays a spokesman of the Stoa in his other dialogues. His own critique of Cato, like Cato's argument, is developed in two parts, the first of which is much weaker than the second. In the first part of his rebuttal Cicero invokes

---

[244] *De fin.* 3.5.16–17, 3.6.21–3.7.25.
[245] *De fin.* 3.12.41–3.18.61, 3.21.69–3.22.73.

the authority of Antiochus and repeats his unpersuasive claim that the Stoics have merely reformulated the teachings of previous schools without adding anything new except a crabbed and confusing terminology. In the field of ethics in particular, he says, the Stoic principle that instinctual goods are just as good for infants as the rational goods are for adults is basically the same as the Peripatetic principle that the bodily goods are goods. Likewise, he argues, the Stoics, in admitting the category of the preferables, are accepting in effect the doctrine of a hierarchy of goods.[246] He adds as an afterthought the feeble point that the Stoics do not all agree on this issue, which is supposed to prove that all the Stoics are wrong.[247] This part of Cicero's attempted refutation is rather unconvincing, relying as it does on illogic and the citation of authority as a substitute for proof. It does not seriously come to grips with the clear distinction that Cato has made between Stoicism and Aristotelianism.

Cicero next shifts his rebuttal to a somewhat weightier strategy, arguing that the Stoic position is absurd or unrealistic and invoking in defense of his case principles drawn from Aristotelianism and common sense in roughly equal proportions. The Stoic definition of reason as the only good is inconsistent with human nature, he charges, for man is a unity of body and soul, a constitution he possesses at all points in the human life cycle. Thus, if there is a *summum bonum* it must be a good that is good for the whole person at all stages of his development.[248] If the Stoics' *summum bonum* is inconsistent with human nature, their doctrine of the equality of all vices and all virtues is inconsistent with common sense. According to such a view, Cicero notes, the move from vice to virtue would require an instantaneous conversion, a possibility belied by experience.[249] Experience also suggests that adherence to certain of the Stoic preferables does indeed conduce to virtue. It is therefore a fallacy to define these preferables as morally neutral. Worse yet, it is unhelpful to do so. If one truly believed that the preferables were useless, Cicero asserts, one would be so demoralized by the gulf between Stoic vice and Stoic virtue that one would abandon all hope of amending one's life. The Stoic doctrine of the preferables is thus a sterile exercise in logic-chopping which lacks the power to command inner assent and to inspire a true desire for self-improvement. Since the axiomatic basis of the Stoic doctrine of the good entails a rejection of human nature, he adds, the syllogisms used to extrapolate conclusions from this doctrine are nothing but word games and the Stoic paradoxes concerning the sage only

---

[246] *De fin.* 4.2.3–4.8.20, 4.20.56–4.22.61, 4.26.72–73.
[247] *De fin.* 4.25.68–69.
[248] *De fin.* 4.10.24–4.16.45.
[249] *De fin.* 4.9.21–23, 4.23.63–4.24.68, 4.28.70–80.

reflect the hiatus between logic and life.[250] On this vigorous note Cicero rests his case.

The anti-Stoic case is actually presented better by Cicero in Book 4 than by Piso in his advocacy of the position of the Old Academy in Book 5, which restates it without adding much to it. Piso reiterates the unconvincing point that the Stoics teach the same doctrine as the Peripatetics and Academics.[251] He also recapitulates and defends the Aristotelian conception of human nature and human development, arguing likewise that the virtues, like the goods, include the body as well as the intellect and may be graded along a continuum. He expresses an Aristotelian preference for the virtue of justice.[252] If one grasps what virtue truly is, he concludes, and if one acknowledges the fact that virtue embraces bodily goods, it is indeed correct to say that virtue alone gives happiness.[253]

It is this conclusion that provides Cicero with his point of attack in his Stoic critique of Piso at the end of Book 5. If virtue alone brings happiness, and if virtue includes bodily goods, how then, Cicero asks, can the kind of virtue advocated by Piso provide us with the strength to withstand bodily misfortunes and sufferings? How can such a concept of virtue truly liberate us from the vicissitudes of fortune? It would not be consistent, Cicero argues, to say that the Aristotelian sage is always happy unless, with the Stoics, one denies that pain is an evil. In that sense the Stoic position is more logical than the one put forth by Piso.[254] Piso responds with the assertion that the Peripatetic philosophy is more bracing than the Stoic. The Peripatetics acknowledge that pain is an evil, but teach the duty of overcoming it through the virtue of fortitude.[255] This response side-steps the issue as Cicero has posed it. The question is left unresolved at the end of the De finibus. None the less, this dialogue presents a clear statement of the ethical problems which Cicero raises in the De amicitia and to which he returns in the Tusculanarum disputationum and the De officiis. On the one hand, there is the Aristotelian conception of human nature and its corollary, a hierarchy of goods, a conception that Cicero finds more satisfying than the Stoic position on the same subject. On the other hand, there is the Stoic conception of moral autarchy, which he finds extremely appealing. As the De finibus suggests, the Stoic doctrine of the preferables is the point at which Cicero will seek to unify

---

[250] De fin. 4.17.46–4.19.55, 4.27.74–76.
[251] De fin. 5.8.22, 5.25.74, 5.26.78, 5.29.86–5.31.94.
[252] De fin. 5.8.24, 5.22.64, 5.23.65–5.24.69.
[253] De fin. 5.24.71.
[254] De fin. 5.27.79–5.28.94.
[255] De fin. 5.31.94.

the Aristotelian principles he supports with the Stoic idea of moral freedom.

In the *Tusculanarum disputationum* the accent is on human nature and its relation to moral autarchy. In this dialogue Cicero moves to a solution of some of the ethical issues raised in the *De finibus*. His position resembles the teaching of the middle Stoa more closely than that of any other school.[256] The political emphasis in this work is muted. Cicero repeats the claim that philosophy needs to be taken out of the hands of the uncommunicative Greeks, especially the Stoics, and rephrased in eloquent Latin form for the service of society.[257] He also refers to the unfortunate loss of his political career.[258] But his primary stress is placed on the value of ethical philosophy as a means of personal consolation. Cicero states in this work that he is merely expounding the views of several schools without espousing any one position, on the grounds that philosophical debate assists us on the path to truth even though the answers it provides may only be probable ones.[259] In actuality, he does arrive at positive conclusions which he professes without doubting either their certitude or their capacity to strengthen the troubled soul.[260] With this emphasis on the consolatory function of philosophy in mind, Cicero, through two unidentified interlocutors, M. and A., turns to the questions of whether pain and death are evils, whether the wise man suffers, and whether virtue is sufficient for the happy life. He relies heavily on the Stoics' analysis of the passions and on their doctrine of *apatheia* in his effort to resolve these questions, mingling them freely with a conception of human nature that allows for irrational faculties within the soul.

Cicero's analysis of pain and death turns on a conception of the soul in which the exclusively rational psychology of the ancient Stoa is revised

---

[256] For the *Quellenforschung* controversy regarding this work see Adelmo Barigazzi, "Sulle fonti del libro I delle Tusculane di Cicerone," *Rivista di filologia e di istruzione classica*, n.s. *76* (1948), 161-203; *78* (1950), 1-29; Bringmann, *Untersuchungen*, pp. 158-59; Bruwaene, *La théologie de Cicéron*, pp. 54-83; Roger Miller Jones, "Posidonius and Cicero's *Tusculan disputations* i.17-18," *CP, 18* (1923), 202-28; A. J. Kleywegt, "Philosophischer Gehalt und persönliche Stellung in *Tusc*. I.9-81," *Mnemosyne*, ser. 4:*19* (1966), 359; Pohlenz, intro. to *Tusc. disp.*, ed. Heines, pp. 31-32; P. H. Poppelreuter, *Quae ratio intercedat Posidonii Peri pathon pragmateias et Tusculanes disputationes Ciceronis* (Bonn, 1883).

[257] *Tusc. disp.* 1.1.1-1.4.8, 2.1.4-2.2.6, 2.3.7, 2.11.26, 2.12.29-2.13.32, 2.18.42, 4.5.9, 5.5.12.

[258] *Tusc. disp.* 1.24.83.

[259] *Tusc. disp.* 1.4.8, 2.1.4-2.2.5, 2.3.9, 4.4.7.

[260] *Tusc. disp.* 2.4.10-2.5.13, 2.12.29-2.13.32, 2.18.42, 3.3.6, 3.5.10, 3.6.13, 3.14.30, 3.16.34, 3.25.60, 3.30.74, 3.31.75-3.32.77, 3.33.79. This emphasis on consolation has been analyzed well by Bringmann, *Untersuchungen*, pp. 158-70; Hildebrecht Hommel, *Ciceros Gebetshymnus an die Philosophie: Tusculanen V, 5*, Sitzungsberichte der Heidelberger Akademie der Wissenschaften, philosophisch-historische Klasse, 3 (Heidelberg, 1968), pp. 26-56, with a good review of the literature on this work, pp. 9-11.

in favor of a psychology admitting the existence of the instincts, along
the lines of the incorporation of Platonic and Aristotelian faculty psychology in the thought of Panaetius and Posidonius. In the mode of the
middle Stoics, Cicero also holds that, despite the presence of these irrational faculties, reason alone is normative in the sphere of ethics. He
agrees with Zeno and Panaetius that the soul is material, composed of
fire or warm air;[261] at the same time, he agrees with Plato and Aristotle
that the soul has two main parts, rational and irrational.[262] Most of the
Stoics, he notes, teach that the soul survives after death. Panaetius alone
rejects this opinion and Cicero disagrees with him.[263] It is because the
soul is immortal, he argues, that death is not an evil. The conclusion he
reaches on this issue is compatible with Stoicism in general, but it is
scarcely unique to the Stoic tradition.

On the other hand, Cicero defines pain unequivocally as one of the
four Stoic passions. Although he accepts the idea of irrational faculties
in the soul, he does not think that the passions arise from them. Rather,
with the Stoics, he holds that the passions spring from false judgments.
Reason is the sole origin of ethical decisions. Man's irrational faculties,
hence, can never be retrained under the rule of reason so as to contribute
to virtue, as the Peripatetics teach. The only way to deal with the passions, says Cicero, is to reject them utterly and to cultivate the state of
apatheia.[264] He agrees with the Stoic view that pain is not an evil. At the
same time, pain is felt and it brings suffering. *Apatheia* is not to be confused
with *anaesthesia*. Rather, the doctrine of *apatheia* recognizes the existence
of pain, takes its measure, and triumphs over it through reason, which
enables man to understand the place of suffering in a wider moral or
cosmic context, as the Stoic example of Hercules makes clear.[265] Thus,
while Cicero does not think that reason is fully descriptive of human
nature he regards it as fully and exclusively normative for the ethical life.
It is reason alone that enables men to be virtuous and the virtues, which
are all equal, are sufficient for the happy life.[266] While noting in his
concluding remarks that the Peripatetics, Academics, and Stoics all agree
in defending virtue as sufficient for the happy life, he ends by elevating
Stoicism above the other schools at this point. He prefers the Stoic so-

---

[261] *Tusc. disp.* 1.9.19, 1.18.42.
[262] *Tusc. disp.* 1.33.80, 2.21.47.
[263] *Tusc. disp.* 1.32.78-1.33.80.
[264] *Tusc. disp.* 1.20.46, 3.6.13-3.10.21, 3.11.24-3.13.27, 3.27.65, 4.5.9. This point has
been developed well by Riccardo Miceli, "La classificazione stoica delle passioni nelle
'Tusculanae' di Cicerone," *Sophia, 3* (1935), 181-86.
[265] *Tusc. disp.* 2.7.17-2.9.22, 2.25.60-61.
[266] *Tusc. disp.* 2.14.32-33, 3.1.2., 3.17.37, 5.28.82.

lution because he thinks that it provides the most certain remedy against suffering and the other vicissitudes of human existence.[267]

The *Tusculanarum disputationum* draw on several of the non-Stoic ideas which the middle Stoics had absorbed into their philosophy, notably in the areas of psychology and eschatology. With the middle Stoics, Cicero associates these principles with Stoic ethics, leaving the Stoic ethics essentially intact. At the same time, he omits a number of related Stoic ideas, such as the conception of the *adiaphora* in his definitions of pain and death and the conception of *eupatheia* in his treatment of the relations between reason and the passions. The most striking contrast between Cicero's position in this work and the ethics of Panaetius and Posidonius is that he does not modify the ethical strategy that he advocates in the light of his admission of the soul's irrational faculties. Nor does he devote attention to the methods by which the seeker attains *apatheia*, a topic which the middle Stoics had discussed in some detail. Cicero deals with some of these practical matters in his final work, the *De officiis*, organizing this entire treatise around the conception of the *honestum* and the *utile*. His plan evokes the Stoic doctrine of the good and the preferables as its framework. Cicero tells us, in the *De officiis* and elsewhere, that he is following the Stoics, especially Panaetius, although not slavishly.[268] The last phrase in this remark is the operative one. The *De officiis*, often called the synthesis of Cicero's ethical thought, is actually far less Stoic in substance than the *Tusculanarum disputationum*, despite its ostensibly Stoic character.

Scholars have generally agreed that Cicero's principal sources for the *De officiis* are middle Stoic[269] and that, although dedicated to his son

---

[267] *Tusc. disp.* 5.8.22, 5.11.32, 5.26.75-76.

[268] *De officiis* 1.1.2, 1.2.6; *Ad Att.* 420.4.

[269] The best recent introduction to the literature on this point is by Testard, intro. to his ed. of *De off.*, *1*, 25-49. See also P. A. Brunt, "Aspects of the Social Thought of Dio Chrysostom and of the Stoics," *Proceedings of the Cambridge Philological Society, 199* (1973), 26-34; Paolo Fedeli, "Il 'De officiis' di Cicerone: Problemi e atteggiamenti della critica moderna," *Aufstieg und Niedergang der römischen Welt, 1*, part 4, 361-75; Philipp Finger, "Das stoische und das akademische Führerbild in Cicero's Schrift De officiis (1. Buch)," *Neue Jahrbücher für Antike und deutsche Bildung, 5* (1942), 1-20; Hans Armin Gärtner, *Cicero und Panaitios: Beobachtungen zu Ciceros De officiis*, Berichte der Heidelberger Akademie der Wissenschaften, philosophisch-historische Klasse, 5 (Heidelberg, 1974), who emphasizes Cicero's methodological differences from Panaetius; Heinrich Jungblut, "Cicero und Panätius im zweiten Buch über die Pflichten," *Beilage zum Program des Lessing-Gymnasiums zu Frankfurt a. M. Ostern 1910* (Frankfurt, 1910); Georg Kilb, "Ethische Grundbegriffe der alten Stoa und ihre Übertragung durch Cicero," in *Das neue Cicerobild*, ed. Büchner, pp. 38-64; McKeon, intro. to *Brutus*, trans. Poteat, pp. 50-51. Scholars emphasizing other sources include Quintino Cautadella, "Sulle fonti del 'De officiis' di Cicerone," *Atti del I congresso internazionale di studi ciceroniani*, Roma, aprile 1959 (Roma, 1961), *2*, 479-91, who stresses Platonism; and Lepore, *Il princeps ciceroniano*, p. 387, who stresses Aristotelianism.

Marcus, the work was intended for the entire younger generation, re-
capitulating his familiar political opinions, rhetorical interests, and personal self-justifications in a proposal that argues for a relative rather than
an absolute ethic, geared primarily toward public service.[270] The rhetorical element in the *De officiis* is certainly unmistakable. Cicero abandons the dialogue form in preference for straightforward advocacy. He
seeks to persuade by appealing simultaneously to the higher aspirations
and the self-interest of his audience. He urges that oratory is useful to
society and refers to his own speeches to illustrate the point.[271] He applies
ethical rules to concrete cases following the mode of rhetorical *controversiae*[272] and liberally besprinkles his argument with historical and literary
exempla. Equally impossible to overlook is Cicero's propaganda and self-
advertisement in the *De officiis*. He cites his own example as a courageous
public servant while castigating his enemies, especially Caesar and Pompey, as tyrants motivated by greed and ambition.[273] He portrays the
Republic as a whole as governed by decency, clemency, and esteem in
contrast to the present arrangements, which are marked by terrorism
and oppression.[274] He fires another salvo against the Gracchi, criticizing
them as hypocrites for supporting agrarian reforms which he opposes.[275]
Cicero also takes occasion to repeat his rationale for *otium litterarium*, observing that philosophy remained his only constructive means of public
service after the state was taken over by autocrats who preferred to destroy it rather than to reform it.[276]

But there is much more at issue in the *De officiis* than the ventilation
of these familiar Ciceronian concerns. Cicero wants to take a definitive
stand on the moral life in this work. Although he sometimes poses as an
Academic skeptic in the *De officiis*, claiming that it would be presumptious
to seek anything but probabilities in the sphere of ethics,[277] and although
he claims only to be refining and extending an unfinished work by Panaetius on duties,[278] he is actually doing neither of these things. Cicero
posits and uses axiomatic ethical principles in the *De officiis* without rais-

---

[270] Good recent assessments include Bringmann, *Untersuchungen*, pp. 229-50; Domenico
Romano, "Motivi politici ed autobiographici nel 'De officiis' di Cicerone," *Annali del
Liceo classico "G. Garibaldi" di Palermo*, n.s. 5-6 (1968-69), 21-31; Testard, intro. to his ed.
of *De off.*, I, 52-66.
[271] *De off.* 2.19.66-68.
[272] *De off.* 3.6.26-32.
[273] *De off.* 1.8.26, 1.14.43, 1.20.58, 1.22.77-78, 1.24.83, 1.39.139, 2.6.20, 2.7.23,
2.8.28-29, 2.13.45, 2.15.54, 2.17.59, 3.20.79-3.22.88.
[274] *De off.* 2.6.21-2.8.29.
[275] *De off.* 2.22.78.
[276] *De off.* 2.1.2-2.2.6, 3.1.1-3.1.4.
[277] *De off.* 3.2.7-8, 3.4.20.
[278] *De off.* 1.2.7-1.3.10.

ing any questions about their epistemological status. And, despite his dependence on Panaetius, he injects a number of non-Stoic principles into the *De officiis* which have the effect of altering Stoic ethical philosophy dramatically. What emerges is a new Ciceronian amalgam in which Stoicism is a critical ingredient but in which it is subordinated to other philosophical insights, to traditional Roman values, and to Cicero's personal vision of politics.

At the beginning of the *De officiis* Cicero observes that duties can be viewed in two ways. There is absolute or perfect duty (*officium perfectum*), which pertains to the supreme good (*finem bonorum*) and there is intermediate duty (*medium officium*), which pertains to utility (*usus vitae*). The second type has the wider practical application, but he proposes to analyze both types and their interrelationships. He makes his point of departure Panaetius' rule that moral choices involve three considerations: Is the act intrinsically right (*honestum*)? Is the act conducive to utility? How can one reconcile the *honestum* and the *utile* when they conflict? Panaetius, Cicero notes, did not finish his treatise on duties and left the third question unanswered. This omission needs to be rectified. There are also two other issues that need to be considered, which Panaetius did not even project: How does one choose between two acts which are both *honeste*? How does one choose between two acts that are both *utile*?[279] Cicero's desire to deal with these two additional questions alerts the reader at once that he has no intention of adhering strictly to the Stoic definition of the good. The *honestum* of the *De officiis* is not going to be a single and indivisible good but rather a category populated by a range of goods graded according to some as yet unspecified criterion of value. The *utilia* of the *De officiis* are susceptible of gradations and may, for this reason, appear to resemble the Stoic *adiaphora*. However, Cicero by no means defines the *utilia* as *adiaphora* and he does not treat them as morally neutral at all.

Cicero's analysis of the *honestum* in Book 1 immediately clarifies what his alternatives or adjuncts to Stoicism are going to be. After making the Stoic point that man is distinguished from the animals by his possession of reason, which gives him the faculty of speech, the desire to seek the truth, a set of social responsibilities, and his moral sensibilities,[280] Cicero moves forthwith to the cardinal virtues. He does not define any of them in a fully Stoic fashion. Wisdom or prudence is not the leading virtue in the group. Furthermore, he defines wisdom as the quest for truth and sees its application lying in the avoidance of credulity and excessive con-

---

[279] *De off.* 1.3.7-10, 3.2.9.
[280] *De off.* 1.4.11-14, 1.16.50.

cern with topics that are obscure or useless.[281] Rather than itself judging what is useful, wisdom is thus judged by its own utility. Justice is the paramount virtue, according to Cicero.[282] Cicero joins to this Aristotelian preference a definition of justice that combines the traditional Platonic-Aristotelian *suum cuique* formula with values drawn from Roman law. Justice, he says, demands that men refrain from harming each other, unless one is trying to protect one's private rights. Justice moreover teaches men how to use common things for the common good as well as private things for individual good. Cicero is aware of the fact that both Plato and the Stoics taught that there is no such thing as private property or social inequity in the natural order. None the less, in discussing the virtue of justice, he argues that the principles of property law currently in force in Rome are the ones to be observed. The ideal of equality should be followed in spirit, but in spirit only. One may sin against justice, he adds, either by force or by fraud. Force suggests the lion and fraud suggests the fox. Both approaches are alien to the nature of man, says Cicero. But nothing suggests to him that his definition of justice is itself incompatible with the law of nature as he conceives it. In effect, the criteria that govern the duties pertaining to justice are non-philosophical ones; they are Roman legal and social conventions and, above all, the duty of patriotism,[283] an obligation which Cicero extends only to his own fellow citizens but which he does not widen to embrace the other members of the Stoic cosmopolis beyond the boundaries of the Roman state.

Cicero's treatment of the other two cardinal virtues is somewhat more Stoic in coloration than his discussion of wisdom and justice. He says that the Stoics define fortitude correctly, but gives as the definition the force of character needed to act justly, which assimilates fortitude to justice rather than to wisdom. However, his actual analysis of fortitude shows clearly Stoic traits, particularly in the distinction he draws between internal and external courage. Inner fortitude, according to Cicero, is a state of mind that counts the *honestum* as the only good and that entails equanimity and forebearance under all circumstances. This condition is characterized by freedom from the passions of pleasure, pain, fear, and desire. Both the active and the contemplative lives can be expressions of inner fortitude, although the contemplative life should not be chosen unless its practitioner can serve his fellow man better by thinking and writing than he could in the forum or if his health prevents him from public service. Cicero groups statesmanship and scholarship together

---

[281] *De off.* 1.6.18-19.
[282] *De off.* 3.6.28. See also 1.43.153-155, 1.45.157-158.
[283] *De off.* 1.7.20-1.17.58.

under the rubric of internal fortitude and contrasts them with external fortitude, which involves exactly the same kind of rationality, *apatheia*, and selflessness but which manifests itself in physical or military activity.[284] The fourth virtue, temperance, is also one that Cicero treats in a relatively Stoic manner. He defines temperance as consistency with nature and reason and states that it involves the complete suppression of the passions. The central term which he uses to define this virtue is *decorum*. Decorum means truthfulness in action and its antithesis is error. Here Cicero follows the Stoics once again in identifying virtue and vice with correct and incorrect intellectual judgments. In this sense, he says, decorum governs all the virtues. He also applies the term decorum to the arts, both literary and musical, acknowledging the aesthetic value of moral decorum and vice versa, as Panaetius had done. Cicero completes his treatment of temperance by noting that this virtue is expressed by moderation in all things and that its function is to subject the instincts to reason.[285] These themes are Aristotelian rather than Stoic strictly speaking, but they are themes that Panaetius had incorporated into his own ethics.

Despite the fact that the definitions Cicero provides for the virtues are not always particularly Stoic, the principles he outlines for applying them in practice are almost totally Stoic. Indeed, the segment of the *De officiis* in which he deals with this topic can be read as a virtual translation of Panaetius' rules of casuistry into Latin. In deciding how to apply ethical rules in practice, Cicero says, one has to take into account several things apart from one's membership in the human race, with the general obligations that this entails. One needs to consider one's individual situation, one's character, talents, status, age, and the circumstances in which one lives, as well as any personal commitments one may have made. Cicero cites the Stoic example of Hercules at the crossroads to illustrate the point that one has to make a deliberate choice concerning one's vocation.[286] All other things being equal, Cicero states a preference, shared by the Stoics, for the vocation of agriculture. But he undermines the Stoic force of this preference by falling back on social prejudices of a sort that no Stoic would tolerate in distinguishing between professions that are vulgar (*sordidi*), including tax-collecting, wage-earning, craftsmanship, and manual labor, and professions that are suitable for a gentleman (*liber-*

---

[284] *De off.* 1.19.62–1.26.92.

[285] *De off.* 1.27.93–1.30.106, 1.35.126–1.41.146. On Panaetian *decorum* as a stylistic principle in Cicero see George Converse Fiske, *Lucilius and Horace: A Study in the Classical Theory of Imitation*, University of Wisconsin Studies in Language and Literature, 7 (Madison, 1920), pp. 85–89.

[286] *De off.* 1.30.107–1.34.125.

ales).[287] If social snobbery modifies the Stoicism of Cicero's casuistry, so does masculine bias. Conspicuous for its absence from his list of casuistic considerations is the variable of sex, in sharp contrast to Panaetius on the same subject. The Ciceronian implication is that virtue is a matter for men only.

The final topic that Cicero treats in his discussion of the *honestum* is the adjudication of conflicts among the virtues and the duties flowing from them, a problem that would not exist for a Stoic, for whom all virtues are one and the same. Here, he returns to the idea of a hierarchical gradation of goods as a means of resolving the difficulty. Justice is the highest virtue, he repeats. It is closest to nature; it governs action and not just theory; and the duties stemming from it are the most exalted, above all the duty of patriotism. There is only one case in which he allows another value to supersede patriotism. This is when temperance prevents the wise man from doing shameful deeds even if the safety of his country is at stake. In general, however, he argues that justice provides the guidelines in this area because it tends to counsel the choice of goods that benefit society as a whole most fully.[288]

Cicero's treatment of the *honestum* in Book I represents a stringent redefinition of this Stoic principle in the light of Aristotelian and Roman values. The gradation of the goods, the norm of moderation, the inclusion of instincts among the ethically relevant faculties of man, and the strong preference for justice as the virtue par excellence are redolent of Aristotelianism. The elevation of legal and social conventions above nature, the limitation of the moral horizon to members of his own polity, class, and sex, and the exaltation of patriotism as the chief criterion of virtue bespeak Cicero's adherence to the Roman tradition. The chief Stoic elements which survive more or less intact are the idea of decorum with its dual moral and aesthetic aspects, the interiorizing of fortitude as the common motive for the active and the contemplative lives with a preference for the active life, the idea that vice and virtue arise from intellectual judgments, and Panaetius' casuistic methodology for applying ethical principles in practice. Despite Cicero's retention of these Stoic teachings, however, he achieves a reformulation of the Stoic idea of the *honestum* so as to include a significant amount of social utility within it, a point that harks back to his treatment of ethics in his rhetorical works. The *honestum*, which he now sets out to compare and relate with the *utile*, has ceased decisively to be the Stoic *summum bonum*.

The contrast between Cicero's *utile* and the Stoic category of the pref-

---

[287] *De off.* 1.42.150–151.
[288] *De off.* 1.43.152, 1.45.160.

erables, which it appears to resemble on the surface, is even more striking. The *utile* is in no sense morally neutral for Cicero. Indeed, he states that things which are *utile* help man to withstand the vicissitudes of fortune,[289] a function traditionally assigned by the Stoics to the *honestum* alone. Cicero's *honestum* has at least some initial connection with the Stoic notion of the good, but his *utilia* merely stand for practical advantages, which he treats in Book 2 of the *De officiis* as ends in themselves, ends, moreover, to which the *honestum* serves as a means. Things that are *utile*, he says, are valuable because they enable one to manipulate others in one's own interest. The possession of virtue, particularly the virtue of justice, inspires confidence and respect, thus allowing one to bend others to one's will more easily. Since virtue is useful, it is important to make it visible to others. Cicero therefore provides rules enabling virtuous persons to publicize their reputations.[290] At the end of Book 2 Cicero poses the question of how to choose between two useful courses of action, a discussion that parallels his consideration of the choice between *honesta* at the end of the first book. The rule he proposes is that of expediency, a norm that has been at work throughout his analysis of the *utile* in Book 2. Cicero's *utilia* are clearly not Stoic *adiaphora*; nor are they evaluated, as are middle Stoic preferables, in the light of their relative conformity to reason or their relative capacity to conduce to the *honestum*. What is perhaps most striking about Cicero's argument in the second book of the *De officiis* is his use of a strategy which he also discusses in his rhetorical works, that of making the good seem attractive by presenting it under the guise of the useful, in order to make it appealing to an audience that can be counted on to respond out of self-interest.

In Book 3 Cicero turns the tables on his audience by attempting to show that there is no real conflict between the *honestum* and the *utile*, from another direction. In the second book, he argues that virtue is expedient; here he argues that immorality is inexpedient. In adopting this position he aligns himself with Panaetius, who asserted, Cicero notes, that there can be no real conflict between these values. But, in so doing, Cicero also expressly dissociates himself from Panaetius' definitions of the *honestum* and the *utile*. Panaetius was a Stoic, he points out, who therefore thought that the *honestum* constituted the only good, and that anything appearing to be good that conflicted with it was morally indifferent. Panaetius also thought that morally indifferent things had no ethical status to speak of; however useful they might be, they could not really be compared in any meaningful sense with the one and only *summum bonum*. For Panaetius,

---

[289] *De off.* 2.6.19–20.
[290] *De off.* 2.9.31–34, 2.11.39.

consequently, the problem of reconciling the *honestum* and the *utile* was a false one. Cicero even hypothesizes that Panaetius probably planned to treat this issue in the unwritten third section of his book on duties in order to expose its very falsity. But Cicero himself rejects the Stoic definition of the *honestum* and the *utile*. For the Stoics, he observes, only a tiny handful of sages are capable of attaining the *honestum* as that school defines the term. Everyone else has to be content with the *media officia*, which represent perfect virtue for most people since they are the highest goods that the majority are capable of attaining. Even recognized sages, such as Cato and Laelius, cannot measure up to the Stoic ideal of virtue. Thus, Cicero says, the *honestum* which he proposes to reconcile with the *utile* in Book 3 is the type of virtue represented by the *media officia*. In the first book he had defined the *media officia* as the duties pertaining to the *utile*. Now, however, he effects a significant reformulation of this conception by defining the *honestum* as the goal served by the *media officia*. Thus, he assimilates the *honestum* to the *utile* by redefining his terms. While he follows Panaetius' principle that the *honestum* and the *utile* cannot conflict, his substitution of different meanings for the terms enables him to develop a different rationale for why they cannot conflict. For Cicero the *honestum* as he sees it in the *De officiis* is the common good and the *utile* is individual interest. The reason why they cannot conflict is that man is part of a larger social and moral whole, which makes radical individualism unacceptable as a basis for ethical action.[291]

Although Cicero has drastically altered the meaning of the Stoic terminology he uses in the *De officiis*, he adopts the rule laid down by the Stoics in resolving the apparent conflict between the *honestum* and the *utile*. The rule is that the *honestum* is always to be preferred to the *utile*, because the *honestum*, or the common good, is more in accordance with nature and reason than is private expediency. He illustrates this point in good Stoic fashion with the example of Hercules, toiling and suffering for the sake of others.[292] Even in cases where an exception can be made to the general rule, the spirit of the rule, that is, social utility, is the criterion to be invoked for departing from it.[293] Cicero notes in this connection that men have moral obligations transcending what the civil law requires. In this context, as in the *De legibus*, he uses the term law of nations (*ius gentium*) and roots it in the moral fellowship binding all men together. He observes that this higher law is not identical with the civil law, although it ought to be.[294] Still, social utility, for the Romans or for some Romans, is what Cicero means even by this term in the *De officiis*.

---

[291] *De off.* 3.3.12–3.4.17, 3.7.34–3.9.39.
[292] *De off.* 3.4.20, 3.5.21–3.6.29.
[293] *De off.* 3.6.30–32.

Cicero's stress on the norm of social utility is evident from his analysis of how the *honestum* and the *utile* are compatible in the case of the cardinal virtues.[295] In discussing these virtues he touches only lightly on the virtue of temperance, which he dismisses rather abruptly with the remark that sensual pleasure is *per se* inconsistent with virtue. Sensual pleasure may give spice to life, at most, but it is in no sense expedient. In this case the *honestum* triumphs on the grounds that the *utile* is not *utile* after all.[296] Cicero does not deal at all with the virtue of wisdom in this connection, but passes on to justice and fortitude. He handles fortitude here, as he had earlier in the work, as a virtue ordered to justice. Its main function is to enable the individual to subordinate private interest to the needs of society. Fortitude, moreover, is not incompatible with private interest in that it yields reputation. It may also entail suffering; but, as Cicero notes, agreeing here with the Stoics, pain is not an evil.[297] His primary attention in this section of the book is focused on the virtue of justice. He agrees that the common good has higher claims than does private interest, but he is actually far more concerned with exploring the harmony that may obtain between these values. In his very definition of justice he includes the conception of private rights, which he does not think need to be sacrificed so long as they do not interfere with the rights of others, the public good, or good faith. The conclusion that Cicero reaches is that a sound public order maintains and protects private rights while a sound moral order eliminates conflicts between the individual and the group.

Cicero's argument in the *De officiis*, for all its dependence on Stoicism, ends by substantially reversing the direction of Panaetius' ethics. Cicero categorically rejects the concept of the *adiaphora*. He also redefines the *honestum* as a species of the *utile*. This being the case, he is forced to reject the Stoic norm of inner intentionality ordered to the *summum bonum* as the criterion of the ethical value of moral choices. By Stoic standards, the desire for the good cannot be virtuous if it is conditioned by any other end. What Cicero does is to posit the intermediate goods or preferables as ends in themselves, making social utility the highest of these values. This procedure entails a major de-Stoicization of Cicero's ethics in the *De officiis*, even in comparison with the modifications of Stoic doctrine that he achieves in his other ethical works. He retains the values of Stoic *apatheia* and autarchy and the casuistical method of Panaetius, but he alters profoundly the nature and relationship of the *honestum* and the *utile* as the Stoics had conceived of them. In one sense the absence of a real

---

[294] *De off.* 3.17.69.
[295] *De off.* 3.10.40–3.33.120.
[296] *De off.* 3.33.116–120.
[297] *De off.* 3.29.105.

conflict between these values is a function of the fact that Cicero regards them both as forms of the *utile,* both as an ethical principle and as a rhetorical strategy. In another sense the harmony between public and private interests which Cicero envisions appears to be predicated on a political and ethical ideal according to which the individual and society are equally bound to the protection of each other's rights. Such an arrangement could obtain only in a good society where all men were good, a utopia in which Cicero's *honestum* and *utile* would truly be reciprocal if not identical. In the end, Cicero's reformulation of Stoic ethics and his effort to bring the Stoic *summum et unicum bonum* down to earth is tied to a political and ethical ideal that, in its own way, is every bit as unattainable as the Stoic ideal that he seeks to Romanize, naturalize, and correct.

VIII. Conclusion

Our analysis of Cicero's philosophical thought has shown considerable variation in his attitude toward Stoicism in the major areas of philosophy which he treats. In rhetoric, he is extremely critical of the Stoics. In legal and political theory, he is warmly favorable to their natural law doctrine, which he appropriates and develops creatively. In epistemology, he communicates a substantial amount of Stoicism although without taking a particularly decisive point of view toward it. In theology he uses the Stoa to symbolize the philosophical approach to religion, which he attacks vigorously, singling out a few Stoic doctrines for praise but only because they correspond with principles he supports for other reasons. In ethics he embraces several major Stoic doctrines enthusiastically and works out his own views in initially Stoic terms. But the main thrust of his ethical thought is to criticize and redefine Stoicism in the light of alternative ethical values. The dialogue form and the rhetorical techniques which Cicero uses in his philosophical works give him repeated opportunities to set forth the Stoic doctrines that he treats in all these areas in a number of ways, overt and covert, positive and negative, accurate and garbled, for whatever purposes he has in mind. Later readers of Cicero could thus learn a tremendous amount about Stoicism from him in one way or another. Since this is the case, it will be useful to recall the major Stoic teachings that Cicero made available to the Latin-speaking world, according to their traditional philosophical subdivisions.

In the sphere of physics, the principal points that emerge are those dealing with the nature of God, the nature of man, and their interrelations. Cicero does refer to a number of other Stoic doctrines pertaining to physics in general. On several occasions he adverts to the Stoics' cyclical cosmology with its recurrent conflagrations, the *vis caloris* as the creative, sustaining, vital force in nature, the idea of *tonos*, or *vinculum* in his terms, which binds all parts of the universe together and which can be illustrated by the nourishment of the stars by exhalations from the earth. He also mentions the doctrine that everything which acts is a body, although he is not particularly interested in its implications and he pays no attention to the Stoic incorporeals.

The main topic in physics on which Cicero focuses is the nature of God. He refers repeatedly to the Stoic conception of God as a material being, composed of aether or fire, immanent in the world, identical with fate, causation, necessity, and providence. On one level he is interested in the idea of God as reason, the *logos* ruling the universe, with which the human *logos*, also material, is consubstantial. This principle explains for Cicero, as for the Stoics, the distinction between men and the sub-human world and is seen as the bond which unites all men with each other and with God. Cicero uses this constellation of ideas as the basis for his theory of natural law, applying it to the concept of the ideal statesman and to the legal norms that ought to govern institutional life, whether in a specific polity or in the wider cosmopolis. On another level, the Stoic doctrine of God is important for Cicero from the standpoint of theodicy and religion. He restates, both positively and negatively, the Stoic idea of God as directly involved in human affairs, manifesting his benevolence symbolically through the many gods of the pantheon, generally through the natural order, and on specific occasions through the signs interpreted by divination. On still another level, Cicero is interested in the Stoic identification of God with fate because of the association of this idea with the problem of free will and determinism. He recapitulates Chrysippus' position on this issue clearly and fully, and cites Chrysippus' metaphor of the rolling cylinder to illustrate it. There is only one aspect of the nature of man which Cicero takes up that he does not relate in some way to the nature of God. This is the theory of human development put forth by the Stoa, which he criticizes heavily, whereby the instinctual life of the child is superseded utterly as man moves into rational adulthood. However, this doctrine, like the other points of Stoic physics which he discusses, is of interest to Cicero primarily because of its ethical implications.

Cicero provides an even more extensive conspectus of Stoic ethical teachings, partly because of his own intense concern with this subject and partly because he deals with ethical issues in some way or other in every segment of his philosophical *oeuvre*. For the sake of convenience, the Stoic ethical doctrines in Cicero may be grouped into two categories, those which Cicero supports consistently and those which he criticizes, modifies, or takes differing stands on in different works. In the first category the most notable doctrines are the theory of the passions, the origin of the vices and virtues, the idea of *apatheia* and autarchy, the principle of decorum, the theory of the active and contemplative life, and the casuistical method. Cicero consistently reports the Stoic view of the four passions fully and accurately, and gives it his support. He invariably depicts the vices as aroused by the passions and sees the vices along with the virtues as arising from intellectual judgments. Although he rejects the exclusively rational definition óf human nature proposed by the ancient Stoa in favor of a more middle Stoic position that includes irrational faculties within the soul, he is consistent in imposing an exclusively rational norm for ethical choices. Cicero is strongly attracted by the doctrine of *apatheia* and autarchy and supports it so vigorously that he tends to ignore the associated doctrine of *eupatheia* in his desire to stress the need to suppress the passions completely as the only way of attaining moral liberty and consolation. He absorbs the Panaetian principle of decorum in both its ethical and its aesthetic dimensions, although it can scarcely be said that his own literary theory corresponds with the Stoics'. Cicero is the chief Latin source for Panaetius' system of casuistry, which he recapitulates quite faithfully, although he omits the variable of sex as a consideration in applying ethical rules to concrete cases. Indeed, sexual equality is an aspect of Stoic ethics that Cicero ignores completely. He is also the first Latin source for the Stoic conception of vocational choice as rooted in public-spirited morality, whatever its form of expression, making both the active and the contemplative lives valid moral choices.

In other areas of ethics, Cicero sometimes advocates Stoic positions in one place and attacks or alters them elsewhere, occasionally modifying them quite dramatically. The most important single example is the Stoic doctrine of the good and the *adiaphora*, which he frequently restates accurately under the labels of *honestum* and *utile* but which he eventually discards, using the same terms to signify an entirely different set of moral categories, introducing gradations into the Stoic *summum bonum*, reducing the good to the useful, and rejecting the idea that the preferables are morally neutral. Similarly, although he often adverts to the Stoic doctrine that all virtues and vices are equal and that their equality consists in their common expression of an inner virtuous or vicious intention, he ultimately departs from this notion in working out his own ethical position. Cicero's definitions of the four cardinal virtues are sometimes Stoic and sometimes not. Thus, while he repeatedly agrees that virtue is sufficient for happiness, he usually means something different from the Stoics by this statement. While he reports the Stoic paradoxes concerning the sage, he also alters the conception of the moral excellence that the sage possesses, attaching his own version of ethical perfection to the traditional Stoic exemplars of the sage, such as Cato, Scipio, Cincinnatus, and Hercules. Similarly, he sometimes supports the ideal Stoic conception of friendship but he tends to devote more attention to revising this theory in the light of traditional Roman attitudes than he does to defending it.

The Stoic position on logic, epistemology, and related subjects is represented somewhat less heavily in Cicero's works than either physics or ethics. There are, still, a number of passages in which he transmits material in this field which cannot be found so fully in other Latin authors. His *Academica* provides a good statement of the Stoic theory of cognition with its three stages of sensation, conceptualization, and the formation of kataleptic presentations. He adds to this the Stoics' emphasis on the will in intellectual judgments and acknowledges the fact that they located the criterion of truth in both sensation and intellectual judgment. The main point that Cicero omits in this connection is the role of the *pneuma* in sensation, flowing from both the sense organ and the sensed object, along with the idea that the *hegemonikon* controls both sensation and intellection. He relates Zeno's metaphor of the open palm, the semi-closed fist, and the clenched fist to illustrate the three stages in the cognitive process, although he interprets the same metaphor incorrectly in specifying his own preference for rhetoric over dialectic.

Cicero is extremely hostile to Stoic rhetoric, whose deficiencies he sees as a function of the Stoics' very eminence as dialecticians. In his repeated explanations of why he thinks that the Stoics fail to communicate effectively he presents a clear if tendentious outline of their preference for the plain style, the *verba antiqua*, a minimum of coloristic decoration, and the exclusive appeal to the intellect of the audience. Intellectualism at the expense of persuasiveness is also the charge that Cicero levels against Stoic dialectic. He depicts the Stoics as acute and relentless debaters but as liable to degenerate into abstruse technical jargon, logical hairsplitting, and irritating word games. Cicero is familiar with the Stoic syllogisms although he seems to have a rather shaky grasp of the essential character of Stoic logic in general. In the *De natura deorum* he has Cotta make a logical leap from a Stoic syllogistic proof to an ontological conclusion, while in the *Academica* he has Catulus assert that logic establishes nothing about the external world, a Stoic logical principle which, however, this speaker uses against Stoicism. Cicero shows little awareness of the fact that the Stoics treated logic as a purely formal art, under the rubric of the *lekta*. None the less, his *Topica* is a major Latin source for four of the five Stoic syllogisms, even though he does not identify them as Stoic in the passage in question.

If Cicero's ability to communicate Stoic philosophy is conditioned by his omissions, his modifications of some of the doctrines at isssue, and the shifting positions that he or the interlocutors in his dialogues take on many of them, there is also another major circumstance that had a decisive effect on his role as a transmitter of Stoicism. Not all of Cicero's philosophical works enjoyed the same level of popularity in later antiquity and in the early Middle Ages. Their availability to post-classical readers thus varied widely.[298] In the first century after his death, Cicero had his supporters and detractors, both on stylistic and political grounds. It was thanks to Quintilian that his place was established as the greatest master of Latin oratory. Thenceforth, both his oratorical theory and his speeches became a standard part of the school tradition, a place of honor which they retained throughout the Middle Ages and beyond. On the other hand, Cicero's philosophical works, except for the *Hortensius*,[299] won few readers and exercised minimal influence in the first two hundred years after his death. It is during that period that many of his philosophical works appear to have degenerated into the fragmentary state in which they still exist to this day.

The revival of interest in Cicero's philosophical works coincided with the age of the western apologists and Church Fathers. It was primarily Lactantius, Augustine, Ambrose, and Jerome who were responsible for putting these works back into circulation and for preserving the fragments of those that had suffered from the neglect of late classical readers. In most cases the first extant manuscripts of Cicero's philosophical writings date from the Carolingian era. This is true for his three theological dialogues, which were probably brought together into one corpus in the ninth century and joined to the *Topica,* the *Paradoxa Stoicorum,* the surviving books of the *De legibus,* the *Timaeus* translation, and Book 2 of the *Academica* in the same period. After that time, these texts were passed down together in the manuscript tradition.[300] The most dramatic ex-

---

[298] The best recent study of Cicero's reputation in antiquity is Will Richter, "Das Cicerobild der römischen Kaiserzeit," in *Cicero,* ed. Radke, pp. 161-97. See also M. L. Clarke " 'Non Hominis Nomen, sed Eloquentiae'," in *Cicero,* ed. Dorey, pp. 81-85; John Ferguson, "Some Ancient Judgments of Cicero," *Studies in Cicero,* pp. 11-33; John C. Rolfe, *Cicero and His Influence* (New York, 1928), pp. 110-19; Ettore Paratore, "Cicerone attraverso i secolo," in *Marco Tullio Cicerone,* pp. 237-44. T. Zieliński, *Cicero im Wandel der Jahrhunderte,* 4th ed. (Leipzig, 1929), pp. 10-130, is very general and has been superseded by the more recent studies.

[299] Ruch, *L'Hortensius de Cicéron,* pp. 37-57.

[300] On Cicero's theological works see T. J. Hunt, "The Medieval Tradition of Cicero's Theological Works," *Pegasus,* University of Exeter Classical Society Magazine, 5 (February 1966), 52-57; also Harris, "Cicero as an Academic," *Univ. of Auckland Bulletin, 58,* Classics ser. 2 (1961), 4; Ilona Opelt, "Ciceros Schrift De natura deorum bei den lateinischen Kirchenvätern," *Antike und Abendland, 12* (1966), 141-55; Bruwaene, intro. to his

ample of a patristic salvage operation on Cicero is the case of the *De republica*.[301] The only known manuscript of this work, an incomplete fourth-century palimpsest, was discovered only in 1819. Apart from this unique exemplar our knowledge of the first five books of the *De republica* is based on the fragments preserved by Lactantius, Augustine, and Ambrose, although there is a separate and extensive tradition of manuscripts and commentaries on Book 6 dating from late antiquity. Some of Cicero's ethical works, such as the short and relatively non-controversial *De senectute*, were read to some extent in later antiquity, cited by authors and noted by scholiasts, as well as enjoying a vogue with the Latin Fathers; there are many manuscript versions in the Middle Ages.[302] But Cicero's most popular and influential work in the Middle Ages, the *De officiis*, received no attention until it was resuscitated by Lactantius and above all by Ambrose.[303]

The general lack of enthusiasm which late classical readers felt for Cicero's philosophical works, apart from his rhetorical theory, can be explained ultimately as a consequence of Cicero's own miscalculations as an author. Despite his own opinions on the subject, Roman readers evidently felt no need or desire to study Greek philosophy in Latin translation, particularly not in a form wedded to Cicero's political attitudes. The Christian apologists and Church Fathers, on the other hand, found in Cicero's dialogues and treatises a convenient shortcut to Greek phi-

---

ed. of *De nat. deor.*, *1*, 34; Arthur Stanley Pease, intro. to his ed. of *De div.*, University of Illinois Studies in Language and Literature, *6*:2 (Urbana, 1920), pp. 29–32. On the *Academica* see Charles B. Schmitt, *Cicero Scepticus: A Study of the Influence of the Academica in the Renaissance*, International Archives of the History of Ideas, 52 (The Hague, 1972), pp. 2–42. On the *De legibus* see Georges de Plinval, "Autour du *De legibus*," *REL*, *47* (1969), 294–309; intro. to his ed. of *De leg.*, pp. lxvii–lxix; Peter Lebrecht Schmidt, *Die Überlieferung von Ciceros Schrift "De legibus" im Mittelalter und Renaissance* (München, 1974). On the *Paradoxa Stoicorum* see Molager, intro. to his ed. of *Par. Sto.*, pp. 80–81.

[301] See the excellent study by Eberhard Heck, *Die Bezeugnung von Ciceros Schrift De re publica* (Hildesheim, 1966), with its useful review of the literature on this issue prior to 1966, pp. 8–10; Boyancé, *Étude sur l'humanisme cicéronien*, pp. 180–87; Schmidt, "Cicero 'De re publica'," *Aufstieg und Niedergang der römischen Welt*, *1*, part 4, 276–79; Konrat Zeigler, trans. and intro., M. T. Cicero, *Staatstheoretische Schriften* (Berlin, 1974), pp. 31–33. On the history of Book 6 see Pierre Courcelle, "La postérité chrétienne du *Songe de Scipion*," *REL*, *36* (1958), 205–34; Paul Lehmann, "Nachrichten und Gerüchte von der Überlieferung der libri sex Ciceronis 'De re publica'," *Studi italiani di filologia classica*, *26–27* (1956), 202–15.

[302] Wuilleumier, intro. to his ed. of *De sen.*, pp. 100–13; "L'Influence du *Cato maior*," *Mélanges de philologie, de littérature et d'histoire anciennes offerts à Alfred Ernout* (Paris, 1940), pp. 383–88.

[303] N. E. Nelson, "Cicero's *De Officiis* in Christian Thought: 300–1300," *Essays and Studies in English and Comparative Literature*, University of Michigan Publications, Language and Literature, 10 (Ann Arbor, 1933), pp. 59, 64–79; Fedeli, "Il 'De officiis' di Cicerone," *Aufstieg und Niedergang der römischen Welt*, *1*, part 4, 376–86, 421–22; Testard, intro. to his ed. of *De off.*, *1*, 67–70.

losophy and a rich source of information on pagan theology and religious practices. Both in his substance and in his style Cicero provided them with numerous arguments and models which they used extensively in their own works of polemical and constructive theology. They mined his philosophical works heavily, particularly those dedicated to theology and ethics. It is largely thanks to the apologists and Church Fathers that Cicero's philosophical works were preserved. It is also thanks to them that he became the most widely read and the most influential ancient Latin prose author during the Middle Ages, whose prominence as a school rhetorician only served to enhance his authority in other fields. Cicero's own misconception of the impact that he was likely to exert on his contemporaries, which inspired him to expound, to debate, and to reformulate Greek philosophy in the Latin tongue, thus became the basis for his later fame among Christian readers and insured for him the place he came to hold in the Middle Ages as the most important single transmitter of Stoicism after the Stoics themselves.

CHAPTER THREE

THE SATIRISTS

The Roman satirists have attracted a good deal of attention on the part of commentators seeking to trace the influence of Greek philosophy in Latin literature. At the same time, scholars primarily concerned with illuminating the essential nature of Roman satire have often stressed the importance of its philosophical content. Whether crudely or subtly, consistently or inconsistently, the satirists, they point out, sought to enforce an ethical viewpoint. This didactic intention, it has been observed, reflects the satirists' application of the Cynic-Stoic diatribe to poetry and likewise inspired its authors to draw heavily on the substance of Stoic ethics in their critiques of individual foibles and social corruption.[1] Some scholars hold that Lucilius (ca. 180-ca. 103/01 B.C.), the first of the Roman satirists, was also the first to have transmuted Stoic philosophy into Latin satiric form. The basis for this view appears to be the fact that Lucilius was acquainted with Scipio and other members of his circle and was a member of it at the same time as Panaetius.[2] From this coincidence, it has been argued that Lucilius was able to absorb a number of Stoic ideas, ranging from the entire philosophy[3] to Panaetius' teachings in general[4] to social and political theory[5] to the doctrine of *humanitas*[6] to the definition of virtue as the *summum bonum*[7] to the theory of grammar,

---

[1] The first major statement of this position as applied to the satirists in general is Clarence W. Mendell, "Satire as Popular Philosophy," *CP*, *15* (1920), 138-57. Mendell's thesis is repeated with greater or lesser emphasis by J. Wight Duff, *Roman Satire: Its Outlook on Social Life*, Sather Classical Lectures, 12 (Berkeley, 1936), pp. 9, 78-83, 117-18; Moses Hadas, *A History of Latin Literature* (New York, 1952), p. 52; and very strongly by the more recent scholars Werner Krenkel, "Römische Satire und römische Gesellschaft," *Wissenschaftliche Zeitschrift der Universität Rostock*, gesellschafts- und sprachwissenschaftliche Reihe, *15*:4-5 (1966), 471-77; Charles Witke, *Latin Satire: The Structure of Persuasion* (Leiden, 1970), pp. 2-3, 5-7.

[2] For the biography of Lucilius see the intro. to Gaius Lucilius, *Fragments*, in *Remains of Old Latin*, ed. and trans. E. H. Warmington, Loeb (Cambridge, Mass., 1961), *3*, vii-xx.

[3] Arnold, *Roman Stoicism*, p. 383.

[4] Brown, *Scipionic Circle*, p. 83.

[5] George Converse Fiske, *Lucilius and Horace: A Study in the Classical Theory of Imitation*, University of Wisconsin Studies in Language and Literature, 7 (Madison, 1920), pp. 68-75.

[6] Ibid., pp. 28, 52-53, 66.

[7] George Converse Fiske, "Lucilius, the *Ars Poetica* of Horace, and Persius," *HSCP*, *24* (1913), 14.

rhetoric, and literary style.[8] However, the fragments of Lucilius which have come down to us are so scanty that the attribution of Stoic stylistic and ethical ideas to him would appear to be a hazardous venture at best. The only fragment preserved in which Lucilius makes any express reference to Stoicism is one in which, according to the scholiast Porphyrio, he satirizes the ancient Stoic conception of the sage, rejecting the claim that the sage alone possesses all things and that he alone is handsome, wealthy, free, and royal.[9] This one fragment does not provide adequate grounds for regarding Lucilius as the founder of Roman satire *more Stoicorum*. Our analysis will therefore begin not with Lucilius, but with Horace.

I. HORACE

The son of a simple freedman, Horace (65-8 B.C.) was brought from his native Venusia to Rome by his father, who provided him with the best schooling available there and who later sent him to Athens to complete his education. Horace's studies in Greek philosophy and literature were interrupted in 44 B.C. when he left Athens in the retinue of Brutus, sharing his defeat at the second battle of Philippi. Shortly thereafter, he returned to Rome, where he was pardoned by the victorious Antony and Octavius and where he sought to recoup the losses which his inheritance had suffered thanks to his participation in the recently crushed rebellion by acquiring a post in the civil bureaucracy.

At the same time that he was taking up his official duties, Horace started to publish his first works of poetry, beginning his literary career with satires. His early poems caught the attention of well-established authors such as Vergil, through whose good offices Horace was introduced to Maecenas and became one of his protégés. This connection soon provided Horace with the leisure and independence which enabled him to devote his full attention to poetry; two years after the publication of his first book of *Satires*, Maecenas presented him with a Sabine farm. For the rest of his life, Horace enjoyed a position of financial security, prestigious associations, artistic freedom, and literary acclaim, numbered along with Vergil as one of the poet laureates of the Augustan age.

Horace's education gave him ample opportunity to familiarize himself with Greek culture. One of his avowed aims, it is generally conceded, was to extend the range of Greek models upon which Roman literature

---

[8] Duff, *Roman Satire*, pp. 43-48, 51; Fiske, *Lucilius and Horace*, pp. 107-18; Hadas, *Hist. of Latin Lit.*, p. 56; Smiley, *Latinitas and Hellenismos*, p. 217.

[9] Lucilius, frag. 1189-1190, ed. Warmington, *3*, 388. This point is also noted by Duff, *Roman Satire*, p. 52.

might draw, accomplishing for several forms of Greek lyric a process of Latinization analogous to that performed by his contemporaries Vergil and Cicero for epic and bucolic poetry and for prose.[10] Far more controversial is the question of Horace's relationship to Greek philosophy.[11] In their efforts to resolve this issue, Horace scholars have produced four distinctly different Horaces: Horace the Stoic, Horace the Epicurean, Horace the eclectic, and Horace the man lacking any sustained interest in philosophy. The claims of these divergent schools of thought will have to be examined as part of the task of assessing the place of Stoicism in Horace's work.

While few of the critics who view Horace as a Stoic go so far as to say that Stoicism was a religion for him, a creed through which he hoped to regenerate the society of his day,[12] the proponents of the Stoic interpretation are united in treating his thought in a developmental or evolutionary manner. According to the dominant position taken by this school, Horace's outlook in his *Satires* (35-30 B.C.) is Epicurean. But, over the next decade, in the course of writing his *Epodes* (ca. 29 B.C.) and the first three books of his *Odes* (ca. 23 B.C.), Horace underwent a gradual conversion brought on by advancing age, ill health, and the place of honor he had come to enjoy in the eyes of the literary and political establishment, which inspired him to abandon the frivolities of his youth in favor of a more mature religious, patriotic, and philosophical attitude toward life. While never abandoning Epicureanism altogether and while continuing to draw on a variety of philosophical schools throughout his life, Horace none the less, according to this view, shows an increasing attachment to Stoicism in his later works. The conversion, announced in the first book of his *Epistles* (ca. 20 B.C.), becomes a progressively deeper commitment in his *Carmen saeculare* (17 B.C.), the second book of *Epistles* (ca. 14 B.C.) and his fourth book of *Odes* (ca. 13 B.C.). A few commentators find evidence of the conversion as early as the first book of *Satires*[13] and

---

[10] This point has been generally accepted by Horace scholars. For excellent recent analyses see Eduard Fraenkel, *Horace* (Oxford, 1959), p. 47 and passim; R. G. M. Nisbet and Margaret Hubbard, *A Commentary on Horace: Odes, Book I* (Oxford, 1970), p. xii; Gordon Williams, *Tradition and Originality in Roman Poetry* (Oxford, 1968), passim and more briefly in *Horace*, Greece & Rome: New Surveys in the Classics, 6 (Oxford, 1972); useful but to a lesser extent is Cornelia C. Coulter, "Aeolian Strains on the Roman Lyre," *CJ*, *31* (1935-36), 175-82.

[11] An effort to catalogue Horace's philosophical ideas was made by Oscar Edward Nybakken, *An Analytical Study of Horace's Ideas*, Iowa Studies in Classical Philology, 5 (Scottsdale, Pa., 1937), but the work is superficial and of marginal utility.

[12] Archibald Y. Campbell, *Horace: A New Interpretation* (London, 1924), p. 234; Tenney Frank, *Catullus and Horace: Two Poets in Their Environment* (New York, 1928), pp. 182-83.

[13] Campbell, *Horace*, p. 164; Ulrich Knoche, *Roman Satire*, trans. Edwin S. Ramage (Bloomington, 1975), p. 86 dates the transition to Book 2 of the *Satires*.

one sees the shift in Horace's attitude as symptomatic of a larger wa-
tershed in Greek and Latin satire as a whole.[14] But the conversion thesis,
with or without these refinements, has been defended repeatedly since
the late nineteenth century.[15]

The interpretation just described depends to a significant degree on
two analytic techniques which may well be questioned as applied to Horace. The first is the extrapolation of Stoic ideas from their contexts in
Horace's works. This approach leads to the conclusion that Horace is
displaying a Stoicizing attitude in many poems where he may actually
be treating the idea in question in an ironic, critical, or incidental manner. It also leads adherents of this position to attribute to Stoicism notions
on which the Stoa held no monopoly and which Horace may in fact be
defending with non-Stoic arguments.[16] The second methodological blind
spot of the pro-Stoic school is one already noted, its insistence on studying
the poems of Horace in chronological order so as to chart his presumed
conversion from Epicureanism to Stoicism. This approach entails the
reading of Horace's works as a source for his autobiography. The autobiographical information which emerges from such a reading is then used
as an interpretive guide to the philosophical content of the poems. Apart
from the obviously tautological character of this method, it can also be
faulted for failing to take sufficient account of the fact that there may be
a difference between poetic truth and historical truth, between the exigencies of a work of imagination, the statement of a credo, and a factual
account.[17] As will be seen from the analysis of the Horatian texts below,
once the matter to be analyzed is confined to those ideas that are unique
to the Stoa and once they are read in the poetic contexts in which Horace

---

[14] Campbell, *Horace*, pp. 121-22.

[15] A useful survey of adherants to this position prior to 1930, among whom he numbers
himself, is provided by A. Rabe, "Das Verhältnis des Horaz zur Philosophie," *Archiv für
Geschichte der Philosophie und Soziologie, 39* (1930), 77-91. Among the more influential pro-
ponents of the conversion theory in the first third of the twentieth century are Campbell,
Horace, pp. 99, 121-22; Edmond Courbaud, *Horace: Sa vie et sa pensée à l'époque des épîtres.
Étude sur le premier livre* (Paris, 1914), pp. 35-196; Duff, *Roman Satire*, pp. 75, 77-83, 117;
Fiske, *Lucilius and Horace*, pp. 68, 75, 219-475; Richard Heinze, Q. *Horatius Flaccus,
Briefe*, ed. Adolf Kiessling and Richard Heinze, 6th ed. (Berlin, 1959), pp. 369-71; Paul
Kohler, *Epikur und Stoa bei Horaz* (Greifswald, 1911), pp. 15-22, 54-67. More recent
scholars who have seconded this view include Karl Hans Abel, "Horaz auf der Suche
nach dem wahren Selbst," *Antike und Abendland, 15* (1969), 34-46; Knoche, *Roman Satire*,
pp. 82-94; Walter Wili, *Horaz und die Augusteische Kultur*, 2nd ed. (Basel, 1965),
pp. 105-07, 109, 123-24, 205, 285, 292-97, 303, 313; Witke, *Latin Satire*, p. 8.

[16] An extremely exaggerated recent example of this tendency can be found in Chester
G. Starr, "Horace and Augustus," *AJP, 90* (1969), 58-64, in connection with Horace's
use of the terms *liber* and *libertas*.

[17] This issue both in general and in specific application to Horace has been ably
treated by Williams, *Tradition and Originality*, pp. 1-29, 443-59, 561-77; *Horace*, pp. 1-5.

placed them, the incidence of Stoic as compared with non-Stoic ideas in Horace's *oeuvre* bears no significant relationship to chronology. Thus, the claim of a developing attachment to Stoicism on Horace's part as put forth by the pro-Stoic school seems ripe for revision or rejection. At the same time, this school has made a permanent contribution to the discussion by focusing attention on many of the Stoic ideas or *topoi* that need to be investigated and by encouraging the reader to examine the entire body of Horace's works for evidences of Stoicism, a procedure that will be followed here even though it involves the consideration of some Horatian works in this chapter which cannot be defined as satires.

The Epicurean interpretation of Horace has fewer adherants than the Stoic one and tends to regard the pro-Stoic view as the principal school to be vanquished. This circumstance may explain the fact that the pro-Epicureans share some of the methodological assumptions of the pro-Stoics. Advocates of the Epicurean interpretation concede that Horace is not always completely Epicurean and that he borrows ideas from the Stoics as well.[18] One member of this school even concurs with the pro-Stoic picture of a Horace moving from the Epicureanism of his early works toward a broader acceptance of Stoicism in his later works, although he maintains that the philosophical balance in Horace continues to be weighted in favor of Epicureanism.[19] In their efforts to disprove the Stoic thesis, one strategy which the pro-Epicureans frequently employ is to underline the repeated occasions on which Horace satirizes or expressly rejects Stoic doctrines, such as the Stoic conception of the sage.[20] A second strategy, analogous to one used by the pro-Stoics, is to focus on ideas extrapolated from Horace's works which can be identified with Epicureanism, the most popular being Horace's praise of pleasure, his enthusiasm for the simple country life, his views on friendship, and his sometimes jaundiced attitude toward the gods.[21] The most eloquent and

---

[18] This position has numbered adherants from the early twentieth century up to the present. See, for example, Robert Philippson, "Horaz' Verhältnis zur Philosophie," *Festschrift dem König Wilhelms-Gymnasium zu Magdeburg zur Feier seines 25 jahrigen Bestehens, Osten 1911* (Magdeburg, 1911), pp. 77-110; Vincenzo Ussani, "Orazio e la filosofia popolare," *Atene e Roma, 19* (1916), 2-5; Mary N. Porter Packer, "The Consistent Epicureanism of the First Book of the Epistles of Horace," *TAPA, 72* (1941), xxxix-xl; Henry Dwight Sedgwick, *Horace: A Biography* (Cambridge, Mass., 1947), pp. 59 ff., 147-51; O. A. W. Dilke, "Horace and the Verse Letter," in *Horace*, ed. C. D. N. Costa (London, 1973), p. 99.

[19] Thadée Zieliński, *Horace et la société romaine du temps d'Auguste*, Collection de l'Institut française de Varsovie, 5 (Paris, 1938), pp. 48, 65-86.

[20] A good recent example is M. Ruch, "Horace, Satires I, 3: Étude littéraire et philosophique," *LEC, 38* (1970), 520-21, 523-24.

[21] This strategy is well illustrated by the series of articles by Norman N. DeWitt, "Parresiastic Poems of Horace," *CP, 30* (1935), 312-19; "The Epicurean Doctrine of Gratitude," *AJP, 58* (1937), 320-28; "Epicurean Doctrine in Horace," *CP, 34* (1939), 127-34.

persuasively argued expression of the Epicurean interpretation treats the poet as inflamed by a yearning for "deliverance and redemption,"[22] a philosophical quest which eventually led him to Epicureanism. The teachings of Epicurus served as a remedy for his sorrows and provided him with a means of legitimizing the *vita privata* given the collapse of the Roman Republic and with it his youthful ideals and values.[23] Whether seeing Horace as a basically wry and dégagé humanist who enjoyed scoring off the pomposities of Stoic extremists or as a deeply committed seeker after truth and meaning, the members of this school agree in taking literally Horace's description of himself as *Epicuri de grege porcum*, a pig from Epicurus' flock,[24] and in reading this phrase as descriptive of his overall philosophical attitude. The pro-Epicurean school has performed a valuable service in directing attention to this component in Horace's thought. But, like the pro-Stoics, they have sometimes been overly zealous in attributing to their chosen philosophy notions which are not always exclusive or even proper to it and in extrapolating doctrines from a surrounding environment of arguments and ideas which often condition or stringently limit their force.

If Horace the Stoic and Horace the Epicurean have drawn a large host of supporters to their ranks, Horace the eclectic is easily the most popular of the Horaces put forth by modern scholarship. In some cases scholars have attached the label of eclectic to Horace because they wish to acknowledge the fact that the sources from which he borrows go well beyond Stoicism and Epicureanism. Horace's works thus need to be viewed, according to one vivid formulation of this position, as "something of an intellectual smorgasbord,"[25] with an assortment of dishes including Aristotelianism, Platonism, Pythagoreanism, and the traditional ethos of Rome side by side with the offerings of the Porch and the Garden.[26]

---

[22] Viktor Pöschl, "Poetry and Philosophy in Horace," in *The Poetic Tradition: Essays on Greek, Latin, and English Poetry*, ed. Don Cameron Allen and Henry T. Rowell (Baltimore, 1968), p. 48.

[23] Ibid., pp. 47-61.

[24] Quintus Horatius Flaccus, *Ep.* 1.4.16 in *Briefe*, ed. Heinze-Kiessling. This edition and the editions of Horace's other works which follow will be referred to throughout: *Ars poetica*, ed. C. O. Brink (Cambridge, 1971); *Oden und Epoden*, ed. Adolf Kiessling and Richard Heinze, 10th ed. (Berling, 1960); *Satires*, ed. Paul Lejay (Hildesheim, 1966 [repr. of 1911 ed.]).

[25] Smith Palmer Bovie, trans. and intro., *The Satires and Epistles of Horace* (Chicago, 1959), p. 96.

[26] Ibid.; Marie-Thérèse LeBon, "La 'vera virtus' chez Horace," *Études Horatiennes: Receuil publié in l'honneur du bimillénaire d'Horace*, Travaux de la Faculté de philosophie et lettres de l'Université de Bruxelles, 7 (Bruxelles, 1937), pp. 141-46; Lejay, intro. to his ed. of *Satires*, pp. vii-xxxvi; Anna Lydia Motto, "Stoic Elements in the *Satires* of Horace," in *Classical, Mediaeval and Renaissance Studies in Honor of Berthold Louis Ullman*, ed. Charles Henderson (Roma, 1964), pp. 133-42; Zoja Pavlovskis, "Aristotle, Horace, and the Ironic

Although deriving from a variety of sources, Horace's philosophical attitude, it is stressed by this school, is "no mere rag-bag of multicolored scraps,"[27] but reflects a serious interest in working out a consistent if personal point of view on his part. Some scholars in this camp, agreeing with the pro-Stoic school to a greater or lesser extent on this point, argue for the amalagamation of Horace's personal philosophy out of its diverse elements within a chronological framework;[28] others reject the conversion thesis embedded in this mode of analysis.[29] Whatever their position on this issue, the proponents of the eclectic interpretation see Horace as a thinker temperamentally repelled by the idea of an orthodox or exclusive adherence to any one philosophical school. Drawing on several philosophies while remaining independent of all of them, he eventually forges an original synthesis of his own, selecting from his sources on the basis of the psychological resonance and ethical relevance which they possess for him.[30] The important question is not the proportion of Stoic or Epicurean or Aristotelian elements in Horace's thought but the freshness and integrity of the new philosophy which Horace creates out of his diverse sources. If indeed Horace's personal philosophy can be identified primarily with any one influence, it has been suggested that the influence in question is most likely to have been middle Stoicism as represented by Panaetius.[31] But more importantly, the final Horatian product is a consistent if idiosyncratic one.

The eclectic interpretation of Horace has the considerable merit of providing a view of the poet which is capable of making sense out of the frequent discrepancies between his Stoic and Epicurean moods, the lack

Man," CP, 63 (1968), 28; Niall Rudd, The Satires of Horace: A Study (Cambridge, 1966), p. 139; Frederick W. Shipley, "The Universality of Horace," CJ, 31 (1935-36), 143; David L. Sigsbee, "The Disciplined Satire of Horace," in Roman Satirists and Their Satire: The Fine Art of Criticism in Ancient Rome, ed. Edwin S. Ramage, David L. Sigsbee, and Sigmund C. Fredericks (Park Ridge, N. J., 1974), pp. 86-87; Charles Newton Smiley, Horace: His Poetry and Philosophy (New York, 1945), pp. 3, 39-40.

[27] Rudd, Satires of Horace, p. 19.

[28] Thus, for instance, Hildebrecht Hommel, Horaz: Der Mensch und das Werk (Heidelberg, 1950), p. 33; W. S. Maguinness, "The Eclecticism of Horace," Hermathena, 52 (1938), 27-46.

[29] Thus, for instance, M. J. McGann, Studies in Horace's First Book of Epistles, Collection Latomus, 100 (Bruxelles, 1969), pp. 96-97; Alfred Noyes, Horace: A Portrait (New York, 1947), p. 194; Rudd, Satires of Horace, p. 20.

[30] Hommel, Horaz, pp. 33, 44-50; Edward Jędrzyński, "Horatii philosophia atque conscientia religiosa," Studia philosophiae christianae, 8 (1972), 25-38; Kohler, Epikur und Stoa bei Horaz, p. 5 and passim; Maguinness, "Eclecticism of Horace," Hermathena, 52 (1938), 27-46; "Friends and Friendship in the Philosophy of Horace," ibid., 51 (1938), 31, 43-45 [both articles are expressly written in opposition to DeWitt; see note 21 above]; Noyes, Horace, pp. xii, 226-27; Rudd, Satires of Horace, pp. 19-20; Grant Showerman, Horace and His Influence (Boston, 1922), pp. 35-38, 54-55; Wili, Horaz, p. 376.

[31] Persuasively argued by McGann, Studies in Horace, pp. 9-32.

of rigor with which he usually professes the doctrines of both of these schools when he does profess them, and the presence in his work of ideas clearly derived from other sources. The insight that Panaetius may have been a major influence on Horace is a plausible suggestion which might help to account for the syncretistic element in Horace as well as for his distaste for the austerities and paradoxes of ancient Stoic ethics. The principal difficulty with the eclectic interpretation is its insistence on the premise that Horace does indeed have a consistent philosophy, however eclectic it may be. This belief in Horace's philosophical consistency and seriousness is a point which the pro-eclectic school shares with the pro-Stoic and pro-Epicurean schools. Yet, no scholar in any one of these groups has thus far succeeded in demonstrating that the entire corpus of Horace's works can be understood in the light of any one set of philosophical principles.

The fourth and final group of commentators is the smallest. Despite a filiation which goes back to the late nineteenth century, its leading exponents are recent scholars who write with an air of self-conscious revisionism. This group, protesting against a preoccupation with *Quellenforschung* in Horace studies which, as they see it, has deflected attention away from his poetic genius, views Horace as a man who was a poet and who therefore was neither deeply nor consistently interested in philosophy of any kind. The earliest modern herald of the unphilosophical Horace, striking a note which reverberates in the work of his successors, dismisses Horace as a philosophical dilletante.[32] "It would be a mistake," says the next important commentator in this school, "to look in Horace for deep or abiding convictions," either in religion or in philosophy.[33] While his analysis leads him to give Stoicism the edge over other philosophies found in Horace, this critic thinks it a fruitless task to try to piece together any kind of coherent philosophy within his works. Being a poet, Horace is a man of shifting moods; he simply makes use of whatever ideas happen to suit his current feelings when he sits down to write a poem.[34]

The most recent supporters of this position have sought to strengthen it by directing attention to the fact that Horace made use of poetic as well as philosophical sources. Greek lyric poetry, in particular, supplied him with a range of ethical attitudes no less than with generic and stylistic models. Many of these ethical attitudes had become commonplaces by the time that Horace received them. But he expresses them less out of an

---

[32] A. Cartault, *Étude sur les satires d'Horace*, Université de Paris, Bibliothèque de la faculté des lettres, 9 (Paris, 1899), pp. 323-46.

[33] J. F. D'Alton, *Horace and His Age: A Study in Historical Background* (London, 1917), p. 76.

[34] Ibid., pp. 76-103, 127, 133-44, 228.

interest in philosophy than out of the desire to follow in the footsteps of his Greek poetic predecessors. While, to a certain extent, these commentators stress the importance of Horace's poetic sources in order to dilute the importance of his philosophical sources, they remain adamant about the independence with which he deployed any sources that he did use. Horace, they emphasize, is an extremely original poet. No sources which he absorbed could survive intact but underwent an inescapable sea change on contact with his unique poetic genius. Horace uses his sources to express his personal feelings even at the price of depriving them of their original meanings;[35] they serve "as the material for poetic composition, ... [being] completely subordinated to the ordinances of imagination and humour."[36] Horace, according to this interpretation, was fully capable of faking an interest in philosophy which he did not really feel in contexts where he thought that such an interest was expected of him by his audience, as a form of *captatio benevolentiae*.[37] His famous proclamation in his first *Epistle* that he was an adherant of no school of thought although a borrower from many means something different for proponents of the unphilosophical Horace than it does for proponents of Horace the eclectic. Rather than signifying a philosophy that is held consistently and with deep conviction for all its being tailor-made to Horace's own order, it points to the substitution of sensibility, wit, and the exigencies of poetic *inventio* as Horace's guiding inspiration. Horace's crucial motivation was not a philosophical yearning for the true or the good; "he was at the core a man who lived for his art, preserving a certain coolness in his relations with everyone and everything but the Muse."[38]

The promoters of the unphilosophical Horace have performed a valuable service in reminding readers of the fact that a work of poetic art is always more than the sum of its parts. But, in reacting against the *Quellenforscher* who have all too often given the impression that the task of literary criticism is to reduce an author to a compendium of his received ideas, the revisionists have tended to succumb to a corresponding form of reductionism by implying that poets may do battle under the banner of imagination or under the banner of intellect but that they cannot serve both allegiances simultaneously. Such a divorce between *ars* and *doctrina*,

---

[35] C. O. Brink, *Horace on Poetry* (Cambridge, 1963-71), *1*, 154-55, 213-14; *2*, 448; Viktor Pöschl, "Horaz," in *L'Influence grecque sur la poésie latine de Catulle à Ovide*, Fondation Hardt, Entretiens sur l'antiquité classique, 2 (Genève, 1956), pp. 93-115; the same position is expressed implicitly in his *Horazische Lyrik: Interpretationen* (Heidelberg, 1970); Williams, *Tradition and Originality*, pp. 315-16, 329-57, 593-96, 599.

[36] Williams, *Tradition and Originality*, p. 599.

[37] Ibid., pp. 28-29.

[38] Joseph B. Clancy, trans. and intro., *The Odes and Epodes of Horace* (Chicago, 1960), p. 4.

whatever its merits may be in the abstract, is not necessarily the most sensible critical perspective to apply to Horace. Also, the separation between art and life, while it eliminates some of the absurdities perpetrated by the autobiographical approach to Horace, ends by imposing the equally absurd hypothesis that the poet's ideas and the circumstances of his life are under no conditions relevant to his poetry.

The critics who have contributed to the debate on Horace's philosophy thus far have all provided helpful insights and have at the same time emitted signals warning the reader of certain debatable preconceptions and methods which he would do well to shun. The analysis of Horace's works which now follows has as its avowed purpose the assessment of Stoicism in Horace. It is possible that this investigation may also shed some light on the larger critical issues concerning Horace which have been discussed above, even though a full resolution of those issues lies beyond the scope of our inquiry.

A considerable number of Stoic themes, primarily in the field of ethics, are present in Horace's poems, sometimes treated sympathetically, sometimes treated unsympathetically, sometimes treated incidentally, and sometimes expressly rejected in favor of an alternative doctrine or attitude. A statistical survey of the incidence of these themes in the Horatian corpus shows that neither their occurrence nor the ways in which the poet handles them can be correlated chronologically with any particular stages of his career. However, if one reads Horace's poems topically and synchronically rather than chronologically one finds that as one moves from favorable to unfavorable references to Stoicism one also moves from the smallest to the largest groups of examples.

There are a few instances in which Horace alludes to Stoicism as a quick and easy way of identifying philosophy as such, or the upright moral life. In one of his odes, he castigates the addressee for allowing his acquisitive instincts to drive out his former interest in philosophy; this benighted soul has sold the books of Panaetius and Socrates to make room in his house for Spanish armor.[39] Here, Panaetius, along with Socrates, simply functions as a readily identifiable personification of the enduring value of philosophy in contrast with material wealth. Likewise, in one of Horace's epodes, he paints a scabrous portrait of a lecherous old society woman conducting her adulterous affairs in the luxurious boudoir beneath whose silken cushions she keeps her Stoic volumes.[40] Horace attacks his subject's hypocrisy no less than her lasciviousness and her repulsive physical appearance. Her Stoic volumes epitomize the

---

[39] *Carm.* 1.29.13–15.
[40] *Epod.* 8.15–16.

ideals of dignity, chastity, and honesty that stand in such sharp contrast to her vicious character and unseemly behavior. In these two poems Horace uses a technique which he and other satirists employ frequently. He seeks to sway the reader toward virtue not by presenting an inspiring example of the ideals he wishes to advance but by depicting the sinner as ludicrous or loathesome. Both poems suggest the high contemporary visibility of Stoicism and its shorthand association with wisdom and virtue, although the philosophical principles involved are not unique to Stoicism.

There is a second although equally small group of poems in which Horace provides information about Stoicism in a somewhat more substantial vein. While Horace does not attach a Stoic label to the ideas in question and while he states maxims without supplying any of the philosophical rationale that support them, he advances principles with which no Stoic would have any difficulty agreeing and he takes a strongly positive attitude toward them. Sometimes these principles are ones that Stoics shared with other philosophical schools. A good case in point is an ode in which Horace elaborates on the theme that the desire for wealth is folly while liberation from greed is a sign of wisdom and virtue, a virtue which endows its possessor with the only form of power that is safe and enduring. He counsels the addressee of the poem to seek this virtue despite its unpopularity with the crowd.[41] A more speculatively oriented treatment of this theme by a Stoicizing poet might also touch on the point that vice and folly result from erroneous judgments, that judgments can be corrected because they are under the control of the *logos*, that the wise man is ruled by the *logos* while the fool is not. None of these specifically Stoic reasons for advancing the advice which Horace proffers are set forth in this poem. Although it provides much more evidence of a potentially Stoic attitude than the two poems just discussed, its philosophical tone coincides with Stoicism while affording no proof that Stoicism is its source.

A much more interesting example is *Epistle* 1.16 because, in addition to expressing doctrines which the Stoics shared with other schools of philosophy, it includes several ideas unique to Stoicism.[42] This poem is also noteworthy in that its argument uses a strategy of persuasion combining the presentation of an edifying model of what to follow with a satirical model of what to avoid. The theme of the poem, as Horace states it to his addressee, is the praise of the wise man: *neve putes alium sapiente bonoque beatum* ("Nor think that anyone but the sage is good and happy,")[43] a

---

[41] *Carm.* 2.2.9-14.
[42] Campbell, *Horace,* pp. 266-67 gives a good content analysis of this poem.
[43] *Ep.* 1.16.20.

typically Stoic maxim. Horace then proceeds to outline some of the characteristics of the man who merely appears to be virtuous, contrasting
them with true virtue. This distinction between illusion and reality might
suggest that Horace intends to orchestrate the theme in Platonic terms.
Rather, he connects it to two interrelated Stoic doctrines, the idea that
one's inner intention is the sole criterion of the virtue of one's actions and
the idea that, since virtue is the only good, the intention to do good is
the only truly virtuous motivation for one's ethical behavior. The man
who is seemingly virtuous, as Horace delineates him, concentrates on the
performance of external acts of the sort that win public approbation. He
is a law-abiding and conventionally pious citizen and an industrious
worker. His error, as Horace exposes it, rests on three foundations: his
industry masks his enslavement by the desire for riches; he believes that
he can manipulate the gods by prayers and propitiations so as to avoid
the consequences of his misdeeds; and he takes credit for his absence of
a criminal record as if this were a positive merit. But, in fact, the only
reason why the seemingly virtuous man obeys the law is because he is
constrained by the fear of punishment, unlike truly good men who shun
crime out of the love of virtue: *oderunt peccare boni virtutis amore:/ tu nihil
admittes in te formidne poenae* ("The good hate to sin out of love of virtue;/
You recognize only the fear of punishment.")[44] If this deterrent were
removed, Horace adds, the seemingly virtuous man would not even
shrink from desecrating holy things. His folly lies in his failure to realize
that his sins, however small, damage him more than they damage his
victims: *nam de mille fabae modiis cum surripis unum,/ damnum est, non facinus,
mihi pacto lenius isto* ("If you should steal but one bean from my thousand
bushels/ You are guilty, though the harm done to me is slight.")[45] Here,
Horace carries the principle of intentionality as the norm of virtue to its
logical Stoic conclusion by acknowledging the doctrine that there are no
gradations of vice; the theft of one bean is just as much a manifestation
of a vicious attitude toward life as an act of sacrilege would be.

At the end of the poem Horace brings forward his model of the truly
virtuous man by means of a dialogue between Dionysus and Pentheus,
ruler of Thebes, paraphrasing Euripides' *Bacchae* 492-98. In selecting a
god who submits himself to the will of a mortal as an example of ideal
human virtue Horace suggests at the same time the value of Stoic forebearance in the face of external vicissitudes and the idea that the sage is
connatural with the deity. Dionysus does not challenge the justice of
Pentheus' decision to confiscate his wealth, to imprison him, and to put

---

[44] *Ep.* 1.16.52-53.
[45] *Ep.* 1.16.55-56.

him to torture. After making the point that wealth, freedom, and physical well-being are matters of indifference he observes in his concluding line that his moral liberty still remains within his own control: *'ipse deus, simul atque volam, me solvet'* (" 'God himself will release me whenever I will it.' ")[46]

This poem is the closest that Horace comes to a full-scale treatment of Stoic ethics presented with wholehearted approbation. He shows his agreement with several central premises of Stoicism, including the self-sufficiency of virtue, the sage as the exclusive possessor of goodness and happiness, inner intention as the criterion of ethical choices and actions, the moral justification of suicide, vice as self-delusion and enslavement to things that are *adiaphora,* the absence of gradations of vice and virtue, and the sage as connatural with the deity. Horace does not refer expressly to Stoicism or to any Stoic philosopher in this poem, nor does he develop all of the anthropological or metaphysical foundations of the ethical doctrines he cites. Yet *Epistle* 1.16 gives clear evidence of the fact that Horace was perfectly capable, when he was so inclined, of appropriating Stoic teachings accurately and of expressing them with an authentically Stoic flavor.

A much more typical method of treating Stoic ideas on occasions when Horace wishes to present them in an ostensibly sympathetic manner is to place them in contexts where they are coupled with or surrounded by other sources which may be non-Stoic or anti-Stoic in character. Horace often advances a Stoic argument as one among a number of good reasons for adopting a particular attitude or course of action. The other sources involved include Epicureanism, Aristotelianism, traditional Roman morés, and themes from Greek lyric poetry, as well as his own personal opinions as to what is sensible or desirable. In organizing the mix of material in poems which fall into this category, Horace rarely allows the Stoic point of view to carry the day. In this way, while he gives Stoic arguments a positive hearing in a significant number of poems, the net result of his handling of this Stoic material is to dilute its force in relation to the other ideas he is propounding. Stoic teachings are thus cited repeatedly and with approval, but the overall effect and tone of this group of poems is not at all Stoic.

This particular approach to Stoicism is visible in Horace's treatment of four major topics which he often connects thematically with each other: the defense of moderation, the praise of the simple country life, the exhortation to patriotic service, and the idea that happiness lies in one's

---

[46] *Ep.* 1.16.78.
[47] *Sat.* 1.1.49–51; trans. Bovie.

inner wisdom and virtue and not in one's physical location or condition. The advocacy of moderation is a commonplace found in many philosophical schools. It would take a particular rationale for moderation to distinguish a Stoic from a non-Stoic treatment of this *topos*. A Stoic would argue that temperance is a corollary of the norm of life in accordance with reason and nature, using an intellectualistic assessment of his natural needs in determining the measure of his indulgence in things that are fundamentally matters of indifference. He would also argue that the attitude of detachment from the *adiaphora* cultivated by moderation helps the sage to preserve his equanimity in the face of life's vicissitudes. These arguments could be adjusted to a more or a less ascetic way of life depending on the Stoic involved.

Horace makes precisely these Stoic points on behalf of moderation in several of his poems. However, in all cases the Stoic argument is submerged in and swallowed up by alternative reasons for living a temperate life, some of which are antipathetic to Stoicism. In *Satire* 1.1, for instance, Horace advocates moderation in the use of wealth. Avarice, he observes, causes people to labor for greater riches than they naturally need: *vel dic quid referat, intra/ naturae finis vivente, iugera centum an/ mille aret?* ("Tell me, if you please, what's the difference /To the man who knows how to live within nature's true limits,/ Between plowing a good hundred acres and plowing a thousand?")[47] Prudence, Horace adds, dictates that there should be a moderate measure in all things. But, having stated this Stoic rationale for moderating one's wealth, he proceeds to list a host of other reasons for following this course of action, approving the Aristotelian doctrine of the golden mean[48] as well as the Epicurean distinction among needs which are natural and necessary, needs which are natural and not necessary, and needs which are neither natural nor necessary.[49] He also cites a large number of practical common-sense reasons for avoiding avarice: the rich man lives in fear of thieves, of the envious, of his heirs; he is beset by cares and worries, etc.,[50] all of which are as much if not more to the point than the norm of life in accordance with nature. He develops the same arguments with regard to wealth in *Epistle* 1.2.

Moderation in the use of wealth merges insensibly into moderation in the quest for power and status. The theme of ambition is treated in a poem which contains one of Horace's most frequently quoted lines: *nil admirari prope res est una, Numici | solaque quae possit facere et servare beatum*

---

[48] Bovie, intro. to his trans. of *Satires and Epistles*, pp. 14–16. See also *Ep.* 1.18.9 and *Carm.* 2.10.5-6 for passages where Horace refers expressly to the golden mean.

[49] Lejay, intro. to his ed. of *Satires*, pp. 3-6.

[50] *Sat.* 1.1.61–105, 1.1.108–119.

("Marvel at nothing, Numicius. This is the only rule to follow/ That can make and keep you happy.")[51] Some scholars identify the *nil admirari* with the Stoic idea of *apatheia*,[52] some with the Epicurean idea of *ataraxia*,[53] and some with both.[54] Whatever Stoic associations the restriction of one's craving for power may have, Horace immediately engulfs them in a wave of arguments based on the criteria of practicality and pleasure. As in the case of wealth, he points out, political power engenders worry and fear in its possessor and envy in others. Better a modest private life, with simple pleasures, with love and laughter—a position which blends common sense and the Epicurean taste for privacy and pleasure with the Greek lyric theme as expressed by Mimnermus that life is not worth living without love.[55]

Intemperance in the use of wealth also leads to luxury and gourmandise at table. In a satire devoted to this topic Horace advances the Stoic principle that moderation in the matter of food and table ware enables one better to accept the vicissitudes of fortune than does luxury.[56] At the same time, he lays down the Aristotelian criterion of the mean, in this case between the extremes of extravagance and parsimony.[57] This Peripatetic doctrine shares the honors with a series of pragmatic and conventional reasons for keeping a modest table: gastronomic temperance is conducive to good health; it forestalls excessive bills which may prove ruinous to one's patrimony; it enables one to devote some of one's income to pious and charitable causes; and it permits one to avoid a vice which makes one ridiculous in the eyes of friend and foe alike.[58]

In a more general vein, Horace expresses a connection between moderation, the doctrine of the *adiaphora*, and the constancy and equanimity of the sage in several poems which combine these Stoic doctrines with Epicurean and Greek lyric themes. It matters not, he says, whether one is poor and lowborn or rich and of high estate; one should cultivate a calm and steady mind in good times as well as bad.[59] This sounds, and is, quite Stoic. But the reasons he advances for maintaining an untroubled mind are antithetical to Stoicism. Horace proposes the policy of mod-

---

[51] *Ep.* 1.6.1-2.
[52] Campbell, *Horace*, p. 274; Wili, *Horaz*, p. 227.
[53] McGann, *Studies in Horace*, p. 46.
[54] Heinze-Kiessling, comm. on ed. of *Briefe*, pp. 55-56; H. Rushton Fairclough, trans., Horace, *Satires, Epistles, and Ars Poetica*, Loeb (Cambridge, Mass., 1961), p. 284, who also attributes this idea to Pythagoras and Democritus.
[55] *Ep.* 1.6.5-68.
[56] *Sat.* 2.2.106-111, 2.2.126-136.
[57] *Sat.* 2.2.66-69.
[58] *Sat.* 2.2.70-111.
[59] *Carm.* 2.3.1-2, 2.3.21-23.

eration as an Epicurean hostage to fortune. Too much gaiety blunts one's sensibilities, ill prepares one for the absence of happiness, and thus is a potential source of grief. Temperate joys provide pleasures that are more enduring.[60] Then, moving on to another line of argument, he adds the point that no pleasure endures forever since death is unavoidable.[61] Therefore, he concludes, bring on the wine and the flowers; enjoy one's youth while one may.[62]

This mélange of themes, combining the autarchy of the Stoic, the calculated hedonism of the Epicurean, and the Greek lyric poets' consciousness of the fear of impending death as a motive for enjoying the evanescent pleasures of the moment ends by conceding the weight of the argument to the lyric stance. No Stoic would regard the inevitability of death as a rationale for moderation, and certainly not as a rationale for pleasure. The sense of the fragility of life and the inescapability of death as a meaningful context for the quest of pleasure has sometimes been seen as an index of Horace's Epicureanism, both in poems where he counsels moderation and in poems where he proposes the *carpe diem* philosophy.[63] However, it has been shown very clearly that this is not an Epicurean attitude at all.[64] For Epicurus, death has no subjective significance. When it occurs, the human ego *ipso facto* ceases to exist. Epicurus' main concern at this point is to disallow the belief in man's posthumous survival and thereby to offer deliverance from the fear of death, not to promote either a bittersweet sensibility or a frantic attempt to grasp at life's pleasures in the fearsome light of life's transiency. For Epicurus, death is a neutral event and the thought of its impending arrival should have no influence on our way of life. It is rather to the Greek lyric tradition, especially as represented by Alcaeus and Simonides, that one must look in seeking Horace's source for the association of transitory pleasure with the fear of death.[65] It is debatable whether Horace succeeds, in poems where he tries to do so such as *Carmina* 2.3, in synthesizing the appeal to moderation on Epicurean grounds with the lyric appeal to the wine and the flowers. But one thing certain is that the Stoicizing elements in poems of this type cede pride of place to either or to both of these motifs.

---

[60] *Carm.* 2.3.3-4; *Carm.* 3.1.14-48.

[61] *Carm.* 2.3.4, 2.3.23-28.

[62] *Carm.* 2.3.13-16; *Carm.* 1.11; *Carm.* 2.16.9-16, 2.16.25-40; *Ep.* 1.4.11-13.

[63] On the three odes just discussed, see Heinze-Kiessling, comm. on ed. of *Oden*, pp. 224-29, 250; W. Kroll, "Horaz' Oden und die Philosophie," *WS, 37* (1915), 223-38.

[64] See the excellent analysis of Epicureanism on this point by Philip Merlan, "Epicureanism and Horace," *JHI, 10* (1949), 445-51, a paper that deserves more attention from Horace critics than it has received.

[65] Heinze-Kiessling, comm. on ed. of *Oden*, pp. 48, 54 à propos of *Carm.* 1.11; Williams, *Tradition and Originality*, p. 114.

An idea closely associated with his advocacy of moderation to which Horace reverts again and again is the praise of the simple country life. Such a mode of life combines frugality and privacy, a style of life to which Stoicism is perfectly amenable so long as it is undertaken in consideration of the unimportance of external circumstances to virtue. Whether the sage follows a public or a private career, he has a duty to serve his fellow men. Either mode of life may be virtuous if it is embraced for the right reasons. While the Stoics on the whole tend to stress public service, they also accept the *vita privata* when it is sought in order to separate oneself from unavoidable dishonor in serving a corrupt regime and as a means of engaging in contemplation and teaching for the benefit of others. Some Stoics connect the life of retirement in the country with the moral value of manual labor, especially agricultural labor on one's own land, an idea that surfaces in the idealization of Cincinnatus at the plow as a Stoic saint. Such a style of life is praiseworthy because it combines closeness to the soil, frugality, and the rejection of self-aggrandizement in the forum.

Horace appears to be well aware of at least some of the grounds on which Stoicism could be brought to bear on the praise of the simple country life. In one poem he correlates simplicity and retirement with the themes of detachment and equanimity in the face of the flux of life.[66] But he immediately assimilates what might otherwise be an assertion of Stoic autarchy to the Epicurean argument that the simple independent life is the true pathway to pleasure and he surrounds it with an appeal to the joys of the country deriving from the bucolic tradition.[67] In another poem dealing with the country life Horace tips his hat to the Stoic interiorizing of ethical values by remarking that the best rule of life is an internal one, not one accepted from without.[68] But what he does in the rest of the poem is to divest the maxim of any specifically Stoic content by using it to justify his preference for the country over the city, a preference springing from his own personal inclinations and not from any philosophical premises. The most striking instance of Horace's capacity for denaturing a Stoic principle while extolling the country life on Epicurean, bucolic, pragmatic, and personal grounds is *Epistle* 1.10. Here, he presents the Stoic rationale straightforwardly: one must live in accordance with nature:

Vivere naturae si convenienter oportet,
ponendaeque domo quaerenda est area primum,
novistine locum potiorem rure beato? ...

---

[66] *Carm.* 3.29.32-56.
[67] *Carm.* 3.29.9-16, 3.29.21-32, 3.29.57-64.
[68] *Ep.* 1.7.98.

Naturam expellas furca, tamen usque recurret,
et mala perrumpet furtim fastidia victrix.[69]

If it is proper to live in accordance with nature
And to build one's house having sought the best location,
Do you know any spot better than the country? ...
Expel nature with a pitchfork; she'll be back again
And triumph over vain contempt.

These Stoic thoughts, however, are set amid bucolic evocations of the scenic beauty of the country, Epicurean allusions to the superior pleasure found in simplicity and privacy, practical considerations such as the uncertainty and expense of the life of the urban striver, and above all Horace's personal tastes. Whatever else may be said for the country, the primordial reason why Horace lives there is because he likes it; his own preferences constitute a moral absolute. Not only does he inundate the Stoic principle which he cites with his other arguments, he also empties it of its specifically Stoic denotation by using it to support a conception of nature that means little else besides a landscape and a life-style which he finds personally congenial. As Gordon Williams has well said in his comment on this poem, "Horace is perpetrating a confidence trick by using 'nature' in the sense in which it is contrasted with convention and society. ... This is a very far cry from the Stoics and from any reasonable sense that could be attached to *naturae convenienter vivere*. Horace has taken philosophical commonplaces and warped them into a new meaning of his own."[70]

There are other poems in which Horace omits the Stoic rationale for the simple country life and contents himself with bending the Epicurean distaste for public life and the conventional wisdom relative to the worry, greed, fear, and insecurity attendant on the life of urban luxury and ambition to the support of his personal proclivities, as, for instance, in *Satire* 1.6, *Satire* 2.6, and *Carmina* 3.16. He even seems willing to trump the argument he gives elsewhere in support of the *carpe diem* position in this connection by placing a speech advocating the enjoyment of fleeting pleasures in the face of the inevitability of death in the mouth of the Town Mouse,[71] in the satire where he exalts the frugality of the Country Mouse. Apart from the subordination of Stoicism, along with Horace's

---

[69] *Ep.* 1.10.12-14, 1.10.24-25.

[70] Williams, *Tradition and Originality*, pp. 594-96. See also pp. 315-16, 593. For other poems in which Horace exalts the simple country life see *Ep.* 1.5 and *Ep.* 1.14. As Williams notes, *Tradition and Originality*, pp. 9, 11-13, 103-31, the emphasis on frugality in such poems can also be seen as a traditional feature of the invitation poem.

[71] *Sat.* 2.6.90-96.

other sources, to his personal tastes when he deals with this theme, many
of the poems in which he extols the simple country life admit of another
possible interpretation. A number of them are either addressed explicitly
to Maecenas[72] or reveal through internal references to him that he is the
intended recipient.[73] These poems might therefore be read as graceful
thank-you notes expressing Horace's gratitude to the patron who had
provided him with the Sabine farm, whose setting he loved and whose
income made possible his financial security and poetic leisure.

Horace is fully capable, when the spirit moves him, of shifting his
emphasis to the praise of the active life. Here, the Stoics had much to
offer in the way of philosophical support. Indeed, Horace seems to be
adverting to the Panaetian norm of decorum in his famous phrase, *dulce
et decorum est pro patria mori* ("it is sweet and fitting to die for one's country,")[74] a thought reiterated in a later ode where Horace avers that true
blessedness consists not in possessions but in satisfaction with what one
has and in the willingness to sacrifice one's life in defense of one's friends
or homeland.[75] These statements have sometimes been read as an expression of Stoic civic spirit,[76] as an index of how Horace's Stoic seriousness
grew with his advancing years. It might be argued, however, that such
sentiments are fully consistent with traditional Roman patriotism and
could be advocated by partisans of that ethos without recourse to the
Stoa. Horace does not refer to any of the metaphysical or anthropological
principles undergirding his injunctions to public service which would
place them unequivocally within a Stoic framework of ideas. At the same
time, there are clear affinities between the message conveyed by Horace
in these two poems and the long-standing Greek lyric tradition of patriotic poetry, represented in particular by Tyrtaeus and Simonides.[77]
Carmina 4.9 provides considerable support for the conclusion that what
Horace was really aiming at in his patriotic odes was a Latinization of
this tradition. Here he praises patriotism in the context of a poem expatiating on the public need for poets. Great men, he notes, must have
poets to sing their praises if their deeds are to be immortalized, a service
which Horace himself, like his Greek predecessors, is prepared to render.[78] In this case, Horace's awareness of himself as a transmitter of the
Greek lyric tradition provides the tone that permeates his patriotic poems
most strongly.

---

[72] *Sat.* 1.6; *Carm.* 3.16; *Ep.* 1.7.
[73] *Sat.* 2.6.
[74] *Carm.* 3.2.13.
[75] *Carm.* 4.9.45-53.
[76] Heinze-Kiessling, comm. on ed. of *Oden*, pp. 441-42.
[77] Ibid., p. 258.
[78] *Carm.* 4.9.5-12.

Contentment with what one has, an attitude inspiring Horace to praise both the simple country life and the life of heroic public service, depending on his mood, is also an element in his treatment of the fourth and last theme in this category of his works. The Stoa linked contentment, on the one hand, with the recognition that a great many things are matters of indifference and, on the other hand, with the notion that the virtue possessed by the sage is a fixed inner intention unaffected by the presence or absence of the *adiaphora*. Horace suggests this constellation of ideas in his handling of a topic later to receive full-scale Stoic treatment by Seneca in his *Ad Helviam matrem*: the idea that one's peace of soul is not a function of one's geographical location but that it resides in one's inner wisdom and virtue. Horace treats this theme in three of his poems, where he argues that exile cannot disturb the equanimity of the wise man and that travel does not enable a disturbed soul to flee from itself. In all cases, however, this Stoic sentiment is associated with Epicurean and lyric themes which succeed in turning it inside out. As Horace puts it in his most quotable line on this subject, *caelum, non animum, mutant qui trans mare currunt* ("They change their skies but not their souls who hasten across the seas.")[79] But the reason why such behavior is misguided is that it neglects what makes life truly worth living; and that, says Horace, is pleasure:

> Tu quamcumque deus tibi fortunaverit horam
> grata sume manu neu dulcia differ in annum,
> ut quocumque loco fueris vixisse libenter
> te dicas;[80]

> Whatever excellent hour a god has bestowed
> Upon you, take it gratefully, graciously take it in hand—
> Do not postpone your pleasure from year to year.
> Thus, you'll be able to say, 'I've *lived* today,'
> Wherever you are.

The constancy of the Stoic sage is thus made an integer in an equation which concludes by supporting the Epicurean criterion of pleasure.

Similarly, in *Carmina* 1.7, Horace presents the Stoic position counseling calmness in the face of exile in the words of Teucer, who exhorts his companions to submit to the decree of heaven without dismay.[81] At the same time, the same speaker as well as Horace speaking in his own persona acknowledge that exile brings sorrow and they advocate wine as the

---

[79] *Ep.* 1.11.27.
[80] *Ep.* 1.11.22-25; trans. Bovie.
[81] *Carm.* 1.7.25-29.

anodyne for it.[82] It has been urged that this counter-argument is an Epicurean one,[83] but it seems equally if not more plausible to see it as a reminiscence of the Greek lyric tradition of the drinking song represented in particular by Alcaeus, which advocates the winecup as the sovereign response to all circumstances, whether sorrowful or joyful. Finally, as Horace notes in a poem already discussed in another connection, neither the traveller nor the exile is able to escape from himself.[84] Tranquillity is fleeting in this life, as life itself is. Happiness is never perfect; but the best way to seek it is through contentment with the simple life.[85] Horace concludes this personal blend of Epicurean *temperantia* and the lyric lament at the inevitability of death with the equally personal advice to his addressee to emulate Horace's own wisdom:

> Mihi parva rura et
> spiritum Graiae tenuem Camenae
> Parca non mendax dedit et malignum
> spernere vulgus.[86]

> I was not cheated by Fate,
> who gave me a little farm and a spirit
> sensitive to Grecian poetry, above
> the crowd and its spite.

In this passage, as in so many of the poems in the category that has just been examined, the reader can observe the freedom with which Horace uses his materials, Stoic, Epicurean, poetic, and traditional, tempering them in the crucible of his own personal taste and using them with great flexibility to meet a variety of poetic occasions. Although Stoicism scarcely predominates in the poems within this group, does this mean that some other school takes pride of place, that a new synthesis has been created, or that philosophy has been used in a purely decorative manner? And can the evidence provided by this large group of poems be generalized to apply to Horace's *oeuvre* as a whole? Before any answer can be given to these questions, one further category of Horatian poems must be considered. In the works just discussed, Stoic ideas are frequently cited with approval although they are even more frequently distorted or emasculated by their association with and subordination to ideas derived from other sources. In the final group of poems to be examined, Stoic ideas

---

[82] *Carm.* 1.7.17–34.
[83] Edmund T. Silk, "Notes on Cicero and the Odes of Horace," *Yale Classical Studies,* *13* (1952), 148–49.
[84] *Carm.* 2.16.18–20.
[85] *Carm.* 2.16.11–15, 2.16.25–32.
[86] *Carm.* 2.16.37–40.

are often presented clearly and forcefully, but only to be satirized, treated ironically, or expressly rejected. But in the name of what alternatives are they rejected?

The group of poems to which we now turn is much smaller than the category just treated, but it provides readers of Horace with the most detailed information on Stoicism found anywhere in his works. In particular, several poems of Horace criticize gleefully the Stoic ideal of the sage and two other ideas connected to this doctrine, the equality of all vices and the notion of friendship as a relationship of which sages alone are capable. In this group of poems Horace often identifies the ideas he is attacking by specific reference to Stoicism, to individual members of the school, or to personages traditionally regarded as exemplars of Stoic virtue. Many of the poems in this group are marked by a fine touch of ironic humor.

Sometimes Horace incorporates an apparently favorable view of the Stoic sage within the poem, only to expose and ridicule his attributes. In *Epistle* 1.1 he outlines at some length the vices which he thinks should be rejected, contrasting the constancy of the sage with the fickleness of the fool, always subject to his latest whims, unable to concentrate, unable to find satisfaction in anything.[87] However, he precedes this disquisition with the question of whether his own recent interest in the pursuit of virtue is an indication of such a lack of constancy in himself. If he were truly constant, he implies, he would not seek to change himself, even in the name of virtue. In any event, he adds, it is silly to believe that one can ever achieve moral perfection.[88] And, he concludes with a witty *reductio ad absurdum* of the Stoic sage who not only claims that such perfection can exist but also that he embodies it:

> Sapiens uno minor est Iove, dives,
> liber, honoratus, pulcher, rex denique regum,
> praecipue sanus, nisi cum pitvita molesta est.[89]

> The wise man is only surpassed by Jove.
> He is well off, respected, handsome, the free king above
> All kings. And above all, being RIGHT in the head,
> He's always quite well ... if a cold doesn't keep him in bed.

In another poem in the same vein, Horace begins by poking fun at Tigellius the singer and his inconsistent style of life, at one moment lavish, at the next miserly.[90] In this case, however, the appeal to the constancy

---

[87] *Ep.* 1.1.31-79.
[88] *Ep.* 1.1.80-106.
[89] *Ep.* 1.1.106-108; trans. Bovie.
[90] *Sat.* 1.3.1-19.

of the sage is a teaser for a lengthy argument opposing the Stoic notion
that friendship can be enjoyed by sages alone. Citing Chrysippus, Horace
rejects the idea that the sage is truly the king, the rich man, the most
handsome, or that he alone knows all things perfectly.[91] The false conception of the sage which he is trying to expose reflects in turn a false
conception of virtue and vice. Virtues and vices, says Horace, here contradicting his position in Satire 1.1, are not devoid of degrees:

> Adsit
> regula, peccatis quae poenas irroget aequas,
> ne scutica dignum horribili sectere flagello.[92]

> There must be a sliding scale
> By which crimes can be punished in the degree they deserve,
> So that what should be whipped is not fanatically flayed.

The Stoic conception of virtue, in addition, is based on the premise that
the sage makes correct judgments, evaluating objects according to their
conformity with reason and their consistency with the idea of the good,
one of the *ennoia* or common notions which all men acquire more or less
automatically. Vices in turn spring from erroneous judgments. For Horace, however, both vice and virtue have different roots. Vices, he asserts,
arise from nature or from habit,[93] not from false judgments. As for virtue,
he paints a picture of man evolving from brutish origins and developing
a moral code only out of a fear of injustice. Man, he says, has no natural
moral sense. Reason in itself is incapable of ascertaining what virtue is,
at least if one defines all virtues as equally virtuous and all vices as equally
vicious.[94] Rather, utility and common sense are the sources of virtue; and
according to these criteria it is impossible to maintain that all virtues are
equally virtuous and all vices equally vicious.[95]

This whole argument discrediting the sage and his virtue is designed
to discredit the Stoic idea of friendship. If the idea of such a sage is itself
senseless, then the claim that sages alone qualify for friendship must be
rejected as well. We ourselves are not perfect, says Horace, but our affection causes us to overlook or even to look fondly on the limitations of
those we love. Thus, we should accept our friends with all their faults if
we wish to be accepted by them in return.[96] This poem has sometimes

---

[91] *Sat.* 1.3.123-142.
[92] *Sat.* 1.3.117-119; trans. Bovie.
[93] *Sat.* 1.3.35-36.
[94] *Sat.* 1.3.98-123.
[95] *Sat.* 1.3.96-98.
[96] *Sat.* 1.3.36-95.

been read as a refutation of Stoicism in favor of the Epicurean doctrine
of friendship.[97] Paul Lejay is undoubtedly correct, however, in describing
Horace in this satire as "encore plus hostile à Zénon que favorable à
Épicure."[98] The dominant note in the poem is less a desire to find a
philosophical counterweight to the Stoic position than to eschew any
form of idealism that might judge Horace adversely and enjoin him to
change his ways. As he puts it, *quam temere in nosmet legem sancimus iniquam!*
("How rash we are to pass a law that punishes, chiefly, ourselves!")[99]
He criticizes the Stoa from the vantage point of a man who is satisfied
with himself the way he is, and who has no intention of reforming.

On two occasions Horace refers specifically to historical personages
who had been invested in the Stoic tradition with an aura of sanctity as
exemplary sages. In both cases he abruptly dissociates himself from the
ethos which they represent, in the name of worldly wisdom or the exigencies of his craft as he chooses to interpret it. In one of his epistles he
takes pains to proclaim the fact that he is a lyric poet. As such, it would
hardly be fitting for him to adopt the ways of the barefoot and abstemious
Cato; a poet, as everyone knows, must drink deeply.[100] Elsewhere he
considers and contrasts the positions of Diogenes, the Cynic-Stoic saint,
and Aristippus, the Cyrenaic hedonist who ridiculed his frugal style of
life. According to Diogenes' position, it is wise to be content with little.
But, according to Aristippus, true wisdom consists in being clever enough
so as not to have to be content with little, a sentiment with which Horace
concurs.[101]

The two poems in this category in which the Stoic sage is analyzed
and satirized the most exhaustively are *Satire* 2.3 and *Satire* 2.7. Both of
these poems are written in the form of dialogues in which Horace takes
part as one of the speakers. In *Satire* 2.3, the other interlocutor is Damasippus, who introduces himself as a recent convert to the Stoic philosophy. Having failed in his own business, he now occupies himself with
other people's,[102] as a disciple of the Stoic Stertinus. The bulk of the
poem consists of a speech in which Damasippus reports Stertinus' teachings to Horace. In addition to conveying the substance of Stoic ethics on
a number of important topics, Damasippus' recapitulation of Stertinus'
speech provides considerable information on the Stoic diatribe style and
on certain Stoic modes of argumentation. The Stoic conception of the

---

[97] Cartault, *Étude sur les satires*, p. 69; Wili, *Horaz*, pp. 91-93.
[98] Lejay, comm. on his ed. of *Satires*, p. 61.
[99] *Sat.* 1.3.67; trans. Bovie.
[100] *Ep.* 1.19.12-14.
[101] *Ep.* 1.17.11-32.
[102] *Sat.* 2.3.18-20.

physical world as a series of concrete events is reflected in the speaker's tendency to enumerate specific examples and to rely on particular proofs rather than to generalize; his appeal to the *consensus omnium* is also an appeal to the doctrine of *ennoia*; he uses hypothetical rather than deductive syllogisms as well as a number of technical Stoic terms.[103]

As far as the content of Damasippus' speech is concerned, he begins by asserting that virtue pertains to the sage alone and that everyone else is a fool and a madman. He then proceeds to analyze four major follies or forms of madness: avarice, ambition, luxury, and superstition. He defines these vices in a typically Stoic sense as arising from erroneous judgments which do not correspond with the truth because the subject's mind has been clouded by his emotions:

> Qui species alias veri scelerisque tumultu
> permixtas capiet, commotus habebitur, atque
> stultitiane erret nihilum distabit an ira.[104]

> The man whose impressions fail to square with the truth
> And are further confused by a tumult of guilty emotions
> I consider somewhat disturbed: it makes no difference
> Whether folly or anger leads him away from the path.

He likewise defines virtue as conformity to what nature requires.[105] Yet, despite the solidly Stoic content of this poem, Horace turns it into an ironic comment on Stoic virtue, both its teachings and the men who claim to exemplify them. His *ad hominem* argument is directed not only against Damasippus, the failed businessman become busybody, but also against his master Stertinus. While Stertinus is not depicted as hypocritical or contradictory in his arguments, his speech as reported lacks stylistic consistency, wavering between mundane examples set forth in colloquial language, technical schoolroom analysis, and high-flown classical allusions. Although the vices dealt with in this satire are clearly and Stoically defined as springing from irrational and unnatural desires, the actual counsels to virtue as developed in the body of Damasippus' speech are not based on appeals to reason and nature but rather on appeals to practical utility, many of which are also found in other poems that treat these same themes. Avarice is to be shunned because of the burdens and worries that wealth places on its possessor, leading to such fear of loss

---

[103] An excellent and detailed analysis of the use of Stoic methods of argument in this satire is provided by Lejay, comm. on his ed. of *Satires*, pp. 356-90. See also Cartault, *Étude sur les satires*, pp. 82-86.

[104] *Sat.* 2.3.208-210.

[105] *Sat.* 2.3.177-178.

and even to the fear for his life that he cannot enjoy what he has. Ambition leads a man to dissipate his patrimony and even to commit impious crimes in order to gain power and political support. Luxury likewise leads to prodigality while its subdivision, lust, makes a man the ridiculous toy of a fickle jade. Superstition is a massive rejection of expediency, encouraging its adherents even to endanger their health in the hope of wresting concessions from the gods. Throughout, the substance of these arguments is an appeal not to Stoic rationalism but to common sense, investing with normative value considerations which a Stoic would regard as vicious or indifferent concerns. At the end of Damasippus' speech he diagnoses Horace as a sufferer from the very maladies which he has been discussing. Horace, in turn, asserts categorically that he has no interest in seeing these judgments applied to himself and dismisses Damasippus as a pompous meddler.[106]

In *Satire* 2.3, Stoicism is satirized by means of an "as told to" treatment in the person of a failed businessman. In *Satire* 2.7 Horace gives his subject analogous treatment, but this time through the arguments of his slave, Davus, who has obtained his information about Stoicism even more indirectly, by means of another slave who serves as doorkeeper to the Stoic preacher Crispinus. As Lejay remarks, "nous descendons d'un degré."[107] The occasion in the poem which allows Davus to express himself with such audacity to his master is the feast of the Saturnalia, when slaves were traditionally granted a good deal of freedom of speech and action. Both the holiday setting of the poem and the content of the dialogue are designed to focus attention on the central point of the satire, the Stoic paradox that only the sage is truly free. Davus' speech develops this point, attempting to show that he, albeit a slave, is morally free, while Horace, his master, is morally enslaved by his vices and passions. Davus offers a full and formal Stoic statement of this theme indicating that he is well aware of its essential nature:

> Quisnam igitur liber? Sapiens, sibi qui imperiosus,
> quem neque pauperies neque mors neque vincula terrent,
> responsare cupidinibus, contemnere honores
> fortis, et in se ipso totus, teres, atque rotundus,
> externine quid valeat per leve morari,
> in quem manca ruit semper fortuna.[108]

---

[106] *Sat.* 2.3.300–326.

[107] Lejay, comm. on his ed. of *Satires*, p. 539.

[108] *Sat.* 2.7.83–88; trans. Bovie. Spherical shape is a standard Stoic image as applied to the sage; see, for example, Seneca, *Apoc.* 8. It is also applied to the deity by Cicero in *De nat. deor.* 2.16.45 ff.

Who, then, is free?
The wise man alone, who has full command of himself,
Whom poverty, death, or chains cannot terrify,
Who is strong enough to defy his passions and scorn
Prestige, who is wholly contained in himself, well rounded,
Smooth as a sphere on which nothing external can fasten.

But in the unravelling of the argument, which reflects some traces of the
Stoic rhetorical style, particularly in the use of concrete examples,[109] the
illustrations which Davus provides and the rationale which he offers both
depart markedly from Stoic doctrine, thereby reducing disastrously his
credibility as a spokesman for Stoic ethics.

Horace tips his hand concerning the outcome of the satire by giving
Davus some introductory lines which raise serious doubts as to whether
he really knows what he is talking about. Davus begins with an encomi-
um on the virtue of constancy as an attribute of the sage[110] before going
on to criticize Horace for his enslavement to adultery, to luxury at table,
to drinking, and to sloth.[111] Inconstancy and perennial dissatisfaction
with what one has, this order suggests, are the sources of these other vices.
Thus, Davus' analysis of inconstancy is a clue to the plausibility which
Horace is going to concede to him as a spokesman of Stoic ethics in the
rest of the poem. In elaborating on the virtue of constancy, Davus contrasts two notorious playboys, Priscus and Voleranius. Priscus, a liber-
tine, is criticized for his short attention span and his precipitous alternations in behavior while Voleranius, a compulsive gambler, is praised
for his unwavering absorption in his vice, to the point of hiring a servant
to rattle the dice for him when his fingers become crippled by gout.
However, for the Stoic, it goes without saying, singlemindedness in the
pursuit of vice is no virtue. The fixed intentionality of the fool which
permeates all of his deeds with evil is not the constancy of the sage but
rather its negative mirror image. The fact that Davus has misunderstood
this point at the very outset of the poem suggests that he is an unworthy
guide indeed in the realms of Stoic ethics which follow.

As Davus proceeds to outline Horace's vices and to explain why they
are morally wrong, he uses a strategy which we have already noticed in
Satire 2.3 and in a number of other works—the defense of Stoic principles
by means of non-Stoic arguments which have the effect of undermining
them. In particular, he relies on utilitarian considerations and the fear
of being thought ridiculous by society, arguments which a Stoic would

---

[109] See Lejay, comm. on his ed. of *Satires*, p. 545, for an analysis of Stoic argumentative
rhetoric in this satire.
[110] *Sat.* 2.7.6-20.
[111] *Sat.* 2.7.22-115.

reject as beneath contempt. Also, some of the examples which Davus
adduces in support of his case are in rather questionable taste, suggesting
the vulgarity of his outlook and the unlikeliness that a hearer with the
slightest degree of fastidiousness could bring himself to agree with him.
Thus, for instance, in treating the topic to which he gives most of his
attention, Davus contrasts his own virtue in sexual matters with Horace's
vicious attachment to adulterous love affairs. However, far from depicting himself as a man who is liberated from the temptations of the flesh,
he proclaims himself morally superior to Horace because he has recourse
to prostitutes when he feels the need while Horace runs after other men's
wives. And why is adultery to be shunned? Here Davus offers a set of
purely pragmatic reasons—the annoyance and indignity of having to
conduct one's sex life in a furtive and clandestine manner, the danger of
prosecution or of summary vengeance on the part of the betrayed husband, and the arrogance, fickleness, and egotism of a free woman as a
mistress. Similarly, in criticizing Horace for his enslavement to his stomach, Davus presents the standard practical arguments against gourmandise, noting that it is bad for one's physical and financial health. But in
elevating himself morally above Horace, he does not claim any indifference to food himself but merely states his personal preference for hearty,
ordinary fare as opposed to the rich cuisine preferred by Horace.

Thus, far from embodying the virtue of the Stoic sage either in his own
behavior or in the rationale for it which he advances,[112] Davus' character
and argument are devices through which Horace achieves an ironic in-
version of the Stoic moral message.[113] Davus is a travesty of that message
rather than an exponent of it. And, given the fact that he has failed to
understand that he himself stands condemned just as much by the rational norms of the Stoa as the master whom he ventures to castigate, it
is not surprising that this satire should conclude, as does Satire 2.3, with
Horace's abrupt dismissal of his vis-à-vis as in no way qualified to ha-
rangue him on virtue and as in no way persuasive. Saturnalia or no Saturnalia, he reminds Davus that he is, in real life, a slave, and orders him
to hold his tongue on pain of being reduced to hard labor as a field
hand.[114]

In both of these satires, replete with Stoic ideas, the claims of Stoicism
are systematically and humorously subverted. On one level, this process
is achieved by the fact that Horace places Stoic arguments in the mouths

---

[112] A point which many scholars have failed to notice. See, for example, Frank, Horace
and Catullus, p. 180; Lejay, comm. on his ed. of Satires, p. 550; M. J. McGann, "The Three
Worlds of Horace's 'Satires'," in Horace, ed. Costa, pp. 73-74.

[113] Noted by Cartault, Étude sur les satires, pp. 94-97.

[114] Sat. 2.7.117-118.

of speakers who are anything but compelling examples of the wisdom and virtue which they profess. On another level, it is achieved by the inability of these speakers to defend the Stoic principles they advocate with anything but non-Stoic arguments. On a third, and probably the most basic level, it is achieved by Horace's presentation of himself as a man who is not fundamentally interested in seeking the *summum bonum* if it involves changing his way of life in any particular. It would be perfectly possible to criticize and to ridicule the paradoxes cloaking the ancient Stoic sage from the standpoint of a competing philosophical position, including that of the middle Stoa. In the group of poems we have just been considering, however, Horace does not do this; he does not attack Zeno or Chrysippus in the name of Epicurus or Aristotle or Panaetius. Rather, he attacks the claims of ancient Stoic ethics in these poems on the grounds that they weigh him in the balance and find him wanting. But he is a man who has no difficulty living with his own foibles. He lacks all interest in becoming his own best self if that means becoming something which he currently is not. The moral stance which Horace adopts here is the same as the one he advertises in his first epistle. There, he announces that his criterion in making his selections from the different schools of philosophy is *mihi res, non me rebus, subiungere conor* ("to fit the world to myself, not me to it.")[115] Or, as he adds elsewhere, he intends to use common sense and his own temperamental affinities as his norms for judging what should be followed and what avoided.[116] In practice what Horace wants is what he already has:

> Frui paratis et valido mihi,
> Latoe, dones, at, precor, integra
> cum mente, nec turpem senectam
> degere nec cithara carentem.[117]

> Apollo, give me joy in what I have,
> I pray, and with good health and a steady mind,
> May my old age be spent without
> Dishonor, and not be deprived of the lyre.

The *mens aequum* for which Horace prays is less the *apatheia* of the Stoic, the tranquillity of the Epicurean, or the equilibrium of the Aristotelian than the undisturbed contentment of a man who lives at ease within his own skin and within his own world, and who would have it no other way.

---

[115] *Ep.* 1.1.19; trans. Bovie.
[116] *Sat.* 1.4.104-137.
[117] *Carm.* 1.31.17-20; trans. Clancy. See also *Ep.* 1.18.106-112.

A final case in which Horace adverts to Stoic doctrines at some points while expressly negating them in the main thrust of the work is in his treatment of poetic theory. Horace brings up this subject in a number of his poems but gives it his most extended treatment in the *Ars poetica*. This work has inspired a larger body of commentary than any of Horace's other poems. As might be expected, the range of opinions as to its meaning parallels the views on Horace's relationship to his sources found on the broader spectrum of Horace criticism.[118] Debate has centered on the ultimate provenance of particular ideas on literary theory which Horace expresses in the *Ars poetica* as well as on the overall tenor of his poetics. Even more debate has been devoted to the identification of the intermediaries through whom Horace may have obtained his ideas. Horace sometimes makes express reference to literary theory which can be identified with that of the Stoa. But here, as in the other works within this category of his *oeuvre*, he counteracts them with other theories to which he subscribes much more enthusiastically. In the case of literary theory, however, his reasons for rejecting Stoic ideas tend to be far more speculative than is the case with the ethical doctrines in the group of poems examined immediately above.

Horace shows a certain familiarity with the Stoic conception of the nature and function of poetic style. As a poet himself, he frequently assumes the stance of an educator, a moralist, and a director of conscience. Sometimes he refers expressly to the power of poetry to promote the virtue of its audience even more efficaciously than philosophical exposition,[119] a position of which the Stoics among all the schools of ancient philosophy were the strongest defenders.[120] Horace also refers expressly to the idea of poetry as a function of wisdom and virtue on the part of the poet, combining in one passage two related themes—the importance of the poet's knowledge of moral truths and the importance of a style in which the language corresponds with things as they truly are, the subject matter dictating the choice of words:

> Scribendi recte sapere est et principium et fons. ...
> Verbaque provisam rem non invita sequentur.

---

[118] Useful guides to the literature devoted to the *Ars poetica* are provided for critics prior to World War I by Roy Kenneth Hack, "The Doctrine of Literary Forms," *HSCP*, 27 (1916), 1-16 and most recently and exhaustively by Brink, *Horace on Poetry, 1*, 15-40.

[119] *Ep.* 1.2.1-4; *Ep.* 2.1.124-138; *Ars Poet.* 391-396.

[120] Noted by Carl Becker, *Das Spätwerk des Horaz* (Göttingen, 1963), p. 38; Courbaud, *Horace*, pp. 202-27; Mary A. Grant and George C. Fiske, "Cicero's 'Orator' and Horace's 'Ars Poetica'," *HSCP, 35* (1924), 66; F. Solmsen, "Drei Rekonstruktionen zur antiken Rhetorik und Poetik, III, Horaz ars poet. 391 ff.," *Hermes, 67* (1932), 154. Cf. Brink, *Horace on Poetry, 1*, 133 n. 2; 136 n. 1, who sees this as a generally traditional idea.

Qui didicit patriae quid debeat et quid amicis,
quo sit amore parens, quo frater amandus et hospes ...
ille profecto
reddere personae scit convenientia cuique.[121]

Knowledge is both the origin and source of good writing. ...
And with the subject matter well in hand, the words will follow freely.
The man who has learned what he owes to his country and what to friends,
The love due to a parent, to a brother, to a guest, ...
He indeed will know how to write suitably
About each of his characters.

This passage conveys clearly the Stoic correlation between the good poet and the good man,[122] as well as providing a verbal reminiscence of the elder Cato's Stoic stylistic maxim, *rem tene verba sequentur*.[123] Finally, as is generally agreed,[124] Horace is referring to Stoicism when he counsels brevity, simplicity, and integrity, stylistic norms which he applies to the visual arts as well as to poetry.[125]

Yet, what happens to this Stoic didacticism served by a rational, simple style? Both in theory and in practice, Horace rejects it in favor of a conception of poetry that derives from sharply contrasting sources and which is expressed in the *Ars poetica* and throughout his works by means of stylistic devices far removed from those propounded by the Stoa. Horace proposes the stylistic norm of appropriateness and decorum, an apparently Stoic idea derived from Panaetian ethics and the plain style of the Scipionic circle.[126] However, when he moves on to a more specific discussion of linguistic and stylistic strategies, Horace firmly rejects the Stoic preference for the *verba antiqua*, arguing that new ideas and new circumstances give rise to new words and that convention or usage are the prime tests of correct language.[127] This notion has been traced by some scholars

---

[121] *Ars poet.* 309–316.

[122] Noted by Becker, *Spätwerk des Horaz*, pp. 97, 198; Fiske, *Horace and Lucilius*, p. 477; Grant and Fiske, "Cicero's 'Orator'," pp. 48–49; Heinze-Kiessling, comm. on ed. of *Briefe*, p. 285. On the other hand, Brink, *Horace on Poetry*, *1*, 131 n. 1, 2; *2*, 338–39 sees this point as a commonplace shared by all philosophical schools.

[123] Noted by Bovie, intro. to trans. of *Satires and Epistles*, p. 242; Fiske, "Lucilius, the *Ars Poetica*, and Persius," *HSCP*, *24* (1913), 11; Heinze-Kiessling, comm. on ed. of *Briefe*, p. 344. Even Brink, *Horace on Poetry*, *1*, 256; *2*, 340–41 acknowledges the reference to Cato although he thinks that it should not be taken too seriously.

[124] Brink, *Horace on Poetry*, *2*, 108; Grant and Fiske, "Cicero's 'Orator'," pp. 22–23.

[125] *Ars poet.* 1–26.

[126] The most fully developed argument on behalf of this claim is by Max Pohlenz, "*To Prepon*: Ein Beitrag zur Geschichte des griechischen Geistes," *Nachrichten von der Gesellschaft der Wissenschaften zu Göttingen*, philologisch-historische Klasse, Fachgruppe I (Altertumswissenschaft), *16* (1933), 53–92. See also Fiske, *Lucilius and Horace*, pp. 84–85, 88–94, 124–34,447; Costil, "L'Esthétique stoicienne." *Actes du 1er congrès ... des Associations d'études classiques* (Paris, 1951, pp. 360–64.

[127] *Ars poet.* 46–72.

to Epicureanism and by others to Aristotelianism,[128] but the critical point is that it stands in sharp contrast to the Stoic theory of words as natural signs, which served as the basis for their linguistic and grammatical doctrines.

Since Horace's conception of language is fully non-Stoic it is not surprising to find that his practical application of the norm of decorum should also depart from the Stoic theory of style despite its associations with middle Stoic ethics. Horace's source for the stylistic norm of decorum has been traced back to Cicero, who is seen in turn as a transmitter of either Platonic[129] or Aristotelian ideas;[130] another school of commentators argues that Horace derived this notion from Aristotle by way of Neoptolemus.[131] While Horace is clearly concerned with the congruity between style and subject matter, he is equally concerned with the congruity between style and audience. This orientation reflects a sharp departure from the Stoic notion that the poet should appeal exclusively to the intellect of his hearers in preference for the Aristotelian and Ciceronian stress on the need to consider the ethos of the audience as well. One reason for this advice is a purely practical one: teaching and persuasion should be accomplished by whatever strategy is most effective, which may well mean an appeal to the hearer's emotions. For Horace, as for Cicero, such an appeal to the non-rational faculties constitutes an aesthetic objective in its own right and cannot be seen merely as a utilitarian device:

> Aut prodesse volunt aut delectare poetae,
> aut simul et iucunda et idonea dicere vitae.
> Quidquid praecipies, esto brevis, ut cito dicta
> percipiant animi dociles teneantque fideles. ...
> Omne tulit punctum qui miscuit utile dulci,
> lectorem delectando pariterque monendo.[132]

> Poets seek both to instruct and to delight their readers,
> To say something both entertaining and relevant to their life.
> And whatever you teach, be brief, so that their minds

---

[128] Pierre Grimal, *Essai sur l'Art poétique d'Horace* (Paris, 1968), pp. 92, 94-98, 128-36.
[129] Grant and Fiske, "Cicero's 'Orator'," pp. 11-21; Hack, "Doctrine of Literary Forms," pp. 38-52.
[130] Grimal, *Essai sur l'Art poétique*, pp. 110-13, 124-27.
[131] Brink, *Horace on Poetry, 1*, 96-100, 228-30, 235, 253-54; *2*, 80, 115-16, 463-64, 465. See also Wilhelm Kroll, "Die historische Stellung von Horazens Ars poetica," *Sokrates: Zeitschrift für das Gymnasialwesen*, n.F. 6 (1918), 91-95; Wolf Steidle, *Studien zur Ars poetica des Horaz: Interpretation des auf Dichtkunst und Gedicht bezüglichen Hauptteils (Verse 1-294)* (Hildesheim, 1967), p. 65 and n. 68.
[132] *Ars poet.* 333-344. For the relevant aspects of Cicero's literary theory see above, ch. 2, part III.

Will grasp readily and retain firmly what you have said. ...
He who combines the sweet with the useful wins every contest,
Delighting the reader and admonishing him at the same time.

Such a theory of poetry scarcely suggests a triumph of Stoicism.[133] Still less is it Epicurean.[134] Rather, it points to the tradition of anti-sophistic rhetoric coupled with the conception of literature as an ethical catalyst achieving its effect through its aesthetic power, a theory of the sort that Cicero had recently synthesized for Latin prose on a largely Aristotelian basis. The Horace of the *Ars poetica* has been aptly described as "an *anima naturaliter Aristotelica*."[135] The leading proponent of this interpretation, C. O. Brink, argues vigorously for Neoptolemus as Horace's source for Aristotelian literary theory, rather than Cicero.[136] Some supporters of the Neoptolemus thesis are less hostile to the idea of Cicero as a possible model for Horace.[137] Whether or not the influence of Neoptolemus can be demonstrated, a moot point indeed, there seems to be no *a priori* reason to rule out the possibility that Horace was applying to Latin poetry a doctrine already made normative for Latin rhetoric by Cicero.[138] Not only in his theoretical statements in the *Ars poetica* but also in the range of stylistic devices which he uses throughout his works, Horace shows his kinship to the Ciceronian-Aristotelian position by combining didacticism with pleasure. He draws on a wide range of arguments and devices to convey both instruction and delight; and the taste with which he applies the criterion of suitability takes equal account of the subject matter and the ostensible audience of his poems.

Horace's consciousness of his place within a poetic tradition stretching back to Greece also inspires him to blend this rhetorical conception of poetry with the lyric appeal to fame as a motive and justification for his art. Poets, as Horace notes, are needed in order to immortalize the deeds of great men.[139] But the writing of great poetry is also a deed which

---

[133] As argued by Grant and Fiske, "Cicero's 'Orator'," p. 63; J. Tate, "Horace and the Moral Function of Poetry," *CQ*, *22* (1928), 68–73.

[134] Kroll, "Die historische Stellung," pp. 88–89.

[135] Brink, *Horace on Poetry*, *2*, 520.

[136] Ibid., *1*, 43–150; *2*, vii–xxi, 132, 182–83, 352–53, 520–22. See also Grimal, *Essai sur l'Art poétique*, pp. 37–225, who argues for a strict and unmediated Aristotelian basis for the *Ars poetica* although he is unconvincing in his effort to demonstrate that the organization of Horace's work is patterned after Aristotle's formal, material, efficient, and final causes.

[137] Otto Immisch, *Horazens Epistel über die Dichtkunst, Philologus*, Supplementband *24*:3 (Leipzig, 1932), 26, 48.

[138] As argued by J. W. H. Atkins, *Literary Criticism in Antiquity: A Sketch of Its Development* (New York, 1952), *2*, 76–77, 100; Charles Sears Baldwin, *Ancient Rhetoric and Poetic Interpreted from Representative Works* (New York, 1924), pp. 246–47.

[139] *Carm.* 4.9.1–12.

brings undying honor to its author, as Horace observes quite propheti-
cally in surveying his own work; *exegi monumentum aere perennius* ("I have
built a monument more enduring than bronze.")[140] All of these
ideas—the poet's desire to delight as well as teach his readers and to win
fame for himself and his departures from a strictly rational address to the
logos of his audience—emerge as the dominant themes of Horace's poetics
and are expressly antithetical to the literary theory of the Stoa, whatever
allusions to Stoicism Horace may include within the *Ars poetica*. And, in
contrast to the group of poems in which Horace satirizes the paradoxes
of ancient Stoic ethics in the name of an ethos rooted less in abstract
philosophical alternatives than in his own personal temperament, the *Ars
poetica* and other works in which Horace develops his theory of poetry
show him rejecting Stoicism from the perspective of a well-developed
literary theory which, while freshly transposed into poetics by Horace
himself, shows his intellectual dependence on other rhetorical and philosophical models and sources.

Horace's works, as we have seen, reflect a variety of approaches to
Stoicism, as well as to the other traditions on which he drew. His attitude
toward Stoicism cannot be correlated with any particular chronological
stage of his career. At times he shows a sensitive, well-informed, and
sympathetic awareness of important ethical doctrines taught by the Stoa.
At other times he draws freely on Stoic arguments for causes that he
favors but mingles them even more freely with arguments drawn from
a host of other sources whose individual and collective effect is to neu-
tralize the Stoic components. At still other times he manifests a familiarity
with Stoicism in depth coupled with the wish to expose it to ridicule and
attack or to reject it in favor of opposing principles. The rationale for
such dismissals of Stoicism is sometimes purely personal and unspecu-
lative while at other times it reflects Horace's preference for a different
but equally theoretical position. It might also be noted that there are a
number of poems, not discussed here, in which Horace takes no position
on Stoicism whatsoever, either positive or negative.

Is there, then, any typically Horatian stance toward philosophy in
general or toward Stoicism in particular? Our investigation has shown
that Horace is capable of a number of different levels of commitment to
Stoicism and to his other sources, ranging from superficial attachment to
deep understanding to deliberate rejection. He expresses all of these attitudes in different poems and in a host of ways, ranging from the playful
to the profound. The fact that Horace is able to assume such a variety
of approaches does not in itself demonstrate that he is not seriously in-

---

[140] *Carm.* 3.30.1.

terested in the ideas he happens to be dealing with in each poem. Part
of his aim as a writer was to experiment with a range of poetic forms,
some of which were new to Latin verse. Sometimes the philosophical
position which Horace takes in a given poem seems to flow from the
traditional associations which poems of that sort brought to his mind,
such as the lyric praise of pleasure in the light of the evanescence of youth.
At other times Horace appears to have adapted a certain poetic form,
such as the satire and the epistle, to serve as an effective medium for his
philosophical leanings or personal preferences. There is certainly no one
philosophical position which Horace maintains consistently or even
preeminently throughout his works. But this fact is not synonymous with
a disinvolvment with philosophy as such, regardless of the ideas that are
at issue and the marks that he gives them in particular poems. The philosophy on which he draws is often commonplace but it is rarely used in
a merely decorative manner. At its weakest it reinforces or supplements
a deeply felt attitude deriving from a non-philosophical source of some
sort; at its strongest it is the stuff and substance of the poem. The one
attitude is fully as characteristic of Horace as the other.

As a chapter in the history of the Stoic tradition, Horace plays a double
role. If one surveys his *oeuvre* from a statistical point of view, one reaches
the inescapable conclusion that he depreciates the philosophy of Stoicism
far more than he supports it, although he does support it generously on
occasion. On the other hand, Horace communicates a good deal of information about Stoicism whether he expressly identifies it as Stoic or
not. He provides much evidence on the Stoic doctrine of the sage, on the
nature of virtue and vice, and on the Stoic mode of preaching and argumentation. Some of the richest sources of Stoicism in Horace's works
are the very poems in which he holds the Stoa up to ridicule in the most
devastating manner. The Stoic doctrines found in Horace are often presented as bare and isolated maxims. On some occasions, however, he
supplies them with the connective tissue that links them to their wider
philosophical context. Horace's poetic reputation attained meteoric
heights in his own age. He became an instant classic and was read in-
tensively during the rest of the classical era. He was also one of the most
widely read of ancient poets during the Middle Ages, an author whose
works were a staple of the grammar school curriculum.[141] Some of his

---

[141] On Horace's posthumous reputation see Giuseppina Crispino, *Le Idee morali e educativi di Orazio* (Napoli, 1935), pp. 17–25, 73–88; Friedrich Klingner, "Über die Recensio
der Horaz-Handschriften," *Studien zur griechischen und römischen Literatur* (Zürich, 1964),
pp. 455–518; Ranier Rauthe, *Zur Geschichte des Horaztextes im Altertum* (Bamberg, 1971),
pp. 213–21; Eduard Stemplinger, *Horaz im Urteil der Jahrhunderte*, Das Erbe der Alten, 2:5
(Leipzig, 1921), pp. 4–10.

post-classical readers read his poems with an integral grasp of what he had sought to achieve. Others used his works as a mine from which to extract well-turned phrases and nuggets of wisdom. As the modern school of pro-Stoic critics has shown, it is not difficult to make a case for Horace's Stoic affinities if one is willing to read the Stoic references in his works out of context. Many medieval readers, using similar critical principles, could and did find in Horace a rich if often inadvertent source of Stoic ethical doctrine.

II. PERSIUS

If the philosophical affinities of Horace have inspired longstanding controversies among his commentators, the same cannot be said for Persius. On the basis of the known facts of his life no less than the internal evidence provided by his works, scholars with almost total unanimity[142] have hailed him as the Stoic satirist par excellence. He has been described repeatedly as the most integrally Stoic of all the ancient Latin authors, the first and most deeply committed of the Stoic satirists, and an ardent missionary of the Stoic gospel who, having welded it to the satirical form developed by Horace, preached it as an unfailing remedy for the social ills and literary decay he saw around him.[143] Although Persius' literary

---

[142] The only significant dissenters are Hugo Beikircher, *Kommentar zur VI. Satire des A. Persius Flaccus, Wiener Studien*, Beiheft *1* (Wien, 1969), 11–15, who offers an Epicurean interpretation but whose literal commentary on *Sat.* 6 does little to prove his point; and Kenneth J. Reckford, "Studies in Persius," *Hermes, 90* (1962), 498–504, who sees Stoicism in Persius as a point of departure but not as a doctrine to which he adhered religiously.

[143] Among the most thorough studies of Persius' philosophy which may be recommended are Charles Burnier, *Le Rôle des Satires de Perse dans le développpment du néo-stoïcisme* (La Chaux-de-Fonds, 1909), esp. pp. 11–32, which also supplies a useful guide to nineteenth-century Persius scholarship; J. Wight Duff, *A Literary History of Rome in the Silver Age from Tiberius to Hadrian* (New York, 1935), pp. 279–95; *Roman Satire*, pp. 114–24; Enzo V. Marmorale, *Persio*, 2ª ed. (Firenze, 1956), pp. 11, 13, 26–27, 30–37, 75–96, 109–73; Ettore Paratore, *Persio e Lucano*, quaderni della *Rivista di cultura classica e medievale, 6* (Roma, 1963), 5–39; and most exhaustively François Villeneuve, *Essai sur Perse* (Paris, 1918), pp. xi, 154, 159–70, 242–313. Less important treatments of Persius which also reflect the consensus include Francesco Ballotto, *Cronologia ed evoluzione spirituale nelle satire di Persio* (Messina, 1964), p. 49; Aloysius Bucciarelli, *Utrum Aulus Persius Flaccus doctrinae stoicae sit sectator idem et interpretes* (Roma, 1888); A. M. Guillemin, "Le satirique Perse," *LEC, 7* (1938), 161–67; Knoche, *Roman Satire*, pp. 130–32; J. M. K. Martin, "Persius— Poet of the Stoics," *Greece & Rome, 8* (1939), 172–82; Clarence W. Mendell, *Latin Poetry: The Age of Rhetoric and Satire* (Hamden, Conn., 1967), pp. 47–48, 57–64; Henry Nettleship, *Lectures and Essays*, 2nd ser., ed. F. Haverfield (Oxford, 1895), p. 43; R. G. M. Nisbet, "Persius," in *Critical Essays on Roman Literature: Satire*, ed. J. P. Sullivan (London, 1963), pp. 39–71; Ettore Paratore, *Biografia e poetica di Persio* (Firenze, 1968), pp. 151–52, 197; Edwin S. Ramage, "Persius, the Philosopher-Satirist," in *Roman Satirists*, pp. 118–27; Rieks, *Homo, Humanus*, pp. 197–201, 256; Rudolf Schottlaender, "Persius und Seneca über die Problematik der Freilassung," *Wissenschaftliche Zeitschrift der Universität Rostock*, gesell-

career was brief and his small number of poems did not provide him with the scope in which to elaborate on a large number of Stoic ideas, the prevailing critical view of his attitude toward Stoicism is substantially correct.

Persius (A.D. 34-62), unlike Horace, came from a wealthy upper-class background.[144] A native of Volaterra, he was the son of an equestrian family connected by ties of blood and marriage to the senatorial class. Persius was sent to Rome for his education and studied with the best teachers of his age: the grammarian Remmius Palaemon, the rhetorician Verginius Flavus, and most importantly Annaeus Cornutus. Cornutus, probably a freedman of Seneca's, was a Stoic philosopher known also as a tragedian. The discussion in his circle, which Persius entered at the age of sixteen, brought together this combined interest in philosophy and literature. Persius' associations from this time onward included Seneca and his nephew Lucan, although he himself remained aloof from politics, rejecting Seneca's moderate Stoicism in favor of the more uncompromising position taught by Cornutus and lived by friends and relatives such as the senator C. Paetus Thrasea and his wife Arria. Arria, a close relative of Persius, possibly his aunt, gained the reputation of a Stoic saint and martyr in A.D. 42, when, in response to an imperial demand that her husband commit suicide, she gave heart to Thrasea by plunging the knife into her own breast first with the words, "See, Paetus, it doesn't hurt." Persius identified himself with Stoicism of the rigorist school and was so identified by his contemporaries. He amassed a library of Stoic works including some seven hundred treatises of Chrysippus, which he bequeathed to Cornutus at his death. Apart from his six satires, he wrote some tragedy early in his career which has not survived.

Persius' satires, begun in A.D. 58/59, were all the products of the last three of four years of his short life. They deal preeminently with Stoic moral themes, treated on a rather general level. Persius singles out only one particular moral issue for extended discussion, the ethics of public service. It is not clear whether his decision to begin writing satires as a vehicle for Stoic ethics in 58/59 was triggered by any external event or by any new development in his own inner life. It is possible that Persius, like other members of Seneca's circle, greeted the accession of Nero in

schafts- und sprachwissenschaftliche Reihe, *15*:4-5 (1966), 533-39; W. H. Semple, "The Poet Persius: Literary and Social Critic," *Bulletin of the John Rylands Library*, 44 (1961), 157-74; Smiley, "Stoicism and its Influence," *CJ*, *29* (1934), 652; Otto Weinreich, trans. and intro., *Römische Satiren* (Zürich, 1949), pp. lv-lviii; Witke, *Latin Satire*, pp. 79-80, 94, 100, 272.

[144] An outstanding discussion of Persius' biography is provided by William S. Anderson, intro. to *The Satires of Persius*, trans. W. S. Merwin (Bloomington, 1961), pp. 7-50. See also Villeneuve, *Essai sur Perse*, ch. 1-3.

A.D. 54 with high hopes for a new era of edifying imperial leadership, hopes which had been betrayed irretrievably by 58/59. This suggestion might account for the fact that Persius' one extended analysis of a specific moral issue deals with political life, but it fails to explain the emphasis on the general shortcomings of mankind which permeates the majority of his satires and the fact that he had never associated himself with the activist stance or the machinations of the court. It is known that Persius' death in A.D. 62 was caused by a stomach ailment, and it is possible that this illness had already begun to prey on his body and to turn his mind to philosophy in a more immediate sense than before. In any event, we are left with the six satires, which convey a spirit of unmistakable seriousness and commitment to the ethics of the Stoa, both as a criterion of the choices to be made in the public arena and as a guide to inner happiness and peace.

Persius makes it clear in a number of his satires that philosophy is the prime source of wisdom and consolation and that the philosophy with which he identifies himself above all is that of the Stoa. His third satire is an exhortation to the youth of his day to concern themselves with philosophy. Their failure to do so he likens, traditionally, to childishness,[145] sickness,[146] aimless dissolution,[147] and madness.[148] Philosophy, he notes, teaches the causes of things, the nature and purpose of human life, and man's moral duties both public and private, acquisitions which constitute true riches, unlike the material goods which the unenlightened seek.[149] The youths whom Persius addresses are not ignorant; they are educated men well aware of the teachings of the various schools of philosophy including those of Pythagoras and Arcesilas.[150] But most blameworthy is their neglect of the Stoic philosophy despite their extensive familiarity with it.[151]

Much fuller and more immediate as an index of Persius' own personal views is his fifth satire, in which he eulogizes his Stoic mentor Cornutus. The author relates how he came to Cornutus as a youth who had just assumed the *toga virilis*:

> Teneros tu suscipis annos
> Socratico, Cornute, sinu. Tum fallere sollers
> adposita intortos extendit regula mores

---

[145] Aulus Persius Flaccus, *Saturae* 3.43-52, ed. W. V. Clausen (Oxford, 1966). All references to Persius will be drawn from this edition.

[146] *Sat.* 3.63-65, 3.88-106.

[147] *Sat.* 3.77-87.

[148] *Sat.* 3.115-118.

[149] *Sat.* 3.66-76.

[150] *Sat.* 3.56-57.

[151] *Sat.* 3.52-55.

et premitur ratione animus vincique laborat
artificemque tuo ducit sub pollice voltum.[152]

    I consigned
Myself to your charge, Cornutus, and you gathered
My tender years to your Socratic heart. And you applied
The rule with unsuspected cunning, straightening
My crooked ways, and my spirit, laboring to be
Subdued, was molded to the cast of your thought, and took
Form and expression under your shaping thumb.

It was indeed Stoicism, and ancient Stoicism at that, which Cornutus
taught:

At te nocturnis iuvat inpalliscere chartis;
cultor enim iuvenum purgatas inseris aures
fruge Cleanthea.[153]

But you have found your joy in growing pale
Over the page night after night, in your ambition
To cultivate the young and in their scrubbed ears sow
The seed of Cleanthes.

    Persius indicates throughout his works the specific teachings in the field
of Stoic ethics which he has learned. He does not merely present a dis-
embodied assortment of maxims and conclusions but reflects an understanding of their underlying rationale and interconnections. Virtue, he
acknowledges, is life in accordance with nature and reason,[154] unlike the
external criterion preferred by the crowd, which *stat contra ratio*; is contrary to reason.[155] Both reason and nature judge the crowd to be fools:
*Publica lex hominum naturaque continet hoc fas,/ ut teneat vetitos inscitia debilis
actus* ("The self-evident law of man and nature limits/The actions of incompetents and half-wits.")[156] Since virtue is conformity to reason, it
requires an assessment of right and wrong which depends on a correct
intellectual judgment[157] and is reinforced by frequent examinations of
conscience.[158] Virtue also entails a fixed inner orientation toward the
good, a pure and constant intentionality.[159] It is in the intention and not

---

[152] *Sat.* 5.36–40; trans. Merwin.
[153] *Sat.* 5.62–64; trans. Merwin.
[154] *Sat.* 2.73.
[155] *Sat.* 5.96.
[156] *Sat.* 5.98–99; trans. Merwin.
[157] *Sat.* 5.120–121.
[158] Noted by Witke, *Latin Satire*, p. 100.
[159] *Sat.* 2.73–74; *Sat.* 4.23, 4.51–52; *Sat.* 5.64–65.

in the act that virtue is found. Frugality, for instance, may be a good way of life, but not if it is embraced for the purpose of saving on one's expenses and leaving a larger inheritance to one's heirs.[160] The sage, who alone possesses a rationally derived morality and a consistent inner commitment to the good, is also the sole possessor of virtue, on an all or nothing basis. Just as one cannot serve two masters, says Persius, so one must be either wholly virtuous or wholly vicious;[161] as with the ancient Stoics, he accepts no gradations of vice or virtue. Likewise, he holds that sages alone are capable of true friendship. Cornutus, he observes with gratitude, has communicated his wisdom to Persius, making him the equal of his master. Master and disciple can now enjoy the total harmony of minds committed to the same truth and same good which marks the perfect friendship between sages.[162]

Such virtue is the only good worth seeking, for Persius. It is its own reward and it produces many other benefits as well. It is the one sure remedy for the miseries of old age[163] and the only true source of the equanimity which enables the wise man to dwell secure amid the vicissitudes of life.[164] In addition to endowing man with security, virtue grants him the only true liberty—not the external emancipation which the praetor can grant to a slave but inner liberation from the passions of luxury, avarice, ambition, and superstition.[165] The way of life which follows from this freedom from the passions may be either a public or a private one. Persius himself opts for the contemplative life, withdrawn from the forum, in which one can live simply, in philosophical calm, engaged in manual labor on one's own land:

> Utar ego, utar,
> nec rhombos ideo libertis ponere lautus
> nec tenuis sollers turdarum nosse salivas.
> Messe tenus propria vive et granaria (fas est)
> emole. Quid metuas? Occa et seges altera in herba est.[166]

> As for me, I try
> To make the most of things, without being so lavish
> As to feed my freedmen on turbot, nor of so
> Sophisticated a palate that I can tell
> Hen thrush from cock thrush by the taste.

---

[160] Sat. 6.61-80.
[161] Sat. 5.154-160.
[162] Sat. 5.30-44.
[163] Sat. 5.65.
[164] Sat. 6.12-14.
[165] Sat. 2.3-72; Sat. 4; Sat. 5.73-192; Sat. 6.14-24, 6.75-80.
[166] Sat. 6.22-26; trans. Merwin.

Live on your own harvest, mill your own grain, that's as it
Should be. Why should you worry? You have only
To harrow again to have another crop on the way.

In *Satire* 4, through the person of Alcibiades, Persius presents a scathing
indictment of a corrupt and hypocritical politician, greedy for power,
praise, and money and willing to perpetrate injustice and to prostitute
himself to the mob in exchange for these false goods. Persius enjoins him
to give up his evil way of life:

Respue quod non es; tollat sua munera cerdo.
Tecum habita: noris quam sit tibi curta supellex.[167]

Reject all that is not
Yourself. Let the mob have back what it gave to you. Live in
Your own house and learn what a bare lodging it is.

However, while his own personal preference is clearly for the life of
retirement, Persius recognizes that it is not public life as such, but public
life entered for the wrong reasons and conducted in the wrong spirit, that
is worthy of blame. In his general exhortation to the youth of his day he
acknowledges the principle that men have public obligations as well as
private ones:

Discite et, o miseri, causas cognoscite rerum:
quid sumus et quidnam victuri gignimur, ordo
quis datus, aut metae qua mollis flexus et unde,
quis modus argento, quid fas optare, quid asper
utile nummus habet, patriae carisque propinquis
quantum elargiri deceat, quem te deus esse
iussit et humana qua parte locatus es in re.[168]

Oh wretches, come learn the causes of things—what we are,
What manner of life we were born for, to what station
Brought forth, how and when to ease around the turning point, and
The limitations of wealth, what it's right to wish for,
The uses of new-minted coin, how much should be spent
On your relatives, how much on your country, to what
Calling God has summoned you, and what your position is
In human affairs.

His own personal choices and antipathies notwithstanding, Persius does
not succumb to the temptation to recast the moral philosophy of the Stoa

---

[167] *Sat.* 4.51–52; trans. Merwin.
[168] *Sat.* 3.66–73; trans. Merwin.

in the mold of his own temperament. While his own tastes lead him to emphasize one among the possible styles of life proposed by the Stoics, he never forgets that there are other acceptable styles which in fact might be more appropriate for other people.

Ethics remains the center of Persius' concern, but it might also be noted that there are some occasions when he reflects a knowledge of Stoic physics and logic. In one passage he asserts that the stars rule men's destinies. This point is, to be sure, not exclusively Stoic; but Persius goes on to correlate the harmony between the stars and human affairs with the bond of friendship between true sages that unites Cornutus and himself, who must have been born under the same stars, for a kindly destiny has bound them together.[169] In another passage Persius refers to a famous *sorites* of Chrysippus, who posed the question of how many grains of sand could be removed from a sand pile without its ceasing to be a sand pile. Here again, he places the doctrine within an ethical context by using it to conclude his attack on avarice. The avaricious man who still claims that he can set limits on his greed, says Persius, is the one who can unravel Chrysippus' paradox.[170]

While it could certainly be argued that Persius is generally indifferent to Stoic physics and logic and while the small size of his *oeuvre* forces him to omit many specific moral teachings of the Stoa as well, those Stoic doctrines which he does draw upon are handled with understanding and sympathy and with a clear recognition of their interconnections. There are only two exceptions to this rule, one major and one minor. The minor point concerns tonsorial practice, an index of the place a thinker occupies on the Stoic ethical spectrum. The more rigorous Stoics with whom Persius identifies himself objected to any tonsorial or cosmetic alterations of one's personal appearance as unnatural, a theme inherited from the Cynics, while the more moderate Stoics taught that philosophers should maintain a clean, neat, and conventional appearance, avoiding both loutishness and dandyism. Persius takes a position on this subject which is consistent with neither of these two approaches. He depicts Stoic philosophers as men with shaven heads,[171] a tonsorial style advocated neither by the rigorists nor the moderates. On the other hand, in sympathy with Seneca, who distinguishes between the depilation of some parts of the male body as comme il faut and the depilation of other parts as effeminate and unseemly, Persius castigates the politician he attacks in *Satire* 4 for depilating his pubic hair,[172] a practice characteristic of the male homo-

---

[169] *Sat.* 5.45-51.
[170] *Sat.* 6.80.
[171] *Sat.* 3.54.
[172] *Sat.* 4.36-37.

sexual prostitute, in his accusation that Alcibiades is selling himself to the crowd. In neither passage, however, does he invoke the Stoic norms of nature or prudence.

The second, and major, departure which Persius makes from the teachings of the Stoa is his theory of poetry. Persius presents a clear conception of himself as a moral counselor and of poetic satire as a vehicle for ethical instruction, themes that are visible in practice throughout his works and which he also discusses expressly in some of them. His message in all important respects is fully Stoic but this is not the case with his medium. In Persius' first satire, aptly described as his *"apologia pro satura sua,"*[173] he explains why he has taken up his pen to write satire and why he writes it as he does. The whole poem exudes his distaste for the shallowness and degeneracy of contemporary poets, concerned only with rehashing stale and trivial themes and with finding ever more florid and empty phrases in which to express them. Such poets are to be rejected because they are simultaneously unedifying and bombastic. Their lack of wisdom and virtue, says Persius, is reflected in their decadent style, so unfaithful to the example of Lucilius and Horace, who used their art to point a lesson whether by invective or by wit.[174] The didactic aims of Stoic literary theory are ventilated here along with the equally Stoic correlation between the good poet and the good man, a principle to which Persius adverts again at some length in *Satire* 5 as a preface to his eulogy of his mentor Cornutus, who taught him to avoid such vapid and flabby writing himself.[175]

Persius appeals to Lucilius, and more importantly, to Horace, as models of didactic poetry; but, as our analysis of Horace has shown, Horace's poetics can scarcely be equated with that of the Stoa, either in theory or in practice. How literally, then, should Persius' citation of Horace in this context be read? Persius does unquestionably borrow a number of stylistic devices from Horace. He follows the Horatian model of the satire written as a monologue[176] and even more frequently the satire written as a missive in which the author wears the mantle of a director of conscience to the addressee. Persius also relies heavily on the device of the internal dialogue with himself as one interlocutor and a second party, whose position he attacks, as the other speaker. Also quite Horatian is his tendency to accomplish his objectives more by painting an unflattering picture of the victim of his own vices than by offering an attractive

---

[173] Duff, *Roman Satire*, p. 119.

[174] *Sat.* 1.14-118.

[175] *Sat.* 5.1-21.

[176] Noted by Gilbert Highet, *The Anatomy of Satire* (Princeton, 1962), p. 41.

picture of the sage. Finally, like Horace, he occasionally uses the diatribe style as a means of developing his arguments.[177]

Yet, it would be a mistake to maintain that Persius took over the aesthetic creed proclaimed by Horace in the *Ars poetica*.[178] A central premise of Horace's poetics is its simultaneous concern with delight and instruction, each to be attained by a variety of aesthetic and emotional strategies appealing to the reader's sensibilities as well as to his mind. Persius, on the other hand, makes no concessions to the reader's emotions and maintains a rigorous adherence to the Stoic insistence that instruction alone is the poet's goal. His aim as a stylist is not to please the reader by the suavity with which his poetry falls on the ear but to win him over by the uncompromising weight of his argument. His response to the question posed by his interlocutor in *Satire* 1, *sed quid opus teneras mordaci radere vero | auriculas?* ("But why/ Harrow delicate ears with your cutting truths?")[179] is the reproach that the poet's duty is to cauterize not to charm the ears of the reader.

It would seem, then, that Stoic intellectualism and the rigors of the plain style are the central ingredients in Persius' poetic creed. Yet, most of Persius' commentators and all of his translators have noted the difficulty of his style, dense to the point of constriction, often lacking in mellifluousness, jarred by abrupt transitions. Some scholars maintain that, despite his obscurity, Persius' conciseness is an authentic reflection of the Stoic stylistic norm of brevity.[180] A more ingenious argument has recently been offered which focuses on the fact that Persius organizes his satires by juxtaposing conflicting ideas in the form of metaphorical contrasts developed consistently throughout each of his poems and even from one satire to another. Persius' reliance on metaphor is seen as an application of the Stoic taste for allegoresis. Allegory, originally used as a means of resolving tensions between Stoic doctrines and the mythological content of ancient poetry, is here extended to metaphor and used by Persius in a non-mythological setting in order to communicate moral truths in a non-literal or deliberately recondite manner.[181] Still other scholars have

---

[177] Cynthia S. Dessen, *Iunctura callidus acri: A Study of Persius' Satires*, Illinois Studies in Language and Literature (Urbana, 1968), pp. 39–47; Marmorale, *Persio*, pp. 12–18, 21–22, 39.

[178] As argued by Fiske, "Lucilius, the *Ars Poetica*, and Persius," *HSCP*, 24 (1913), 19, 21, 23.

[179] *Sat.* 1.106–107; trans. Merwin.

[180] Witke, *Latin Satire*, p. 112.

[181] This interpretation has been defended most ably by Dessen, *Iunctura callidus acri*. See also Reckford, "Studies in Persius," *Hermes*, 90 (1962), 490–98; Witke, *Latin Satire*, p. 102. Most recently J. C. Bramble, *Persius and the Programmatic Satire* (Cambridge, 1974), pp. 2–12, agrees that Persius adopts a deliberately difficult style combining common diction with unusual combinations of words for didactic purposes, although he makes no effort to relate this strategy to Stoic literary theory.

interpreted Persius' style as a sincere effort to express the Stoic appeal to the mind rather than to the passions, but one that is carried to such extremes in its departures from clarity and simplicity that it ends by obstructing the very didactic objectives intended.[182] This latter interpretation seems to be the most plausible one. It is difficult to accept as Stoic in execution a style whose harshness and complexity stand as far away from the plain style as the Alexandrian grandiloquence which Persius himself attacks. Despite his praise of Horace as a model and the many satirical devices which he borrows from him, despite his announced adherence to Stoic didacticism, Persius' literary style is ultimately neither Horatian nor Stoic, but Persius' own.

Persius' satires had not been completed at the time of his death.[183] Along with his library, they were willed to Cornutus, who had them edited by Persius' friend Caesius Bassus. They aroused immediate interest as soon as they were published. Martial and Quintilian commented on them and at the end of the first century a biography of Persius was written, excerpted from a commentary of Valerius Probus, which came to be appended to manuscripts of the Satires. During the remainder of the classical era Persius' works stayed in constant circulation. They appealed greatly to the taste of the second century, when they were made a school text; and scholars and moralists continued to read and refer to him in the third and fourth centuries. In the patristic and early medieval era Persius remained well known through the writings of apologists and theologians as well as through the works of commentators. The manuscript tradition of Persius runs unbroken from antiquity through the Carolingian renaissance, with the filiation of the earliest complete manuscript, of the ninth century, being traceable with confidence back to the original first-century edition. The very difficulty of Persius' style helped to stimulate the continuing interest of his classical commentators and admirers no less than the uncompromising austerity of his moral outlook, which commended itself as well to his Christian readers in the patristic era. Persius thus stands as a faithful exponent of the assimilation of Stoic ethics into ancient Latin satire and as an important vehicle of its transmission to the early Middle Ages.

---

[182] Anderson, intro. to Merwin's trans. of Satires, pp. 34-45; Highet, Anatomy of Satire, p. 41, who, however, confuses the issue somewhat by claiming that the Stoics were disinterested in the question of literary style.

[183] On Persius' posthumous reputation, see Anderson, intro. to Merwin's trans. of Satires, pp. 46-49; Dessen, Iunctura callidus acri, pp. 2, 4-5.

III. Juvenal

Much less is known about the life of Juvenal than is the case with Horace and Persius; after almost two millenia the details of his biography remain largely conjectural.[184] Juvenal (A.D. ca. 60–ca. 140) was born in Aquinum, possibly the son of a wealthy freedman. His cognomen "Iuvenalis" suggests on the one hand a lower-class or foreign origin and there were two freedmen by that name known to have been residents of Aquinum during his lifetime. On the other hand, one of the consuls during this period possessed the same name. An inscription found at Aquinum commemorates one Juvenal, quite possibly the poet himself, as a priest, a joint mayor and benefactor of the town, and as the commander of the Dalmatian cohort, a military post likely to have been held by a young officer of the equestrian class. It is probably safe to guess that Juvenal came from a comfortable *rentier* background, whatever its ultimate origins. Nothing is known about his education and the presumption is that he received the instruction usual for an upper-class youth. Either military and civil offices which he was able to acquire or his private income enabled Juvenal to make his way in Rome up to the 90s. But he was exiled by the emperor Domitian, probably to Egypt and probably between A.D. 93 and 96, either for attacking an imperial favorite or for criticizing the emperor's policy of selling commissions. Juvenal was brought back to Rome by the emperor Nerva, only to find his estate apparently irretrievable and his career in ruins. Now, aged about forty, he was no longer able to attain civil or military preferment. He made his living as the dependent of a series of wealthy and arrogant patrons. Juvenal appears to have received a gift from the emperor Hadrian which gave him a certain amount of financial security toward the end of his life, enabling him to purchase a small farm in Tivoli. His sixteen satires date from his middle age onward, being published in five books between ca. 110 and ca. 130. They are all vituperative indictments of the vices of society. Lacking Horace's self-satisfaction and wry humor and Persius' earnest yet detached idealism, Juvenal's satires read as if they have been brewed in the bitter cauldron of his own personal frustrations and resentments.

All commentators have noticed the strongly moralistic tone of Juvenal's satires but they have by no means interpreted them in the same way.[185] The scarcity of reliable external evidence for Juvenal's life has

---

[184] The most thorough recent analyses of the information on which a life of Juvenal might be based are Peter Green, intro. to his trans. of Juvenal, *The Sixteen Satires* (Baltimore, 1967), pp. 9–22; and Gilbert Highet, *Juvenal the Satirist: A Study* (Oxford, 1954), pp. 4–41.

[185] For an excellent survey of the various schools of Juvenal criticism see David Wiesen, "Juvenal's Moral Character, an Introduction," *Latomus, 22* (1963), 440–71; less detailed but also useful is E. J. Kenney, "Juvenal: Satirist or Rhetorician?" ibid., pp. 704–20.

encouraged critics to turn to his satires as a source for his biography, leading in turn to a tendency to interpret the ethical content of the satires in the light of the biographical information thus obtained. This procedure leads to the same sort of circular reasoning as it does in the case of Horace criticism, although in Juvenal studies the prime exponent of the biographical method sees Epicureanism rather than Stoicism as the philosophy which changes in his subject's life situation presumably encouraged him to adopt.[186] The main critics who have reacted against the biographical approach are those stressing the Stoic coloration of Juvenal's thought. As these scholars have shown, Stoic elements are present in roughly equal strength throughout Juvenal's works, a fact which belies the theory of an Epicurean conversion. A number of these commentators underline the close textual parallels between Juvenal and Seneca and argue plausibly for Seneca as the most likely source for his Stoicism,[187] although some of the older proponents of this view identify as Stoic many ideas in Juvenal which are commonplaces lacking a discernibly Stoic rationale, an oversight which weakens the thrust of their argument.[188] It has also been asserted that many of the themes in Juvenal which others attribute to Stoicism are actually rhetorical *topoi* and that he should be read in the context of the oratorical tradition rather than as an exponent of one school of philosophy or another.[189] As has been noted by opponents of this view, the rhetorical thesis simply pushes the issue of sources one step backward to the question of the ultimate philosophical provenance of the rhetorical *topoi* involved. A lateral attack on the rhetorical thesis has also been offered by scholars holding that Juvenal was indeed a serious moralist and no mere rhetorician, but that his ethical principles are eclectic.[190] Finally, there is a group of commentators who see Juvenal as lacking any real interest in or aptitude for sustained philosophical reasoning and as devoid of any coherent speculative orientation. His moralism, they argue, is simply an appeal to the traditional virtues of

---

[186] Gilbert Highet, *Juvenal the Satirist*, pp. 93, 123, 130, 133, 135; "Juvenal's Bookcase," *AJP*, 72 (1951), 374; "The Philosophy of Juvenal," *TAPA*, 80 (1949), 254-70.

[187] The most important and most recent exponent of this view is Bernard F. Dick, "Seneca and Juvenal 10," *HSCP*, 73 (1969), 237-46. See also Duff, *Silver Age*, pp. 620, 622; *Roman Satire*, pp. 154, 155, 161-62; Ludwig Friedlaender, comm. on his ed. of D. Junii Juvenalis, *Saturam libri V* (Amsterdam, 1962 [repr. of Leipzig, 1895 ed.]), pp. 39-42; Carl Schneider, *Juvenal und Seneca*, (Würzburg, 1930), pp. 9-91; Reinoldus Schuetze, *Juvenalis Ethicus* (Greifswald, 1905), pp. 70-74.

[188] Schneider, *Juvenal und Seneca*, pp. 9-60; Schuetze, *Juvenalis Ethicus*, pp. 70-74.

[189] The most important statement of this thesis is by Josué DeDecker, *Juvenalis Declamans: Étude sur la rhétorique déclamatoire dans les satires de Juvénal* (Gand, 1912).

[190] Enzo V. Marmorale, *Giovenale*, 2ª ed. (Bari, 1950), pp. 27-81; Augusto Serafini, *Studio sulla satira di Giovenale* (Firenze, 1957), pp. 97-160, 229-48; Wiesen, "Juvenal's Moral Character," *Latomus*, 22 (1963), 470-71.

Rome or is a vindictive reaction against changing currents in Roman society that had robbed Juvenal of the opportunities which he felt that he and members of his own class had an automatic right to enjoy.[191]

Our own analysis of Juvenal suggests that the insights of some of these varied schools of criticism can be substantiated and harmonized with each other. The pro-Stoic critics are correct in pointing to the limitations of the biographical approach as it has been applied to Juvenal. If one reads his satires in chronological order it is difficult to see any significant development taking place or any shift to a more Epicurean or a less acerbic attitude as the presumed result of an improvement in his material circumstances. At the same time, the critics who read Juvenal's satires as the expression of the snobbism of a déclassé gentleman forced to live in an inhospitable social environment can point to the fact that his irritation on this score likewise characterizes his satires both early and late. Juvenal's personal or class-based social attitudes may well be the most plausible source of the criteria he uses in selecting the ethical problems on which he chooses to focus. However, neither Stoicism nor Epicureanism nor eclecticism nor an appeal to the *mos maiorum* supplies him with any consistent means of solving these same problems.

In dealing with the Stoic component in his thought Juvenal manifests three distinct attitudes.[192] On some occasions he views Stoic ideas with sympathy. On other occasions he takes a position strongly opposed to Stoicism. In some of his satires he appears to give Stoic teachings his approval but, when the argument of the poem is considered as a whole, his orientation is clearly non-Stoic or anti-Stoic. In each of these three cases Juvenal confines his attention to a limited number of ethical themes. Sometimes he expressly attributes the Stoic ideas cited to that school while at other times he does not. There is only one passage where he provides incidental information about Stoicism, at least as it was evidently regarded in his day, without taking a position for or against. In *Satire* 5, he refers to two well-known statesmen of the previous generation generally associated with Stoicism, P. Fannius Thrasea Paetus and Helvidius Priscus, as nostalgic partisans of the Roman Republic, in the context of a complaint against a stingy patron who serves a rotgut vintage to his dependents while saving for himself the kind of wine that Thrasea and Helvidius would have drunk to commemorate the birthdays of Bru-

---

[191] Ulrich Knoche, "Juvenals Mass-stäbe der Gesellschafts-kritik," in *Die römische Satire*, ed. Dietmar Korzeniewski, Wege der Forschung, 138 (Darmstadt, 1970), pp. 513, 515; Peter Green, *The Shadow of the Parthenon: Studies in Ancient History and Literature* (London, 1972), pp. 230, 255-56; intro. to his trans. of *Satires*, pp. 22-63.

[192] John James Bodoh, "An Analysis of the Ideas of Juvenal," (University of Wisconsin Ph.D. diss., 1966), is minimally analytical and cannot be recommended.

tus and Cassius.[193] This passage is the exception which proves the rule. In all other cases where Stoicism or Stoic ideas are involved Juvenal makes his position, whatever it may be, perfectly clear.

In those poems where Juvenal refers to Stoicism or to Stoic ideas with approval, he sometimes cites ideas characteristic of the ancient Stoa, sometimes those of the middle or Roman Stoa, but most typically doctrines to which all members of the school adhered. In the most general sense he depicts Stoicism as a teaching identifiable with austere and upright morality. His second satire is directed against contemporary hypocrites and perverts who claim to be Stoics but who disgrace themselves and besmirch the Stoa by their actual behavior. These targets of Juvenal's ire try to pass themselves off as philosophers; they decorate their homes with statues of Chrysippus and pictures of Cleanthes and other sages[194] and they adopt tonsorial styles for those parts of their bodies visible when they are clothed which are associated with the Stoa.[195] But they are frauds, "Stoicidae" or make-believe Stoics[196] who denounce others for the same vices in which they themselves wallow. The most specific moral principle which surfaces in this poem as a rationale for the rectitude which these false Stoics so notoriously fail to manifest is the middle Stoic idea that ethical development is a gradual process; *nemo repente fuit turpissimus* ("no one becomes all bad all of a sudden,")[197] which Juvenal uses to defend the point that one should not overlook small departures from the narrow path since they lead step by step to more serious vices. In *Satire* 2 he singles out lust as the vice that tempts man toward his moral downfall although elsewhere he fastens on avarice as the most likely root of folly and wrongdoing.[198]

In *Satire* 2 Juvenal does not speculate on the origins of vice and virtue as such but he suggests some Stoic answers to that question in other poems. In his sixth satire he deals at length with the vice of lasciviousness in women, a failing which they share with the *Stoicidae* of *Satire* 2. It is the unbridled expression of the passions, he says, which incites the lust of these indecent women, the passions being four in number: joy, fear, wrath, and worry,[199] which approximate the classic Stoic quartet of pleasure, pain, fear, and desire. In *Satire* 6 Juvenal does not go on to contrast this free reign of the passions with virtuous action arising from judgments

---

[193] Decimus Iunius Iuvenalis, *Saturae* 5.36-37, ed. W. V. Clausen (Oxford, 1966). All references to Juvenal will be drawn from this edition.
[194] *Sat.* 2.4-7.
[195] *Sat.* 2.11-13. Noted by Friedlaender, comm. on his ed. of *Satires*, p. 165.
[196] *Sat.* 2.65.
[197] *Sat.* 2.83.
[198] *Sat.* 6.295-300; *Sat.* 14.173-175.
[199] *Sat.* 6.189-190.

conformable with reason, as a more thoroughgoing Stoicizer might do. However, he does do so in *Satire* 10, where he notes the antithesis between reason and two of the passions as defined by the Stoics, fear and desire: *quid enim ratione timemus | aut cupimus?* ("Since when were our fears or desires / Ever dictated by reason?")[200]

In another poem he deals at length with the important Stoic idea that humanitarianism and benevolence are based on reason and that it is man's rational endowment that distinguishes him from the animals:

> Mollissima corda
> humano generi dare se natura fatetur,
> quae lacrimas dedit. Haec nostri optima sensus. ...
>   Quis enim bonus et face dignus
> arcana, qualem Cereris volt esse sacerdos,
> ulla aliena sibi credit mala? Separat hoc nos
> a grege mutorum, atque ideo verabile soli
> sortiti ingenium divinorumque capaces
> atque exercendis pariensque artibus apti
> sensum a caelesti demissum traximus arce,
> cuius egent prona et terram spectantia. Mundi
> principio indulsit communis conditor illis
> tantum animas, nobis animum quoque, mutuus ut nos
> adfectus petere auxilium et praestare iuberet ...[201]

> When Nature
> Gave tears to mankind, she proclaimed that tenderness was endemic
> To the human heart: of all our impulses, this
> Is the highest and best. ...
>   What good man, worthy to bear
> The mystic's torch, and such as the Corn Mother's priest would wish him,
> Thinks any human ills outside his concern? It's this
> That sets us apart from dumb brutes, it's why we alone
> Have a soul that's worthy of reverence, why we're imbued
> With a divine potential, the skill to acquire and practise
> All manner of arts: we possess that heaven-sent faculty
> Denied to the creeping beasts with their eyes on the ground.
> To them, when the world was still new, our common Creator granted
> The breath of life alone, but on us he further bestowed
> Sovereign reason, the impulse to aid one another. ...

Reason, then, is a distinctive possession of man, the source of his arts, his moral sense, his *eupatheia,* and the mutual obligations that bind all men together.[202] This impulse toward mutual assistance, Juvenal adds, is also

----

[200] *Sat.* 10.4–5; trans. Green.

[201] *Sat.* 15.131–133; 15.140–150.

[202] Friedlaender, comm. on his ed. of *Satires,* p. 590, has noted the Stoic affinities of this passage.

the foundation of political society and civic virtue.[203] The same sense of humanity rooted in the common possession of reason by all men is probably what inspires Juvenal to espouse fair treatment for slaves, although, like the Stoics, he never advocates the overthrow of slavery as an institution.[204] He criticizes a harsh master, setting a sadistic example to his children by treating his slaves as if their souls and bodies were not composed of the same substance as those of free men;[205] and he sides with a long-suffering husband against his merciless wife who rejects the idea that a slave is also a human being.[206]

Juvenal's *Satire* 15, where he provides his most extended discussion of the subject of humanity and inhumanity, is also the place where he deals with the topic of cannibalism. Among the ancient schools of philosophy the Stoa was virtually unique in its willingness to provide a moral justification for this practice. Juvenal supports the Stoic position and in so doing communicates more information about the Stoa's views on cannibalism than any other classical Latin author. The entire satire is an attack on the Egyptians because of their cannibalistic customs. But, while he criticizes the Egyptians severely for their inhumanity on this account, Juvenal adds that cannibalism is not necessarily a vice under all circumstances. He contrasts the cannibalism of the Egyptians with that of the ancient Spaniards, which he thinks was justified because the Spaniards only ate the flesh of persons who had died a natural death and only as a last resort, to sustain life while they were under siege. Their behavior, he concludes, would have been acceptable to Zeno even though the Spaniards in question had had no opportunity to familiarize themselves with his teachings on this point.[207]

By all accounts, the poem of Juvenal that is the most deeply imbued with Stoicism, both in substance and in outlook, is his tenth satire.[208] The main body of this satire is devoted to a recitation of the follies and vices of men, which derive from their tendency to follow their passions rather than their reason. Men foolishly pray to the gods for such false goods as wealth, fame, power, comfort, longevity, and children of fair form. Juvenal argues that the craving for all of these apparent goods is in fact contrary to reason. In developing his argument he makes frequent use of a technique often employed by Horace; he puts forth various prac-

---

[203] *Sat.* 15.151-158.

[204] Friedlaender, intro. to his ed. of *Satires*, p. 308; Green, intro. to his trans. of *Satires*, p. 23.

[205] *Sat.* 14.15-18.

[206] *Sat.* 6.222.

[207] *Sat.* 15.93-109.

[208] Noted by Dick, "Seneca and Juvenal," *HSCP, 73* (1969), 237-46; Duff, *Roman Satire*, p. 155; Friedlaender, comm. on his ed. of *Satires*, pp. 39-42, 486.

tical reasons for shunning the desires in question and holds up the example of individuals who have made themselves ridiculous by their enslavement to them. However, in contrast to Horace, Juvenal also has recourse to a line of reasoning which supplies a fully Stoic foundation for the course of action he is advocating. He makes the point repeatedly in this satire that the false values under consideration all involve an erroneous attribution of goodness to things that lie outside our control. If we treat these things as goods we will be desolated if they should be stricken from us as a consequence of our inability to control the people and events around us. The ambitious politician, for instance, may suffer a sudden reversal in his fortunes thanks to the fickleness of the crowd or the policy of an arbitrary emperor;[209] the mightiest of conquerers may be felled by a chance illness;[210] the man who rejoices at his length of life may face the sorrowful task of burying his descendants and other loved ones;[211] however handsome and well brought up a child may be, no parent receives a guarantee that he will not disgrace himself and his family through his own weaknesses or because he attracts the lust of a tyrannical ruler whose whims brook no opposition.[212] The central point which Juvenal is making in all these examples is the thoroughly Stoic one that the good is what lies within our control and that there is no security in those things that lie outside our control; such external things are either evils or matters of indifference.

In addition to advancing this fully Stoic argument for abandoning one's dependence on the *adiaphora* Juvenal also offers his prescription for what one should pray for instead, a passage worth quoting at length:

Nil ergo optabunt homines? Si consilium vis,
permittes ipsis expendere numinibus quid
conveniat nobis rebusque sit utile nostris;
nam pro iucundis aptissima quaeque dabunt di.
Carior est illis homo quam sibi. Nos animorum
inpulsu et caeca magnaque cupidine ducti
coniugum petimus partumque uxoris, at illis
notum qui pueri qualisque futura sit uxor.
Ut tamen et poscas aliquid voveasque sacellis
extra et candiduli divina tomacula porci,
orandum est ut sit mens sana in corpore sano.
Fortem posce animum mortis terrore carentem,
qui spatium vitae extremum inter munera ponat
naturae, qui ferre queat quoscumque labores,

---

[209] *Sat.* 10.66-77.
[210] *Sat.* 10.168-173.
[211] *Sat.* 10.240-265.
[212] *Sat.* 10.289-345.

nesciat irasci, cupiat nihil et potiores
Herculis aerumnas credat saevosque labores
et venere et cenis et pluma Sardanapalli.
Monstro quod ipse tibi possis dare; semita certe
tranquillae per virtutem patet unica vitae.
Nullum numen habes, si sit prudentia: nos te,
nos facimus, Fortuna, deam caeloque locamus.[213]

Should men then pray for nothing? If you want my advice,
Let the gods themselves decide what is fitting for us
And what things are useful to us. For the gods give
What is most suitable rather than what we most enjoy.
Man is dearer to them than he is to himself.
We are led by irrational impulses and by great blind desires
To pray for marriage and children, while they alone know
What our future wives and offspring will be like.
And still, if you want to pray for anything and to offer
Sacrifices of entrails and sacred pork sausages at the altars,
Pray for a sound mind in a healthy body.
Pray for a brave soul free from the fear of death,
Which holds long life as the least of Nature's gifts,
Which bears calmly all sorts of labors,
Which knows not wrath and desires nothing
And holds the sorrows and labors of Hercules dearer
Than the loves and feasts and downy cushions of Sardanapalus.
You can give yourself what I am showing you;
For the one sure path to a tranquil life runs through virtue.
If we had prudence, Fortune, you would have no divinity.
It is we who place you in heaven as a goddess.

Juvenal's positive advice in this passage, like his critique of folly in the rest of *Satire* 10, is rich with Stoic doctrine. Virtue alone, he asserts, is the source of tranquillity and happiness; and the attainment of virtue lies within our own power. It can be acquired through the exercise of a sound mind, the development of prudence or practical wisdom being the key virtue on which all others depend. Through virtue we can overcome the passions, which incline us to error and vice. Hercules plays his classic Stoic function in this poem as a symbol of the constancy of the sage and the successful though toilsome struggle of reason against the passions. Physical health, one of the preferables in Stoic ethics, is also admitted as a desideratum. Finally, the entire passage is set in the context of a prayer in which Juvenal rationalizes the gods, raising them to the level of the providential Stoic *logos*, whose rule of the cosmos is always reasonable and beneficent. All the external vicissitudes of life are a function of its causative agency, for it knows what is good for men better than they

---

[213] *Sat.* 10.346-366.

know it themselves. The concluding address to the goddess Fortuna is an appeal to the Stoic principle that fortune is not an arbitrary power, as is believed in popular mythology; if properly understood, she is the servant rather than the master of the providential *logos* which controls the circumstances of our lives.

An overzealous advocate of biographical criticism or of the view that Juvenal's philosophy must perforce be consistent might be tempted to conclude on the basis of *Satire* 10 that, by ca. A.D. 123, the approximate middle of his literary career and the point at which he wrote this poem, Juvenal had experienced a conversion to Stoicism which enabled him to acquire the detachment he needed to confront the distasteful features of the world in which he lived. The Stoic content and Stoic sensibility of this poem are both profound and unmistakable. Yet, both before and after *Satire* 10, Juvenal's works provide equally unmistakable evidence of a strongly anti-Stoic point of view. With comparable frequency and feeling he takes up his pen to oppose or to distort Stoic principles, sometimes point blank and sometimes in a more oblique manner.

A straightforward illustration of the cut direct can be found in Juvenal's third satire, where he lashes out at the Stoic teacher Publius Egnatius Celer, who betrayed his friend and pupil Barea Soranus in A.D. 66:[214] *Stoicus occidit Baream delator amicum/ discipulumque senex* ("that old Stoic delator, who was responsible for the death of Barea, his friend and pupil.")[215] The *ad hominem* argument in this passage coupled with the express reference to Stoicism but without specific reference to Stoic doctrine gives way to a different strategy in Juvenal's handling of two other topics, where he takes a position antithetical to that of the Stoa but without mentioning the school. One such barometer of his anti-Stoicism is his hostile attitude toward homosexuality, a theme that crops up in a number of his poems but which he treats most fully in his second and ninth satires. In *Satire* 2, as noted above, Juvenal attacks false philosophers, men claiming to live by the ethics of the Stoa but who practice the same vices they condemn. All of these pseudo-philosophers are homosexuals, a fact which renders them still more despicable in Juvenal's eyes. They offend him more than the eunuch priests of Isis, who at least are frank about their *morbum* or pathological condition.[216] Likewise, in *Satire* 9 he treats as more loathesome than pathetic the misfortunes of the overaged bi-sexual prostitute Naevolus, cast out by his former protector. This conception of homosexuality as disgusting and abnormal is a position well opposed to

---

[214] Identified by Friedlaender, comm. on his ed. of *Satires*, p. 206; Green, comm. on his trans. of *Satires*, p. 101.
[215] *Sat.* 3.115-116.
[216] *Sat.* 2.16-17.

Stoicism. While the Stoics drew the line at adultery and while Musonius Rufus taught that sexual intercourse should be ordered exclusively to the procreation of offspring within the bonds of matrimony, the school on the whole regarded the means by which an individual satisfied his sexual needs as a matter of indifference, so long as he did not become enslaved by his passions. For the Stoics, then, homosexuality in itself is neither better nor worse than heterosexuality.

A second case in which Juvenal departs markedly from a distinctive Stoic doctrine is his lengthy broadside against women in *Satire* 6, written in the form of advice to a friend to dissuade him from marriage. While it is true that Juvenal states elsewhere that men are much more reprehensible as a group than women[217] and while he devotes much more attention throughout his *oeuvre* to the foibles of men than to those of women, *Satire* 6 none the less is a vituperative outburst of unmitigated misogyny, leaving no glimmer of hope for the moral salvation of the female sex as such. Most of Juvenal's attention is focused on the vice of lasciviousness in women, but he finds room to denounce their luxury, extravagance, avarice, irresponsibility, jealousy, insubordination, arrogance, capriciousness, contentiousness, sloth, drunkenness, vanity, cruelty, and superstition as well. Juvenal lists as vices in women some traits which the Stoics, especially those of the Cynic-Stoic persuasion, would regard as positive indices of the moral and intellectual equality between the sexes—the enjoyment of physical exercise, the wearing of unisex clothing, a lively intelligence, a taste for learning, and the desire to take an active part in the conversation.[218] Juvenal does grudgingly admit that a virtuous women of the old school might conceivably be found, although she would be *rara avis in terris nigroque simillima cycno* ("a rare bird in this world, something like a black swan.")[219] Yet, even if one could marry such a pure and dignified woman, a veritable Cornelia, her very uprightness would smother her husband in a blanket of priggishness, making her impossible to live with.[220] Thus, Juvenal decisively reverses the egalitarianism which undergirds the Stoics' treatment of women. While agreeing that most women, like most men, can be written off as vicious and foolish, he goes on to argue that capacities and activities which are virtuous in men are vicious in women. Even those qualities which, he acknowledges, constitute virtue for a woman end by making her intolerably haughty. In effect, then, Juvenal treats women as a class

---

[217] *Sat.* 2.47-48.
[218] *Sat.* 6.245-267, 6.398-412, 6.434-456.
[219] *Sat.* 6.165.
[220] *Sat.* 6.161-169.

of people whose sex *ipso facto* deprives them of the potentialities for moral excellence possessed by men.[221]

Is it personal idiosyncracy, the preference for an opposing philosophical doctrine, or simply the opportunity to excoriate groups or individuals who he thought merited a tongue lashing that inspires Juvenal to take the anti-Stoic stance which he assumes in the poems just discussed? With respect to the misogyny expressed so exhaustively in *Satire* 6, it is certainly true that Juvenal could draw on a longstanding tradition of rhetorical *controversiae* on the praise and dispraise of women. It is worth noting, however, that in all of these cases Juvenal's critique is surrounded by a broader analysis of the major social problems of his day. The culprits responsible for the vicious tendencies which he castigates are foreigners, especially Greeks, who have become so influential in Rome, and the Roman aristocracy, which has failed in its social obligation to provide a model of rectitude for its inferiors. As he says before introducing his treacherous Stoic philosopher in *Satire* 3, *non possum ferre, Quirites | Graecam urbem* ("I cannot, citizens, stomach / A Greek-struck Rome.")[222] He then proceeds to list his objections to the Greeks, whom he attacks as sycophants and opportunists of the worst sort, engaged in a cabal to infiltrate all the professions in Rome. And, what is worse, so wily and unprincipled are they that they have succeeded in snaring all the patrons.[223] The betrayer of Barea, to be sure, was a Roman, but he was perverted by his education in Greece.[224] As for homosexuality, Juvenal sees it as an oriental vice[225] which has so enfeebled the Roman upper classes from the emperor to the scions of the most famous Republican families down to the more recent possessors of wealth and social prominence[226] that they can now give lessons in effeminacy to the Armenians and outstrip even Cleopatra in their luxurious degeneracy.[227]

A similar capitulation to insidious foreign customs, undermining the ethos of those classes with the duty to set a good moral example, is reflected in the iniquitous women of *Satire* 6. When Juvenal mentions individuals in illustrating the various modes of female vice in this poem, he chooses women whose names reveal their membership in the most distinguished of senatorial families.[228] These highborn women are only mini-

---

[221] The only exception in Juvenal is his praise of the virgin Cloelia, who swam the Tiber to save the city of Rome from attack, in *Sat.* 8.265.

[222] *Sat.* 3.60–61; trans. Green.

[223] *Sat.* 3.61–114, 3.119–121.

[224] *Sat.* 3.116–117.

[225] *Sat.* 2.163–170.

[226] *Sat.* 2.99–101, 2.126–132, 2.143–148, 2.170; *Sat.* 9.54–62, 9.84–85.

[227] *Sat.* 2.108–109, 2.163–170.

[228] *Sat.* 6.72, 6.82–114, 6.136, 6.265–267, 6.306–308, 6.320–322, 6.385, 6.566, 6.638.

mally exculpated by the fact that they are imitating the deplorable example set for them by the still more august and reprehensible ladies of the imperial household, from the nymphomaniac Messalina to the cold-blooded poisoners Caesonia and Agrippina.[229] If empresses behave this way, Juvenal asks, what can one expect?[230] But why should such well bred women have departed from the chaste, frugal, and hardworking ethos of their ancestors? The answer, for Juvenal, is all too plain. Oriental corruption is to blame, from the superstitious foreign cults of Cybele, Isis, Osiris, and Ammon and the pseudoscientific claptrap of the magi of Chaldea, Armenia, Syria, Egypt, Thessalonia, and Phrygia[231] to the suggestive fashions and meretricious vocabulary that Roman women have learned from the Greeks.[232] But how in turn did this foreign depravity succeed in taking hold? Juvenal is equally sure of where to point the accusing finger. It is the commercial expansion of Rome which opened her society to the corrupting influence of the east:

> Hinc fluxit ad istos
> et Sybaris colles, hinc et Rhodos et Miletos
> atque coronatum et petulans madidcumque Tarentum.
> Prima peregrinos obscena pecunia mores
> intulit, et turpi fregerunt saecula luxu
> divitiae molles.[233]

> Sybaris, Rhodes,
> Miletus, shameless Tarentum, drunk and garlanded—all
> Come pouring in upon our Seven Hills. But filthy
> Lucre it was that first brought these loose foreign
> Morals amongst us, enervating wealth that
> Destroyed us, over the years, through shameless self-indulgence.

Ultimately avarice, and by implication the commercial middle classes, have been responsible for turning Rome into a cosmopolitan society in which oriental turpitude has gained the upper hand, seducing the aristocratic matrons of Rome away from their ethical obligations. This constellation of upper-class and xenophobic values explains the hostile and un-Stoic attitude which Juvenal takes not only toward women but also toward homosexuality and Greek education in the poems just examined.

In some of his satires, finally, Juvenal includes some passages which

---

[229] *Sat.* 6.115–132, 6.615–626.
[230] *Sat.* 6.617.
[231] *Sat.* 6.512–516, 6.527–529, 6.531–534, 6.538–541, 6.548–550, 6.553–556, 6.580–581, 6.585–588.
[232] *Sat.* 6.185–199.
[233] *Sat.* 6.295–300; trans. Green.

appear to support Stoic principles; but these principles are in turn crushed under the weight of arguments reflecting non-Stoic perspectives of various kinds. This way of treating Stoicism, as well as some of the moral themes for which Juvenal reserves it, is reminiscent of one group of Horace's poems. An excellent case in point is Juvenal's handling of the related topics of moderation and the simple country life. Like Horace, he repeatedly expresses his dislike of the city and his personal preference for the country, often setting forth a rationale for this taste which has a Stoic coloration on the surface. In one of his poems, written in the form of a dinner invitation to a friend, he bids the addressee to join him at his modest table, taking this occasion to castigate other hosts for their luxury, gluttony, and unedifying parlor entertainments. The Stoics would of course support the appeal to moderation. In addition, the *topos* of friendship making up for a rich cuisine and elegant accoutrements is a commonplace in the genre of the invitation poem. But Juvenal concludes the satire with a straightforward appeal to Epicureanism as his culminating argument: *voluptates commendat rarior usus* ("Pleasures rarely indulged in are more enjoyable.")[234]

This is the sole instance in this group of poems, however, where Juvenal's reasoning depends on Epicureanism. Sometimes he simply argues in terms of practical utility. In another poem praising moderation, he raises the question of how much is enough, answering it with the Stoic criterion of nature as the guide to what is sufficient to our needs.[235] And nature counsels frugality. Juvenal illustrates this point by relating the story of how Alexander the Great grasped the lesson conveyed by Diogenes with his one pottery bowl, which could be mended easily if it broke, and realized that the man who has little and who desires nothing is wiser and happier than the greedy man.[236] For good measure, Juvenal adds the point that the frugal life enables us to free ouselves from the superstitious attempt to forestall or to propitiate the goddess Fortuna.[237] Yet, despite these concessions to Stoicism,[238] the main argument throughout the body of *Satire* 14 is a rehearsal of the traditional practical disadvantages, worries, and fears which flow from wealth.[239] Again, in Juvenal's most acidulated broadside against city life, after describing in electrifying detail the demeaning and uncomfortable existence of the city

---

[234] *Sat.* 11.208.
[235] *Sat.* 14.321.
[236] *Sat.* 14.308-314.
[237] *Sat.* 14.315-316.
[238] Duff, *Silver Age,* p. 620 notes the Stoic elements in this poem but not its non-Stoic content.
[239] *Sat.* 14.284-308.

dweller, he urges the addressee of the poem to live in the country where, by cultivating his garden with his own hands he will obtain enough to live on,[240] a position quite amenable to Stoicism. But the finishing touch to his argument is the point that in the country at least one can be the lord of one lizard,[241] which relocates the issue within the context of his complaint against a society where the people who ought to receive deference and respect are continually being pushed aside by upstarts and foreigners.

This strain of social snobbery in Juvenal also results in a conception of nobility against which the principle, taught by the Stoics and others, that nobility is an ethical rather than a genetic endowment, struggles in uncertain hope of victory. Juvenal devotes *Satire* 8 to the theme that *nobilitas sola est atque unica virtus* ("virtue is the one and only nobility.")[242] Having made this point early in the poem, he goes on to list a number of virtues which should be cultivated, including justice, military valor, trustworthiness, honesty, respect for the law, honor, temperance, and kindness.[243] In addition to lamenting the fact that the descendants of the leading Roman noble families have failed to live up to these ideals, he cites by comparison examples of men of lesser birth who displayed their moral excellence and who demonstrated their claims to the praises of their fellow citizens.[244] Yet, Juvenal is far from attacking the system of privilege which surrounds the aristocracy whether their behavior is exemplary or not, as he shows in a passage sneering at a dissolute nobleman who goes slumming, drinking in lowbrow taverns with escaped convicts, navvies, roughnecks, executioners, coffin-makers, and unfrocked priests: *aequa ibi libertas, communia pocula, lectus/ non alius cuiquam, non mensa remotior ulli* ("Here is freedom and equality: they share a common cup and bed and board.")[245] While a Stoic might agree that some of the drinkers around the table are indeed equal in their vice and folly, Juvenal includes others in the group merely because of their low social status; even an immoral aristocrat possesses nobility as a corollary of his birth and should not lower his dignity by associating with the dregs of society.[246]

Juvenal's most elaborate subversion of Stoicism in the context of a poem where he ostensibly supports it is *Satire* 13, written in the persona

---

[240] *Sat.* 3.222–230.
[241] *Sat.* 3.231.
[242] *Sat.* 8.20.
[243] *Sat.* 8.79–94.
[244] *Sat.* 8.236–268.
[245] *Sat.* 8.177–178.
[246] The anti-Stoic element in this satire has been noted by Duff, *Roman Satire*, p. 154; Friedlaender, comm. on his ed. of *Satires*, p. 121; Green, comm. on his trans. of *Satires*, p. 191.

of a counselor advising a friend who has been defrauded and whom the judicial process has provided no satisfaction. In the course of this poem Juvenal sets forth some important Stoic ethical principles, although he disavows adherence to any one philosophical school and although he departs from the sense of the Stoic doctrines he cites in his handling of his friend's problem. The organization of Juvenal's brief in this poem is somewhat convoluted and it may be well to summarize the main points he makes before subjecting them to analysis.

Juvenal begins by stating that vice is its own punishment; an evildoer, such as the criminal responsible for his friend's dilemma, will suffer pangs of conscience even if he manages to clear himself of guilt in court by suborning the judge.[247] Thus, he advises, do not be upset at the existence of fraud and dishonesty and at the failure of the judicial system to punish the guilty and to make restitution to their victims. In any case, he adds, apart from the internal punishment which the guilty will endure, other innocent victims have suffered from worse crimes;[248] and crime, after all, is a normal feature of Roman life, nothing to be surprised at nowadays,[249] a point which he illustrates lavishly. People are dishonest whatever they claim to believe in; religion supplies no deterrent.[250] Those who believe in fortune think that everything is predetermined and that this relieves them of all personal responsibility for their actions; those believing in the gods think that they can escape retribution by prayers and propitiations. Given the fact that society is corrupt and that its official creeds serve as no brake to wrongdoing, the victimization of the innocent is inevitable. The solution is not to try to reform society but to reconcile oneself to misfortune and thereby to overcome it. While he himself disclaims membership in either the Cynic, the Stoic, or the Epicurean schools,[251] Juvenal argues that philosophy is a means of learning how to triumph over misfortune—but so, he adds, is ordinary common-sense experience:

> An nihil in melius tot rerum proficis usu?
> Magna quidem, sacris quae dat praecepta libellis,
> victrix fortunae sapientia, ducimus autem
> hos quoque felices, qui ferre incommoda vitae
> nec iactare iugum vita didicere magistra.[252]

> Or has a lifetime's experience taught you nothing at all?
> Philosophy's fine, its scriptures provide you with precepts

---

[247] Sat. 13.1-4.
[248] Sat. 13.5-18, 13.124-158.
[249] Sat. 13.23-85, 13.159-173.
[250] Sat. 13.86-119.
[251] Sat. 13.120-123.
[252] Sat. 13.18-22; trans. Green.

For rising above misfortune: but those who have learnt the hard way
In the school of life, to bear all vicissitudes
Without fret or resentment—don't we admire them too?

Having established that crime is rampant and having given the fore-
going advice, Juvenal then moves on to explain more concretely how his
counsel can be applied to his friend's situation. Criminals, as he has
noted, are rarely punished as they deserve, owing to the corruption of
the courts. And, even when one is punished, the money which he has
defrauded is rarely restored to the victim. Still, the contemplation of the
condemned man's sufferings is sweet vengeance.[253] But stop—Juvenal
interrupts himself. This delight in vengeance is a very unenlightened
attitude which wins no support at all from the philosophers, among
whom he names Chrysippus.[254] The true aim of philosophy is to strip
away such ignorant errors, not to reinforce them:

[Plurima felix
paulatim vitia atque errores exuit, omnes
prima docens rectum, sapientia.][255]

Benign
Philosophy, by degrees, peels away our follies and most
of our vices, gives us a grounding in right and wrong.

The lust for vengeance is a moral error, a sign of weakmindedness and
meagerness of spirit.[256] Actually, says Juvenal, reminding the addressee
of a point he made earlier, the guilty man will be punished by his own
conscience more than by an external judicial penalty and even in its
absence; his conscience will cause him to suffer from fear and worry and
their psychosomatic effects, such as insomnia, nightmares, and the inability to eat.[257] These penalties levied on the criminal by his own conscience
increase with the seriousness of the crime. While one's inner intention
alone makes one guilty of a crime, Juvenal acknowledges, the internal
punishment of conscience is even greater if one translates intention into
action.[258]

Juvenal at this point seems to have realized that he has erected such
a strong case for the Stoic principle that vice is its own punishment that
he has made it difficult to understand why, in that event, anyone would

---

[253] *Sat.* 13.174-180.
[254] *Sat.* 13.184.
[255] *Sat.* 13.187-189; trans. Green.
[256] *Sat.* 13.189-192.
[257] *Sat.* 13.192-207, 13.210-238.
[258] *Sat.* 13.208-210.

ever be motivated to commit a crime. He tries to repair this deficiency
in his argument by shifting the burden of proof to another Stoic principle.
Criminals, he says, while they may feel the scruples of conscience immediately after committing a crime, all too soon return to their immoral
ways. They are evil men at heart and an evil man has a basically vicious
intention which defines his moral state as such:

> Cum scelus admittunt, superest constantia; quod fas
> atque nefas tandem incipiunt sentire peractis
> criminibus. Tamen ad mores natura recurrit
> damnatos fixa et mutari nescia. Nam quis
> peccandi finem posuit sibi? Quando recepit
> eiectum semel attrita de fronte ruborem?
> Quisnam hominum est quem tu contentum videris uno
> flagitio?[259]

> Bad men, by and large, display shifty, capricious natures:
> They're bold enough in action: it's afterwards, when the crime's
> Accomplished, that notions of right and wrong begin to
> Assail their minds. But soon they're back to the same old tricks
> They so lately abjured—they can't change their nature: who
> Ever set limits upon his programme of crime? When did
> A hardened brow recover the capacity for blushing
> Once it was lost? What man have you ever seen satisfied
> With a single villainous action?

This observation seems to offer cold comfort to the victim, now that the
previous thought of the criminal's ongoing punishment by his own conscience has been withdrawn. But Juvenal rallies with a new point on
which he triumphantly concludes. Even though the criminal returns to
his evil ways, crime will out, eventually. And even if society is too corrupt
to penalize him, he will ultimately be punished by the gods. Thus, the
victim will get his revenge in the end in the assurance that the gods do
justice even if men do not.[260]

As can be seen from this brief summary of Satire 13, Juvenal draws on
a number of Stoic doctrines but he uses them inconsistently, undermining
them by the contradictory manner in which he handles them and by
their association with the non-Stoic principles to which they are subordinated. He asserts, to begin with, that vice is its own punishment, the
second half of the Stoic maxim that virtue is its own reward. However,
he goes on to show that this is not really the case. The sinner's punishment
at the bar of his own conscience is merely a momentary departure from

---

[259] *Sat.* 13.237-244; trans. Green.
[260] *Sat.* 13.244-249.

his ongoing moral outlook, by no means a deterrent strong enough to prevent recidivism. The truly enduring punishment received by the guilty is not the internal punishment imposed by his own conscience but the external punishment imposed by the gods.

A second major Stoic principle which Juvenal first supports and then perverts is the idea that one's moral ego resides in one's intention. In the case of criminals, he says, a fixed intention to do evil defines their moral character. Juvenal appears to recognize that this fixed intention to do evil is the opposite of the fixed intention to do good which goes by the name of the constancy of the sage; in line 237 he explicitly rules out the application of the term *constantia* to the behavior of criminals. But in developing his picture of the psychology of vice, he contradicts the premise that the criminal has a fixed intention to do evil in his argument that criminals do feel pangs of conscience, even if briefly. Such conscientious self-recognition on the part of the sinner suggests that a person can will to do evil, having judged it to be evil. It further implies that the fool can become wise spontaneously, if momentarily, and that a man once converted to the status of a sage could voluntarily regress to the status of a fool, theories that would be hotly contested by the Stoa. Another distortion of Stoicism in Juvenal's treatment of this topic is his use of the term *natura* in line 239. The sinner sins, he says, because he acts in conformity with his own nature. The implication of this statement is that the criminal would be acting unnaturally if he abandoned the life of crime. For the Stoa, of course, virtue is life in accordance with nature. "Nature" is always used in a normative as well as a descriptive sense when the Stoics apply this notion to ethics. But Juvenal here uses the term in a purely descriptive sense and thereby manages to substitute a functional conception of nature for the normative Stoic identification of nature with the rational good.

Finally, there is Juvenal's promotion of philosophy as a source of consolation in the midst of injustices which one cannot change, as a cure for the base and smallminded desire for vengeance. As an effort to come to grips with the psychology of the criminal and to put it into some sort of manageable perspective through a rational understanding of it, Juvenal's argument is manifestly a failure. He does not succeed in unsnarling the contradictions in which he entangles himself in his juxtaposition of the two Stoic principles that vice is its own punishment and that vice lies in a fixed evil intention. As far as achieving a substitution of forebearance for vengeance, all that Juvenal really attempts to do in *Satire* 13 is to shift the locus of vengeance from one point to another in his addressee's expectations. The first stage of the argument counsels him not to hope for vengeance through the prosecution of the criminal by the courts; the corruption of the judicial system is such that it cannot predictably supply satisfaction to the victim. Next, he asserts that vengeance will be obtained by the contemplation of the torments of conscience suffered by the criminal. But he immediately abandons this position in his counter-claim that these torments of conscience are only a passing aberration in the criminal's basic psychology. His ultimate effort is not to persuade the addressee to give up the desire for vengeance, although he has previously argued that this desire is irrational and immoral. Rather, Juvenal shifts the task of wreaking vengeance to the gods, making them stand in contempt of the wisdom taught by philosophy instead of treating them as exponents of the *logos* that permeates the moral as well as the natural order. The only real consolation which *Satire* 13 provides lies in Juvenal's effort to palliate his friend's indignation by reminding him of all the other people who have suffered injustices worse than his. This argument points to the fact that Juvenal's real purpose in *Satire* 13 is to flay his contemporaries for the injustices which they perpetrate or tolerate rather than to provide a coherent Stoic formula for reducing them to *adiaphora*. For Juvenal these social and moral ills are not matters of indifference at all. They are not to be addressed with equanimity but with righteous indignation.

The contradictions in *Satire* 13 point to some of the broader contradictions in Juvenal's thought as a whole, as well as providing the most elaborate example of his conversion of an ostensible apologia for Stoicism into something quite different. In the last group of poems which we have considered, the alternative rationale which Juvenal offers is at one point Epicurean and at several points utilitarian, but most frequently it expresses the frustrated anger of a man who feels helpless in the midst of a society which he sees as disintegrating from within thanks to the irresponsibility of its leaders and their willingness to collaborate with arrivistes who pander to their worst instincts. A socially based critique is even more evident in the second group of poems examined, where Juvenal's substitutes for Stoicism, whether idiosyncratic or traditional, are supported by an analysis of Rome's historical development from a small Italic community to a heterogeneous commercial empire as he seeks the causes of her moral decline. Even in some of the poems in the first group, where Juvenal takes a warmly sympathetic attitude toward a number of Stoic doctrines, his remarks are often set in the context of poems whose main theme is this same moral decline of Roman society. The influx of foreigners, the upsurge of nouveaux riches, and the demoralization of the patrician class combine to explain this decline, not the proliferation of judgments contrary to nature in the Stoic sense.

If this is the moral problem he sees, what is Juvenal's solution? Although his diagnosis is rarely Stoic, might not the cure be Stoic, considering the deep appreciation of Stoicism which he reveals in some of his poems? Or, is his solution a reversal of the historical process that has brought Rome to its present condition, a return to a Golden Age in the ancient Roman past? Although Stoicism is represented more strongly in Juvenal than the teachings of any other philosophical school, it is not present in sufficient density or consistency to provide a positive corrective for the ills he analyzes. Despite Juvenal's acceptance of the principles of humanitarianism and benevolence based on the recognition of the common rational endowment shared by all human beings, his egalitarianism and fellow-feeling in practice are contained within certain elastic limits marked off by class, nationality, and sex. His appeal to moral autarchy, his injunction that men disengage themselves from the things beyond their own control, are in the end not persuasive enough to temper the wrath he heaps on a historical development which he can in no sense control and on a social world within which he feels powerless. His prayer for equanimity in *Satire* 10 seems written as much to convince Juvenal himself as to sway the reader. Whether he does succeed in convincing himself is debatable. But a return to an ideal Roman past is neither fully possible nor fully desirable.[261] Juvenal holds up as exemplary the ancient virtues but he cannot always repress a grimace at the primitivism of life in those days, at the oppressiveness of its unrelieved righteousness, and at the superstitious character of Roman religion. In the end, Juvenal neither swallows his own Stoic prescriptions nor resolves the tensions implicit in his appeal to the *mos maiorum*. Juvenal's moral optimism is guarded and only partially Stoic at best.

Juvenal met a post-mortem fate rather different from that of either Horace or Persius.[262] Neglected for 250 years after his death, his works became known again largely through the efforts of commentators and grammarians such as Servius, Donatus, Probus, and Priscian. The first Latin authors to cite him with approval were the Christian apologists Tertullian and Lactantius. By the end of the fourth century a reference in the historian Ammianus Marcellinus indicates that some non-Christians were reading him as well. Christian Latin poetry between the fourth

---

[261] Juvenal's inconsistency on this point has been noted by Green, comm. on his trans. of *Satires,* pp. 38-39.

[262] On this topic see Friedlaender, intro. to his ed. of *Satires,* pp. 80-92; Highet, *Juvenal the Satirist,* pp. 2, 180-90; and Paul Wessner, "Lucan, Statius, und Juvenal bei den römischen Grammatikern," *Philologische Wochenschrift, 49* (1929), 296-303, 328-35. Ferdinando Gabotto, "Appunti sulla fortuna di alcuni autori romani nel medioevo: Giovenale," *Biblioteca delle scuole italiane, 3:*17 (16 giugno 1891), 260-64 has been superseded. J.-A. Hild, "Juvénal dans le moyen âge," *Bulletin de la Faculté des lettres de Poitiers, 8* (1890), 177-89; *9* (1891), 39-54, 106-22, 235-52 contains some useful information although it is presented in a rather disorganized manner.

and sixth centuries contains a number of reminiscences of Juvenal and he was used fairly extensively by St. Augustine as a source for the decay of Roman morals under paganism. St. Jerome; in his stance as a satirist, found him even more appealing as a model. But it is Servius above all who receives the credit for putting Juvenal back in circulation, both through his own commentaries, which quote him over seventy times, and through the work of his disciple Nicaeus, who produced the first known textual rescension of Juvenal. The manuscript tradition remained very scanty until the fifth century. Carolingian efforts to rescue the text of Juvenal were intensive and serve as the basis of all modern editions; but many problems with the text still remain unresolved to this day.

Conceivably Juvenal received less attention from his immediate posterity than did Persius because his style, although brilliant, was easier to read, less challenging, and less controversial. After the ninth century his fortunes were often coupled with those of Persius and the works of the two satirists are sometimes found in the same manuscripts from the Carolingian era onward. A poorer source of Stoicism than either Persius or Horace in terms of the range of doctrines he communicates, Juvenal none the less plays a significant role in the transmission of Stoicism to the medieval period. On a number of points he reinforces the information on Stoicism found in previous authors. There are also some Stoic positions he communicates, notably the school's teaching on cannibalism, that are difficult to find at all or so well expressed anywhere else in Latin literature. Juvenal brings a passionate intensity to the advocacy of Stoic moral teachings at the points in his works where he professes them, a conviction which could endow them with a compelling appeal to his medieval readers even when they are isolated from the less rigorously Stoic body of his writings. Like his fellow satirists, Horace and Persius, Juvenal did much to strengthen the medieval impression of Stoicism as a philosophy identifiable preeminently with ethics.

CHAPTER FOUR

THE EPIC POETS

Classical Latin epic, no less than satire, lent itself to the expression of philosophical ideas and attitudes. In Romanizing this genre, the Latin epic poets could and did bring a certain amount of Stoicism to bear on their material. The Stoic elements that occur most typically in Latin epic poetry are relatively few in number. They touch mainly on the themes of fate, the gods, and the interaction of the divine will with human choices, and on the moral character of the epic hero as well as the personages with whom he is contrasted. There are striking differences in the success with which individual authors in this tradition assimilated the Stoic ideas on which they drew and integrated them effectively with their other sources. Stoicism is sometimes presented in its most overt form by those Latin epic poets who were the least accomplished practitioners of their art. On the other hand, Stoicism is sometimes appropriated with much more sensitivity and with a far greater sense of its own latent ambiguities by those poets who were the most gifted exponents of the classical Latin epic.

I. Vergil

This judgment certainly holds true for Vergil. Acclaimed since his own day as the Latin epic poet par excellence, Vergil displays a profound and perceptive feeling for the ethical and metaphysical implications of Stoic philosophy. To the extent that he appeals to Stoic principles in the *Aeneid* he internalizes them thoroughly and weaves them seamlessly into the web of his epic. Yet, he subordinates them ultimately to his own personal poetic vision. Vergil's ability to grasp the inner significance of the Stoic doctrines which he uses points to the pervasive influence which this philosophy had attained in the Roman culture of his own day, for there is nothing in Vergil's own education, associations, or style of life that suggests any Stoic inclinations on his part. Indeed, his biography would lead one to expect him to have a much more Epicurean cast of mind.

A great deal of evidence about Vergil's life was gathered in antiquity, thanks to his immediate and enduring fame as a literary figure.[1] Vergil

---

[1] Good treatments of Vergil's biography can be found in Jean-Paul Brisson, *Virgile: son temps et le nôtre* (Paris, 1966), pp. 15-56; Karl Büchner, *P. Vergilius Maro: Der Dichter der Römer* (Stuttgart, 1966), cols. 2-41; Tenney Frank, *Vergil: A Biography* (New York, 1922); W. F. Jackson Knight, *Roman Vergil*, rev. ed. (Harmondsworth, 1966), pp. 52-64.

(70/71-19 B.C.) was the son of a small but prosperous farmer who attained some eminence in the region near Mantua. The education he provided for Vergil was designed to elevate his son still higher through a career as an advocate and politician. Vergil was sent to school at Cremona, Milan, and eventually Rome to study rhetoric, with the best teachers available. Vergil did make a maiden speech in court but left the forum abruptly thereafter, presumably because the career of advocacy did not appeal to him. He may have taken part in the civil war between Caesar and Pompey, conceivably participating in the battle of Pharsalus in 48 B.C. However, Vergil suffered from poor health throughout his life, which may have led to his discharge after a brief tour of duty or to his exemption from military service altogether.

In 35 B.C. Vergil settled in Campania, where he spent the rest of his days. He joined a philosophical circle of Epicurean stamp, founded by Phaedrus and continued by Philodemus and Siro, Siro being the current leader of that school in Italy. Vergil remained in this group for six years until Siro's death. He took no further part in public life except for an appeal to the government for the restoration of certain family lands near his birthplace, which had been confiscated and redistributed to the demobilized troops following Octavius' victory at Philippi in 42 B.C. Vergil stayed at home, cultivated his privacy, and devoted himself to his poetry. His *Eclogues*, published in 40 B.C., earned him immediate acclaim and the patronage of Maecenas. His position as an imperial protégé after this time involved occasional trips to Rome, but he preferred to live quietly and modestly at his villa in Campania. There, between 37 and 30 B.C., he also wrote the *Georgics* and then the *Aeneid*, which he composed between 30 and 19 B.C. and on which he undertook revisions between 21 and 19 B.C. In 19 B.C. Vergil travelled to Greece to visit the sites mentioned in his epic. At Megara he fell ill. He returned home at once, died at Brundisium, and was buried near his house in Campania. Vergil did not want his *Aeneid* to be published in its imperfectly revised state. Augustus, however, either overruled this wish or persuaded Vergil to let his friends Lucius Varius and Plotius Tucca edit the work if he were unable to finish it himself. Varius and Tucca took on this task and published the *Aeneid* in 15 B.C. It was hailed at once as the crowning literary achievement of the Augustan age and as the greatest masterpiece of Latin epic poetry, gaining for Vergil the undisputed pride of place in the school tradition from which no subsequent shifts in taste were capable of dislodging him.

It is generally agreed that Vergil's *Georgics* mark an important stage in his development from a lyric to an epic poet and in the emergence of the characteristic Vergilian attitude toward life which he expresses in the

Aeneid. His *Eclogues* represent an entirely successful reexpression of Greek pastoral poetry in the Latin idiom, but their philosophical content is negligible. The *Georgics,* however, do reflect a distinct philosophical perspective. In some quarters this point of view has been interpreted as Stoic, although there is little basis for the opinion. The particular aspects of the *Georgics* that have been singled out for comment in this connection are worth examining because they have parallels in the *Aeneid,* where Vergil sometimes handles the same themes similarly and sometimes does not. Of primary interest are the themes of work, the nature of the deity and his relationship to the created universe, the connection between animals and men, and the quest for an understanding of the laws of nature. The Stoics held distinctive views on all of these subjects, which are not the views that Vergil chooses to express on them in the *Georgics.* He relies instead on insights drawn from Lucretius, from Hesiod, and from his own personal conception of life.

No doubt the most famous line in Vergil's *Georgics* is *felix qui potuit rerum cognoscere causas,* which has sometimes been read as a statement of Stoic theodicy or of the Stoic's responsibility to apply his knowledge to the service of others.[2] This same line has also been read as a forthright Epicurean attempt to demythologize nature.[3] The text suggests that the Epicurean interpretation has much more to be said for it than the Stoic, a point that seems evident when the whole passage in which the line occurs is considered:

> Felix qui potuit rerum cognoscere causas
> atque metus omnis et inexorabile fatum
> subiecit pedibus strepitumque Acherontis avari:
> fortunatus et ille deos qui novit agrestis
> Panque Silvanumque senem Nymphasque sorores.
> Illum non populi fusces, non purpura regum
> flexit et infidos agitans discordia fratres, ...[4]

> That man is happy who can understand
> The nature of the world and crush all fears
> Of ruthless fate and unrelenting hell.
> But happy too, who knows the country gods,
> Pan, old Sylvanus and the sister Nymphs.
> No magistral power nor royal pomp
> Disturbs his peace, nor fratricidal strife, ...

---

[2] E.g. Pierre Boyancé, "Le sens cosmique de Virgile," *REL, 32* (1954), 232, 235; Smith Palmer Bovie, intro. to his trans. of *Georgics* (Chicago, 1956), pp. xvi–xx.

[3] Friedrich Klingner, *Virgil: Bucolica, Georgica, Aeneis* (Zürich, 1967), p. 271; L. P. Wilkinson, *The Georgics of Virgil: A Critical Survey* (Cambridge, 1969), p. 121.

[4] Publius Vergilius Maro, *Georgica* 1.490–497, in *Opera,* ed. R. A. B. Mynors (Oxford, 1969), trans. K. R. Mackenzie (London, 1969). All references to Vergil's works will be taken from the Mynors ed. and translations of the *Georgics* from Mackenzie.

Here we see the Lucretian idea of scientific knowledge freeing the mind
from fear of the gods and from a conception of fate as hostile and implacable, an Epicurean rationalization of an otherwise confusing and
terrifying world order. While Vergil does not abandon the gods themselves, the deities he mentions are the patrons of the countryside, a device
which he uses to emphasize the Epicurean preference for the rustic private life as contrasted with the ambitions and contentions of the forum.
At another point in the *Georgics* he returns to the Epicurean theme of
scientific knowledge as a means of liberation from superstition, in criticizing the attitude of shepherds who shrink from applying the proper
precautions and remedies for the diseases attacking their flocks, praying
to the gods instead.[5] One should, he therefore urges, seek to learn the
causes of things, or at least the practical applications of such knowledge.
Still, in the *Georgics* man lives in a world where nature cannot be understood and controlled entirely. Plagues and storms may carry off one's
livestock and crops unpredictably. A complete rationalization of the
forces of nature is thus impossible, either in Epicurean or in Stoic terms.

None the less, the leading theme of the *Georgics* is man's obligation to
master his natural environment to the extent that he can. This task is a
necessity which, for Vergil, arises from divine fiat, as a consequence of
man's fall from the Golden Age. Before the reign of Jove, the earth delivered her fruits to man without human toil, and men shared all their
possessions in common. But in the present state of human existence, man
must wrest a livelihood from the earth with hardship, developing the
crafts and techniques he needs by his own efforts:

> Pater ipse colendi
> haud facilem esse viam voluit, primusque per artem
> movet agros, curis acuens mortalia corda
> nec torpere gravi passus sua regna veterno.[6]

> The father of mankind himself has willed
> The path of husbandry should not be smooth;
> He first disturbed the fields with human skill,
> Sharpening the wits of mortal men with care,
> Unwilling that his realm should sleep in sloth.

Whatever man gains in this process is his only at a heavy cost: *labor
omnia vicit/ improbus et duris urgens in rebus egestos* ("Work conquered all,/
Relentless work and harsh necessity.")[7] It is not only man himself but

---

[5] *Georg.* 3.440-456.
[6] *Georg.* 1.121-124.
[7] *Georg.* 1.145-146.

also other creatures who must pay the price for every agricultural advance, like the little birds fluttering about in dismay when the plow uproots their long familiar homes[8] and the ox that is bludgeoned to death so that its carcass may generate a swarm of bees.[9] Vergil, it is true, alludes to the labors of Hercules in this connection[10] and a number of commentators have suggested that he is replacing an Epicurean love of *otium* with the Stoic gospel of work.[11] However, it has been noted correctly that Vergil's conception of work in the *Georgics* is not basically a Stoic one. He does not depict nature as beneficent, but as an obstacle with which man must struggle. Man seeks to master the laws of nature in order to overcome nature. Man does not live in a state of harmony with nature but in a state of tension with it, a vision of reality owing a great deal to Hesiod. From this perspective, man may recognize and appreciate the beauty of a landscape ordered by human cultivation, but the work of cultivating it is imposed on man as an onerous duty, not as an ethical value in itself.[12] In the *Georgics* man is obliged to work as a matter of external practical necessity. Despite his allusion to Hercules, Vergil makes no attempt in the *Georgics* to explore the inner, moral implications which human labor may possess.

The same deity who legislates the harsh obligation of labor is also seen in the *Georgics* as a being immanent in nature, arranging all things by his providence, the vital force which permeates the universe and unites all living beings. This feature of the poem is visible above all in the passages where Vergil treats animal husbandry and bee-keeping, and it has inspired many scholars to argue for a Stoic conception of God in the *Georgics*.[13] A closer look at the passages in question belies this interpretation.

---

[8] *Georg.* 2.207-210.
[9] *Georg.* 4.280-558.
[10] *Georg.* 3.4-5.
[11] E.g. A. M. Guillemin, *Virgile: poète, artiste et penseur* (Paris, 1951), pp. 115-28; Josef Lünenborg, *Das philosophische Weltbild in Vergils Georgika* (Bochum, 1935), pp. 21-22, 23, 26, 78-82; L. P. Wilkinson, "Virgil's Theodicy," *CQ*, n.s. *13* (1963), 75-84.
[12] The best discussions of this point are found in Brooks Otis, *Virgil: A Study in Civilized Poetry* (Oxford, 1966), pp. 157-59, who none the less speaks of "Virgil's Stoic philosophy" in this connection, p. 158; W. Y. Sellar, *The Roman Poets of the Augustan Age; Virgil*, 3rd ed. (Oxford, 1908), pp. 211-12. See also Büchner, *P. Vergilius Maro*, col. 315; Jacques Perret, "The *Georgics*," in *Virgil: A Collection of Critical Essays*, ed. Steele Commager (Englewood Cliffs, 1966), p. 33, whose remarks are vitiated by his belief that the Stoics viewed man's material nature as inferior to his spirit.
[13] E.g. Boyancé, "Le sens cosmique de Virgile," *REL, 32* (1954), 235; Brisson, *Virgile*, p. 221; Hellfried Dahlmann, "Der Bienenstaat in Vergils Georgica," *Kleine Schriften* (Hildesheim, 1970), pp. 192-96; T. J. Haarhoff, "Virgil's Garden of Flowers and His Philosophy of Nature," *Greece & Rome*, ser. 2:5 (1958), 77, 78; *Vergil the Universal* (Oxford, 1949), pp. 77, 78; Guillemin, *Virgile*, pp. 124, 128-131; Lünenborg, *Das philos. Weltbild*, pp. 21-22, 23, 26, 78-82; Hermann Raabe, *Plurima mortis imago: Vergleichende Interpretationen zur Bildersprache Vergils* (München, 1974), pp. 59-60; Wolfgang Schadewaldt, "Sinn und

In discussing the bees, their mode of organization, and its parallels with human society, for example, Vergil states a point of view but he does not say whether he personally subscribes to it:

> His quidam signis atque haec exempla secuti
> esse apibus partem divinae mentis et haustus
> aetherios dixere; deum namque ire per omnis
> terrasque tractusque muris caelumque profundum;
> hinc pecudes, armenta, viros, genus omne ferarum,
> quemque sibi tenuis nascentem arcessere vitas:
> scilicet huc reddi deinde ac resoluta referre
> omnia, nec morti esse locum, sed viva volare
> sideris in numerum atque alto succedere caelo.[14]

> Inferring from these signs and instances,
> Some men have argued that the bees received
> A share of the divine intelligence,
> A spark of heavenly fire. For God, they say,
> Pervades all things, the earth and sea and sky.
> From Him the flocks and herds, and man and beast,
> Each draws the thin-spun stream of life at birth;
> To Him all things return, at last dissolved:
> There is no place for death, but living still
> They fly to join the number of the stars.

Certainly the notion of God as all-pervading is Stoic, as is the conception of God as fire. However, for the Stoics man is the only creature who is granted a share of the divine *logos,* an attribute which is located in the very faculty of reason that differentiates man so decisively from the sub-human world. Similarly, insofar as the Stoics support the idea of life after death and the elevation of souls to the realm of the stars, this is a posthumous honor accorded to man only, specifically to those individuals who have manifested the virtues of the sage.[15]

Vergil's tendency to blur the distinctions between men and animals is also visible in his treatment of the sexual and social instincts. In livestock and in human beings, he says, the mating instinct is the same: *amor omnibus idem.*[16] This notion empties human nature of its distinctively rational character, denying to man the capacity to control and direct his passions. Insofar as Vergil draws a parallel between animal society and human

---

Werden der vergilischen Dichtung," in *Wege zu Vergil: Drei Jahrzehnte Begegnungen in Dichtung und Wissenschaft,* ed. Hans Oppermann, Wege der Forschung, 19 (Darmstadt, 1963), pp. 58-59; Sellar, *Roman Poets,* p. 213; Wilkinson, *Georgics of Virgil,* pp. 122-24, 140, 152.

[14] *Georg.* 4.219-227.

[15] This point is well developed by Büchner, *P. Vergilius Maro,* col. 315.

society in his analysis of the bees, the message he has to communicate is a demoralizing one for mankind. The bees, however well adapted to harmonious group behavior they may be, are subject in turn to the will of a higher power, in this case, man himself, who is capable of manipulating and punishing them at his own discretion. Even when an external human agent does not intervene, the bees are totally dependent on their leader, at whose death they go berserk, losing all their community spirit, turning on their own hive and honey and destroying them.[17] The claim that animals possess a share of the divine mind thus appears to be refuted by Vergil's observation of the way that animals actually behave. And if man is placed on a continuum that includes animals, his capacity to exert any special intelligence deriving from his consubstantiality with the divine nature is likewise cast seriously in doubt.

There are, thus, a number of ambiguities in the *Georgics*, arising from the tension between man's rationality and his participation in the subhuman order and from the tension between his obligation to apply his constructive energies to the taming of the earth and the fact that his efforts are always conditioned by forces greater than himself which he cannot control. It certainly cannot be said that Vergil resolves these tensions in the *Georgics* or that he looks to Stoicism as a possible source of assistance. Ambiguities and unresolved tensions remain a feature of Vergil's vision of life in the *Aeneid* as well. In the epic they are centered on a number of the same themes: the gods' governance of the universe and their relationship to human effort and will, and human reason and its relationship to the irrational passions and instincts. In the *Aeneid* Vergil occasionally alludes to motifs that he had raised earlier in the *Georgics*. He also gives significantly greater scope to Stoicism as a framework within which he deals with some of these themes in the *Aeneid*. But in the end he does not adopt Stoicism as a philosophical solution capable of dealing satisfactorily with the complex historical and ethical problems which he has elected to treat in his epic.

Stoicism in the *Aeneid* is represented most strongly in Vergil's depiction of the gods as agents of destiny and their relation to human effort and choice. Vergil devotes a great deal of attention to the topic of *fatum* or *fortuna* on the one side and to human *labor* on the other. His conception of fate has drawn much scholarly attention, largely because Vergil does not always use the relevant terms in the same way. Fate, for him, sometimes means simply the circumstances of life,[18] the luck or happiness of

---

[16] *Georg.* 3.244.
[17] *Georg.* 4.86–87, 4.212–214.
[18] *Aen.* 1.454.

an individual or group,[19] which may conflict with that of another individual or group.[20] It is sometimes identified with the will of Jove[21] which he may or may not reveal to the lesser gods or to men.[22] Sometimes the lesser gods can act as agents of fate in advancing their own desires over against Jove's will, but at most they can only deflect or delay fate, for it is ineluctable.[23] Yet, there appears to be a need for human cooperation with fate in order for it to be effective;[24] and at one major point in the epic Jove appears to dissociate himself from his own control over events.[25] A number of commentators have noted these apparent discrepancies in Vergil's treatment of fate and have concluded that his conception of fate and the gods is simply not clear and that he hesitates on this subject because of his own uncertainties,[26] because he was writing the *Aeneid* as a work of propaganda and wanted to avoid offending people with differing beliefs,[27] or because he deliberately wanted to convey a sense of unreconciled tension or to express a pessimistic view of life.[28]

What is actually at issue in Vergil's treatment of fate is the Stoic doctrine of necessity and contingency. In human terms, this doctrine means that there is a mutual relationship between fate, as administered by the gods, and human free will. Fate is, to be sure, inexorable. But in asserting this principle Vergil is not saying that man must subordinate himself to destiny by the abnegation of his free will. Rather, with the Stoics, Vergil holds that man's virtuous acceptance of his fate involves a voluntary choice on his part, a choice that is itself a necessary ingredient in the causation of events. In some respects, man is limited and controlled by fate; but fate does not operate without contingency. It, too, is controlled to some extent by the decisions and actions of men.

A number of scholars have noted the Stoic dimensions of this point

---

[19] *Aen.* 1.1-7, 1.18, 1.22, 1.32, 1.38, 4.653, 12.435-436.

[20] *Aen.* 2.385.

[21] *Aen.* 1.238-241, 1.257-295, 3.375-376, 12.503-594.

[22] *Aen.* 1.257-295, 1.299, 4.110-111.

[23] *Aen.* 1.1-7, 1.18, 1.22, 1.32, 1.38, 3.395, 5.604, 7.294-295, 7.313-316, 8.334, 10.62-95, 10.621-627.

[24] *Aen.* 2.54-56.

[25] *Aen.* 10.1-15, 10.35, 10.107-112.

[26] See, for example, W. A. Camps, *An Introduction to Virgil's Aeneid* (London, 1969), pp. 42-43; John M. Dougherty, "Vergilian 'Fate' as Cosmic," *CB, 34* (1958), 65, 67; Jacques Perret, *Virgile,* nouvelle éd. (Paris, 1965), pp. 130-35.

[27] J. D. Jefferis, "The Theology of the *Aeneid*: Its Antecedents and Developments," *CJ, 30* (1934), 28-38.

[28] The most detailed expressions of this position are Louise E. Matthaei, "The Fates, the Gods, and the Freedom of Man's Will in the *Aeneid*," *CQ, 2* (1917), 11-25 and H. L. Tracy, "*Fata Deum* and the Action of the *Aeneid*," *Greece & Rome,* ser. 2:*11,* (1964), 188-95. See also Pierre Boyancé, *La Religion de Virgile* (Paris, 1963), pp. 42-57; Francis A. Sullivan, "Virgil and the Mystery of Suffering," *AJP, 90* (1969), 165-72.

correctly,[29] and it is certainly borne out by the epic itself. Fortune is all-powerful, Vergil states repeatedly, and fate is inescapable; *fortuna omnipotens et ineluctabile fatum*.[30] The lesser deities, especially Juno and Venus, appear to function as hypostases of the passions that conflict with rational providence. Juno personifies wrath, hatred, and vengefulness, as she seeks to inflict sufferings on the Trojans, to place obstacles in their path, and to assist their enemies, even though she is aware of the fact that she cannot impede their destiny in any final sense.[31] Venus no doubt has a broader significance in the *Aeneid*, but in this contrast with Juno she personifies the immediate gratification of desire, impatience, impulsiveness, inconstancy, and the unwillingness to subordinate passing interests to larger goals. While she feels free to criticize Jove for the delays experienced by the Trojans in their passage to Italy and for the hardships that he lays upon them,[32] she herself engineers the love affair between Dido and Aeneas, even though it can only lead to suffering for Aeneas and delay in his attainment of the ends which she desires for him. Where Venus reflects a lack of singlemindedness and the triumph of the pleasure principle, Juno reflects obstinacy, the misdirected will persisting stubbornly in a lost cause. This conflict between passion and reason manifests on a divine level the kinds of moral struggles experienced by mortals on a human level. The ability of these goddesses to impose their will on the course of events, temporarily at least, signifies the capacity of the passions to deflect men from a rational acceptance of what must be. But the inability of both gods and men to contravene the decrees of fate perma-

---

[29] The most sensitive treatment of this question is in Otis, *Virgil*, pp. 226-30, 234-37. See also Cyril Bailey, *Religion in Virgil* (Oxford, 1935), pp. 208-34. Other scholars with less detailed treatments of the topic, some of whom do not identify the Stoic elements involved, include Brisson, *Virgile*, pp. 288-91; Karl Büchner, "Der Schicksalsgedanke bei Vergil," in *Wege zu Vergil*, ed. Oppermann, pp. 270-300; *P. Vergilius Maro*, cols. 438-40; Gunnar Carlsson, "The Hero and Fate in Vergil's *Aeneid*," *Eranos*, 43 (1945), 119-20; George E. Duckworth, "Fate and Free Will in Vergil's *Aeneid*," *CJ*, 51 (1956), 357-64; Guillemin, *Virgile*, pp. 213-18; John MacInnes, "The Conception of *Fata* in the *Aeneid*," *Classical Review*, 24 (1910), 169-74; Brooks Otis, "The Originality of the *Aeneid*," in *Virgil*, ed. D. R. Dudley (London, 1969), p. 61; Henry W. Prescott, *The Development of Virgil's Art* (Chicago, 1927), pp. 250-53, 423; R. D. Williams, *Aeneas and the Roman Hero* (London, 1973), pp. 31-32. A number of other authors have identified Vergil's conception of fate as Stoic, but only in the sense that man must bow to it. See, for example, Boyancé, *La Religion de Virgile*, p. 56; Robert Seymour Conway, "The Philosophy of Vergil," in *Harvard Lectures on the Vergilian Age* (New York, 1967 [repr. of Cambridge, Mass., 1928 ed.]), p. 102; M. Ruch, "Le destin dans l'*Énéide*: Essence et réalité," in *Vergiliana: Recherches sur Vergile*, ed. Henry Bardon and Raoul Verdière (Leiden, 1971), pp. 312-21; Terrot Reavely Glover, *Studies in Virgil* (London, 1904), pp. 279-81.

[30] *Aen.* 8.334.

[31] *Aen.* 1.1-7, 1.22, 5.604, 7.313-316, 10.62-95.

[32] *Aen.* 1.238-241, 10.35.

nently points in turn to the idea that providence is the ruling principle of the universe.

This ruling principle is one that, for Vergil as for the Stoics, is not only capable of being deflected at times by the passions but is a force that also requires man's active rational collaboration in order to be efficacious. Fate will, to be sure, drag man along if he fails to assent to it. But, at the same time it often operates with and through human agency and choice. In relating the story of how the Trojans admitted the Trojan horse within their gates, Aeneas notes that they would have destroyed it, if fate had not dictated otherwise and if their minds had not been deluded.[33] The Trojans' own judgment, as well as their destiny, accounts for their decision. The most impressive elaboration of this idea in the *Aeneid* occurs in Jove's speech to the assembly of gods in Book 10, at which he berates his subordinates for encouraging the war between the Trojans and the Latins. Although he has frequently stated earlier in the epic that the Trojans are fated to defeat the Latins and to found Rome, Jove says at this point that he will favor neither side. Whatever rights or wrongs have brought the belligerents to their present pass, from here on their own actions and the results of the choices that they themselves have made will determine the outcome: *sua cuique exorsa laborem/ fortunaque ferent.*[34]

This speech points to the necessary and reciprocal relationship between divine *fatum* and human *labores* which Vergil treats as the causative force in his epic. *Labor* is certainly a theme which he had developed in the *Georgics,* although in a purely external sense. In the *Aeneid* he expands this notion considerably, endowing it with an inner moral meaning as well as using it to denote physical hardships. He also associates it in a clearly Stoic sense with the figure of Hercules. *Labor* in the *Aeneid* thus bears with it the multiple meaning of difficult exploits, usually of a military nature, and of the inner sufferings which men must endure. In both of these denotations, *labor* stands for the human effort and sacrifice that must be united with providence in accomplishing the goals that life sets before individuals and nations. The processes set in motion by these twin divine and human causes entail endurance both objective and subjective, a conception that has some affinities with the middle Stoic notion of moral progress through the use of, and the willingness to abandon, the preferables,[35] but which is more perfectly expressed in Vergil's own philosophy of *sunt lacrimae rerum.*

Vergil uses the term *labor* in several ways, all of which bear on this

---

[33] *Aen.* 2.54–56.

[34] *Aen.* 10.111–112.

[35] This point has been noted by Heinrich Altevogt, *Labor improbus: Eine Vergilstudie* (Münster i. Westf., 1952).

central idea. *Labor,* in its simplest sense, denotes toilsome constructive activity in general. Thus, when Aeneas arrives in Carthage he sees the Tyrians busy at work in building their city, dredging its harbor, raising its walls, laboring as diligently as bees among the summer flowers.[36] He is amazed by the artistry of their *labores* on their temple of Juno[37] and is impressed by the judiciousness and leadership shown by Dido in assigning the *labores* to her people.[38] Similarly, the commission which Vulcan and his helpers accept in forging arms for Aeneas at Venus' behest is called *labor.*[39] In a much more specific, but still external sense, Vergil uses *labor* to denote military activity and the struggles it entails.[40] In a more general sense, *labor* also refers to physical hardships and obstacles of a material nature, from plague to the passage over uncharted seas to the hazards involved in undertaking untried ventures.[41] On a more subjective level, *labor* stands for the moral triumph over grief, suffering, and sorrow. It denotes inner fortitude and constancy in the face of these trials.[42] Even more typical of Vergil's conception of *labor* are the passages where he uses it to suggest several of these senses of the term at once, as when Helenus, in prophesying to Aeneas the sign indicating where he should found his new city, tells him, *is locus urbis erit, requies ea certa laborum* ("here will be the place for your city, a certain peace and an end to struggle")[43] or when the Sybil tells him how to bear or avoid each of the *labores* that he will encounter enroute to the goal.[44]

Vergil's association of all of these senses of *labor* with each other and his placement of this idea within a Stoic causal framework is also suggested forcibly by his linking of both the concept of *labor* and the character of Aeneas with the myth of Hercules.[45] Hercules, to be sure, signifies

[36] *Aen.* 1.430–431.
[37] *Aen.* 1.455–456.
[38] *Aen.* 1.507–508.
[39] *Aen.* 8.439, 8.442–444.
[40] *Aen.* 2.11, 2.284, 2.385, 6.890–892, 10.111, 10.759.
[41] *Aen.* 1.10, 1.241, 1.627–630, 3.145, 3.367.
[42] *Aen.* 3.714, 11.182–183, 12.435–436.
[43] *Aen.* 3.393, restated 8.46, although Clausen brackets the latter passage.
[44] *Aen.* 3.459.
[45] This theme has received careful study by several scholars, above all Robert W. Cruttwell, *Virgil's Mind At Work: An Analysis of the Symbolism of the Aeneid* (Oxford, 1946), pp. 69–82; Galinsky, *The Herakles Theme,* pp. 132–38, 143–49; "The Hercules-Cacus Episode in *Aeneid* VIII," *AJP, 87* (1966), 18–51; P. McGushin, "Virgil and the Spirit of Endurance," *AJP, 85* (1964), 225–43, 253. Less detailed treatments can be found in Guillemin, *Virgile,* pp. 274–82; Otis, *Virgil,* pp. 330–32; Kenneth Quinn, *Virgil's Aeneid: A Critical Description* (London, 1969), pp. 123–24; Hermann Schnepf, "Das Herculesabenteuer in Virgils Aeneis (VIII 184 f.)," *Gymnasium, 66* (1959), 250–68, who de-emphasizes the Stoic associations; Williams, *Aeneas and the Roman Hero,* p. 52. With this prevailing opinion may be contrasted John W. Zarker, "The Hercules Theme in the 'Aeneid'," *Vergilius, 18* (1972), 34–48, who argues that Vergil intended to oppose the Hercules model with the more civilized and humane Aeneas as an epic hero.

more to Vergil and to his Roman audience than just the Stoic saint and apotheosized sage who endured hardships for the sake of others, hardships which he internalizes as moral virtues through his own voluntary choice. In addition, there are other parallels that Vergil suggests between Hercules and Aeneas. Both are persecuted by Juno;[46] both triumph over rivals who are, or who are compared with, savages, animals, or semi-human beings;[47] both are associated with Atlas, as heroes who figuratively shoulder the weight of the universe;[48] both are inflamed by madness, a *furor* that is not inconsistent with their inner virtuous ethos;[49] both visit and return from the underworld;[50] and both win apotheosis, although in Aeneas' case this honor is reserved for his descendants.[51]

Beyond this, the cult of Hercules is a bond that unites the Trojans and the Latins. In forging his alliance with Evander, Aeneas observes that they share a common descent from Atlas and a common reverence for Hercules.[52] Aventinus, another of the Latin kings, is portrayed as a son of Hercules, wearing a lion-skin,[53] an attribute also attached to Aeneas and Evander.[54] The many-leveled associations conjured up by the myth of Hercules thus serve to reinforce the kinship between the Trojans and the Latins as well as the moral similarities between Aeneas and Hercules as heroic figures characterized by *labor*.[55] Like Aeneas himself, Hercules stands at the same time under the law of fate and under the necessity of free choice and willing self-sacrifice. He, like the other gods, can feel grief at the death of brave warriors[56] just as mortals can feel sorrow for the valiant youths cut down in their flower[57] in imagery reminiscent of the blossoms destroyed by the advance of the plow in the *Georgics*. Even at the moment when Rome's future greatness is being revealed to Aeneas in the underworld, the same note of sadness creeps in, as he sees Marcellus, hope of the nation, who died young.[58] The greatest, as the least, suffer grief and loss. Triumph is ever shadowed by sorrow; and victory, no less than defeat, demands the oblation of some of man's basic human values.

---

[46] *Aen.* 8.820–305.
[47] *Aen.* 8.194, 8.267, 12.94–106.
[48] *Aen.* 6.803, 8.133–142.
[49] *Aen.* 10.758–759, 12.464–467, 12.494–499, 12.525–528, 12.938–951.
[50] *Aen.* 6.119–123.
[51] *Aen.* 6.791–803, 9.641–642.
[52] *Aen.* 8.133–142.
[53] *Aen.* 7.655–658, 7.669.
[54] *Aen.* 2.721–723, 8.177–178, 8.552–553.
[55] *Aen.* 8.291–293.
[56] *Aen.* 10.457–472, 10.758–759, 11.836–840.
[57] *Aen.* 9.435–437, 11.67–71.
[58] *Aen.* 6.865–886.

Vergil's poignant awareness that a heavy price must be paid for all human achievements, his sense of the irreducible tensions in human life, is a perception that he expresses on a cosmic, a historical, and a personal ethical level. It is also the overriding quality in the *Aeneid* which moves the poem out of a Stoic context despite the homage that Vergil pays to the Stoic doctrine of causation. The merging of Stoic motifs into perspectives more fundamental to Vergil can be seen, on the cosmic level, in Book 6, where Aeneas learns about the nature of human souls from Anchises:

> Igneus est ollis vigor et caelestis origo
> seminibus, quantum non noxia corpora tardant
> terrenique hebetant artus moribundique membra.
> Hinc metuunt cupientque, dolent gaudentque, neque auras
> despiciunt clausae tenebris et carcere caeco.[59]

> Their vigor springs from fiery seeds of celestial origin,
> So long as they are not weighed down by harmful bodies
> And earthly members doomed to die. For this reason
> Men fear and desire, they suffer and rejoice. But, they cannot see
> The bright air, shut up in their dark and windowless prison.

The divine being is described here in Stoic terms, as fire and as seminal reasons immanent in creation as the souls of men. Also Stoic are the four passions of fear, desire, pleasure, and pain. But these doctrines are associated with a non-Stoic physics and psychology.[60] Vergil distinguishes between mind and matter. Although he sees God and the human soul as consubstantial and as made up of fiery matter, he views the human body as a prison, the source of the passions and hence the source of sin and suffering. Some features of the eschatology which he attaches to this notion were shared by certain Stoics, although not the critical idea that the body is the essential cause of human vice, which forces men to undergo the purgation of their sins in the next life, until their souls are purified. At that point, according to Vergil, the purified souls can be reembodied,

---

[59] *Aen.* 6.730–734.

[60] Eduard Norden, intro. to his ed. of *Aeneis Buch VI*, 2nd ed. (Leipzig, 1916), pp. 20–48, argues that the sources for this book are primarily Posidonian. The generally accepted view, which is much more plausible, sees Vergil as drawing on diverse Hellenistic philosophical and theological traditions. Excellent studies are provided by M. R. Arundel, "'Principio caelum' (Aeneid vi. 724–751)," *Proceedings of the Virgil Society, 3* (1963–64), 27–34; Friedrich Solmsen, "Greek Ideas of the Hereafter in Virgil's Roman Epic," *Proceedings of the American Philosophical Society, 112* (1968), 8–14; "The World of the Dead in Book 6 of the *Aeneid*," *CP, 67* (1972), 31–41. See also Bailey, *Religion in Virgil*, pp. 241–81; Büchner, *P. Vergilius Maro*, cols. 361–62; Duff, *Golden Age*, p. 334; Rosa Lamacchia, "Ciceros Somnium Scipionis und das sechste Buch der Aeneis," *RM*, n.F. *107* (1964), 261–78; Otis, *Virgil*, pp. 300–01.

not freed forever from the cycle of the cosmos, *more Stoicorum*. Given Vergil's belief that the possession of a body is itself the chief condition from which man needs to be saved, the idea that souls are ordained to a perpetual transmigration from body to body, never attaining a complete liberation from the flesh, is no cause for optimism. On a lesser scale, the level of history, Vergil strikes a similarly grim note in comparing the nations of mankind which Aeneas sees in the underworld with swarms of bees,[61] a thought which reminds the reader of the blind instinct that regulates the bees' society, their completely regimented existence, and their subjection to an omnipotent ruler as the only escape from chaos, anarchy, and group annihilation.

It is on the level of ethics, however, that Vergil orchestrates most fully the ambiguities between man's strivings and his limitations, between the rational pursuit of constructive goals and the destructive force of passion, between hard-won gains and the unavoidable human losses that they entail. His treatment of the major characters in the epic, and above all Aeneas, reflects a moral perspective which cannot be identified either with Stoicism or with any other school of philosophy. For Vergil no character is entirely wise or entirely foolish; no one is completely a saint or a sinner. His most harshly drawn portraits are softened by redeeming traits of some kind, while the figures he depicts most sympathetically also possess some unredeemed weaknesses. Aeneas himself, ideal hero though he may be, is by no means a perfect sage.

The major characters with whom Aeneas engages and with whom Vergil contrasts him are Dido and Turnus. Both of these individuals are enslaved by passions of one sort or another; both are limited in their choices to a significant extent by the will of the gods and by the fact that they constitute obstacles over which Aeneas must triumph in order to fulfill his destiny. Both, at the same time, possess a kind of greatness; and both are capable of exercising free will. Vergil endows each of them with a final dignity, but it is one whose ultimate victory over error remains in doubt. Of the two, Vergil gives a far more compassionate treatment to Dido. At her first appearance in the epic he describes her as beautiful, dignified, magnanimous, a just and competent ruler who inspires her people to constructive activity.[62] Her reception of the shipwrecked Trojans is gracious and hospitable.[63] She is attracted to Aeneas by his moral character, his inner fortitude, and his fatherly affection for his son no less than by his valor at arms, his eloquence, and his masculine charm. At

---

[61] *Aen.* 6.706-709.
[62] *Aen.* 1.436, 1.497, 1.503-504, 1.507-508.
[63] *Aen.* 1.561-578, 1.613-614, 1.727-636.

the same time she is impressed by the Trojans' lavish gifts and her maternal feelings are stirred by Ascanius, or by Cupid in Ascanius' guise.[64] In advancing the idea of a union between Dido and Aeneas, her sister Anna points out in its favor that Carthage is a new settlement surrounded by hostile or savage neighbors. An alliance with the Trojans would enhance the city's security and glory. Anna appeals simultaneously to Dido's womanly feelings, her desire for a husband and children, as well as speaking to her political prudence. Both sets of arguments inflame Dido's mind.[65] Thus, it is not merely her capitulation to *amor* and to the maternal instinct that motivates Dido's decision but also the reasonable concern of a responsible ruler for the well-being of her city.

None the less, when Dido commits herself to the affair with Aeneas she forswears her pledge of fidelity to her deceased husband Sychaeus and entangles herself in a web of dishonesty, neglect of her public duty, small-mindedness, and the loss of her self-control, suggesting the Stoic principle that one vice entails the other vices. Dido's first lapse is the neglect of her political responsibilities. Lacking her active supervision, the work of building her city comes to a standstill.[66] Her people, earlier compared to bees energetically pursuing their *labores,* now resemble the aimless swarm bereft of its leadership. Further, once she consummates her affair with Aeneas, she sinks into hypocrisy and self-delusion, calling the union a marriage although it is not one.[67] When Dido learns that Aeneas intends to leave her, she loses all control of herself: *saevit inops animi totamque incensa* ("she raged helplessly, like a complete madwoman.")[68] In her efforts to stop Aeneas from leaving, she resorts to accusations of bad faith, insulting aspersions on his lineage, hopes that he will be shipwrecked, threats from beyond the tomb, revealing a mean and petty side to her character.[69] Again, she makes a demeaning appeal for delay which she knows is futile, losing all sense of her own dignity;[70] then, sinking into madness in capitulation to her grief, she decides to commit suicide.[71]

Dido's decision to do away with herself, although it is aroused by irrational grief, serves not only to end her sufferings but also enables her to reclaim a measure of the self-respect that she has abandoned. In deciding on suicide she admits that she has been guilty of weakness of will

---

[64] *Aen.* 1.712-722, 4.3-19.
[65] *Aen.* 4.31-54.
[66] *Aen.* 4.86-89.
[67] *Aen.* 4.170-173.
[68] *Aen.* 4.300.
[69] *Aen.* 4.362-387.
[70] *Aen.* 4.412-438.
[71] *Aen.* 4.465-475.

and infidelity to Sychaeus' memory.[72] She accepts the blame for her own actions even though her sister had encouraged her. At the same time she considers her alternatives and their public implications, thereby returning to an awareness of the fact that her personal choices affect the city which she rules. When Dido finds that Aeneas' fleet has set sail, however, she suffers a moral lapse, during which she contemplates the things she might have done to punish him. But she soon rejects these thoughts as unworthy,[73] accepting the fact that Aeneas is obliged to pursue his destiny, whose fixed ordinances neither of them can avert.[74] None the less, Dido relapses once again, praying for vengeance and invoking curses on Aeneas and his mission.[75] Then again, she repudiates vengeance, adverting as before to the constructive, public accomplishments of her reign, as a means of transcending her rage and pettiness.[76] In her final speech, Dido says that she has adjusted her perspective to fate at last and that she has lived out her life as fortune has decreed.[77] Yet, there remains some doubt as to whether the shifting emotions she experiences as she prepares for death really bespeak a soul reconciled to fate and at peace with itself. Vergil notes at the end of Dido's story that she did not, in fact, die at her fated hour, but untimely, for Proserpina had not yet cut the lock of her hair that would release her soul from her body, and Iris had to be sent by Juno for this purpose.[78] When Aeneas looks back at Carthage from his ship, he sees the flames of Dido's funeral pyre, which seem to set the walls of the city afire, suggesting that Dido's suicide will indeed have a destructive effect on Carthage as a whole.[79] She leaves no successor to rule after her. Nor is Dido's claim that she has reconciled herself to fate and to Aeneas' need to bow to his own destiny borne out in the sequel. When Aeneas encounters Dido's shade in the underworld, his plea for forgiveness leaves her unmoved. She regards him with disdain and hatred, hard as stone, and then looks away, turning from him without acknowledging his words.[80] Just as Dido's initial motivation cannot be seen as an unmixed capitulation to passion, so her end cannot be seen as an unmixed triumph over her unreasonable desires. She does not fully recover the greatness of which she is capable.[81]

---

[72] *Aen.* 4.534-552.
[73] *Aen.* 4.584-606.
[74] *Aen.* 4.612-614.
[75] *Aen.* 4.615-629.
[76] *Aen.* 4.651-662.
[77] *Aen.* 4.651-653.
[78] *Aen.* 4.696-705.
[79] *Aen.* 5.3-4.
[80] *Aen.* 6.469-474.
[81] This point is developed most sensitively by Brooks Otis, "Virgil and Clio," *Phoenix*, 20 (1966), 62. Compare, on the other hand, Camps, *Intro. to Virgil's Aeneid*, pp. 34-35, 40;

Turnus, from the beginning, is a much less appealing character than Dido. His behavior throughout the last six books of the *Aeneid* is marked by violence, selfishness, and wrath. These unattractive traits overbalance the sympathy which the reader is inclined to feel for him as a man whose promised bride and whose political expectations are snatched from him by an interloper. Vergil's first introduction of Turnus effectively delineates his strengths and weaknesses. On Juno's instructions, the Fury Allecto appears to Turnus in the form of an aged prophetess, in the effort to incite enmity between him and the Trojans. When he hears her Turnus adopts an arrogant, patronizing, and discourteous attitude, refusing to take her seriously and dismissing her communication as an old wives' tale beneath the consideration of men and rulers.[82] When Allecto reveals her identity and expresses her anger at his reaction, his next response is one of terror, which then sweeps him into a totally irrational lust for war and bloodshed. Turnus is overpowered by his rage:

> Arma amens fremit, arma toro tectisque requirit;
> saevit amor ferri et scelerata insania belli,
> ira super.[83]

> Madly he roared for arms, searching both bed and house
> For weapons; lusting for his sword, his rage mounted wildly
> For the insane wickedness of war.

At the same time, Turnus is depicted a few lines later as a man who commands the respect, loyalty, and love of his followers on account of his youth, his beauty, his royal lineage, his bravery, and his military prowess.[84] Turnus, then, is an inspiring and noble leader. In contrast to Dido, however, his virtues are purely external and adventitious. He is not presented as possessing any inner virtues at all, and his moral weaknesses are far more pronounced than his admirable traits.

Vergil takes frequent occasion to portray Turnus in a state of irrational passion. He is bloodthirsty, exulting in Book 11 at the thought that the battle will be rejoined after the truce.[85] His blood lust sometimes causes him to lose all sense of military perspective, as in the incident in Book 9 where he finds himself locked into the Trojan camp all by himself. Having killed the Trojan who first challenges him to fight, his wits flee from him,

---

Viktor Pöschl, *The Art of Vergil: Image and Symbol in the Aeneid*, trans. Gerda Seligson (Ann Arbor, 1962), pp. 76-77, 86-91.

[82] *Aen.* 7.435-444.
[83] *Aen.* 7.460-462.
[84] *Aen.* 7.473-474, 7.650, 7.783-784, 9.126-127, 9.797-816.
[85] *Aen.* 11.491.

and, instead of opening the gates of the camp to his army, thereby enabling his forces to defeat the enemy in one swift stroke, his bloodthirsty
folly leads him on to single combat against the entire Trojan host,[86] a
situation from which he extricates himself only with extreme difficulty.
Turnus' pride and ambition often motivate him more than any selfless
concern for others, even for those whom he loves and leads. His love for
Lavinia is tinctured by his concern for his own political aggrandizement,
at the expense of the lives of his followers and despite the disrespect for
the gods that it involves. He insists that Lavinia's hand be the condition
on which he will engage in single combat with Aeneas, even though her
father Latinus protests that the marriage would be a sacrilege and even
though the alternatives to single combat would be an ignoble surrender
or the condemnation of more of the Latins to death by prolonging the
war.[87] His very love for Lavinia spurs him on, but it is associated with
his lust for battle,[88] one passion entailing the other in his case as in Dido's.
On another occasion Turnus shows himself to be more concerned with
the figure he cuts than with the fate of his troops. Having been fooled by
an illusory image of Aeneas sent by Juno, he attacks it, pursuing it by
jumping on a ship whose moorings, thanks to Juno, break loose, taking
him away from the battle. When Turnus realizes that he is being carried
away from the front, leaving his men without a leader, his principal
concern is the loss of reputation he will suffer, rather than what may
befall his troops and his cause as a result.[89]

    Turnus' character is also flawed by malice and gratuitous incivility
toward others. When Drances, counselor to Latinus, criticizes him for
running away from the battle and sacrificing the lives of his men for the
sake of his own personal gain, urging him to make peace or at least to
agree to single combat in order to end the war, Turnus turns on him
with a series of invidious remarks, attacking him as a coward rich in
words, not in deeds or arms. He speaks in a violent rage but does not
address himself to the charge that he is using the war to advance his own
interests.[90] Turnus' most despicable manifestation of ill will is his expression of *Schadenfreude* as he prepares to engage young Pallas in combat, in
regretting that Pallas' father is not present to witness the slaughter of his
son.[91] Turnus' behavior in this contest with Pallas reveals his inability
to observe moderation and decency. Having issued taunts, threats, and

---

[86] *Aen.* 9.756–761.
[87] *Aen.* 12.1–53.
[88] *Aen.* 12.10–11.
[89] *Aen.* 10.665–688.
[90] *Aen.* 11.336–337, 11.376–444.
[91] *Aen.* 10.443.

insults before the combat, he is boastful of his triumph and afterwards despoils the body of the vanquished Pallas of the sword belt[92] which is eventually to deprive Turnus himself of Aeneas' mercy.

The traits on which Vergil focuses the most repeatedly in depicting Turnus in action are not his malice, his ambition, or even his bloodthirstiness but rather his violence, his wrath, and his rage, the implacable fury that is totally incompatible with reason and humane feelings. The terms that Vergil applies to Turnus most consistently are *ira*, *violentia*, and *furor*. Turnus burns with wrath, which inflames his bones;[93] he changes his strategy abruptly, inspired by unreasoning and monstrous *ira*.[94] He is a man of violent temper, *violentaque pectora*,[95] whose violence in speech matches his violence in action.[96] His *furor* possesses him with the desire to inflict pain, a characteristic which leads Vergil to compare him with a wild bull.[97] The death of Camilla, his comrade-in-arms, and the defeat of her Volscians, arouses his *furor*;[98] Turnus never expresses grief or sympathy at anyone's death, only rage. Vergil's final description of Turnus, as he goes into battle, having treacherously violated his agreement to meet Aeneas in single combat, displays him riding forth like Mars, with fear, wrath, and treason in his suite.[99]

Vergil gives Turnus so few redeeming features that he appears to resemble, much more than does Dido, the Stoic fool, whose every inclination betrays a vicious intentionality. Turnus' passions seem to be innately ungovernable, even without the incitement of Juno to spur him on to the *furor* and *superbia* that it is Aeneas' mission to put down. Yet, Turnus has inspired sympathy from some readers of the *Aeneid*, who have argued that his zeal for the defense of his homeland is perfectly understandable and that he is a tragic figure not because his motives are complex or confusing but because Vergil disapproves of them. Turnus, like Dido, is held to have attained a measure of dignity and self-knowledge in the manner in which he meets his death.[100]

When he realizes that he has been defeated, Turnus does steel himself to die with bravery. He says, to the spirits of the dead, that he goes to meet them with a blameless soul.[101] Is this assertion a reflection of a

---

[92] *Aen.* 10.502, 10.514–515.
[93] *Aen.* 9.66.
[94] *Aen.* 9.694–695.
[95] *Aen.* 10.151.
[96] *Aen.* 12.9, 12.45–46.
[97] *Aen.* 12.94–106.
[98] *Aen.* 11.901.
[99] *Aen.* 12.331–338.
[100] Camps, *Intro. to Virgil's Aeneid*, pp. 38–40; Otis, "Virgil and Clio," p. 62; Pöschl, *Art of Vergil*, pp. 92–138.
[101] *Aen.* 12.646–649.

moral conversion at the eleventh hour, or is it an expression of Turnus'
self-delusion, his desire to attitudinize even before the shades in the underworld? When Turnus learns of Latinus' horror at his own violation
of the agreement to end the war by single combat with Aeneas, and of
Amata's suicide, he experiences for the first time some compunction, some
intellectual enlightenment, some uncertainty about his behavior:

> Obstipuit varia confusus imagine rerum
> Turnus et obtutu tacito stetit; aestuat ingens
> uno in corde pudor mixtoque insania luctu
> et furiis agitatus amor et conscia virtus.
> Ut primum discussae umbrae et lux reddita menti,
> ardentis oculorum orbis ad moenia torsit
> turbidus eque rotis magnam respexit ad urbem.[102]

> Stunned by the confused and shifting image of events,
> Turnus stood staring and silent. Shame flared up in his heart,
> Madness mixed with grief, love driven by fury
> And self-conscious worth. When the light first returned to his mind
> And dispersed the shadows, he turned his blazing eyes to the walls,
> And looked back in dismay from his chariot wheels
> To the great city.

Returning to the city, he sees that the Trojans have put it to the torch
and he accepts his fate, in full knowledge of the fact that it means his
death. Dashing into the battle, he stops the fighting by announcing that
he will engage Aeneas in single combat. When the end comes, he does
not plead with Aeneas for mercy. He acknowledges the fact that he has
earned what he has received. Thus, he dies with nobility. Still, while
Turnus' voluntary submission to fate restores to him some of the dignity
of which his irrational vices have deprived him during the previous action, the last lines of the *Aeneid* leave the question of his moral redemption
ambiguous:

> Ast illi solvuntur frigore membra
> vitaque cum gemitu fugit indignata sub umbras.[103]

> Then his members went slack with the chill of death
> And his soul, with a groan, fled indignant to the shades.

His soul, at the end, does not acquiesce, but protests as it flees to the
underworld.

On a less elaborate level, some of the same tensions visible in the char-

---

[102] *Aen.* 12.665-671.
[103] *Aen.* 12.951-952.

acters of Dido and Turnus can be seen in a number of subordinate figures in the epic, who also manifest the Vergilian idea that reason and passion, virtue and vice, are never pure states. The brave Euryalus, disregarding his companion Nisus' plea for moderation, takes as booty the shining helmet which betrays their presence to the enemy and leads to their death.[104] The savage Mezentius, who rules his people through terror and torture[105] and who is compared with a wild animal in battle, is yet an honorable fighter who refuses to take advantage of his enemy by attacking him from behind.[106] When the corpse of his son Lausus is brought to him, he is struck with guilt over his own injustice as a ruler, feeling that his son has paid the price for his father's crimes. His grief over the loss of his son is mixed with shame, and he is redeemed to some extent by this moral realization.[107] The warrior maiden Camilla is contrasted with her ally Turnus in that she fights purely for love of country and not for any personal gain.[108] Yet, for all her selfless valor, she is tempted by a love of finery, and in quest of booty she loses her caution, and hence her life.[109] Camilla, like Dido, is judged by the same ethical standards which Vergil applies to his masculine characters, and his lesser characters, like their betters, manifest the same kinds of moral complexities.

The character who expresses Vergil's ethical philosophy above all is his hero, Aeneas. Just as his opponents cannot be disposed of by classifying them as Stoic fools, so it is equally impossible to force Aeneas into the Procrustean bed of the Stoic sage. This point may need to be asserted with some force because of the long-standing interpretation of Aeneas as a Stoic sage, which was first put forth by St. Augustine and which has continued to win many adherents in modern Vergil criticism. Augustine's estimate of Aeneas is set in the context of his discussion of the various schools of philosophy on the subject of the passions in the *City of God*. According to Augustine, the Stoics teach that the sage may indeed experience the passions but that he judges them to be errors and controls them by means of reason. The sage, moreover, does not regard external vicissitudes as important enough to allow them to disturb his equanimity, sacrificing preferables freely if they obstruct his path toward virtue. Augustine cites Aeneas as a model Stoic sage in this respect, stressing that, in his decision to leave Dido, he reflects the sage's fixed inner intention to follow the good, despite the sorrow that it may cause him.[110]

---

[104] *Aen.* 9.353–356.
[105] *Aen.* 8.472–502.
[106] *Aen.* 10.731–735.
[107] *Aen.* 10.832–871.
[108] *Aen.* 11.892.
[109] *Aen.* 11.678–782.
[110] St. Augustine, *De civitate dei* 9.4, ed. Bernardus Dombart and Alphonsus Kalb, Corpus christianorum, series latina, 47 (Turnholt, 1965), *1*, 253.

The same conception of Aeneas as a Stoic sage, the ideal manifestation of rationality and *apatheia*, has appealed to many modern commentators, some of whom attach to it the other elements of Stoicism present in the *Aeneid*.[111] It is true that a few scholars stress Vergil's debts to Epicureanism,[112] Platonism,[113] or Pythagoreanism.[114] Still, the Stoic view of Aeneas has proved to be the most durable one. The major issue in the more recent criticism, taking this Stoic interpretation as a given, has been the question of whether Aeneas' character as a Stoic sage is expressed consistently throughout the epic[115] or whether he undergoes a gradual development, showing an imperfect grasp of his duty in the first half of the *Aeneid*, then undergoing a conversion experience on his trip to the underworld in Book 6, and finally emerging as a perfected sage in the second half of the epic.[116] Both of these views present difficulties. It can be admitted, in support of the developmental interpretation, that an education of the hero does indeed take place. However, the theory of a conversion from folly to wisdom cannot be sustained. Vergil describes Aeneas as *pius* throughout the epic, both before and after Book 6. Yet, Aeneas manifests not only virtue but also uncontrolled emotions in both halves of the *Aeneid*. At the same time, it can be admitted that the balance between passion and reason in Aeneas' character shifts from the first to the second half of the poem. However, it must also be noted that Vergil

---

[111] See, for instance, R. S. Conway, "The Philosophy of Vergil," *Bulletin of the John Rylands Library*, 6 (1922), 390-98; Clarence A. Forbes, "The Philosophy of Vergil," *Vergilius*, 10 (1964), 8-10; Glover, *Studies in Virgil*, pp. 204-05; Haarhoff, *Vergil the Universal*, pp. 6-7, 78-80, 95, 110; Richard Heinze, *Vergils epische Technik* (Leipzig, 1903), pp. 266, 268-73, 286-89, 293-310, 324-25; Otis, "Virgil and Clio," p. 62; Prescott, *Development of Virgil's Art*, pp. 478-81; Edward Kennard Rand, *The Magical Art of Virgil* (Cambridge, Mass., 1931), p. 29, who also represents the Victorian attitude toward Aeneas, seeing him as a cad and a prig in the Dido episode because his Stoicism causes him to abandon her; Sikes, *Roman Poetry*, pp. 184-85, 188-89; Charles N. Smiley, "Vergil—His Philosophical Background and His Relation to Christianity," *CJ*, 26 (1931), 664-71.

[112] Tenney Frank, "Epicurean Determinism in the *Aeneid*," *AJP*, 41 (1920), 115-26; *Vergil*, pp. 101-09, 183-92, who argues for Epicureanism on the grounds that the gods are not omnipotent in the *Aeneid*; Knight, *Roman Vergil*, pp. 19-21, 183-84, 395, who supports this view because he feels that the emotional tenor of the epic is more Epicurean than Stoic. Sullivan, "Virgil and the Mystery of Suffering," *AJP*, 90 (1969), 172, argues unconvincingly that Aeneas is not a Stoic hero because he must overcome temptations.

[113] Viktor Pöschl, "The Poetic Achievement of Virgil," *CJ*, 66 (1961), 290-99.

[114] Josette Lallemant-Maron, "Architecture et philosophie dans l'oeuvre virgilienne," *Euphrosyne*, n.s. 5 (1972), 447-55.

[115] The most important and eloquent defense of this interpretation is Pöschl, *Art of Vergil*, pp. 42-60.

[116] The major modern exponent of this view is Otis, *Virgil*, pp. 219-32, 236, 241-46, 250, 270, 306-08, 314-17, 348, 361, 380-82, 391-93. See also R. P. Bond, "Aeneas and the Cardinal Virtues," *Prudentia*, 6 (1974), 67-91; C. M. Bowra, "Aeneas and the Stoic Ideal," *Greece & Rome*, 3 (1933), 8-22.

does not portray all of Aeneas' passions in Books 7 through 12 as incompatible with his *pietas*.

In dealing with this issue, it is necessary to recognize the fact that Vergil justifies as *pius* certain passions in Aeneas which no Stoic would regard as *eupatheia* in accordance with reason. Equally important, it cannot really be said that Aeneas internalizes fully his submission to fate or that he rationalizes completely the sacrifices which the acceptance of his destiny entails. In Anchises' prophesies and instructions to Aeneas, he joins his description of Rome's mission, to put down the proud,[117] with the injunction to be merciful.[118] It is debatable whether Aeneas accomplishes both of these goals. Dido's dying wish that he may never come to rule the land to which he goes is actually heard and answered by Vergil. Although Aeneas defeats his enemies and founds his Italian kingdom, he never establishes a perfect kingship over himself. He never attains an inner peace flowing from the total surrender of his emotions to reason. Despite his external victory and the frequent assurances he receives about his capacity to attain it, he repeatedly feels the need to steel himself to the task, to quell his own doubts, and to wrestle with his feelings. Internally, he never arrives in the promised land. He remains, morally, *in via* throughout the poem. Vergil never resolves this tension. Indeed, a number of scholars have emphasized the idea that it is this very lack of a resolution that gives the *Aeneid* its tragic vision and its special greatness,[119] a critical perspective which is extremely persuasive. In terms of Vergil's philosophy, it means that Stoicism cannot and does not provide the ethical matrix around which Aeneas' character is constructed. The rigorous

---

[117] *Aen.* 6.853.

[118] *Aen.* 6.834–835.

[119] Good statements of this position can be found in William Hardy Alexander, "Maius opus (*Aeneid* 7-12)," *University of California Publications in Classical Philology, 14* (1950–52), 193–214; Robert A. Brooks, "*Discolor Aura*: Reflections on the Golden Bough," in *Virgil*, ed. Commager, p. 162; Conway, "Philos. of Vergil," in *Harvard Lectures*, pp. 108–09; Mark W. Edwards, "The Expression of Stoic Ideas in the *Aeneid*," *Phoenix, 14* (1960), 151–65; Brian Morris, "Virgil and the Heroic Ideal," *Proceedings of the Virgil Society, 9* (1969-70), 20–34; Adam Parry, "The Two Voices of Virgil's *Aeneid*," in *Virgil*, ed. Commager, pp. 107–23; C.-A. Sainte-Beuve, *Étude sur Virgile*, 4me éd. (Paris, 1883), pp. 186–87; Williams, *Aeneas and the Roman Hero*, pp. 46, 49–60, 62, 69–70; R. D. Williams, intro. to his ed. of *Aeneid*, Books 1-6 (London, 1972), pp. xx-xxv; *Virgil*, Greece & Rome: New Surveys in the Classics, 1 (Oxford, 1967), pp. 34–35. Michael C. J. Putnam, *The Poetry of the Aeneid: Four Studies in Imaginative Unity and Design* (Cambridge, Mass., 1965), pp. 151–201 and W. R. Johnson, *Darkness Visible: A Study of Vergil's Aeneid* (Berkeley, 1976), pp. 15–16, 74–75 have taken this interpretation to the point of substituting pessimism and futility for Vergil's pathos and tension. A much less convincing explanation of the tensions in the *Aeneid* is offered by Tracy, "*Fata Deum*," *Greece & Rome*, ser. 2:*11* (1964), 188–89, who argues that they stem from the disjunction between Vergil's belief in fate and the traditional materials concerning the myth of Aeneas and the founding of Rome which he used.

Stoic rationality, the obligation to cultivate *apatheia* and even *eupatheia*, give way ultimately to Vergil's sense of pathos and to his recognition of the ambiguities and fallibilities that permeate the human condition.

It is certainly true that Vergil depicts Aeneas in the first half of the epic as simultaneously virtuous and humane, yet as given over at times to irrational passions. Aeneas is called *pius* from the very outset.[120] He is first introduced in a storm at sea, shuddering and groaning as he implores heaven for a safe passage.[121] He is easily moved, by Dido's gracious welcome,[122] by the memory of the sufferings evoked by his narration of the fall of Troy and by pictorial representations of it,[123] and by the death of his friend Palinurus.[124] He is offended by brutal and unsportsmanlike behavior at the funeral games for Anchises and intervenes to prevent the loser in a boxing match from being beaten to a pulp.[125] This concern for others is also reflected in Aeneas' behavior after landing on the coast of north Africa, where his first action is to reconnoitre, to provide food for his men, and to speak words of cheer to them. Although inwardly he is deeply worried, he hides his fears from his followers lest he demoralize them[126] and lies awake at night preoccupied by his responsibilities as their leader.[127] In the underworld, he is bemused and saddened by the inequities of death, as he contemplates the souls who must wait for passage across Cocytus because their bodies went unburied.[128] Aeneas' *pietas*, for Vergil, is in complete conformity with his sensitivity to the sorrowful dimensions of life, an irreducible sorrow that cannot be assuaged by reason.

Aeneas' sensibility, his doubts and fears, go far beyond what a Stoic would regard as acceptably reasonable emotions. At the same time, Aeneas manifests passions which are decidedly antithetical to reason and which are described as irrational by the poet. In the battle of Troy, when he sees the city burning, Aeneas seizes his sword without thinking, swept along by mindless anger: *arma amens capio, nec sat rationis in armis.*[129] As he rushes back to his own family, he meets Helen, who has sought sanctuary at the shrine of Vesta, and considers killing her, despite the fact that the killing of an unarmed woman at a sanctuary would be a violation of his

---

[120] *Aen.* 1.10, 1.220, 1.305, 1.378.
[121] *Aen.* 1.92–93.
[122] *Aen.* 1.579–581.
[123] *Aen.* 1.485, 2.3, 2.6–8, 2.12–13.
[124] *Aen.* 5.868–871.
[125] *Aen.* 5.461–464.
[126] *Aen.* 1.180–209.
[127] *Aen.* 1.305–308.
[128] *Aen.* 6.332–333.
[129] *Aen.* 2.314.

warrior's code and a gross sacrilege. He is dissuaded only by the intervention of Venus.[130] Not only is Aeneas deflected from reasonable behavior by the crisis conditions of battle, he is, more seriously, hesitant to accept as true the communications made to him by the gods or their representatives. Although the Sybil in Book 6 has told him that he will, in fact, be admitted to the underworld, Aeneas gives way to discouragement when he faces the forest in which he must look for the golden bough.[131]

Vergil's chief illustration of the irreconcilable tension between Aeneas' reason and his passions in the first half of the epic is his behavior in the affair with Dido. Like Dido, Aeneas in love neglects his responsibilities and is enslaved by desire.[132] However, once Mercury's message has made him realize that he must leave Dido, he tries to effect the break so as to inflict the least possible pain on her.[133] When she refuses to accept the necessity of his departure, Aeneas himself feels pain, but controls it, pointing out that he must obey the will of heaven and seeking, by gentle implication, to call her back to her own dignity as a queen who had also founded a new city and who had earlier sympathized with his wanderings. Yet, he does not completely internalize his own obligations; as he says, *Italiam non sponte sequor* ("I do not seek Italy of my own free will.")[134] Although he remains unmoved by Dido's plea, he lacks equanimity, for he sheds a futile tear at the same time.[135] Despite his wish to console Dido, at the last minute he has no words for her, but turns and goes to his ships.[136] Even when the affair has been terminated irrevocably, Aeneas cannot relegate it to the past. As he sails away from Carthage, he looks back;[137] and his love for Dido as well as his desire to commiserate with her flame up again when he meets her shade in the underworld.[138] Aeneas does not, therefore, succeed either in bringing his feelings into perfect conformity with his reason or in consigning them to the category of *adiaphora*.

Even after Aeneas has returned from the other world with his personal destiny and its place in the fated history of Rome fully revealed to him, his behavior gives evidence of the difficulties he finds in reconciling himself to the will of heaven and to the criterion of reason. He still draws

---

[130] *Aen.* 2.567–621.
[131] *Aen.* 6.185–186.
[132] *Aen.* 4.193–194.
[133] *Aen.* 4.293–294.
[134] *Aen.* 4.461.
[135] *Aen.* 4.438–449.
[136] *Aen.* 4.390–392, 4.393–396.
[137] *Aen.* 5.3–4.
[138] *Aen.* 6.455–468, 6.475–476.

apart from his men, worried and uncertain about the future despite the divine assurances he has been given.[139] Although he bears the image of Cato on the shield that Vulcan has forged for him,[140] Aeneas is not transformed into a Stoic sage. The need to do battle entailed by his commission to *debellare superbos* means that he must manifest all the courage and leadership required of the warrior. He does not hesitate to deal out death to his enemies, and, in so doing, he displays many of the same passions on the field of battle which the poet charges to Turnus' discredit. Aeneas, like Turnus, is possessed by *ira* and *furor*. He rages in terrible wrath against his foes;[141] he exults with irrational fury;[142] he rejoices at Mezentius' challenge and at the fact that he has drawn his enemy's blood.[143] Yet, in several of these passages where Vergil shows Aeneas swept away by irrational *furor* he also describes him as *pius*.[144] In Turnus' case, *furor* and *pietas* are mutually exclusive, but in Aeneas' case they are not. The association which Vergil evokes is that of Hercules *furens*, whose insane rage is a necessary stage in his moral perfection. Aeneas must wage war, because war is the only way that he can impose peace and contain *furor impius* at last.[145] *Furor pius* is the weapon which Vergil places in Aeneas' hands for this purpose. Aeneas' rage, therefore, is a passion permitted to him in the service of his destiny.

The question still remains whether, in accepting this charge, Aeneas does not have to abandon some of his humanity and whether he succeeds in fulfilling the entire commission laid upon him by Anchises. To be sure, Aeneas manifests many of the same signs of sensibility in the second half of the *Aeneid* as he reflects in the first five books. He weeps for the friends fallen on his own side[146] and shows grief and sympathy over the death of his enemies; he shows his willingness for a truce, or a peaceful settlement, or anything that will bring the war to a speedy end with as few fatalities as possible.[147] He takes the time before his final engagement with Turnus to comfort and counsel his son and his associates and to send messengers to Latinus with the terms of peace.[148] He restrains his troops when Turnus breaks his agreement to do single combat.[149] He waits until

---

[139] *Aen.* 8.18-30, 10.159-60, 10.217.
[140] *Aen.* 8.670.
[141] *Aen.* 10.569, 12.106.
[142] *Aen.* 10.812-814, 12.525-528, 12.494-495, 12.938-951.
[143] *Aen.* 10.787, 10.874.
[144] *Aen.* 10.591, 10.783, 11.291-292, 12.311.
[145] *Aen.* 1.294.
[146] *Aen.* 11.29, 11.40.
[147] *Aen.* 10.812, 10.821-832, 11.94-96, 11.100-120.
[148] *Aen.* 12.106-112.
[149] *Aen.* 12.311-317.

he is provoked; and, in the final battle, he refuses to attack anyone whose back is turned, or anyone who offers to engage him save Turnus, whom he alone has agreed to fight.[150] Still, all is not honor on the Trojan side. Arruns, Aeneas' captain, stabs Camilla in the back[151] and Aeneas himself mocks his opponent Lucagus, insulting him when he is thrown from his chariot. More important, in the light of Anchises' charge, he rejects the pleas of Lucagus and Magus for clemency.[152] And, in the end, he dispatches Turnus without pity, although his enemy has already acknowledged defeat. Some of these actions may conceivably be explained in the light of Aeneas' need to punish violence by violent means. But some of them strike the reader not only as gratuitous but also as an index of Aeneas' ultimate inability to unite force with mercy and to resolve the conflict between reason and the passions. The final lines of the *Aeneid* refer not to Aeneas' victory or to the historical triumph of Rome but to the soul of Turnus, fleeing in protest to the shades. If Turnus in the end fails to accept his destiny wholeheartedly, Aeneas too fails to achieve a perfect synthesis between his commitment to duty and his compassion. Her certainly fails to attain a Stoic resolution of the tensions between these conflicting motivations.

Stoic with respect to his conception of fate and free will, yet un-Stoic in the delineation of the epic hero, Vergil faced no obstacles in the transmission of his perspectives on either of these topics after his death. He enjoyed the well-deserved reputation, attained in his own day and never challenged since then, of being the best loved, best preserved, and most widely read Latin poet in antiquity and in the Middle Ages.[153] The popularity of the *Georgics*,[154] the later reputation acquired by his fourth *Eclogue* as a prophesy of Christianity,[155] and the legend of Vergil as a magician that grew up in the Middle Ages[156] only served to enhance the

---

[150] *Aen.* 12.464-467.

[151] *Aen.* 11.759-767.

[152] *Aen.* 10.531-534, 10.591-601.

[153] The most detailed and up-to-date discussion of the textual tradition of the *Aeneid* is provided by Williams, intro to his ed. of *Aeneid*, Books 1-6, pp. xxviii-xxx. The best general treatment of Vergil's posthumous reputation is provided by Büchner, *P. Vergilius Maro*, cols. 441-59. See also D. Comparetti, *Virgilio nel medio evo*, nuova ed., ed. Giorgio Pasquali, 2 vols. (Firenze, 1937-46); A. J. Gossage, "Virgil and the Flavian Epic," in *Virgil*, ed. Dudley, pp. 67-93; Perret, *Virgile*, p. 152; Knight, *Roman Vergil*, pp. 262-63, 342-45, 370-80; E. K. Rand, "The Mediaeval Virgil," *Studi medievali*, n.s. 5 (1932), 418-42; Sellar, *Roman Poets*, pp. 59-66; Vincenzo Ussani, "In margine al Comparetti," *Studi medievali*, n.s. 5 (1932), 1-42.

[154] Wilkinson, *Georgics of Virgil*, pp. 270-90.

[155] The best study is Pierre Courcelle, "Les exégèses chrétiennes de la quatrième Églogue," *REA, 59* (1957), 294-319.

[15] The standard study remains John Webster Spargo, *Virgil the Necromancer: Studies in Virgilian Legends*, Harvard Studies in Comparative Literature, 10 (Cambridge, Mass., 1934).

already towering influence which his *Aeneid* exerted on all readers educated in the Latin language in that era. St. Augustine's estimate of
Aeneas as a Stoic sage may have led his own immediate posterity to
exaggerate or to misinterpret this aspect of the epic. The place of the
Aeneid in the history of the Stoic tradition should not be assessed on that
basis, but rather in terms of Vergil's success in integrating the Stoic doctrine of fate and free will into a non-Stoic vision of life that is completely
his own.

II. Lucan

If any Latin poet can lay claim to the reputation of uniting Stoicism
with the epic genre, that poet is Lucan. The nephew of Seneca, raised
and educated in a Stoic milieu with which he expressly identified himself,
Lucan has long been read as a poet whose *Pharsalia* attains its chief epic
unity in its fidelity to Stoic philosophy. Lucan certainly includes far more
Stoic material in the *Pharsalia* than can be found in any other classical
Latin epic, material that spans the fields of theology, cosmology, physics,
eschatology, anthropology, and ethics. In addition, his characterization
of Cato of Utica is the most detailed and circumstantial portrait of the
Stoic sage to be found anywhere in Latin literature.[157] None the less,

---

[157] The most detailed analyses, citing the relevant passages, are by W. E. Heitland,
intro. to M. Annaei Lucani, *Pharsalia*, ed. C. E. Haskins (London, 1887), pp. xlii-xlviii;
Kay Don Morris, "A Comparative Study of Marcus Annaeus Lucanus and Seneca the
Philosopher," (Ohio State University Ph.D. diss., 1959), pp. 90-120; René Pichon, *Les
Sources de Lucain* (Paris, 1912), pp. 165-216. On physics and related issues the most detailed
study is Hans-Albert Schotes, *Stoische Physik, Psychologie und Theologie bei Lucan* (Bonn,
1969), pp. 15-166. On physics, see also M. P. O. Morford, *The Poet Lucan: Studies in
Rhetorical Epic* (Oxford, 1967), pp. 42-43, 47-50, 54. On theology see also A. Bourgery,
"Lucain et la magie," *REL, 6* (1928), 302-13; Jacqueline Brisset, *Les Idées politiques de
Lucain* (Paris, 1964), pp. 65-89; Bernard F. Dick, "The Role of the Oracle in Lucan's de
Bello Civili," *Hermes, 93* (1965), 463-66; Henri LeBonniec, "Lucain et la religion," in
Lucain, Fondation Hardt: Entretiens sur l'antiquité classique, 15 (Paris, 1970), pp. 174-
94; Morford, *The Poet Lucan*, pp. 63-65, 73-76.

   On ethical themes in general see Paratore, *Persio e Lucano*, p. 39; Rieks, *Homo, Humanus*,
pp. 167-96, 256; Werner Rutz, "Amor Mortis bei Lucan," *Hermes, 88* (1960), 462-75. On
fate and free will see Erich Burck, "Vom Menschenbild in Lucans Pharsalia," in *Lucan*,
ed. Werner Rutz, Wege der Forschung, 235 (Darmstadt, 1970), pp. 157-58; Wolf-Hart-
mut Friedrich, "Cato, Caesar und Fortuna bei Lucan," ibid., pp. 81-102. On Cato specifically see Jean-Marie Adatte, "Caton ou l'engagement du sage," *Études de lettres*, Bulletin de la Faculté de lettres de l'Université de Lausanne, sér. 2:8 (1965), 232-40; William
Hardy Alexander, "Cato of Utica in the Works of Seneca Philosophus," *Proceedings and
Transactions of the Royal Society of Canada*, 3rd ser., *40*,, section 2 (1946), 72-74; Pierre
Grimal, "L'Épisode d'Anthée dans la 'Pharsale'," *Latomus, 8* (1949), 60-61; A. W. Lintott,
"Lucan and the History of the Civil War," *CQ*, n.s. *21* (1971), 499-500; M. P. O. Mor-
ford, "The Purpose of Lucan's Ninth Book," *Latomus, 26* (1967), 123-29; Georg Pfligers-
dorfer, "Lucan als Dichter des geistigen Widerstandes," *Hermes, 87* (1959), 346-51; Sikes,
Roman Poetry, pp. 194-209.

Lucan's Stoicism is not always orthodox or consistent. The *Pharsalia* is pervaded by an atmosphere of irony, pessimism, and doubt that modifies the force of Lucan's Stoic convictions in a number of ways. Lucan, like Vergil, leaves a number of major philosophical questions unanswered. While there is much more Stoicism in Lucan than there is in Vergil, it is not capable of resolving completely all of the problems which the *Pharsalia* raises.

Lucan (A.D. 39-65) was the son of Seneca's brother, Marcus Annaeus Mela, who moved his family from his native Córdoba to Rome, where Lucan was educated.[158] His teachers in grammar and rhetoric were the best available and included the Stoic Cornutus, in whose circle Lucan met the poet Persius. Lucan became an intellectual and political associate of Seneca, and it was through his uncle's influence as well as for his own poetic talent that he was called from his studies in Greece in about A.D. 59 to take up a privileged position at Nero's court. Lucan was a supporter of Nero early in his reign and wrote an oration in his honor in A.D. 60. Shortly after that time he became a quaestor and then an augur. However, Lucan soon fell into Nero's disfavor and was forbidden to publish, perhaps because the emperor envied his literary talent. Lucan became involved in the Pisonian conspiracy. When the plot was discovered, he was denounced and ordered by Nero to commit suicide, a fate which

For a less detailed treatment of Lucan's Stoicism see Otto Steen Due, "Lucain et la philosophie," *Lucain*, Fondation Hardt, pp. 210-14; John Ferguson, "Lucan and His Epic," *Durham University Journal*, 49, n.s. *18* (1956-57), 116-25; Enrica Malcovati, *Lucano*, 2nd ed. (Brescia, 1947), pp. 50-54; Berthe M. Marti, "Cassius Scaeva and Lucan's *Inventio*," *The Classical Tradition*, ed. Wallach, pp. 254-56; "The Meaning of the *Pharsalia*," *AJP*, *66* (1945), 352-57; which is substantially repeated in "La structure de la Pharsale," *Lucain*, Fondation Hardt, pp. 3-34; Mendell, *Latin Poetry*, pp. 66, 72, 75, 85-87, 109, 120; David Vessey, *Statius and the Thebaid* (Cambridge, 1973), pp. 1, 57. Frederick M. Ahl, *Lucan: An Introduction*, Cornell Studies in Classical Philology, 39 (Ithaca, 1976), pp. 7, 56-57, expresses caution on the degree to which Lucan's Stoicism can be taken seriously, but his own attribution of Stoicism to Lucan at specific points, pp. 100, 121 n. 2, 241 n. 11, 240-44, 281-305, raises some doubts as to whether he understands the Stoic doctrines involved.

Seneca has traditionally and plausibly been regarded as Lucan's major source, although Posidonius as well as historical and poetical models have also been noted. On the *Quellenforschung* issue see Julius Baeumer, *De Posidonio Megasthene Apollodoro M. Annaei Lucani auctoribus* (Münster i. W., 1902), pp. 7-20; Hermann Diels, "Seneca und Lucan," *Philosophische und historische Abhandlungen der königlichen Akademie der Wissenschaften zu Berlin*, 1885, Abhandlung 3 (Berlin, 1886); Carl Hosius, "Lucan und seine Quellen," *RM*, *48* (1893), 380-97; "Lucanus und Seneca," *Neue Jahrbücher für Philologie und Paedagogik*, *145* (1892), 337-56.

[158] Good treatments of Lucan's biography can be found in J. D. Duff, intro. to his trans. of the *Pharsalia*, Loeb (London, 1928), vii-ix; Brisset, *Les Idées politiques de Lucain*, pp. 5-26; A. Bourgery, intro. to his ed. and trans. of *La Guerre civile*, Budé (Paris, 1926-29), *1*, v-xi; Paolo Tremoli, *M. Anneo Lucano: L'ambiente familiare e letterario*, Università degli studi di Trieste, Facoltà di lettere e filosofia, Istituto di filologia classica, 8 (Trieste, 1961).

Lucan sought unsuccessfully to avert by implicating others in his guilt, including his own mother. Lucan's talent appeared early and he wrote several works of prose and poetry besides the *Pharsalia,* which have not survived. He had not completed his epic at the time of his death. Only the first three books had been published at the point when Nero proscribed his work. The remaining six books appeared posthumously, possibly at the initiative of Polla Argentaria, his widow.

For Lucan, as for the other epic poets, the chief points of interaction between his poetry and his Stoic sources are the relationship between fate and free will and the ethical characterization of the epic hero. Where Vergil's debt to Stoicism can be seen most clearly in his handling of the first of these themes, Lucan's case is exactly the reverse. His treatment of Cato as the ideal Stoic sage and of Caesar and Pompey as morally flawed characters is entirely consistent with Stoic ethics. The ambiguities and unresolved tensions in the *Pharsalia* lie, on the other hand, in the poet's difficulties with the idea of fate, seen from one perspective as an all-embracing providence which is yet conditioned by human choices and, from another perspective, as an arbitrary and capricious force, the fate that brings about the fratricidal civil war responsible for the death of the Roman Republic, the triumph of Caesarism, and the loss of political liberty. Lucan struggles to rationalize this conception of fate in order to come to grips with a historical reality in which the virtuous are defeated, the vicious succeed, and the sufferings brought about by the civil war are unredeemed. In the end, he cannot find consolation in the Stoic doctrine of fate as rational and beneficent.[159] But, unlike Vergil, Lucan never substitutes for the Stoicism he rejects a personal philosophy of his own.

Before addressing these major themes in the *Pharsalia,* it is worth noting that there are a number of other areas in which Lucan's use of Stoicism is less clear-cut than has sometimes been thought. His very conception of the epic style is a case in point. Lucan refers to the gods more or less interchangeably with fate as a causal agent. However, he departs both from the previous epic tradition and from the Stoic conception of poetry

---

[159] The limitations in Lucan's Stoicism with respect to these issues have been well developed by Adatte, "Caton ou l'engagement du sage," *Études de lettres,* sér. 2:8 (1965), 232–40; Arthur Bachmayer, *Die Motivierung in Lukans Pharsalia* (Freiburg [Schweitz], 1940), pp. 1–7, 25–85; Bernard F. Dick, "*Fatum* and *Fortuna* in Lucan's *Bellum civile*," *CP,* 62 (1967), 235–42; Otto Steen Due, "An Essay on Lucan," *Classica et mediaevalia, 23* (1962), 86; "Lucain et la philosophie," *Lucain,* Fondation Hardt, pp. 220–24; Duff, *Silver Age,* p. 322; Malcovati, *Lucano,* pp. 46–49; Morris, "M. A. Lucanus and Seneca," pp. 103–05; James Raymond Murdock, "Fatum and Fortuna in Lucan's Bellum civile," (Yale University Ph.D. diss., 1970), the fullest study of this subject; Heitland, intro. to *Pharsalia,* ed. Haskins, pp. xlviii–xlix; Schotes, *Stoische Physik,* p. 75; Antony Snell, "Lucan," *Greece & Rome, 8* (1939), 90.

and theology in his disinclination to personify the gods and to treat them as characters who interact with human beings on an individual basis.[160] In addition, Lucan takes a certain amount of poetic license with the facts of history, which he manipulates for his own purposes. This tendency conflicts with the Stoic stylistic concern for verisimilitude and accurate reporting. The *Pharsalia* is also marked by extended digressions, excessively long amplifications, and the multiplication of illustrative examples, a trait at odds with the Stoics' norm of brevity and their distaste for coloristic elaboration. Lucan's most noticeable departure both from previous canons of epic style and from a Stoic literary sensibility lies in his relish for the grotesque. His taste for the horrible, his *terribilità*, is, in part, a device which he uses to emphasize the frightfulness of civil war itself; but, at the same time, he revels in his own aptitude for ghastly descriptiveness as a literary end in itself. It is true that Lucan also displays at times some of Seneca's flair for crisp, epigrammatic expression, and his epic is indeed a cautionary tale with a strongly didactic flavor. At the same time, the prevailing style and tone of the *Pharsalia* can scarcely be described as an expression of Stoic literary theory.

While no critics have defended the thesis that Lucan's style is Stoic, many have viewed him as an orthodox Stoic in his physical, cosmological, and theological beliefs. There is a good deal of room for doubt in this area. In the *Pharsalia*, Pompey attains apotheosis after his death. As the poet describes this event, the shade of Pompey flies upward from the grave to abide in the region between the earth and the moon, at the frontier of the celestial zone where the souls of the heroes dwell because their fiery nature is connatural with that of the heavenly bodies.[161] This eschatology accords with what some Stoics taught, although the ideas involved are not uniquely Stoic. The point that Lucan fails to clarify, however, is why Pompey is apotheosized in the first place, given the fact that he has scarcely been depicted as a model of Stoic virtue in the *Pharsalia*. If Lucan's treatment of Pompey's posthumous fate is perplexing, his Stoicism is even less solid in other quarters. In three passages Lucan refers to the destruction of the universe, a notion that some critics have seen as an expression of the Stoics' cyclical cosmology. One of the reasons he gives for the outbreak of the civil war is the idea that the world itself has reached its final hour and that it now must revert to primeval chaos.[162] He makes the same point in setting the stage for the decisive battle of Pharsalus.[163] The upheavals of a storm through which Caesar

---

[160] This point has been well developed by Malcovati, *Lucano*, pp. 24-28.

[161] Marcus Annaeus Lucanus, *Pharsalia* 9.1-18, trans. Duff. All citations to and translations of the *Pharsalia* will be taken from this edition.

[162] *Phars.* 1.73-80.

[163] *Phars.* 7.46-47.

ventures in a small boat are also compared with the return of chaos, the destruction of the concord of the elements, the universal catastrophe.[164] These lines no doubt reflect Lucan's desire to endow the historical events he relates with a cosmic significance. However, they lack the specific Stoic notes of the sequence in which fire absorbs the other elements and, even more important, there is no sense at all of any cyclical renewal of the universe.[165]

Lucan is also unclear or inconclusive about a number of theological matters, including the utility of prophesies and portents, features of his thought that have often led to his facile identification as a Stoic. In a passage in Book 5, where Appius goes to consult the Delphic oracle about the outcome of the war, the poet reports certain theories about the deity, the world, and his relationship to it, although he refrains from committing himself. There is indeed a god who dwells at Delphi, he says, who reveals the future to man, although whether the future is identical with his will or whether he merely communicates future events which he himself does not determine cannot be ascertained. Possibly, Lucan adds, this deity is immanent in the universe and rules it from within, upholding the earth in empty space. This immanent spirit, if it exists, may be the vapor that issues from the caves at Cirrha, which is inhaled by the oracle and inspires her prophetic outpourings.[166] Some of the content of this cosmology and theology is clearly Stoic, but Lucan does not indicate whether he thinks the doctrine is true or false.

Lucan sprinkles his epic liberally with dreams, portents, augury, and divination, but it is debatable whether he sees the divine messages conveyed by these means as reliable indices of future events. Signs of this sort frequently do indicate the future in the *Pharsalia*. Ominous portents occur when Caesar arrogates the title of consul to himself in a managed election.[167] They herald the outbreak of hostilities[168] and recur in large numbers immediately before the battle of Pharsalus itself,[169] indicating that something disastrous is about to take place. Messages received in dreams are sometimes correct, as in the dream where Pompey sees the shade of his second wife, Julia, who prophesies his downfall[170] and the dream

---

[164] *Phars.* 5.634-636.

[165] This point has been noted by Émile Campiche, "Les causes de la guerre civile d'après Lucain," *Études de lettres,* Bulletin de la Faculté de lettres de l'Université de Lausanne, sér. 2:8 (1965), 224-31, esp. p. 227; Lintott, "Lucan and the History of the Civil War," *CQ,* n.s. *21* (1971), 493.

[166] *Phars,* 5.91-99.

[167] *Phars.* 5.395-396.

[168] *Phars.* 1.526-694.

[169] *Phars.* 7.151-206.

[170] *Phars.* 3.8-40.

received by his third wife, Cornelia, fraught with dire forebodings about his fortunes at Pharsalus.[171] Still, there are situations where this is not the case. Caesar has a dream before crossing the Rubicon in which he sees a female figure representing Rome, who urges him not to proceed with his rebellion.[172] He disregard this message, and his position seems vindicated given the fact that he emerges as the victor. Pompey also has a dream on the night before the battle of Pharsalus in which he sees himself sitting in the theatre he had built in Rome, receiving the plaudits of the crowd. This dream is in direct opposition to Pompey's actual fate, a circumstance which Lucan himself is hard put to explain.[173] In one significant case, furthermore, the merits of oracles in general are held up to criticism, and by Cato, the epic's exemplar of perfect Stoic virtue. When his army in Libya comes to the temple of Ammon, he refuses to consult the oracle there; for Cato, *deo plenus* ("filled with the god within,")[174] this is not necessary. He knows already, he says, that the moral quality of one's life is more important than its length or its external success. He also knows that men and gods form one community and that the will of providence governs all things. God, in any case, dwells immanently in the world and is to be found also in the souls of virtuous men, which is where men should seek him, rather than in oracles.[175] Here, Lucan's chief model of Stoicism provides a fully Stoic rationale for avoiding a practice that most of the Stoics sanctioned. Elsewhere, also, Lucan expresses regret at the fact that portents exist at all, arguing that men would be happier if they were not aware of their doom ahead of time,[176] an observation that conflicts with the Stoic desire to know what is to be so that the mind can reconcile itself with dignity to its inevitable fate.

From a Stoic standpoint, the least orthodox attitude toward prophesy expressed by Lucan in the *Pharsalia* is no doubt his treatment of the visit of Sextus, the son of Pompey, to the witch of Thessaly, an event which may by contrasted with Cato's refusal to consult the oracle of Ammon in Book 9. Lucan voices two principal criticisms of Sextus' action, criticisms with which no Stoic would disagree. In the first place, Sextus' motivation is morally improper. He consults the witch unworthily because he is inspired by cowardice and fear concerning the issue of events.[177] This observation reflects the importance to the Stoics of a cor-

---

[171] *Phars.* 8.43-45.
[172] *Phars.* 1.185-203.
[173] *Phars.* 7.7-33.
[174] *Phars.* 9.564.
[175] *Phars.* 9.566-584.
[176] *Phars.* 2.14-15.
[177] *Phars.* 6.413-423.

rect inner intention as the criterion of ethical behavior. In the second
place, Lucan blames Sextus for consulting the wrong kind of source—not
a legitimate oracle or a conventional augur but a witch, although nec-
romancy is loathsome to the gods.[178] While Lucan may castigate witches
as fonts of superstition, illicit and detestable to the gods, it is none the
less true that he believes that they possess supernatural powers. He asserts
that the potions, philtres, and charms of witches can control the gods,
the forces of nature, and the behavior of men,[179] a claim which he vin-
dicates immediately by enabling the witch of Thessaly to raise from the
dead a soldier recently fallen in battle in order to question him about
what is transpiring in the other world. The tale told by the dead man is,
in fact, what comes to pass.[180] In trying to deal with the inconsistencies
of his position on the subject of witchcraft, Lucan raises several questions
about the relationship between the gods and the witches. Are the gods
forced to heed and to obey the witches? Is their obedience extorted from
them by some higher power? Or, do they obey willingly, and if so, why?
The poet fails to answer any of these questions, although he clearly shows
that the witches, despite the Stoics' distaste for them, are more powerful
than the gods and that they are more consistently in control of events
than the augurs and the oracles.

In turning to the great theme of causation in history, however, Lucan's
recourse to Stoicism is much more systematic, even though he remains
incapable of appropriating the Stoic doctrine completely. The most important philosophical questions that Lucan raises in the *Pharsalia* are
questions of causation. Why did the civil war break out? Why did it
proceed and conclude as it did? It is true that the political result of the
war in Lucan's own day was a dictatorship to which he objected. Yet,
the *Pharsalia* is much more than an outburst of anti-Neronian propaganda.[181] It is also a searching effort to understand the dynamics of
historical events. There are three types of causes to which Lucan adverts
in this connection: fate, understood as a rational and ineluctable force;
fate, understood as a capricious and irrational force, although one that
is no less ineluctable; and voluntary human choices. Many of the commentators who read the *Pharsalia* as a drama of Stoic fatalism emphasize
the first of these causes without taking sufficient account of the other two.

---

[178] *Phars.* 6.425-432.
[178] *Phars.* 6.450-451, 6.454-506, 6.827-830.
[180] *Phars.* 6.620-820.
[181] This interpretation has been emphasized by Brisset, *Les Idées politiques de Lucain*,
passim and esp. pp. 186-230; Richard T. Bruère, "The Scope of Lucan's Historical Epic,"
CP, 45 (1950), 217-35; Achim Kopp, *Staatsdenken und politisches Handeln bei Seneca und Lucan*
(Heidelberg, 1969), pp. 91-131; Enrica Malcovati, "Lucano e Cicerone," *Athenaeum*, 41,
n.s. *31* (1953), 288-97.

Those who wish to stress the limitations of Lucan's Stoicism emphasize the importance of fickle fortune. Scholars who place the accent on human agency as a cause in the *Pharsalia* have been all too inclined to treat it as Lucan's only or major cause.[182] It is certainly possible to reconcile Lucan's providential fate and his appeal to human choices and actions within the framework of a Stoic conception of the necessary interaction between destiny and free will.[183] Lucan's most original contribution to this Stoic doctrine is his inclusion of the choices and actions of ordinary people, masses of men, entire communities, along with those of great men and leaders as factors in the causal equation.[184] The area where his theory of causation breaks down is in his occasional treatment of fate as irrational and arbitrary. There is no room for such a notion in Stoicism. More important, from the standpoint of Lucan's handling of the problem of causation in his own terms, he does not find a personal resolution of the tensions between this concept of chance and his Stoic amalgam of determinism and free will.

Lucan makes it clear that a combination of causes, not all of them fully knowable, was involved in the outbreak of the civil war. It was fortune, he says, that provoked the war and reversed the destiny of Rome, leading not merely to fratricidal strife and Caesarian tyranny but to the decline of Rome's economic and political position in the world.[185] Can this fate or fortune be equated with the gods? At one point Lucan says no, asserting that there are no gods who govern the world of men.[186] However, in general, he uses the gods, or heaven, as a term interchangeable with fate or fortune. More important, he raises the question of whether this fate constitutes a fixed and reasonable law of nature or whether it is blind chance that controls human life. Lucan does not answer this question.[187] Both conceptions of fate come into play, leaving Lucan incapable of deciding whether they are equally powerful or whether one is paramount over the other.

---

[182] Good examples of this tendency are Ahl, *Lucan*, pp. 281-305; Ugo Piacentini, *Osservazioni sulla tecnica epica di Lucano*, Deutsche Akademie der Wissenschaften zu Berlin, Schriften der Sektion für Altertumswissenschaft, 39 (Berlin, 1963), pp. 12-18; Ettore Paratore, "Seneca e Lucano," *Accademia nazionale dei Lincei*, Problemi attuali di scienza e di cultura, *363*, no. 88 (1966), p. 21; Giovanni Tria, *Un poema repubblicano ai tempi di Nerone* (Trani, 1891), pp. 17-19.

[183] This point has been given a sensitive appreciation by Campiche, "Les causes de la guerre civile," *Études de lettres*, sér. 2:8 (1965), 224-31; Max Pohlenz, "Causa civilium armorum," *Kleine Schriften, 2*, 139-48.

[184] Lucan's skill in dealing with men in groups and the importance he attaches to this dimension of his epic has been noted by Malcovati, *Lucano*, pp. 81-82; Tria, *Un poema repubblicano*, pp. 17-19, although neither author has connected this point with the fatalism-free will issue.

[185] *Phars.* 1.33-38, 1.44-66, 7.410-427, 7.440-445.

[186] *Phars.* 7.445-459.

If he is uncertain on this point, however, he is fully convinced that it is not fate alone that was responsible for the war. Outside of fate, he notes, Rome's fall was Rome's own fault, the fault of the entire society as well as that of its leaders. Rome herself had grown too great and was bound to collapse, like a building too weighty for its own foundations.[188] The prosperity that Rome had come to enjoy, he says, led to luxury and extravagance, with a consequent decline in the moral fiber of the nation. The Romans could not remain in peace and enjoy their prosperity, but became contentious and prone to violence as a means of settling disputes, regulating their affairs by force and greed, not by law and justice and good faith. These failings, for Lucan, were visible throughout Roman society from the rulers down to the plebeians.[189] A variety of vicious motives is attributed to the men who have promoted and tolerated the war by Brutus, in a speech he makes to Cato. Some men, he says, guilty of private crimes, have been willing to overthrow the law lest it be enforced against them; others are motivated by need or avarice. Whatever the reason, all have sought their own self-interest and none is engaged in the struggle for reasons of principle.[190]

The leaders of the state manifest the same vices as the rest of Roman society, only more conspicuously. The triumvirs, says Lucan, had no interest in cooperating with each other for the sake of the common weal. It was personal advantage and nothing else that impelled them to seize power:

> Facta tribus dominis communis, Roma, nec unquam
> in turbam missi feralia foedera regni.
> O male concordes nimiaque cupidine caeci
> quid miscere iuvat vires orbemque tenere
> in medio?[191]

> The doom of Rome was due to Rome itself, when she became
> The joint property of three masters, and when despotism,
> Which never before was shared among so many,
> Struck its bloody bargain. Blinded by excess of ambition,
> The Three joined hands for mischief.

As far as the immediate causes of the civil war are concerned, Lucan mentions the deaths of Crassus and Julia, who could have served as moderating influences among the triumvirs.[192] But the chief immediate caus-

---

[187] *Phars.* 2.7–15.
[188] *Phars.* 1.70–80.
[189] *Phars.* 1.158–182.
[190] *Phars.* 2.251–255.
[191] *Phars.* 1.85–90.
[192] *Phars.* 1.99–120.

es, in human terms, are the same as the causes that led to the initial establishment of the triumvirate, the overweening ambition and jealousy of the leaders: *Nec quem quam iam ferre potest Caesarve priorem/ Pompeiusve parem* ("Caesar could no longer endure a superior, nor Pompey an equal.")[193] Both Pompey and Caesar, Lucan stresses, are equally at fault. It is impossible to say which of them had the better cause. Each had strong support on his side and high authority: *victrix causa deis placuit, sed victa Catoni* ("for, if the victor had the gods on his side, the vanquished had Cato.")[194]

Once the civil war is set in train, the same causes that inspired it, both human and divine, continue to control its progress and to direct its outcome. This is true both for the agency of fate and for the agency of human groups and individuals. Fate, Lucan asserts, sometimes acted capriciously. Fortune had favored Pompey in the earlier stages of his career, but after the battle of Pharsalus she chose to crush him with the weight of his former fame.[195] The message that Appius receives from the Delphic oracle is so cryptic that it suggests to Lucan the irrationality of a system in which divine prophesies are given to men which cannot be understood or which reflect a possible frivolity or even unclarity in the minds of the deities themselves.[196] In the thick of battle at Pharsalus, some of the soldiers try to bury the points of their spears in the ground to avoid killing their fellow citizens on the opposing side. But not all who seek this escape from wrongdoing achieve it: *Rapit omnia casus/ atque incerta facit quos volt fortuna nocentes* ("but chance and haste are supreme, and random Fortune makes whom she will guilty.")[197]

Fate is not always capricious in the *Pharsalia*, but even when it is not, it grants the victory to the wrong side. On a few occasions, it is true, destiny favors the cause of Pompey with which Lucan sympathizes.[198] But it is Caesar who is fortune's favorite, even though Lucan can find no fully convincing reason why this should be the case. Fortune is behind Pompey's failures and those of his lieutenants.[199] It is responsible for his loss of Italy[200] and for his defeat at Pharsalus.[201] It is even the cause of his securing so many allies, so that, in vanquishing Pompey, Caesar could

---

[193] *Phars.* 1.125-126.
[194] *Phars.* 1.128.
[195] *Phars.* 8.21-23.
[196] *Phars.* 5.19-208.
[197] *Phars.* 7.487-488.
[198] *Phars.* 8.204-207, 9.890-893.
[199] *Phars.* 4.342-344, 4.351, 4.787-790.
[200] *Phars.* 2.726-728, 2.732-735.
[201] *Phars.* 7.503-505, 7.543-544, 7.600-602, 7.645-646, 7.666, 7.668, 7.685-686, 7.705, 7.796.

conquer the whole world at one stroke.[202] It was a decree of destiny, ordained from all time, that drew Pompey after his defeat at Pharsalus to Egypt and to his death.[203] Fortune's last blow against Pompey was to direct that his body be dismembered and beheaded and his remains unburned and cast into the sea.[204] Pompey himself is incapable of perceiving that fate favors his opponent's cause. He repeatedly tries to revive the flagging zeal of his troops by arguing that fate no longer attends Caesar, despite the evidence to the contrary.[205] Others, however, have no difficulty in seeing that fortune has abandoned Pompey, and the Egyptians in particular are able to base a successful strategy on that fact.[206]

On the other hand, fate regularly comes to Caesar's aid, inspiring him to initiate his rebellion, enabling him to overcome bad weather and to break the siege of Alexandria.[207] Caesar is aware of his favored status, and repeatedly succeeds in inspiring his troops by adverting to it.[208] Caesar's fortune leads to the destruction and dishonor of other men.[209] Fortune causes him to depart from all sense of shame and reverence, and even leads him to commit a sacrilege in cutting down a sacred grove near Marseilles, a deed for which he is not punished.[210] Lucan cannot really explain why this should be the case. The closest he comes to an explication is that Caesar's own boldness attracted the favor of destiny: *temeraria prono/ expertus cessisse deo* ("rashness succeeds when Heaven favours.")[211]

While fortune in general organizes both the sequence of events in the war and its final outcome,[212] fate does not simply act through men who are puppets manipulated by metaphysical forces behind the scenes. The moral characteristics and voluntary choices of the groups and individuals involved are also a prominent feature of Lucan's analysis of causation. The most original feature of the *Pharsalia* in this respect is not the fact that Lucan accords a significant role to human free will but that he considers the behavior and attitudes of groups as well as those of individuals. For Lucan, history is not made only by leaders. Leaders could not lead unless they could command followers; and the followers, no less than the leaders, possess moral freedom and the capacity to choose vice or

---

[202] *Phars.* 3.290–292, 2.296–297.
[203] *Phars.* 8.568–570.
[204] *Phars.* 8.692–711.
[205] *Phars.* 2.544–546, 2.555–556.
[206] *Phars.* 8.484–535.
[207] *Phars.* 1.262–265, 4.212–213, 5.510, 5.536, 5.581–582, 10.485.
[208] *Phars.* 1.309–311, 1.358–366, 5.325–332.
[209] *Phars.* 1.151–153, 1.256–257, 2.517–518.
[210] *Phars.* 1.264–265, 3.447–449.
[211] *Phars.* 5.501–502.
[212] *Phars.* 4.243–245, 5.1–3, 7.46–47.

virtue. Men in the mass are the molders of events just as much as their captains. In a speech to his troops, Caesar rightly states that they, with their swords, can summon fate; his destiny lies in their hands.[213] At another point, Caesar reverses this position, arguing that it is the leaders not the masses who control events;[214] but the soldier who protests this interpretation makes the argument borne out by the *Pharsalia*.[215] Ordinary people in the mass sometimes command fate by their endurance of hardships[216] or by their steadfast refusal to compromise their principles.[217] More typically, however, it is corporate vice rather than corporate virtue that is at issue, vices such as fear, cowardice, disloyalty, fickleness, treachery, or greed.[218] Lucan repeatedly depicts groups of men deflected from their rationality and humanity by the appeals of demagogic oratory.[219] What he is trying to underline is not only the causal importance of group decisions and attitudes but also the idea that the masses, as well as the leaders, are capable of choice and that they are therefore also morally responsible for the outbreak and outcome of the war.

Still, Lucan gives much more specific attention to the behavior of the leaders as causal agents in history. Since the leaders possess greater authority, they bear a proportionately greater share of the blame. Lucan finds the entire senatorial class guilty of cowardice and irresponsibility. When the senate first learns that Caesar is poised to attack, it adjourns precipitously and many of its members flee from the capital, each thinking only of where he can run and hide.[220] Even before the outbreak of the war, the senate had disregarded the law by threatening and then expelling two of the tribunes.[221] When Caesar arrives in Rome with no senate in session, a rabble of senators emerges from hiding, convenes itself with no real legality, and hands over to Caesar whatever powers he requests, not scrupling even at granting him the treasure in the temple of Saturn.[222] Those senators who had fled the city before Caesar's advance likewise assemble in contravention of lawful procedure and lay upon Pompey his own commission to defend the state and themselves.[223] The entire ruling class, in Lucan's view, has simply abandoned its duty to govern the people and to control factionalism through the enforcement

---

[213] *Phars.* 7.252, 7.285-286.
[214] *Phars.* 5.339-343.
[215] *Phars.* 5.291-295.
[216] *Phars.* 4.388-392.
[217] *Phars.* 3.298-357.
[218] *Phars.* 1.469-486, 1.502-513, 2.446-461, 2.507-509, 2.704-707, 10.402-411.
[219] *Phars.* 4.169-252, 5.365-366.
[220] *Phars.* 1.486-493.
[221] *Phars.* 1.266-267.
[222] *Phars.* 3.103-153.
[223] *Phars.* 5.5-70.

of the law. The senate instead has made itself the tool of the partisans, thereby collaborating in their guilt.

Unedifying behavior on the part of individual leaders is also one of Lucan's principal themes, a topic that brings us at length to the character of the epic hero and his antitheses. Personal valor is, it is true, at times capable of thwarting fortune. The most dramatic example in the *Pharsalia* is Scaeva's defense of his position on the ramparts under Pompey's siege. Even though, as Lucan says, fortune would not permit this position to hold if it had been manned by a thousand soldiers and Caesar himself, Scaeva holds it thanks to his magnificent bravery.[224] But Lucan more usually stresses the vices and weaknesses of individual leaders. Pompey's lieutenants take to their heels and flee before Caesar's advances in north Africa, leaving their posts undefended.[225] The fall of the consul Curio is even more deplorable, for he has been an honorable and praiseworthy leader. But he betrays the state for money, allowing himself to be bought by Caesar,[226] thus standing in Lucan's view as a particularly telling example of the moral corruption into which Roman society in general had fallen.

It is above all in the figures of Caesar and Pompey that Lucan dramatizes the interaction of fate and character. He depicts Caesar as an archvillain and as the man who initiated the sequence of events that had led in Lucan's own day to Neronian despotism.[227] At the same time, his actions in the epic show him as a bold, decisive, and imaginative general whose successes may be attributed to his own genius as a strategist and politician and not merely to the favor of fortune. Lucan makes this clear in his initial description of Caesar. Caesar, he notes, has a well-earned military reputation. He is possessed of a restless energy, a vitality that makes it impossible for him to stand still. He is bellicose by nature, esteeming a victory no victory unless he wins it by force of arms. He is bold and sharp, quick to respond with violence to anything that inspires his ambition or arouses his anger. He is prompt in seizing and capitalizing on his advantage, joyously annihilating any obstacle in his path. Lucan compares Caesar with a bolt of lightning, for his quickness, his capacity to strike fear in the hearts of men, for his dazzling and irresistible power.

---

[224] *Phars.* 5.140-142.

[225] *Phars.* 2.462-477.

[226] *Phars.* 4.811-824.

[227] On the character of Caesar see particularly Robert Graves, intro. to his trans. of *Pharsalia* (Harmondsworth, 1956), p. 13; O. A. W. Dilke, "Lucan's Political Views and the Caesars," in *Neronians and Flavians*, ed. Dudley, pp. 62-69; Aurèle Cattin, "Une idée directrice de Lucan dans la *Pharsale*," *Études de lettres*, sér. 2:8 (1965), 219, 222; Morford, *The Poet Lucan*, pp. 15-19.

He is like a force of nature flashing across the heavens to its ordained destination, uncontrollable, brilliant, and terrible.[228]

The vices that emerge from this characterization of Caesar are topics to which Lucan frequently adverts in the course of the epic. He repeatedly shows Caesar leading and manipulating his men and his victims through terrorism and demagoguery, appealing to their fear, their greed, their shame, and their blind loyalty.[229] Since his recourse is always to the baser emotions, he finds it impossible to believe that anyone can truly be inspired by high ideals, regarding this claim on the part of the citizens of Marseilles as nothing but a ploy to block his advance.[230] He himself is bloodthirsty, treacherous, an adulterer,[231] a would-be tyrant who seeks his affinity in the memory of Alexander the Great,[232] and who dissimulates his ambitions to his men.[233] He enjoys posing as a magnanimous conqueror knowing full well that by granting clemency to Domitius he is forcing him to live in dishonor according to his own lights.[234] Caesar is impious, not only in destroying the sacred grove outside of Marseilles and in seizing the treasure of the temple of Saturn in Rome but also in failing to burn the corpses of the fallen decently after the battle of Pharsalus.[235] His only pious act is to pray to the gods when he goes to Troy, but his main concern in this episode is to assert the claim that he is the descendant of the Trojans who founded Rome, who will fulfill their destiny by establishing his own dictatorship.[236]

Lucan, however, does not neglect to note Caesar's positive talents as a politician and strategist. As a general Caesar repeatedly demonstrates his decisiveness, his refusal to brook delay or idleness, his intelligence, and his ability to improvise. He is capable of envisioning his campaign as a whole, which leads him to undertake the battles in Spain which, as Lucan says, were *maxima sed fati ducibus momenta daturum* ("destined to turn decisively the scales of fate for the rival leaders.")[237] His swift and shrewd action often enables Caesar to seize the initiative and to forward the course of fortune.[238] He is a masterful tactician, devising schemes of military engineering that can trap his enemy and delimit the battle area to

---

[228] *Phars*, 1.143-157.

[229] *Phars*. 1.244-247, 1.257-261, 1.299-386, 3.399-452, 5.301-303, 5.319-402.

[230] *Phars*. 3.358-374.

[231] *Phars*. 1.222-227, 2.439-446, 10.73-77.

[232] *Phars*. 10.14-23. This point has been developed well by Ahl, *Lucan*, p. 224; Morford, *The Poet Lucan*, pp. 15-19.

[233] *Phars*. 7.266-269.

[234] *Phars*. 2.509-525.

[235] *Phars*. 7.794-808.

[236] *Phars*. 9.964-999.

[237] *Phars*. 4.3.

[238] *Phars*. 1.391-394, 2.650-652, 5.481-484.

his own advantage.[239] He uses his own cavalry as a protective line thrown at an angle across the current of the Rubicon, permitting his infantry to cross safely; he constructs rafts of willow boughs covered with ox hides to ferry his army across the river Sicoris.[240] His lieutenants show the same flair for strategic extemporization.[241] Lucan's most brilliantly realized depiction of Caesar's generalship is in his description of the battle of Marseilles, where Caesar plans an attack that places his camp on a fortified height behind the city. He builds a huge rampart from his camp to the sea, thereby preventing escape from the town in all directions and cutting off its inhabitants from their water and food supply. He then constructs a causeway from his camp to the city on which his army can advance and from which it can attack the city walls, attaching to it twin towers that match the citadel in height, from which missiles can be fired into the city. These constructions also allow Caesar's troops to launch their own offensive out of the range of the defenders' catapults. Simultaneously, Caesar organizes an attack from the sea, devising a naval strategy which turns the heavier and less maneuverable Roman ships into an advantage, as well as permitting him to trap the city in a pincer movement by land and sea at once.[242]

Lucan's remarkable skill at describing military maneuvers enhances, if anything, the portrait he paints of Caesar as a general, but he does not neglect to delineate Caesar's strengths as a politician and diplomat as well. Caesar neither wastes time nor forgets the practical necessities of war; nor does he permit anyone else to take credit for events that accrue to his own advantage. Cheated of his prey by Pompey's escape from Italy, Caesar makes use of the time provided by his inability to do battle by seizing control of the grain supply from Sicily and Sardinia, both in order to provision his troops in the future and because he is aware of the fact that he can command the loyalty of the civilian population by controlling the price of bread.[243] When the severed head of Pompey is brought to him by the Egyptian envoys he responds with duplicitious but highly pragmatic diplomacy, attacking the Egyptians for breaking their alliance with Rome and for desecrating Pompey's body. Although he is inwardly delighted with what has come to pass, he charges the Egyptians with treachery because he has no intention of allowing them to make any political capital out of the fact that they have dispatched his rival.[244] As

---

[239] *Phars.* 2.668-728, 6.29-65.
[240] *Phars.* 1.213-222, 4.130-133.
[241] *Phars.* 4.404-473.
[242] *Phars.* 3.375-582.
[243] *Phars.* 2.71-168.
[244] *Phars.* 9.1035-1104.

one considers the total character of Caesar presented by Lucan in these passages, one is struck by the inescapable conviction that, much as the poet may have been unwilling to admit it, he could not help admiring Caesar's striking gifts as a leader and his equally impressive deployment of them, which function as a critical factor in his victories. Despite his wish to treat Caesar as an incarnation of vice, Lucan cannot prevent himself from showing that Caesar deserved what he won.

Although Lucan personally favors Pompey's cause over Caesar's and despite the fact that he accords Pompey the singular honor of apotheosis in the *Pharsalia*, he depicts Pompey as consistently vicious, and with fewer admirable traits than Caesar. Pompey has sometimes been regarded as the hero of the *Pharsalia*. It is more plausible to regard him as a man condemned by a collection of moral failings which are not really mitigated by his past accomplishments or present virtues.[245] Lucan's initial characterization of Pompey shows him to be a man content to rest on his laurels, a leader who courts his reputation and who is gratified by his popularity with the masses. Trusting entirely in this previous greatness, he does nothing to keep his power alive. Lucan compares him with a mighty oak, venerated and laden with trophies, whose roots have lost their resilience, whose branches offer no shade, an oak kept standing only because of its own massiveness, not because of its vitality or its capacity for organic growth.[246] Where Caesar is dynamic and aggressive, Pompey is lethargic and self-satisfied; where Caesar is a force brooking no opposition, Pompey's strength is the strength of inertia. He is able to stand when no one opposes him, but he is vulnerable in the face of a countervailing force.

Pompey's behavior in the epic certainly bears out this assessment of his character. There is only one point at which Lucan shows him mastering his feelings. When he sees Caesar's army advancing against him at Pharsalus, his blood runs cold in fright, but he controls himself.[247] Pompey is much more frequently depicted as acting out of fear and concern for his own safety. In his first reference to Pompey following his initial description of the rivals Lucan shows him fleeing from Caesar, like the senators and the populace, terrified by the news that Caesar is invading Italy.[248] Pompey's first reaction to Caesar's breach of the peace is thus a cowardly and irresponsible one, which increases the fear of the people

---

[245] An excellent discussion of this point with an analysis of the previous literature is supplied by Lintott, "Lucan and the History of the Civil War," *CQ*, n.s. *21* (1971), 494-95, 501-03.

[246] *Phars.* 1.129-143.

[247] *Phars.* 7.337-342.

[248] *Phars.* 1.522.

who look up to him for guidance. When he sees that his cause is hopeless at Pharsalus, Pompey likewise flees. Lucan tries to exculpate him,[249] but Pompey none the less abandons the remnant of his army, leaving his men behind him to die. On this flight, he is subject to irrational terror, frightened by the sound of the wind in the trees and by the appearance of his own comrades who arrive to join him.[250] In parting from his wife before the battle, he tells her that he is sending her to a safe place, not only to protect her from harm but also so that, if his army is destroyed, he will by able to join her there himself, escaping the wrath of the victor.[251] Pompey thus reveals that he has no intention of holding his ground in battle, even to death. He prefers safety and dishonor to a noble death in the face of defeat. He also indulges in rationalizations of his less than courageous behavior in abandoning Italy to Caesar, claiming that he chose to move his troops to the east in order to avoid the destruction of the homeland that warfare on Italian soil would bring about.[252]

Pompey's self-justifications, although they may permit him to delude himself, do not persuade his followers, or Lucan either. He is repeatedly shown, and is seen to be, a weak leader, guided by self-interest and possessed of an unrealistic conception of his own importance. Before the battle of Pharsalus, his own troops and allies regard him as having delayed matters for selfish reasons and call him a coward, concerned mainly with his own power and the prosperity of his own family, who has dragged them into war to serve his own ambitions.[253] This judgment is confirmed by Cato, who agrees to side with Pompey because he thinks that Pompey's legal position is better than Caesar's, but who recognizes in Pompey a man equally avid for political aggrandizement.[254] Pompey frequently manifests poor judgment as a general and as a politician. At a critical point in the battle of Pharsalus he holds back his troops, a serious tactical error in Lucan's view, since he might have won the battle had he urged them forward, thereby ending the civil war and saving Rome from tyranny.[255] Unlike Caesar, he neither attracts good fortune nor acts so as to control or direct it. He procrastinates when his forces wish to press onward and at length gives way to them, making no effort to dominate or persuade them, turning himself into their follower rather than acting as their leader.[256] He lacks the ability to command and the

---

[249] *Phars.* 7.677-684.
[250] *Phars.* 8.5-8.
[251] *Phars.* 5.756-759.
[252] *Phars.* 6.322-326.
[253] *Phars.* 7.52-123.
[254] *Phars.* 2.319-323.
[255] *Phars.* 6.299-312.
[256] *Phars.* 7.52-123.

knowledge of how to encourage his troops. In his first speech to his men, he rehearses his past triumphs and asserts that he is the chosen instrument for repressing Caesar's revolt, Caesar's crime being his audacious wish to be greater than Pompey. His soldiers are not impressed by this argument. It is fear of Caesar, not love of Pompey, that spurs them on.[257] In his speech to his troops just before the battle of Pharsalus, Pompey notes that he himself will be disgraced and exiled if his side loses,[258] a remark which shows his inability to subordinate his personal interest to any loftier cause, even for the immediate rhetorical purposes at hand.

The same poor judgment, self-delusion, and weak leadership are reflected in Pompey's coordination of his alliances and his plans and prospects both before and after his defeat at Pharsalus. After giving up Italy to Caesar without a struggle, his next move is to form alliances with the subject kings and client states of Rome in the southern Mediterranean. He commissions his son Gnaeus to visit these areas and to propose alliances. Gnaeus' instructions indicate that Pompey expects these kings and states to flock to his banner because of his erstwhile fame, in the belief that they would rather help him against Caesar than use the opportunity of the civil war to make a bid for their own independence.[259] This notion reveals both his own lack of political sagacity and the fact that he is so bewitched by his own past glory that he assumes that everyone else shares his own opinion of himself. After his defeat at Pharsalus, Pompey debates with his followers as to which foreign ally they should repair to in seeking a haven from which they may retrieve their position. Pompey argues for Parthia, on the grounds that his exploits have been greatest in the east. Lentulus, one of his captains, demurs, pointing out that, unlike the Parthians, Pompey's western allies owe their thrones to him and might therefore be more inclined to assist him. Since the king of Parthia is more independent, he observes, Pompey could only secure his support by becoming his client. If Pompey is prepared to accept such terms, why not submit to Caesar and end the war? In any case, Lentulus adds, although the king of Parthia might have been impressed by Pompey's reputation in the past, what possible reason does he have to retain this opinion in the present? Lentulus' reasoning prevails.[260] This episode not only shows Pompey as a leader with less intelligence than his subordinates but also as a man incapable of accepting reality. His pride and obtuseness are carried over into his final moments. He leaves a dying message with his sons, adjuring them never to make peace with Caesar, to continue the

---

[257] *Phars.* 2.531–609.
[258] *Phars.* 7.379–382.
[259] *Phars.* 2.632–649.
[260] *Phars.* 8.211–455.

war, to continue to seek allies, and to concern themselves above all with forwarding the power and prestige of the family.[261] In his ultimate breath Pompey thus shows the dominion over common sense which his ambition exercises and his complete inability to grasp the realities of the political situation.

Pompey's passions, at least with respect to ambition, are the same as Caesar's. However, unlike Caesar, he possesses neither the intelligence, the toughmindedness, nor the capacity to advance them coherently nor the boldness and resolution necessary to associate fortune with his own will. These failings are visible also in Pompey's private life. He is, at least in Stoic terms, excessively uxorious. His love for Cornelia is immoderate, arousing the passions of fear, anxiety, and doubt on the eve of Pharsalus. His love also makes him indecisive and he delays sending Cornelia away, even though this is advisable for her safety, out of his desire to keep her with him.[262] He wishes, in this way, *tempus subducere fatis* ("to steal a reprieve from destiny;")[263] but this private desire, like his public actions and like his conception of himself, reflects a vain illusion. Where Caesar's brilliance, despite the vices stimulated by his passions, enables him to collaborate with fortune in his own interests, Pompey's vices merely cause him to make decisions that hasten his own doom and that facilitate Caesar's victory. Both Caesar and Pompey are characterized by Lucan as Stoic fools. Pompey's folly is the more immediately visible. Caesar's folly resides in his belief that he will be able to retain the power that he has won; his victory in the *Pharsalia* is always shadowed for Lucan and his readers by their knowledge of Caesar's subsequent assassination. Pompey suffers defeat on all levels. If Caesar enjoys a political triumph, it can scarcely be said that he attains anything like a moral one. The one character in the *Pharsalia* who does achieve a moral victory and whom Lucan contrasts with both Caesar and Pompey is Cato of Utica.

Unlike Caesar, Cato is on the losing side. His fondest hopes do not flow in the same direction as destiny. However, his moral excellence enables him to manifest *apatheia* in the face of a hostile fortune. Like Pompey, Cato supports the Republican cause. But, while Pompey represents its external form, Cato represents its animating spirit; his inner moral freedom is the ethical correlative of the *libertas* doomed to destruction in the political arena.[264] Lucan depicts Cato, from the very first, and consistently throughout the epic, as a model Stoic sage. He shows Cato, at the outbreak of the civil war, as completely unconcerned with his own

[261] *Phars.* 9.87-97.
[262] *Phars.* 5.728-733.
[263] *Phars.* 5.733.
[264] Lintott, "Lucan and the History, of the Civil War," *CQ*, n.s. *21* (1971), 503.

safety but as preoccupied with the fate of the nation; *uni quippe vacat studiis odiisque carenti/ humanum lugere genus* ("for he alone, free from love and free from hate, had leisure to wear mourning for mankind.")[265] Lucan describes Cato as a staunch adherent of Stoic ethical principles in their most rigorous form:

> Hi mores, haec duri inmota Catonis
> secta fuit, servare modum finemque tenere
> naturamque sequi patriaeque inpendere vitam
> nec sibi sed toti genitum se credere mundo.
> Huic epulae, vicisse famem; magnique penates,
> summovisse hiemem tecto; pretiosaque vestis,
> hirtam membra super Romani more Quiritis
> induxisse togam; Venerisque hic unicus usus,
> progenies; urbi pater est urbique maritus,
> iustitiae cultor, rigidi servator honesti,
> in commune bonus; nulloque Catonis in actus
> subrepsit partemque tulit sibi nata voluptas.[266]

> Such was the character, such the inflexible rule of austere Cato—
> To observe moderation and hold fast to the limit,
> To follow nature, to give his life for his country,
> To believe that he was born to serve the whole world
> And not himself. To him it was a feast to banish hunger;
> It was a lordly palace to fend off hard weather
> With a roof over his head; it was fine raiment
> To draw over his limbs the rough toga
> Which is the Roman's dress in time of peace. In his view
> The sole purpose of love was offspring; for the State
> He became a husband and father; he worshipped justice
> And practiced uncompromising virtue; he reserved his kindness
> For the whole people; and there was no act of Cato's life
> Where selfish pleasure crept in and claimed a share.

Cato is clearly free from the irrational passions and he unites Stoic *apatheia* with Stoic *eupatheia*. He is no partisan. He agrees to join in the civil war only out of his love of country, despite his serious misgivings about the motives of both Caesar and Pompey, submitting himself to the will of fate: *quo fata trahunt, virtus secura sequentur* ("virtue will follow fearless wherever destiny summons her.")[267] If he could, Cato states, he would offer up his life, if his own death were capable of reconciling the warring factions and redeeming the vices of Roman society. Since this is impossible, the best plan is to join Pompey, despite his adverse judgment of

---

[265] *Phars.* 2.377-378.
[266] *Phars.* 2.380-395.
[267] *Phars.* 2.287.

Pompey's character, in the hope of moderating his ambition should his cause prevail, and bending his victory to the general good.[268] Cato's entire attitude toward the civil war bespeaks the triumph of Stoic detachment from ambition and the exercise of the rational emotions flowing from the sage's obligation to his fellow man. Similarly, Cato's attitude toward sexuality reflects the strict Stoic view, as developed by Musonius Rufus, that love and marriage are justified only by the sage's social duty to procreate offspring. Lucan also emphasizes this position by retelling the story of Cato's divorce of his wife Marcia so that she could marry and bear children to his friend Hortensius, and of their remarriage, in a celibate union, after Hortensius' death.[269]

The primary impression that Lucan wishes to give of Cato, however, is as a leader of men. The contrasts he draws here between Cato and the passive and cowardly Pompey and the demagogic and terrifying Caesar are crisp and unmistakable. When Pompey's troops indicate the wish to surrender after his death, Cato dissuades them in a speech which stresses that the *casus belli* is not private interest or personal loyalty but rather a matter of principle; what is at stake is freedom, law, and patriotism.[270] He appeals, in other words, to his hearers' better nature, to their rational ideals and moral sensibilities, not, as Caesar and Pompey do in their speeches to their troops, to fear, hero-worship, greed, or some other base motive. Cato assumes the leadership of the anti-Caesarian cause for the sake of liberty, seeking no political dominion for himself, fearing no defeat.[271] He decides to march his army across the Libyan desert. In steeling his men for this ordeal, he delivers another speech, which, like his earlier appeal, addresses them as rational beings. He makes no attempt to minimize the hardships they will face, urging those who choose to accompany him to do so with a full knowledge of what lies ahead. He himself, he notes, will share their dangers and deprivations, assuming no privileges in his capacity as their leader. He adds, finally, that the men should view the sufferings they will endure as a test of their virtue and as a penance for having fled after the battle of Pharsalus.[272] This appeal to reason and virtue is successful and his troops willingly follow him.

The fact that the historical Cato actually did march across Libya provides Lucan with a ready-made means of achieving a Stoic association of his hero with the myth of Hercules, for one of Hercules' labors was his contest with the giant Antaeus, who was identified with Libya.[273] The

---

[268] *Phars.* 2.288-323.
[269] *Phars.* 2.236-380.
[270] *Phars.* 9.222-283.
[271] *Phars.* 9.28-30.
[272] *Phars.* 9.379-406.
[273] An excellent study of this point is provided by Grimal, "L'Épisode d'Anthée," *Latomus, 8* (1949), 60-61.

concept of the progressive development of virtue through voluntary submission to suffering may apply to Cato's troops but it does not apply to
Cato himself. Throughout the entire Libyan episode he reveals himself
to be a fully perfected Stoic sage. He marches on foot at the head of his
men, giving no orders but showing his followers how to bear their hardships by his own example. He is the last to drink when water is found;
indeed, the only time he refreshes himself first is at a stream frequented
by snakes, whose water the men would have otherwise been afraid to
drink.[274] When his army is beset by an attack of poisonous snakes whose
bites result in a horrible death, the only thing that keeps the group together is Cato's heroic endurance. He stands guard over the sick and
strengthens the dying by his own courage, thereby enabling them to die
bravely: *casus alieno in pectore vincit/ spectatorque docet magnos nil posse dolores*
("He conquered calamities in the hearts of others, and proved by his own
mere presence that sore pain was powerless.")[275] He also, it will be remembered, disdains to consult the oracle of Ammon on the grounds that
the deity dwells within the soul of the virtuous man, a thesis which he
demonstrates by the rule of the *logos* in his own behavior.

Cato's end is left in suspense in the *Pharsalia,* since the epic is unfinished. After traversing the desert, he does engage in combat, manifesting
clemency in victory and exacting no revenge, since he thinks that conquest is a bitter enough cup for anyone to drink and that nothing further
should be demanded of the vanquished.[276] Although Lucan and his readers were well aware of how Cato met his death, the epic, as we have it,
does not include this event. It seems highly likely that Lucan intended
to depict Cato's suicide. Cato's own words clearly express the Stoic estimate of suicide: *scire mors sors prima viris, sed proxima cogi* ("Happiest of
all men are those who know when to die.")[277] Lucan gives voice to the
same sentiments in a personal observation interjected into the story and,
in negative terms, in the example of Vulteius, who encourages his men
to take their own lives, but for the wrong kinds of reasons.[278] Vulteius'
rationale for suicide is by no means a Stoic one. But Cato, when the time
comes, will end his life because he refuses to serve a tyrant. Even without
Cato's final Stoic coup de grâce, his character as a totally realized example of Stoic virtue in its most stringent form is beyond question.

Lucan thus succeeds admirably in depicting the Stoic ethical ideal in
action in the figure of Cato, as well as its antithesis in the characters of

---

[274] *Phars.* 9.500–509, 9.587–604, 9.607–618.
[275] *Phars.* 9.888–889.
[276] *Phars.* 9.398–399.
[277] *Phars.* 9.211.
[278] *Phars.* 4.473–520, 8.31–32.

Caesar and Pompey. The one signal departure that he makes from Stoic ethics can be seen in the fact that none of his female characters serve as vehicles for his moral message. In this respect, Vergil is more Stoic than Lucan. Unlike Dido and Camilla, whose virtues and vices are assessed according to the same moral criteria that Vergil applies to his masculine characters, the chief female figures in the *Pharsalia* are all flat and philosophically uninteresting. They are either vindictive, like Julia, long-suffering but sentimental, like Cornelia, or inserted into the action, like Marcia, merely to illustrate the moral traits of their husbands. Apart from this, Lucan achieves a thoroughgoing realization of the Stoic sage in Cato. In choosing to idealize a figure on the losing side, he is able to develop the theme of voluntary submission to fate, delineating the necessary conjunction of free will and fatalism on the level of Cato's inner life just as he expresses the same idea on an external, historical level in the case of the other leaders and groups who populate the epic. On the plane of history, however, Lucan never succeeds in reconciling his Stoic theory of necessity and contingency with his conception of fate as capricious. He does not manage to adjust the Stoic notion of a benevolent and rational providence with a set of historical facts in which the vicious are rewarded and the rise of tyranny is fostered. To the extent that this tension is resolved, and Lucan does not resolve it perfectly, it is resolved in his acceptance of the principle, through his characterization of Cato, that power and glory and even political *libertas* are ultimately *adiaphora* whose loss can only be sustained by the possession of Stoic autarchy and *apatheia*.

The richness of its Stoic content is only one reason why Lucan's *Pharsalia* appealed to readers in later antiquity and the Middle Ages. Their interest in his historical subject matter, in the natural history and magical lore he includes in his epic, and in the original features of his literary style also accounts for his popularity.[279] Lucan was read extensively by later Latin epic poets and by historians and was cited frequently by grammarians and scholiasts. He became a school author in the fourth century. The *Pharsalia* is second only to Vergil's *Aeneid* in the number of pre-Car-

---

[279] On Lucan's posthumous reputation see Bourgery, intro. to his ed. of *La Guerre civile*, *1*, xi–xiv; Jessie Crosland, "Lucan in the Middle Ages, with Special Reference to the Old French Epic," *Modern Language Review*, *25* (1930), 32–51; Due, "Essay on Lucan," *Classica et mediaevalia*, *23* (1962), 78; Harold C. Gotoff, *Transmission of the Text of Lucan in the Ninth Century* (Cambridge, Mass., 1971); Walter Fischli, *Studien zum Fortleben der Pharsalia des M. Annaeus Lucanus* (Luzern, n.d.), pp. 7–17, 19–44; Haskins, intro. to his ed. of *Pharsalia*, pp. 1–5; Margaret Jennings, "Lucan's Medieval Popularity: The Exemplum Tradition," *Rivista di cultura classica e medioevale*, *16* (1974), 215–33; Víctor-José Herrero Llorente, "Lucano en la literatura hispano-latino," *Emerita*, *27* (1960), 19–52; Malcovati, *Lucano*, pp. 109–22; Lao Paoletti, "La fortuna di Lucano dal medioevo al romanticismo," *Atene e Roma*, *7* (1962), 144–48; R. B. Steele, "Lucan's *Pharsalia*," *AJP*, *25* (1924), 305–28.

olingian manuscripts in which it is found. Lucan takes his place next to the satirists, if on a lower step than Vergil, as a favorite among the classical Latin poets studied and admired in the Middle Ages. In his portrait of Cato Lucan supplied his later readers with the most graphic, the most extended, and the most compelling model of the Stoic sage realized anywhere in classical Latin literature. Lucan's Cato is his most important and enduring contribution to the history of the Stoic tradition.

III. Statius

The *Thebaid* of Statius is by no means as significant a vehicle for philosophical thought as Lucan's *Pharsalia*. Yet, it has received an inflated amount of attention from commentators who wish to read it as an expression of Stoicism. The features of the *Thebaid* on which they have fastened are the typical epic themes of fate and the moral traits of the principal characters. The leading proponent of the Stoic interpretation of the *Thebaid* does not see Statius' attachment to the Stoa as overtly propagandistic, but as none the less pervasive, "coherent but not doctrinaire."[280] However, if one submits this estimate of Statius to the evidence, he emerges as far less coherent and as far less Stoic than the theory asserts.

Statius (A.D. 40/50–95/96) was born in Naples to an equestrian family in straightened circumstances.[281] His education, which he received from his father, and his interests throughout his life, appear to have been exclusively poetical. Statius began publishing his occasional poems, the *Silvae*, in A.D. 69, receiving a poet's crown in Naples for them in A.D. 78 or 80. At around that time he acquired some land at Alba, moved north, and married a wife from a wealthy Roman family in A.D. 80. Ten years later Statius won a second poet's crown for a poem, now lost, celebrating the exploits of the emperor Domitian. This honor seems to have won him entrée into the highest social circles in Rome. He published his major work, the *Thebaid,* in A.D. 91/92. It did not receive the reception that Statius would have liked. This fact, along with his failure to win a poetic competition which he had entered in A.D. 94 and possibly also declining health, encouraged him to return to Naples for part of the following year. He continued to produce *Silvae* and began a second epic, the *Achillaid,* of which he had completed slightly more than one book at the time of his death.

---

[280] Vessey, *Statius,* p. 59, and passim. Another, but very general, assessment which agrees with this view, is Sikes, *Roman Poetry,* pp. 212-13.

[281] On Statius' life see Jean Méheust, intro. to his ed. of P. Papinius Statius, *Achilléide,* Budé (Paris, 1971), pp. vii–xvi; J. H. Mozley, intro. to his ed. and trans. of *Thebaid,* Loeb (London, 1967), *1,* vii–ix.

The *Thebaid* retells the story of the downfall of the house of Oedipus, the enmity between his sons Eteocles and Polynices, and the destructive conflict between Thebes and Argos which results from it. The line of Oedipus bears a curse, laid on them and executed by the gods, whom, primarily in the person of Jove, Statius identifies with fate. Neither human beings nor the lesser deities can alter the inexorable decrees of destiny. The punishment that falls on Oedipus and his descendants can in no way be averted. All the members of his house must suffer and be destroyed, whether guilty of any crime or not, along with a great many other innocent people. Statius' rigidly fatalistic outlook has been seized on by many critics as an important index of his adherence to Stoicism,[282] coupled with the fact that the gods in the *Thebaid* often manifest their will in the form of omens.[283] This interpretation, however, fails to note the absence from the epic of a number of other ingredients that would need to be present in order for the presence of fatalism and divination to be pronounced authentically Stoic.

Statius' treatment of divination, to begin with, is anything but consistent. At one point, the poet says that augury truly presages the will of the gods.[284] But in the same incident, the very priest who performs the rites criticizes his fellow men as credulous and depraved for seeking to probe the future in this way.[285] Elsewhere, Statius offers an even more curious estimate of omens and portents:

> Quis fluere occultis rerum neget omina causis?
> fata patent homini, piget inservare, peritque
> venturi praemissa fides: sic omina casum
> fecimus et vires hausit fortuna nocendi.[286]

> Who will deny that omens flow from hidden causes of things to come?
> The fates lie open to mankind, but we choose not to take heed,
> And the proof foreshown is wasted; thus turn we omens into chance,
> And from hence Fortune draws her power to harm.

---

[282] Erich Burck, "Die Schicksalsauffassung des Tacitus und Statius," *Studies Presented to David Moore Robinson on His Seventieth Birthday*, ed. George E. Mylonas and Doris Raymond (St. Louis, 1953), 2, 702–06; Mozley, intro. to his ed. of *Thebaid*, *1*, xvi; Paola Venini, "Ancora sull'imitazione senecana e lucana nella *Tebaide* di Stazio," *Studi staziani* (Pavia, 1971), pp. 77–80; Vessey, *Statius*, p. 166; L. Watkiss, "The 'Thebaid' of Statius: A Reappraisal," (University of London Ph.D. diss., 1966), pp. 199–207.

[283] Vessey, *Statius*, pp. 152–54, 156–57, 227–28.

[284] Publius Papinius Statius, *Thebais* 3.450–451, ed. Alfredus Kotz, curavit Thomas C. Klinnert (Leipzig, 1973). All references to the *Thebaid* will be taken from this edition and the Mozley translation will be cited in all passages quoted.

[285] *Theb.* 3.465–565.

[286] *Theb.* 6.934–937.

In this passage the poet first states that omens do indeed foretell the future. At the same time he asserts that men, by choosing to ignore these messages, can convert fate into chance. Statius seems to be implying that fate and chance are not the same thing, suggesting that fate itself, or the will of Jove, rules the world reasonably, in contrast to capricious fortune. He also implies that men have the power to exercise free will in the position they choose to take toward fate or fortune. Such an association of ideas, were it developed systematically in the *Thebaid*, would indeed support the thesis that Statius was giving poetic expression to the Stoic conception of providence and free will. But, the weight of the evidence in the text of the epic makes this thesis impossible to sustain.

Statius does not show the gods, or fate, as reasonable, just, or benevolent. Jove enforces his will to the bitter end, regardless of how much innocent blood is shed. Statius makes no effort whatsoever to develop a theodicy or to show that any worthwhile political or moral ends are served thereby.[287] Both the virtuous and the vicious are crushed indiscriminately. The gods at times appear to be quite arbitrary. Early in the epic, the Argive king Adrastus explains to Polynices why his people celebrate certain rites in honor of Apollo. The daughter of an earlier king, he relates, was ravished by Apollo and bore a son. She hid the child with a shepherd, but wild dogs killed him. In her grief she revealed her secret to her father, who condemned her to death. Apollo, angered by this treatment of the lady, punished the community by sending a monster which attacked their children. A youth named Coroebus killed this monster, thereby arousing Apollo's wrath once more and causing the god to lay a pestilence on the land. Then Coroebus volunteered to sacrifice his life to Apollo if the god would lift the plague. At the last minute, Apollo spared his life.[288] This nude summary of the tale shows Apollo displaying little of the rationality or consistency that the Stoics attributed to the divine *logos*. Rather, Statius depicts him as violent and capricious.

Jove himself also manifests logical inconsistency. He enforces the destiny that he chooses, he explains, in order to do justice, in the name of piety and good faith:

> Ast ego non proprio diros inpendo dolori
> Oedipodionidas: rogat hoc tellusque polusque
> et pietas et laesa fides naturaque, et ipsi
> Eumenidum mores.[289]

---

[287] This point is developed well by Otto Schönberger, "Zum Weltbild der drei Epiker nach Lucan," *Helikon*, 5 (1965), 132-37.

[288] *Theb.* 1.557-672.

[289] *Theb.* 7.215-218.

> But it is to glut no private wrath that I sacrifice the sons of Oedipus:
> Earth and heaven demand it, and natural piety and injured faith,
> And the laws of the Avenging Powers themselves.

Jove none the less does not withhold his wrath from individuals who have in no sense been guilty of bad faith or impiety. The daughters of Oedipus are characterized by *pietas*, yet they suffer along with the rest of the family, not to mention the hosts of blameless Thebans and Argives who lose their lives in the conflict. Fate does not spare the virtuous: *Invida fata piis et fors ingentibus ausis/ rara comes* ("Fate is envious of devoted souls, and good luck goes rarely with great ventures.")[290] Senseless and malicious fate even goes to the lengths of mocking the grief-stricken survivors who make mistakes in identifying the mangled corpses of the fallen on the field of battle.[291]

Statius' fate thus has nothing of the benevolence and rationality of the Stoic conception of providence. At the same time, his treatment of the role of human free will in relation to fate marks a sharp departure both from Stoicism and from his Latin epic predecessors. The human agents in the *Thebaid* actually possess no free will at all.[292] The ineluctable fate that controls the entire course of events in the epic stems from a divine curse laid on Oedipus and his descendants well before the action begins. Oedipus' own tragedy is pre-ordained; and he himself lays a curse on his sons for their lack of filial piety in response to his sufferings. Oedipus implores the gods to punish Eteocles and Polynices by inciting bitter hatred between them that will lead to their destruction. The Fury Tisiphone hears this prayer and casts a spell on the sons, afflicting them with the family curse and arousing their mutual hostility and jealousy. It is this situation that leads Polynices to go to Argos, where he marries a daughter of Adrastus and involves the Argives in his fratricidal war with Eteocles. Jove underwrites the Fury's decision, adding that he himself will foment the war between Argos and Thebes. The gods, essentially, sow the seeds of war by granting Oedipus' appeal.[293] Both Oedipus and his sons are guilty of unfilial behavior, according to Statius' analysis of the circumstances precipitating the action in the *Thebaid*. Eteocles and Polynices are blameworthy for mocking their father and Oedipus is blameworthy for cursing his sons, even overlooking his previous behavior toward his parents. Yet, neither the father nor the sons is free not to act

---

[290] *Theb.* 10.384-385.
[291] *Theb.* 12.34-36.
[292] Schönberger, "Zum Weltbild der drei Epiker nach Lucan," pp. 132-37; Willey Schetter, *Untersuchungen zur epischen Kunst des Statius* (Wiesbaden, 1960), pp. 15-16.
[293] *Theb.* 1.212-247, 2.235-236.

as he does. All of them live under the constraints of a hereditary curse, a curse laid on the family before Oedipus himself was born.[294] In that sense, while Oedipus and his sons can be condemned for their vices, these vices do not spring from intellectual misjudgments or from the voluntary decision to give in to their passions. It is fate alone that determines their ethical behavior and it is fate that unilaterally causes the events in the epic to take place.

Statius' delineation of Oedipus and the members of his family is the closest he comes to providing anything resembling a psychological or moral analysis of any of his characters. The other figures in the Thebaid are one-dimensional stereotypes, portrayed without any nuances or insights into their inner ethical workings. Statius presents the other leading figures as all good or all bad, in terms of some one besetting sin or prominent virtue. Among the vicious characters, Oedipus is typified by bitterness, Etoecles by the lust for power, Polynices by envy, Tydeus by wrath, Hippomedon by brutality, and Capaneus by impiety. Among the more virtuous characters, Adrastus is typified by equanimity, Amphiarius by piety, Parthenopaeus by innocence, and Theseus by justice. It has been argued that the two most praiseworthy of these personages, Adrastus and Theseus, represent Stoic sages, and that Statius' juxtaposition of so many polar opposites among his characters is designed to express the ancient Stoic conception of the complete antithesis between wisdom and folly. It is asserted, furthermore, that the vicious characters reflect the Stoic doctrine that one vice entails all the other vices, since all the vicious are destroyed whatever their preeminent weaknesses may be.[295] However, a great many virtuous people are destroyed as well. The possession of one virtue or vice, for Statius, does not necessarily entail the other virtues or vices. Rather, his treatment of his characters reflects his relative disinterest in the dynamics of the human psyche, not the express desire to contrast Stoic sages with Stoic fools. Moreover, Statius is often inconsistent or vague in handling his characters, raising doubts about the significance of the seemingly Stoic associations which he attaches to some of them.

A glance at a few such characters from the Thebaid will illustrate this point. Theseus is referred to in a speech by Evadne as a second Hercules.[296] There are also a number of allusions made to Hercules in connection with other, lesser characters. Some of them merely share a geo-

---

[294] Theb. 2.460–467, 4.426–644.

[295] Vessey, Statius, pp. 58, 64–67, 76–91, 95–98, 151. On the regal figures see also Paola Venini, "Echi senecani e lucani nella Tebaide: Tirannia e tirranide," Studi staziani, pp. 62–64.

[296] Theb. 12.546–586.

graphical association with him, as is the case with the contingent from
Tiryns that engages in the war. With others, Statius pays so little attention to their moral traits that they are mere names, making the theory
that he is deliberately clothing them in a mantle of Stoic virtue seem
extremely forced. In one case, Statius even links Hercules with Tydeus,
whose criminal and irrational character has already been noted.[297] All
of this suggests that Statius' references to Hercules are accidental and
decorative and are not clues to any vital relationship in his mind between
his epic characters and Stoic sages. The behavior of a minor figure, Me-
neceus, who falls on his sword, has also been cited as evidence of Statius'
support for the Stoic doctrine of suicide.[298] If suicide were all that was
needed in antiquity to earmark an individual as a Stoic, the ranks of that
school would have been swollen beyond all recognizable limits. Thyestes
has also been identified as a Stoic sage because of his calm acceptance of
exile and his willingness to give up his political power in exchange for a
simple private life. Yet, Thyestes lacks the central virtue of the Stoic sage,
prudence, for he fails to see through Atreus' disingenuous offer of re-
conciliation and he is therefore sucked back into a life of passion and
intrigue.[299]

The behavior of Adrastus, the leading claimant for the title of Stoic
sage, is likewise crosshatched with ethical traits that are scarcely conso-
nant with that conception. He welcomes Tydeus to Argos, even though
he knows him to be a fratricide.[300] When he discovers Tydeus and Polynices fighting in a bloodthirsty rage in front of his palace gates, he
invites them to tell their tale, although their activities warrant rebuke
rather than curiosity.[301] He is quick to accept them as husbands for his
daughters once he sees their cloaks, which correspond with the attributes
which he believes his future sons-in-law will possess, despite the inaus-
picious evidence of their moral character which they have just given
him.[302]

The Stoicism that has been alleged to exist in the *Thebaid* is thus more
of an illusion than a reality. Fate, for Statius, is not the beneficent Stoic
logos. His gods are arbitrary and vindictive rather than reasonable. Statius' fatalism completely obliterates contingency and free will. His characters are instruments of destiny, deprived of choice. Their capacity to

---

[297] The relevant passages are assembled complete with overinterpretation by Vessey,
Statius, pp. 112-13, 114-16, 129, 131, 199-200, 204, 229.
[298] Henri Glaesener, "Les caractères dans le Thébaïde de Stace," *Le Musée Belge, 3*
(1899), 116.
[299] Vessey, *Statius*, p. 140, who does not note this inconsistency.
[300] *Theb.* 1.401-403, 2.111-113.
[301] *Theb.* 1.408-413, 1.435-446.
[302] *Theb.* 1.482-496, 2.167-172.

judge and to master their passions lies entirely outside of their own control, making it impossible for them to function as responsible moral agents in anything resembling a Stoic sense. Statius makes no attempt to rationalize the moral and metaphysical universe which he depicts in the *Thebaid* in any way, Stoic or otherwise. Statius was widely read and frequently commented on in later antiquity, holding a place close to Lucan's. His popularity continued in the Middle Ages, enhanced by the legend that he was a Christian.[303] But his *Thebaid* is best understood as an effort to translate the theme of nemesis from Greek tragedy into Latin epic, rather than as a chapter in the Latin appropriation and transmission of Stoic philosophy.

IV. SILIUS ITALICUS

The *Punica* of Silius Italicus enjoys the dubious distinction of being the longest and certainly the dullest of all classical Latin epics. It has not inspired a great deal of enthusiasm on the part of modern critics. On purely literary grounds, this estimate can evoke few arguments. However, from the standpoint of the history of the Stoic tradition, a study of the *Punica* has a great deal to be said for it. Although nothing is known of Silius' education and early life, he appears to have learned much from Vergil and Lucan about the ways in which Stoic philosophy might be integrated with epic poetry. Despite its heavy-handedness, its repetitiousness, and its occasional infelicities of style, the *Punica* does a good job of illustrating in epic form both the Stoic conception of causality and the virtue of the Stoic hero.

The life of Silius Italicus (A.D. 26-101) is known mainly from casual references in the works of Pliny and Martial.[304] His parentage and education are unknown, but he must have come from a wealthy, prominent, and cultivated family. He was a distinguished advocate in his youth, holding high political offices including the consulate in A.D. 68 and later the proconsulate of Asia. He was a connoisseur, assembling a large collection of books and works of art. Silius was also a dévoté of Vergil,

---

[303] The most detailed treatment of Statius' posthumous reputation, although it does not discuss the manuscript tradition, is Zoja Pavlovskis, "The Influence of Statius upon Latin Literature before the Tenth Century," (Cornell University Ph.D. diss., 1962). See also Méheust, intro. to his ed. of *Achilléide*, p. x n. i; Mozley, intro. to his ed. of *Thebaid*, *1*, xxvi-xxvii, xxx-xxxi; Luigi Valmaggi, "La fortuna di Stazio nella tradizione letteraria latina e bassolatina," *Rivista di filologia e d'istruzione classica*, *21* (1892), 409-62, 481-554; diffuse but still useful; Vessey, *Statius*, p. 311 n. 4.

[304] The fullest study of Silius' biography is Onorato Occione, *Cajo Silio Italico e il suo poema*, 2ª ed. (Firenze, 1871), pp. 15-33. See also J. D. Duff, intro. to his ed. and trans. of Silius Italicus, *Punica*, Loeb (London, 1934), *1*, ix-x; *Silver Age*, p. 453.

restoring his tomb at Naples and making pilgrimages to it, observing Vergil's birthday faithfully. He also venerated Cicero and made a point of buying a certain villa for no other reason than the fact that it had once belonged to Cicero. Silius' *Punica* is the work of his old age, written after he had retired from political life. Its theme recalls one of the most glorious moments in the history of the Roman Republic, the defeat of Hannibal in the second Punic war. Silius gives a decidedly Stoic cast to this tale. It is not clear whether he was a professed Stoic himself. He is thought to have been an acquaintance of Epictetus; and, when he found himself suffering from an incurable disease, he took his own life by starving himself to death. Whether Silius' attraction to Stoicism was in fact personal as well as literary, he does succeed in giving it expression in his epic.

There is a general consensus among the commentators that the ethical delineation of his characters is the place to look for Silius' Stoicism.[305] This judgment is perfectly correct. There is, however, another important area in which Silius shows a sensitive appropriation of Stoicism, the theme of causation. Silius carefully preserves a balance between divine and human agency in his analysis of the causes and progress of the Punic war. The gods, especially Jove and Juno, are the embodiments of fate or fortune, who initiate and direct the course of events. The war begins because of Juno's hatred of Rome's success. It is she who stirs up anger and the desire for war among the Carthaginians. After the failure of the first Punic war, she finds a fit instrument of her purpose in Hannibal.[306] Jove, more all-seeing than Juno, knows that the Romans will prevail. He executes the overall plan of destiny and prevents small obstructions from interfering with it.[307] Lesser gods can delay the outcome of a strategy imposed by a major god, but cannot avert it.[308] Silius gives credit as well to human choices and actions. Both the vices of the Carthaginians and the virtues of the Romans come into play. It is Hannibal's bellicose passions, as well as his election by Juno, which account for his initiation of the war.[309] It is Scipio's superior generalship and not just the favor of fortune that enables him to defeat Hanno in Spain.[310] It is their fear and

---

[305] The only alternative view is that of Edward L. Bassett, "Scipio and the Ghost of Appius," *CP*, *58* (1963), 73-92, who argues for the influence of Stoic cosmology and eschatology. This thesis, however, depends on the idea that Silius was influenced by Cicero's *Tusculan disputations* and that Cicero's work is a Stoic statement, a highly debatable opinion.

[306] Silius Italicus, *Punica* 1.26-37, ed. and trans. Duff. All citations and translations will be taken from this edition.

[307] *Pun.* 6.595-618.

[308] *Pun.* 2.506-512.

[309] *Pun.* 1.38-39, 1.56-63.

[310] *Pun.* 16.28-37.

cowardice, acting as evil counselors deflecting them from correct judgment, and not only divine wrath, that cause Tauranus and his comrades to flee into a wood during the course of battle, where they are trapped by the enemy.[311] Human actions, like those of the lesser gods, may accelerate or delay fortune, as is the case with Fabius' delay.[312] In all these examples, Silius reveals a conception of the forces motivating the action that preserves in full strength the Stoic relationship between destiny and free will.

Still, there is much more evidence that can be brought forward concerning his use of Stoic ethics as the framework in which he treats his leading characters. His epic heroes sometimes undergo a psychomachia, facing the need to make choices between moral alternatives. Silius is deeply interested in their psychology, recognizing, *more Stoicorum*, the importance of internal motivation and the exercise of free will in assessing the value of ethical decisions.[313] His use of Stoic modes of ethical analysis is visible in his treatment of the Carthaginians, who are mostly vicious, as well as the Romans, who are mostly virtuous. He also seems to have borrowed from Lucan the idea that the vices and virtues relevant to the action can be manifested by groups and by lesser characters as well as by the leaders in the front ranks.

The principal figure on the Carthaginian side is Hannibal, who sums up the moral characteristics of his nation, especially the Carthaginians' proclivity toward the passions of wrath and cruelty. For Silius the Carthaginians in general are faithless, breaking the treaty they had made with Rome, which they had sworn to Jove to uphold.[314] As a group they are given to brutality, particularly in their tendency to torture captives and hostages.[315] The leaders of Carthage manifest jealousy and miserliness after Hannibal's defeat, refusing him the supplies he would need to renew the war and forcing him to retire from the field.[316] The ruling family, composed of Hamilcar and his sons Hasdrubal and Hannibal, reflect these national traits even more vividly. Silius depicts Hamilcar as a man governed by his warlike passions, who raises his sons to be violent and vindictive men, nurturing these vices in them deliberately.[317] Hasdrubal, who first takes over the leadership of the Carthaginian cause after

---

[311] *Pun.* 5.475–479.

[312] *Pun.* 7.10–15.

[313] The best general study is Michael von Albrecht, *Silius Italicus: Freiheit und Gebundenheit römischer Epik* (Amsterdam, 1964), pp. 69–71, 87–89. In very general terms, see also Mendell, *Latin Poetry*, pp. 140, 146.

[314] *Pun.* 1.8–11, 1.694.

[315] *Pun.* 1.169–178, 6.535–544.

[316] *Pun.* 16.1–22.

[317] *Pun.* 1.70–71, 1.79–80, 2.349–352.

his father's death, is shown to be motivated by *ira, furor*, impiety, savagery, aggressiveness, bloodthirstiness, and tyranny. He seeks and enjoys political power primarily because of the opportunity it affords him to indulge in these passions.[318]

Hannibal shares all the same vices; but Silius portrays him much more subtly than he does the other members of Hannibal's family and nation. His Hannibal emerges as a man with admirable traits as well as moral weaknesses. To be sure, Hannibal is bellicose, full of *ira*, faithless to his word, crafty, shameless toward the gods, vindictive, vain-glorious, hypocritical, treacherous, and a true son of his father in his desire to raise his own son to be a warlike man with an implacable hatred of Rome.[319] Yet, despite the domination which these irrational passions exercise over him, Silius shows Hannibal as motivated by humane and reasonable feelings as well. Unlike Turnus, he is capable of feeling sorrow and not merely rage at the death of his relatives and comrades-in-arms.[320] When he learns of Hasdrubal's death, he masters his grief courageously: *compressit lacrimas Poenus minuitque ferendo/ constanter mala* ("Hannibal suppressed his tears, and made the disaster less by bearing it bravely.")[321] He is a patriot, willing to sacrifice himself for his cause, preferring to fight to the death rather than to accept terms of surrender that would subject his country to Rome.[322] Hannibal is also a man of sensibility and depth of feeling as a husband, consoling and strengthening his wife in his parting speech to her just before leaving for his campaign over the Alps.[323] In this famous venture, Hannibal invokes the memory of Hercules and his crossing of the Pyrenees as a justification for his strategy.[324] This association with Hercules is ironic, for Silius depicts Hannibal as an anti-type of Hercules.[325] Yet, the irony is not total. Hannibal does not lack praiseworthy traits. His error lies in the fact that he applies these qualities in the defense of a reprehensible cause, for his initiation and prosecution of the war forces him to perjure himself before both gods and men, subverting a peace and undermining a treaty.[326] For Silius, Hannibal emerges as a tragic figure but as an ultimately blameworthy man in Stoic terms because his inner intentions are evil. Hence his marks of greatness,

---

[318] *Pun.* 1.144–168.

[319] *Pun.* 1.38–39, 1.56–63, 1.187, 1.239–240, 1.533–534, 2.18–35, 3.75–86, 12.473–478.

[320] *Pun.* 2.209–210, 15.819–820.

[321] *Pun.* 15.819–820.

[322] *Pun.* 2.364–367.

[323] *Pun.* 3.131–154.

[324] *Pun.* 2.356–357, 3.420–439, 3.512–515, 4.4–5.

[325] Noted by Albrecht, *Silius Italicus*, pp. 47–51. This author also makes some penetrating remarks about other Carthaginian figures, p. 68.

[326] *Pun.* 1.239–270.

while they make him a worthy opponent for the Romans, cannot be accounted to his righteousness.

The Romans, for their part, manifest many signs of Stoic virtue, a characteristic that Silius illustrates on several levels, ranging from groups to individuals of various kinds, but which he delineates most sharply in his portraits of the three main heroes, Fabius, Regulus, and Scipio. It is not only the Romans themselves but even their allies who exemplify Stoic moral excellence. Silius holds up for praise the behavior of the servant of the Spanish king Tagus, who undergoes horrible torture for killing Hasdrubal in order to avenge the death of his master:

> Mens intacta manet; superat ridetque dolores,
> spectanti similis, fessoque labore ministros
> increpitat dominique crucem clamore reposcit.[327]

> But the man's spirit remained unbroken; he was the master still
> And despised the suffering; like a mere looker-on he blamed the myrmidons
> Of the torturer for flagging in their task and loudly demanded
> To be crucified like his master.

What is particularly noticeable here is not so much the man's heroism *per se* as his Stoic *mens intacta* triumphing over the passion of *dolor*.

Groups, also, are capable of manifesting Stoic virtue. Silius' image of the Roman senate, which may be contrasted strikingly with the picture of this body found in Lucan's *Pharsalia,* is made up of men uniting the virtues of the Stoic sage with those of traditional Republican worthies, all, to a man, evocations of Cincinnatus:

> Concilium vocat augustum castaque beatos
> paupertate patres ac nomina parte triumphis
> consul et aequantem superos virtute senatum.
> Facta animosa viros et recti sacra cupido
> attolunt; hirtaque togae neglectaque mensa
> dexteraque a curvis capulo non segnis aratris;
> exiguo facilis et opum non indigna corda,
> ad parvos curru remeabant saepe penates.[328]

> The consul summoned the worshipful assembly—the Fathers rich
> In unstained poverty, with names acquired by conquests—a senate
> Rivalling the gods in virtue. Brave deeds and a sacred passion for justice
> Exalted these men; their dress was rough and their meals simple,

---

[327] *Pun.* 1.179-181.
[328] *Pun.* 1.608-616.

And the hands they brought from the crooked plough were ready
With the sword-hilt; content with little, uncovetous of riches, they
Often went back to humble homes from the triumphal car.

Silius' chief medium for the delineation of the Stoic sage is the individual Roman leader. The three major figures of this type whom he depicts
are all associated with Hercules, either as examples of *fides* and *patientia*,
as victors over terrifying monsters, as men confronted with moral choices,
or as heroes struggling through their *labor* to attain wisdom, autarchy,
and ultimate apotheosis.[329] Fabius, to whom Silius refers several times
as a descendant and a protégé of Hercules,[330] is portrayed as godlike in
his fixed resolve[331] and as completely free from irrational emotions.[332]
This estimate of his character is shared by Jove, who notes, when Fabius
is chosen as commander of the Roman army by his own divine inspiration, that Fabius lacks all personal ambition; he has no interest in court-
ing popularity, no jealousy, no desire for booty. He is capable of dealing
with all that war or peace may require, *quieta/ mente*, and is proof against
all the passions.[333] Jove's opinion is certainly borne out in the scenes
where Silius shows Fabius in action. His chief characteristic as a politician
is thoughtful deliberation and a disinclination toward bloodshed. When
the news is first brought to Rome that Hannibal has attacked Saguntum
and the senate has to decide whether to declare war on him, Fabius
argues that they should first ascertain whether Hannibal has the support
of his own people or is acting on his personal whim. He advocates war
only if negotiation fails to restore peace.[334] As a senator he exerts himself
to hearten and encourage the populace.[335] Fabius' leading trait as a
military commander is also circumspection. He repeatedly devises strategies that enable him to wear out or outwit his enemy so as to achieve
victory without spilling blood if possible.[336] As a general no less than as
a statesman, he knows how to inspire and to discipline the men he
leads,[337] by his example as much as by his words.

---

[329] Excellent treatments of this point are provided by Vittorio d'Agostino, "La favola
del bivio in Senofonte, in Luciano, e in Silio Italico," *RSC, 2* (1954), 177-84; Albrecht,
Silius Italicus, pp. 45-46, 68, 76, 82-88; Andrew Runni Anderson, "Hercules and His
Successors," *HSCP, 39* (1928), 35-36; Edward L. Bassett, "Hercules and the Hero of the
Punica," *The Classical Tradition*, ed. Wallach, pp. 258-73; "Regulus and the Serpent in the
Punica," *CP, 50* (1955), 1-20.
[330] *Pun.* 2.3, 6.640, 7.35, 7.43-44, 7.592.
[331] *Pun.* 7.9-10.
[332] *Pun.* 7.26, 7.577-579.
[333] *Pun.* 6.613-617.
[334] *Pun.* 1.679-694.
[335] *Pun.* 10.592-622.
[336] *Pun.* 6.619-640, 7.123-126, 7.267-275, 15.320-333.
[337] *Pun.* 7.91-95, 7.707-713.

Fabius presents the aspect of the fully perfected sage, never troubled by doubt or inner turmoil. Silius' other heroes are much more compelling in that they undergo a certain amount of moral tension and development. Regulus, on one level, is identified as a Herculean figure because he kills a monstrous serpent.[338] He is more interesting, however, as a hero who attains mastery over himself and who sacrifices himself for the good of the nation. When he first introduces Regulus, Silius describes him as a man who has a mistaken trust in the god of war, *fallax fiducia Martis*, and who tends to be carried away by his yearning for fame.[339] Regulus is captured by the Carthaginians and subjected to torture, a fate he learns to accept, maintaining his dignity with an untroubled mind. But a fresh temptation awaits him. He is sent back to Rome by Hannibal, who offers to release him in exchange for a number of Carthaginian prisoners of war whom the Romans have captured. It is Regulus' view that this exchange would be detrimental to the Romans' war effort. He maintains this position resolutely, despite the emotions that his return arouses among the senators, the people, and his own family. The difficulties which this situation imposes on him are greater even than the trials he suffered under torture, but he endures them without wavering, urging the senate to reject Hannibal's offer and to send him back to Carthage as a sacrifice to the Roman cause.[340] He persuades the senate to adopt this policy in a speech that takes place at dawn, the hour, as the poet notes, when the sun began to shine on Hercules' funeral pyre.[341] With the reproaches of his uncomprehending wife as the last Roman voice to sound in his ears as he sails away[342] and with the certainty of being tortured to death on his return to Carthage,[343] Regulus can truly be said to have earned the title of Stoic sage through a trial by fire.

Scipio is the hero whose inner psychology Silius explores the most extensively and whose behavior as a leader he delineates the most sympathetically. Scipio's principal traits are magnanimity and a will instructed by reason. He has a parallel in the lesser figure of Marcellus. Surveying the city of Syracuse which he has just conquered, Marcellus must decide whether to destroy it or to spare it. He chooses to spare it, in a tense moment when the decision might have gone the other way, leading him to groan aloud at the thought of the violence and impiety that would have resulted had he exercised the power which fell to him

---

[338] *Pun.* 6.145-260.
[339] *Pun.* 6.332-333.
[340] *Pun.* 6.381-388, 6.394-396, 6.451-489.
[341] *Pun.* 6.451-454.
[342] *Pun.* 6.519-520.
[343] *Pun.* 6.535-550.

by right of conquest.[344] By his clemency toward Syracuse Marcellus
shows himself equal to the gods in spirit, *aemulus ipse/ ingenii superum*.[345]
Scipio has more than one choice to make. The first, and the most dramatic, is his decision to take on the leadership of the Romans' campaign
in Spain. As Scipio considers this matter, two allegorical figures, Virtus
and Voluptas, appear to him, personifying the inner debate going on in
his mind. Voluptas is richly dressed, perfumed with Persian scents, her
tresses flowing freely. She regards Scipio with a wanton gaze as she tries
to persuade him to follow her by refusing the commission. Virtus, dressed
in a plain white robe, with her hair severely dressed and a straightforward
expression on her face, offers her own arguments. Man, she says, is created with an intellect which is a seed of the divine nature and which distinguishes him decisively from the animals. Those who fail to cultivate
this divine gift of reason are condemned to Avernus, while those who do
cultivate it are apotheosized, like Hercules, Castor, and Pollux. One
should make moral choices in accordance with reason, she adds, not only
because of the posthumous rewards and punishments involved. Reason
also enjoins man to accept his duty for his own happiness in this life and
for the service of his fellow man. Virtue, thus, is its own reward as well
as an expression of *humanitas* and a source of future honor and glory. The
path of virtue, she emphasizes, is a difficult one, requiring hard and un-
remitting effort and self-discipline. But, Virtus concludes, this effort is
rewarded not only by the positive benefits it enables the virtuous man to
confer on others but also, and more importantly, by the autarchy it makes
possible for himself.[346] Scipio is won over by this argument, which is as
concise and thorough a summary of Stoic ethics as one can find anywhere
in Latin epic poetry.

Scipio then displays his Stoic virtue in action. He is a man capable of
warlike passion, having shown this characteristic much earlier in the *Punica* as a general spurred on by righteous indignation in the midst of
battle.[347] When he has defeated Hanno in Spain and the booty is being
divided up by the conquerors, a captive maiden betrothed to the ruler
of one of the Spanish tribes is brought to him. Her rank and beauty make
her a prize of war fit for the commander in chief. But Scipio decides not
to exercise the rights that law and custom grant him. He returns her
unsullied to her fiancé.[348] Scipio thus exhibits the virtues of clemency
and self-restraint as well as those of selfless leadership. At the very end

---

[344] *Pun.* 14.670-674.
[345] *Pun.* 14.580-681.
[346] *Pun.* 15.18-123.
[347] *Pun.* 4.642-648.
[348] *Pun.* 15.268-276.

of the epic, when he makes his triumphal entry into Carthage, Silius compares him with Hercules after he had slain the giants.[349] The giants which Scipio has bested are internal as well as external ones. The Herculean and Stoic resonances evoked by Scipio go well beyond this. Like Hercules and like Aeneas, Scipio makes a trip to the underworld, in Book 13 of the epic. For Silius, Scipio unites the Stoic victory of reason, *apatheia*, and *eupatheia* over the irrational passions with the Roman victory of civilization over barbarism. Silius' Scipio bears comparison not only with Vergil's Aeneas but also with the Scipio of the sixth book of Cicero's *De republica*.[350] In concept, if not always in execution, Silius' portrayal of Scipio and the other heroes of the *Punica* shows that his epic is a legitimate heir of the literary models which he venerated and of the Stoic philosophy which served as its inspiration.

In the sequel to this tale, however, we encounter a paradox. There can be no question of the sympathy and fidelity with which Silius expresses his Stoic values in depicting his epic heroes or in his handling of the problem of fatalism and free will. The *Punica* in this sense earns him an entirely respectable place in the history of the appropriation of Stoicism by the Latin epic poets. On the other hand, Silius does not play a commensurate role as a transmitter of Stoicism to the Middle Ages. There is no evidence that he was read or copied in late antiquity or in the early Middle Ages.[351] The first known exemplar of the *Punica* is a manuscript, no longer extant and probably from St. Gall, which was discovered by Poggio Bracciolini in 1416 or 1417. Sixteenth-century scholars preserve a few readings from another medieval copy, a Cologne manuscript of the ninth century, which has not survived. Apart from these scanty indications, there is no medieval or late classical history of the *Punica*. Silius' importance as an exponent of Stoicism is thus limited to his own time, and had no discernible influence on his medieval posterity.

---

[349] *Pun.* 17.649-650.

[350] See the excellent study of this point by Richard Heck, "Scipio am Scheideweg: Die Punica des Silius Italicus und Ciceros Schrift De re publica," *WS*, n.F. *4* (1970), 156-80.

[351] On Silius' posthumous reputation see Duff, intro. to his ed. of *Punica, 1*, xvi; Rudolf Schieffer, "Silius Italicus in St. Gallen: Ein Hinweis zur Lokalisierung des 'Waltharius'," *Mittellateinisches Jahrbuch, 10* (1975), 7-19.

CHAPTER FIVE

HISTORIANS, LESSER POETS, SCHOLIASTS, PEDAGOGUES, AND ENCYCLOPEDISTS

The authors to be considered in this chapter are a diverse group both with respect to the genres in which they wrote and in the degree to which they reflect the influence of Stoicism. In some cases their debts to Stoic philosophy have been the subject of flamboyant exaggeration on the part of commentators. In other cases their use and transmission of important Stoic doctrines have remained all but unnoticed. Their late classical and medieval fortunes, also, vary widely. Some of the figures discussed in this chapter whose Stoic affinities have been inflated the most wildly enjoyed an extensive post-classical reputation. But this is even more true of others who made significant contributions to the forwarding of the Stoic tradition and who occupied a place of considerable authority in medieval scholarship and education, although they have been less appreciated for their literary merits and less exhaustively studied for their philosophical content.

I. The Historians

As a group, the Roman historians have suffered more violence at the hands of modern commentators anxious to recast them as Stoics than is true for any of the other types of authors considered in this chapter. Critics are well aware of the fact that the Stoa was the only school of ancient philosophy to produce historiography. We know that Posidonius wrote a history, now unfortunately lost, and that he took it upon himself to serve as Polybius' continuator. There has been a powerful inclination to assume that the Latin historians in general were informed by Stoic principles. This temptation has been strengthened by the commentators' recognition of the fact that other Latin writers, such as the epic poets, were capable of expressing a Stoic position on matters integrally related to the philosophy of history. Although no actual Stoic historiography survives, it has been argued quite plausibly that an attachment to Stoicism would result in a distinctive point of view toward history.[1] We might outline such a Stoic philosophy of history, although it is admittedly a

---

[1] On this point see the useful analysis by Gérard Verbeke, "Stoïciens et le progrès de l'histoire," *Revue philosophique de Louvain*, 62 (1964), 5-38.

hypothetical extrapolation from Stoic doctrines in other areas or from Stoicizing authors in other genres, simply to provide a yardstick against which the work of the Roman historians can be measured.

A historian imbued with Stoicism would have a decidedly metahistorical outlook, reflecting a physics in which change is the paramount reality and in which the deity is identical with the material world. Historical phenomena, no less than natural phenomena, would therefore be viewed as manifestations of the immanent divine *logos,* at the same time a benevolent providential force and the rational yet ineluctable cause of historical events. This divine *logos* ruling history from within would also be identified with the cosmic process of *ekpyrosis* and *diakosmesis*. The historical order would therefore be governed by a cyclical pattern of disintegration and reintegration. Just as the cosmos and its natural laws are eternal, so history would be understood as a temporal extension without limits, a continuous process of cyclical change in which all stages are equally perfect because they are equally identified with the divine *logos*.

For the Stoics, time is an incorporeal. This fact, coupled with the cyclical pattern of destruction and recreation, would tend to deprive individual historical events of their uniqueness. History would appear to shrink to the status of a sequence of recurrent moments in a metaphysical process whose ultimate meaning lies beyond them. But, at the same time, these individual events in human history parallel a physics of concrete, ever-changing realities making up a natural order that is in no sense distinct from God. Thus, despite the elements in Stoicism that might pull him in that direction, a Stoicizing historian would not be able to regard the historical process as metaphysically inferior to the divine reality which is its true meaning. Indeed, the chief philosophical interest in this sort of historical theory would lie in the tension, or harmony, which it posits between historical events which contain their own causes and the metahistorical framework of recurrent cycles in which these same events would also have to be viewed.

On another level, the Stoicizing historian would be deeply concerned with the implications of Stoic anthropology, psychology, and ethics for the understanding of history. Agreeing that all men share in the common possession of reason and are therefore bound together in a cosmopolitan moral community, the historian would adopt a universal perspective. He would not regard any one class or nation as intrinsically more interesting or more important than any other. He would be able to find edifying examples of vice and virtue in whatever historical quarter he might look. Responsive to the principle that vices and virtues arise out of intellectual judgments and inner motivations, the historian would seek to plumb the psychology of the individuals and groups whose history he related. His analysis would also embrace the question of free will as a critical ingredient in intellectual decision and moral choice. He would find a place for human free will in relation to divine causation in the historical order analogous to the relationship between necessity and contingency in the natural order. The Stoicizing historian, finally, would have a didactic conception of his craft. He would seek to inculcate an attitude of *apatheia* and detachment in his reader, given the nature of historical reality as a never-ending flux, in which kingdoms and empires inevitably rise and fall. But beyond this, the necessary collaboration between divine causation and human free will coupled with the cyclical conception of history would urge him to instill in his readers an attitude of ethical activism and philosophical optimism inspired by a vision of the future in which the world itself, and human possibilities, are constantly renewing themselves. Such, it might plausibly be suggested, might be the philosophy of history resulting from the assimilation of Stoicism into the operative mentality of the historian.

In turning from this hypothesis to the actual historiography produced by the Romans, we come down from the clouds with a rude shock. While the Roman historians are unquestionably didactic in orientation, none of them displays the slightest trace of the metaphysical or ethical attitudes that might entitle us to describe his work as an application of Stoicism to historiography. None of them has a universal scope, a cyclical view of history, a providential conception of historical causation, or a Stoic analysis of the inner dynamics of man's ethical choices. They all confine themselves to the history of one single community, Rome. While they tend to criticize the present as a degeneration from the past, they neither depict nor envision any possibility of future regeneration. They concentrate on the actions of men rather than on the workings of the divine *logos* as the primary or exclusive causal agency in history, however much they may bow to religious conventions. The vices and virtues of their human agents are neither specifically Stoic for the most part nor are they subjected to much psychological analysis. The historians delineate individuals and groups from the skin out, being concerned less with the causes of their behavior than with its effects on events. None the less, and despite the need to refute the unfounded claims of scholars urging a Stoic interpretation of the Roman historians, several of them do preserve a few elements of Stoic thought which are worth noting.

A) Sallust

Sallust is the earliest of the Roman historians to have been interpreted in a Stoic light, although there is very little reason to support such a reading. Sallust touches on a number of apparently Stoic themes but he subordinates them completely to a non-Stoic point of view. He rigorously excludes divine and metaphysical causes and, when he introduces the theme of fortune, he treats it as a manifestation of human decisions and actions rather than as a superhuman force. Born in Amiternum to a family of uncertain rank, Sallust (86-36/34 B.C.) led an active life in both the military and the civil service.[2] A supporter of Caesar, he retired from politics after his mentor's assassination, producing his histories between 44 B.C. and the year of his death. His subjects were the Catilinarian conspiracy and the Jugurthine war. There is also an oration on the republic dedicated to Caesar which most scholars attribute to him. Sallust's works enjoyed a good deal of popularity in late antiquity and the early Middle Ages, being cited by many historians and a wide range of prose authors both pagan and Christian.[3] Manuscripts of both of his histories are well represented in the Middle Ages, going back to Carolingian exemplars. Well read and much admired as he undoubtedly was, however, Sallust did not really appropriate or transmit Stoicism in any meaningful sense. This is a myth that deserves to be laid to rest.

The chief issue in Sallust scholarship relative to his philosophical orientation is the doctrine he sets forth in the prologues to his *Bellum Catilinae* and his *Bellum Iugurthinum*. In the *Catilinae*, Sallust begins, all men, unlike the beasts, possess minds as well as bodies. The mind, created to rule the body, is a faculty that man shares with the gods. Through the use of his intelligence or *ingenium* man may attain lasting *gloria*.[4] Although in warfare, physical prowess is needed along with *ingenium*, intelligence is the more important of these two qualities. It is still more critical in the career of statesmanship, where, if *ingenium* or *animi virtus* were more in evidence, political life would be far more tranquil than it is.[5] *Virtus*, Sallust adds, is necessary in all human endeavors. Those who fail to exercise it pass through life half asleep; but those who make use of it attain distinction

---

[2] For Sallust's life see Ettore Albino, *L'uomo Sallustio* (L'Aquila, 1966), pp. 59-109; D. C. Earl, *The Political Thought of Sallust* (Amsterdam, 1966 [repr. of London, 1961 ed.], p. 1; Michel Grant, *The Ancient Historians* (New York, 1970), pp. 198-99; Ettore Paratore, *Sallustio*, Quaderni della *Rivista di cultura classica e medioevale*, 12 (Roma, 1973), 35-47, which has an up-to-date survey of the literature; Ronald Syme, *Sallust*, Sather Classical Lectures, 33 (Berkeley, 1964), pp. 5-15, 29-59.

[3] On Sallust's posthumous reputation see Karl Büchner, *Sallust* (Heidelberg, 1960), pp. 356-61; Alfred Ernout, intro. to his ed. and trans. of *Catilina, Jugurtha, Fragments des Histoires*, Budé (Paris, 1947), pp. 36-46; Grant, *Ancient Historians*, p. 395; Beryl Smalley, "Sallust in the Middle Ages," *Classical Influences on European Culture A.D. 500-1500*, ed. R. R. Bolgar (Cambridge, 1971), pp. 165-75; Syme, *Sallust*, pp. 274-301.

[4] C. Sallustius Crispus, *Bellum Catilinae* prooemium, 1.1.4, in *Bellum Catilinae, Bellum Iugurthinum, Orationes et epistulae excerptae de historiis*, trans. J. C. Rolfe, Loeb (London, 1931). All citations to and translations of Sallust's works will be taken from this edition.

[5] *Cat.* 1.5-2.6.

in whatever career they choose.[6] This observation serves as Sallust's transition to a defense of his own *otium litterarium*. It is a fine thing, he notes, to serve one's country in public life by one's deeds. So also is it noble to serve it by one's words. Thus, when he himself retired from politics, he chose to devote himself to the writing of history, rather than passing his time in idleness or in hunting or farming or some such servile pursuits (*servilibus officiis*).[7]

Sallust repeats and elaborates on some of the same ideas in the prologue to the *Iugurthinum*. People complain, he says, that chance (*fors*) not virtue rules their lives. But in fact, he counters, it is human intelligence that governs human affairs: *sed dux atque imperator vitae mortalium animus est*.[8] Possessing *ingenium*, men have the capacity to attain glory and they have no need of *fortuna*; for fortune cannot provide them with honesty, industry, and the other virtues and achievements which they acquire through the use of their minds. This being the case, Sallust says, men are responsible for their own successes and failures.[9] If men would only use their talents, *neque regerentur magis quam regerent casus et eo magnitudinis procederent, ubi pro mortalibus gloria aeterni fierent* ("they would control fate rather than being controlled by it, and would attain to that height of greatness where from mortals their glory would make them immortals.")[10] The reason underlying this possibility, Sallust explains, is that the *anima* and *ingenium* rule the body, which is inferior to the mind. Intellect alone endures, incorruptible and eternal, animating the body yet not controlled by it.[11] The need to use one's intelligence once more serves him as a transition to the praise of historiography, which he elevates here above civil and military service. Magistracy is wearisome, he notes, leading to intrigue, jealousy and even the forced association with dishonorable men, while military command involves danger to life and limb.[12] A safer form of public service is to write history, providing one's fellow citizens with examples of vice and virtue to avoid and to emulate.[13] In the body of his history, Sallust makes it clear that he plans to concentrate on the vices which his reader should disdain. This, he notes, is why he has chosen to write about the Jugurthine war, for it initiated the series of events leading to the domestic turmoil and factionalism that have brought Rome to her present sorry pass.[14]

---

[6] *Cat.* 2.7-9.
[7] *Cat.* 3.1-4.5.
[8] *Iug.* prooemium, 1.3.
[9] *Iug.* 1.1-4.
[10] *Iug.* 1.5.
[11] *Iug.* 2.3.
[12] *Iug.* 2.4-3.3.
[13] *Iug.* 4.1-9.
[14] *Iug.* 5.2-3.

The basic ideas articulated in these two prefaces are carried forward consistently throughout Sallust's works. He treats the vices of Catiline as both the symptoms and the causes of the moral decline of the later Roman Republic.[15] Catiline's downfall is thus a cautionary tale illustrating how a man with a certain number of virtues chose to exercise his *ingenium* viciously, thereby providing leadership for the immoral tendencies in society at large. These evil inclinations on one level seem to be a matter of fortune, which, says Sallust, dominates all things and accounts for the moral and intellectual endowments of entire peoples.[16] The Romans, for instance, were invested with the virtues of vigorous activity. But, once they had conquered and pacified the world, their fortune grew cruel and they developed the vices of avarice, lust for power, hardheartedness, and impiety,[17] which Catiline precipitated and raised to new heights of destructiveness. Fortune, as Sallust uses it here, does not denote a superhuman metaphysical force that may intervene into human affairs. Rather, it stands for the virtues and vices of men, or the way they choose to employ their talents and opportunities. Catiline symbolizes the evil fortune that Rome brought on herself by abandoning the virtues of the early Republic in preference for the vices of luxury and power. On the other hand, Gaius Marius, in the *Iugurthinum*, exemplifies an individual whose fortune is identified with his virtues. Early in his career, a soothsayer prophesies that a happy issue and a great career await him and counsels him to put his fortune to the test. He does so, attaining the consulate and winning supporters by exercising his political skill, by seizing the initiative, and by making clever use of circumstances.[18] His fortune, like Catiline's, is equated with his own abilities and the ways he chooses to deploy them. Sallust sums up the same message with regard to causation in history in his speech dedicated to Caesar. In former times, he says, men thought that fortune held kingdoms and empires in her gift. But experience shows that each man is the maker of his own fortune: *fabrum esse suae quemque fortunae.*[19]

Now what philosophical attitudes, if any, can be detected in these passages? Proponents of the Stoic interpretation, who point to Posidonius and Panaetius as Sallust's presumed sources, cite his moralistic outlook, his distinction between mind and body, his praise of the active life, his justification of *otium litterarium*, his notion that decline inevitably follows the rise of a civilization, and his idea that virtue attained through the

---

[15] *Cat.* 5.1-9.
[16] *Cat.* 8.1-9.3.
[17] *Cat.* 10.2.
[18] *Iug.* 65.4-5, 73.1-7, 84.1, 144.4.
[19] *Ad Caesarem senem de re publica* 1.2.

exercise of *ingenium* yields glory, even unto eternity.[20] Opponents of the
Stoic thesis, however, have emphasized quite correctly that the dualism
of mind and body on which Sallust bases his ethics is a Platonic not a
Stoic idea and that the immortality of the soul is not a uniquely Stoic
doctrine. Even in the case of the middle Stoics who absorbed a certain
amount of Platonic anthropology, a psychosomatic dynamic is preserved
in their ethics which is absent from Sallust. Also, in contrast to the Stoics,
who analyzed virtue and vice on the basis of absolute ethical categories,
Sallust's treatment of ethics is relative and existential. Finally, Sallust
views constitutional forms as dogmatic first principles and not as Stoic
adiaphora.[21]

There is also a third school of thought which depreciates the idea that
there is any philosophical influence at all in Sallust's histories. Sallust's
emphasis on intelligence and its capacity to produce glory is seen instead
as a traditional Roman attitude, reflecting an extroverted, family-orient-
ed ethos concerned with achievement in public service and which also
entails the ability of a *novus homo* to win reputation through his own talent
and industry.[22] Sallust's stress on *ingenium*, moreover, is viewed as a statement about the power of men to mold events, to seize the propitious
moment, and to command a fortune that is no metaphysical force but a
reflection of man's own activity, a notion that can be seen either as an
index of Sallust's originality[23] or as a function of his imitation of Thu-
cydides.[24] The dualism between mind and body has also been interpreted
with more ingenuity than persuasiveness as a device which Sallust uses

---

[20] André, *L'Otium*, p. 373; Franz Altheim, "Poseidonios und Sallust," *Studi in onore di
Pietro de Francisi* (Milano, 1956), *1*, 104-14; F. Klingner, "Über die Einleitung der Historien Sallusts," *Hermes, 63* (1928), 182-89; Antonio LaPenna, "Il significato dei proemi
sallustiani," *Maia, 11* (1959), 89-106; S. Pantzerhielm Thomas, "The Prologues of Sallust," *Symbolae Osloenses, 15-16* (1936), 140-62; Werner Schur, *Sallust als Historiker* (Stuttgart, 1934), pp. 6-7, 61-103; Syme, *Sallust*, pp. 241-43, who, however, notes that the
ethical ideas involved are all commonplaces; Étienne Tiffou, *Essai sur la pensée morale de
Salluste à la lumière de ses prologues* (Paris, 1974), pp. 80-117.
[21] The best analysis along these lines is by Tiffou, *Essai*, pp. 38-55, 57-74, 159-78 and
especially "Salluste et la tradition stoïcienne," *Echoes du monde classique, 12* (1968), 13-19.
See also Ezio Bolaffi, "I proemi delle monografie di Sallustio," *Athenaeum, 16* (1936),
128-57; Franz Egermann, *Die Proömien zu den Werken des Sallust*, Sitzungsberichte der
Akademie der Wissenschaften in Wien, philosophisch-historische Klasse, *214*:3 (Wien,
1932), pp. 7, 23-81; A. D. Leeman, "Sallusts Prologe und seine Auffassung von der
Historiographie," *Mnemosyne*, ser. 4:7 (1954), 327; *8* (1955), 39, although ibid., p. 40 he
states that Sallust could have gotten his Platonic anthropology by way of Posidonius.
[22] Earl, *Political Thought of Sallust*, pp. 6, 10-11, 16-17, 24-40, 111, 113; M. L. W.
Laistner, *The Greater Roman Historians* (Berkeley, 1963), pp. 45-57; Paratore, *Sallustio*, pp.
48, 57-59; Gerd Schweicher, *Schicksal und Glück in den Werken Sallusts und Caesars* (Köln,
1963), pp. 9-72; Tiffou, *Essai*, pp. 144-54.
[23] Douglas J. Stewart, "Sallust and *Fortuna*," *History and Theory, 7* (1968), 298-317.
[24] Syme, *Sallust*, pp. 246-48.

to distinguish people into two categories, those apt for politics and those not. The former use their intelligence and lead fortune while the latter are carried along on the current of their age but can never serve as its helmsmen.[25]

It may not be quite so easy to dispose of Sallust's mind-body split in these terms, since it is difficult to explain why he takes such pains to elaborate on this Platonic doctrine in two of his prefaces unless he wishes it to be taken seriously in its own terms. In considering his attachment to this doctrine it is also difficult to see him as an adherent either of Stoicism or of the unreconstructed *mos maiorum*. The thesis that Sallust was justifying the rise of the *novus homo* is linked to the view that he was a *novus homo* himself, a premise that has not won universal credence among his biographers. Sallust's rationale for *otium litterarium* as the conduct of public life by other means is the most overtly Stoicizing element in his thought. It appears to be an application to historiography of Cicero's justification of philosophical *otium*. However, this seemingly Stoic theme is subordinated to a notion of self-aggrandizing *gloria* that any Stoic would regard as a matter of indifference at best and as an unacceptable motive for public service at worst. Sallust furthermore attaches this notion to the idea of eternal *gloria,* which not all Stoics supported and which those who did shared with many other philosophical schools. Moreover, Sallust contrasts *otium litterarium* with idle and base pursuits, among which he lists agriculture, a profession praised by the Stoics and the Roman traditionalists alike. His analysis of the choice of professions, also, includes the idea that magistracy and military service should be avoided because of their dangers and hardships, an attitude that both the *maiores* and the Stoics would have regarded as cowardly and self-indulgent. Sallust's alleged equation of the active and passive types of human personality with the mental and physical faculties is impossible to square with Stoicism even in its middle Stoic forms. Sallust shows no interest in the psychogenesis of virtue, except for his statement that it arises from *ingenium* and *industria*. Nor does he discuss the psychogenesis of vice and the means by which it may be counteracted or converted into virtue.

This lack of interest in the dynamics of ethical behavior is particularly striking given the fact that Sallust locates the causal forces of history so exclusively in human choices. He does not invoke a theodicy of any kind to explain the degeneration of Rome; nor does he envision any coming renewal. He advances no cyclical theory to explain the more depressing

---

[25] Michel Rambaud, "Les prologues de Salluste et la démonstration morale dans son oeuvre," *REL, 24* (1946), 115-30.

events in history or to offer hope for the future. There is only man. And man, for Sallust, is available for inspection only in terms of his external behavior, despite the importance of his vices and virtues in motivating historical events. Neither his debts to Platonism nor his allusions to the traditional Roman ethos nor his passing evocation of Stoicism enables Sallust to produce a philosophy of history that is ultimately satisfactory in terms of any of these perspectives. Sallust may well be a moralist, but he makes no systematic effort to apply any particular ethical theory, Stoic or otherwise, to his analysis of causation in history.

B) Livy

Livy (59 B.C.-A.D. 12) has received even more attention in connection with Stoicism than has Sallust, partly because of the scope and influence of his history and partly because of his known dependence on Polybius, whose work was continued by the lost history of Posidonius. Practically nothing is known of Livy's life,[26] except for the fact that he was born in Patavium, that he took no part in public affairs, and that he confined himself to literary pursuits. Livy wrote some philosophical works that have not survived as well as his lengthy history, *Ab urbe condita*, which he started publishing in 27/25 B.C. It is known, however, that his success as a historian was immediate and lasting from the century of his death up through the fifth century A.D.[27] Livy was cited frequently during this period as an authority, by writers of all kinds, and was often excerpted and epitomized. His fortunes fell after the patristic era and only two and one half decades of his history, Books 1-10 and 21-45, survived in the Middle Ages, each segment deriving from manuscripts dating from the fourth and fifth centuries, respectively.

There are a number of features of Livy's history that have led commentators to argue for the importance of Stoicism in his thought, either as the principal ingredient in his philosophy of history or in association with traditional Roman values. According to the leading proponent of the Stoic interpretation,[28] Livy's dependence on Stoicism is visible most

---

[26] An excellent biographical study is provided by P. G. Walsh, *Livy: His Historical Aims and Methods* (Cambridge, 1961), pp. 1-19.

[27] On Livy's posthumous fame see B. O. Foster, intro. to his ed. and trans., with others, of *Ab urbe condita*, Loeb (Cambridge, Mass., 1919-59), *1*, xxii-xxiv, xxxii-xxxiii; *5*, vii-xi; Grant, *Ancient Historians*, p. 396.

[28] P. G. Walsh, *Livy*, Greece & Rome: New Surveys in the Classics, 8 (Oxford, 1974), p. 12; "Livy," in *Latin Historians*, ed. T. A. Dorey (New York, 1966), pp. 116, 120; "Livy and Stoicism," *AJP*, *79* (1958), 355-75; *Livy* (1961), pp. 26-27, 46-81, 272-73; "Livy's Preface and the Distortion of History," *AJP*, *76* (1955), 369-83. See also Duff, *Golden Age*, p. 474; Leonardo Ferrero, "Attualità e tradizione nella praefatio Liviana," *RFC*, 77, n.s.

clearly in his didactic and moralistic outlook. His stress on human vices and virtues reflects a belief in the need for ethical struggle, but without ruling out the power of supernatural forces to predetermine the outcome of events. Thus, it is argued, for Livy divine patronage protects Rome from dangers and ensures her success. The very virtues that the Romans develop are an index of the fact that they live, *more Stoicorum*, in harmony with their fated natural destiny. The intervention of the gods in forwarding Rome's destiny, which Livy frequently depicts in conventional terms by means of portents and augury, is an idea that he sometimes treats with noticeable coolness, it is acknowledged. But more often he uses this same idea to symbolize a higher and more philosophical conception of the deity as the norm of reason with which man must conform if he is to succeed in his enterprises. All of these aspects of Livy's historical thought are seen as Stoic in inspiration, but it is the cosmological aspect that is regarded as the true test of Livy's Stoicism.

Livy himself, however, makes it clear that he has no overarching metaphysical theory to vindicate and no consistent theology or cosmology to advance. Human behavior receives most of his attention. He treats ethical issues and moral *exempla* in a decidedly non-Stoic way, for the most part. As he tells the reader in his preface, the aim of his history is to show what life and morals were like in the early days of Rome, how her empire was established, and how moral discipline was then relaxed, leading to the vicious behavior characterizing Roman society in the present. His goal, as he makes quite plain, is to set forth moral lessons so that the reader will know what virtues to imitate and what vices to shun.[29] Livy's treatment of the gods, fate, and fortune reveals no coherent attitude toward supernatural causation. At some points he depicts fate or the gods as providentially guiding and protecting Rome and her founder Aeneas.[30] Sometimes the gods collaborate with men in attaining victory.[31] But the relations among the gods, fate, and human action are not clear. While Livy sometimes associates the gods with fate or with human choices, there are also occasions when fate outwits human planning or when the gods overturn fate.[32] Most of the time Livy attaches no providential or metaphysical meanings at all to fate or fortune, using these terms simply to denote chance or luck,[33] or as a synonym for the outcome

---

27 (1949), 21-25; Grant, *Ancient Historians*, pp. 241-42; Laistner, *Greater Roman Historians*, pp. 69-77.

[29] Titus Livius, *Ab urbe condita* praefatio, 1.9-11, ed. and trans. Foster et al. All citations to and translations of Livy will be taken from this edition.

[30] *Ab urbe cond.* 1.1.4, 3.7.1.

[31] *Ab urbe cond.* 7.26.8.

[32] *Ab urbe cond.* 1.4.1-2.

[33] *Ab urbe cond.* 1.23.10, 2.5.6, 3.7.1, 3.8.11, 4.32.2, 4.42.10, 9.14.7, 21.1.2, 21.43.4, 22.29.2, 30.15.4, 30.42.15-17.

of human decisions.[34] This stress on the causal role of human action, to
the point of identifying fortune with its consequences or concomitants,
suggests that Livy shares with Sallust the view that the proper role of
the historian is not to speculate on metaphysics but to analyze the ethos
of political action.[35]

Although the gods, for Livy, do not intervene to direct the course of
history in any meaningful sense, he still devotes a great deal of attention
to recording religious events. To be sure, his views on religion are not
entirely consistent, but at no point does he offer a Stoic rationale for
traditional religious practices. There are passages in which Livy identifies
the oracles of the gods as synonymous with justice[36] and where he treats
religious rites as necessary in order to propitiate the gods and to avert
divine punishments.[37] At other times he notes the apparent or alleged
significance of omens whose validity he neither supports nor attacks
overtly, keeping his distance by reporting them in the form of indirect
statements.[38] Generally speaking, Livy contents himself with recording
auguries, portents, and propitations in a straightforward and laconic
style, making no comment of any kind about them. The annalistic form
which he espouses in his history leads him to list the religious events that
marked the times, along with the names of the reigning consuls, in a
purely conventional manner, in passages too numerous to cite. Livy is
interested neither in attacking or rationalizing the traditional religion of
Rome nor in acting as its defender and apologist.[39]

The reason for Livy's attitude toward religion is that he sees himself
as neither a philosopher nor a theologian manqué but as a historian. He
is not concerned with demonstrating or refuting the truth of religious

---

[34] *Ab urbe cond.* 6.9.4–5, 9.18.11, 9.18.17, 21.43.5, 21.43.10, 42.62.4.

[35] This point has been made well by Jean Bayet, intro. to his ed. and trans. of *Histoire romain*, Budé (Paris, 1947), *1*, 38–41; E. Burck, "The Third Decade," in *Livy*, ed. Dorey, pp. 31–36; Gaetano Curcio, "La filosofia della storia nell'Opera di T. Livio," *Rivista indo-greco-italica di filologia-lingua-antichità*, *1* (1917), 323–29; Iiro Kajanto, "Die Götter und das Fatum bei Livius," in *Wege zu Livius*, ed. Erich Burck, Wege der Forschung, 132 (Darmstadt, 1967), pp. 475–85; Mario Mazza, *Storia e ideologia in Tito Livio: Per un'analisi storiografica della Praefatio ai Libri ab urbe condita* (Catania, 1966), pp. 130–49. Walsh, *Livy* (1974), pp. 12–13 appears to reverse his position here.

[36] *Ab urbe cond.* 3.34.1.

[37] *Ab urbe cond.* 1.31.8, 5.15.1–2, 5.16.8, 5.17.5, 8.6.9–14, 9.1.3–7, 9.2.1, 22.9.7–22.11.1, 22.67.2–7, 28.11.6–7.

[38] *Ab urbe cond.* 1.31.2–4, 7.3.2, 38.36.4.

[39] The best treatment of this issue is W. Liebeschuetz, "The Religious Position of Livy's History," *JRS, 57* (1967), 45–55. See also Bayet, intro. to his ed. of *Hist. rom.*, *1*, 38–41; José Jiménez Delgado, "Clasificación de los prodigios titolivianos," *Helmantica, 12* (1961), 441–61; "Importancia de los prodigios en Tito Livio," ibid., pp. 27–46; "Postura de Livio frente al prodigio," ibid., *14* (1963), 381–419; Grant, *Ancient Historians*, pp. 240–41; Franklin Brunell Krauss, *An Interpretation of the Omens, Portents, and Prodigies Recorded by Livy, Tacitus, and Suetonius* (Philadelphia, 1930), pp. 26–29 and passim.

doctrines or in commenting on the appropriateness of religious rituals but rather with examining religious beliefs and practices as social facts. As a historian he finds religious attitudes of interest because they affect and are affected by historical events. The tensions caused by a protracted and inconclusive state of war, he notes, led to a mood of nervousness in Rome and a hunger for certitude which the traditional religion could not assuage, with a consequent proliferation of demagogues and false prophets who preyed on the fears of the credulous masses.[40] Livy is also sensitive to the fact that religion can be used for political purposes, both good and bad. Reflecting his patrician bias, he objects to a scheme permitting marriages between patricians and plebeians, which would obliterate social distinctions while at the same time polluting the auspices, rites performed by patricians alone.[41] He shows how skillful political leaders appeal to the religious scruples of the people in promoting the election of their favored candidates.[42] In the most interesting example of this type, Livy explains how Numa Pompilius, an early king of Rome, created new religious rites and laws, claiming to have received instructions during nocturnal meetings with the goddess Egeria, in order to instill civic virtue, trustworthiness, pacific behavior, and *pietas* in his people, a policy which succeeded to the point where neighboring tribes looked with reverence on the Romans as a holy nation.[43] The piety of the Romans, for Livy, is a virtue which prevents them from believing in false portents[44] and from succumbing to depraved foreign cults.[45] Piety and impiety, moreover, are moral states that affect the lives of individuals and nations, piety curing illness[46] and determining the outcome of battles[47] while impiety results in the fall from political power.[48] In all of these instances, religion is historically significant as an index of Roman virtue and as a function of Roman convictions and psychological needs. It is relevant, in Livy's eyes, both as a historical cause and as a historical effect, whatever the truth of the doctrines in question may be.

In bringing religion down to earth in this manner, Livy reinforces the importance of human attitudes, choices, vices, and virtues as the moving causes of historical events. His treatment of ethics, like his treatment of fate and the gods, shows few signs of Stoicism. Indeed, he handles a

---

[40] *Ab urbe cond.* 25.1.6–12.
[41] *Ab urbe cond.* 4.2.5–6.
[42] *Ab urbe cond.* 5.13.2–5.
[43] *Ab urbe cond.* 1.19.1–5, 1.20.1–17, 1.21.1–5.
[44] *Ab urbe cond.* 42.37.5–9.
[45] *Ab urbe cond.* 39.8.1–39.19.17.
[46] *Ab urbe cond.* 2.36.1–8.
[47] *Ab urbe cond.* 10.41.1–4.
[48] *Ab urbe cond.* 1.46.6–7, 1.48.7, 1.49.1–2, 3.2.4.

number of traditional Stoic *topoi* in a decidedly non-Stoic way, a fact
which is immediately apparent when one compares his presentation of
the relevant personages and issues with the way in which they are treated
by other Latin authors. In dealing with women, for instance, Livy has
ample opportunity to depict female characters like Lucretia, who, like
men, exemplify the virtues as well as the vices. However, on the few
occasions where Livy adds a personal comment, he tends to reflect the
un-Stoic conception of women as morally weaker than men. Their lack
of self-control, he says, leads women to give way more readily to grief
than men do.[49] Also, in reporting a speech made by Cato opposing the
idea that women should be given greater rights to participate in public
life, Livy makes this well known proponent of Stoicism attack the policy
not only in the light of the traditional Roman conception of women as
purely domestic beings but also in terms of their nature as uncontrollable,
licentious, luxurious, irrational, and morally inferior to men.[50]

If Cato's reputation for Stoicism cedes to his concern for conservative
Roman values in Livy's portrayal of him, the same can be said for Cincinnatus and Scipio Africanus, two other figures often treated as Stoic
sages in Latin literature. Livy introduces Cincinnatus' recall to political
leadership by describing him as a man who spurns riches, a virtue which
the Stoics shared with the ancient Romans. However, Livy is far less
concerned with Cincinnatus' inner psychology than with the reaction of
the Romans to his selection as dictator. Although his friends and kinsmen
greet him warmly and escort him to his house on his arrival in the capital,
the plebeians are by no means overjoyed by this turn of events. They
remember only too well the harangues to which he subjected them on
the vices of the tribunes of the people during his previous term as consul.[51] It is not so much Cincinnatus' virtues that interest Livy as the
political implications and results of his rule.

Livy also reports the famous incident reflecting the clemency of Scipio
after his victory in Spain, which is given such full-dress Stoic treatment
in Silius Italicus' *Punica*. As an introduction to Scipio's release of the
captive maiden, Livy shows his response to a Spanish matron who begs
him to respect the honor of the female prisoners. Scipio replies that he
will do so, disdaining violence and lust, *meae populique Romani disciplina
causa facerem* ("thanks to my own training and that of the Roman
people.")[52] In his subsequent decision to return the noble maiden to her
fiancé, Scipio treats the question from the standpoint of the rights of the

---

[49] *Ab urbe cond.* 3.48.8–9.
[50] *Ab urbe cond.* 34.2.7–34.3.9.
[51] *Ab urbe cond.* 3.26.7–12.
[52] *Ab urbe cond.* 26.49.14.

fiancé, which merit his respect, adding that he himself is not legally free to marry the girl. He donates the money collected by her relatives in order to ransom her to the young couple as a wedding gift, hoping thereby to gain the fiancé's good will as a friend and ally of Rome.[53] In this passage it is not so much Scipio's forebearance or his sacrifice of his personal pleasure that Livy emphasizes as his liberality, his traditional Roman respect for the honor of the marriage bond and for the chastity of women, and his desire to capitalize on the event for Rome's political advantage. Scipio serves as an exemplar of Roman corporate values and interests, not as an exemplar of heroic Stoic virtue.

In Livy's history, however, there are three individuals, Fabius, Hannibal, and Lucretia, who are treated from a Stoic ethical perspective to some extent. These personages represent the one and only point where Livy can be said to reflect a Stoic attitude. He depicts Fabius' policy of delay as an exercise of rationality. Fabius wins glory through the saving of lives; he triumphs over fortune through his prudence,[54] that critical Stoic virtue. Livy's picture of Hannibal corresponds in many ways with that of Silius Italicus. Livy's Hannibal possesses physical courage and endurance, uniting these external attributes with the inner qualities of judgment and equanimity. He lives in accordance with reason; his use of food and drink, says Livy, *desiderio naturali non voluptate modus finitus* ("was determined by natural desire, not by pleasure.")[55] Yet, these virtues are perverted by the fact that Hannibal puts them to the service of his even more impressive vices of cruelty, perfidy, and impiety.[56] Thus, Livy suggests, a man's inner intention specifies the meaning of his moral acts. This Stoic principle, implied in his portrait of Hannibal, is stated plainly in Livy's treatment of Lucretia, or, more precisely, in his treatment of her husband and father when they discover that she has been raped by Sextus Tarquinius. Horrified as they are, her relatives regard her as the innocent victim of a tyrant's lust. They seek to console her by stressing that *mentem peccare, non corpus*;[57] it is the mind that sins, not the body. She did not consent to the deed and hence bears no guilt for it. Unfortunately for Lucretia, she is not convinced by this Stoic argument and kills herself rather than live in dishonor. But Livy at least pays a certain amount of lip service to Stoic ethical values in his delineation of Fabius, Hannibal, and Lucretia's father and husband, although these passages constitute the sole evidences of Stoicism in an extremely lengthy

---

[53] *Ab urbe cond.* 26.50.1-14.
[54] *Ab urbe cond.* 22.18.8, 22.25.14-15.
[55] *Ab urbe cond.* 21.4.6.
[56] *Ab urbe cond.* 21.4.5-10.
[57] *Ab urbe cond.* 1.58.9.

history that elsewhere reveals no traces of Livian sympathy with the philosophy of the Stoa.

C) Tacitus

If Sallust adverts to a single Stoic *topos* only to handle it in a non-Stoic manner and if Livy transmits a few traces of Stoic ethics, Tacitus communicates more overt information about Stoicism than either of them while at the same time assuming an attitude toward the Stoa that ranges from the noncommittal to the actively hostile. Tacitus (A.D. 54/56–ca. 120), although probably a *novus homo*, received a patrician education and made his way in the world early, marrying the daughter of the consul Agricola in A.D. 78.[58] He served in the army, possibly in northern Europe, and held a number of important civil offices including consul suffectus and proconsul of Asia. Tacitus began his career as a historian during his period of active political service, writing his *Agricola* and *Germania* in A.D. 98 and his *Histories* between A.D. 98 and 110, beginning his *Annals* after his return from Asia in A.D. 114. He also wrote a *Dialogus* on oratory in ca. A.D. 100 which has no interest for our present purposes. Tacitus attained both literary eminence and political success in his own day. Politically, he identified himself with the senatorial party which resented growing autocracy of the Principate, although he took no part in the abortive anti-imperial plots of the period. He retired from political life after his governership of Asia and his exact date of death is not known.

Tacitus' histories enjoyed much less popularity in late antiquity and the early Middle Ages than those of Sallust and Livy.[59] Some readers objected to his rather archaizing style and his anti-imperial sympathies, while the early Christian writers and Church Fathers occasionally took

---

[58] The best treatment of Tacitus' biography is B. Walker, *The Annals of Tacitus: A Study in the Writing of History* (Manchester, 1952), pp. 162-86. See also Grant, *Ancient Historians*, pp. 271-78.

[59] The fullest treatment of Tacitus' posthumous reputation, covering both *testimonia* and the manuscript tradition, is Clarence W. Mendell, *Tacitus: The Man and His Work* (New Haven, 1957), pp. 225-55. See also Herbert W. Benario, *An Introduction to Tacitus* (Athens, Ga., 1975), pp. 159-62; Grant, *Ancient Historians*, p. 401; F. Haverfield, "Tacitus during the Late Roman Period and the Middle Ages," *JRS*, 6 (1916), 196-201; Ludwig Pralle, *Die Wiederentdeckung des Tacitus*, Quellen und Abhandlungen zur Geschichte der Abtei und der Diözese Fulda, 17 (Fulda, 1952), pp. 10-13; Kenneth C. Schellhase, *Tacitus in Renaissance Political Thought* (Chicago, 1976), ch. 1. On the *Agricola* see also R. M. Ogilvie, intro. to his ed. of *De vita Agricolae* (Oxford, 1967), pp. 1, 80-85. On the *Germania* see J. C. G. Anderson, intro. to his ed. of *De origine et situ Germanorum* (Oxford, 1938), pp. lxii-lxiv; Jacques Perret, intro. to his ed. and trans. of *La Germanie*, Budé (Paris, 1949), pp. 45-51; Michael Winterbottom, "The Manuscript Tradition of Tacitus' *Germania*," *CP*, 70 (1975), 1-7; on the *Annals* see Erich Klostermann, intro. to his ed. of *Annales* (Leipzig, 1965), pp. v-xxii.

exception to his treatment of Judaism and Christianity. There are references to his works in both pagan and Christian authors up through the seventh century, after which time a gap opened that was not bridged until the Carolingian era. The earliest extant manuscripts of Tacitus' works are few and date from the ninth century, although the text of the *Germania* goes back to a fifth century version, now lost. After a brief flurry of interest in the ninth century, medieval readers tended to ignore Tacitus, and he did not come into his own until the Renaissance.

Despite his somewhat checkered fortunes in comparison with other Roman historians, Tacitus' treatment of certain topics and personages has stimulated an interest in his relation to the Stoic tradition. There are a number of issues in this connection that can be disposed of rapidly. Tacitus includes a great deal of information about the customs of the Germans in his *Germania*. He might have visited the Rhineland during his youthful tour of military duty. One scholar at least argues that the content of the work is based on Tacitus' personal observation.[60] The majority of commentators think that his sources for the *Germania* were purely literary, deriving from the ethnographic tradition in which Posidonius occupies a significant position.[61] This latter view may well be correct. However, Posidonius' taste for ethnography was one that he did not share with the other Stoics, and there is nothing specifically Stoic in his views on that subject. Thus, while Tacitus' *Germania* may be dependent to some extent on Posidonius, this dependence cannot really be viewed as a Stoic influence. Also, in his other histories, Tacitus takes frequent occasion to praise or blame certain individuals for their virtues or vices. This fact has led some critics to the overenthusiastic conclusion that Tacitus espouses Stoic moral values.[62] However, the moral traits in question are either commonplaces or else they reflect the virtues attributed to the emperors in imperial propaganda, expressed in official iconography and the state cult, with the vices Tacitus stresses being their parodic opposites.[63]

There are several other areas of Tacitus' thought where he addresses

---

[60] E. A. Thompson, *The Early Germans* (Oxford, 1965), pp. vi-vii, 51 n. 1.

[61] Anderson, intro. to his ed. of *Germ.*, pp. xiv-xv, xix-xxii; Benario, *Intro. to Tacitus*, pp. 30-31; Eduard Norden, *Die germanische Urgeschichte in Tacitus Germania* (Leipzig, 1920), pp. 59-84, 105-15, 118-24, 137-38, 142-69; Perret, intro. to his ed. of *La Germ.*, pp. 16-24; Ronald Syme, *Tacitus* (Oxford, 1958), *1*, 126-27.

[62] John Paul Armleder, "Tacitus' Attitude to Philosophy," *CB, 38* (1962), 89-91; Maximilianus Zimmerman, *De Tacito Senecae philosophi imitatore*, Breslauer philologische Abhandlungen, 5:1 (Breslau, 1889).

[63] See the excellent study by Albert Dwight Castro, "Tacitus and the 'Virtues' of the Roman Emperor: The Role of Imperial Propaganda in the Historiography of Tacitus," (University of Indiana Ph.D. diss., 1972).

issues of a more substantial philosophical nature. One is the topic of religion and the related question of fatalism and free will. Another concerns Tacitus' portrayal of a number of personages who were identified as Stoics or as members of the so-called Stoic opposition to the emperors. Tacitus is by no means consistent in his treatment of religion. At the beginning of the *Histories,* he observes that the period covered by the book was one of frequent calamity. There were many portents in those times, showing *non esse curae deis securitatem nostram, esse ultionem* ("that the gods care not for our safety, but for our punishment.")[64] Likewise, he asserts that heaven set its seal on the shameful deeds of Nero by sending destruction and plague to punish mankind.[65] But, although the gods may be harsh and uncaring, Tacitus sometimes promotes the traditional religion of Rome, attacking as debased and impious certain acts which neglect or distort the ancient rites.[66] Even more frequently he contents himself with a bare listing of auguries, propitiations, and other religious rites, reporting them in a completely noncommittal manner.[67] There are also points at which he criticizes certain religious practices as superstitious or erroneous. With the exception of the belief in astrology,[68] the creeds involved are all foreign to Rome.[69] Much more noticeable are the occasions where he follows Livy's lead in treating religious belief and practice as a historical cause or effect. He sometimes generalizes on the psychological significance of religion, noting that people accept prophesies and omens *cupidine ingenii humani libentius obscura credendi* ("for human nature is especially eager to believe the mysteries,")[70] a trait exacerbated by situations of crisis.[71] Tacitus occasionally characterizes individuals and groups by their tendency to be frightened or encouraged by omens, both to underline their credulity and to show how their beliefs affect their motivations to act.[72] Whatever the theological truth of religious beliefs may be, a matter on which Tacitus rarely speculates, they are relevant to the historian because religion is a psychological and social phenomenon that affects human behavior.

---

[64] P. Cornelius Tacitus, *The Histories* 1.3, ed. and trans. Clifford H. Moore, Loeb (Cambridge, Mass., 1956–58). All citations to and translations of the *Histories* will be taken from this edition.

[65] *Annales* 16.12, ed. Klostermann. Citations will be taken from this edition and translations from *The Annals,* trans. John Jackson, Loeb (Cambridge, Mass., 1956).

[66] *Hist.* 3.71–72; *Ann.* 2.32.

[67] *Hist.* 1.18, 2.3, 2.50, 4.53, 4.83–84, 15.44, 15.47, 15.74, 16.14; *Ann.* 1.10–11, 2.41–48, 2.86, 4.70, 11.15, 12.43, 14.12.

[68] *Hist.* 1.22.

[69] *Hist.* 2.4, 4.54, 4.81–83, 5.13.

[70] *Hist.* 1.22.

[71] *Hist.* 1.27, 4.26; *Ann.* 2.24.

[72] *Hist.* 1.62, 1.84, 2.1, 2.91, 16.1–2; *Ann.* 2.14, 2.17, 6.20–21, 14.32.

Closely allied to his views on the gods is Tacitus' treatment of fate. In this case, his attitude is somewhat less ambiguous. At his most typical he simply uses the terms fate or fortune as synonyms for circumstance or opportunity,[73] accident or chance,[74] or sheer luck.[75] His manner of expressing himself on this subject makes it clear what he really thinks about the relations between fortuitous gifts or events and the moral character of individuals. Nero's mistress Poppaea, he says, enjoyed the favors of fortune, as a substitute for virtues,[76] a remark which trades on his own and the reader's knowledge of Poppaea's sorry end at the hands of her capricious consort. In a similarly acerbic tone reinforced by his taste for either/or constructions which make his preferences plain, Tacitus notes that Asinius Gallo died of starvation, but whether by his own free will or from necessity no one knows: *sponte an necessitate, incertum habebatur,*[77] a formula suggesting that his subject lacked the moral courage to take his own life.

In his most extended discussion of fate and related matters, Tacitus, having mentioned the emperor Tiberius' use of astrology, raises the question of whether human affairs are ruled by fate (*fato*) and necessity (*necessitas*) or by chance (*fors*). He says that his own opinion wavers but that different schools of philosophy maintain different positions on the subject. He does not identify these schools by name but they are patently the Epicureans and Stoics. Some philosophers, Tacitus notes, assert that heaven does not concern itself in any way with mankind. Others hold that a fate exists which harmonizes all events in the universe, and that it should be sought not in astrology but in the principles and connections among natural causes. This second school of thought also admits the existence of human free will. Its proponents maintain that men may make free choices but that these choices, once made, create a chain of events that cannot be altered. This same latter school, he adds, rejects the goods praised by the multitude, stressing instead the importance of equanimity in the face of life's vicissitudes. In contrast to this view, Tacitus observes, most people believe that the fate of an individual is ordained at his birth and that he has no freedom to change it. It is true that later events may fail to bear out a person's fate as prophesied, a circumstance that points not to the fallaciousness of the theory but to the ineptitude or inconsistent perceptiveness of the prophet. He ends by citing as an example the fact

---

[73] *Hist.* 1.56, 2.1, 15.61, 16.1.
[74] *Hist.* 4.5; *Ann.* 2.84, 3.24, 4.62, 6.5.8, 6.22.
[75] *Hist.* 1.65, 2.11, 4.24, 4.34, 5.21.
[76] *Hist.* 16.6.
[77] *Hist.* 6.23.

that the same astrologer who made a correct forecast for Galba also made a prediction concerning Nero which did not come true.[78]

Tacitus does not take a stand on the respective merits of the Epicurean and Stoic views of fate, although he does indicate something of his opinion regarding both philosophy and popular religion in this passage. On the one hand, he claims that the fallibility of prophets and astrologers should not cause skepticism toward prophesy as such; on the other hand, his very mention of the unpredictability of the astrologers' art raises the very doubts that Tacitus is ostensibly seeking to allay. If the credulity of the masses, and of the emperors, is placed in doubt, do the philosophers offer a better approach? On one level, this seems to be Tacitus' implication. However, he does not clarify the relationship between fate and free will as taught by the Stoics, and his introduction of the point that they shun the goods prized by most people may be designed to weaken the appeal of their position. He also presents this school as opposed to astrology, a practice which the Stoics were willing to justify. He withholds his own judgment on the comparative merits of Epicureanism and Stoicism in this passage. But, as his treatment of action and motivation throughout the body of his historical *oeuvre* shows, he does not conceive of fate as an ineluctable superhuman force. Rather, with Sallust and Livy, he concentrates on human character and choice as the prime moving forces in history. Unlike his predecessors, however, he focuses almost preclusively on human weaknesses and vices as the dominant causes of historical events.

The scholarship on this aspect of Tacitus' thought is as lacking in consistency as is Tacitus himself. There is one, aberrant, view which sees Tacitus' conception of fate as primarily Neoplatonic.[79] A significant number of commentators depict his attitude toward fate and the gods as Stoic, a position that depends on their willingness to ignore the passages where he calls the gods indifferent or where he speaks of fortune as blind, or where he fails to come to grips with the problem of evil.[80] In one case the thesis of Tacitus' Stoicism is based on the author's willingness to ignore the fact that the historian is reporting the views of this school in *Annales* 6.22, among others, without taking a stand on them.[81] A number

---

[78] *Ann.* 6.22.

[79] Willy Theiler, "Tacitus und die antike Schicksalslehre," *Phyllobolia für Peter von der Mühl zum 60. Geburtstag am 1. August 1945* (Basel, 1946), pp. 35-90.

[80] P. Beguin, "Le 'fatum' dans l'oeuvre de Tacite," *LAC, 20* (1951), 315-34; "Le positivisme de Tacite dans son notion de 'fors'," *LAC, 24* (1955), 352-71; Pierre Grenade, "Le pseudo-épicurisme de Tacite," *REA, 55* (1953), 36-57; Janine Lacroix, "'Fatum' et 'Fortuna' dans l'oeuvre de Tacite," *REL, 29* (1951), 247-64; Alain Michel, *Tacite et le destin de l'Empire* (Paris, 1966), pp. 229-35; Ettore Paratore, *Tacito* (Milano, 1951), p. 558; J. S. Reid, "Tacitus as a Historian," *JRS, 11* (1921), 191-92.

[81] Alain Michel, "La causalité historique chez Tacite," *REA, 61* (1959), 96-106.

of other commentators argue that Tacitus is a skeptic, a taste reinforced by his use of irony in discussing religious matters. But this position can be maintained only by ignoring the many passages where he reports omens and religious rites noncommittally, treating them as a normal and unexceptionable feature of Roman public life, or where he depicts the gods as active in the world, although not as benevolent, or where he mentions religious behavior not in order to weigh its plausibility but merely to consider its historical impact.[82] Faced with these discrepancies, another group of scholars has argued that Tacitus is basically unsystematic,[83] whether because he was disinterested in metaphysical questions[84] or because he was led eventually to a pessimistic vision of history that called into question its very didactic utility[85] or because his conception of history expressed his alleged neurotic ambivalences.[86]

The evidence of Tacitus' works supports the view that he is neither systematic nor consistent in his attitude toward the gods, fate, and causation in history. He does supply a certain amount of information on Stoicism in this connection, above all in *Annales* 6.22. He may indeed have concluded that the world was "a moral chaos, deserted by God."[87] At the same time Tacitus' defects as a philosopher of history may have actually enhanced his capacity to function as a historian. His lack of a doctrinaire metaphysical system can be seen as an asset, since he is not constrained by any preconceived dogma, and his emphasis on human action as the chief cause in history is not obstructed by any gloom or bitterness he may have felt.[88] Whatever may be the causes and effects of Tacitus' lack of a coherent theory of historical causation, he is anything but a proponent of theodicy, Stoic or otherwise.

---

[82] P. Fabia, "L'irréligion de Tacite," *Journal des savants*, 12 (1914), 250-65; Mendell, *Tacitus*, pp. 51-55, 59, 61, 62, 63; Syme, *Tacitus*, 2, 521-25.

[83] Excellent recent reviews of the literature are provided by Jürgen Kroymann, "Fatum, Fors, Fortuna und Verwandtes im Geschichtsdenken des Tacitus," in *Tacitus*, ed. Viktor Pöschl, Wege der Forschung, 97 (Darmstadt, 1969), pp. 130-60; Russell T. Scott, *Religion and Philosophy in the Histories of Tacitus*, Papers and Monographs of the American Academy in Rome, 22 (Rome, 1968), 5-8. See also Benario, *Intro. to Tacitus*, pp. 151, 154; Gaston Boissier, *Tacitus and Other Roman Studies*, trans. W. G. Hutchison (New York, 1906), pp. 115-19; S. Borzák, "P. Cornelius Tacitus," *Paulys Realencyclopädie der classischen Altertumswissenschaft* (Stuttgart, 1968), Supplementband, *11*, cols. 494-96; Reinhard Häussler, *Tacitus und das historische Bewusstsein* (Heidelberg, 1965), pp. 380-408; Robert von Pöhlmann, *Die Weltanschauung des Tacitus*, Sitzungsberichte der königlich Bayerischen Akademie der Wissenschaften, philosophisch-philologische und historische Klasse, 1 (München, 1910); Richard Reitzenstein, "Tacitus und sein Werk," *Neue Wege zur Antike*, 2nd ed. (Leipzig, 1924), *4*, 28; Syme, *Tacitus*, 2, 526-27.

[84] Scott, *Religion and Philos.*, pp. 45-106.

[85] Walker, *Annals of Tacitus*, pp. 11, 245-54.

[86] Joseph Lucas, *Les obsessions de Tacite* (Leiden, 1974), pp. 55-56, 131-47.

[87] Walker, *Annals of Tacitus*, p. 253.

[88] Syme, *Tacitus*, 2, 526-27.

There is one final area where Tacitus' attitude toward Stoicism requires comment, his treatment of historical figures who were themselves
partisans of that school. In this case Tacitus reveals his opinions somewhat more overtly than he does in connection with religion and fate,
although there is still a certain amount of ambiguity in his handling of
the topic. The Stoics he discusses receive both praise and blame. Some
commentators think that Tacitus emphasizes their virtues over their vices
and that his attitude toward them is a favorable one on balance.[89] Other
scholars stress his hostility toward men identified with Stoicism, particularly those associated with plots against the emperors. This hostility, they
note, is something that Tacitus not only expresses outright; it is also reflected in his ironic use of certain themes and *topoi* in connection with
these personages. His point of view, they argue, stems from the opinion
that the Stoics' political opposition was immoderate, impractical, and
self-serving, and possibly also from the need to justify his own inaction
despite his personal objections to imperial absolutism.[90]

Tacitus usually depicts men associated with Stoicism as a mixture of
virtue and vice, with the vice predominating or leaving the more pervasive impression in the reader's memory. He castigates some Stoics un-
ambiguously as hypocrites. Such, for example, is Publius Egnatius, who
*auctoritatem Stoicae sectae praeferebat, habita et ore ad exprimendam imaginem
honesti: exercitus, ceterum animo perfidiosus, subdolus, avaritiam ac libidinem oc-
cultans* ("affected the grave pose of the Stoic school, trained as he was to
catch by manner and by look the very features of integrity while at heart
treacherous, wily, a dissembler of cupidity and lust.")[91] Another case is
Plautus, who, as Tigellinus charges, *sed veterum Romanorum imitamenta prae-
ferre, adsumpta etiam Stoicorum adrogantia sectaque, quae turbidos et negotiorum
adpetentis faciat* ("not content to parade his mimicries of the ancient
Romans, had taken upon himself the Stoic arrogance and the mantle of
a sect which inculcated sedition and an appetite for politics.")[92] Tacitus
himself makes no comment on this charge and makes no attempt to refute
it, but lets the reader judge the character and credibility of Plautus and
Tigellinus alike.

---

[89] William Hardy Alexander, "The Tacitean *non liquet* on Seneca," *University of California Publications in Classical Philology, 14*:8 (1952), 269-386; John Paul Armleder, "Tacitus and Professional Philosophers," *CB, 37* (1961), 90-93; Benario, *Intro. to Tacitus*, pp.
29-30, 116; Scott, *Religion and Philos.*, p. 110.

[90] Stephen L. Dyson, "The Portrait of Seneca in Tacitus," *Arethusa, 3* (1970), 71-83;
Elizabeth Bunting Fine, "The Stoic Opposition to the Principate as Seen in Tacitus,"
(Yale University Ph.D. diss., 1932), pp. 324-27; A. Sizoo, "Paetus Thrasea et le stoïcisme," *REL, 4* (1926), 230-31; Walker, *Annals of Tacitus*, pp. 221, 223, 225, 230-32,
239-40, 242.

[91] *Ann.* 16.32.

[92] *Ann.* 14.57.

There are several other cases in which Tacitus contrasts the qualities to which he objects in the Stoic politicians with the virtues which they undeniably manifested. In these instances he supplies a bit more information on the ethical content of Stoicism, while at the same time undercutting whatever admiration it may inspire in him by his ironic contrast between what the Stoics preached and what they practiced. Helvidius Priscus, the son-in-law of Paetus Thrasea, he notes, followed the sect of philosophers who regard only the *honesta* as good, the base things (*turpia*) as evil, and all other things, which lie beyond man's voluntary control, as neither good nor bad. Armed with this philosophy, Helvidius performed all of life's duties well, *opum contemptor, recti pervicax, constans adversus metus* ("despising riches, determined in the right, unmoved by fear.")[93] However, Tacitus reports that some people thought that Helvidius was not proof against the desire for fame, since, as the historian notes with a touch of venom, *quando etiam sapientibus cupido gloriae novissima exuitur* ("the passion for glory is that from which even philosophers last divest themselves.")[94]

This passion for glory, and in some cases the lust for wealth and power as well, afflict three other members of the Stoic opposition of even greater eminence. Tacitus depicts their shortcomings in this connection with combined irony and malice. In describing Lucan's suicide he observes that Lucan, in his last moments, chose to recite a passage from his own *Pharsalia* which recalled a similar death,[95] a choice suggesting a note of pretentious self-advertisement even in Lucan's ultimate hour. Paetus Thrasea certainly merits praise in Tacitus' eyes for his equanimity and his uncompromising defense of principle. He bears insults calmly; he pointedly walks out of the senate house during the speech justifying Nero's matricide; he abstains from the vote according divine status to the recently deceased Poppaea; and he meets his death bravely.[96] Yet he is not free from the vices of ambition and imprudence. As the leader of a military campaign against the Parthians, Thrasea crosses the Taurus mountains leaving his winter quarters undefended and making no provision for his grain supply. He achieves some conquests, gaining a certain amount of plunder and glory; or, as Tacitus suggests, he would have gained still greater glory had he moderated his plunder, given the fact that he failed to retain control of the areas he captured; and he did not even manage to protect the foodstuffs he seized against spoilage. Thrasea's greed and lack of foresight are coupled in this incident with ambi-

---

[93] *Hist.* 4.5.
[94] *Hist.* 4.6.
[95] *Ann.* 15.70.
[96] *Ann.* 15.23, 15.28, 16.21-22, 16.24-29, 16.34-35.

tion. Despite the limited gains he had made in his campaign, he writes a letter to the emperor, full of empty and grandiloquent self-congratulation, announcing his success.[97] Whether the virtues manifested by Thrasea in his later opposition to Nero serve to mitigate these vices is a matter on which Tacitus declines to comment. But the implication is clear that the same concern for self-aggrandizement and the same lack of prudence exemplified by Thrasea the general were at the root of his policy as Thrasea the conspirator.

The most powerful of all the members of the Stoic opposition and the one whom Tacitus charges with the most elaborate and disgusting hypocrisy is Seneca. Given his importance as Nero's tutor and minister of state, Seneca had ample opportunity to enrich himself. Tacitus relates in detail the charges of graft leveled against Seneca and pointedly refuses to comment on them.[98] Seneca was known for his learning, his eloquence, and his philosophical commitments; yet, Tacitus shows, he debases these abilities in the service of Nero while at the same time using his position to parade his moral and intellectual superiority. Thus, Seneca writes a series of speeches on clemency for Nero to deliver, *quam honesta praeciperet, vel iactandi ingenii* ("either to attest the exalted qualities of his teaching or to advertise his own ingenuity.")[99] When he receives Nero's order to kill himself, Seneca meets his fate with calmness, steeling his friends and his wife to fortitude. Yet, even here, Tacitus suggests that Seneca's remarks *velut in communi disseruit* ("might have been intended for a wider audience.")[100] Like his nephew, Seneca lacks the virtue of self-transcendence even at the very moment of death.

Tacitus' depiction of the Stoics he portrays is of considerable importance for their later reputations, for his histories were major sources for the period in which they lived and for their own historical characterization. He specifies little of the doctrinal content of their Stoic creed in most cases. What emerges much more clearly is their inability to live up to the ideals they professed. Tacitus cites their example not so much to comment on the fact that human beings are imperfect as to puncture the Stoics' pretensions. His overall treatment of these personages is a hostile one even though he acknowledges some of their virtues and sympathizes in some respects with the political values which they sought to defend. In mentioning a few points relative to the Stoic conception of fate and free will, although he does not ascribe the doctrine to the Stoa, and in presenting the Stoics whose careers he treats in both their strengths and

---

[97] *Ann.* 15.8-9.
[98] *Ann.* 14.52-56.
[99] *Ann.* 13.11.
[100] *Ann.* 15.63.

their weaknesses, Tacitus conveys more about Stoicism to his readers than is true for any of the other Roman historians. The material, however, is seasoned with more than a grain of salt and is associated with other features of Tacitus' style and mentality that rendered his works less influential than those of his predecessors in the late classical and early medieval period.

II. Minor Poets: Manilius

There are a few Latin poets, apart from those discussed in other chapters, who have been singled out for scholarly attention because their works contain passages which allude to the Stoics as a school of philosophy[101] or which refer to commonplace ideas which the Stoics shared with other schools.[102] There is also one poet, distinctly minor both in his intrinsic literary merit and in his later influence, who shows a heavy dependence on a number of Stoic principles. He is Manilius, of whose biography little is known except for the fact that he lived in the first century A.D. His poem, the *Astronomicon,* is referred to by a number of later classical authors but it was not known between the time of Martianus Capella and the eleventh century, when the first extant archetypes of the work were written. Nor, evidently, was the *Astronomicon* read to any extent until it was rediscovered by Poggio Bracciolini in 1417.[103] None the less, the few scholars who have commented on this work have noted correctly Manilius' use of Stoic physics in his poem.[104]

There are three major points at which Manilius draws upon Stoic physics: the concept of God as the cosmic *logos* or world soul, rationally

---

[101] Marcus Valerius Martial, *Epigrams* 7.64, 7.69, trans. Walter C. A. Ker, rev. ed., Loeb (Cambridge, Mass., 1968).

[102] Two poets who have been overinterpreted in this way are Plautus and Ovid. On Plautus, see for example Frederick Leo, *Plautinische Forschungen: Zur Kritik und Geschichte der Kömodie* (Berlin, 1895), p. 117; on Ovid see for example Luigi Alfonsi, "Ovidio e Posidonio," *Aevum, 28* (1954), 276–77; "L'Inquadramento filosofico delle Metamorfosi Ovidiane," in *Ovidiana: Recherches sur Ovide,* ed. N. I. Herescu (Paris, 1958), pp. 268–71; Wade C. Stephens, "Two Stoic Heroes in the *Metamorphoses*: Hercules and Ulysses," ibid., pp. 273–82; L. P. Wilkinson, *Ovid Recalled* (Cambridge, 1955), pp. 213–19.

[103] The best treatment of Manilius' life, influence, and posthumous reputation is Jacob van Wageningen, "Manilius," *Paulys Realencyclopädie der classischen Altertumswissenschaft,* ed. Wilhelm Kroll (Stuttgart, 1928), *14*:1, cols. 1130–31. On Manilius' Stoicism the best study to date is Michael Lapidge, "A Stoic Metaphor in Late Latin Poetry: The Binding of the Universe," *Latomus, 39* (1980), 819–20.

[104] See, for instance, Thomas Creech, intro. to his trans. of Manilius, *The Five Books, containing a System of the Ancient Astronomy and Astrology together with the Philosophy of the Stoicks* (London, 1697), pp. 60–65; Duff, *Golden Age,* pp. 452–54; *Silver Age,* p. 154; Mendell, *Latin Poetry,* pp. 35, 38, 42; Eduinus Mueller, *De Posidonio Manilii auctore* (Borna, 1901); Rieks, *Homo, Humanus,* pp. 43–50; Wageningen, "Manilius," cols. 1121, 1123–25.

ordering the universe from within, and, indeed, identical with the world; the idea of universal harmony illustrated by the doctrine that the heavenly bodies are fed by vapors arising from the waters on the earth's surface; and the notion of the cyclical renewal of the cosmos through a universal conflagration and recreation during which the world remains in being although it undergoes a continuous process of change. Manilius repeats these ideas in a number of places. One rather lengthy passage may be cited to illustrate his handling of most of these themes:

> Hic igitur deus et ratio, quae cuncta gubernat,
> ducit ab aetheris terrena animalia signis,
> quae, quamquam longo, cogit, summota recessu
> sentire tamen, ut vitas ac fata ministrent
> gentibus ac proprios per singula corpora mores.
> Nec nimis est quaerenda fides: sic temperat arua
> caelum, sic varias fruges redditque rapitque,
> sic pontum movet at terris inmittet et aufert,
> atque haec seditio pelagus nunc sidere lunae
> mota tenet, nunc diverso stimulata recessu,
> nunc anni Phoebum comitata volantem;
> sic submersa fretis, concharum et carcere clausa,
> ad lunae motum variant animalia corpus
> et tua damna, tuas imitantur, Delia, vires;
> tu quoque fraternis sic reddis curribus ora
> atque iterum ex isdem repetis, quantumque reliquit
> aut dedit ille refers et sidus sidere constas;
> denique sic pecudes et muta animalia terris,
> cum maneant ignara sui legisque per aevum,
> natura tamen ad mundum revocante parentem
> attolunt animos caelumque et sidera servant
> corporaque ad lunae nascentis cornua lustrant
> venturusque vident hiemes reditura serena.[105]

> I'll sing how God the World's Almighty Mind
> Thro' All infus'd, and to that All confin'd,
> Directs the Parts, and with an equal Hand
> Supports the whole, enjoying his Command:
> How All agree, and how the Parts have made
> Strict Leagues, substiting by each other's Aid;
> How All by Reason move, because one Soul
> Lives in the Parts, diffusing thro' the whole.
> For did not the Friendly Parts conspire
> To make one Whole, and keep the Frame intire;
> And did not Reason guide, and Sense control

---

[105] M. Manilius, *Astronomicon* 2.82-104, ed. Fabricius Serra, Scriptorum Romanorum quae extant omnia, 224-225 (Pisa, 1975). This edition will be the one cited. The trans. is that of Creech and retains his original spelling and punctuation.

The vast stupendous Machine of the whole,
Earth would not keep its place, the Skies would fall,
And universal Stiffness deaden All;
Stars would not wheel their Round, nor Day, nor Night,
Their course perform, be put, and put to flight:
Rains would not feed the Fields, and Earth deny
Mists to the Clouds, and Vapors to the Sky;
Seas would not fill the Springs, not Springs return
Their grateful Tribute from their flowing Urn:
Nor would the All, unless contrived by Art,
So justly be proportion'd in each part,
That neither Seas, nor Skies, nor Stars exceed
Our Wants, nor are too scanty for our Need:
Thus stands the Frame, and the Almighty Soul
Thro' all diffus'd so turns, and guides the whole,
That nothing from its setled Station swerves,
And Motion alters not the Frame, but still preserves.

The seventeenth-century translation cited, although scarcely literal, conveys both the sense of Manilius and his rather long-winded style. The poet makes the same point elsewhere, by way of a Stoic theodicy designed to rebut the Epicurean theory of chance and universal chaos.[106] In another passage he adverts even more specifically to the idea that the stars are nourished by vapors arising from the earth.[107] Manilius is the only Latin poet treating cosmological themes who refers expressly to the Stoic conception of *ekpyrosis* and *diakosmesis*, depicting not only the destruction of the universe but also its subsequent renewal: *longo mutantur tempore cuncta atque iterum in semet redeunt* ("at length all things change and return again to their former state.")[108] A final point of interest in Manilius' physics is his conception of human nature, which reflects the middle Stoic absorption of Platonic and Aristotelian anthropology to the extent of admitting some distinctions between mind and body, but which at the same time preserves the normative character of the intellect as the ruling faculty in man, corresponding with the rule of the divine *logos* in the universe.[109] Manilius' only departure from Stoicism at this point is the fact that he does not view the human soul as consubstantial with God. Man's mind is the image of the divine *logos, cognatamque sibi mentem*; man is related to God but not identical with him.[110] Aside from this, Manilius provides an accurate and extended expression of the Stoic physical teach-

---

[106] *Astron.* 1.246–254, 1.474–531.
[107] *Astron.* 1.157–158.
[108] *Astron.* 3.838. My translation is given. For the whole doctrine see 3.818–865.
[109] *Astron.* 2.122–135, 4.866–935.
[110] *Astron.* 2.123. Rieks, *Homo, Humanus*, p. 50 fails to note this lapse in Manilius' Stoic anthropology.

ings on which he draws, if one that failed to attract enough readers after his own day to serve as a significant vehicle of intellectual transmission.

III. THE SCHOLIASTS

Two of the Latin scholiasts, Servius and Macrobius, communicate a certain amount of information about Stoicism in the course of commenting on Vergil's poetry and Cicero's *Dream of Scipio*. It may be debated how much their annotations contribute to an understanding either of Stoicism or of their chosen authors. None the less, both of these scholiasts enjoyed a considerable medieval reputation. Their works bear scrutiny for the Stoic material that they contain, whatever their fidelity to Stoicism, to Vergil, and to Cicero may be.

A) Servius

Apart from his fourth-century date, nothing is known about Servius except for that fact that he gained instant renown as the outstanding ancient commentator on Vergil. Servius was cited without remission from his own day up through the time of Isidore of Seville. Alongside of these repeated *testimonia*, the rich manuscript tradition of his works from the eighth century onward reflects his eminence as a critic of Vergil in the Middle Ages.[111] The esteem which Servius enjoyed is, from the standpoint of the transmission of Stoicism, something of a mixed blessing. His philosophical outlook is best described as eclectic, involving a good deal of Neoplatonism, Epicureanism, and Pythagoreanism as well as Stoicism. His perspective as a critic is shaped as much by his mixture of these philosophical traditions as it is by a sense of what Vergil himself actually thought.[112] Thus, while Servius refers to a number of Stoic doctrines, some of which he identifies expressly as Stoic, his attribution of ideas to that school and to Vergil is often blurred and incorrect. Some of the passages in which Servius invokes Stoicism to explain Vergil's meaning obscure the poet as much as they shed light on him. None the less, Servius' references to Stoicism, whether accurate or inaccurate, are occasionally yoked with his own opinion and thereby associated with his authority as a commentator.

---

[111] Georgius Thilo, intro. to his ed. with Hermannus Hagen of Servius, *In Vergilii carmen commentarii* (Leipzig, 1923), pp. xxii–xxvii, xxxv–lxxvii. This is the edition that will be cited.

[112] The chief study of Servius' philosophical opinions is Edith Owen Wallace, *The Notes on Philosophy in the Commentary of Servius on the Eclogues, the Georgics, and the Aeneid of Vergil* (New York, 1938), pp. 70-175, 182-85, who also cites all the relevent passages of his work in this connection.

The main areas into which Servius introduces Stoicism are cosmology, physics, theology, anthropology, and ethics. Acknowledging at *Georgics* 2.336 that Vergil is exercising poetic license on the subject of the immortality of the universe, Servius asserts that the poet is wrong and cites the views of a number of philosophical schools on this topic, including the position of Zeno who, he notes, teaches that the universe is immortal as a whole because of the economy of matter, although its arrangement is perpetually shifting.[113] The pattern which the world describes in going through its material changes, he says in commenting on *Eclogues* 4.4, is, according to the *philosophi*, a cyclical one: *completo magno anno omnia sidera in ortus suos redire et ferri rursus eodem motu* ("at the end of the great year all the heavenly bodies return to their source and then reinitiate the same movements;") a circumstance which, if true for the stars, applies also to everything else in the universe.[114] At *Aeneid* 11.186, he attributes to Heraclitus the notion that all things return to fire because they were originally constituted out of fire.[115] This Heraclitean doctrine, of course, is the ultimate source of the Stoic *ekpyrosis* and *diakosmesis*, although Servius does not make the connection. At several points, also, he refers to the Stoics' doctrine of fate as ineluctable, although he omits their correlative doctrine of free will within specific limits and in one passage he criticizes this position as incompatible with moral freedom and responsibility.[116]

In moving from cosmology to theology, Servius reports a number of Stoic teachings quite accurately. At *Aeneid* 4.379 he asserts, following Cicero's *De natura deorum*, that there are three positions on the gods: the view that they do not exist, the Epicurean view that they exist but pay no attention to man, and the Stoic view that the gods exist and do concern themselves with man.[117] Elsewhere he notes that the Stoics believe in one God and attach to him the names of the various gods of the pantheon.[118] In commenting on the sixth book of the *Aeneid*, he mentions an unnamed group of thinkers who believe the deity to be a corporeal being, an *ignem sensualem*, or fire endowed with sensation and intelligence. He offers this view noncommittally in one place although he states it elsewhere as a fact.[119]

There are a number of physical, anthropological, and ethical topics on

---

[113] Thilo-Hagen, *3*, 248; Wallace, pp. 16–17.
[114] Thilo-Hagen, *3*, 45–46; Wallace, p. 17.
[115] Thilo-Hagen, *2*, 498; Wallace, p. 16.
[116] *In Aen.* 1.257, 2.689, 8.334, 10.467; Thilo-Hagen, *1*, 96, 319; *2*, 248, 439–40; Wallace, pp. 63–64, 65.
[117] Thilo-Hagen, *1*, 532. See also *In Aen.* 1.11, 1.227; Thilo-Hagen, *1*, 86, 532; Wallace, p. 57.
[118] *In Aen.* 4.638; *In Georg.* 1.5; Thilo-Hagen, *1*, 574; *3*, 130; Wallace, p. 57.
[119] *In Aen.* 6.727, 6.747; Thilo-Hagen, *2*, 102, 105; Wallace, pp. 13, 14.

which Servius either misconstrues Stoic doctrine or treats it uncritically or attributes it erroneously to some other school. At *Georgics* 1.249 he states that the Stoics think that the sun revolves around the earth,[120] which is true but which is a position that is not unique to the Stoa. Servius attributes a few anthropological ideas mistakenly to the Stoics. In commenting on the disposal of the dead at *Aeneid* 3.68, he ascribes to the Stoics the view that the soul remains united with the body after death, so long as the body does not decompose. This belief, he says, is what inspires the Egyptians to mummify corpses, in contrast with Roman funerary practice. He adds that Vergil subscribes to this allegedly Stoic opinion in the passage in question.[121] Elsewhere Servius distinguishes between two aspects of the soul: *animus,* or intellect, which is localized, and *anima,* or life, which is diffused throughout the body. The Epicureans, he says, call the *animus* the *hegemonikon;*[122] here he associates with Epicureanism a Stoic term and the Stoic conception of the function of reason in man's constitution.

Finally, in commenting on Vergil's claim in *Georgics* 4.219 that the bees possess a share of the divine nature, Servius agrees that they do. All animals no less than men, he argues, are composed of the four elements and the divine spirit. Men and animals thus have exactly the same kind of physical composition. They also share the same passions; and here Servius cites the Stoic quartet as Vergil had formulated it: *namque metuunt, cupiunt, dolent, gaudentque* ("for they fear, desire, suffer, and rejoice,")[123] thus using a Stoic ethical idea to support a physical doctrine to which the Stoics took sharp exception. Servius also adverts to the same four Stoic passions at the point where Vergil himself introduces them, *Aeneid* 6.733, as well as at *Georgics* 2.499. However, in the first case he attributes them to *Varro et omnes philosophi* and in the second case he gives them to Cicero rather than to the Stoics directly. He follows Vergil in conceiving of the body as the source of the passions, a non-Stoic idea.[124] Aside from this, Servius makes only two other, minor observations about Stoic ethics, both of which are commonplaces which they shared with other schools. At *Aeneid* 3.90, he notes that the Stoics and the Academics objected to magic, as contrary to nature,[125] and at *Aeneid* 1.604 he states that the Stoics taught that virtue is its own reward.[126]

---

[120] Thilo-Hagen, *3,* 189; Wallace, p. 20.
[121] Thilo-Hagen, *1,* 350; Wallace, p. 45.
[122] *In Aen.* 10.487; Thilo-Hagen, *2,* 422; Wallace, p. 37.
[123] Thilo-Hagen, *3,* 337; Wallace, p. 13.
[124] Thilo-Hagen, *2,* 103; *3,* 267; Wallace, pp. 41, 131.
[125] Thilo-Hagen, *1,* 357; Wallace, p. 63.
[126] Thilo-Hagen, *1,* 178; Wallace, p. 43.

As can be seen from Servius' references to Stoicism, he is concerned primarily with physical and theological doctrines. In the majority of his citations of Stoic teachings he mentions the school expressly. In a good many of these passages he sets forth the Stoic doctrine with a fair degree of accuracy, although there are also a number of rather garbled opinions which he attributes to the Stoic school as well.

B) Macrobius

Macrobius provides much less access to Stoicism than does Servius. His *floruit* is probably the late fourth century and his medieval fortunes were quite extensive. Macrobius' chief allegiance is to the Platonic tradition. Indeed, his principal function in medieval intellectual history was to transmit Neoplatonism and related doctrines.[127] Yet, a few traces of Stoicism appear in his two main works, the *Commentary on the Dream of Scipio* and the *Saturnalia*, the latter of which is largely a series of *scholia* on Vergil's *Aeneid*.

Macrobius refers to several points that are not unique to the Stoa and cites a few Stoic ideas with imperfect accuracy. His correct references to Stoic doctrine are in the nature of reports of what the Stoics teach, set forth without much comment on his part. In his *Commentary on the Dream of Scipio* he reviews opinions on the nature of the Milky Way and gives Posidonius' view, which he says conforms to the prevailing consensus, that the Milky Way is a stream of starry heat crossing the zodiac obliquely, whose function is to temper the universe by its warmth.[128] In the same work, in the context of discussing a Platonic proof of the immortality of the soul, he notes that the Platonists developed a syllogistic argument for this purpose whose major premise asserted that the soul is self-moving, a principle that the Stoics accepted although the Aristotelians did not.[129] At another point, probably under the influence of Servius, Macrobius quotes Vergil's *Aeneid* at 6.733, defining the four passions as fears, desires, griefs, and joys, a Stoic notion which he then proceeds to denature by

---

[127] The main author to dissent from the consensus dating Macrobius to the fourth century is Alan Cameron, "The Date and Identity of Macrobius," *JRS*, *56* (1966), 25–38, who prefers a fifth century date and who reviews the previous literature on the subject. On Macrobius' posthumous fortunes see Richard Bernabei, "The Treatment of Sources in Macrobius' Saturnalia, and the Influence of the Saturnalia during the Middle Ages," (Cornell University Ph.D. diss., 1970), part 2. On Macrobius' sources see Bernabei, part 1 and Pierre Courcelle, *Late Latin Writers and Their Greek Sources*, trans. Harry E. Wedeck (Cambridge, Mass., 1969), p. 36.

[128] Macrobius, *In Somnium Scipionis* 1.15.7, in *Opera quae supersunt*, ed. Ludwig von Jan, 2 vols. (Quedlinburg, 1848–52). This edition will be cited for both of Macrobius' works.

[129] *In Somn. Scip.* 2.14.1.

analyzing the virtues in a completely non-Stoic fashion.[130] A more elaborate example of an incomplete treatment of a Stoic idea is Macrobius' discussion of the myth of the castration of Cronus and the birth of Venus, which he introduces in the *Saturnalia* as a means of explaining the doctrine of seminal reasons. All the elements, he observes, draw their sources from seeds that originate in heaven, so that the individual things in creation can be brought into being at their appointed times in the future. Since Venus presides over love, the manner in which seminal reasons operate is through the sexual union of male and female.[131] This idea may be Stoic so far as it goes, but in its application it confines the doctrine of seminal reasons to the animal world alone.

There are only two fully accurate and straightforward references to the Stoics in Macrobius. In both cases he cites the positions of individual members of the school without taking a stand on their opinions. In one passage, while discussing the etymology of the name of Apollo, he notes what different authorities have had to say, including the Stoics Cleanthes and Antipater.[132] At another point, in reviewing how different philosophers define the nature of the soul, he states that Zeno regards it as a spirit grown into the body while Boethus teaches that it is composed of air and fire and Posidonius holds it to be spirit only.[133] As one can see from these references, the Stoic allusions in Macrobius are rather sketchy and rarely touch on the school's most distinctive teachings.

IV. THE GRAMMARIANS

The major contribution made by the Latin grammarians to the history of the Stoic tradition is their preservation of certain features of the Stoic philosophy of language. They provide information about the Stoic conception of language as sound which naturally signifies real objects. They refer to the etymological conception of the derivation of words which stems from this theory and to the debate over analogy and anomaly in constructing the rules of grammatical declination. There is one overriding trait shared by all the grammatical writers. However faithfully they may have reproduced the Stoic doctrines which they received and transmitted, they saw their task as a purely pedagogical one, confined to elaborating the rules of their particular scholastic discipline. Rarely if ever do they display any interest in the connections between the Stoic theory of language and the physical and metaphysical foundation on

---

[130] *In Somn. Scip.* 1.8.11.
[131] *Saturnalia* 1.8.6.
[132] *Sat.* 1.17.36.
[133] *In Somn. Scip.* 1.14.19.

which the Stoics had originally erected it. Thus, the fidelity of the grammarians to their Stoic sources is limited by the non-philosophical mentality which they bring to bear on their subject.

A) Varro

Varro is both the earliest and the most influential writer on the Latin language to incorporate Stoic ideas within his work. There is little known about his origins or youth, but Varro (116–27 B.C.) received an extensive education in literature and philosophy, leading an active life in politics as well as producing some seventy-four treatises on a wide range of subjects.[134] Of these numerous writings only his *De re rustica* has survived intact. Varro's major work on language, the *De lingua latina,* was written in 47/45 B.C. It originally contained twenty-five books, of which only Books 5 through 10 have been preserved, with some gaps in the text. The *De lingua latina,* despite its fragmentary state, was destined to play a formative role in shaping the attitudes towards Latin and towards linguistic theory which Varro bequeathed to his successors in the late classical and medieval eras.

Aside from a passing allusion to Zeno's statement that the seed of animate beings is the fire that is life and mind[135] and a reference, in his lost *Disciplinarum,* to the metaphor of the closed fist and the open palm to suggest the differences between dialectic and rhetoric,[136] Varro's debts to Stoicism are visible in three areas: the definition of language as sound, the etymological derivations of words, and the analogy-anomaly debate. His definition of language, preserved in a fragment from a lost work by the fourth-century grammarian Diomedes, is important both for its expressly Stoic content and its later influence:

> Vox est, ut Stoicis videtur, spiritus tenuis auditu sensibilis,
> quantum in ipso est. Fit autem vel exilis aurae pulsu vel verberati
> aeris ictu. Omnis vox aut articulata est aut confusa. Articulata est
> rationalis hominum loquellis explanata. Eadem et litteralis vel
> scriptilis appellatur, quia litteris comprehendi potest. Confusa est

---

[134] On Varro's life see Vittorio d'Agostino, "Sulla formazione mentale di Varrone Reatino," *RSC, 3* (1955), 28; Hellfried Dahlmann, "M. Terentius Varro," *Paulys Realencyclopädie der classischen Altertumswissenschaft,* (Stuttgart, 1935), Supplementband, *6,* cols. 1173-81; Roland G. Kent, intro. to his ed. and trans. of *On the Latin Language,* Loeb (London, 1938), *1,* vii–xii.

[135] M. Terentius Varro, *De lingua latina* 5.10.59, ed. Kent. This will be the edition cited.

[136] Quintilian, *Institutio oratoria* 2.22.7, trans. H. E. Butler, Loeb (London, 1966); Cassiodorus Senator, *Institutionum* 2.3.2, ed. R. A. B. Mynors (Oxford, 1937).

inrationalis vel inscriptilis, simplici vocis sono animalium effecta, quae scribi non potest, ut est equi hinnitas, tauri mugitas.[137]

Utterance, according to the Stoics, is a subtle breath perceptible to the ear, according to its power. Now it is made either by an impulse of rarefied air or by a blow of air that has been struck. All utterance is either articulate or confused. The articulate is what is expressed by rational human speech. It is called literal or written because it involves letters. The confused is irrational or unwritten, the simple noises made by animals, which cannot be written, such as the neigh of a horse or the bellow of a bull.

There are several important Stoic elements in this definition. First of all, Varro distinguishes clearly between rational human speech and the sounds made by irrational animals. Only the first is regarded as language properly speaking. Secondly, in his use of the terms *spiritus tenuis* and *exilis aurae* to denote utterance, Varro seems to be pointing to the Stoic conception of *pneuma*, although without speculating on its physical composition or its functions in human psychology. Finally, he suggests that sound has a two-fold origin, being either an apparently active impulse arising from rarefied air itself or an impulse arising elsewhere that is transmitted mechanically on the air waves.[138] Varro does not make explicit the idea that *pneuma* flows both from the sense organ and the sensed object and that this double flow of *pneuma* forms a material bridge on which sense data travel to the hearer. But, so far as he goes, his description of sound and the way it is perceived, if incomplete, is authentically Stoic.

Varro is far more eclectic in treating etymology. He is sympathetic to the principle that language signifies real objects naturally, so that etymologies can be analyzed according to the correspondences between words and places, bodies, times, and actions, a system of classification which he says he has derived from Pythagoras.[139] While he cites Cleanthes, Chrysippus, and the Stoics in general as authorities on the subject of etymology, he cites non-Stoic authorities as well.[140] Moving from the rationale

---

[137] Hyginus Funaioli, ed., *Grammaticae romanae fragmenta*, *238 [42] (Stuttgart, 1969 [repr. of 1907 ed.]), p. 268.

[138] Jean Collart, *Varron: Grammarien latin*, Publications de la Faculté des lettres de l'Université de Strasbourg, 121 (Paris, 1954), pp. 57-63 notes the Stoic origins of Varro's definition but fails to note this double source of sound and its possible connection with the doctrine of *pneuma*.

[139] *De ling. lat.* 5.1.11-12. This derivation seems to have escaped most commentators. Agostino, "Formazione mentale di Varrone," p. 29 and Hellfried Dahlmann, *Varro und die hellenistische Sprachtheorie*, 2nd ed. (Berlin, 1964), pp. 16-24, 38-41, identify it as Stoic while Daniel J. Taylor, *Declinatio: A Study of the Linguistic Theory of Marcus Terentius Varro* (Amsterdam, 1975), p. 68 argues that it is an arbitrary idea designed only to serve programmatic ends.

[140] *De ling. lat.* 5.1.9, 6.1.1; *Gram. rom. frag.*, 265 [32.1.2], p. 283.

to the practical analysis, Varro is willing to accept conventional derivations of words along with derivations presumed to be natural. His approach, therefore, is by no means dogmatically Stoic. Notwithstanding the attention he pays to the theory of the natural correspondences between words and things, the most striking feature of his treatment of etymology is his complete lack of interest in using this theory to attain an insight into the physical reality which, it teaches, words reflect. Varro's concern in this area is entirely that of a grammarian, not that of a philosopher, Stoic or otherwise.[141]

Varro deals at considerable length with the analogy-anomaly debate, devoting three books of the De lingua latina to this question. In explaining the positions taken on this issue by previous thinkers, he expressly identifies Chrysippus and Crates as the chief defenders of the anomaly theory.[142] When he has reviewed the arguments for and against both positions, Varro subjects each of them to an empirical test. His criterion here, as in his analysis of etymology, is not the correspondence of grammatical rules with physical or metaphysical realities as they may be conceived to be by any particular philosophical school, but rather on their correspondence with the nature of the Latin language as it is spoken. On the basis of actual linguistic usage, he concludes that both theories are correct in part and that they are not mutually exclusive, since the Latin language has both regular and irregular forms.[143] It is certainly true that the Stoics' advocacy of anomaly was based on their vision of physical reality as a series of unique and ever-changing events, just as the analogists' position could be based on a physics of fixed essences. But this kind of perspective is completely alien to Varro's mentality. The Latin language, as it is currently spoken and used, is the one and only norm that he invokes.[144]

---

[141] This point is developed well by Dahlmann, Varro, pp. 4–14, 26–29. See also Collart, Varron, pp. 258–78, 341–42. Less critical treatments of Varro's Stoicism in this respect include Nettleship, Lectures and Essays, p. 171; Myra L. Uhlfelder, "'Nature' in Roman Linguistic Texts," TAPA, 97 (1966), 584–87. Gaston Boissier, Étude sur la vie et les ouvrages de M. T. Varron (Paris, 1861), pp. 112–19 and Duff, Golden Age, p. 249 n. 4 see Varro as an adherent of the Old Academy on this point.

[142] De ling. lat. 9.1.1.

[143] De ling. lat. 8.9.22–23, 8.18.34–8.21.4, 9.1.3, 9.27.34–35, 10.3.59.

[144] The best treatment of this subject is Collart, Varron, pp. 132–57. None of the other commentators has acknowledged the fact that, for the Stoics, the theory of anomaly was based on physical laws and did not reflect an arbitrary conception of grammar. Other scholars, however, have noted Varro's synthetic approach to the anomaly-analogy issue. See also Atkins, Literary Criticism in Antiquity, 2, 19; Dahlmann, Varro, pp. 52–87; Adriana della Casa, Il libro X del De lingua latina di Varrone (Genova, 1969), pp. 5–8, 37–45; Francesco della Corte, Varrone: Il terzo gran lume romano (Genova, 1954), pp. 200–05; R. J. Dam, De analogia: Observationes in Varronem grammaticamque Romanorum (Campis, 1930), pp. 24–27, 36–48; Detlev Fehling, "Varro und die grammatische Lehre von der Analogie und

The position taken by Varro on all three of these issues proved to be extremely influential. Although the manuscript tradition of the *De lingua latina* is quite scanty, all texts deriving from a single codex written at Monte Cassino in the eleventh century, Varro had attained recognition as the leading authority on Latin grammar within twenty years after the publication of his *magnum opus*, a status he retained in later antiquity and in the early Middle Ages.[145] Varro was cited and quoted repeatedly by later grammarians and pedagogues from his own day through the time of Isidore of Seville. His ideas recur frequently in manuals and school-books and his treatment of language, etymology, and the analogy-anomaly debate became canonical. Later grammarians, as the sequel will shortly reveal, retained many of Varro's formulae on these topics as well as his non-philosophical orientation toward them.

B) *Nigidius Figulus*

A few fragments preserve the grammatical ideas of Nigidius Figulus, a contemporary and friend of Cicero, known in the first century B.C. and later as a man of considerable learning. Nigidius' philosophical leanings are distinctly in the direction of Pythagoreanism and Neoplatonism, but his work shows some significant traces of Stoic linguistic theory as well.[146] Nigidius is familiar with the analogy-anomaly debate. He departs completely from analogy, siding entirely with the Stoics on this issue. He likewise holds that words are exclusively natural signs.[147] Both of these topics had been treated by Varro, but in a less preclusively Stoic sense. Nigidius also raises a question which Varro does not discuss: How does one define a liar, and in what sense can words, which signify realities by nature, be used in a false statement? This question interests Nigidius on both moral and linguistic grounds. He distinguishes making a false statement, *medacium dicere*, from lying, *mentire*. In both cases there is a linguistic

---

der Flexion," *Glotta*, *35* (1956), 264-70; *36* (1957), 48-60; Taylor, *Declinatio*, pp. x-xi, 51-52, 70; Antonio Traglia, intro. to his ed. and trans. of *De ling. lat.*, liber X, Scriptores latini, 7 (Roma, 1967), pp. 5-29. Two authors who have misinterpreted the physical and logical reasons behind the Stoic espousal of anomaly are F. H. Colson, "The Analogist and Anomalist Controversy," *CQ*, *13* (1919), 25-26; and Uhlfelder, " 'Nature' in Roman Linguistic Texts," pp. 590-91.

[145] On Varro's posthumous fortunes see Jean Collart, "Analogie et anomalie," in *Varron*, Fondation Hardt: Entretiens sur l'antiquité classique, 9 (Genève, 1963), pp. 119-32; *Varron*, pp. 342-46; Traglia, intro. to his ed. of *De ling. lat.*, lib. X, pp. 35-36.

[146] For the *testimonia* on Nigidius' life and reputation see *Gram. rom. frag.*, pp. 158-60; Adriana della Casa, *Nigidio Figulo* (Roma, 1962), p. 66; Antonius Swoboda, *Quaestiones Nigidianae* (Vienna, 1890), pp. 4-6.

[147] Publius Nigidius Figulus, *Operum reliquae*, frags. 4, 5, ed. Antonius Swoboda (Vienna, 1889), pp. 67-68, 76-77.

problem stemming from the fact that the speaker's statement is objectively false. In the latter case, there is also a moral defect, for the speaker misuses language deliberately with the intent to mislead or deceive. In the former case the speaker also fails to tell the truth but he does so as a consequence of ignorance, with no intent to deceive; his statement thus possesses at least a subjective truth in that it corresponds with what he really thinks and means.[148] This problem, and the way in which Nigidius handles it, reflect a Stoic concern with ethical intentionality along with a Stoic commitment to the idea of words as natural signs, even though he does not refer expressly to the Stoics in his analysis.

C) Lesser and Later Grammarians

Most of the Latin grammarians after Varro are of interest from the standpoint of the Stoic tradition because they repeat his definition of *vox* in one form or another. However, with only one exception they fail to attribute it to the Stoics and they omit its distinctively Stoic features. Instead of treating sense perception as a phenomenon with a double source in the sense organ and the sensed object, they tend to confine the origin of sound to the sensed object alone, treating the human ear as an essentially passive receptacle of data that are impressed on it from outside. A few of the grammarians include one or two other points of Stoic linguistic theory, but, for the most part, it is their denatured perpetuation of Varro's definition of *vox* that constitutes their sole connection with Stoicism; and a feeble connection it is at best.

The two exceptions to this rule are Didymus and Valerius Probus. We learn from Priscian that Didymus (ca. 80–10 B.C.), who wrote a treatise in Greek on the Latin language, states that the Stoics regard articles and pronouns as a single part of speech, which they call the infinite article.[149] Probus, who lived in the late first century A.D., reviews the analogy-anomaly debate, agreeing with Varro that both approaches are valid, based on the test of linguistic usage.[150]

Probus also supplies the first example of the dilution of Varro's definition of *vox* that was to become typical of his successors with only one exception: *Vox sive sonus est aer ictus, id est percussus, sensibilis auditu, quantum in ipso est, hoc est quam diu resonat* ("Utterance or sound is a striking of the air, that is, a pulsation, perceptible to the hearing according to its

---

[148] Frag. 49, Swoboda, p. 78.

[149] *Gram. rom. frag.*, 2 [2], pp. 447-48.

[150] Valerius Probus, *Instituta artium* 2, in *Grammatici latini*, ed. Heinrich Kiel, 8 vols. (Leipzig, 1867-70), *4*, 47-48.

strength, that is, so long as it resounds.")[151] Following a gap of three centuries, Aelius Donatus reiterates the same idea, even more simply: *Vox est aer ictus sensibilis auditu, quantum in ipso est* ("Utterance is a striking of the air perceptible to the hearing according to its strength.")[152] Also from the fourth century A.D. come the definitions of Marius Victorinus and probably that of Maximus Victorinus. Marius' formula parallels Donatus': *Vox est aer ictus auditu perceptibilis, quantum in ipso est*. It is distinguished only by the fact that Marius also supplies a rendition of this sentence in Greek as well as Latin.[153] Maximus' definition is virtually identical: *Aer ictus sensibilisque auditu, quantum in ipso est*.[154] The only fourth-century departure from the norm is Diomedes, who quotes Varro's original definition verbatim,[155] a circumstance that is not altogether surprising when one recalls that Diomedes is the source for the fragment of the lost work of Varro containing the formula in the first instance. The last grammarian in the sequence, Priscian, reverts to type and reveals how far away from its original Stoic sense the definition of *vox* had migrated by the sixth century A.D.:

> Philosophi definiunt, vocem esse aerem tenuissimum ictum vel suum sensibile aurium, id est quod proprie auribus accidit. Et est prior definitio a substantia sumpta, altera vero ... ab accidentibus. Accidit enim voci auditus, quantum in ipsa est.[156]

> The philosophers define utterance as air very subtly struck or its sensible effect on the ears, that is, what actually impinges on the ears. The first definition is derived from substance while the second ... is derived from accidents. For utterance falls upon the sense of hearing according to its force.

What we see here is the recasting of an originally Stoic definition of sound and sense perception into an Aristotelian definition based on the Peripatetic distinction between substance and accident. This definition deprives the ear of any active role in sensation, leaving it a purely passive recipient of the data impressed upon it by the sensed object. In Priscian's hands, Varro's formula, already converted into a shell emptied of its Stoic

---

[151] Probus, *Inst. art.* 1, *Gram. lat.*, 4, 47.

[152] Aelius Donatus, *Ars grammatica* 1.1, *Gram. lat.*, 4, 367.

[153] Marius Victorinus, *Ars grammatica* 1.2.2, ed. Italo Mariotti (Firenze, 1967). The Stoic basis of this doctrine is noted by Hellfried Dahlmann, *Zur Ars Grammatica des Marius Victorinus*, Akademie der Wissenschaften und der Literatur, Abhandlungen der geistes- und sozialwissenschaftlichen Klasse, 1970, no. 2 (Mainz, 1970), pp. 13-17.

[154] Maximus Victorinus, *De arte grammatica*, *Gram. lat.*, 6, 189.

[155] Diomedes, *Artis grammaticae* 2, *Gram. lat.*, 1, 420.

[156] Priscian, *Institutionum grammaticarum* 1.1.1, ed. Martin Hertz, in *Gram. lat.*, 2, 5.

content by the post-Varronian grammarians, has now become the vehicle for an Aristotelian conception of sensation.

V. RHETORICIANS, DIALECTICIANS, AND OTHER PEDAGOGUES

A) Quintilian

Quintilian (A.D. ca. 40-ca. 96) attained great prominence in his own day as a rhetorician, both as a practicing advocate and as a teacher endowed with a state chair. He was also named tutor to the heirs of the emperor Domitian. He was praised and cited by many authors of his own century and honored by Suetonius, who devoted a biography to him, now lost, among his lives of the most eminent men of letters. Between the third and the fifth centuries Quintilian's *Institutio oratoria* perpetuated his fame as a rhetorical authority. He was used and adapted by Christian educators from the patristic era up through the seventh century, although his fortunes declined somewhat after the Carolingian age and the full recovery of the text of his major work had to await the energetic reconnaissance of Poggio Bracciolini in the early fifteenth century.[157]

Quintilian's debts to Stoicism are visible in the fields of linguistic theory and ethics and not merely in the discipline of rhetoric. As a rhetorician Quintilian stands firmly in the anti-sophistic tradition. He agrees with the Stoics, and others, on the importance of uniting wisdom and virtue to eloquence. This fact had led one commentator to overinterpret Quintilian fairly drastically as an adherent of Stoicism.[158] The more balanced and accurate picture of Quintilian sees him as an heir to Cicero and as an educator concerned not with philosophy but with the practical needs of rhetorical instruction, who views theoretical speculation with impatience[159] and who, at the same time, attacks the orators of his own age as opportunists detached from moral concerns.[160]

Quintilian certainly argues that the orator should be familiar with philosophy since it contains material relevant to his discipline. With Cic-

---

[157] The best treatment of Quintilian's biography and posthumous reputation is George Kennedy, *Quintilian* (New York, 1969), pp. ix, 15-30, 139-40. See also Giuseppe G. Bianca, *La pedagogia di Quintiliano* (Padova, 1963), pp. 207-32; Jean Cousin, intro. to his ed. and trans. of *Institution oratoire*, livre I, Budé (Paris, 1975), *1*, vii-xxvi, xcvi, cxviii.

[158] Cousin, intro. to his ed. of *Inst. or.*, *1*, xlvi-xlvii, lxxii, lxxvii-xcii; *Études sur Quintilien* (Amsterdam, 1967 [repr. of Paris, 1935 ed.]). Cousin has been seconded by Bruno Zucchelli, "Il destino e la providenza in Quintiliano (A proposito del proemio del VI libro dell'*Istituto*)," *Paideia*, *29* (1974), 3-17.

[159] Kennedy, *Quintilian*, pp. 32-35, 58-59, 124, 126-27; Bianca, *La pedagogia di Quintiliano*, pp. 234-52.

[160] Michael Winterbottom, "Quintilian and the *Vir Bonus*," *JRS*, *54* (1964), 90-97.

ero, he urges the orator to reappropriate such material from the philosophers who, like the Stoics, may debate with great acuteness but who orate with uninspiring aridity.[161] Quintilian also reflects the influence of Cicero in his criticism of the Stoics as rigid, harsh, and unrealistically severe in their ethical standards.[162] At the same time, he praises the Stoics, at the expense of the Peripatetics, for treating rhetoric as a virtue and an art rather than as a science, citing Cleanthes and Chrysippus as authorities on this point and quoting the elder Cato's maxim, *vir bonus dicendi peritus*, as his definition of the orator.[163] Quintilian defends Stoicism still further by arguing that no man can speak well unless he is morally upright. In developing this thesis, deriving from the Stoic doctrine that the sage possesses all the perfections, he departs sharply from Cicero: *In eodem pectore nullum est honestum turpiumque consortium, et cogitare optima simul ac deterrima non magis est unius animi quam eiusdem hominis bonum esse ac malum* ("Vileness and virtue cannot jointly inhabit in the selfsame heart and ... it is as impossible for one and the same mind to harbour good and evil thoughts as it is for one man to be at once good and evil.")[164]

Quintilian makes a few other references to Stoic teachings as well. In discussing the rearing of infants, he cites Chrysippus as an authority on the qualities that parents should seek in a nurse, although he disagrees with Chrysippus' advocacy of corporal punishment for children.[165] Like Nigidius Figulus, he raises the question of the linguistic and moral implications of lying, asserting that it is permissable to tell a lie in a rhetorical context or in order to shield the sensibilities of a person too weak to be told the truth. What is important is the speaker's motivation. If he has the correct moral intention, if his cause is a good one, then his lie is morally defensible.[166] Quintilian adverts to only one topic in the sphere of linguistic theory properly speaking, the analogy-anomaly debate. Here, he follows Varro wholeheartedly, arguing that usage and not abstract theory is the test of grammatical rules, on which basis both analogy and anomaly are admissible.[167]

There are, then, a number of references to the Stoics and to their rhetorical, pedagogical, linguistic, and ethical ideas in Quintilian's work.

---

[161] Quintilian, *Institutio oratoria* 10.1.35–36, trans. Butler. This will be the edition and translation cited.
[162] *Inst. or.* 1, prooemium, 9–20, 11.1.70, 12.1.18.
[163] *Inst. or.* 2.15.20, 2.15.34–35, 3.1.15, 7.17.41.
[164] *Inst. or.* 12.1.4–5. The argument is developed further, 12.1.3–13.
[165] *Inst. or.* 1.1.4, 1.1.16, 1.3.13.
[166] *Inst. or.* 12.1.37–38.
[167] *Inst. or.* 1.6.1–27; Kennedy, *Quintilian*, p. 44.

However, while he gives a sympathetic hearing to the Stoic doctrine of the sage as possessing all the virtues and to the correlative doctrine of vice and virtue as rooted in the subject's inner intention, the virtues which he discusses are all commonplaces. On occasion, also, he takes exception to Stoic virtue as excessively stringent and impractical. Like Cicero, Quintilian thinks that the philosophical *topoi* of interest to the orator should be removed from the philosophers' jurisdiction and handled instead by the rhetoricians. The main substance of Quintilian's actual teaching in his chosen discipline lies in the Aristotelian and Ciceronian tradition rather than in the Stoic tradition, a fact which can be seen clearly in his counsels for moving the audience through emotional appeals and through the use of coloristic embellishment. The framework in which Quintilian introduces the Stoic points that he makes is thus a fundamentally non-Stoic one.

B) Augustine

St. Augustine of Hippo (A.D. 354-430) wrote a logical treatise, the *De dialectica*, as part of a series of works on the liberal arts which he projected shortly after his conversion to Christianity.[168] This treatise preserves several elements of Stoic linguistic and logical theory, some of which are available elsewhere in Latin but some of which are presented more clearly here than in any other Latin work of later antiquity.[169] Augustine's principal contribution is the distinction he draws between speech and meaning, a distinction critical for conveying the Stoics' contrast between language and logic which reflects in turn the idea that logic deals with *lekta*, or meanings, which are incorporeals, while speech is corporeal. Following this understanding, Augustine compares a word (*verbum*), which is a sound, with an idea (*dicible*), which is perceived by the mind but not by the ear, noting that ideas or intentions are the proper subject matter of dialectic.[170] It is on the basis of this distinction between words and mean-

---

[168] The authorship has been debated. On this issue see B. Darrell Jackson, intro. to his trans. of Augustine, *De dialectica*, ed. Jan Pinborg (Dordrecht, 1975), pp. 1-5, 43-71. Pinborg supplies an extensive survey of the literature on this issue, pp. 138-42. See also Jan Pinborg, "Das Sprachdenken der Stoa und Augustins Dialektik," *Classica et mediaevalia*, 22 (1962), 149-51.

[169] The Stoic elements have been noted clearly by Balduinus Fischer, *De Augustini disciplinarum libro qui est de dialectica* (Jena, 1912), pp. 32, 36-39; Pinborg, comm. on his ed., pp. 123 n. 2, 124 n. 3, 125 n. 4, 126 n. 7, 131 n. 2; "Das Sprachdenken der Stoa," pp. 158-74; Uhlfelder, "'Nature' in Roman Linguistic Texts," p. 588.

[170] Augustine, *De dialectica* 5, ed. Pinborg, pp. 86-90. This will be the edition cited. The connection between Augustine's *dicibile* and the Stoic *lekton* has been noted by B. Darrell Jackson, "The Theory of Signs in St. Augustine's *De Doctrina Christiana*," in *Augustine: A Collection of Critical Essays*, ed. R. A. Markus (Garden City, N.Y., 1972), pp.

ings that one can explain in Stoic terms how ambiguities can exist in the denotations of words despite the natural derivation of language. As Augustine notes, different speakers may apply different intentions to the same words.[171] With this principle in mind, Augustine also follows the Stoics in stressing natural word origins and devotes a good deal of attention to their etymological and onomatopoetical derivations, observing that *Stoici autumant ... nullum esse verbum, cuius non certa explicari origo possit* ("the Stoics ... think that there is no word whose origin cannot be explained [in this way].")[172] Augustine includes a discussion of the conditional "if-then" syllogism in illustrating the differences between simple and compound sentences,[173] but his chief importance lies in his preservation of the Stoic conception of *lekta* in Latin form, along with the Stoic notion that logic deals with *lekta* and not merely with language.

The *De dialectica* received comparatively little notice from medieval readers.[174] There is one possible allusion to it in the ninth-century *Libri Carolini* attributed to Alcuin; but the first clear reference occurs in John of Salisbury. None the less, the work is found in library catalogues starting in the ninth century and the extant manuscripts go back to the seventh or eighth century, with the bulk of the exemplars dating from the ninth through the eleventh century. Their locations represent the great educational establishments of the Carolingian and Ottonian period. Some of the dialectical ideas in this work also received attention from Augustine himself in other contexts, recurring in treatises such as his *De magistro*, *De doctrina christiana*, *De trinitate*, *De mendacio*, and *Contra mendacium*, where he has occasion to analyze language and its role in communicating ideas. Augustine the theologian and Christian educator is thus the most immediate heir to the Stoic linguistic and dialectical themes in his own *De dialectica*.

C) Martianus Capella

Martianus Capella, the fourth or fifth-century author whose *Marriage of Mercury and Philology* was to become a standard textbook in medieval

---

123-25; Alain LeBoulluec, "l'Allégorie chez les Stoïciens," *Poétique*, 23 (1975), 307; Jean Pépin, *Saint Augustin et la dialectique* (Villanova, 1976), pp. 72-98; Alfred Schindler, *Wort und Analogie in Augustins Trinitätslehre* (Tübingen, 1965), pp. 76-77, 104; Eugene TeSelle, *Augustine the Theologian* (New York, 1970), p. 225. Each of these authors explores Augustine's use of this idea in his other works. For a more extended discussion see Marcia L. Colish, *The Stoic Tradition from Antiquity to the Early Middle Ages* (Leiden, 1985), II, ch. 4, part II, C.

[171] *De dial.* 9, pp. 106-12.

[172] *De dial.* 7.9, trans. Jackson, p. 93. The same idea is repeated, 7.11, pp. 96-98.

[173] *De dial.* 2.3, pp. 83-86.

[174] On the posthumous fortunes of this work see Jackson, intro. to his trans., pp. 6-20.

schools, a popular source of iconography, and the frequent subject of commentaries from the Carolingian era onward,[175] includes some significant points of Stoic philosophy in the sections of his work dedicated to grammar and dialectic. He makes a few passing references to the Stoics as well, including Zeno among the wedding guests in the allegorical prologue[176] and mentioning the Stoics, especially Chrysippus, as prone to sophistical quibbling in the poetic introduction to his treatment of dialectic.[177] More importantly, Martianus draws on Stoicism in three more substantive areas. In the section on grammar he refers to the analogy-anomaly debate, leaning more heavily toward analogy than toward anomaly himself,[178] in a passage that repeats material available elsewhere in other Latin authors. He is, however, the only Latin writer on logic before Boethius to cite the Stoics' technique of using *non* before a proposition in order to negate the entire proposition, rather than merely attaching the negative particle to the verb.[179] Equally impressive is Martianus' detailed listing of the Stoic hypothetical syllogisms. He is the first author since Cicero to transmit these syllogisms so fully.[180] Moreover, he is the first Latin author to discuss them in a dialectical rather than a

---

[175] On Martianus' fortunes and the conjectures concerning his life see Eleanor Shipley Duckett, *Latin Writers of the Fifth Century*, intro. by Eric Milner-White (Hamden, Conn., 1969 [repr. of New York, 1930 ed.]), pp. 230-32; Nuchelmans, "Philologia et son mariage avec Mercure jusqu'à la fin du XIIe siècle," *Latomus*, *16* (1957), 84-107; Jean Préaux, intro. to his and Adolfus Dick's ed. of *De nuptiis Philologiae et Mercurii* (Stuttgart, 1969), pp. xxxvii-liv; William H. Stahl, "To a Better Understanding of Martianus Capella," *Speculum*, *40* (1965), 104-15; James A. Willis, "Martianus Capella and His Early Commentators," (University of London Ph.D. diss., 1952); "Martianus Capella und die mittelalterliche Schuldbildung," *Das Altertum*, *19* (1973), 215-22. The most recent general study, with an up-to date bibliography, is Fanny LeMoine, *Martianus Capella: A Literary Re-evaluation*, Münchener Beiträge zur Mediävistik und Renaissance-Forschung, *10* (München, 1972). An excellent survey of the recent literature with a state of the question analysis of Martianus scholarship is provided by Luciano Lenaz, "Marziano Capella," *Cultura e scuola*, *11* (1972), 50-59. The most systematic treatment of Martianus' sources is Hans-Werner Fischer, *Untersuchungen über die Quellen der Rhetorik des Martianus Capella* (Breslau, 1936), pp. 5-9.

[176] Martianus Capella, *De nuptiis Philologiae et Mercurii* 2.213.19, ed. Dick-Préaux. This edition will be the one cited.

[177] *De nupt.* 4.327.7-9.

[178] *De nupt.* 3.324.13-18. On this question see Richard Johnson with E. L. Burge, "A Study of Allegory and the Verbal Disciplines," in William Harris Stahl, Richard Johnson, and E. L. Burge, trans., *Martianus Capella and the Seven Liberal Arts* (New York, 1972), *1*, 100-01.

[179] *De nupt.* 4.402. Noted by Johnson and Burge, "A Study of Allegory," p. 108.

[180] On Martianus' possible sources see Fischer, *De Augustini disciplinarum*, pp. 18-31, 54, who opts for Varro; Pierre Hadot, *Marius Victorinus: Recherches sur sa vie et ses oeuvres* (Paris, 1971), pp. 150-56 and appendix 2, pp. 324-26, who opts for Victorinus; and Johnson and Burge, "A Study of Allegory," pp. 108-09, who emphasize the possibility that Martianus drew on Theophrastus as well as on Stoic or Stoicizing sources.

rhetorical context. Martianus' handling of the syllogisms may be rendered schematically in the following manner:

> If it is day, it is light. Now it is day; therefore it is light.
> If it is not day, it is not light. Now it is light; therefore it is day.
> It is not day without being light. Now it is day; therefore it is light.
> It is either day or it is night. Now it is day; therefore it is not night.
> It is either day or it is night. Now it is not day; therefore it is night.
> It is not both day and night. Now it is day; therefore it is not night.
> It is not both day and night. Now it is not day; therefore it is night.[181]

In comparison with the five traditional Stoic syllogisms, Martianus' scheme preserves the conditional, the causal, and the disjunctive forms. His second syllogism is simply the negative of the first, his fifth the negative of the fourth, and his seventh the negative of the sixth. He shows a strong interest in the logical implications of negation in connection with these syllogisms, although he omits the Stoics' conjunctive and likely syllogisms. Elsewhere in the same book Martianus uses the Stoic contrast between wisdom and folly as an example of the disjunctive syllogism in both its positive and negative forms. What is most striking about this analysis is that he acknowledges the fact that hypothetical syllogisms of this kind make no claims about extramental reality.[182] However, Martianus is not always faithful to the Stoic position on this point. Elsewhere he analyzes the disjunctive syllogism as a means of establishing physical facts,[183] an approach far more Aristotelian than Stoic. Martianus thus preserves a number of authentic features of Stoic logic, although his use of them is not always consistently Stoic by any means.

D) Cassiodorus

Cassiodorus Senator (A.D. ca. 480–ca. 575) is one of the most influential of the late classical and early medieval educators and transmitters.[184] The descendant of a distinguished aristocratic family, Cassiodorus enjoyed a long and productive career as a statesman, author, and pedagogue. He served under Theodoric after the Ostrogothic conquest of Italy, holding many important offices including that of chancellor. Among his writings are histories, the *De bello gothico*, the *Historia tripartita*,

---

[181] *De nupt.* 4.414-422. See the analysis by Hadot, *Marius Victorinus*, pp. 150-56.
[182] *De nupt.* 4.387.
[183] *De nupt.* 4.418-421.
[184] On Cassiodorus' life and posthumous reputation see Leslie Webber Jones, intro. to his trans. of Cassiodorus Senator, *An Introduction to Divine and Human Readings* (New York, 1946), pp. 3-36, 41-42, 44-53, 58-63.

and the *Chronicon*; works of philosophy and Scriptural exegesis, such as the *De anima* and commentaries on the Psalms and Epistles; *Variae* or letters; and a treatise on orthography. Cassiodorus' chief work as an educator arose from his foundation of a monastery, school, and library at Vivarium in about A.D. 540 after his retirement from politics. In his efforts to develop his monastery as a school of both Christian and classical learning he composed his most famous work, the *Institutes*, at some point after A.D. 551. Viewed from one perspective, Cassiodorus' *Institutes* is a bibliography, listing what every well equipped monastic library should contain. Even more important, Cassiodorus decided to provide a brief summary of the contents of the works which he recommended and of the disciplines which they represented. In so doing, he preserves a good deal of information about the substance of certain writings on the liberal arts which have not survived, as well as offering his own opinions on the authors and subjects in question. The future of Cassiodorus' own work was never in doubt. He exerted a massive impact on medieval thought and education from the seventh century onward, attested both by extensive citations and verbatim quotations on the part of later authors and by a rich manuscript tradition starting in the eighth century, which is especially strong for Book 2. Cassiodorus' *Institutes* remained a venerated authority and a basic tool for medieval encyclopedists, pedagogues, and writers on the liberal arts. From the standpoint of the Stoic tradition, his importance lies mainly in the fact that he, like Martianus Capella and Cicero, provides access in rather full-scale Latin form to the Stoic hypothetical syllogisms. In addition, Cassiodorus gives some indication of the channels by which this information had been transmitted in Latin up to his own time.

Cassiodorus bows in the direction of Donatus in defining *vox* in the usual diluted form it had been given by the Latin grammarians,[185] but his most significant and circumstantial connection with Stoicism is his presentation of seven hypothetical syllogisms which, he notes, are of express Stoic derivation. The Stoics, he explains, have discussed the topic of the hypothetical syllogism in innumerable weighty tomes. He refers readers seeking a treatment of the subject in greater detail than he himself provides but still within a relatively manageable compass to the now lost *De syllogismis hypotheticis* of Marius Victorinus[186] and to a work, whose

---

[185] Cassiodorus, *Institutionum* 2.1.2, ed. Mynors; trans. Jones, pp. 146-47.

[186] On Victorinus' dialectic, the ancient *testimonia*, and his later influence, see J. de Ghellinck, "Réminiscences de la dialectique de Marius Victorinus dans les conflits théologiques du XIme et du XIIme siècle," *Revue néo-scolastique de philosophie, 18* (1911), 432-35; Hadot, *Marius Victorinus*, pp. 22-25, 172-73, 197-98, 310, 347, who includes an edition of Marius' *De definitionibus*, pp. 331-65.

title he does not give, by the Carthaginian Tullius Marcellus. Cassiodorus
is the only author to mention this figure, whose writings cover categorical
and dialectical as well as hypothetical syllogisms. Cassiodorus' own formulation of the hypothetical syllogisms may be schematized as follows:

> If it is day, it is light. But it is day; therefore it is light.
> If it is day, it is light. But it is not light; therefore it is not day.
> It is not day without being light. Now it is day; therefore it is light.
> It is either day or night. Now it is day; therefore it is not night.
> Is is either day or night. Now it is not night; therefore it is day.
> It is not day without being light. But it is day; therefore it is not night.
> It is not both day and night. Now it is not night; therefore it is day.[187]

Like Martianus, Cassiodorus preserves the Stoics' conditional, disjunctive, and causal syllogisms. He also includes the conjunctive form,
omitting only the likely syllogism. His third and seventh syllogisms have
no exact parallels with the Stoic formulation, although they are modeled
closely after Cicero's. It may be plausibly hypothesized that Cassiodorus
derived his schema from Victorinus, who in turn may have derived it
from Cicero himself. In any event, Cassiodorus' treatment of the syllogisms is somewhat closer to the original Stoic version than is Martianus'.
Departing from Cicero, who presents the Stoic syllogisms in a rhetorical
context, Cassiodorus joins Martianus in restoring them to a logical context. But unlike both Martianus and Cicero, he credits them to the Stoics
and he provides information on their transmission by his own Latin predecessors.

VI. The Encyclopedists: Aulus Gellius

Aulus Gellius is not the only classical Latin author who could be
termed an encyclopedist, but he is the only one who preserves and com-
ments on ideas that are of interest for a history of the Stoic tradition. The
Natural History of Pliny the Elder, for instance, who comes to mind as a
far more systematic compiler than Gellius, is disappointing in this connection. Pliny's references to Stoicism are confined to Posidonius, whom
he mentions merely as a well known philosopher or whom he cites on
points of astronomy and geography that are not specifically Stoic.[188] In

---

[187] *Inst.* 2.3.13. Cassiodorus refers to Victorinus' work also at 2.3.18 and in *Expositio psalmarum* 7.137, ed. M. Andriaen, Corpus Christianorum, series latina, 97–98 (Turnholt, 1958). See also Hadot, *Marius Victorinus*, pp. 143–56 for a comparative analysis of Cicero, Martianus, Cassiodorus, and the Stoics on the hypothetical syllogisms. Cassiodorus' formula is repeated verbatim by Isidore of Seville, as noted by Jones, *Intro. to Divine and Human Readings*, p. 167 n. 44.

[188] C. Plinius Secundus, *Naturalis historia* 2.21.85, 2.30.189-190, 6.21.57, 7.30.112, ed. L. Jan and C. Mayhoff (Stuttgart, 1967–70 [repr. of 1898 ed.]).

contrast, Gellius (second century A.D.) could best be described as a dilettante, but one who transmits a good deal of authentic Stoic doctrine in a number of different areas.[189] The son of a wealthy family, Gellius studied widely in both Rome and Greece, dabbling in a number of philosophical schools including Platonism, Aristotelianism, Skepticism, Cynicism, and Stoicism. He began writing his *Attic Nights* in his youth and produced it gradually, publishing it eventually in ca. A.D. 175. The *Attic Nights* is a compilation of facts and fables whose presence in the work stems simply from the circumstance that they happened to interest the author. His random method of organization and his anecdotal approach, whatever their deficiencies may be as modes of philosophical exposition, do not prevent Gellius from seasoning his literary ragoût with liberal pinches of Stoicism, in fields as diverse as biographical notes on individual Stoics, physics, ethics, epistemology, logic, rhetoric, and linguistic theory.[190] Much of this material he reports accurately and in detail.

Passing briefly over the biographical allusions, which simply mention Persaeus and Epictetus among philosophers who suffered the condition of slavery early in life,[191] Gellius devotes a good deal of attention to physics, in the form of the doctrine of providence and free will. He cites Chrysippus as his chief authority in this field, with Cicero's *De fato* as an intermediary source. As Gellius notes, providence, according to Chrysippus, is compatible with the presence of evil in the world, on two grounds. First, since evil is the opposite of good and since nothing can be conceived to exist without its contrary, evil must exist and its existence proves rather than negating the existence of good. Secondly, certain evils proceed from goods, and may be rationized as the concomitants or unavoidable side effects of those goods. Providence, Gellius adds, is equated by Chrysippus with fate, which the Stoics see as an orderly, rational, and unalterable chain of causes. At the same time, Chrysippus teaches, fate governs individual beings according to the laws of their own particular natures and qualities. Human beings, for example, possess free will and the capacity to choose vice or virtue. The exact relationship between fate and human free will can be understood by means of Chrysippus' metaphor of the

---

[189] Gellius' dates are debated. On his life see Barry Baldwin, *Studies in Aulus Gellius* (Lawrence, Kansas, 1975), pp. 5-20; Josef Gassner, "Philosophie und Morale bei Gellius," *Innsbrucker Beiträge zur Kulturwissenschaft, 17*, Serta philologica Aenipontana, 2, ed. Robert Muth (1972), 196-201; René Marache, intro. to his ed. and trans. of *Les nuits attiques*, livres I–IV, Budé (Paris, 1967), *1*, vii-xii; John C. Rolfe, intro. to his ed. and trans. of *The Attic Nights*, Loeb (Cambridge, Mass., 1961), *1*, xi-xviii.

[190] The best study of Gellius' Stoic interests thus far is Gassner, "Philos. und Morale," pp. 207-11, 213-18, 234-35.

[191] Aulus Gellius, *Noctes atticae* 2.18.8, 2.18.10. ed. P. K. Marshall (Oxford, 1968). This edition will be the one cited.

rolling cylinder, which Gellius cites. His entire presentation of the Stoic position on providence, fate, and free will is quite correct, although Gellius makes no personal comment on it except to tax Chrysippus with an involuted style of reasoning.[192]

Gellius adverts much more frequently to Stoic ethical themes. Some of his citations in this area are fairly trivial, such as his references to Panaetius and Musonius Rufus on the importance of vigilance and effort in the moral life[193] and to Chrysippus' visualization of justice as a maiden which a stern but kindly countenance.[194] There is even one passage where he attributes to Epicurus the Stoic doctrine that the sage cannot teach erroneous doctrine, just as the fool cannot teach the truth, along with the Stoic slogan, "bear and forebear."[195] Most of the time, however, he refers to solid Stoic ethical ideas and he ascribes them accurately to their Stoic sources. In one anecdote Gellius contrasts true Stoic virtue with a hypocritical attachment to the school, in depicting a youth who claimed to be a Stoic but who is put to shame by a quotation from Musonius. The youth's superficial connection with the Stoa is manifested in his praise of the doctrine of equanimity and more noticeably in his use of jargon, dialectical tricks, and logical riddles. The Musonian counterattack stresses the importance of ethical behavior as a test of the true Stoic. A real Stoic, according to Musonius, reveals in his life and not just in his words a state of moral freedom and equanimity. He practices and does not merely preach the doctrine that virtue alone is good, vice is evil, and all else is indifferent, placing such things as wealth, health, pleasure, pain, life, and death among the *adiaphora*.[196] This is a rich passage, but it is limited as a vehicle for the transmission of Stoicism in the Latin tradition by the fact that Gellius gives the relevant quotation from Musonius in Greek.

This limitation does not condition his discussion of the issue of pleasure and pain and their relation to virtue, a topic to which Gellius adverts on several occasions. He tells the reader that he witnessed a debate between a Stoic and a Peripatetic on virtue and the happy life, in which the Stoic argued that virtue alone leads to happiness while the Peripatetic argued that physical well-being is also required for the happy life. The Stoic sought to rebut this position by asserting that his vis-à-vis had defined

---

[192] *Noct. att.* 7.1-2. Noted by Pier Luigi Donini, "Fato e voluntà umana in Crisippo," *Atti della Accademia delle scienze di Torino,* classe di scienze morali, storiche e filologiche, 109:2 (1975), pp. 109, 196-203.

[193] *Noct. att.* 13.28, 16.1.

[194] *Noct. att.* 14.4.

[195] *Noct. att.* 17.19.1-6.

[196] *Noct. att.* 1.2.

bodily well-being as a good when it is not a good in fact. Gellius presents the contrast between these two schools clearly, but he does not indicate the outcome of the debate or whether he personally subscribes to either opinion.[197] He is well aware of the fact that the Stoics classified as *adiaphora* things which other philosophical schools regarded as goods. Gellius makes this plain in another passage where he expressly cites Zeno's definition of pleasure as a matter of indifference. For the Stoics, he notes, pleasure is therefore an utterly unworthy end, a view to which Hierocles the Stoic subscribes as well.[198]

Pain, likewise, is a matter of indifference for the Stoic. In explaining this idea, Gellius devotes his attention to the process by which the virtuous man masters his sorrows. He offers the view of Taurus the Stoic, who, he observes, teaches that the sage indeed feels pain but that he overcomes it. Taurus outlines the stages of human development from infancy to the age of reason in analyzing the psychological and moral dynamics of this process. Nature, he states, implants in the infant the instincts of self-love and self-preservation, which incline man at that age to seek those things agreeable to the body and to flee from pain. But, when man attains the age of reason a purely rational criterion supplants his previously instinctual psychology. Man henceforth must evaluate his experience in the light of reason alone. So judged, all experience will be classified either as good, bad, or indifferent. In the latter category things may further be evaluated as more or less preferable. Now pleasure and pain, Taurus continues, are both *adiaphora*. Each adult has both the rational capacity to judge pleasure and pain correctly and the power of will to triumph over them. While the wise man continues to experience pain, he judges it either as morally indifferent or as the unavoidable accompaniment of a process that is natural and hence reasonable. This rational evaluation and the virtue of fortitude which it enables the sage to exercise will enable him to endure pain even though he cannot prevent himself from feeling it.[199] This exposition is extremely full and accurate and is marred only at the end by Taurus' definition of *apatheia* as insensibility, an idea which conflicts with the substance of the rest of his argument.[200] Gellius, or Herodes Atticus, to whom he gives the floor on another, similar occasion, repeats the same error in asserting that Stoic *apatheia* is complete insensitivity to the passions of *aegritudinis, cupiditatis, timoris, irae, voluptatis* ("sorrow, desire, fear, anger, and pleasure,")[201] a

---

[197] *Noct. att.* 18.1.
[198] *Noct. att.* 9.5.5–6, 9.5.8.
[199] *Noct. att.* 12.5.
[200] *Noct. att.* 12.5.10.
[201] *Noct. att.* 19.12.

formula which also adds anger to the standard Stoic quartet. Aside from these lapses, however, Gellius' presentation of the Stoic position is fundamentally correct.

The capacity of the Stoic sage to control his passions is also shown to be connected to the topic of Stoic epistemology, which Gellius treats, as is so often the case, in anecdotal form. A Stoic on board a ship during a storm at sea manifests fear and pallor. When Gellius questions him about his reactions, he gives a lengthy answer, citing Zeno, Chrysippus, and Epictetus as his sources, describing the process by which the *phantasia*, which man receives involuntarily, is converted into a *synkatathesis*, or an impression to which the knower gives his voluntary assent. Once an impression has been judged by the reason, it becomes subject to man's will and he can control his attitude toward it. Now, the Stoic explains, this process is not an instantaneous one. Initially, he responded involuntarily to the *phantasia* of danger impressed on him by the storm, before he had had a chance to reflect on it rationally, to judge it, to classify it as a matter of indifference rather than as an evil, and to develop a proper virtuous response to it.[202] Outside of the fact that Gellius, or his speaker, telescopes a three-stage epistemic process into two stages, omitting the idea of the *phantasia kataleptike*, the epistemological analysis he provides is substantially correct.

Another piece of information about Stoic epistemology which Gellius transmits, significant because so few Latin authors record it, is the idea that sense perception entails the active involvement of the sense organ as well as that of the sensed object:

> Stoici causas esse videnti ducunt radiorum ex oculis in ea quae videri queunt emissionem aerisque simul intentionem.[203]

> The Stoics say that the causes of sight are the emission of rays from the eyes to those objects which can be seen, and the simultaneous expansion of the air.

The only major element missing from this explanation is the idea that *pneuma* flows outward from the eye and that the expansion of the air which the eye encounters is caused by a correlative flow of *pneuma* from the sensory object.

Gellius also reports a number of isolated doctrines in the fields of lin-

---

[202] *Noct. att.* 19.1. Both Gassner, "Philos. und Morale," p. 216 and Neal W. Gilbert, "The Concept of Will in Early Latin Philosophy," *Journal of the History of Philosophy, 1,* (1963), 28–29 have emphasized the element of free will in this passage but have underrated the Stoic epistemological message it contains.

[203] *Noct. att.* 5.16.2–3, trans. Rolfe.

guistic theory, grammar, logic, and rhetoric. These citations tend to be brief and dissociated from their philosophical substrata. None the less, Gellius' *testimonia* in these areas are all correct. He refers to the debate as to whether utterance is corporeal or incorporeal, observing that the Stoics hold utterance to be corporeal, the air that resonates when it has been struck.[204] In the field of grammar, he adverts to the analogy-anomaly debate, giving a reprise of Varro's position and supporting his conclusions on Varronian grounds.[205] He reflects implicitly a Stoic understanding of the distinction between words and *lekta* in discussing Chrysippus' position that words may be ambiguous because they signify a speaker's intention as well as possessing objective natural denotations. He does not, however, go on to explain Chrysippus' distinction between logic and language.[206] In a more general vein, he mentions that, among the syllogisms developed by the Greek logicians, there are the conditional and disjunctive forms, although he does not attribute them to any particular school.[207] In the sphere of rhetoric, however, his identification of Stoic principles is more specific. He gives Musonius' view that an audience hearing a philosophical discourse should respond with a gravity commensurate with a speech which seeks to edify and not to entertain;[208] and, in referring to the orations of three philosophers who visited Rome several centuries previously, he notes that the Academic spoke with vehemence, the Peripatetic with elegance, and the Stoic with modesty and sobriety.[209]

Although Aulus Gellius is essentially a reporter, citing assorted bits and pieces of information on a wide range of subjects with no particular agenda or emphasis, he does manage to communicate a respectable body of Stoic doctrine. His attitude, to the extent that he has one, is an attitude of tolerance and curiosity. He is not interested in assessing the philosophical truth of any of the views he brings forward and he rarely states a personal opinion. He confines himself, for the most part, to assembling material, often at second hand, simply because it appeals to his collector's instinct. He rarely supplies any insights into the connections between one philosophical idea and another. What interest him, rather, are the individual nuggets of philosophical lore, which, prised from their mother lode, happen to strike his fancy. He shows little awareness of philosophy as a sustained or systematic intellectual enterprise in dealing with the Stoics or with any of the other philosophical schools whose doctrines he

---

[204] *Noct. att.* 5.15.6-7.
[205] *Noct. att.* 2.25.
[206] *Noct. att.* 11.12.1.
[207] *Noct. att.* 16.8.9, 16.8.12-15.
[208] *Noct. att.* 5.1.
[209] *Noct. att.* 6.14.10.

mentions. The scope of Gellius' interests is wide and he does succeed in transmitting a substantial number of Stoic teachings much more correctly and in a broader range of areas than is true for many other Latin authors whose philosophical pretensions may have been more overt or elevated than his own. Although Gellius occasionally omits ideas relevant to the Stoic doctrines he discusses and while he errs pointedly on the subject of Stoic *apatheia*, his level of accuracy is quite high.

The *Attic Nights* has the unmistakable appearance of a mixed bouquet. This being the case, it may not be surprising to learn that Gellius appealed especially to the tastes of late classical and early medieval compilers and scholiasts as well as to the usual catalogue of pagan and Christian authors. He started to become popular with this audience in the fourth century and not before.[210] *Testimonia* to the *Attic Nights* occur from Servius through Einhard with the earliest manuscripts of the work deriving from a fifth-century archetype. Gellius' reputation grew even more markedly once the golden age of the *florilegium* had given way before the reinvigorated interest in classical studies of the twelfth century. The late classical and medieval readers who consulted the *Attic Nights* could find considerable information about Stoicism, much of which has remained buried treasure, its presence unsuspected by modern historians of the survival of classical philosophy in the Latin west. Aulus Gellius, like many of the other authors treated in this chapter, thus suggests the utility of studying Latin writers of a lesser breed as intermediaries between ancient Stoicism and the post-classical era.

---

[210] On Gellius' posthumous fortunes see Marache, intro. to his ed. of *Les nuits att.*, *1*, xlii-lvii; Rolfe, intro. to his trans. of *Attic Nights*, *1*, xviii-xxiii.

CHAPTER SIX

STOICISM IN ROMAN LAW

Roman law is always cited, and with justice, as one of the most characteristic products of Roman civilization and as one of the most enduring forms in which that civilization was transmitted to medieval and modern Europe. Despite its importance as such, however, Roman law is rarely treated as itself a vehicle for the transmission of Greek philosophical thought either to Rome or to the Middle Ages. The exception to this rule is the study of the Stoic tradition. For many years scholars have seen in Stoicism the source for some of the most distinctive and influential concepts in Roman legal thought. There has also been a repeated tendency to explain certain changes which particular Roman legal institutions underwent in the course of time as the practical application of Stoic principles to Roman legislative history. The conclusion that Stoicism played a major role in Roman legal thought and practice, and that Roman law is thus an important channel in the transmission of Stoicism to the medieval and modern world, has achieved the status of a textbook commonplace, repeated again and again in the works of historians of philosophy, law, and general European culture. When examined in the light of the evidence, however, this conclusion does not warrant the credence it has enjoyed. The influence of Stoicism on Roman law is far more limited than has been thought. One must look primarily to sources other than the edicts of legislators and the opinions of jurisconsults to find the theory of law inspired by Stoicism which was transmitted to the post-Roman world.

I. Historiographical Introduction

The areas of Roman law in which Stoic influence has traditionally been seen are three in number. First, there are such general principles as natural law, humanitarianism, equity, and egalitarianism. Next, there is the area of legal reform as it applies to persons in a dependent and inferior legal position, such as women, children, and slaves. Enactments improving the status of these persons and granting them a fuller measure of legal rights have been regarded as applications of the general principles of Stoicism to concrete social issues. Finally, there has been a tendency to confuse the Stoic idea of natural law as well as statements of Roman law believed to embody it with strictly modern conceptions of natural law, such as the idea of absolute political and legal equality, the idea of an international law based on rational principles, which transcends without obliterating the laws enacted by sovereign states, and the idea of inalienable natural rights which limit the authority of civil law over the individual and which justify civil disobedience or even revolt if the state fails to respect them.

The scholars who have adhered to one or another of these opinions, like the areas of influence they wish to treat, fall into three categories. First may be mentioned the historians of ancient philosophy in general and of Stoicism in particular. Scholars in this group are well trained in classical philology and literary history, but they are not equally conversant with the science of Roman jurisprudence, a highly specialized discipline practiced in school of law or faculties of jurisprudence. The study of Roman law thus tends to remain a *terra incognita* for the humanistically trained experts in other fields of classical studies. The judgments of the classical philologists and historians of ancient philosophy on Stoicism in Roman law are often based on a few superficial quotations from the *Corpus iuris civilis*, or from authors like Cicero, who was not a jurisconsult. They do not deal with the question of Stoic influence through a systematic study of the juristic sources themselves. The classicists tend to confine their attention to the principles of Stoicism which they see as having been adopted by Roman legal theory, although a few of them argue for the application of these principles to the reform of the law of persons as well.[1]

The second group of scholars who have addressed themselves to the question of Stoic influence in Roman law are specialists in Roman jurisprudence. As a group the Roman legal scholars show a remarkably consistent tendency to locate historical causation in ideological forces alone. Such a stance seems particularly strange for members of a profession given over to the training of lawyers, a group usually sensitive to the

---

[1] These remarks hold true for some of the leading authorities on ancient Stoicism as well as for classicists applying themselves more specifically to Stoicism and Roman law. See, for example, Arnold, *Roman Stoicism*, pp. 20, 384-85; Edelstein, *Meaning of Stoicism*, p. 83; Long, *Hellenistic Philosophy*, p. 231; Sandbach, *The Stoics*, p. 16 among the former and among the latter Emilio Costa, *Cicerone giureconsulto*, 2ª ed., 2 vols. (Bologna, 1927); *La filosofia greca nella giuresprudenza romana* (Parma, 1892), pp. 29-32; *Storia delle fonti del diritto romano* (Torino, 1909), pp. 70-78, 213-19; Hirzel, *Agraphos nomos*, p. 59; H. C. Montgomery, "The Development of Humanitarianism in Roman Law," *Classical Studies in Honor of William Abbot Oldfather* (Urbana, 1943), pp. 104-21; Rodier, *Études de philos. grecque*, p. 219; Charles N. Smiley, "Stoicism and Its Influence on Roman Life and Thought," *CJ*, *29* (1934), 645-57; Salvatore Talamo, *Il concetto della schiavitù da Aristotele ai dottori scolastici* (Roma, 1908), pp. 71-72, 75-78; Franz Vollmann, *Über das Verhältnis der späteren Stoa zur Sklaverei im römischen Reiche* (Stadtamhof, 1890); Watson, "Natural Law," in *Problems in Stoicism*, ed. Long, pp. 232-35; Robert N. Wilkin, "Cicero and the Law of Nature," *Origins of the Natural Law Tradition*, ed. Arthur L. Harding (Dallas, 1954), pp. 12-25.

correlation between their craft and political and social reality. None the less, scholars in this field persistently rule out, or more usually, disregard entirely, the possible impact of social, economic, and political circumstances and needs in explaining the development of Roman law. Exceptions to this pervasive orientation can, almost literally, be numbered on the fingers of one hand. There have been passing reactions against it in the form of Marxist histories of Roman law which explain all developments in the light of the most orthodox economic determinism.[2] *Odium philosophicum* toward the Marxists perhaps explains the widespread scholarly disinterest in considering the possible connections between Roman law and Roman society, even when those connections are divested of the trappings of dialectical materialism. A few recent studies in the areas of litigation[3] and ownership[4] have gone a long way toward reversing the trend in those fields. But only one scholarly effort has been made to do the same for any of the aspects of Roman legal history which jurists have traditionally analyzed in terms of Stoicism or other ideological influences.[5]

The entrenched view that ideas alone caused things to happen in Roman legal history is probably attributable to the Hegelianism of Moritz Voigt, whose mid-nineteenth century study on the legal philosophy of the Romans at one acquired a canonical status in the field, influencing Roman legal scholarship in the most formative stage of the modern development of the discipline. In addition to the idea of preclusively intellectual causation, Voigt also laid down the principle that Stoicism was responsible for the conceptions of natural law, natural reason, *ius gentium*, and equity in Roman jurisprudence as well as for the translation of these conceptions into institutions in the history of Roman legislative reform.[6] Voigt's position continues to enjoy the support of many recent and contemporary authorities in the field.[7] The general disinclination of the legal

---

[2] Stephan Brassloff, *Sozialpolitische Motive in der römischen Rechtsentwicklung* (Wien, 1933); Ettore Ciccotti, *Il tramonto della schiavitù nel mondo antico* (Udine, 1940), pp. 231-441.

[3] Peter Garnsey, *Social Status and Legal Privileges in the Roman Empire* (Oxford, 1970); Erich S. Gruen, *Roman Politics and the Criminal Courts, 149-78 B.C.* (Cambridge, Mass., 1968); J. M. Kelly, *Roman Litigation* (Oxford, 1966).

[4] György Diósdi, *Ownership in Ancient and Preclassical Roman Law* (Budapest, 1970).

[5] John Crook, *Law and Life of Rome* (Ithaca, 1967). Crook deals with the period ca. 81 B.C. to A.D. 224 and his treatment of the law of persons diverges sharply from traditional assessments in this respect. See especially pp. 56-57, 103-08, 111, 114-15.

[6] Moritz Voigt, *Das jus naturale, aequum et bonum, und jus gentium der Römer*, 4 vols. in 7 (Leipzig, 1856-76), passim and esp. *1*, ¶52-64, 89-96.

[7] The following specimens may be cited without exhausting the literature: Maurice-Philibert Guibal, *De l'influence de la philosophie sur le droit romain et la jurisprudence de l'époque classique: Essai de synthèse historique* (Paris, 1937), pp. 67, 78-82, 128-55, 166, 174-94; P. W. Kamphuisen, "L'influence de la philosophie sur la conception du droit naturel chez les jurisconsultes romains," *Revue historique de droit française et étranger*, 4ᵉ sér., *11*, (1932),

scholars to treat Roman law as a phenomenon bearing any relation to historical circumstances and practical daily needs and to view it instead as a mirror capable of reflecting only the philosophical attitudes of the community or the legislator has thus remained the typical approach to the subject on the part of most of its leading practitioners. The effect of this approach has been to divorce legal history from history *tout court*.

A perspective much more widespread and familiar to the general reader than the interpretations of the historians of ancient philosophy and the specialists in Roman legal history is one found in many authors who treat Stoicism and Roman law as sources of the medieval, early modern, or modern theories of natural law. Writers in this category have frequently credited the Stoics, aided by the Roman jurists, with having invented ethical and political theories which in fact owe their origins to later times. Ideas which have been attributed to the Stoics and their presumed Roman legal perpetuators include the Christian and later Enlightenment notions of a transcendent realm of conscience or of rights seen as a norm of the claims to obedience of the civil state and civil law, the Roman Catholic scholastic and neo-scholastic natural law ethical theory, the seventeenth and eighteenth-century idea of a universal rational law of nations which may serve as a basis for diplomatic agreements among a congeries of sovereign states based on differing constitutional and theological foundations without invalidating their sovereignty, and the rejection of a social order which institutionalizes slavery

---

389-412; Bernhard Kuebler, "Griechische Einflüsse auf die Entwicklung der römischen Rechtswissenschaft gegen Ende der republikanischen Zeit," *Atti del congresso internazionale di diritto romano*, Bologna e Roma, 17-27 aprile 1933, 2 vols. (Pavia, 1934-35), I, 79-98, who also discusses the literature of the subject from the sixteenth to the nineteenth century, pp. 84-85 n. 4; M. F. Laferrière, "De l'influence du stoïcisme sur la doctrine des jurisconsultes romains," *Compe-Rendu de l'Académie des sciences morales et politiques*, Séances de juin et juillet, 1859 (Paris, 1860), pp. 5-109; Fritz Pringsheim, "The Legal Policy and Reforms of Hadrian," *JRS, 34* (1934), 141-53, reprinted in *Gesammelte Abhandlungen*, 2 vols. (Heidelberg, 1961), *1*, 91-101; Salvatore Riccobono, "L'influsso del cristianesimo sul diritto romano," *Atti del CIDR, 2*, 73-77; Johann Sauter, "Die philosophischen Grundlagen des antiken Naturrechts," *Zeitschrift für öffentliches Recht, 10* (1931), 74-75, 80; Félix Senn, "De l'influence grecque sur le droit romain de la fin de la République (Les principes du droit)," *Atti del CIDR, 1*, 99-110; Fritz Schulz, *Classical Roman Law* (Oxford, 1951), pp. 103 ff., 117, 134, 152; *Principles of Roman Law*, rev. ed., trans. Marguerite Wolff (Oxford, 1936), pp. 192-97; Artur Steinwenter, "Utilitas publica-utilitas singulorum," *Festschrift Paul Koschaker* (Weimar, 1939), *1*, 84-102; Johannes Stroux, "Griechiche Einflüsse auf die Entwicklung der römischen Rechtswissenschaft gegen Ende der republikanischen Zeit," *Atti del CIDR, 1*, 111-32; Leopold Wenger, "Naturrecht und römisches Recht," *Wissenschaft und Weltbild, 1* (1948), 148-54.

There is a minor current in Roman legal scholarship which disavows any and all Greek philosophical sources for the jurisprudential idea of natural law and which dates the use of that idea to the end of the Imperial era only. A good example is Guglielmo Nocera, *Jus naturale nella esperienza giuridica romana* (Milano, 1962).

or any other legal inequalities among human beings, religious intolerance, or even the absolute right to private property.[8] These principles are, of course, anachronisms as applied either to the Stoics or to Roman law. They are none the less widely regarded as aspects of Stoic influence in general treatments of the idea of natural law in medieval and modern European thought.

The main camp from which criticism of the traditional views on Stoic influence in Roman law has come has been the camp of Roman legal scholarship itself. While adhering firmly to the theory of intellectual causation, many legal scholars, their ranks occasionally swelled by classicists, have sought to de-emphasize Stoicism and to elevate other intellectual sources for the theories and policies of Roman jurists and legislators. It has been noted that ideas such as the notion of distributive justice and the notion of a law common to all men were not unique to Stoicism but were shared with the Platonic and Aristotelian schools.[9] In analyzing particular definitions given by ancient Roman jurists, scholars have also observed that the Pythagoreans and Aristotelians, unlike the Stoics, viewed man as part of a biological continuum which includes animals, and that Aristotle, unlike the Stoics, held that slavery was in accord with natural law.[10] Aristotelian physics, with its doctrine of an enduring substance that can be defined essentially and with its ability to treat incorporeals as real things, is seen by some writers as providing a more plausible basis for Roman legal thought than the Stoic physics of dynamic materialism,[11] although the teleological orientation of Aristotelian phys-

---

[8] Two of the most typical and influential examples of this kind of thinking are John E. E. D. Acton, *Essays on Freedom and Power*, ed. Gertrude Himmelfarb (London, 1956), pp. 75-77 (I am indebted to Jaroslav J. Pelikan for this reference) and Ernst Troeltsch, "Das christliche Naturrecht;" "Das stoisch-christliche Naturrecht und das modene profane Naturrecht," *Gesammelte Schriften*, ed. Hans Baron (Tübingen, 1925) *4*, 156-66, 174-80. The views represented by these works have been perpetuated well into recent scholarship, as, for example, by Adams, "Law of Nature," *J. of Religion*, 25 (1945), 114-16; Anton-Hermann Chroust, "The Function of Law and Justice in the Ancient World and the Middle Ages," *JHI*, 7 (1946), 298-304; Bernhard Kopp, "Zur Geschichte der Naturrechtsidee," *Begegnung*, 23 (1968), 76-77.

[9] Emilio Albertario, "Concetto classico e definizioni postclassiche del *ius naturale*," *Studi di diritto romano* (Milano, 1937), 5, 281-90; Helmut Coing, "Zum Einfluss der Philosophie des Aristoteles auf die Entwicklung des römischen Rechts," *ZSS*, 69 (1952), 24-59; H. F. Jolowicz, *Historical Introduction to the Study of Roman Law* (Cambridge, 1932), p. 104; John Walter Jones, *The Law and Legal Theory of the Greeks: An Introduction* (Oxford, 1956), pp. 20-21, 59-62; Barry Nicholas, *An Introduction to Roman Law* (Oxford, 1962), p. 56; Fritz Pringsheim, "Bonum et aequum," *ZSS*, 52 (1932), 78-155, repr. in *GA, 1*, 173-223; "Jus aequum et jus strictum," *ZSS*, 42 (1921), 643-68, repr. in *GA, 1*, 131-53; Senn, "De l'influence," *Atti del CIDR, 1*, 99-110; Wenger, "Naturrecht," *Wissenschaft u. Weltbild, 1* (1948), 148-54.

[10] Brink, "*Oikeiosis* and *oikeiotes*," *Phronesis, 1* (1956), 123-45; Nicholas, *Introduction*, p. 56.

[11] Eugène Vernay, *Servius et son école: Contribution à l'histoire des idées juridiques à la fin de la République romaine* (Paris, 1909), pp. 99-153.

ics, which defines things in terms of their potentially best nature instead of according to the way they currently happen to be, is also seen as antipathetical to the mentality of the Roman lawyers.[12]

Still other scholars argue that it is not the physical or ethical content of Greek philosophy but its dialectical rules which influenced Roman law, providing the jurists with a terminology and a method for analyzing and categorizing legal ideas and giving them a style in which to express themselves. The emphasis here is entirely on form rather than on content; the content of Roman law is and remains Roman, but it draws upon Greek philosophy, Stoic and Aristotelian primarily, to systematize itself formally.[13] Aristotle is definitely the most important alternative to Stoicism in the opinion of scholars who deny that Stoicism is the primary or exclusive philosophical influence in Roman law. A significant number of scholars have also urged that the channel by which these philosophical ideas passed to the jurists was rhetoric, in particular the Latinized Greek rhetoric absorbed in late Republican Rome and represented most fully by Cicero.[14] Even larger are the numbers of legal scholars who see rhetoric not merely as the transmitter of philosophical ideas but as itself the source for the formal modes of analysis, synthesis, and categorization of cases practiced by the jurists.[15]

---

[12] Jones, *Law and Legal Theory*, pp. 41-44.

[13] Pietro Bonfante, *Storia del diritto romano*, 4ª ed., in *Opere di Pietro Bonfante*, vols. *1-2* (Milano, 1958-59), *1*, 399-404; W. W. Buckland, "Classical Roman Law," *Cambridge Ancient History*, ed. S. A. Cook, F. E. Adcock, and M. P. Charlesworth (Cambridge, 1936), *11*, 806-07, 818; Giubal, *De l'influence*, pp. 83, 87-122; Elemér Pólay, "Zur Geschichte der Rechtswissenschaft im republikanischen Rom," *Gesellschaft und Recht im griechisch-römischen Altertum*, ed. Mihail N. Andreev et al., Deutsche Akademie der Wissenschaft zu Berlin, Schriften der Sektion für Altertumswissenschaft, 52 (Berlin, 1968), pp. 167-69; Fritz Schulz, *History of Roman Legal Science* (Oxford, 1946), pp. 62-69, 84, 85-86, 98; Vernay, *Servius*, pp. 51-69; Michel Villey, "Logique d'Aristote et droit romain," *R. historique de droit franç. et étrang.*, 4ᵉ sér., *29* (1951), 309-28; Hans Julius Wolff, *Roman Law: An Historical Introduction* (Norman, Okla., 1951), pp. 98-102; F. de Zulueta, "The Development of Law under the Republic," *Cambridge Ancient History*, 9, 869-71.

[14] The most extensive expressions of this viewpoint are Costa, *Cicerone; Storia delle fonti*, pp. 70-78, 213-19 and Maurice Pallasse, *Cicéron et les sources de droits*, Annales de l'Université de Lyon, 3ᵐᵉ sér., droit, 8 (Paris, 1946). See also Adams, "Law of Nature," *J. of Religion*, *25* (1945), 114-16; Chroust, "Law and Justice," *JHI*, 7 (1946), 307-08; Constantin Stelian Tomulescu, "Der juridische Wert des Werkes Ciceros," *Gesellschaft und Recht im griechisch-römischen Altertum*, ed. Andreev et al., pp. 226-67; Watson, "Natural Law," in *Problems in Stoicism*, ed. Long, pp. 225-35; Wilkin, "Cicero and the Law of Nature," *Origins of the Natural Law Tradition*, ed. Harding, pp. 12-25.

[15] Although they may disagree on the precise details of rhetorical influence, scholars upholding this view all follow in the footsteps of Johannes Stroux, "Summum ius summa iniura: Un capitolo concernante la storia della interpretatio iuris," trans. G. Funaioli, *Annali del Seminario giuridico di Palermo*, *12* (1929), 639-91; "Griechische Einflüsse," *Atti del CIDR*, *1*, 111-32. Important followers of Stroux include Adolf Berger, *Encyclopedic Dictionary of Roman Law*, Transactions of the American Philosophical Society, n.s. *43*:2 (1953), s. v. "rhetor;" Buckland, "Classical Roman Law," *CAH*, *11*, 806-07, 818; Coing, "Zum

Finally, while still adhering to the traditional view of intellectual causation, a number of legal scholars argue that the theoretical notions and practical alterations of Roman law which others attribute to Stoic influence should be attributed to Christianity instead.[16] Scholars who reject the view that Christianity is the major causative force in Roman legal history do not do so because the Christian interpretation neglects the more mundane forms of historical causation. Rather, they attack it on the grounds that Stoics and other philosophers taught the same ideas as the Christians on the points in question. They also note that the humanizing of the law involved in the legal reforms at issue began before Rome adopted Christianity as its state religion. Or else, they content themselves with the observation that the Christians did not aim at disrupting Roman society either in theory or in practice.[17] From whatever perspective the

---

Einfluss der Philos.," *ZSS*, *69* (1952), 24–59; Richard M. Honig, *Humanitas und Rhetorik in spätrömischen Kaisergesetzen: Studien zur Gesinningsgrundlage des Dominats* (Göttingen, 1960); Jones, *Law and Legal Theory*, pp. 313-14; Kamphuisen, "L'influence de la philosophie," *R. historique de droit franç. et étrang.*, 4ᵉ sér., *11* (1932), 392–93, 404-08; Pringsheim, "Bonum et aequum," *ZSS*, *52* (1932), 78-155; "Jus aequum et ius strictum," *ZSS*, *42* (1921), 643-68, repr. in *GA*, *1*, 173-223, 131-53; José Santa Cruz Teijeiro, "El influjo de la retórica en el derecho romano," *Revista de estudios políticos*, *44* (1952), 109-24; Leopold Wenger, *Die Quellen des römischen Rechts*, Österreiche Akademie der Wissenschaften, Denkschriften der Gesamtakademie, 2 (Wien, 1953); Zulueta, "Development of Law," *CAH*, *9*, 869–71. The most recent works in this group, which give a useful retrospective on the whole school, are Bernard Vonglis, "Droit romain et rhétorique," *Tijdschrift voor Rechtsgeschiedenis*, *37:2* (1969), 247-56; *La lettre et l'ésprit de la loi dans la jurisprudence classique et la rhétorique* (Paris, 1968); Uwe Wesel, *Rhetorische Statuslehre und Gesetzauslegung der römischen Juristen* (Köln, 1967).

[16] The most extensive elaboration of this view is found in Biondo Biondi, *Il diritto romano* (Bologna, 1957), passim and esp. pp. 46, 72-76, 199-210; *Il diritto romano cristiano* (Milano, 1952), *1*, passim and esp. pp. 1-27, where the recent literature on the subject is discussed, and pp. 65, 96, 102-14. See also Emilio Albertario, "I fattori della evoluzione del diritto romano post-classico e la formazione del diritto romano giustineano," *SDHI*, *1* (1935), 3-41; *Introduzione storica allo studio del diritto romano giustineano*, parte 1 (Milano, 1935), ch. 4; Constantin Hohenlohe, *Einfluss des Christentums auf das Corpus iuris civilis: Eine rechtshistorische Studie zum Verständnisse der sozialen Frage* (Wien, 1937), pp. 100-81; Melchiore Roberti, "Cristianesimo e collezioni giustineane," *Cristianesimo e diritto romano* (Milano, 1935), pp. 1-65; M. Troplong, *De l'influence du christianisme sur le droit civil des Romains* (Paris, 1843), pp. 44-365.

[17] The most vigorous and resourceful attack on the preclusively Christian interpretation is Giovanni Baviera, "Concetto e limiti dell'influenza del cristianesimo sul diritto romano," *Mélanges P. F. Girard* (Paris, 1912), *1*, 67-121, who gives a useful bibliographical conspectus of this issue from Montesquieu through the nineteenth century, pp. 68-74, 109-10. See also Vincenzio Arangio-Ruiz, *Istituzioni di diritto romano*, 9ᵃ ed. (Napoli, 1947), p. 28; E. J. Jonkers, "De l'influence du christianisme sur la législation relative à l'esclavage dans l'antiquité," *Mnemosyne*, ser. 3:*1* (1933-34), 241-80; Kamphuisen, "De l'influence de la philos.," *R. historique de droit franç. et étrang.*, 4ᵉ sér., *11* (1932), 389–91, 393–96; Montgomery, "Humanitarianism," *Oldfather Studies*, p. 120; Riccobono, "L'Influsso del cristianesimo," *Atti del CIDR*, *2*, 73-77; Salvatore Riccobono Jr., "L'idea di *humanitas* come fonte di progresso del diritto," *Studi in onore di Biondo Biondi*, *2*, 582-614; Smiley, "Stoicism," *CJ*, *29* (1934), 645-57.

question has been approached, the stress on ideological causation remains generally unchallenged among most of the serious students of Roman jurisprudence.

This picture of Roman jurisconsults and legislators as legal philosophers who sought to work out an abstract theory of law and a systematic methodology for analyzing it under the influence of Greek philosophy or rhetoric or Christian theology, as the case may be, modifying the law from time to time in response to the stimulus of these ideas, contrasts markedly with a rather different picture of the Roman legal mind at work which is presented, with great plausibility, by many modern legal scholars. Their starting point is the truism that, while the Greeks were speculative, the Romans were practical. This hard-headed Roman practicality, a chorus of scholarly voices agrees, found its quintessential expression in Roman jurisprudence, in a marriage made in heaven between the *Volksgeist* and the *Berufsgeist*. Readers are told repeatedly that Roman lawyers had a constitutional distaste for abstract speculation and general definitions. Roman jurists adhered to a case-by-case approach, stating only the rules needed for solving the particular problem at hand, without any interest in elevating particular solutions to the level of universal principles. They were disinclined to provide moral or philosophical reasons for why a law was binding; it was binding because it was the law, *ipso facto*. The jurists were men with the usual general education of their age and had thus come into contact with rhetorical and philosophical notions, but their more specialized training in the law and the orientation to it enforced by the practice of their profession made them rigorously practical. Where ideas from philosophy or rhetoric do crop up in their writings they are used unsystematically and without personal reflection in an essentially decorative way, to prop up extrinsically a legal principle regarded as valid in any case, without any integral connection with the law as such. The jurisconsults of ancient Rome possessed the least philosophical minds imaginable. They "never showed more than a superficial interest in purely philosophical problems. ... Their efforts were directed not at building a purely theoretical jurisprudence, but at demonstrating from every possible angle the practical use to which the institutions of the law could be put."[18]

---

[18] Wolff, *Roman Law*, p. 92. This view is shared widely. See also ibid., pp. 104–05, 123; Berger, *Encyclopedic Dictionary*, s. v. "jurisprudentia;" Franz Blatt, "Written and Unwritten Law in Ancient Rome," *Classica et mediaevalia*, 5 (1943), 142–46; Buckland, "Classical Roman Law," *CAH, 11,* 821; Nicholas, *Introduction,* p. 56; Schulz, *Classical Roman Law,* pp. 6–7; *Hist. of Roman Legal Science,* pp. 69–80, 135–37; Vernay, *Servius,* p. 51; Alan Watson, *Law in the Making in the Later Roman Republic* (Oxford, 1974), pp. 186–93; Zulueta, "Development of Law," *CAH, 9,* 869. The only historian of Stoicism who has noted this point is Bréhier, *Hellenistic and Roman Age,* p. 153.

The contrast between the Roman lawyer as a legal philosopher and the Roman lawyer as a more or less literal minded case lawyer which is presented by the scholarly literature makes this literature a sometimes confusing guide to the possible impact of Stoicism on Roman law, not to mention the difficulties it creates for anyone seeking to grasp the essential nature of Roman law as such. At this point it will be well to turn to the historical facts of the matter, so far as they can be ascertained, and to the jurisprudential texts themselves.

II. THE DEVELOPMENT OF ROMAN JURISPRUDENCE

We may begin with a consideration of the broad outlines of legal development in Rome and the role which the jurisconsult played in it. Students of Roman law divide its history into three main periods following the archaic era: the late Republican period (third to late first century B.C.), the classical period, in which the most authoritative jurisconsults flourished (late first century B.C. to mid-third century A.D.), and the post-classical period, from the later third century through Justinian's redaction of the *Corpus iuris civilis* in the early sixth century A.D.[19] Jurisprudence, or the *responsa* of the jurisconsults, began to become an important feature of Roman legal history in the last centuries of the Republic. Earlier, priests had functioned as interpreters of the law. In the third and second centuries B.C., however, jurisprudence emerged as a distinct secular profession. The *responsa* of the late Republican jurisconsults acquired a great deal of authority, to the point where they were regarded as sources of law. At the time when the Republican jurists became active, Rome was undergoing a transition from a small, purely agricultural and military state to a commercial and plutocratic Mediterranean empire. The laws were in a state of confusion. Many of them were based on conditions which had ceased to exist, and new laws were needed to meet new conditions. It was also seen as desirable to modify or to discard the rigid, ritualistic, and formulaic approach to law which had characterized the archaic period. In these circumstances the function of the jurisconsults went beyond the mere interpretation and organization of the law in the modern sense. They took on the task of being depositories

---

[19] This general historical outline is based on the following: Berger, *Encyclopedic Dictionary*, s. v. "advocatus," "orator;" Bonfante, *Storia del diritto romano*, 1, 273-78; Jolowicz, *Historical Introduction*, pp. 85-99, 369-72, 384-403, 470-84, 517-38; Wolfgang Kunkel, *Herkunft und soziale Stellung der römischen Juristen*, 2nd ed. (Graz, 1967); *An Introduction to Roman Legal and Constitutional History*, 2nd ed., trans. J. M. Kelly (Oxford, 1973), pp. 98-104; Schulz, *Hist. of Roman Legal Science*, pp. 40-59, 99-140, 262-99; Watson, *Law in the Making*, pp. 99-110; Wolff, *Roman Law*, pp. 95-133, 145-57.

of legal norms and formulae for current use, playing a role which was almost legislative in nature.

Republican jurisconsults did not require any formal accreditation. Jurisprudence was a profession composed of men who engaged in their science at will, acquiring their knowledge of the law through their own private study or, toward the end of the Republican era, through apprenticeship to an older jurist. Their authority stemmed from the high quality of their work and from the fact that there was a need for legal specialists, since the magistrates and judges who administered the law did not necessarily have any legal training. Jurisconsults functioned as private citizens with no official position. They confined themselves to studying the law and to giving legal advice on request both to public officials and to individual litigants who might seek them out. The jurisconsults themselves did not try cases in court. Nor did they represent parties in a lawsuit in court. The advice given by the jurisconsults was free. Their profession was a gentleman's avocation entered into out of a commitment to public service as well as for the love of the art. The Republican jurisconsults came from the senatorial class. They had generally followed the *cursus honorum*, but this was by no means a prerequisite; the field was open to anyone with the talent and interest who was wealthy enough to devote himself to legal study and counseling without the need for remuneration. A number of the eminent jurists of the second century B.C. are known to have been members of the Scipionic circle.[20] Their writings have not survived, so it is impossible to evaluate the degree to which they may have drawn upon Stoicism or any other philosophical or rhetorical materials. What we do know of the jurists of the Republican era, mainly, is that they enjoyed a great deal of prestige, deriving no doubt from their social and political eminence as well as from the distinguished and important legal work which they did.

The period called "classical" in Roman legal history is much better documented than the Republican era. The classical period was the age in which authoritative *responsa* were made on all the major areas which the law treated by the jurists who were the most widely quoted in their own day and afterward. During the first century of the classical era, legal education began to crystallize in a more formal manner than had characterized it earlier. While the apprenticeship system continued, the jurists now tended to congregate at one or another of two distinct schools of jurisprudence, the Proculians and the Sabinians. No information survives about the organization of these schools or about the teaching methods which they used. It is most likely that they were clubs or associations of

---

[20] Brown, *The Scipionic Circle*, gives a detailed list of the membership.

jurists and apprentices, supervised by heads. Some scholars have sought
to prove that these two schools represented distinct philosophical orien-
tations, the Proculians being Aristotelians and the Sabinians Stoics.[21]
This view has not b :n demonstrated and receives little general support.
Most authorities hold that the divergences between the two schools reflect
personal rather than philosophical differences, and point out that their
presumed doctrinal opposition cannot explain many of the stands that
their members actually took.[22]

In any case, the drawing together of the jurisconsults as a professional
class with a distinct educational experience in the first century A.D.
widened the gap that had already existed between jurists on the one hand
and advocates or rhetors on the other. The advocate or rhetor was hired
by a litigant to defend him in court. The advocate might confine himself
to helping his client prepare his case; the rhetor or orator was the one
who actually argued his client's case. An orator might indeed have a
good knowledge of the law. His first step in preparing his oration, however, was to consult a specialist, the jurisconsult. From him the orator
received an expert opinion on the nature of the law which pertained to
his client's case. The use which the orator made of this expert knowledge
depended on his judgment as to what would convince the court in his
client's favor. While the jurisconsult's concern was to state what the law
was as objectively as possible, the orator's concern was to win his client's
case. Orators for this reason were perfectly willing to contrast what they
thought or wanted or what they felt would be persuasive with the letter
of the law itself. They argued for a strict or a lenient application of the
law as the circumstances warranted. They were sometimes guilty of voluntary or involuntary omissions or mistakes in their handling of the law,
reflecting either their lack of technical knowledge or their desire to pass
over points harmful to their clients' interests.[23] There was, of course, a
certain amount of legal content in rhetoric as a school discipline, since
one of the pedagogical goals of rhetoric was to teach students forensic
oratory by having them argue pro and con a particular verdict or by
having them resolve a dilemma flowing from a legal situation, real or
fictitious. However, while rhetoricians and jurisconsults came from the
same social class as a rule and while they had been through the same
educational system in their youth, the habits of mind and the conven-

---

[21] Two leading scholars who adhere to this view are Vernay, *Servius*, pp. 90-95 ana
F. de Zulueta, trans. and ed., *The Institutes of Gaius*, 2 vols. (Oxford, 1946-53), *1*, 79.

[22] See, for example, Jolowicz, *Historical Introduction*, pp. 384-85; Schulz, *Hist. of Roman
Legal Science*, p. 123; Wolff, *Roman Law*, p. 106.

[23] The fullest treatment of this subject is Fabio Lanfranchi, *Il diritto nei retori romani:
Contributo alla storia dello sviluppo del diritto romano* (Milano, 1938).

tional activities imposed on them by their respective professions generated a difference of attitude between them about the law. Where the rhetor moralized and attempted to play on the feelings of the court, pleading for mercy or harshness according to the needs of the case, the jurisconsult stated the legal rule pertaining to a specific case straightforwardly, without defending or criticizing it. The claim that the legal ideas of the rhetors are an adequate index of the philosophical content and temper of Roman jurisprudence is thus tenuous indeed.

As we move into the second century A.D. we find the earlier schools of jurisprudence in decline. This development is a reflection of the shifting status of the senatorial class in relation to the emperor. The political initiative of the aristocracy had by now been depressed decisively. The emperor played an increasingly autonomous role both in legislation and in the according of authoritative status to the *responsa* of the jurists. At this time an individual jurist could still acquire great personal prestige, but only if he had imperial backing. The practice of granting the right to give legal opinions with the emperor's authority on application by a jurist began under Augustus. While this policy may originally have been intended to lend additional weight to the jurists' *responsa*, its effect by the second century was to destroy the professional independence of the jurisconsults and to reduce them to the status of servants of the all-powerful emperor, permitted to practice only if their views corresponded with his. The reign of Hadrian (A.D. 117-38) is seen as a turning point in this respect. The emperor's control over jurisprudence in this period paralleled his wider use of prerogative jurisdiction and his increased intervention into suits pending trial and other such matters.

Also, starting from the latter part of the classical period, the jurists came increasingly from sub-senatorial families. Their prestige came from their skill and their imperial authorization, not from their social class. Their sense of professional identity was even more marked in this era than before. The jurists of the second century cited and discussed the opinions of members of their own group but ignored the views of everyone outside it. In their writings they cultivated their own distinct Latin style, solid, unembellished, idiomatic, terse, with a fixed terminology and a plain, clear, and objective manner of expression, which further divided them from the professional rhetoricians.[24] The elaborateness of the technical education of the second-century jurist can be seen by the fact that tasks requiring a less profound knowledge of the law, such as the drafting of wills and business agreements, were relegated to jurists of inferior train-

---

[24] On this point see Schulz, *Hist. of Roman Legal Science*, p. 98, who also gives some examples of juristic prose, ibid., n. 2 and 3.

ing and status. Starting in the late second century, provincial law schools
were established by the state, which trained men for the civil service as
well as for legal careers. The jurists trained in the capital looked down
on the alumni of the provincial schools and tended to ignore their opinions. The only provincial jurist from this period who became famous was
Gaius. Many of his *responsa* were later held authoritative, but he was not
quoted by other jurists of his own era.

The shift to the post-classical period began in the middle of the third
century A.D. This development is generally regarded as a collapse rather
than as the fulfillment of classical jurisprudence. Post-classical jurists became even less autonomous than their classical predecessors, since the
emperor's assumption of more and more jurisdiction left less and less
scope for *responsa*. The authority of magistrates to expand and develop
the law by issuing edicts at the beginning of their term of office stating
what sorts of cases they would hear was terminated by imperial edict,
which now became the sole source of law. The imperial government did
not consult jurists extensively when it wished to legislate in the latter
centuries of the Empire; the jurists became faceless bureaucrats who
drafted edicts in the name of the emperor. The scope of their initiative
narrowed almost to the vanishing point, as the imperial chancery became
the most important center for the formulation and interpretation of the
law. Legal writing in this period was confined to editing, compiling, and
abridging. Its greatest monuments are the *Theodosian Code* of the fifth
century and Justinian's *Corpus iuris civilis* of the sixth.

The language of post-classical legislation, particularly toward the end
of the period, grew verbose, decorative, and bombastic, with fine sentiments and vague feelings of good will substituted at many points for the
precise legal reasoning and the laconic style of the classical era. It became
much more usual in the post-classical period for legislators to endow their
edicts with prefaces giving a moral rationale for the law which followed.
The level of legal thinking appears to have been higher in the eastern
part of the Empire than the west, a plausible fact in the light of their
relative political positions at this time. The law schools of the east, particularly Beirut and Constantinople, tended to produce the best regarded
scholars. From the fifth century onward it was necessary to have attended
one of the official law schools, at Rome, Constantinople, or Beirut, to be
admitted to legal practice.

A great deal of legal activity took place in the post-classical era. Many
earlier laws were modified and many new laws were enacted. On the
whole, the emphasis in this legislative activity did not fall on the modification of old rules of private law. The main concern of post-classical
legislation was rather the issuing of administrative regulations which were

geared to the fiscal and military interests of the state. To a lesser extent, post-classical legislation concerned itself with criminal law, both its substance and its procedure. It was of course also necessary, given the legitimizing of the Christian Church and the emperor's assumption of state control over it, to elaborate new rules pertaining to the Church, specifying the rights of religious institutions as legal corporations as well as the legal rights and duties of ecclesiastical personnel. The ideological influence of Christianity on Roman law is a subject of debate, as we have noted above. To the extent that Christianity can be shown to have influenced legislation and legal thinking, this influence is confined to the post-classical era, when Christianity was the state religion of Rome. The degree to which Christian influence can be seen will await the analysis of the texts below. It should be noted at this point, however, that Roman legal institutions which were expressly antithetical to Christian doctrine, such as divorce, remained in force throughout the history of the Empire.

The tendency of post-classical legislation to employ moral sentiments and abstract ideas as justifications for enactments has led many scholars to treat this final period of ancient Roman legal history as the main era in which one can appropriately speak of philosophical and rhetorical influences in Roman jurisprudence. Unlike Christianity, however, philosophy and rhetoric were part of the established culture of Rome from the late Republic onward. It is therefore not at all clear why they should have played a more important role at the end of Roman legal history than they had played earlier. Various explanations of this phenomenon have been offered. It is argued that the political and social crises of the third century caused moral sensitivity to burgeon in fields which had been relatively barren before.[25] Another view attributes these shifts to the personal proclivities of individual emperors as legislators.[26] Yet another interpretation, ingenious although admittedly impossible to demonstrate, is that philosophy and rhetoric had a delayed impact on Roman law because they were introduced into it through the agency of Christian theology, which is why they are apparent mainly in the post-classical period.[27] The most usual explanation is that the schools which played the strongest role in post-classical jurisprudence were those in the eastern part of the Empire, where the classical school tradition was perpetuated while it was collapsing in the west in the wake of the Germanic conquests. The inherent conservatism of classical education in general and of legal education in particular perpetuated philosophy and rhetoric in the east

---

[25] Honig, *Humanitas und Rhetorik*, p. 4.

[26] Fritz Pringsheim, "The Character of Justinian's Legislation," *GA*, 2, 73–85.

[27] René Voggensperger, *Der Begriff des "Jus naturale" im römischen Recht* (Basel, 1952), pp. 22–28.

in the fourth to sixth centuries.[28] This argument is not very logical. If classical education was available throughout the Empire, both east and west, up to the fourth century, why was it less manifest in classical jurisprudence than in the jurisprudence emanating from the eastern schools in the later Empire? None of the explanations that have been offered so far is entirely convincing on this point.

The most pressing problem in the scholarly literature has not been the question of why post-classical jurisprudence was more given over to philosophical prefaces and moralizing than was classical jurisprudence. Rather, the main problem springs from the fact that this, indeed, was the case, and from the fact that most of the ideas of the classical jurisconsults are available only in the form in which they were put by sixth-century editors. Justinian, after ordering the compilation of the *responsa* of the classical jurisconsults who he thought were most important in the *Digest* and the *Institutes,* also ordered the originals destroyed. Here and there modern scholarship has brought to light the text of a classical jurist which somehow managed to slip through the Justinianic net. Still, modern reconstructions of classical jurisprudence are heavily dependent on the citations of the classical jurists in the *Corpus iuris civilis.* The fact that Justinian wished to destroy the works of the classical jurists after compiling them has led to the plausible suspicion that he would not have done this had he not doctored them so that his version would not bear comparison with the original texts. The few classical texts which have been found that are independent of the *Corpus iuris civilis* show, at some points, that the Justinianic editors quoted them verbatim. At other points, they show that this is by no means the case. There has been a tendency on the part of some legal scholars to infer that all references to abstract philosophical ideas and moral values found in the classical *responsa* present in the *Corpus iuris civilis* are Justinianic interpolations. This position has been taken very forcefully by Emilio Albertario, a scholar who has exerted a great deal of influence in the complex modern science of interpolation research in Roman law.[29] However, Albertario has been criticized heavily by other outstanding authorities on the ground that the *Corpus iuris civilis* does not always alter the *responsa* of the classical jurists and that the independent classical texts show that classical jurisprudence was not entirely devoid of philosophical content. Albertario's critics have also ar-

---

[28] See, for example, Bonfante, *Storia del diritto romano, 1,* 404; Schulz, *Hist. of Roman Legal Science,* pp. 295-99.

[29] Albertario has written repeatedly to this effect. See, for example, "Concetto classico e definizioni postclassiche," *Studi di diritto romano, 5,* 277-90; "Etica e diritto nel mondo classico latino," *Rivista internazionale di filosofia del diritto, 12* (1932), 3-20; "I fattori," *SDHI, 1* (1935), 3-41; *Introduz. storica,* pp. 81-134.

gued that not all the texts that he rejects as interpolations are, in fact, interpolations.[30] No solution to this problem based on universally acceptable premises is in sight and one is not offered here. For our purposes the statistical presence of philosophical tags, in and of itself, is less important than the use which the jurists actually make of philosophical ideas.

III. DEFINITIONS OF ABSTRACT LEGAL PRINCIPLES

In turning from the historical outline of Roman law to the texts themselves, we may begin by noting that the jurists on some occasions do provide general definitions of abstract ideas, such as law, justice, equity, natural law, natural reason, and the law of nations. A close scrutiny of these definitions shows that they are not always consistent with each other. To the extent that any of these definitions has a Stoic content, it is incidental and unsystematically developed, whether this content may have been introduced by classical or post-classical jurists. There are also some philosophical conceptions to be found in these general definitions which are expressly antithetical to Stoicism.

There is, indeed, some evidence that the classical jurists were aware of Stoic philosophy as it pertained to law. The jurist Marcianus cites a definition of law which he attributes to Chrysippus by name: law is the ruler of divine and human affairs; it ought to be what controls man in distinguishing good from evil, the just from the unjust, and what is to be followed from what is to be avoided.[31] There are reminiscences of this definition in statements defining law given by other jurists. What is immediately striking about these reminiscences is that they omit Chrysippus' distinction between what is and what ought to be. In contrast to Chrysippus, the jurists simply state that law is the science or art of justice, goodness, and equity,[32] implying thereby that a rule of Roman law is just and fair in virtue of the fact that it is legal. *Iustitia* is seen as flowing logically from *ius*, not the other way around.

---

[30] See, for example, Berger, *Encyclopedic Dictionary*, s. v. "aequitas," "humanitas," "ius naturale;" Wolfgang Kunkel, "Civilis und naturalis possessio: Eine Untersuchung über Terminologie und Struktur der römischen Besitzlehre," *Symbola friburgenses in honorem Ottonis Lenel* (Leipzig, 1931), pp. 40–79; Fritz Pringsheim, "Aequitas und bona fides," *Conferenze per il XIV centenario delle Pandette, 15 dicembre 530–15 dicembre 1930*, Pubblicazioni della Università Cattolica del Sacro Cuore, 2ª ser., 33 (Milano, 1931), pp. 183–214; "Bonum et aequum," *ZSS, 52* (1932), 78–155, repr. in *GA, 1,* 173–223; Stroux, "Griechische Einflüsse," *Atti del CIDR, 1,* 111–32.

[31] *Digesta* 1.3.2, in *Corpus iuris civilis*, 16th ed., ed. T. Mommsen, 3 vols.(Berlin, 1954).

[32] *Dig.* 1.1.1.1, 1.1.10.2, 1.1.11; *Institutiones* 1.1.1, in *Corpus iuris civilis*, 16th ed., ed. P. Krueger.

This conclusion is reinforced by another famous text, the definition of justice attributed to the jurist Ulpian. Ulpian is quoted at the beginning of the *Digest* and the *Institutes* as follows: "Justice is the constant and perpetual will to render to each what is his *(suum cuique tribuens)*."[33] The same idea recurs in a definition of the precepts of the law, cited in the *Institutes* as being "to live honestly, not to harm another, to render to each what is his."[34] The notion of rendering to each what is his is found in Platonic and Aristotelian conceptions of justice as well as in Stoicism. The meaning of this concept in practice depends on what "each man's own" is conceived to be. For the Stoics, all human beings are morally equal on the basis of their common possession of reason, which is identical with God, the *logos* of the universe. The *logos* which connects all men with each other and with the natural order entails mutual obligations among men which are pre-legal and supra-legal. To what extent do the jurists really reflect this conception of human nature and human obligations?

There is one jurist, Florentius, who acknowledges that all men share a common nature. "Nature forms a certain kinship among us," he notes, and he then goes on to observe that it is wrong and against the law for one man to lie in wait for another for the purpose of killing him.[35] Florentius does not, however, indicate the basis upon which men enjoy their natural kinship. Neither is it clear from his *responsum* whether the thing he is objecting to is homicide as such, or merely the lack of fair play involved in an ambush. It would, in any case, be difficult to prove that Florentius regards the binding force of the Roman law against ambush as dependent on the existence of some sort of unspecified natural kinship among men. His use of this notion in this particular context appears to be purely decorative, not very well thought out, and not necessarily Stoic. Ulpian, the jurist who defines justice in the elevated philosophical terms noted above, treats the concept of justice in practice in a far less philosophical manner. The "things which are his" turn out to be the specific legal rights which a person possesses as a consequence of his legal status in Roman law, a legal system not notoriously egalitarian in nature. For Ulpian, what is just or unjust refers in practice to what is legitimate or illegitimate according to the rules actually governing Roman legal institutions.[36]

Stoic conceptions of justice and fairness based on the natural kinship of all men do not seem to exercise a particularly vigorous influence on the jurists' definitions of these ideas. The same may also be said for the

---

[33] *Dig.* I.1.10.1; *Inst.* I.1.pr.
[34] *Inst.* I.1.3.
[35] *Dig.* I.1.3.
[36] *Dig.* 38.11.1.

jurists' definitions of natural law and related abstractions. The jurists do provide abstract definitions of natural law, natural reason, and *ius gentium*. These definitions range from an outright rejection of the way in which the Stoics treated the idea of natural law to an apparent acceptance of the Stoic position which breaks down on closer examination. Ulpian produced one famous definition of natural law which is cited in both the *Institutes* and the *Digest*: "Natural law is what nature teaches all animals," in contrast to the law of nations (*ius gentium*), which applies only to men. From this rule flows the observation that throughout the animal kingdom male and female unite to procreate offspring and to raise them, an institution which, among men, is called marriage.[37] The whole passage so far is designed to serve as an introduction to a series of remarks that Ulpian wishes to make on the subject of the Roman law of marriage. There is, indeed, a Stoic side to Ulpian's definition of natural law, since the Stoics, unlike previous ancient philosophers who talked about a universal law of nature, taught that the laws of the physical universe had a normative value in man's ethical life. It is, however, the non-Stoic aspects of Ulpian's definition that are the more striking. The Stoics rejected entirely the idea that man can be seen as part of a biological continuum which includes subhuman beings. For the Stoics animals in no sense form a moral community with men, for animals do not possess reason. Reason alone is the relevant norm for human moral behavior, even for those Stoics who include irrational faculties within their descriptive anthropology. That marriage, procreation, and the rearing of children, moral duties rationally incumbent upon the sage and activities which are to be carried on and regulated by a conscious act of reason and will, should be treated logically as one species within the general category of instinctual animal life would have been totally unacceptable to the Stoics. The principle stated by Ulpian's definition, in fact, is far more akin to an Aristotelian biological view of man than it is to the Stoic view.

Ulpian, in the definition just discussed, distinguishes natural law from the law of nations in terms of the sorts of creatures to which they apply, men and animals in the first case and men alone in the second. There were other jurists besides Ulpian who defined *ius naturale* and *ius gentium*, both in relation to each other and in relation to *ius civile*, without expatiating on the biological similarities between men and animals. They draw rather on such concepts as reason and goodness as constitutive

---

[37] *Dig.* 1.1.1.3-4; *Inst.* 1.2.pr. The non-Stoic character of Ulpian's dictum has been noted by Brunt, "Aspects of the Social Thought of Dio Chrysostom and the Stoics," *Proceedings of the Cambridge Philological Society, 199* (1973), 18 n. 2.

principles in their analyses of these terms. It would seem, then, that their definitions would provide a more fruitful field for the detection of Stoic influences. It should be noted before proceeding any further in this connection that Roman jurisprudence did not deal as a rule with the relations between the individual and the state or with international agreements signed by sovereign states in the contexts where the jurists discuss natural law and natural reason. The distinction among the three kinds of law, natural, common to all nations, and civil, is defined in the first instance as pertaining to private law.[38]

Roman jurists on more than one occasion define natural law as that which is consistent with natural reason, or as that which is good and fair under all circumstances.[39] There is also a tendency on the part of some jurists, especially Gaius, to identify natural law or natural reason with *ius gentium*. There is one famous text in the *Institutes* in which the natural law, defined as the law observed by all nations, is also described as having been appointed by "a divine providence, which always remains firm and immutable."[40] This text is one of the few which, all commentators agree, is a Justinianic interpolation. Whether it was inspired by Stoicism or Christianity has been debated. Stoicism certainly shares with Christianity the idea of a divine providence. The lapidary character of the text does not permit the reader to discern whether its author meant by divine providence an ordinance which transcends the natural world or a divine law which is identical and coterminous with the natural world, as the Stoics taught. The bare connection of the order of nature with the deity's disposition of all events in the universe might be equally Stoic or Christian. A certain un-Stoic touch, however, is present in the description of the divine order as immutable. The Stoic order of the universe is dynamic and ever-changing. Since the Stoic God is material and corporeal, the substance as well as the ordering principle of the natural universe, God likewise changes. The contrast between an immutable deity and the fluctuating institutions of men suggested by the text seems to imply a Platonic or Aristotelian source for this passage, if indeed philosophy rather than Christian theology is the source.

It is more usual for the jurists, in contrasting the *ius gentium* and its backdrop of natural reason with the civil law, to develop the contrast without adverting to the deity. *Ius civile* refers simply to the local law peculiar to a particular community, whose sanction lies in the enactments and reigning customs of that community.[41] *Ius gentium*, on the other hand,

---

[38] *Inst.* 1.1.4.
[39] Gaius, *Institutes* 1.1, ed. Zulueta; *Dig.* 1.1.9, 1.1.11.
[40] *Inst.* 1.2.11.
[41] Gaius, *Inst.* 1.1; *Dig.* 1.1.9.

refers to the laws actually in force, or what the jurists assumed were in force, among all nations, which happen to agree with each other. Roman jurisconsults do not use the term "positive law," but it is a convenient if anachronistic tool for understanding their approach to *ius gentium*. All laws in the *ius gentium*, they held, were institutions actually embodied *de iure* in the positive law of all known peoples, which happen to agree with each other. The two operative principles are the fact that the legal rules in question are identical in all communities, and that these communities have institutionalized them in their own respective civil systems. Legal rules which do not enjoy universal assent are not part of the *ius gentium*. They are irrelevant unless one is interested in the science of comparative law, which the Romans were not. The *ius gentium*, although it does enjoy universal assent, does not acquire its relevance to Roman jurisprudence on that account. For the rules which make up the *ius gentium* are also rules which are embodied in the Roman civil law; and all rules of Roman civil law are *ipso facto* relevant and binding.

The Roman jurists, none the less, identify natural law or natural reason as the underlying principle which establishes the commonly shared civil laws which make up the *ius gentium*.[42] Since some of the laws enacted in Rome are the same as laws possessed by everyone else, Roman law is based partly on the civil law and partly on the *ius gentium*, which is naturally reasonable. Examples cited by the jurists are the principle that minors should have legal guardians[43] and the principle that an item cannot be said to have been legally transferred from the owner to someone else unless the recipient pays for it or makes some kind of pledge or deposit.[44] The natural reason in back of the *ius gentium* is everyday common sense, not an ideal abstraction which serves as the criterion of and justification for the civil law.

The Romans convey the sense that both their own civil law and the *ius gentium* are reasonable, on the whole. In any case, it is the authority of the civil law which makes it binding, whether the civil law itself and the *ius gentium* which may correspond with it at some points are, in fact, rational or not. Roman jurisprudence rarely suggests that the Roman civil law and the *ius gentium* may conflict, a circumstance probably attributable to the fact that the main area in which *ius gentium* was developed in practice was commercial law, whose principles the Romans shared with other Mediterranean peoples. The framework in which the Romans' treatment of *ius gentium* arose was the court of the peregrine praetor.[45]

---

[42] Gaius, *Inst.* 1.1, 1.189; *Dig.* 1.1.9; *Inst.* 1.20.6, 2.1.11, 2.1.41.

[43] Gaius, *Inst.* 1.189; *Inst.* 1.20.6.

[44] *Inst.* 2.1.41.

[45] On this subject most of the authorities are in agreement. See Arangio-Ruiz, *Istitu-*

In late Republican times there were many traders of diverse nationalities in Roman territory doing business with each other and with Roman citizens. Foreigners who were freemen and who lacked Roman citizenship were called *peregrini*. It became necessary to establish courts in which cases involving peregrines could be tried and in which rules relating to their legal problems could be laid down. The Republican constitution authorized magistrates charged with the adjudication of court cases to announce by edict at the beginning of their terms of office what kinds of cases they would hear. This power was enjoyed by the praetors, a magistracy established in 367 B.C. to relieve the consuls of the administration of justice, and by the peregrine praetorship, an office created in 242 B.C. to deal with cases between peregrine and peregrine and between peregrine and citizen. Praetors frequently repeated the statements of their predecessors in issuing their own praetorian edicts, but they were by no means bound to preserve tradition and often did not do so. It was through this discretionary authority to admit new kinds of cases that the peregrine praetors expanded the jurisdiction of the civil law to include persons and matters which it had not originally treated. In so doing, the peregrine praetors drew upon the commercial law current in the Mediterranean world, practices defined as falling under the *ius gentium* because they were common among the peoples of the region.

The activities of the peregrine praetors account for a substantial volume of the litigation on commercial law and related subjects which was

---

zioni, pp. 25-38; Berger, *Encyclopedic Dictionary*, s. v. "ius gentium;" Biondi, *Il diritto romano*, pp. 136-40; *Istituzioni di diritto romano*, 3ᵃ ed. (Milano, 1956), pp. 68-70; Buckland, "Classical Roman Law," *CAH, 11*, 810; David Daube, "Greek and Roman Reflections on Impossible Laws," *Natural Law Forum, 12* (1967), 14; "The Peregrine Praetor," *JRS, 41* (1951), 66-70; Paolo Frezza, "Ius gentium," *Nuova rivista di diritto commerciale, diritto dell'economia, diritto sociale, 2* (1949), 26-51; Jolowicz, *Historical Introduction*, pp. 103-05; Gabrio Lombardi, "Diritto umano e 'ius gentium'," *SDHI, 16* (1950), 254-68; *Ricerche in tema di "ius gentium"*, Università di Roma, pubblicazioni dell'Istituto di diritto romano, dei diritti dell'oriente mediterraneo e di storia del diritto, 21 (Milano, 1946), passim and esp. pp. 192, 231, 271; *Sul concetto di "ius gentium"*, Università di Roma, pubblicazioni dell'Istituto di diritto romano, dei diritti dell'oriente mediterraneo e di storia del diritto, 20 (Milano, 1947), passim and esp. pp. ix-xiv, 3-8, where he discusses the literature on this subject, pp. 17-18, 124 ff., 345-53; Francesco de Martino, "Variazioni postclassiche del concetto romano di ius gentium," *Annali della Facoltà di giurisprudenza dell'Università di Bari*, n.s. 7-8 (1947), 107-39; Nicholas, *Introduction*, pp. 54-58; Félix Senn, "De la distinction du *ius naturale* et du *ius gentium*," in *De la justice et du droit* (Paris, 1927), pp. 63-72; Wolff, *Roman Law*, pp. 70-83; Zulueta, "Development of Law," *CAH, 9*, 867-88; *Institutes of Gaius, 1*, 12-13.

Mario Lauria, "Ius gentium," *Festschrift Paul Koschaker, 1*, 258-65 thinks that the idea of *ius gentium* developed before the institution of the peregrine praetors although he is not clear on how it was administered if such was the case. The only leading authority to reject the idea that the theory of *ius gentium* developed out of the magistracy of the peregrine praetors is Schulz, *Hist. of Roman Legal Science*, pp. 73, 137.

added to the body of Roman civil law in the late Republic and early
Principate. The magistracy of the peregrine praetors continued until the
third century A.D. In 212, the emperor Caracalla extended Roman citizenship to all freemen residing within the Empire. After this time, persons
with the status of *peregrini* tend to disappear from the scene, and with this
development the need for a special magistracy to deal with them disap-
peared as well. The *ius gentium* is a topic to which late Imperial jurisprudence adverts very rarely. While the peregrine was made a Roman
citizen at a specific point in time, the *ius gentium* which the peregrine
praetors had invoked in dealing with his legal problems had always fallen
under the aegis of the civil law. It was the civil law which endowed the
peregrine praetors with the authority to try cases involving foreigners; it
was the civil law which made their judicial decisions legally binding; and
it was to the body of the civil law of Rome that the rules they elaborated
were added.

In the case of the law developed by the peregrine praetors, no tension
was seen between the *ius gentium*, with its theoretical foundation of natural
reason, and the Roman civil law which assimilated it. There were some
points, however, at which Roman jurisprudence did perceive a disparity
between these types of law. In cases where they were not perfectly iso-
metric, it was invariably the civil law that was binding. Roman jurists
saw their task as the identification of what the civil law enjoined. They
willingly admitted that there might well be philosophical principles, principles which they might even subscribe to themselves, which were at
variance with the civil law. If such were the case, the civil law was none
the less binding. The demands of civil law transcended the demands of
natural law and natural reason. Ulpian provides a crisp statement of the
attitude generally taken by the jurists: "The civil law is something which,
on the one hand, is not completely independent of natural law and *ius
gentium*, nor, on the other hand, is it subordinate to it in all respects."[46]
The points at which Roman jurists saw the civil law as incommensurate
with, and superior to, the *ius gentium* or natural reason are points relating
to the law of persons where Roman law is often seen as reflecting the
rationalizing and humanizing influence of Stoicism. The jurists' treatment of these conflicts of laws shows that the reverse is the case; the
abstract principle always yields to the law currently in force. Gaius notes,
for instance, that there is a difference between *ius civile* and *ius gentium* on
the legal status of a child born out of lawful wedlock. In the *ius gentium*,
he points out, the child always follows the legal status of his mother.
Roman law adheres to this rule in some cases, but not in all cases, and

---

[46] *Dig.* 1.1.6.

Gaius goes on to specify the circumstances in which an illegitimate child follows his father's status in the Roman *ius civile*. Gaius also observes that an emperor may depart from the *ius gentium* in this area and cites an example of such an enactment, which remained binding until it was repealed by the edict of a later emperor. Thus, Gaius concludes, the *ius gentium* can be and has been modified by the *ius civile*, and when this happens it is the civil law that binds.[47]

The civil law may also supercede reason. In another *responsum* of Gaius, he notes that, in contrast with the guardianship of minors, a practice whose reasonableness is self-evident and which is found among all nations, the legal tutelage of adult women cannot be justified on any rational grounds. He refers here to the Roman institution of *tutela mulierum*, according to which women who were not under the legal control of their fathers or husbands had to have guardians to supervise their legal business, an institution which will be discussed further below. As Gaius sees it, there is no reasonable basis for the view, taught by the ancient jurists, that women as a class lack the mental capacity to transact their own affairs. He also observes that the Roman institution of *tutela mulierum* finds no support in the *ius gentium*, since not all peoples regard women as legally incompetent. None the less, he concludes, *tutela mulierum* is an institution of the Roman civil law, despite its lack of correspondence with reason and the law of nations; hence it binds.[48] The idea that women by nature are just as capable of transacting their own business as men might have occurred to Gaius as a result of Stoic influence, since sexual equality is one of the school's distinctive teachings. It may also have been a conclusion which he drew from his observation of those women whose business sense happened to come to his attention. In any event, the egalitarianism reflected in Gaius' treatment of the topic of *tutela mulierum* does not suggest to him that the civil law on this question is in any way invalid.

An even more striking example of the tendency to elevate civil law above natural reason in Roman jurisprudence can be seen in the jurists' treatment of the institution of slavery. They note repeatedly that slavery is in accordance with the *ius gentium*; everyone practices it, including the Romans.[49] And the *ius gentium*, they frequently observe, is established by natural reason. However, several jurists point out that slavery is contrary to the law of nature, for all men by nature are free.[50] There is an obvious contradiction here. Some classical jurists even state these points all within

---

[47] Gaius, *Inst.* 1.78-88.
[48] Ibid., 1.190, 1.193.
[49] Ibid., 1.52; *Dig.* 1.1.4, 1.5.4.1-2, 50.17.32.
[50] *Dig.* 1.1.4, 1.5.4.1-2, 50.17.32; *Inst.* 1.2.1-2, 1.3.1-2, 1.5.pr.

the same passage, showing no concern with the fact that they cancel each other out. Post-classical law reiterates the same inconsistent reasoning.[51] Whether rationally justifiable or not in the eyes of the jurists, the institution of slavery endured throughout the history of Rome. Even those jurists who advert to the unnaturalness of slavery do not shrink on that account from outlining the legal rules pertaining to it in a perfectly matter-of-fact way. The idea that all men are naturally free and that slavery is contrary to the law of nature is certainly a distinctively Stoic principle. The treatment of this topic by the jurists, however, shows a complete disregard for the institutional implications of adherence to this principle. They accept natural law and natural reason as abstractions relevant to their consideration when they support the institutions which Rome already possesses, either alone or in company with other nations. However, neither natural law nor the practices of the rest of mankind have any normative force if they conflict with the *ius civile*. The civil law in all cases is the criterion of the degree to which natural law or natural reason is admissible in jurisprudential reasoning. There is one point at which a jurist appears to hold that an exception to the civil law can be made because adherence to the pertinent legal formula would be against natural fairness (*contra naturalem aequitatem*). But a dispensation may be made only if the exceptional procedure does not violate the premise which the formula reflects.[52] Even here, consistency with the intention of the civil law is the basis for the exception to it. The civil law in Roman jurisprudence is the judge of natural law, not vice versa.

IV. LEGAL PRINCIPLES IN PRACTICE

In the general definitions of abstract principles which have been considered so far, there are some ideas which may well have been derived from Stoicism. There are also ideas which are patently non-Stoic. The content of these definitions and the ways in which the jurists use them do not lend much weight to the view that Roman jurisprudence had a systematic theory of law, Stoic or otherwise. The most systematic feature of Roman legal thinking to emerge from the passages referred to so far is an adherence to the concrete rules of the civil law just as it stands in preference to the notion that it can be invalidated in any way by allusion to abstract philosophical principles. But general definitions by no means exhaust the relevant information on this point. The occasions on which jurisconsults and legislators actually put terms such as natural law, nat-

---

[51] *Novellae* 89.9.pr., in *Corpus iuris civilis*, 6th ed., ed. R. Schoell and G. Kroll.

[52] *Dig.* 63.4.1.1-2.

ural reason, and humanity to work far outnumber the occasions when they feel called upon to define them. An examination of the uses to which these terms were put in the juristic literature affords a good deal of evidence as to how Roman law employed these conceptions in practice.

The study of the uses to which terms such as natural law, natural reason, and their cognates were put in practice in Roman law was set on a fresh and solid basis by the work of C. A. Maschi in 1937. Against scholars who argued that the idea of natural law had a primarily theoretical importance in Roman jurisprudence and that it had been interpolated into the citations of classical jurists by the compilers of the *Corpus iuris civilis*, Maschi demonstrated that there were clearly classical uses of the terms "natural law" and "natural reason" and that they had a largely down-to-earth meaning. As Maschi has shown, "nature" for the Roman lawyer meant simply "that which is." "Nature" is a statement about the physical and biological universe and about man's physical and psychological constitution as they can be observed to be. Far from being a supra-legal norm, the basis upon which the civil law in force is to be criticized or altered, "nature" is an intra-legal principle, a corollary of the civil law as it is currently defined. "Nature" also has a sub-legal meaning, in which case it is inferior to the civil law as a source of right. "Natural," finally, is also a term used to describe what is self-evident, be it unquestioned social conventions or common-sense possibilities. Maschi's conclusions have received a good deal of support from his fellow juridical scholars,[53] although his work has hitherto been neglected by historians of philosophy. It remains to be seen whether any Stoic influ-

---

[53] Carlo Alberto Maschi, *La cocezione naturalistica del diritto e degli istituti giuridici romani* (Milano, 1937). Forerunners of Maschi in one particular or another include Otto Gradenwitz, "Natur und Sklave bei der naturalis obligatio," *Festgabe der juristichen Facultät zu Königsberg für ihren senior Johann Theodor Schirmer zum 1. August 1900* (Königsberg, 1900), pp. 137-79; Hirzel, *Agraphos nomos*, pp. 14-15; J. de Koschembahr-Lyskowski, *"Naturalis ratio en droit classique romain,"* *Studi in onore di Pietro Bonfante*, ed. E. Albertario et al. (Milano, 1930), *3*, 471-73; Jan Vážný, *"Naturalis obligatio,"* ibid., *4*, 129-80; Vernay, *Servius*, pp. 90-153, 186-89. An outstanding post-Maschi summary of the conclusions of modern research on this subject is Ernst Levy, "Natural Law in Roman Thought," *SDHI, 15* (1949), 1-23. Two more recent summaries are provided by Peter Stein, "The Development of the Notion of *Naturalis Ratio*," *Daube Noster: Essays in Legal History for David Daube*, ed. Alan Watson (Edinburgh, 1974), pp. 305-16 and Watson, *Law in the Making*, pp. 173-77. An even more concise summary is provided by Berger, *Encyclopedic Dictionary of Roman Law*, s. v. "ius naturale," "natura." Scholars reiterating one or more of the points established by Maschi include Arangio-Ruiz, *Istituzioni*, p. 28; Alberto Burdese, "Il concetto di 'ius naturale' nel pensiero della giurisprudenza classica," *Rivista italiana per le scienze giuridiche*, ser. 3:7 (1954), 407-21; *La nozione classica di naturalis obligatio*, Università di Torino, memorie dell'Istituto giuridico, ser. 2:92 (Torino, 1955); Daube, "Impossible Laws," *Natural Law Forum, 12* (1967), 3; Nicholas, *Introduction*, pp. 54 ff.; Voggensperger, *Der Begriff des "Ius naturale"*.

ences are perceptible in the practical applications of the concept of nature in Roman legal thought following Maschi's demythologizing of it.

It would be gratuitous to recapitulate the entire contents of Maschi's book. It will be helpful, however, to illustrate the main points of his thesis with examples drawn from the texts. There are indeed a great many passages in the juristic sources which reflect the idea that "nature" means simply the commonly visible properties of things. These natural characteristics of physical realities are mentioned by the jurisconsults at points where there are legal consequences that flow from them. There is no basic difference between classical and post-classical legal thought on this point. The *Novels* of Theodosius provide one of the clearest definitions of nature in this sense: nature is the universe, the things in it, and the order that it follows; for Justinian, nature is simply the intrinsic character of a thing, be it a practice, a policy, an object, or a circumstance.[54] To be *in rerum natura* is simply to exist, according to the classical jurist Julianus; and for Ulpian what is natural is simply what, in fact, is.[55]

There are certain natural characteristics of inanimate objects or physical processes which have legal implications. In most cases these implications fall under the heading of property rights. By their very nature air, running water, the sea, and the shore it touches are not amenable to private ownership; thus, they are owned in common by all men according to natural law.[56] Rivers by nature may change their courses or may overflow their banks seasonally, thus washing away the soil upstream and making alluvial deposits downstream. Since this is a natural process, Gaius, Pomponius, and Justinian observe, persons whose land is increased by alluvial deposits have a natural claim to the ownership of their new acquisition, while persons whose land is washed away by the action of the river have no legal right to sue for the recovery of their losses.[57] The exact same reasoning applies to land washed away or increased naturally by the action of rainstorms or hailstorms, as Ulpian and Paulus point out.[58]

The physical characteristics of animals are also described as natural and explored in relation to their legal consequences. The jurists agree

---

[54] Theodosius, *Novellae* 3.1.1, 3.1.8 in Clyde Pharr et al., trans., *The Theodosian Code and Novels and the Sirmondian Constitutions*, The Corpus of Roman Law, 1 (Princeton, 1952), pp. 489, 490; *Codex* 4.35.23.pr., 6.51.2a, 6.51.9c, in *Corpus iuris civilis*, 11th ed., ed. P. Krueger; *Nov.* 73.pr., 84.pr., 90.5.1.

[55] *Dig.* 1.5.26, 50.1.6.1.

[56] *Dig.* 1.8.2, 1.8.3; *Inst.* 2.1.pr., 2.1.1.

[57] Gaius, *Inst.* 2.79; *Dig.* 41.1.7.5, 41.1.30.2; *Inst.* 2.1.23; *Cod.* 7.41.1.

[58] *Dig.* 3.1.1, 3.22-23, 39.2.6. For other examples of this type see *Dig.* 41.1.44, 43.20.6, 50.16.38.

that wild animals are naturally free, belonging to nobody in particular in their natal state. Thus, the first person to capture a wild animal acquires ownership of it by natural reason. Should the animal escape and recover its natural freedom, its former owner loses his property rights to it and the animal will belong by natural reason to anyone else who captures it.[59] It is also noted that, since animals are not human beings, they do not by nature have legal capacities or rights, an observation made by Ulpian in explaining that the owner of an animal which is injured by someone else must sue the injurer if he wishes to collect damages, since the animal cannot take legal action itself.[60]

The physical and psychological makeup of man, his actual behavior as it is observed to be rather than his ideal moral possibilities, and the limitations of the human condition are also natural realities with legal consequences. A good deal of attention is paid to man's reproductive nature by the jurists because of its implications for filiation and inheritance rights. It is natural, the jurists tell us, for man to produce his posterity sexually, a procedure in which male and female each play their naturally assigned reproductive roles, twins being natural as well as single births.[61] Natural children are repeatedly defined as those who are generated physically by their parents, in contrast to adopted children; natural bonds are the biological ties which unite parents and children, brothers and sisters, and other blood relatives.[62] Human nature also may refer more broadly to the way people behave, to their emotional as well as their physical needs. The jurists refer, in discussing human nature in this broader sense, to man's liability to disease, man's need to feel that he is being treated kindly, and the fact that one is naturally drawn to love some people and to fear others.[63] Man's professional activities also fall within the category of nature. Navigation is by nature dangerous,

---

[59] Gaius, *Inst.* 2.66–68; *Dig.* 9.2.2.2, 41.1.1.pr, 41.1.1.53, 41.1.3.1–2, 41.1.5.pr., 41.2.5.6; *Inst.* 2.1.12, 2.1.14–16.

[60] *Dig.* 9.1.1.10.

[61] *Dig.* 38.16.3.10; *Inst.* 2.13.5; Theod., *Nov.* 1.4.1.pr., Pharr, p. 498; *Cod.* 5.13.1.5c–d; *Nov.* 2.2.pr.

[62] Gaius, *Inst.* 1.97, 1.104, 2.36, 2.37, 3.2, 3.31, 3.41; Paulus, *Sententiae* 3.46.1; Ulpian, *Tituli* 8.1, 22.14, 28.3, 29.1, in *Fontes iuris romani antejustiniani*, ed. S. Riccobono et al., 3 vols. (Florentiae, 1940–43), 2, 271–72, 286–98, 300, 359; *Dig.* 1.6.5, 1.7.1, 1.7.16, 1.7.17.1, 1.7.31, 1.7.40, 1.8.5, 1.8.10, 2.4.8, 28.6.40, 37.4.6.4, 37.8.1.2, 37.10.4.7, 38.8.1.4, 38.16.1.3, 38.16.1.11, 38.17.2.6, 40.1.19, 45.1.132.pr., 50.1.17–19, 50.16.195.2; *Inst.* 1.6.5, 1.10.3, 1.11.2, 1.11.4, 2.13.4, 3.1.10, 3.1.11–15, 3.10.2; Theod., *Cod.* 16.2.44; *Sirmondian Const.* 10, Pharr, pp. 448, 482; *Cod.* 1.3.19, 6.51.1, 8.47(48).2, 8.47(48).5, 8.47(48).10; *Nov.* 84.1.pr., 89.1, 89.9.

[63] Allan Chester Johnson et al., trans., *Ancient Roman Statutes*, no. 312, The Corpus of Roman Law, 2 (Austin, 1961) p. 245; Theod., *Nov.* 16.1.1, Pharr, p. 501; *Cod.* 1.17.1; *Nov.* 7.2.pr., 39.pr., 44.1.4.

and hence pinning one's hopes on a safe voyage is a gamble;[64] magicians by nature wander from place to place.[65]

The jurists do not confine their interest to the legal consequences of physical and human realities; they also define as natural those consequences which flow from the civil law itself. Both classical and post-classical jurists share this tendency to identify nature with the law of the Roman state. Ulpian gives the opinion that a bad law is no less binding by nature than a good one.[66] For Justinian, Roman law is natural and the laws of other peoples are unnatural to the extent that they conflict with the laws of Rome. On this basis, he notes, he proposes to reform the laws of the Armenians on such matters as dowries and inheritance rights so that nature be not dishonored.[67] The jurists declare various rules of law natural because they are consistent with or are corollaries of the legal conventions of Rome. This approach can be seen in the areas of property rights,[68] personal legal status,[69] the ever-popular fields of marriage, wardship, and inheritance,[70] and a wide assortment of other institutions ranging from usufructs[71] to servitudes[72] to obligations[73] to administrative regulations.[74]

Roman jurists add to this list of natural legal rules a number of moral and social conventions which they hold to be natural as well as being lawful. Theft, for instance, is as naturally offensive to good morals as it is illegal; the right to private property flows from the law of nature.[75] Marital fidelity[76] and filial piety[77] are likewise natural moral and social values which are enshrined in the law. It is also natural, according to the law of the later Empire, to behave in a manner consistent with piety and the precepts of the Christian religion. The pagans, notes the emperor Theodosius, depart from the true religion through their "natural insanity and stubborn insolence;"[78] and for Justinian molesting dead bodies and

---

[64] *Dig.* 6.1.62.
[65] *Cod.* 9.18.6.
[66] *Dig.* 2.2.3.7.
[67] *Nov.* 21.pr., 136.5.
[68] *Dig.* 9.2.50, 41.1.7.7–13, 41.1.9.3, 41.2.1.pr., 41.2.1.1, 43.26.2.2.
[69] Gaius, *Inst.* 1.89; *Dig.* 1.5.24; *Inst.* 3.20.1; *Cod.* 1.3.36(37).1–2; *Nov.* 1.2.1, 58.5, 91.1; *Appendix constitutionum dispersum* 1, in *Corpus iuris civilis, 3,* 796.
[70] *Dig.* 10.2.35, 25.2.1.17, 36.1.49(48), 37.5.1, 38.16.6–7, 45.1.72.pr., 50.17.85; *Inst.* 1.10.pr.; *Cod.* 5.35.3, 6.51.6, 6.51.6a; *Nov.* 22.44.8.
[71] *Inst.* 2.4.2.
[72] *Dig.* 8.3.22.
[73] *Dig.* 41.1.6, 41.8.8.1–2, 50.17.84.
[74] *Nov.* 20.7(7–8).
[75] *Dig.* 47.2.1.3, 50.16.42.
[76] *Dig.* 50.16.42.
[77] *Dig.* 37.15.1.1; Theod., *Nov.* 22.2.12, Pharr, p. 509; *Cod.* 2.41(42).2.
[78] Theod., *Nov.* 3.1.8, Pharr, p. 489.

practicing the vice of luxuriousness are contrary to nature, and, in the latter case, diabolically inspired as well.[79]

If nature means conformity to the civil law and its corollaries, as well as to the moral conventions which the law acknowledges and reinforces, it also means conformity to the intentions behind legal institutions and legal actions. It is naturally reasonable and naturally fair to return goods held for safekeeping in their original condition, to receive the fruits of the land one has cultivated after acquiring it in good faith even if it turns out that one has acquired it from a person who did not have legal title to it, and to possess by right a treasure which one finds in one's own field.[80] It is likewise fair and in accordance with natural law to carry out the intention of a testator in distributing the property to his designated heirs or the intention of an owner in the transfer of his goods to another.[81]

While the Romans clearly identify nature with their own legal system on many occasions, the jurists at the same time see a category of natural reality which is sub-legal and which is a source of rights inferior to those provided by the civil law. A physical reality which the jurists describe as natural and legal in one connection may be described as natural and sub-legal in another, as in the case of the blood ties between parents and children, and other blood relationships. Thus, the law speaks frequently of natural children, so called because they are born out of lawful wedlock. While their physical relationship to their parents is exactly the same as the tie between legitimate children called natural in contradistinction to adopted children, their inheritance rights are substantially different, and inferior. Legitimate children have a natural and a legal right to inherit from their fathers, and adopted children are "naturalized" to share in the same legal inheritance rights as legitimate heirs of the body. Bastards, on the other hand, are deprived of inheritance rights in earlier Roman law, although some rights to inherit were extended to them by imperial legislation. Imperial law also provided for the legitimization of bastards; thus the civil law could annul their natural legal inferiority.[82] At the bottom of the heap are those persons so unfortunate as to have been born of incestuous or other forbidden unions. Since the law regarded incest as both illegal and unnatural, its unhappy fruits were held to be

---

[79] *Nov.* 60.1.pr., 77.1.pr.

[80] *Dig.* 49.15.9.pr.; *Inst.* 2.1.35, 2.1.39.

[81] *Dig.* 45.1.115.2, 47.4.1.1; *Inst.* 2.1.40; *Fragmenta quae dicitur Vaticana* 238, in *Fontes iur. rom. antejust.*, 2, 518.

[82] *Dig.* 1.6.11, 2.4.6, 9.2.33, 17.1.54, 28.6.45; *Inst.* 1.10.13; Theod., *Cod.* 4.6.3–6; Theod., *Nov.* 22.1.3–9, 22.2.11, Pharr, pp. 86–88, 506–07, 509; *Cod.* 5.27, 5.35.3, 6.25.7(6).2, 6.55.5; *Nov.* 18.5, 38.1, 74.pr., 74.1–3, 74.5–6, 79.pr., 79.1–2, 79.4, 79.6–7, 79.9–15. On this point see Daube, "Impossible Laws," *Natural Law Forum*, 12 (1967), 1–84.

neither natural nor legitimate children. These forgotten ones were truly outcasts in Roman law; with respect to their parents they possessed neither natural nor legal rights.[83]

Roman jurisprudence also made it possible for relationships between persons which are natural by blood to be sub-legal even when they spring from legitimate unions. Rome was strongly patriarchal, both legally and socially; relationships that entailed legal rights to succession passed through the male line. Agnates bore a civil relationship while cognates bore a merely natural relationship.[84] Moving away from the field of personal relationships, the jurists also drew a distinction between civil and natural possession in which natural possession is inferior to civil possession. Natural possession may occur, for example, when a person acquires something through the agency of someone under his authority, such as a slave, who does not himself have the right to possess any property by law, although he is allowed to do so customarily. Such possession is natural, not civil, because it is *de facto* but not *de jure*.[85] Then too a natural obligation is sometimes defined in a sub-legal sense. Slaves, for instance, since they are not technically persons at law cannot contract civil obligations, but they can have natural obligations to their masters which adhere to them even if they are manumitted.[86]

We may note, finally, that the juridical texts on some occasions use the term "natural" in a purely logical or even grammatical sense. Ulpian, for instance, feels called upon to define good things as those things which by nature are good,[87] a tautological observation whose sole interest lies in the fact that he derives the noun grammatically from the verb. Justinian explains that he is reforming the law of lapsed bequests because some parts of the law as it currently stands contradict other parts. Such contradictions are contrary to natural reason,[88] logical consistency being a manifest characteristic of nature. In a less trivial vein, the jurists taught that rules which were humanly as well as logically impossible to honor ceased to be binding.[89] The classic example is the will of a father who made a bequest to his daughter on the condition that she marry with the consent of a man whom he names in his will. The man so designated predeceased the testator, who neglected to alter his will before he himself died. Since it was obviously impossible by nature for the daughter to

---

[83] *Cod.* 1.3.44.3; *Nov.* 12.1.
[84] Gaius, *Inst.* 1.156, 1.158; *Dig.* 38.10.4.
[85] *Dig.* 41.1.53, 41.2.24, 41.5.2.1–2, 43.16.9, 43.18.2.
[86] *Dig.* 43.7.14.
[87] *Dig.* 50.16.49.
[88] *Cod.* 6.51.3a.
[89] See, for example, *Dig.* 43.7.1.9, 45.1.137.4, 45.1.137.6.

marry with the consent of a man who was already dead, the condition in her father's will was ruled invalid by the jurists and she inherited the bequest outright. It is in the context of a series of texts dealing with questions of this sort that the jurist Celsus states that what nature forbids, no law can confirm.[90] With the exception of those areas of the law in which nature is regarded as sub-legal, this dictum might well stand as a monument to the literalmindedness and concreteness of the Roman juristic view of nature in practice. As we have seen, the vast majority of meanings which the jurists attribute to nature are banal in the extreme. It was not the business of the law to contravene propositions self-evident to the jurists, whether their self-evidence lay in the realm of physical fact or in the realm of legal, moral, and social conventions whose status as givens in the fabric of reality was equally beyond question.

The very obviousness of the practical applications of the idea of nature in the juristic literature does not provide much scope for the perception of philosophical qualities within them. Outside of revealing the fact that the Romans succumbed to the general temptation to equate one's own legal, moral, and social institutions with the structure of the universe, the main attitude that the jurists exude is one of down-to-earth, common sense empiricism. In dealing with physical nature, whether inanimate, animal, or human, they betray no particular affinities with Stoicism, or with any other philosophical school, for that matter. They do not reflect any professed doctrine about the universe, its structure, or its functions. Rather, they confine themselves to individual phenomena, describing their character in ways too commonplace to excite the interest of a philosopher of nature. There is a good deal of similarity between classical and post-classical jurisprudence on this point, the post-classical era showing no greater propensity for the elaboration of a synthetic physics than does the earlier period. The main differences between the two periods are three in number. Post-classical law, first of all, is more given over to the use of terms such as "natural" in prefatory remarks designed to justify the edicts which follow. Secondly, post-classical law sometimes uses the same definitions but alters the legal consequences flowing from them, as in the granting of wider inheritance rights to "natural" relations, that is to say, to illegitimate and cognatic ones. Finally, post-classical law on occasion identifies "nature" with the precepts of the Christian religion, thus giving its own contemporary slant to the natural piety acknowledged and enjoined throughout the legal literature.

---

[90] *Dig.* 50.17.188.

V. LEGAL REFORMS

A major difference between the law of the Roman Empire and that of the Republic was a tendency on the part of the emperors to alter various legal institutions through their edicts. Such legislative reform, above all in the post-classical period, is another area in which scholars of Roman jurisprudence have seen the hand of Stoic and/or Christian ethics at work. Emperors, it is argued, if not the entire Roman community, were motivated by ethical considerations in their reforming legislation. They sought to make the civil law conform to transcendent moral values. According to the traditional view, this tendency can be seen most clearly in two aspects of post-classical legislation. One is the extensive use of *humanitas, benevolentia,* and related abstract terms as legal criteria. The second is the actual improvement in the legal status of persons whom the earlier law had held as inferior: woman, children under the authority of their fathers, illegitimate children, and slaves. The amelioration of the legal position of these classes of persons, like the introduction of moral values into the legal vocabulary, is viewed as a reflection of the ideological causation explaining all developments in Roman legal history.

It is indeed true that there is a noticeable increase in the incidence of terms such as *humanitas* in the legal literature of the post-classical era, particularly between the fourth and the sixth centuries. A scrutiny of the texts indicates, however, that this usage cannot be ascribed preclusively to any one ideological cause. Nor is *humanitas* always used with reference to a transcendent moral order in any case. The term is used inconsistently and, on the whole, decoratively.

Humanitas is sometimes merely a short-hand term for human nature and its needs. In this connection it refers most usually to the physical and moral limitations which mark the human condition and it is used to justify policies which the emperors institute in their efforts to cope with human weakness. Thus, Theodosius tells us that he is decreeing, out of humanity, that funerary monuments be set up for the edification of his subjects, whose frivolous tendencies he evidently hopes to check by these grim reminders of mortality. Elsewhere Theodosius observes that the law he is enacting is humane in that it imposes a remedy for human fallibility by admonishing potential malefactors and deterring them from crime.[91] The people possess *humanitas* in these examples in their common weaknesses; the emperor possesses *humanitas* in his desire to correct that weakness. *Humanitas* in the latter sense is a way of describing the emperor's will as embodied in the laws he creates. Since *humanitas* flows from the emperor, whatever he decrees can be called humane, and frequently is,

---

[91] Theod., *Cod.* 9.17.6; Theod., *Nov.* 8.1.pr., Pharr, pp. 240, 495.

regardless of its content. The emperor's grants and concessions are called humane, whether they benefit society as a whole, as in the case of provisions for poor relief[92] and the remission of tax delinquencies,[93] or whether they exclusively benefit privileged corporations, secular or religious.[94] The index of the *humanitas* of imperial grants and edicts is not whether they genuinely serve social needs but the fact that they emanate from the emperor's good will.

Humanitas is also used to denote moral virtues which all men should practice, and not just the emperor, whether or not these virtues are institutionalized in the law. In this context, *humanitas* is often seen as a highly desirable but supererogatory virtue. It goes beyond what the law requires; it is voluntary and not enforceable by law because of its extraordinary quality. Consequently, it would be unrealistic to penalize the citizenry for not manifesting it.[95] As a moral virtue, however, *humanitas* is elsewhere made legally obligatory, particularly in cases where it is identified with piety, whether pagan or Christian. At one point Justinian defines *humanitas* as God's love for man; by implication, it is an attribute of the divine nature which mankind is expected to emulate.[96] Theodosius puts himself forth as an exponent of humanity inspired by the divine example by his clemency during the Easter season.[97] Various texts can be cited where humanity is equated with the religious sensibilities instilled by the Christian faith: respect for religion, for consecrated persons, places, and things,[98] as well as with more substantive doctrines such as the value of human life; Justinian prohibits infanticide as inhuman and unChristian alike.[99] The Christian emperors have no monopoly on the identification of *humanitas* with religious values. Julian the Apostate, in his legislation on the subject of priestly duties, cites humanity, love of mankind, and piety as essential virtues to be sought in appointees to the priesthood and indicates that these qualities may be developed by a study of Pythagoreanism, Platonism, Aristotelianism, and Stoicism.[100]

Humanitas also appears in imperial legislation in contexts where it has a more limited institutional significance. Like its fellow abstraction, natural reason, *humanitas* sometimes means little more than consistency with

---

[92] *Cod.* 1.2.12.

[93] Theod., *Nov.* 1.1.pr., Pharr, p. 515.

[94] Theod., *Cod.* 4.2.1, Pharr, pp. 405–06; *Cod.* 1.3.55(57).pr.

[95] Valentinian, *Novellae* 17.1.2; Theod., *Cod.* 7.9.1, Pharr, pp. 550, 168; *Cod.* 3.33.12.1, 4.35.23.pr., 5.12.30.2, 5.27.8.pr., 5.35.3.2, 6.56.5.1, 8.50(51).20.

[96] *Cod.* 1.17.2.pr.

[97] *Sirmondian Const.* 8, Pharr, p. 480.

[98] Theod., *Cod.* 9.25.3, Pharr, p. 246; *Cod.* 1.12.3.2–3, 8.50(51).20.

[99] *Nov.* 153.

[100] Johnson et al., *Ancient Roman Statutes*, no. 308, 314, pp. 243, 246–48.

the intrinsic character of the civil law. Since certain legal rights flow from certain legal institutions, the task of judges is to see to it that the nature and intention of these rights and institutions are respected, especially in cases where failure to observe some technicality of the law is unintentional or not the fault of a litigant. Emperors use *humanitas* in this connection both in directing instructions to magistrates and in referring to their own humane policies.[101] Perhaps the most interesting example of this type of usage, largely as a sign of the times, is a ruling of Theodosius which states that litigants should not be penalized for governmental incompetence and dishonesty. If a document necessary as evidence in a lawsuit is shown to have been forged by a government official, and not by either of the litigants, the judge may suspend the formalities out of *humanitas* and make the judgment that seems fairest to him.[102]

Still another use of *humanitas* is one which suggests a distinctly propagandistic orientation on the part of imperial legislative rhetoric. *Humanitas* occasionally appears as a justification for those policies which accord with the best interests of the state, in particular, its military, fiscal, and administrative needs. Inflationary prices are inhumane, we are told in an edict of Diocletian, the reason being that inflation is bad for the soldiers, who are on fixed salaries.[103] Diocletian shows no interest in the deleterious effects which inflation may be having on less favored elements in the community. The policies which the emperors attempt to embellish by labeling them as humane often show a facile willingness to convert a moral end into a political means. It is humane to codify and emend the laws not because law-abiding citizens may be benefited by legal reform but because it will make it easier to punish criminals; it is humane to reorganize the appellate courts not because this will speed up the settlement of disputes but because it will enable the administration to make do with fewer judges.[104] The emperor Justinian explains without mincing words that the reason why the law should be adminstered humanely, tempering justice with mercy, is that this policy in the long run will keep the people quiet more effectively than will a policy of harshness.[105] Theodosius agrees with Justinian's utilitarian approach. He is equally blunt in treating *humanitas* as a calculated strategy for buying political support from the restive populace. With regard to the unmanageable provincials, he observes, "the more humanity is shown them, the more is love of loyal

---

[101] *Dig.* 2.14.8, 13.7.6.1; Theod., *Cod.* 9.19.4; Theod., *Nov.* 11.1.1, Pharr, pp. 241, 497; *Cod.* 1.3.52(53).12, 1.12.6.9, 1.24; *Nov.* 159.pr.

[102] Theod., *Cod.* 9.19.4, Pharr, p. 241.

[103] Johnson et al., *Ancient Roman Statutes*, no. 299, pp. 335–37.

[104] *Cod.* 1.14.9; *Nov.* 23.4.

[105] *Nov.* 30.11.

devotion incumbent upon them."[106] *Humanitas* is also the gratitude which the citizens are expected to feel toward an emperor who takes pressure off their pocketbooks.[107] It is clear from these examples of *humanitas* used to dignify what is essentially a political quid pro quo that it is necessary to examine the use of the term in its context, and not merely its statistical incidence, in order to sense the real degree to which it has a transcendent moral meaning in the law.

A final, and extensive, use of *humanitas* in imperial legislation is as a rationale for changes in the law which extended the rights of certain persons beyond their previous limits. In evaluating the degree to which *humanitas* is used in this context in a decorative or a substantive manner, one has to consider the historical reasons why emperors at certain points in time may have found it desirable to extend these rights. Was an emperor responding to a flash of moral enlightenment vouchsafed in his reign but not before, or was he responding to some social need? One area in which imperial reform is very noticeable is the area of inheritance rights. Emperors frequently cite *humanitas* as the motive for new laws enabling illegitimate children to inherit under certain circumstances, laws permitting children born of servile unions to inherit, and laws permitting inheritance through the cognatic as well as the agnatic line.[108] It is fully possible that this desire to extend inheritance rights reflects more than just imperial generosity. In the light of the social and political climate of the late Empire, it may well have seemed prudent to maintain succession to the large landed estates by these devices, rather than allowing the fortunes which enabled them to function to disintegrate through lack of heirs. The villa owners played a vital economic and administrative role in the life of the Empire which no one else had the resources to play. It would have been contrary to the interests of the state had this class been allowed to die out.

Another institution which is frequently linked to *humanitas* in imperial legislation is slavery. While slavery remained fully lawful throughout Roman history, despite what Stoic sages might have had to say about it, there is a marked tendency on the part of the later emperors to enact laws facilitating the manumission of slaves and limiting the master's power over his slaves.[109] The power of the master over his slaves had

---

[106] Theod., *Nov.* 37.1.pr., Pharr, p. 538.

[107] Theod., *Cod.* 11.7.3, Pharr, p. 299.

[108] See, for example, *Inst.* 3.6.10; Theod., *Nov.* 14.1.7, Pharr, p. 499.

[109] On slavery in Roman history see especially R. H. Barrow, *Slavery in the Roman Empire* (London, 1928); Marc Bloch, "Comment et pourquoi finit l'esclavage antique," in M. I. Finley, ed., *Slavery in Classical Antiquity: Views and Controversies* (Cambridge, 1960), pp. 204–18; W. W. Buckland, *The Roman Law of Slavery: The Condition of the Slave in Private Law from Augustus to Justinian* (Cambridge, 1908); A. H. M. Jones, "Slavery in the Ancient

been absolute in Republican law, but from the first through the sixth centuries A.D. a significant number of limitations were placed on the master's right to mistreat his slaves, to harm them physically, to punish them, and to kill them. Manumission was also practiced extensively in the later Empire, and procedural reforms instituted by the emperors made it progressively much easier to accomplish. The emperors repeatedly advert to *humanitas* in explaining why they are making these enactments pertaining to slavery.[110] At the same time there were telling practical reasons for these developments, a conclusion which a brief glance at the patterns of slave use in relation to the economic and political history of Rome makes inescapable.

The main source of slaves in the Republican period was imperial expansion. Captives from the thickly populated Mediterranean world poured into Rome. The supply of slaves was huge and their price was low. Wealthy landowners who ran their villas on the basis of slave labor found it practical to purchase fully grown slaves, to work them as hard as possible, and then to replace them. The initial capital investment in the slave labor force and the need to replace the slaves periodically was less costly than it would have been to breed slaves and to raise them from infancy. Furthermore, if one were to breed a healthy slave stock it would be necessary to purchase more female slaves than were needed for the work of the villa and to provide slaves with a costlier quality of food, shelter, and care. Since slaves were cheap and plentiful it was more feasible economically to get as much work as possible out of an adult slave and then to replace him.

By the first century A.D. the territorial boundaries of the Roman Empire had been stabilized. The Romans fought fewer aggressive wars after this time. Such new territory as they absorbed was thinly populated. While capture had been the primary source of slaves in Republican times, most of the slaves in Rome now acquired their servile status in other ways. Having been born of a slave mother was the most common means

---

World," in Finley, *Slavery*, pp. 8-15. Also useful are J. P. V. D. Balsdon, *Life and Leisure in Ancient Rome* (New York, 1969), pp. 109-10; Arthur E. R. Boak, *Manpower Shortage and the Fall of the Roman Empire in the West*, Jerome Lectures, 3rd ser. (Ann Arbor, 1955), pp. 17, 32-33; P. A. Brunt, *Italian Manpower, 225 B.C.-A.D. 14* (Oxford, 1971), p. 124; A. H. M. Jones, *The Decline of the Ancient World* (New York, 1966), pp. 296-98, 307-09; Adolphe Landry, "Quelques aperçus concernant la dépopulation dans l'antiquité gréco-romain," *Revue historique, 177* (1936), 4-5, 7; Alan Watson, *The Law of Persons in the Later Roman Republic* (Oxford, 1967), pp. 159-72; *Roman Private Law around 200 B.C.* (Edinburgh, 1971), pp. 43-47. Among the handful of juristic scholars who have attempted to view slavery in an economic and political context are Albertario, "I fattori," *SDHI, 1* (1935), 10-11; Bonfante, *Storia del diritto romano, 2,* 3-5; Jonkers, "De l'influence du christianisme," *Mnemosyne,* ser. 3:1 (1933-34), 241-80; Nocera, *Jus naturale,* pp. 69-71.

[110] See, for example, *Inst.* 1.6.1, 2.7.4.

of enslavement. Others were the penal servitude meted out to political prisoners and to *humiliores* convicted of serious crimes, the taking of exposed children as slaves by those who found them, and the selling of one's child or even of oneself into slavery. Despite these variegated means of enslavement, the slave population grew much smaller during the Principate than it had been during the Republic, and the price of slaves climbed dramatically. It ceased to be profitable to buy slaves in large numbers, work them to death or exhaustion, and then replace them. Since slaves were becoming scarcer, they were also becoming more valuable not only as an initial investment but as a continuing investment. The large *latifundia* which had become the dominant mode of organizing agriculture were geared to their use; it was impossible to revert to the small free farmer as the basic unit of agrarian labor. At this point it became logical to treat slaves less harshly and to start protecting them by law against cruelty on the part of their masters. The objective was to maintain the vigor of the agrarian labor force, since agriculture was the foundation of the Roman economy. The slave still remained the private property of his owner, but limits on the owner's power over his slaves were seen as consistent with the common good, as Justinian remarks in reinforcing the second-century laws of Antoninus Pius on this subject, "this rule is just, for it is a matter of public concern that no one should make evil use of his property."[111]

Outside of the inescapable importance of agriculture to the health of the Roman economy, there was yet another practical reason why the Romans were moved to accord to slaves a limited recognition as persons as the Republic gave way to the Principate. A great many of the slaves who were imported from the Mediterranean world at this time had commercial skills which the Romans had not bothered to develop so extensively. Roman slaveowners rapidly saw the advantages of using slaves as agents for all kinds of business operations. Slaves served as shopkeepers, merchants or factors in the wholesale trade, brokers, accountants, shipping agents, bankers, bailiffs, and secretaries to their masters. For these purposes it was necessary to accord them the legal capacity to transact business in the name of their masters, and it was practical to let them have a *peculium*, or fund of money, which, while technically belonging to the master just as the slave himself did, gave the slave the financial flexibility he needed to transact the business he was charged with conducting on his master's behalf. The existence of the *peculium* made third parties more willing to deal with slave agents. Although the master remained liable for the slave's actions, the *peculium* was a guarantee of the slave's

---

[111] *Inst.* 1.8.1.

good faith. The *peculium* would not have endured as an institution unless the slaves to whom it was granted showed themselves to be reliable and trustworthy in the business committed to their charge.

A slave with a *peculium* could speculate with it, if it was not otherwise engaged, and could buy his freedom with the profits he made. The more usual means by which slaves acquired freedom was manumission. Slaves were manumitted for all kinds of reasons. It is important to note that when a slave was manumitted during the Roman Empire he did not automatically receive complete legal freedom from his master. Various obligations and *opera* were demanded of the freedman, and he might be granted a more or less dependent position with respect to his former master in the act of manumission. In some cases, no doubt, piety or affection or gratitude toward the slave was the inspiration for emancipating him on the part of his master. The desire to buy a posterity to mourn him was sometimes the motive of a master's deathbed manumissions. Sometimes a slave was freed so that he could be made his master's heir, or with a view to making possible a legal marriage with a slave. Being a hard-headed people, the Romans also manumitted slaves if they became too expensive to keep, bearing in mind that the ex-slave still owed many services to his former owner and his heirs. The master who freed his slaves in such a situation could thus enjoy the best of both worlds: the devoted service during his lifetime of slaves who knew that they stood to benefit by his testament, the satisfaction of enabling his heirs to enjoy the services of his grateful freedman, and the warm feeling of having done a good deed.

While there was an increased tendency toward manumission in the later Empire, this tendency cannot be described as a curve going ever upward. The manumission rate in the reign of Augustus, at the very beginning of the Principate, was extremely high. The curve then sinks in the post-Augustan age, and starts to rise again dramatically from the third century onward. In understanding the reasons for these ups and downs, the theory of ideological causation is not very helpful. If Christianity was what inspired manumission, why was the manumission rate so high in the first century B.C.-A.D., when the Christian religion had just been born and well before it had attracted a substantial number of propertied converts to the fold? Why should non-Christian emperors have encouraged manumission and the better treatment of slaves later in the Imperial era? If Stoicism is seen as the cause, it is impossible to explain convincingly why Stoicism should have been influential at the beginning and the end of the Roman Empire, but not in the middle. A much more plausible explanation of the manumission curve in the Roman Empire can be found by looking at economic and political realities.

The first question to be considered is why so many Romans manumitted slaves during the late Republic and the early Augustan period
and why manumission fell off after the reign of Augustus. The answer to
this question can be seen in the rich source of captives available at this
time and in the policy of Augustus himself. For most large slaveowners
the first century B.C. was a period of easy come, easy go. They did not
hesitate to manumit slaves who had outlived their usefulness since it was
easy to replace them. Augustus objected to this ready manumission. He
was the author of a number of edicts on a variety of apparently unrelated
subjects which, when looked at together, reveal a consistent social policy.[112] Aware of the fact that Rome was the mistress of a vast multi-ethnic
empire, he wanted to make sure that Roman citizens of Latin stock remained the predominant social element within it. He did not wish to see
Roman citizenship diluted through the emancipation and enfranchise-
ment of slaves from other parts of the empire. Augustus also wanted to
build up the senatorial class, which had declined in numbers as a result
of the civil wars of the late Republican period. He opposed the dilapi-
dation of the estates that gave this class its status, a process which was
occurring through legacies bequeathed to freedmen. Augustus therefore
restricted the number of manumissions that it was legal to make and also
imposed a tax of 5% of a slave's value to be paid by his ex-master, in
order to discourage manumission and at the same time to profit from
what there was of it. Augustus also instituted the principle that a freedman had certain duties and obligations with respect to his former master.
As a result of Augustus' legislation, then, it was no longer lawful to manumit slaves *ad libitum*, and a social and legal distance was preserved between the free-born citizen and the freedman.

The imperial legislation of the later Empire, which loosened Augustus'
restrictions on manumission, was a response to the fact that slavery as an
economic institution was no longer viable. In addition to the drying up
of the supply of slaves, the decline in numbers of the slave population,
and the increased price of slaves, the villa owners of the late Empire were
faced by the host of economic problems immortalized under the title of
"The Fall of Rome" in every elementary textbook of European history.
On the one hand they were confronted by the scarcity and high price of
slaves. On the other hand, rampant inflation and the ever-increasing
burdens of imperial taxation ate away at their resources, which were
frozen in agricultural assets that could not be expanded to meet their

---

[112] On Augustus' social policy as it pertains to slaves see Barrow, *Slavery*, pp. 179–82;
Landry, "Quelques aperçus," *R. historique*, *177* (1936), 11–12; Hugh Last, "The Social
Policy of Augustus," *Cambridge Ancient History*, *10*, 429–34.

rising economic needs. The results, for the landowners, are well known. Smaller landholders went bankrupt and sank to the class of *coloni,* forced to become the semi-free tenants of their wealthier neighbors. The larger landowners found that it was more profitable to upgrade their slaves to the status of semi-free tenants, resembling that of the *coloni,* than to keep them as slaves. In this way the villa owner could still get the labor performed on his estates while no longer having to bear either the initial and recurrent capital investment in slaves or the expenses for their food, clothing, and housing. The decline of slavery in the later Roman Empire was a spontaneous response to the economic conditions of the period. It was paralleled by the spontaneous rise of a semi-free, semi-servile labor force which was its economic and social surrogate. It is just as difficult to argue that the upgrading of slaves which occurred at this time was an expression of Stoic humanitarianism as it is to argue that the proto-serf was, in a real sense, any more autonomous than the slave had been. An instructive analogy has been drawn between the trend toward manumission in the later Empire and the extension of citizenship to all freemen in the third century. In both cases a right was made available whose advantages were more apparent than real thanks to the imperial absolutism and fiscal oppression which accompanied them.[113]

There are two other categories of persons whose legal rights were enhanced during the course of Roman legal history, women and sons under the control of their fathers. In both cases, the greater measure of freedom which they came to enjoy has been attributed to Stoic humanitarianism or egalitarianism, although, unlike the laws on slavery, the legislation and jurisprudence on the subjects of female and filial rights do not employ philosophical terminology. In order to appreciate the significance of these changes it will be useful to outline some features of the late Republican law concerning the family and marriage.[114]

Rome was a strongly patriarchal society, and the Republican law vested virtually unrestricted power over his children in the *paterfamilias.* His *patria potestas* was exercised over all the children he might have, either by birth or adoption. The *paterfamilias* had the power of life and death over his children, the right to sell them into slavery, the right to betroth, marry, and divorce them. He also had legal ownership over any property in the possession of children who were under his authority. Persons subjected to *patria potestas* were *alieni iuris*; they were not free agents at law and had no right to the legal ownership of their own property. The

---

[113] Nocera, *Jus naturale,* pp. 69–70.

[114] A concise and up-to-date treatment is provided by Watson, *Law of Persons,* pp. 19–69, 77–98, 147–54; *Roman Private Law,* pp. 17–33, 39–41. On marriage see also Percy Ellwood Corbett, *The Roman Law of Marriage* (Oxford, 1930), ch. 3–5.

authority of the male head of the family did not terminate when his sons reached their majority. It lasted ordinarily until the death of the *paterfamilias*, although there were several ways in which it could be terminated voluntarily by him. A *filiusfamilias*, however, might be fully adult, a married man with his own children, and even an important officer of state, while still remaining under the control of his *paterfamilias* in all matters of private law. It was customary to give a son *alieni iuris* a *peculium* analogous to that of a slave. This property remained within the legal ownership of the *paterfamilias*. It could be used by the son, but the right to dispose of it by gift or testament remained in the father's hands.

This lack of independence on the part of the *filiusfamilias* does not seem to have been regarded as oppressive by the Romans, since it persisted in most respects until the end of Roman history. There were two features of *patria potestas*, however, which did undergo significant change between the end of the Republic and the later Empire. One was the institution of the *peculium* and the other was the life and death power of the *paterfamilias* over his children.

In early classical law the principle of the *peculium castrense* was developed. This was the *peculium* of a *filiusfamilias* who was a member of the armed forces. His property and any wealth he might acquire through his military service could now be disposed of freely by him without his father's approval, although the *peculium* still remained technically his father's legal property. In the later Empire an analogous institution, the *peculium quasi-castrense*, was developed for sons in the civil service. It is difficult to regard the limited recognition of property rights to sons who were functionaries in the army and the civil bureaucracy as a new general recognition of the moral equality of descendants and ascendants. The rights involved in the *peculium castrense* and *quasi-castrense*, such as they were, applied only to sons in two particular careers, not to all sons under *patria potestas*. Furthermore, even those men who enjoyed the right to the *peculium castrense* or *quasi-castrense* in the light of their professions remained under *patria potestas* in all other respects. Rather than being a recognition of the full legal personhood of sons under *patria potestas*, the institution of the *peculium castrense* and *quasi-castrense* was a perfectly transparent effort on the part of the emperors to encourage members of the propertied classes to enter and to remain in the service of the state as military and civil officials. The *peculium castrense* was instituted at the end of a period of civil wars which had decimated the upper classes from which the army officer corps was drawn; and while all male citizens had the duty to serve for a time in the army, the officer corps was composed of men who made it a voluntary career choice. The early Principate was also an era when the glamorous wars of conquest were giving way to the less lucrative and publicity-fraught defense of the frontiers. It was thought necessary, therefore, to make permanent careers of military service more attractive. The *peculium quasi-castrense* was instituted in a period when recruits to the civil service were less numerous, not merely because of the demographic attrition of the upper classes, as well as all other classes in the later Empire, but because of the demoralization and unwillingness to serve on the part of the aristocrats who were the backbone of the imperial bureaucracy. The upper classes did the work of implementing the law and executing the emperor's policies, but they received in return only an ever-lessening role in actual decision making and an ever-increasing burden of taxation. It was thus not a humanitarian revulsion against the subordinate position of the *filiusfamilias* but the need to make civil and military service more appealing which inspired the granting of these new property rights.[115]

It is much more likely, on the other hand, that the termination of the father's life and death power over his children reflects the impact of more genuine moral feelings. While it may be argued that the prohibition of the exposure of unwanted infants was a feature of the demographic policy of the later emperors, who were waging a losing battle against the decline of the population, their opposition to infanticide on moral and religious grounds seems to be clearly indicated. In classical law, infants, even those still in the womb, were regarded as existing *in rerum natura* and as having legal rights in most branches of the civil law.[116] One might see the new definition of infanticide as homicide as a logical extension of that principle. If so, it was a corollary of the civil law which did not occur to the Romans until the later Empire. When the emperors do get around to prohibiting infanticide, they expressly condemn it as unnatural and un-Christian, as an edict on this subject by Justinian, cited above, illustrates. While it is possible that the demographic problems of the later Empire may have served as a catalyst to the emperors' Christian enlightenment in this connection, there would seem to be no basis for attributing the prohibition of infanticide to Stoicism, which, unlike Christianity, was a constant potential influence throughout the history of Roman family law.

In the case of the Roman law of marriage what is at issue is the shift from one form of marriage to another and the alteration of the married woman's rights to manage her own property. In both cases the significant changes occurred in the late Republican period or in the reign of Augustus, too early to make Christianity a possible cause. The changes in-

---

[115] Virtually the only legal scholars who have connected the *peculium castrense* with the military needs of the early Empire are Arangio-Ruiz, *Istituzioni*, pp. 476-77; Crook, *Life and Law of Rome*, p. 111; and Schulz, *Classical Roman Law*, p. 154.

[116] *Dig.* 1.5.26.

volved have, instead, been assigned to a new enlightened awareness of sexual equality stemming from the Stoic philosophy.

In the Roman Republic there were two forms of marriage, marriage *cum manu*, which placed the wife entirely under her husband's legal control, and marriage *sine manu*, which did not. The husband might acquire *manus* by one of three ways: *confarreatio*, *coemptio*, and *usus*. *Confarreatio* was a religious ceremony involving the sacrifice of a cake, the *farreus panis* which gave its name to the rite. The sacrifice was made to Jupiter in the presence of ten witnesses as well as the *flamen dialis* and *pontifex maximus*, the priest of Jupiter and the high priest. Certain ritual words had to be spoken to effect the marriage. *Confarreatio* was a form of marriage necessary for certain priests and it was confined in practice if not in law to patricians. *Coemptio* was the transfer of the bride to the bridegroom by means of a fictitious sale. It was probably a survival of the earlier practice of actually selling the bride to her husband. *Manus* was acquired by *usus* simply through the cohabitation of husband and wife for one year. It was very easy to avoid *manus* by *usus* since it could not be established if the wife absented herself for three days and nights before the year was up. With regard to property and inheritance rights, the status of a wife *in manu* was exactly analogous to that of a female descendant of her husband under *patria potestas*; her marriage transferred her legally as well as ritually from her father's family to her husband's family, and she inherited from her husband and not from her father.

A woman might also be married *sine manu* in Republican law. A marriage *sine manu* required no special formalities and no sanction by any kind of public official to be valid. It was customary for the bride to be led to her husband's house, but the omission of this ceremony in no sense invalidated the marriage; a marriage *sine manu* could even take place when the couple were *in absentia*. The legal status of a wife in a marriage *sine manu*, with respect to property and inheritance rights, was either that of a *filiafamilias* in the household of her own father or that of a woman *sui iuris* with a *tutor* or legal guardian, depending on whether or not she had been under *patria potestas* before her marriage. In other words, a marriage *sine manu* did not alter the legal status with regard to property rights which the bride had possessed before her marriage. She remained a member of her paternal family by law.

The rights of the concerned parties to create and to terminate a marriage depended to some extent on whether the marriage were *cum manu* or *sine manu*. In either case the marriage could take place only with the consent of the *patresfamiliarum* if both the bridegroom and bride were *alieni iuris*. The bridegroom's consent was also necessary in either form of marriage, whether he was *alieni iuris* or *sui iuris*. If the bride were *alieni iuris* she could be married in either form of marriage without her consent. The bride's consent was necessary only if she were *sui iuris*, but in this event she needed the consent of her *tutor* to contract a marriage *cum manu*. Her *tutor*'s consent was not needed for a marriage *sine manu*, since her property rights were not altered in this case. In either form of marriage, the husband and his *paterfamilias*, if he were *alieni iuris*, had the right to initiate divorce. Either the father or the son could initiate the divorce against the will of the other, the crucial factor appearing to have been the first call. Neither the wife nor her *paterfamilias* could initiate divorce in a marriage *cum manu*. However, in a marriage *sine manu*, the wife could initiate divorce if she were *sui iuris*. If she were a *filiafamilias* her father could initiate divorce against her will, although the reverse was not the case as far as one can tell. In a marriage *cum manu* a divorce required a ceremony reversing the mode by which *manus* had been acquired in the first place. No formalities were required for divorce in a marriage *sine manu*, although it was customary for the party who had initiated the divorce to utter the phrase *"res tuas tibi habeto"* to the spouse who was being divorced. It was very easy to split up a household when a marriage *sine manu* was terminated by divorce, since the property of the spouses had been kept separate by law during the course of the marriage. It was unnecessary to give grounds for a divorce in a marriage *sine manu*. The marriage could be terminated by one side or the other or by mutual consent, without showing cause, although it was to the advantage of the husband with regard to his legal claims to his wife's dowry if he could prove infidelity on her part.

In the later Republic, marriage *sine manu* tended to replace marriage *cum manu*. It is argued that this development reflects a more egalitarian view of women, inspired by Stoicism. Scholars have made this point who at the same time recognize that the legal inferiority of women is still quite apparent in marriage *sine manu*.[117] The wife can still be married and divorced against her will. She remains legally just as dependent on her *pater* or *tutor* as she had been before her marriage. It is thus difficult to see any great leap forward toward the legal autonomy of women in marriage *sine manu*. If a shift in the moral attitude toward women is not the explanation for the growing popularity of marriage *sine manu* in the late Republic, what is? The answer is manifest to anyone who casts a glance at the social and political history of the late Republic.[118] It was

---

[117] See, for example, Guibal, *De l'influence de la philos.*, pp. 135-55; Laferrière, "De l'influence du stoïcisme," *Compte-Rendu de l'Acad. des sciences morales et politiques* (1860), pp. 46-55; Schulz, *Classical Roman Law*, pp. 103 ff., 117; *Principles of Roman Law*, pp. 192-97.

[118] See on this subject Balsdon, *Life and Leisure*, p. 87; *Roman Women*, (London, 1962), pp. 47, 216-17; Ronald Syme, *The Roman Revolution*, 2nd ed. (Oxford, 1960), ch. 2; pp.

an era of incessant civil war. Marriage was an essential means by which the aristocrats cemented together and realigned their political parties. The divorce rate, unsurprisingly, rose considerably in the last century of the Republic. Since they used marriage and divorce as instruments of policy, the political dynasts of this period preferred that form of marriage which gave them the maximum maneuverability. Marriage *sine manu* required no formalities to contract or to terminate. Each of the two fathers-in-law had an equal right to terminate the marriage when it ceased to be useful; and, since the property of the spouses remained separate, the wife staying under the control of her *paterfamilias* or *tutor*, the household could be split up without any inconvenient losses of property on either side. The spouses were pawns on the chessboard of Republican politics. A great many of the important men of the late Republican period married and divorced repeatedly in their efforts to gain a yet more advantageous social and political position in the contest. It is this situation, and not any new philosophical perceptions about the dignity of women, which explains the decline of marriage *cum manu* and the popularity of marriage *sine manu* in the late Republic.

The second change pertaining to the legal status of women which has frequently been seen as a recognition of Stoic sexual egalitarianism on the part of the Romans is the limitation of a woman's dependence on her *tutor* in the handling of her own property. An important change in this field of the law was instituted by Augustus, who made noteworthy inroads into the previous rules. The Republican law regarding *tutela mulierum* had been clear, unambiguous, and, from the point of view of egalitarianism, deplorable.[119] All women at any time of their lives were regarded as legally incompetent. If they were not under *patria potestas* or the *manus* of their husbands, they had to have a *tutor* to supervise their business activities. The only women exempted from this rule were the Vestal Virgins. *Tutors* were appointed for women in many of the same ways in which they were appointed for other legal incompetents, such as minors, prodigals, and lunatics. The main difference between *tutela mulierum* and these other forms of legal tutelage is that it was permanent. Minors could cast off tutelage when they reached their majority; prodigals might do so if they mended their ways; and lunatics were allowed

---

12, 20, 33, 34, 40, 43, 64, 69, 84, 112, 189, 340-41, 345, 373, 376, 377-79, 424, 492, 500; Lily Ross Taylor, *Party Politics in the Age of Caesar*, Sather Classical Lectures, 22 (Berkeley, 1949), passim and esp. pp. 33-34. The only legal scholars to have noted the connection between contemporary politics and the growing popularity of marriage *sine manu* are Crook, *Law and Life at Rome*, pp. 104-06, 108; and Schulz, *Classical Roman Law*, p. 133.

[119] See on this subject Watson, *Law of Persons*, pp. 106-11, 146-58; *Roman Private Law*, pp. 35-41.

to manage their own affairs in their moments of lucidity. Women, however, were regarded by Republican law as legally incompetent from birth to death. A woman's *tutor* exercised extensive control over his ward. His consent was needed for any legal action that could diminish her patrimony. The woman could not make a binding stipulation, mancipation, manumission, or will without her tutor's consent. His consent was also necessary for her to enter a marriage *cum manu*, since this would transfer the right to control her property to her husband. Indeed, any diminution of his ward's civil rights, the most usual form of which was marriage *cum manu*, required his consent. A woman under *tutela mulierum* was called *sui iuris* in Roman law, a euphemism as it applies to a status which is clearly not autonomous.

Major changes in the institution of *tutela mulierum* set in during the early Principate. Agnatic *tutela* was abolished and women were given much broader rights to choose their own *tutors*. But the most significant change was the one decreed by Augustus. Augustus devoted a good deal of legislative attention to matrimony. His most extensive decree on this subject was the *Lex Papia Poppaea* of A.D. 9, which states that a matron will henceforth be freed from *tutela mulierum* if she is the mother of three children, or four children if she is a freedwoman. While it has been hailed as a major step in the direction of sexual equality before the law, Augustus' policy is far more comprehensible within the context of his social legislation as a whole. Augustus' goal in a great deal of his social legislation was to stimulate the birth rate, especially among the upper classes of the Latin stock, a motivation which has been as crystal clear to modern historians of his reign[120] as it was to his contemporaries.[121]

The objective of Augustus was to counteract the trend toward the dying out of upper-class families which had characterized the late Republican era. The civil wars had taken their toll for generations. It was also increasingly more expensive to bear the costs of public life in the first century B.C. Another financial drain was the practice of leaving large bequests to one's friends. A certain economic level was necessary for the enjoyment of the status of patrician, with the political rights it entailed. Members of this class wished to insure the transmission of these rights to their children. Their marital behavior reflects the deliberate attempt to limit the number of their offspring in order to guarantee this result. A

---

[120] See on this point Balsdon, *Life and Leisure*, pp. 82–87; *Roman Women*, pp. 76–79; Last, "Social Policy of Augustus," *CAH*, *10*, 437–56; Syme, *Roman Revolution*, pp. 44–45, 452, 498. The only juristic scholar to have noted the connection between Augustus' social policy and his relaxation of the law of *tutela mulierum* is Crook, *Law and Life of Rome*, p. 115.

[121] Balsdon, *Roman Women*, p. 79.

good many late Republican aristocrats were reluctant to marry at all, an attitude castigated as early as 131 B.C. by the Censor Metellus Macedonius. Those who did marry sought to limit the size of their families. It was unusual for an upper-class family of the first century B.C. to have more than two or three children. One fool-proof method of population control was the exposure of unwanted children, a right which the *paterfamilias* possessed absolutely at this time. Abortion may well have been practiced as well as contraception, although it is difficult to know with what success. Contemporary medical authorities listed various recipes for contraceptives, all of which are scientifically ineffective, and did not distinguish between contraceptives and abortifacients. Whatever methods were employed to limit family size, they achieved the desired results. Noble families regularly died out through lack of heirs, and the *novi homines* who filled their places, faced with the same conditions, followed suit. Some childless families that wished to perpetuate themselves did so through adoption. If they followed this route, they tended to adopt boys and they waited until their adoptive son had reached puberty before adding him to the family. In this way they could avoid the costs and hazards of raising children from infancy as well as picking the kind of son they wanted.

Now Augustus took a firm stand against the reproductive parsimony of the patrician class. He wished to regenerate this group for he wished to make it the most important social and political element in his regime. Augustus castigated the upper classes for not having more children in a speech to the senate which reiterated the exhortations of Metellus Macedonius. More concretely, he enacted a series of laws to encourage this end, of which the *Lex Papia Poppaea* is only one salient example. Augustus' first step was to encourage marriage itself. He prohibited fathers from placing vexatious obstructions in the path of children who wanted to marry and he removed some of the legal obstacles to marriage that had existed before. He also encouraged marriage by penalizing bachelors, spinsters, widows, and widowers. Marriage became a legal duty for men between the ages of twenty-five and sixty and for women between the ages of twenty and fifty. Single persons within these age limits had to pay a special tax. He also decreed that both spouses in a new marriage had to be within these age limits on pain of forfeiture of the wife's dowry to the state after the husband's death, in order to obviate marriages in which one spouse was too old to have children. People who had no children were deprived of certain inheritance rights up to the age of sixty, for men, and fifty, for women. Augustus made it politically as well as economically advantageous for patricians to bear children. Public offices were filled by members of this class, and philoprogenitive fathers were given preference in the staffing of both elective and appointive offices. If there were a tie vote for an elective office, the candidate with the most children would be returned. The seniority of the consuls was fixed on the same basis. Men with children were given preference in appointments to provincial governorships, and were allowed to stand for offices before the minimum age limit by as many years as they had children. The overall tenor of this legislation is impossible to misconstrue. So was the need for it, in Augustus' estimation. An unmistakable index of that need was the fact that the consuls during whose term his most far-reaching demographic ordinance was passed, Papius and Poppaeus, were both bachelors. They thus enjoy the unique distinction of having been part of the problem and part of the solution at the same time.

The conditional removal of *tutela mulierum* by Augustus was therefore merely one facet of an elaborate policy which aimed at enlarging the birth rate among the propertied classes, who stood most to benefit from his legislative package. It would certainly be difficult to interpret his ruling on *tutela mulierum* as a recognition of sexual equality, for it does not pertain to all women, nor even to those who might plausibly be expected to have the most practical business sense. If women as a class, or women of a certain age, are competent to handle their own legal affairs, this capacity has no logical connection with their sex lives. As a social strategy, the *Lex Papia Poppaea*, like other features of Augustus' demographic legislation, appears to have been a failure. A large number of emperors after Augustus, including Tiberius, Claudius, Nero, Vespasian, Hadrian, the Antonines, and the Severi, found it desirable to reinforce his ordinances on this subject, but upper-class families continued to breed themselves into extinction with depressing regularity throughout the history of the Roman Empire.

Our consideration of the reforms which took place in late Republican and Imperial law has shown that the thesis of Stoic inspiration cannot be seriously maintained. In a few cases, there are traces of Christian concern, as in the prohibition of infanticide. The use of philosophical language in the prefatory justifications for legal enactments bears little or no organic relationship to the content of the enactments themselves. On the other hand, the improvements ordained in the legal status of persons in a dependent and inferior position can in all cases be correlated with well known political, social, and economic conditions, which account for their timing as well as their content. One cannot sustain the view that the reforms of the emperors reflect a systematic effort to Stoicize Roman society. While the emperors did show concern for social welfare, their response to human suffering was a stop-gap and superficial effort to alleviate the symptoms of social problems. They never envisioned a reform of basic institutions which might uproot the problems at their sources. While discoursing freely about humanity and equity in connection with policies of all kinds, whether related to these ideals or not, the emperors also showed a great deal of insensitivity to these same ideals in the way they reacted to the institutions which they inherited and did not abolish and in the new laws which they enacted themselves. It never occurred to them, for instance, to regard judicial torture as inhumane. They never abolished as inequitable the criminal law which condemned *humiliores* to penal servitude in the imperial mines for the exact same crimes which merely banished *honestiores* to islands in the Mediterranean. They did not regard the progressive regimentation of their subjects, which fills the codes of the later emperors, as incompatible with human dignity. Their test for whether a law should be abolished, retained, or enacted was not its conformity with the moral values of Stoicism but its conformity with the interests of the state.

VI. CONCLUSION

The investigation of the extent of Stoic influence in Roman law which has concerned us in the preceding pages has led us, in effect, to end this book on a somewhat negative note. The main contribution to the history of the Stoic tradition which this chapter can hope to make is to lay to rest at long last the widespread but unsubstantiated myth regarding its impact on the Roman jurisconsults and emperors. Stoicism had only a tangential and superficial relationship to Roman jurisprudence. A few general principles and definitions attributable to Stoicism can be found in the juristic literature, but they are treated unsystematically in theory and applied inconsistently in practice, to the marginal extent to which there are any efforts to apply them at all. Theories of law inspired by the distinctive Stoic amalgam of natural law and ethics are to be found, rather, in the writings of professional orators, and preeminently in the rhetoric and political theory of Cicero,[122] not in the *responsa* of the jurisconsults or in the legislative prefaces and practices of the emperors. It was through Latin literature far more than through Roman law that Stoicism was transmitted to the Latin Christian Fathers and to the intellectual world of western Europe in the Middle Ages.

---

[122] See above, ch. 2, parts III and IV, and in particular the literature cited in part IV, p. 96 n. 110.

BIBLIOGRAPHY

Bibliographies and Works of Reference

Berger, Adolf, *Encyclopedic Dictionary of Roman Law,* Transactions of the American Philosophical Society, n.s. *43,* part 2 (1953), 333-808.

Büchner, Karl and Hofmann, J. B., *Lateinische Literatur und Sprache in der Forschung seit 1937,* Wissenschaftliche Forschungsberichte, 6, Bern, A. Franke, 1951.

Cabrol, Fernand and Leclercq, Henri, *Dictionnaire d'archéologie chrétienne et de liturgie,* Paris, Librairie Letouzey et Ané, 1939.

Collart, Jean, "Varron grammarien et l'enseignement grammatical dans l'antiquité romaine 1934-1963," *Lustrum, 9* (1964), 213-42.

Fedeli, Paolo, "Il 'De officiis' di Cicerone: Problemi e attegiamenti della critica moderna," *Aufstieg und Niedergang der römischen Welt: Geschichte und Kultur Roms im Spiegel der neueren Forschung,* ed. Hildegard Temporini, Berlin, Walter de Gruyter, 1973, *1,* part 4, 376-87.

Gigon, Olof, "Cicero und die griechische Philosophie," *Aufstieg und Niedergang der römischen Welt: Geschichte und Kultur Roms im Spiegel der neueren Forschung,* ed. Hildegard Temporini, Berlin, Walter de Gruyter, 1973, *1,* part 4, 226-61.

Holsinger, George Robert, "Seneca's Use of Stoic Themes, with an Index of Ideas to Books I-VII of the Epistulae Morales," Ohio State University Ph.D. diss., 1952.

Leeman, A. D., *A Systematic Bibliography of Sallust (1879-1964),* rev. and augmented ed., Leiden, E. J. Brill, 1965.

Legg, J. Wickham, "A Bibliography of the *Thoughts* of Marcus Aurelius Antoninus," *Transactions of the Bibliographical Society, 10* (1910), 15-81.

Motto, Anna Lydia, "Recent Scholarship on Seneca's Prose Works, 1940-1957," *Classical World, 54* (1960-61), 37-48, 70-71, 111-12.

—, *Seneca Sourcebook: Guide to the Thought of Lucius Annaeus Seneca,* Amsterdam, Adolf M. Hakkert, 1970.

—, "Seneca's Prose Writings: A Decade of Scholarship, 1958-1968," *Classical World, 64* (1971), 141-58, 177-91.

Oldfather, W. A., *Contributions toward a Bibliography of Epictetus,* Urbana, University of Illinois Press, 1927.

—, *Contributions toward a Bibliography of Epictetus,* Supplement, ed. Marian Harman, with a preliminary list of Epictetus manuscripts by W. H. Friedrich and C. U. Faye, Urbana, University of Illinois Press, 1952.

Rawson, Elizabeth, "The Interpretation of Cicero's 'De legibus'," *Aufstieg und Niedergang der römischen Welt: Geschichte und Kultur Roms im Spiegel der neueren Forschung,* ed. Hildegard Temporini, Berlin, Walter de Gruyter, 1973, *1,* part 4, 334-56.

Rutz, Werner, "Lucan 1943-1963," *Lustrum, 9* (1964) 243-334.

—, "Zweiter Nachtrag zum Lucan-Bericht Lustrum 9, 1964," *Lustrum, 10* (1965), 246-56.

Schmidt, Peter L., "Cicero 'De re publica': Die Forschung der letzten fünf Dezennien," *Aufstieg und Niedergang der römischen Welt: Geschichte und Kultur Roms im Spiegel der neueren Forschung,* ed. Hildegard Temporini, Berlin, Walter de Gruyter, 1973, *1,* part 4, 262-333.

Smethurst, S. E., "Cicero's Rhetorical and Philosophical Works: A Bibliographical Survey," *Classical World, 51* (1957), 1-4, 24; *58* (1964), 36-45; *61* (1967), 125-33.

Primary Sources

Anastasi, Rosario, trans., *I frammenti degli stoici antichi, 3*, Pubblicazioni dell'Istituto universitario di magistero di Catania, serie filosofica, testi e documenti, 8, Padova, CEDAM, 1962.

Arnim, Hans F. A. von, ed., *Stoicorum veterum fragmenta*, 4 vols., Leipzig, B. G. Teubner, 1903-24.

Augustinus, Aurelius, *De civitate dei libri I-X*, ed. Bernardus Dombart and Alphonsus Kalb, Corpus christianorum, series latina, 47, Turnholt, Brepols, 1960.

—, *De dialectica*, ed. Jan Pinborg, trans. B. Darrell Jackson, Synthese Historical Library, 16, Dordrecht, D. Reidel Publishing Company, 1975.

Barlow, Claude W., ed., *Epistolae Senecae ad Paulum et Pauli ad Senecam 'quae vocantur'*, Papers and Monographs of the American Academy in Rome, *10*, Horn, Austria, Ferdinand Berger, 1938.

—, ed., *Martini Episcopi Bracarensis Opera omnia*, Papers and Monographs of the American Academy in Rome, *12*, New Haven, Yale University Press, 1950.

Blin, G. and Keim, M., trans., "Chrysippe: De la partie hégémonique de l'âme," *Mesures*, 5:2 (1939), 163-74.

Bowra, C. M. and Higham, T. F., eds., *The Oxford Book of Greek Verse in Translation*, Oxford, Clarendon Press, 1938.

Bréhier, Émile and Schuhl, Pierre-Maxime, ed. and trans., *Les Stoïciens*, Bibliothèque de la Pléiade, 156, Paris, Éditions Gallimard, 1962.

Cassiodorus Senator, *Expositio psalmarum*, ed. M. Andriaen, Corpus christianorum, series latina, 97-98, Turnholt, Brepols, 1958.

—, *Institutionum*, ed. R. A. B. Mynors, Oxford, Clarendon Press, 1937.

—, *An Introduction to Divine and Human Readings*, trans. Leslie Webber Jones, Records of Civilization, Sources and Studies, 40, New York, Columbia University Press, 1946.

Cicero, Marcus Tullius, *Academica*, ed. James S. Reid, Hildesheim, Georg Olms Verlagsbuchhandlung, 1966 [repr. of London, 1885 ed.].

—, *L'Amitié*, ed. and trans. L. Laurand, Collection des Universités de France, publiée sous le patronage de l'Association Guillaume Budé, Paris, Les Belles Lettres, 1928.

—, *Brutus*, trans. G. L. Hendrickson; *Orator*, trans. H. M. Hubbell, Loeb Classical Library, Cambridge, Mass., Harvard University Press, 1962.

—, *Brutus, On the Nature of the Gods, On Divination, On Duties*, trans. Hubert M. Poteat, intro. by Richard McKeon, Chicago, University of Chicago Press, 1950.

—, *Caton l'Ancien (De la vieillesse)*, ed. and trans. P. Wuilleumier, Collection des Universités de France, publiée sous le patronage de l'Association Guillaume Budé, Paris, Les Belles Lettres, 1940.

—, *De divinatione*, ed. Arthur Stanley Pease, University of Illinois Studies in Language and Literature, 6:2-3; 8:2-3, Urbana, 1920-23.

—, *De fato*, ed. and trans. Karl Bayer, Tusculum-Bücherei, München, Heimeran-Verlag, 1963.

—, *De fato, Paradoxa Stoicorum, De partitione oratoria*, trans. H. Rackham, Loeb Classical Library, Cambridge, Mass., Harvard University Press, 1960.

—, *De finibus bonorum et malorum*, trans. H. Rackham, Loeb Classical Library, Cambridge, Mass., Harvard University Press, 1961.

—, *De finibus bonorum et malorum*, libri I et II, ed. Antonius Selem, Roma, Edizioni dell'Ateneo, 1962.

—, *De inventione, De optimo genere oratorum, Topica*, trans. H. M. Hubbell, Loeb Classical Library, Cambridge, Mass., Harvard University Press, 1960.

—, *De natura deorum*, livre premier, ed. and trans. M. van den Bruwaene, Collection Latomus, 107, Bruxelles, Latomus, 1970.

—, *De natura deorum, Academica*, trans. H. Rackham, Loeb Classical Library, London, William Heinemann Ltd., 1961.

—, *De officiis*, trans. Walter Miller, Loeb Classical Library, Cambridge, Mass., Harvard University Press, 1961.

—, *De oratore*, trans. E. W. Sutton and H. Rackham, 2 vols., Loeb Classical Library, Cambridge, Mass., Harvard University Press, 1959-60.
—, *De re publica*, ed. Petrus Krarup, Firenze, Mondadori, 1967.
—, *De re publica*, ed. K. Ziegler, Leipzig, B. G. Teubner, 1964.
—, *De re publica, De legibus*, trans. Clinton Walker Keyes, Loeb Classical Library, Cambridge, Mass., Harvard University Press, 1959.
—, *De senectute, De amicitia, De divinatione*, trans. William Armistead Falconer, Loeb Classical Library, London, William Heinemann Ltd., 1959.
—, *Hortensius*, ed. Albertus Grilli, Testi e documenti per lo studio dell'antichità, Milano, Cisalpino, 1962.
—, *Les devoirs*, livres I-III, ed. and trans. Maurice Testard, Collection des Universités de France, publiée sous le patronage de l'Association Guillaume Budé, Paris, Les Belles Lettres, 1965-70.
—, *Letters to Atticus*, ed. D. R. Shackleton Bailey, 6 vols., Cambridge Classical Texts and Commentaries, 3-8, Cambridge, The University Press, 1965-68.
—, *The Letters to His Friends*, trans. W. Glynn Williams, 3 vols., Loeb Classical Library, Cambridge, Mass., Harvard University Press, 1958-60.
—, *On the Commonwealth*, trans. George Holland Sabine and Stanley Barney Smith, Columbus, Ohio State University Press, 1929.
—, *On Old Age and On Friendship*, trans. Frank O. Copley, Ann Arbor, University of Michigan Press, 1967.
—, *Paradoxa Stoicorum*, ed. A. G. Lee, London, Macmillan & Co. Limited, 1953.
—, *Les paradoxes des stoïciens*, ed. and trans. Jean Molager, Collection des Universités de France, publiée sous le patronage de l'Association Guillaume Budé, Paris, Les Belles Lettres, 1971.
—, *Pro Murena*, trans. Louis E. Lord, Loeb Classical Library, Cambridge, Mass., Harvard University Press, 1959.
—, *Staatstheoretische Schriften*, trans. Konrat Ziegler, Schriften und Quellen der alten Welt, 31, Berlin, Akademie-Verlag, 1974.
—, *Traité des lois*, ed. and trans. Georges de Plinval, Collection des Universités de France, publiée sous le patronage de l'Association Guillaume Budé, Paris, Les Belles Lettres, 1959.
—, *Traité du destin*, ed. and trans. Albert Yon, Collection des Universités de France, publiée sous le patronage de l'Association Guillaume Budé, Paris, Les Belles Lettres, 1933.
—, *Tusculan Disputations*, trans. J. E. King, 2 vols., Loeb Classical Library, Cambridge, Mass., Harvard University Press, 1960.
—, *Tusculanarum disputationum libri V*, ed. Otto Heines, comm. by Max Pohlenz, Stuttgart, B. G. Teubner, 1957 [repr. of 5th ed., 1912].
Clark, Gordon H., trans., *Selections from Hellenistic Philosophy*, New York, F. S. Crofts & Co., 1940.
Clement of Alexandria, *Stromateis*, ed. D. Nicolai le Nourry, *Patrologia graeca, 8*, ed. J. P. Migne, Paris, 1857.
Corpus iuris civilis, ed. P. Krueger, T. Mommsen, R. Schoell, and G. Kroll, 3 vols., Berlin, Weidemann, 1954.
Diogenes Laertius, *Lives of Eminent Philosophers*, vol. 2, trans. R. D. Hicks, Loeb Classical Library, London, William Heinemann, 1925.
Epictetus, *The Discourses as Reported by Arrian, the Manual, and Fragments*, trans. W. A. Oldfather, 2 vols., Loeb Classical Library, London, William Heinemann, 1926.
Festa, Nicola, ed. and trans., *I frammenti degli stoici antichi*, 2 vols., Bari, Gius. Laterza & Figli, 1932-35.
Fontes iuris romani antejustiniani, ed. S. Riccobono, J. Baviera, C. Ferrini, J. Furlani, and V. Arangio-Ruiz, 3 vols., Florentiae, S. A. G. Barbèra, 1940-43.
Franceschini, Ezio, ed., *Il Commento di Nicola Trevet al Tieste di Seneca*, Orbis Romanus, 11, Milano, Vita e Pensiero, 1938.

Funaioli, Hyginus, ed., *Grammaticae romanae fragmenta*, Stuttgart, B. G. Teubner, 1969 [repr. of 1907 ed.].

Gellius, Aulus, *The Attic Nights*, ed. and trans. John C. Rolfe, 3 vols., Loeb Classical Library, Cambridge, Mass., Harvard University Press, 1961.

—, *Noctes atticae*, ed. P. K. Marshall, 2 vols., Oxford, Clarendon Press, 1968.

—, *Les nuits attiques*, livres I–IV, ed. and trans. René Marache, Collection des Universités de France, publiée sous le patronage de l'Association Guillaume Budé, Paris, Les Belles Lettres, 1967.

Guasti, Cesare, ed., *L'Epistole di Seneca a S. Paolo e de S. Paolo a Seneca, volgarizzate nel secolo XIV, Miscellanea di opuscoli inediti o rari dei secoli XIV e XV*, Prose, *1*, Torino, Unione Tipografico-Editrice, 1861, pp. 289–302.

Hadas, Moses, ed., *The Greek Poets*. New York, Modern Library, 1953.

Horatius Flaccus, Quintus, *Ars poetica*, ed. C. O. Brink, Cambridge, The University Press, 1971.

—, *Briefe*, ed. Adolf Kiessling and Richard Heinze, 6th ed., Berlin, Weidmannsche Verlagsbuchhandlung, 1959.

—, *Oden und Epoden*, ed. Adolf Kiessling and Richard Heinze, 10th ed., Berlin, Weidmannsche Verlagsbuchhandlung, 1960.

—, *Odes, Épodes et Chant séculaire*, ed. Frédéric Plessis, Hildesheim, Georg Olms Verlagsbuchhandlung, 1966 [repr. of 1924 ed.].

—, *The Odes and Epodes of Horace*, trans. Joseph P. Clancy, Chicago, University of Chicago Press, 1960.

—, *Satires*, ed. Paul Lejay, Hildesheim, Georg Olms Verlagsbuchhandlung, 1966 [repr. of 1911 ed.].

—, *The Satires and Epistles of Horace*, trans. Smith Palmer Bovie, Chicago, University of Chicago Press, 1959.

—, *Satires, Epistles, and Ars poetica*, trans. H. Rushton Fairclough, Loeb Classical Library, Cambridge, Mass., Harvard University Press, 1961.

Johnson, Allan Chester, Coleman-Norton, Paul Robinson, and Brown, Frank Card, trans. and comm., *Ancient Roman Statutes*, The Corpus of Roman Law, 2, Austin, University of Texas Press, 1961.

Justinian, *Digest*, trans. Charles Henry Monro, 2 vols., Cambridge, The University Press, 1904.

—, *Institutes*, trans. J. T. Abdy and Brian Walker, Cambridge, The University Press, 1876.

Juvenalis, Decimus Iunius, *The Satires*, trans. Hubert Creekmore, New York, New American Library, 1963.

—, *The Satires*, trans. Rolfe Humphries, Bloomington, Indiana University Press, 1958.

—, *Saturae*, ed. Ulrich Knoche, Das Wort der Antike, 2, München, Max Hueber Verlag, 1950.

—, *Saturarum libri V*, ed. Ludwig Friedlaender, Amsterdam, Verlag Adolf M. Hakkert, 1962 [repr. of Leipzig, 1895 ed.].

—, *The Sixteen Satires*, trans. Peter Green, Baltimore, Penguin Books, 1967.

Keil, Heinrich, ed., *Grammatici latini*, 8 vols., Leipzig, B. G. Teubner, 1867–70.

Livius, Titus, *Ab urbe condita*, trans. B. O. Foster, Frank Gardner Moore, Evan T. Sage, and Alfred C. Schlesinger, 14 vols., Loeb Classical Library, Cambridge, Mass., Harvard University Press, 1919–59.

—, *Histoire romaine*, vol. 1, ed. and trans. Jean Bayet, Collection des Universités de France, publiée sous le patronage de l'Association Guillaume Budé, Paris, Les Belles Lettres, 1947.

Lucanus, Marcus Annaeus, *The Civil War*, trans. J. D. Duff, Loeb Classical Library, London, William Heinemann, 1928.

—, *La Guerre civile (La Pharsale)*, ed. and trans. A. Bourgery, 2 vols., Collection des Universités de France, publiée sous le patronage de l'Association Guillaume Budé, Paris, Les Belles Lettres, 1926–29.

—, *Pharsalie,* ed. C. E. Haskins, intro. by W. E. Heitland, London, George Bell and Sons, 1887.
—, *Pharsalia: Dramatic Episodes of the Civil Wars,* trans. Robert Graves, Harmondsworth, Penguin Books, 1956.
Lucilius, Gaius, *Fragments,* in *Remains of Old Latin,* vol. 3, ed. and trans. E. H. Warmington, Loeb Classical Library, Cambridge, Mass., Harvard University Press, 1961.
Lutz, Cora E., ed., "Musonius Rufus, 'The Roman Socrates'," *Yale Classical Studies, 10* (1947), 3-147.
Macrobius, *Commentary on the Dream of Scipio,* trans. William Harris Stahl, Records of Civilization, Sources and Studies, 48, New York, Columbia University Press, 1952.
—, *Opera quae supersunt,* ed. Ludwig von Jan, 2 vols., Quedlinburg, Godofredus Bassius, 1848-52.
—, *The Saturnalia,* trans. Percival Vaughan Davies, Records of Civilization, Sources and Studies, 79, New York, Columbia University Press, 1969.
Manilius, M., *Astronomicon,* ed. Fabricius Serra, Scriptorum romanorum quae extant omnia, 224-225, Pisa, Giardini, 1975.
—, *The Five Books, containing a System of the Ancient Astronomy and Astrology together with the Philosophy of the Stoicks,* trans. Thomas Creech, London, Jacob Tonson, 1697.
Marcus Aurelius Antoninus, *The Communings with Himself together with His Speeches and Sayings,* ed. and trans. C. R. Haines, Loeb Classical Library, London, William Heinemann, 1930.
Martial, Marcus Valerius, *Epigrams,* rev. ed., trans. Walter C. A. Ker, 2 vols., Loeb Classical Library, Cambridge, Mass., Harvard University Press, 1968.
Martianus Capella, *De nuptiis Philologiae et Mercurii,* ed. Adolfus Dick and Jean Préaux, Stuttgart, B. G. Teubner, 1969.
Musonius Rufus, C., *Le diatribe e i frammenti minori,* ed. and trans. Renato Laurenti, Roma, Angelo Signorelli, 1967.
—, *Reliquiae,* ed. Otto Hense, Leipzig, B. G. Teubner, 1905.
Nigidius Figulus, Publius, *Operum reliquae,* ed. Antonius Swoboda, Vienna, 1889.
Oates, Whitney, J., ed., *The Stoic and Epicurean Philosophers,* New York, Random House, 1940.
Persius Flaccus, A., *The Satires,* ed. H. Nettleship, trans. John Conington, Hildesheim, Georg Olms Verlagsbuchhandlung, 1967 [repr. of Oxford, 1893 ed.].
—, *The Satires,* trans. W. S. Merwin, intro. by William S. Anderson, Bloomington, Indiana University Press, 1961.
— and Juvenalis, Decimus Iunius, *Saturae,* ed. W. V. Clausen, Oxford, Clarendon Press, 1966.
Pharr, Clyde, trans. and comm. with Davidson, Theresa Sherrer and Pharr, Mary Brown, *The Theodosian Code and Novels and the Sirmondian Constitutions,* The Corpus of Roman Law, 1, Princeton, Princeton University Press, 1952.
Places, Édouard des, ed., "Un poème 'stoïcien' du IIIe siècle avant Jésus-Christ," *L'Homme devant Dieu: Mélanges offerts au père Henri de Lubac,* Théologie: Études publiées sous la direction de la Faculté de théologie S. J. de Lyon-Fourvière, 58, Paris, Aubier, 1964, *3,* 43-49.
Plinius Secundus, C., *Naturalis historia,* ed. L. Jan and C. Mayhoff, 6 vols., Stuttgart, B. G. Teubner, 1967-70 [repr. of 1896 ed.].
Pohlenz, Max, trans. and intro., *Stoa und Stoiker. Die Gründer. Panaitios. Poseidonios,* Die Bibliothek der alten Welt, Zürich, Artemis-Verlag, 1950.
Posidonius, *The Fragments,* vol. 1, ed. L. Edelstein and I. G. Kidd, Cambridge Classical Texts and Commentaries, 13, Cambridge, The University Press, 1972.
Prato, Carlo, ed., *Gli epigrammi attribuiti a L. A. Seneca,* Biblioteca di letterature classiche, N. p., Adriatica Editore, 1955.
Quintilian, *Institutio oratoria,* trans. H. E. Butler, 4 vols., Loeb Classical Library, London, William Heinemann, 1966.
—, *Institution oratoire,* tome 1 livre 1, ed. and trans. Jean Cousin, Collection des Universités

de France, publiée sous le patronage de l'Association Guillaume Budé, Paris, Les Belles Lettres, 1975.

Sallustius Crispus, C., *Bellum Catilinae, Bellum Iugurthinum, Orationes et epistulae excerptae de historiis*, trans. J. C. Rolfe, Loeb Classical Library, London, William Heinemann, 1931.

—, *Catilina, Jugurtha, Fragments des Histoires*, ed. and trans. Alfred Ernout, Collection des Universités de France, publiée sous le patronage de l'Association Guillaume Budé, Paris, Les Belles Lettres, 1947.

Saunders, Jason L., ed., *Greek and Roman Philosophy after Aristotle*, Readings in the History of Philosophy, ed. Paul Edwards and Richard H. Popkin, New York, Free Press, 1966.

Seneca, Lucius Annaeus, *Ad Lucilium epistulae morales*, trans. Richard M. Gummere, 3 vols., Loeb Classical Library, London, William Heinemann Ltd., 1925-34.

—, *Apocolocyntosis*, trans. W. H. Rouse, Loeb Classical Library, London, William Heinemann Ltd., 1913.

—, *Moral Essays*, trans. John W. Basore, 3 vols., Loeb Classical Library, London, William Heinemann Ltd., 1928-35.

—, *Naturales quaestiones*, trans. Thomas H. Corcoran, 2 vols., Loeb Classical Library, Cambridge, Mass., Harvard University Press, 1971-72.

—, *Tragedies*, trans. Frank Justus Miller, 2 vols., Loeb Classical Library, London, William Heinemann Ltd., 1929-38.

Servius, *In Vergilii carmina commentarii*, ed. Georgius Thilo and Hermannus Hagen, Leipzig, B. G. Teubner, 1923.

Sextus Empiricus, *Against the Logicians*, ed. and trans. R. G. Bury, Loeb Classical Library, Cambridge, Mass., Harvard University Press, 1935.

—, *Against the Physicists. Against the Ethicists*, ed. and trans. R. G. Bury, Loeb Classical Library, Cambridge, Mass., Harvard University Press, 1936.

—, *Against the Professors*, ed. and trans. R. G. Bury, Loeb Classical Library, Cambridge, Mass., Harvard University Press, 1949.

—, *Outlines of Pyrrhonism*, ed. and trans. R. G. Bury, Loeb Classical Library, London, William Heinemann Ltd., 1933.

Silius Italicus, *Punica*, ed. and trans. J. D. Duff, 2 vols., Loeb Classical Library, London, William Heinemann Ltd., 1934.

Stahl, William Harris, Johnson, Richard, and Burge, E. L., trans. and intro., *Martianus Capella and the Seven Liberal Arts*, vol. 1, Records of Civilization, Sources and Studies, 84, New York, Columbia University Press, 1971.

Statius, P. Papinius, *Achilléide*, ed. and trans. Jean Méheust, Collection des Universités de France, publiée sous le patronage de l'Association Guillaume Budé, Paris, Les Belles Lettres, 1971.

—, *Thebaid*, ed. and trans. J. H. Mozley, 2 vols. Loeb Classical Library, London, William Heinemann Ltd., 1967.

—, *Thebais*, ed. Alfredus Klotz, curavit Thomas C. Klinnert, Leipzig, B. G. Teubner, 1973.

Sullivan, J. P., trans., "Seneca: The Deification of Claudius the Clod," *Arion, 5* (1966), 378-99.

Tacitus, P. Cornelius, *Annales*, ed. Erich Koestermann, Leipzig, B. G. Teubner, 1965.

—, *The Annals*, trans. John Jackson, 3 vols., Loeb Classical Library, Cambridge, Mass., Harvard University Press, 1956.

—, *La Germanie*, ed. and trans. Jacques Perret, Collection des Universités de France, publiée sous le patronage de l'Association Guillaume Budé, Paris, Les Belles Lettres, 1949.

—, *The Histories*, ed. and trans. Clifford H. Moore, 2 vols., Loeb Classical Library, Cambridge, Mass., Harvard University Press, 1956-58.

—, *De origine et situ Germanorum*, ed. J. G. C. Anderson, Oxford, Clarendon Press, 1938.

—, *De vita Agricolae*, ed. R. M. Ogilvie and Ian Richmond, Oxford, Clarendon Press, 1967.

Todd, Robert B., ed., *Alexander of Aphrodisias on Stoic Physics: A Study of the De mixtione with Preliminary Essays, Text, Translation and Commentary*, Philosophia Antiqua, 28, Leiden, E. J. Brill, 1976.

Traversa, Augustus, ed., *Index stoicorum Herculanensis*, Università di Genova, Facoltà di lettere, pubblicazioni dell'Istituto di filologia classica, 1, Genova, 1952.

Troost, Karl, ed., *Zenonis Citiensis de rebus physicis doctrinae fundamentum ex adiectis fragmentis*, Berliner Studien für classische Philologie und Archaeologie, *12*:3, Berlin, S. Calvary & Co., 1891.

Van Straaten, Modestus, ed., *Panaetii Rhodii fragmenta*, 3rd ed., Philosophia Antiqua, ed. W. J. Verdenius and J. H. Waszink, 5, Leiden, E. J. Brill, 1962.

Varro, M. Terentius, *On the Latin Language*, ed. and trans. Roland G. Kent, 2 vols., Loeb Classical Library, London, William Heinemann Ltd., 1938.

—, *De lingua latina*, liber X, ed. and trans. Antonio Traglia, Scriptores latini, 7, Roma, Edizioni dell'Ateneo, 1967.

Vergilius Maro, Publius, *Georgics*, trans. Smith Palmer Bovie, Chicago, University of Chicago Press, 1956.

—, *The Georgics*, trans. K. R. Mackenzie, London, The Folio Society, 1969.

—, *The Aeneid*, Books 1-6, ed. R. D. Williams, London, Macmillan, 1972.

—, *Aeneis Buch VI*, 2nd ed., ed. Eduard Norden, Leipzig, B. G. Teubner, 1916.

—, *Opera*, ed. R. A. B. Mynors, Oxford, Clarendon Press, 1969.

Victorinus, Marius, *Ars grammatica*, ed. Italo Mariotti, Firenze, Le Monnier, 1967.

—, *Traités théologiques sur la Trinité*, ed. Paul Henry and Pierre Hadot, 2 vols., Sources chrétiennes, 68-69, Paris, Éditions du Cerf, 1960.

Vogel, C. J. de, ed., *Greek Philosophy: A Collection of Texts with Notes and Explanations*, vol. 3, Leiden, E. J. Brill, 1959.

Zulueta, Francis de, ed. and trans., *The Institutes of Gaius*, 2 vols., Oxford, Clarendon Press, 1946-53.

Secondary Sources

Aall, Anathon, *Der Logos: Geschichte seiner Entwicklung in der griechischen Philosophie und der christlichen Litteratur*, 2 vols., Leipzig, O. R. Reisland, 1896-99.

Abel, Karlhans, "Die kulturelle Mission des Panaitios," *Antike und Abendland*, *17*:2 (1971), 119-43.

—, "Horaz auf der Suche nach dem wahren Selbst," *Antike und Abendland*, *15* (1969), 29-46.

—, "Poseidonios und Senecas Trostschrift an Marcia (dial. 2, 24, 5 ff.)," *Rheinisches Museum für Philologie*, n.F. *107* (1964), 221-60.

Actas del congreso internacional de filosofía en conmemoración de Séneca, en el XIX centenario de su muerte, 2 vols., Córdoba, Congreso Internacional de Filosofía, 1965-66.

Actas del congreso internacional de filosofía en conmemoración de Séneca, en el XIX centenario de su muerte: Ponencias y conferencias para las sesiones plenarias, Madrid, Librería Editorial Augustinus, 1966.

Acton, John Emrich Edward Dalberg, *Essays on Freedom and Power*, selected with intro. by Gertrude Himmelfarb, London, Thames and Hudson, 1956.

Adam, James, *The Vitality of Platonism and Other Essays*, ed. Adela Marion Adam, Cambridge, The University Press, 1911.

Adamczyk, Stanley J., "Political Propaganda in Cicero's Essays, 47-44 B.C.," Fordham University Ph.D. diss., 1961.

Adamietz, Joachim, *Untersuchungen zu Juvenal*, Hermes Einzelschriften, *26*, Wiesbaden, Franz Steiner Verlag GMBH, 1972.

Adams, James Luther, "The Law of Nature in Greco-Roman Thought," *Journal of Religion*, *25* (1945), 97-118.

Adatte, Jean-Marie, "Caton ou l'engagement du sage," *Études de Lettres*, Bulletin de la Faculté de lettres de l'Université de Lausanne, sér. 2:*8* (1965), 232-40.

Adorno, Francesco, "Sul significato del *huparchon* in Zenone stoico," *La parola del passato*, *12*:61 (1957), 362-74.

—, "Sul significato del termine *hegemonikon* in Zenone stoico," *La parola del passato*, *14*:64 (1959), 26-41.

Africa, Thomas W., "The Opium Addiction of Marcus Aurelius," *Journal of the History of Ideas*, *22* (1961), 97-102.

Ahl, Frederick M., *Lucan: An Introduction*, Cornell Studies in Classical Philology, 39, Ithaca, Cornell University Press, 1976.

Akinpelu, Jones A. "Stoicism and a Future Existence," *Classical Bulletin*, *45* (1969), 67-68, 76-77.

Albrecht, Michael von, *Silius Italicus: Freiheit und Gebundenheit römischer Epik*, Amsterdam, P. Schippers, 1964.

Albertario, Emilio, "Caritas nei testi giuridici romani," *Reale istituto Lombardo di scienze e lettere, Rendiconti*, ser. 2:*64*, 6-10 (1931), 375-92.

—, "Concetto classico e definizioni postclassiche del *ius naturale*," *Studi di diritto romano*, Milano, Antonio Giuffrè, 1937, *5*, 277-90.

—, "Etica e diritto nel mondo classico latino," *Rivista internazionale di filosofia del diritto*, *12* (1932), 3-20.

—, "I fattori della evoluzione del diritto romano postclassico e la formazione del diritto romano giustinianeo," *Studia et documenta historiae et iuris*, *1* (1935), 3-41.

—, *Introduzione storica allo studio del diritto romano giustiniano*, parte 1, Milano, Antonio Giuffrè, 1935.

—, Ciapessoni, Pietro, and De Francisi, Pietro, eds., *Studi in onore di Pietro Bonfante*, vols. 4 and 5, Milano, Fratelli Treves, 1930.

Albertini, Eugène, *La composition dans les ouvrages philosophique de Sénèque*, Bibliothèque des Écoles françaises d'Athènes et de Rome, 127, Paris, E. de Boccard, 1923.

Albino, Ettore, *L'uomo Sallustio*, L'Aquila, L. U. Japadre Editore, 1966.

Alexander, William Hardy, "Cato of Utica in the Works of Seneca Philosophus," *Proceedings and Transactions of the Royal Society of Canada*, 3rd ser., *40*:2 (1946) 59-74.

—, "Maius opus (*Aneid* 7-12)," *University of California Publications in Classical Philology*, *14* (1950-52), 193-214.

—, "The Tacitean *non liquet* on Seneca," *University of California Publications in Classical Philology*, *14*:8 (1952), 269-386.

Alfonsi, Luigi, "Contributo allo studio delle fonti del pensiero di Marco Aurelio," *Aevum*, *28* (1954) 101-17.

—, "Ovidio e Posidonio," *Aevum*, *28* (1954), 376-77.

—, "Il pensiero ciceroniano nel *De senectute*," *Studi letterari: Miscellanea in onore di Emilio Sentini*, Palermo, U. Monfredi, 1956, pp. 1-16.

Allers, Rudolf, "Microcosmus from Anaximandros to Paracelsus," *Traditio*, *2* (1944), 319-407.

Altevogt, Heinrich, *Labor improbus: Eine Vergilstudie*, Orbis antiquus, 8, Münster i. Westf., Aschendorffsche Verlagsbuchhandlung, 1952.

Altheim, Franz, "Poseidonios und Sallust," *Studi in onore di Pietro de Francisi*, Milano, Antonio Giuffrè, 1956, *1*, 104-14.

Altman, Marion, "Ruler Cult in Seneca," *Classical Philology*, *33* (1938), 198-204.

Amand, David, *Fatalisme et liberté dans l'antiquité grecque: Recherches sur la survivance de l'argumentation morale antifataliste de Carnéade chez les philosophes grecs et les théologiens chrétiens des quatre premiers siècles*, Université de Louvain, Recueil de travaux d'histoire et de philologie, 3me sér., 19, Louvain, Bibliothèque de l'Université, 1945.

Anderson, Andrew Runni, "Heracles and His Successors," *Harvard Studies in Classical Philology*, *39* (1928), 7-58.

André, Jean-Marie, *L'Otium dans la vie morale et intellectuelle romaine des origines à l'époque augustéenne*, Publications de la Faculté des lettres et sciences humaines de Paris, sér. "Recherches," 30, Paris, PUF, 1966.

Andriopoulos, D. Z., "The Stoic Theory of Perceiving and Knowing," *Philosophia, 2* (1972), 305-26.

Anquin, Nimio de, "Sobre la lógica de los Estoicos," *Sapientia, 11* (1956), 166-72.

Arangio-Ruiz, Vincenzo, *Istituzioni di diritto romano,* 14ᵃ ed. riv., Napoli, Dott. Eugenio Jovene, 1960.

Ardley, G. W. R., "Cicero on Philosophy and History," *Prudentia, 1* (1969), 28-41.

Armleder, John Paul, "Tacitus and Professional Philosophers," *Classical Bulletin, 37* (1961), 90-93.

—, "Tacitus' Attitude to Philosophy," *Classical Bulletin, 38* (1962), 89-91.

Arnold, E. Vernon, *Roman Stoicism: Being Lectures on the History of the Stoic Philosophy with Special Reference to Its Development within the Roman Empire,* New York, The Humanities Press, 1958 [repr. of Cambridge, 1911 ed.].

Arundel, M. R., " 'Principio caelum' (Aeneid vi, 724-751)," *Proceedings of the Virgil Society, 3* (1963-64), 27-34.

Association Guillaume Budé, *Actes du VIIᵉ congrès,* Aix-en-Provence, 1-6 avril 1963, Paris, Les Belles Lettres, 1964.

Astin, A. E., *Scipio Aemilianus,* Oxford, Clarendon Press, 1967.

Atkins, J. W. H., *Literary Criticism in Antiquity: A Sketch of Its Development,* vol. 2, New York, Peter Smith, 1952.

Atti del congresso internazionale di diritto romano, Bologna e Roma, 17-27 aprile 1933, Roma, Istituto di studi romani, 2 vols., Pavia, Prem. Tipografia Successori F.lli Fusi, 1934-35.

Atti del I congresso internazionale di studi ciceroniani, Roma, aprile 1959, 2 vols., Roma, Centro di Studi Ciceroniani, 1961.

Atzert, C., *Die Apotheose der Virtus Romana in Ciceros Schrift "De re publica": Ein Beitrag zur Würdigung Ciceros,* 2nd ed., Breslau, Frankes Verlag, 1933.

Aubenque, Pierre and André, Jean-Marie, *Sénèque,* Paris, Éditions Seghers, 1964.

Babut, D., "Les Stoïciens et l'amour," *Revue des études grecques, 76* (1963), 55-63.

Bachmayer, Arthur, *Die Motivierung in Lukans Pharsalia,* Freiburg (Schweitz), Paulus-druckerei, 1940.

Baeumer, Julius, *De Posidonio Megasthene Apollodoro M. Annaei Lucani auctoribus,* Münster i. W., Typograph, Guestf., 1902.

Bailey, Cyril, *Religion in Virgil,* Oxford, Clarendon Press, 1935.

Bailey, D. R. Shackleton, *Cicero,* London, Duckworth, 1971.

Baillot, A.-F., "Aperçus sur le stoïcisme," *Revue philosophique de la France et de l'étranger, 142* (1952), 14-30.

Baldry, H. C., "The Idea of the Unity of Mankind," *Grecs et barbares,* Fondation Hardt: Entretiens sur l'antiquité classique, 8, Genève, Fondation Hardt, 1962, pp. 167-95.

—, *The Unity of Mankind in Greek Thought,* Cambridge, The University Press, 1965.

—, "Zeno's Ideal State," *Journal of Hellenic Studies, 79* (1959), 3-15.

Baldwin, Barry, *Studies in Aulus Gellius,* Lawrence, Kansas, Coronado, Press, 1975.

Baldwin, Charles Sears, *Ancient Rhetoric and Poetic Interpreted from Representative Works,* New York, The Macmillan Co., 1924.

Ballotto, Francesco, *Cronologia ed evoluzione spirituale nelle satire di Persio,* Messina, Casa Editrice G. D'Anna, 1964.

Balsdon, J. P. V. D., *Life and Leisure in Ancient Rome,* New York, McGraw-Hill Book Company, 1969.

—, *Roman Women,* London, Bodley Head, 1962.

Banner, William A., "Origen and the Tradition of Natural Law Concepts," *Dumbarton Oaks Papers, 8* (1954), 49-82.

Barigazzi, Adelmo, "Sulle fonti del libro I delle Tusculane di Cicerone," *Rivista di filologia e di istruzione classica,* n.s. *76* (1948), 161-203; *78* (1950), 1-29.

Barlow, Claude W., "Seneca in the Middle Ages," *Classical Weekly, 34* (1940-41), 257-58.

Barra, Giovanni, *La figura e l'opera di Terenzio Varrone Reatino nel "De civitate dei" di Agostino,* Napoli, Istituto Editoriale del Mezzogiorno, 1969.

Barrow, R. H., *Slavery in the Roman Empire*, London, Methuen & Co., Ltd., 1928.

Barth, Paul, *Die Stoa*, Stuttgart, Frommanns Verlag, 1903.

—, *Die Stoa*, 6th ed., ed. Albert Goedeckemeyer, Stuttgart, Frommanns Verlag, 1946.

Barwick, Karl, *Probleme der stoischen Sprachlehre und Rhetorik*, Abhandlungen der sächsischen Akademie der Wissenschaft zu Leipzig, philologisch-historische Klasse, *49*:3, Berlin, Akademie-Verlag, 1957.

Barzellotti, Giacomo, *Delle dottrine filosofiche nei libri di Cicerone*, Firenze, G. Barbèra, 1867.

Barzin, Marcel, "La signification du Stoïcisme," *Académie royale de Belgique, Bulletin de la classe des lettres et des sciences morales et politiques*, 5ᵉ sér., *35* (1949), 94-105.

Bassett, Edward L., "Hercules and the Hero of the *Punica*," *The Classical Tradition: Literary and Historical Studies in Honor of Harry Caplan*, ed. Luitpold Wallach, Ithaca, Cornell University Press, 1966, pp. 258-73.

—, "Regulus and the Serpent in the *Punica*," *Classical Philology, 50* (1955), 1-20.

—, "Scipio and the Ghost of Appius," *Classical Philology, 58* (1963), 73-92.

Baudry, J., *Le problème de l'origine et de l'éternité du monde dans la philosophie grecque de Platon à l'ère chrétienne*, Collection d'études anciennes publiée sous le patronage de l'Association Guillaume Budé, Paris, Les Belles Lettres, 1931.

Baviera, Giovanni, "Concetto e limite dell'influenza del Cristianesimo sul diritto romano," *Mélanges P. F. Girard*, Paris, Librairie Arthur Rousseau, 1912, *1*, 67-121.

Becker, Carl, *Das Spätwerk des Horaz*, Göttingen, Vandenhoeck & Ruprecht, 1963.

Becker, Oskar, *Zwei Untersuchungen zur antiken Logik*, Klassisch-philologische Studien, ed. Hans Herter and Wolfgang Schmid, 17, Wiesbaden, Otto Harrassowitz, 1957.

Beguin, P., "Le 'fatum' dans l'oeuvre de Tacite," *L'Antiquité classique, 20* (1951), 315-34.

—, "Le positivisme de Tacite dans sa notion de 'fors'," *L'Antiquité classique, 24* (1955), 352-71.

Beikircher, Hugo, *Kommentar zur VI. Satire des A. Persius Flaccus*, Wiener Studien, Beiheft 1, Wien, Hermann Böhlaus Nachf., 1969.

Bellincioni, Maria, *Struttura e pensiero del Laelius ciceroniano*, Antichità classica e cristiana, 9, Brescia, Paideia, 1970.

Beltrami, Achille, "Seneca e Frontone," *Raccolta di scritti in onore di Felice Ramorino*, Pubblicazioni della Università cattolica del Sacro Cuore, ser. 4ᵃ, scienze filologiche, 7, Milano, Vita e Pensiero, 1927, pp. 508-14.

Benario, Herbert W., *An Introduction to Tacitus*, Athens, Ga., University of Georgia Press, 1975.

Benoît, Pierre, "Les idées de Sénèque sur l'au-delà," *Revue des sciences philosophiques et théologiques, 32* (1948), 38-51.

Benz, Ernst, *Das Todesproblem in der stoischen Philosophie*, Tübinger Beiträge zur Altertumswissenschaft, 7, Stuttgart, W. Kohlhammer, 1929.

Bernabei, Richard, "The Treatment of Sources in Macrobius' *Saturnalia*, and the Influence of the *Saturnalia* during the Middle Ages," Cornell University Ph.D. diss., 1970.

Berti, Enrico, *Il "De re publica" di Cicerone e il pensiero politico classico*, Pubblicazioni della Scuola di perfezionamento in filosofia dell'Università di Padova, 1, Padova, CEDAM, 1963.

Bevan, Edwyn, *Stoics and Sceptics: Four Lectures Delivered in Oxford during Hilary Term, 1913, for the Common University Fund*, New York, Barnes & Noble, Inc., 1959.

Bianca, Giuseppe G., *La pedagogia di Quintiliano*, Pubblicazioni dell'Istituto universitario di magistero di Catania, serie pedagogica, monografie, 1, Padova, CEDAM, 1963.

Bickel, Ernst, "*Metaschematizesthai*: Ein übersehener Grundbegriff des Poseidonios," *Rheinisches Museum für Philologie*, n.F. *100* (1957), 98-99.

—, "Die Schrift des Martinus von Bracara formula vitae honestae," *Rheinisches Museum für Philologie*, n.F. *6* (1905), 505-51.

—, "Seneca und Seneca-Mythus," *Das Altertum 5* (1959), 90-100.

Bidez, J., "La Cité du monde et la cité du soleil chez les Stoïciens," *Bulletins de l'Académie royale de Belgique*, Classe des lettres, 5ᵉ sér., *18*:7-9 (Paris, 1932), 244-91.

Biondi, Biondo, *Il diritto romano*, Istituto di studi romani, Bologna, Licino Cappelli, 1957.

—, *Il diritto romano cristiano*, 3 vols., Milano, A. Giuffrè, 1952.

—, *Istituzioni di diritto romano*, 3ª ed. riv., Milano, A. Giuffrè, 1956.
Birley, Anthony, *Marcus Aurelius*, London, Eyre & Spottiswoode, 1966.
Birt, Theodor, "Was hat Seneca mit seinen Tragödien gewollt?" *Neue Jarhbücher für das klassische Altertum, 27* (1911), 336-64.
Blatt, Franz, "Written and Unwritten Law in Ancient Rome," *Classica et mediaevalia, 5*:2 (1943), 137-58.
Blomgren, Sven, "De Venantio Fortunato Lucani Claudianique imitatore," *Eranos, 48* (1950), 150-56.
—, "De Venantio Fortunato Vergilii aliorumque poetarum priorum imitatore," *Eranos, 42* (1944), 81-88.
Bloos, Lutz, *Probleme der stoischen Physik*, Hamburger Studien zur Philosophie, 4, Hamburg, Helmut Buske Verlag, 1973.
Boak, Arthur E. R., *Manpower Shortage and the Fall of the Roman Empire in the West*, Jerome Lectures, 3rd ser., Ann Arbor, University of Michigan Press, 1955.
Bodoh, John James, "An Analysis of the Ideas of Juvenal," University of Wisconsin Ph.D. diss., 1966.
Bodson, Arthur, *La morale sociale des derniers stoïciens, Sénèque, Épictète et Marc Aurèle*, Bibliothèque de la Faculté de philosophie et lettres de l'Université de Liège, 176, Paris, Les Belles Lettres, 1967.
Bocheński, I. M., *Ancient Formal Logic*, Studies in Logic and the Foundations of Mathematics, ed. L. E. J. Brouwer, E. W. Beth, and A. Heyting, Amsterdam, North-Holland Publishing Company, 1951.
Boissier, Gaston, *Étude sur la vie et les ouvrages de M. T. Varron*, Paris, Hachette, 1861.
—, *L'Opposition sous les Césars*, 6ᵐᵉ éd., Paris, Hachette, 1909.
—, *Tacitus and Other Roman Studies*, trans. W. G. Hutchison, New York, G. P. Putnam's Sons, 1906.
Bolaffi, Ezio, "I proemi delle monografie di Sallustio," *Athenaeum, 16* (1938), 128-57.
Bolla, Ermenegildo, *Arriano di Nicomedia: Saggio storico-filologico*, Torino, Carlo Clausen, 1890.
Bonaria, Mario, "Echi lucanei in Paneg. lat. X (4), 29, 5," *Latomus, 17* (1958), 497-99.
Bond, R. P., "Aeneas and the Cardinal Virtues," *Prudentia, 6* (1974), 67-91.
Bonfante, Pietro, *Storia del diritto romano*, 4th ed., 2 vols., Opere di Pietro Bonfante, *1-2*, Milano, A. Giuffrè, 1958-59.
Bonhöffer, Adolf, *Epiktet und die Stoa: Untersuchungen zur stoischen Philosophie*, Stuttgart, Ferdinand Enke, 1890.
—, *Die Ethik des stoikers Epiktet*, Stuttgart, Ferdinand Enke, 1894.
—, "Zur stoischen Psychologie," *Philologus, 54* (1895), 403-29.
Bonnard, André, "Marc-Aurèle," *Revue de théologie et de philosophie*, n.s. *17* (1929), 217-36.
Born, Lester Kruger, "Animate Law in the Republic and the Laws of Cicero," *Transactions of the American Philosophical Association, 64* (1933), 128-37.
Borzsák, S., "P. Cornelius Tacitus," *Paulys Realencyclopädie der classischen Altertumswissenschaft*, Stuttgart, Alfred Druckenmüller Verlag, 1968, Supplementband *11*, cols. 373-512.
Bosshard, Ernst, "Épictète," *Revue de théologie et de philosophie*, n.s. *17* (1929), 201-16.
Bouché-Leclercq, A., *Histoire de la divination dans l'antiquité*, vol. 1, Paris, 1879.
Bourgery, A., "Lucain et la magie," *Revue des études latines, 6* (1928), 299-313.
—, *Sénèque prosateur: Études littéraires et grammaticales sur la prose de Sénèque le philosophe*, Collection d'études anciennes publiée sous le patronage de l'Association Guillaume Budé, Paris, Les Belles Lettres, 1922.
Bourne, Randolph S., "Stoicism," *The Open Court, 27*:6 (1913), 364-71.
Bovis, André de, *La sagesse de Sénèque*, Théologie: Études publiées sous la direction de la Faculté de théologie S. J. de Lyon-Fourvière, 13, Paris, Aubier, 1948.
Bowra, C. M., "Aeneas and the Stoic Ideal," *Greece & Rome, 3* (1933), 8-22.
Boyancé, Pierre, "Cicéron et la vie contemplative," *Latomus, 26* (1967), 3-26.
—, "Cum dignitate otium" *Revue des études anciennes, 43* (1941), 172-91.

—, *Études sur l'humanisme cicéronien*, Collection Latomus, 121, Bruxelles, Revue d'Études Latines, 1970.

—, *La Religion de Virgile*, Paris, PUF, 1963.

—, "Le sens cosmique de Virgile," *Revue des études latines*, 32 (1954), 220-49.

Bramble, J. C., *Persius and the Programmatic Satire*, Cambridge Classical Studies, Cambridge, The University Press, 1974.

Brassloff, Stephan, *Sozialpolitische Motive in der römischen Rechtsentwicklung*, Wien, Moritz Perles, 1933.

Bréhier, Émile, *Chrysippe et l'ancien Stoïcisme*, nouv. éd., Paris, PUF, 1951.

—, "La cosmologie stoïcienne à la fin du paganisme," *Revue de l'histoire des religions*, 64 (1911), 1-20.

—, *Études de philosophie antique*, Publications de la Faculté des lettres de Paris, 1, Paris, PUF, 1955.

—, *The Hellenistic and Roman Age (The History of Philosophy, 2)*, trans. Wade Baskin, Chicago, University of Chicago Press, 1965.

—, "Posidonius d'Apamée, théoricien de la géométrie," *Revue des études grecques*, 27 (1914), 44-58.

—, "La théorie des incorporeals dans l'ancien stoïcisme," *Archiv für Geschichte der Philosophie*, 22, n.F. *15* (1909), 114-25.

Bridoux, André, *Le Stoïcisme et son influence*, Paris, J. Vrin, 1966.

Brinckmann, Wolfgang, *Der Begriff der Freundschaft in Senecas Briefen*, Dissertation, Köln, Gouder u. Hansen, 1963.

Bringmann, Klaus, *Untersuchungen zum späten Cicero*, Hypomnemata: Untersuchungen zur Antike und zu ihrem Nachleben, 29, Göttingen, Vandenhoeck & Ruprecht, 1971.

Brink, C. O., *Horace on Poetry*, vol. 1, Cambridge, The University Press, 1963.

—, "*Oikeiosis* and *oikeiotes*: Theophrastus and Zeno on Nature in Moral Theory," *Phronesis*, *1* (1956), 123-45.

Briot, Paul, "Cicéron: Approches d'une psychanalyse," *Latomus*, 28 (1969), 1040-49.

Brisset, Jacqueline, *Les Idées politiques de Lucain*, Collection d'études anciennes publiée sous le patronage de l'Association Guillaume Budé, Paris, Les Belles Lettres, 1964.

Brisson, Jean-Paul, "Carthage et le *fatum*: Réflexions sur un theme de l'Énéide," *Hommages à Marcel Renard*, ed. Jacqueline Bibauw, Collection Latomus, 101, Bruxelles, Latomus, 1969, *1*, 162-73.

—, *Virgile: Son temps et le nôtre*, Paris, François Maspero, 1966.

Brochard, V., *Études de philosophie ancienne et de philosophie moderne*, nouv. éd., Paris, J. Vrin, 1926.

Brown, Ruth Martin, *A Study of the Scipionic Circle*, Iowa Studies in Classical Philology, 1, Scottsdale, Pa., Mennonite Press, 1934.

Bruère, Richard T., "The Scope of Lucan's Historical Epic," *Classical Philology*, 45 (1950), 217-35.

Brugnoli, Giorgio, "La tradizione manoscritta di Seneca tragico alla luce delle testimonianze medioevali," *Atti della Accademia nazionale dei Lincei*, classe di scienze morali, storiche e filologiche, *354*, ser. 8, *8*:3, Roma, Accademia Nazionale dei Lincei, 1957, pp. 199-287.

Brummer, Rudolf, "Auf den Spuren des Philosophen Seneca in den romanischen Literaturen des Mittelalters und des Frühhumanismus," *Romanica: Festschrift Prof. Dr. Fritz Neubert*, ed. Rudolf Brummer, Berlin, Stunderglas-Verlag, 1948, pp. 55-84.

Brun, Jean, *Le Stoïcisme*, "Que sais-je?" 770, Paris, PUF, 1958.

Brunschwig, Jacques, ed., *Les stoïciens et leur logique*, Actes du Colloque de Chantilly, 18-22 septembre 1976, Paris, J. Vrin, 1978.

Brunt, P. A., "Aspects of the Social Thought of Dio Chrysostom and of the Stoics," *Proceedings of the Cambridge Philological Society*, 199 (1973), 9-34.

—, *Italian Manpower, 225 B.C.-A.D. 14*, Oxford, Clarendon Press, 1971.

—, "Marcus Aurelius in His *Meditations*," *Journal of Roman Studies*, 64 (1974), 1-20.

Bruwaene, Martin van den, *La théologie de Cicéron*, Université de Louvain, Recueil de travaux publiés par les membres des conférences d'histoire et de philologie, 2ᵉ sér., 42, Louvain, Bureaux du Recueil, 1937.

Bucciarelli, Aloysius, *Utrum Aulus Persius Flaccus doctrinae stoicae sit sectator idem et interpretes*, Roma, E. Mantegazza, 1888.

Büchner, Karl, *Cicero*, Studien zur römischen Literatur, 2, Wiesbaden, Franz Steiner Verlag GMBH, 1962.

—, *Cicero: Bestand und Wandel seiner geistigen Welt*, Heidelberg, Carl Winter, 1964.

—, "Humanum und humanitas in der römischen Welt," *Studium Generale, 14* (1961), 636-46.

—, *P. Vergilius Maro: Der Dichter der Römer*, Stuttgart, Alfred Druckenmüller, 1966.

—, *Resultate römischen Lebens, in römischen Schriftwerken*, Studien zur römischen Literatur, 6, Wiesbaden, Franz Steiner Verlag GMBH, 1967.

—, "Römische Konstanten und De legibus," *Werkanalysen*, Studien zur römischen Literatur, 8, Wiesbaden, Franz Steiner Verlag GMBH, 1970, pp. 21-39.

—, *Sallust*, Heidelberg, Carl Winter, 1960.

—, *Somnium Scipionis: Quellen, Gestalt, Sinn*, *Hermes* Einzelschriften, 36, Wiesbaden, Franz Steiner Verlag GMBH, 1976.

—, ed., *Das neue Cicerobild*, Wege der Forschung, 27, Darmstadt, Wissenschaftliche Buchgesellschaft, 1971.

Buckland, W. W., "Classical Roman Law," *Cambridge Ancient History*, ed. S. A. Cook, F. E. Adcock, and M. P. Charlesworth, Cambridge, The University Press, 1936, *11*, 806-44.

—, *The Roman Law of Slavery: The Condition of the Slave in Private Law from Augustus to Justinian*, Cambridge, The University Press, 1908.

Buckley, Michael J., "Philosophical Method in Cicero," *Journal of the History of Philosophy*, 8 (1970), 143-54.

Burck, Erich, "Die Schicksalsauffassung des Tacitus und Statius," *Studies Presented to David Moore Robinson on His Seventieth Birthday*, ed. George E. Mylonas and Doris Raymond, St. Louis, Washington University, 1953, 2, 693-706.

—, ed., *Wege zu Livius*, Wege der Forschung, 132, Darmstadt, Wissenschaftliche Buchgesellschaft, 1967.

Burdese, Alberto, "Il concetto di 'ius naturale' nel pensiero della giurisprudenza classica," *Rivista italiana per le scienze giuridiche*, ser. 3:7 (1954), 407-21.

—, *La nozione classica di naturalis obligatio*, Università di Torino, memorie dell'Istituto giuridico, ser. 2:92, Torino, G. Giappicelli, 1955.

Burkert, Walter, "Cicero als Platoniker und Skeptiker: Zum Platonverständnis der 'Neuen Akademie'," *Gymnasium, 72* (1965), 175-200.

Burnier, Charles, *Le Rôle des Satires de Perse dans le développement du néo-stoïcisme*, La Chaux-de-Fonds, Imprimerie du National Suisse, 1909.

Busch, Gerda, "Fortunae resistere in der Moral des Philosophen Seneca," *Antike und Abendland, 10* (1961), 131-54.

Bussell, F. W., *Marcus Aurelius and the Later Stoics*, New York, Charles Scribner's Sons, 1910.

Busuttil, Joseph, "Cicero: *De Legibus* Book I, An Introduction, a Translation and a Commentary," University of London Ph.D. diss., 1964.

Cameron, Alan, "The Date and Identity of Macrobius," *Journal of Roman Studies, 56* (1966), 25-38.

Campbell, Archibald Y., *Horace: A New Interpretation*, London, Methuen & Co. Ltd., 1924.

Campiche, Émile, "Les causes de la guerre civile d'après Lucain," *Études de Lettres*, Bulletin de la Faculté de lettres de l'Université de Lausanne, sér. 2:8 (1965), 224-31.

Camps, W. A., *An Introduction to Virgil's Aeneid*, London, Oxford University Press, 1969.

Cancelli, Filippo, "Sull'origine del diritto secondo un motivo ricorrente in scrittori ellenistico-romani, e Cicerone 'De re publica' 5.3," *Studia et documenta historiae et iuris, 37* (1971), 328-37.

Cancik, Hildegard, *Untersuchungen zu Senecas Epistulae morales*, Spudasmata, 18, Hildesheim, Georg Olms Verlagsbuchhandlung, 1967.

Capes, W. W., *Stoicism*, London, SPCK, 1880.

Carlsson, Gunnar, "The Hero and Fate in Virgil's *Aeneid*," *Eranos*, 43 (1945), 111-35.

Cartault, A., *Étude sur les satires d'Horace*, Université de Paris, Bibliothèque de la Faculté des lettres, 9, Paris, Félix Alcan, 1899.

Casa, Adriana della, *Il libro X del De lingua latina di Varrone*, Genova, Libreria Editrice Mario Bozzi, 1969.

—, *Nigidio Figulo*, Roma, Edizioni dell'Ateneo, 1962.

Castro, Albert Dwight, "Tacitus and the 'Virtues' of the Roman Emperor: The Role of Imperial Propaganda in the Historiography of Tacitus," Indiana University Ph.D. diss., 1972.

Cattin, Aurèle, "L'âme humaine et la vie future dans les textes lyriques des tragédies de Sénèque," *Latomus*, 15 (1956), 359-65, 544-50.

Cazeneuve, Jean, "Les cadres sociaux de la doctrine morale stoïcienne dans l'empire romain," *Cahiers internationaux de sociologie*, 34 (1963), 13-26.

Charlesworth, Martin Percival, *Five Men: Character Studies from the Roman Empire*, Martin Classical Lectures, 6, Cambridge, Mass., Harvard University Press, 1936.

Cherniss, Harold, "Galen and Posidonius' Theory of Vision," *American Journal of Philology*, 54 (1933), 154-61.

Chevallier, R., "Le milieu stoïcien à Rome au 1er siècle après Jésus-Christ ou l'âge héroïque du stoïcisme romain," *Bulletin de l'Association Guillaume Budé*, supplément *Lettres d'humanité*, 19 (1960), 534-62.

Christensen, Johnny, *An Essay on the Unity of Stoic Philosophy*, Copenhagen, Munksgaard, 1962.

Chroust, Anton-Hermann, "The Ideal Polity of the Early Stoics: Zeno's Republic," *Review of Politics*, 27 (1965), 173-83.

Ciaceri, E., "Il trattato di Cicerone *De re publica* e le teorie di Polibio sulla costituzione romana," *Rendiconti della reale Accademia dei Lincei*, classe di scienze morali, storiche, e filologiche, ser. 5:27 (1918), 237-49, 266-78, 303-15.

Ciccotti, Ettore, *Il tramonto della schiavitù nel mondo antico*, Udine, Istituto delle Edizioni Accademiche, 1940.

Ciulei, Georges, *L'Équité chez Cicéron*, Amsterdam, Adolf M. Hakkert, 1972.

Clarke, M. L., *The Roman Mind: Studies in the History of Thought from Cicero to Marcus Aurelius*, Cambridge, Mass., Harvard University Press, 1956.

Cocchia, Enrico, "Cicerone oratore e giureconsulto," *Atti della reale Accademia di archeologia, lettere e belli arti di Napoli*, n.s. 9 (1926), 421-59.

Coing, Helmut, "Zum Einfluss der Philosophie des Aristoteles auf die Entwicklung des römischen Rechts," *Zeitschrift der Savigny-Stiftung für Rechtsgeschichte*, romanistische Abteilung, 69 (1952), 24-59.

Colardeau, Th., *Étude sur Épictète*, Paris, Albert Fontemoing, 1903.

Coleman, R. G. G., "The Dream of Cicero," *Proceedings of the Cambridge Philological Society*, 190, n.s. 10 (1964), 1-14.

Colish, Marcia L., "The Roman Law of Persons and Roman History: A Case for an Interdisciplinary Approach," *American Journal of Jurisprudence*, 19 (1974), 112-27.

—, "Seneca's *Apocolocyntosis* as a Possible Source for Erasmus' *Julius Exclusus*," *Renaissance Quarterly*, 39 (1976), 361-68.

—, "The Stoic Hypothetical Syllogisms and their Transmission in the Latin West through the Early Middle Ages," *Res Publica Litterarum*, 2 (1979), 19-26.

—, *The Stoic Tradition from Antiquity to the Early Middle Ages*, II: *Stoicism in Christian Latin Thought through the Sixth Century*, Studies in the History of Christian Thought, 35, ed. Heiko A. Oberman, Leiden, E. J. Brill, 1985.

Collart, Jean, "Analogie et anomalie," *Varron*, Fondation Hardt: Entretiens sur l'antiquité classique, 9, Genève, Vandoeuvres, 1963, pp. 119-32.

—, *Varron: Grammarien latin*, Publications de la Faculté des lettres de l'Université de Strasbourg, 121, Paris, Les Belles Lettres, 1954.

Colson, F. H., "The Analogist and Anomalist Controversy," *Classical Quarterly, 13* (1919), 24-36.

Commager, Steele, ed., *Virgil: A Collection of Critical Essays,* Twentieth Century Views, Englewood Cliffs, N. J., Prentice-Hall, Inc., 1966.

Comparetti, D., *Virgilio nel medio evo,* nuova ed., ed. Giorgio Pasquali, 2 vols., Firenze, La Nuova Italia, 1937-46.

Conway, Robert Seymour, *Harvard Lectures on the Vergilian Age,* New York, Biblo and Tannen, 1967 [repr. of Cambridge, Mass., 1928 ed.].

—, *Makers of Europe: Being the James Henry Morgan Lectures in Dickinson College for 1930,* Cambridge, Mass., Harvard University Press, 1931.

—, "The Philosophy of Vergil," *Bulletin of the John Rylands Library, 6* (1922), 384-401.

Corbett, Percy Ellwood, *The Roman Law of Marriage,* Oxford, Clarendon Press, 1930.

Corte, Francesco della, *Varrone: Il terzo gran lume romano,* Genova, Pubblicazioni dell'Istituto universitario di magistero, 1954.

Costa, C. D. N., ed., *Horace,* London, Routledge & Kegan Paul, 1973.

—, ed., *Seneca,* London, Routledge & Kegan Paul, 1974.

Costa, Emilio, *Cicerone giureconsulto,* 2ª ed., 2 vols., Bologna, Nicola Zanichelli, 1927.

—, *La filosofia greca nella giurisprudenza romana,* Parma, Luigi Battei, 1892.

—, *Storia delle fonti del diritto romano,* Torino, Fratelli Bocca, 1909.

Costil, P., "L'Esthétique stoïcienne," *Actes du 1ᵉʳ congrès de la fédération internationale des Associations d'études classiques,* Paris, 28 août-2 septembre 1950, Paris, C. Klincksieck, 1951, pp. 360-64.

Couissin, Pierre, "Le Stoïcisme de la nouvelle Académie," *Revue d'histoire de la philosophie, 3* (1929), 241-76.

Coulter, Cornelia C., "Aeolian Strains on the Roman Lyre," *Classical Journal, 31* (1935-36), 175-82.

Courbaud, Edmond, *Horace: Sa vie et sa pensée à l'époque des épîtres. Étude sur le premier livre,* Paris, Librairie Hachette et Cie., 1914.

Courcelle, Pierre, "Les exégèses chrétiennes de la quatrième Églogue," *Revue des études anciennes, 59* (1957), 294-319.

—, *Late Latin Writers and Their Greek Sources,* trans. Harry E. Wedeck, Cambridge, Mass., Harvard University Press, 1969.

—, "La postérité chrétienne du *Songe de Scipion*," *Revue des études latines, 36* (1958), 205-34.

Cousin, Jean, *Étude sur Quintilien,* Amsterdam, P. Schippers N. V., 1967 [repr. of Paris, 1935 ed.].

Cresson, André, *Marc-Aurèle: Sa vie, son oeuvre avec un exposé de sa philosophie,* Paris, Félix Alcan, 1939.

Crispino, Giuseppina, *Le Idee morali e educativi di Orazio,* Napoli, Francesco Perrella A. S., 1935.

Croisille, J.-M., "Lieux communs, *sententiae* et intentions philosophiques dans la *Phèdre* de Sénèque," *Revue des études latines, 42* (1964), 276-301.

Crook, John, *Law and Life of Rome,* Ithaca, Cornell University Press, 1967.

Crosland, Jessie, "Lucan in the Middle Ages, with Special Reference to the Old French Epic," *Modern Language Review, 25* (1930), 32-51.

Cruttwell, Robert W., *Virgil's Mind at Work: An Analysis of the Symbolism of the Aeneid,* Oxford, Basil Blackwell, 1946.

Cumont, Franz, *After Life in Roman Paganism,* New Haven, Yale University Press, 1922.

—, *Lux Perpetua,* Paris, Librairie Orientaliste Paul Geuthner, 1949.

Curcio, Gaetano, "La filosofia della storia nell'opera di T. Livio," *Rivista indo-greco-italica di filologia-lingua-antichità, 1* (1917), 321-29.

Currie, Bethia S., "God and Matter in Early Stoic Physics," New School for Social Research Ph.D. diss., 1971.

D'Agostino, Vittorio, "Il contrapposto fra l'uomo e gli animali nelle opere di Cicerone," *Rivista di studi classici, 12* (1964), 150-59.

—, "La favola del bivio in Senofonte, in Luciano, e in Silio Italico," *Rivista di studi classici, 2* (1954), 173-84.

—, *Studi sul neostoicismo: Seneca, Plinio il giovane, Epitteto, Marco Aurelio*, 2ª ed. riv., Torino, Presso l'Autore, 1962.

—, "Sulla formazione mentale di Varrone Reatino," *Rivista di studi classici*, *3* (1955), 24-31.

Dahlmann, Hellfried, *Kleine Schriften*, Collectanea, 19, Hildesheim, Georg Olms Verlag, 1970.

—, "M. Terentius Varro," *Paulys Realencyclopäide der classischen Altertumswissenschaft*, new ed., ed. Wilhelm Kroll, Stuttgart, J. B. Metzlersche Verlagsbuchhandlung, 1935, Supplementband *6*, cols. 1172-1277.

—, *Varro und die hellenistische Sprachtheorie*, 2nd ed., Berlin, Weidmannsche Verlagsbuchhandlung, 1964.

—, *Zur Ars Grammatica des Marius Victorinus*, Akademie der Wissenschaften und der Literatur, Abhandlungen der geistes- und sozialwissenschaftlichen Klasse, 1970, no. 2, Mainz, Akademie der Wissenschaften und der Literatur, 1970.

Dailly, Robert and Effenterre, Henri van, "Le cas Marc-Aurèle: Essai de psychosomatique historique," *Revue des études anciennes*, *56* (1954), 347-65.

D'Alton, J. F., *Horace and His Age: A Study in Historical Background*, London, Longmans, Green and Co., 1917.

Dam, R. J., *De analogia: Observationes in Varronem grammaticamque Romanorum*, Campis, J. H. Kok, 1930.

Daniélou, Jean, *Message évangelique et culture hellénistique aux IIᵉ et IIIᵉ siècles*, Bibliothèque de théologie: Histoire des doctrines chrétiennes avant Nicée, 2, Tournai, Desclée & Cie., 1961.

Daube, David, "Greek and Roman Reflections on Impossible Laws," *Natural Law Forum*, *12* (1967), 1-84.

—, "The Peregrine Praetor," *Journal of Roman Studies*, *41* (1951), 66-70.

Davidson, William L., *The Stoic Creed*, Edinburgh, T. & T. Clark, 1907.

Davies, J. C., "The Originality of Cicero's Philosophical Works," *Latomus*, *30* (1971), 105-19.

Davis, Charles H. Stanley, *Greek and Roman Stoicism and Some of Its Disciples: Epictetus, Seneca, and Marcus Aurelius*, Boston, Herbert B. Turner & Co., 1903.

Déchanet, J.-M., "Seneca Noster: Des lettres à Lucilius à la Lettre aux Frères de Mont-Dieu," *Mélanges Joseph de Ghellinck, S. J.*, Museum Lessianum, section historique, 14, Gembloux, J. Duculot, 1951, *2*, 753-66.

DeDecker, Josué, *Juvenalis Declamans: Étude sur la rhétorique déclamatoire dans les satires de Juvénal*, Gand, A. Vander Haeghen, 1912.

Defourny, Pierre, "Les fondements de la religion d'après Cicéron," *Les Études classiques*, *22* (1954), 241-53, 366-78.

DeLacy, Phillip, "The Logical Structure of the Ethics of Epictetus," *Classical Philology*, *38* (1943), 112-25.

—, "The Stoic Categories as Methodological Principles," *Transactions and Proceedings of the American Philological Association*, *76* (1945), 246-63.

—, "Stoic Views of Poetry," *American Journal of Philology*, *69* (1948), 241-71.

Delatte, A., "Le sage-témoin dans la philosophie stoïco-cynique," *Académie royale de Belgique, Bulletin de la classe des lettres et des sciences morales et politiques*, 5ᵉ sér., *39* (1953), 166-86.

Delgado, José-Jiménez, "Clasificación de los prodigios titolivianos," *Helmantica*, *12* (1961), 441-61.

—, "Importancia de los prodigios en Tito Livio," *Helmantica*, *12* (1961), 27-46.

—, "Postura de Livio frente al prodigio," *Helmantica*, *14* (1963), 381-419.

Dermience, Alice, "La notion de 'libertas' dans les oeuvres de Cicéron," *Les Études classiques*, *25* (1957), 157-67.

Dessen, Cynthia S., *Iunctura callidus acri: A Study of Persius' Satires*, Illinois Studies in Language and Literature, Urbana, University of Illinois Press, 1968.

Devine, Francis Edward, "Stoicism on the Best Regime," *Journal of the History of Ideas*, *31* (1970), 323-36.

DeWitt, Norman N., "Epicurean Doctrine in Horace," *Classical Philology, 34* (1939), 127-34.
—, "The Epicurean Doctrine of Gratitude," *American Journal of Philology, 58* (1937), 320-28.
—, "Parresiastic Poems of Horace," *Classical Philology, 30* (1935), 312-19.
Dhile, A., "Posidonius' System of Moral Philosophy," *Journal of Hellenic Studies, 93* (1973), 50-57.
Diano, Carlo, *Forma ed evento: Principii per una interpretazione del mondo greco*, Venezia, Neri Pozza, 1952.
Dick, Bernard F., "*Fatum* and *Fortuna* in Lucan's *Bellum civile*," *Classical Philology, 62* (1967), 235-42.
—, "The Role of the Oracle in Lucan's de Bello Civili," *Hermes, 93* (1965), 460-66.
—, "Seneca and Juvenal 10," *Harvard Studies in Classical Philology, 73* (1969), 237-46.
Diehl, Georg Joseph, *Zur Ethik des Stoikers Zenon von Kition*, Programm des Grossherzog-lichen Gymnasiums zu Mainz, Schuljahr 1876-77, Mainz, Heinrich Prickarts, 1877.
Diels, Hermann, *Seneca und Lucan*, Philosophische und historische Abhandlungen der kö-niglichen Akademie der Wissenschaft zu Berlin, 1885, *3*, Berlin, 1886.
Dill, Samuel, *Roman Society from Nero to Marcus Aurelius*, New York, Meridian Books, 1956.
Dillon, John, *The Middle Platonists, 30 B.C. to A.D. 220*, Ithaca, Cornell University Press, 1977.
Diósdi, György, *Ownership in Ancient and Preclassical Roman Law*, Budapest, Akademiai Kiado, 1970.
Dobson, J. F., "Boethus of Sidon," *Classical Quarterly, 8* (1914), 88-90.
—, "The Posidonius Myth," *Classical Quarterly, 12* (1918), 179-95.
Dodds, E. R., *Pagan and Christian in an Age of Anxiety: Some Aspects of Religious Experience from Marcus Aurelius to Constantine*, Wiles Lectures, Queen's University, Belfast, 1963, Cambridge, The University Press, 1965.
Döllinger, John J. I., *The Gentile and the Jew in the Courts of the Temple of Christ: An Intro-duction to the History of Christianity*, vol. 1, trans. N. Darnell, London, Longman, Green, Longman, Roberts, and Green, 1862.
Donini, Pier Luigi, "Chrisippo e la nozione del possibile," *Rivista di filologia e di istruzione classica, 101* (1973), 333-51.
—, "Fato e volontà umana in Crisippo," *Atti della Accademia delle scienze di Torino*, classe di scienze morali, storiche e filologiche, *109*:2 (1975), 187-230.
Doppioni, Lino, *Virgilio nell'arte e nel pensiero di Seneca*, Firenze, Libreria Editrice Fioren-tina, 1939.
Dorey, T. A. ed., *Cicero*, London, Routledge & Kegan Paul, 1965.
— ed., *Latin Historians*, New York, Basic Books, Inc., 1966.
— ed., *Livy*, London, Routledge & Kegan Paul, 1971.
Döring, U., "Zeno, der Gründer der Stoa," *Preussische Jahrbücher, 107* (1902), 213-42.
Dougherty, John M., "Vergilian 'Fate' as Cosmic," *Classical Bulletin, 34* (1958), 65, 67.
Douglas, A. E., *Cicero*, Greece & Rome: New Surveys in the Classics, 2, Oxford, Clar-endon Press, 1968.
Drabkin, I. E., "Posidonius and the Circumference of the Earth," *Isis, 34* (1942-43), 509-12.
Dragona-Monachou, Myrto, *The Stoic Arguments for the Existence and Providence of the Gods*, National and Capodistrian University of Athens, Faculty of Arts, S. Saripolos' Li-brary, 32, Athens, 1976.
Duckett, Eleanor Shipley, *Latin Writers of the Fifth Century*, intro. by Eric Milner White, Hamden, Conn., Archon Books, 1969 [repr. of New York, 1930 ed.].
Duckworth, George E., "Fate and Free Will in Vergil's *Aeneid*," *Classical Journal, 51* (1956), 357-64.
Dudley, Donald R., *A History of Cynicism from Diogenes to the 6th Century A.D.*, London, Methuen & Co. Ltd., 1937.

—, ed., *Neronians and Flavians: Silver Latin I*, London, Routledge & Kegan Paul, 1972.

—, ed., *Virgil*, London, Routledge & Kegan Paul, 1969.

Due, Otto Steen, "An Essay on Lucan," *Classica et mediaevalia*, *23* (1962), 68–132.

—, "Lucain et la philosophie," *Lucain*, Fondation Hardt: Entretiens sur l'antiquité classique, 15, Vandoeuvres-Genève, 26–31 août 1968, Paris, Librairie Klincksieck, 1970, pp. 203–24.

Duff, J. Wight, *A Literary History of Rome from the Origins to the Close of the Golden Age*, 3rd ed., ed. A. M. Duff, London, Ernest Benn Ltd., 1967.

—, *A Literary History of Rome in the Silver Age from Tiberius to Hadrian*, New York, Charles Scribner's Sons, 1935.

—, *Roman Satire: Its Outlook on Social Life*, Sather Classical Lectures, 12, Berkeley, University of Claifornia Press, 1936.

Duhem, Pierre, *Le Système du monde: Histoire des doctrines cosmologiques de Platon à Copernic*, vols. 2 and 3, Paris, Librairie Scientifique A. Hermann et Fils, 1913-14.

Duprat, G.·L., "La Doctrine stoïcienne du monde, du destin, et de la providence d'après Chrysippe," *Archiv für Geschichte der Philosophie*, 33, n.F. *16* (1910), 472–511.

Dyroff, Adolf, *Die Ethik der alten Stoa*, Berliner Studien für classische Philologie und Archaeologie, n.F., *2*:2-4, Berlin, S. Calvary & Co., 1897.

Dyson, Stephen, L., "The Portrait of Seneca in Tacitus," *Arethusa*, *3* (1970), 71–83.

Earl, D. C., *The Political Thought of Sallust*, Cambridge Classical Studies, Amsterdam, Adolf M. Hakkert, 1966 [repr. of London, 1961 ed.].

Eckstein, Walther, *Das antike Naturrecht in sozialphilosophischer Beleuchtung*, Soziologie und Sozialphilosophie, 2, Wien, Wilhelm Braümuller, 1926.

Edelstein, Ludwig, *The Meaning of Stoicism*, Martin Classical Lectures, 21, Cambridge, Mass., Harvard University Press, 1966.

—, "The Philosophical System of Posidonius," *American Journal of Philology*, *57* (1936), 286–325.

Edlow, R. Blair, "The Stoics on Ambiguity," *Journal of the History of Philosophy*, *13* (1975), 423–36.

Edsman, Carl-Martin, *Ignis Divinus: Le feu comme moyen de rajeunissement et d'immortalité. Contes, légendes, mythes et rites*, Skrifter utgivna av Vetenskaps-Societeten i Lund, 34, Lund, C. W. K. Gleerup, 1949.

Edwards, Mark W,. "The Expression of Stoic Ideas in the *Aeneid*," *Phoenix*, *14* (1960), 151-65.

Egermann, Franz, *Die Proömien zu den Werken des Sallust*, Sitzungsberichte der Akademie der Wissenschaften in Wien, philosophisch-historische Klasse, *214*:3, Wien, Hölder-Pichler-Tempsky A. G., 1932.

—, "Seneca als Dichterphilosoph," *Neue Jahrbücher für Antike und deutsche Bildung*, *3* (1940), 18-36.

Egli, Urs, *Zur stoischen Dialektik*, Inaugural-Dissertation, Universität Bern, Bern, Eigenverlag Sandoz AG, 1967.

Ehrenberg, Victor, "Anfänge des griechischen Naturrechts," *Archiv für Geschichte der Philosophie*, 35, n.F. *28* (1923), 119-43.

Eliade, Mircea, *The Myth of the Eternal Return*, trans. Willard R. Trask, Bollingen Series, 46, New York, Pantheon Books, 1954.

Elorduy, Eleuterio, "La lógica en la Estoa," *Revista de filosofía*, *3* (1944), 7-66, 222-66.

—, *Séneca: Vida y escritos*, Madrid, Consejo Superior de Investigaciones Científicas, Instituto "Luis Vives" de Filosofía, 1965.

—, *Die Sozialphilosophie der Stoa*, Philologus, Supplementband *28*:3, Leipzig, Dieterich'sche Verlagsbuchhandlung, 1936.

English, Robert B., "A Brief Comparison of Stoic and Epicurean Psychology," *Transactions and Proceedings of the American Philological Association*, *41* (1910), xxviii-xxxi.

Erbse, Hartmut, "Die Vorstellung von der Seele bei Marc Aurel," *Festschrift für Friedrich Zucker zum 70. Geburtstag*, Berlin, Akademie-Verlag, 1954, pp. 127-52.

Estudios sobre Séneca: Ponencias y communicaciones, Octava Semana Española de Filosofía,

Madrid, Consejo Superior de Investigaciones Científicas, Instituto "Luis Vives" de Filosofía, 1966.

Étienne, Jacques, "Sagesse et prudence selon le stoïcisme," *Revue théologique de Louvain, 1* (1970), 175-82.

Evans, J. D. G., "The Old Stoa and the Truth-Value of Oaths," *Proceedings of the Cambridge Philological Society, 200* (1974), 44-47.

Fabia, Philippe, "L'irréligion de Tacite," *Journal des savants, 12* (1914), 250-65.

—, *Les sources de Tacite dans les Histoires et les Annales*, Paris, Imprimerie National, 1893.

Faggi, Adolfo, "Il 'somatismo' o 'corporalismo' degli stoici," *Atti della Reale Accademia delle scienze di Torino*, classe di scienze morali, storiche e filologiche, *67* (1931-32), 59-70.

Faider, Paul, *Études sur Sénèque*, Université de Gand, Recueil de travaux publiés par la Faculté de philosophie et lettres, 49, Gand, Van Rysselberghe & Rombaut, 1921.

Farrington, Benjamin, *The Faith of Epicurus*, London, Weidenfeld and Nicholson, 1967.

Favez, Charles, "Un féministe romain: Musonius Rufus," *Bulletin de la Société des Études de Lettres de Lausanne, 8* (1933), 1-8.

—, "Le pessimisme de Sénèque," *Revue des études latines, 25* (1947), 158-63.

—, "Le sentiment dans les *Consolations* de Sénèque," *Mélanges Paul Thomas*, Bruges, Imprimerie Sainte Catherine, 1930, pp. 262-70.

Fehling, Detlev, "Varro und die grammatische Lehre von der Analogie und der Flexion," *Glotta, 35* (1956), 214-70; *36* (1957), 48-100.

Ferguson, John, "Cicero's Contribution to Philosophy," *Studies in Cicero*, Collana di studi ciceroniani, 2, Roma, Centro di Studi Ciceroniani, 1962, pp. 99-111.

—, "Lucan and His Epic," *Durham University Journal*, 49, n.s. *18* (1956-57), 116-25.

—, "The Religion of Cicero," *Studies in Cicero*, Collana di studi ciceroniani, 2, Roma, Centro di Studi Ciceroniani, 1962, pp. 83-96.

—, "Some Ancient Judgments of Cicero," *Studies in Cicero*, Collana di studi ciceroniani, 2, Roma, Centro di Studi Ciceroniani, 1962, pp. 11-33.

—, *Utopias of the Classical World*, London, Thames and Hudson, 1975.

Ferrary, Jean-Louis, "Le discours de Laelius dans le troisième livre du *De re publica* de Cicéron," *Mélanges d'Archéologie et d'histoire de l'École française de Rome, 86* (1974), 745-71.

Ferrero, Leonardo, "Attualità e tradizione nella praefatio Liviana," *Rivista di filologia classica*, 77, n.s. *27* (1949), 1-47.

Ferrill, Arthur, "Seneca's Exile and the *Ad Helviam*: A Reinterpretation," *Classical Philology, 61* (1966), 253-56.

Festa, Nicola, "Ortodossia e propaganda nello stoicismo antico," *Mélanges offerts à M. Octave Navarre par ses élèves et ses amis*, Toulouse, Édouard Privat, 1935, pp. 169-80.

—, La *"Repubblica" di Zenone*, Roma, Tipografia Poliglotta Vaticana, 1928.

—, *L'Uomo e l'universo nella dottrina di Zenone Cizio*, Roma, Tipografia Poliglotta Vaticana, 1929.

Festugière, A.-J., *Liberté et civilisation chez les grecs*, Initiations, 14, Paris, Éditions de la Revue des Jeunes, 1947.

—, *Personal Religion among the Greeks*, Sather Classical Lectures, 26, Berkeley, University of California Press, 1954.

—, *La révélation d'Hermès Trismégiste*, vol. 2, 2ᵐᵉ éd., Paris, Librairie Lecoffre, 1949.

—, "Le symbole du Phénix et le mysticisme hermétique," *Fondation Eugène Piot*, Monuments et mémoires publiés par l'Académie des Inscriptions et Belles-Lettres, *38* (1941), 147-51.

La filosofia della natura nel medioevo, Atti del 3° congresso internazionale di filosofia medioevale, Passo della Mendola (Trento), 31 agosto-5 settembre 1964, Milano, Vita e Pensiero, 1966.

Fine, Elizabeth Bunting, "The Stoic Opposition to the Principate as Seen in Tacitus," Yale University Ph.D. diss., 1932.

Finger, Philipp, "Die beiden Quellen des III. Buches der Tusculanen Ciceros," *Philologus, 84* (1928-29), 51-81, 320-48.

—, "Die drei Grundlagen des Rechts im I. Buche von Ciceros Schrift De legibus," *Rheinisches Museum für Philologie*, n.F. *81* (1932), 155-77, 243-62.

—, "Die drei kosmologischen Systeme im zweiten Buch von Ciceros Schrift über das Wesen der Götter," *Rheinisches Museum für Philologie*, n.F. *80* (1931), 151-200, 310-20.

—, "Das stoische und das akademische Führerbild in Ciceros Schrift De officiis (1. Buch)," *Neue Jahrbücher für Antike und deutsche Bildung*, 5 (1942), 1-20.

Finley, M. I., ed., *Slavery in Classical Antiquity: Views and Controversies*, Cambridge, W. Heffer & Sons Ltd., 1960.

Fisch, M. H., "Alexander and the Stoics," *American Journal of Philology*, *58* (1937), 59-82, 129-51.

Fischer, Balduinus, *De Augustini disciplinarum libro qui est de dialectica*, Jena, G. Neuenhahn, 1912.

Fischer, Hans-Werner, *Untersuchungen über die Quellen der Rhetorik des Martianus Capella*, Inaugural-Dissertation, Breslau, Breslau, Hermann Eschenhagen K. G., 1936.

Fischli, Walter, *Studien zum Fortleben der Pharsalia des M. Annaeus Lucanus*, Luzern, Eugen Haag, n.d.

Fiske, George Converse, *Lucilius and Horace: A Study in the Classical Theory of Imitation*, University of Wisconsin Studies in Language and Literature, 7, Madison, University of Wisconsin Press, 1920.

—, "Lucilius, the *Ars Poetica* of Horace, and Persius," *Harvard Studies in Classical Philology*, *24* (1913), 1-36.

—, "The Plain Style in the Scipionic Circle," *Classical Studies in Honor of Charles Forster Smith*, University of Wisconsin Studies in Language and Literature, 3, Madison, 1919, pp. 62-105.

Flintoff, Everard, "New Light on the Early Life of Juvenal," *Wiener Studien*, n.F. *8* (1974), 156-59.

Flückiger, Felix, *Geschichte des Naturrechtes*, vol. 1, Zürich, Evangelischer Verlag AG, 1954.

Foerster, Otto, *Handschriftliche Untersuchungen zu Senecas Epistulae morales und Naturales quaestiones*, Würzburger Studien zur Altertumswissenschaft, 10, Stuttgart, W. Kohlhammer, 1936.

Forbes, Clarence A., "The Philosophy of Vergil," *Vergilius, 10* (1964), 7-11.

Forschner, Maximilian, *Die stoische Ethik: Über den Zusammenhang von Natur-, Sprach- und Moralphilosophie im altstoischen System*, Stuttgart, Klett-Cotta, 1981.

Forstner, Michael, "Silius Italicus und Poseidonios," *Bayer. Blätter für das Gymnasial-Schulwesen*, hg. vom Bayer. Gymnasiallehrverein, *54* (1918), 79-86.

Fraenkel, Eduard, *Horace*, Oxford, Clarendon Press, 1959.

Fraisse, Jean-Claude, *Philia: La notion d'amitié dans la philosophie antique. Essai sur un problème perdu et retrouvé*, Paris, J. Vrin, 1974.

Frank, Richard I., "Augustus' Legislation on Marriage and Children," *California Studies in Classical Antiquity*, 8 (1975), 41-52.

Frank, Tenney, *Catullus and Horace: Two Poets in Their Environment*, New York, Henry Holt and Company, 1928.

—, "Cicero," *Proceedings of the British Academy*, 1932, London, Oxford University Press, 1932, pp. 111-34.

—, "Epicurean Determinism in the *Aeneid*," *American Journal of Philology*, *41* (1920), 115-26.

—, "Horace's Definition of Poetry," *Classical Journal*, *31* (1935-36), 167-74.

—, *Vergil: A Biography*, New York, Henry Holt and Company, 1922.

Franceschini, Ezio, *Studi e note di filologia latina medievale*, Pubblicazioni della Università cattolica del Sacro Cuore, ser. 4ª: science filologiche, 30, Milano, Vita e Pensiero, 1938.

Frede, Michael, *Die Stoische Logik*, Abhandlungen der Akademie der Wissenschaften in Göttingen, philosophisch-historische Klasse, 3:*88*, Göttingen, Vandenhoeck & Ruprecht, 1974.

—, "Stoic vs. Aristotelian Syllogistic," *Archiv für Geschichte der Philosophie*, *56* (1974), 1-32.

Frezza, Paolo, "Ius gentium," *Nuova rivista di diritto commerciale, diritto dell'economia, diritto sociale, 2* (1949), 26-51.

Fritz, K. von, "Zenon von Kition," *Paulys Realencyclopädie der classischen Altertumswissenschaft,* 2nd ed., München, Alfred Druckenmuller Verlag, 1972, *19,* cols. 83-121.

Fuchs, Harald, "Ciceros Hingabe an die Philosophie," *Museum Helveticum, 16* (1959), 1-28.

Fuhrmann, Manfred, "Cum dignitate otium: Politisches Programm und Staatstheorie bei Cicero," *Gymnasium, 67* (1960), 481-99.

—, "Die Alleinherrschaft und das Problem der Gerechtigkeit (Seneca: De clementia)," *Gymnasium, 70* (1963), 481-514.

Gabotto, Ferdinando, "Appunti sulla fortuna di alcuni autori romani nel medioevo: Giovenale,"*Biblioteca delle scuole italiane, 3*:17 (16 giugno 1891), 260-64.

Galinsky, G. Karl, *The Herakles Theme: The Adaptations of the Hero in Literature from Homer to the Twentieth Century,* Oxford, Basil Blackwell, 1972.

—, "The Hercules-Cacus Episode in *Aeneid* VIII,'" *American Journal of Philology, 87* (1966), 18-51.

Ganss, Wilhelm, *Das Bild des Weisen bei Seneca,* Schaan, Buchdruckerei Gutenberg, 1952.

García-Borrón Moral, Juan C., *Séneca y los estoicos: Una contribución del senequismo,* Consejo Superior de Investagaciones Científicas, Instituto "Luis Vives" de Filosofia, Delegación de Barcelona, Estudios, 6, Barcelona, Gráficas Marina S. A., 1956.

Garnier, J., "Observations sur quelques ouvrages du Stoïcien Panétius," *Histoire et Mémoirs de l'Institut royale de France,* Classe d'histoire et de littérature ancienne, *2* (1815), 81-110.

Garnsey, Peter, *Social Status and Legal Privilege in the Roman Empire,* Oxford, Clarendon Press, 1970.

Gärtner, Hans Armin, *Cicero und Panaitios: Beobachtungen zu Ciceros De officiis,* Sitzungsberichte der Heidelberger Akademie der Wissenschaften, philosophisch-historische Klasse, 5, Heidelberg, Carl Winter, 1974.

Gasquy, Armand, *Cicéron jurisconsulte,* Paris, Ernest Thorin, 1887.

Gassner, Josef, "Philosophie und Moral bei Gellius," *Innsbrucker Beiträge zur Kulturwissenschaft, 17, Serta philologica Aenipontana,* 2, ed. Robert Muth (1972), 197-235.

Gauthier, R.-A., *Magnanimité: L'Idéal de la grandeur dans la philosophie païenne et dans la théologie chrétienne,* Bibliothèque thomiste, 28, Paris, J. Vrin, 1951.

Gawlick, G., "Cicero in der Patristik," *Studia Patristica,* 9, Texte und Untersuchungen zur Geschichte der altchristlichen Literatur, 94, Berlin, Akademie-Verlag, 1966, pp. 57-62.

Geffcken, Johannes, *Kynica und Verwandtes,* Heidelberg, Carl Winters Universitätsbuchhandlung, 1909.

Geigenmuller, Paul, "Stellung und Pflichten des Menschen im Kosmos nach Epiktet," *Neue Jahrbücher für Wissenschaft und Jugendbildung, 5* (1929), 529-42.

—, "Vernunft und Affect in der Philosophie Senecas," *Neue Jarhbücher für Wissenschaft und Jugendbildung, 3* (1927), 641-57.

Gelsomino, Remo, "Studi sulle fonti di Vibio Sequestre: Lucano e gli scholi perduti a Lucano," *Helikon, 1* (1961), 645-60; *2* (1962), 131-61.

Gelzer, Matthias, *Cicero: Ein biographischer Versuch,* Wiesbaden, Franz Steiner Verlag GMBH, 1969.

—, "Ciceros 'Brutus' als politische Kundgebung," *Philologus, 93* (1938), 128-31.

Gentile, Marino, "Etica e metafisica nel pensiero die Seneca," *Rivista di filosofia neo-scolastica, 23* (1931), 479-83.

—, *I fondamenti metafisici della morale di Seneca,* Pubblicazioni della Università cattolica del Sacro Cuore, serie prima, scienze filosofiche, 19, Milano, Vita e Pensiero, 1932.

Georgesco, Valentin-Al., " 'Nihil ad ius, ad Ciceronem!' Note sur les relations de M. T. Cicéron avec la *iurisprudentia* et la profession de *iuris consultus,*" *Mélanges de philologie, de littérature et d'histoire anciennes offerts à J. Marouzeau,* Paris, Les Belles Lettres, 1948, pp. 189-206.

Germain, Gabriel, *Épictète et la spiritualité stoïcienne*, Paris, Éditions du Seuil, 1964.

Geytenbeek, A. C. van, *Musonius Rufus and Greek Diatribe*, rev. ed., trans. B. L. Hijmans, Wijsgerige Teksten en Studies, 8, Assen, Van Gorcum & Comp. N.V., 1962.

Ghellinck, J. de, "Réminiscences de la dialectique de Marius Victorinus dans les conflits théologiques du XIme et du XIIme siècle," *Revue néo-scolastique de philosophie*, 18 (1911), 432-35.

Giancotti, Francesco, *Cronologia dei "Dialoghi" di Seneca*, Torino, Loescher, 1957.

—, *Saggio sulle tragedie di Seneca*, Roma, Società Editrice Dante Alighieri, 1953.

—, "Seneca amante di Agrippina?" *La parola del passato*, 8:28 (1953), 53-62.

Gigon, Olof, "Cicero und Aristoteles," *Hermes*, 87 (1959), 143-62.

—, "Posidoniana-Ciceroniana-Lactantiana," *Romanitas et Christianitas: Studia J. H. Waszink*, ed. W. den Boer et al., Amsterdam, North-Holland Publishing Company, 1973, pp. 145-80.

Gilbert, Neal W., "The Concept of Will in Early Latin Philosophy," *Journal of the History of Philosophy*, 1 (1963), 17-35.

Gilson, E., "Éloquence et sagesse selon Cicéron," *Phoenix*, 7 (1953), 1-19.

Giuffrida, Pasquale, "La dottrina stoica della *phone* e l'*Orator* di Cicerone," *Scritti vari pubblicati dalla Facoltà di magistero dell'Università di Torino*, 1 (1950), 115-28.

—, *Ricerche sull'ecletticismo ciceroniano*, ed. Felicità Portalupi, Torino, G. Giappichelli, 1963.

Glaesener, Henri, "Les caractères dans la Thébaïde de Stace," *Le Musée Belge*, 3 (1899), 97-117.

Gilbert-Thirry, Anne, "La théorie stoïcienne de la passion chez Chrysippe et son évolution chez Posidonius," *Revue philosophique de Louvain*, 75 (1977), 395-435.

Glover, Terrot Reaveley, *Studies in Virgil*, London, Edward Arnold, 1904.

Goar, R. J., *Cicero, and the State Religion*, Amsterdam, Adolf M. Hakkert, 1972.

Goldschmidt, Victor, "*Huparchein* et *huphistanai* dans la philosophie stoïcienne," *Revue des études grecques*, 85 (1972), 331-44.

—, "Logique et rhétorique chez les Stoïciens," *Logique et analyses*, n.s. 6 (1963), 450-56.

—, *Le système stoïcien et l'idée de temps*, 2me éd., Paris, J. Vrin, 1969.

Gomoll, Heinz, *Der stoische Philosoph Hekaton: Seine Begriffswelt und Nachwirkung unter Beigabe seiner Fragmente*, Bonn, Friedrich Cohen, 1933.

Gonnet, J.-P., "Épictète directeur de conscience," *L'Université catholique*, n.s. 35 (1900), 23-61.

Görler, Woldemar, *Untersuchungen zu Ciceros Philosophie*, Bibliothek der klassischen Altertumswissenschaft, n.F. 2:50, Heidelberg, Carl Winter, 1974.

Gotoff, Harold C., *The Transmission of the Text of Lucan in the Ninth Century*, Loeb Classical Monographs, Cambridge, Mass., Harvard University Press, 1971.

Gould, Josiah B., "Chrysippus: On the Criteria for the Truth of a Conditional Proposition," *Phronesis*, 12 (1967), 152-61.

—, "Deduction in Stoic Logic," *Ancient Logic and Its Modern Interpretations*, Proceedings of the Buffalo Symposium on Modernist Interpretations of Ancient Logic, 21 and 22 April 1972, ed. John Corcoran, Synthese Historical Library, 9, Dordrecht, D. Reidel Publishing Company, 1974, pp. 151-68.

—, *The Philosophy of Chrysippus*, Albany, State University of New York Press, 1970.

—, "Reason in Seneca," *Journal of the History of Philosophy*, 3 (1965), 13-25.

—, "The Stoic Conception of Fate," *Journal of the History of Ideas*, 35 (1974), 17-32.

Gradenwitz, Otto, "Natur und Sklave bei der naturalis obligatio," *Festgabe der juristichen Fakultät zu Königsberg für ihren Senior Johann Theodor Schirmer zur 1. August 1900*, Königsberg i Pr., Hartungsche Verlagsdruckerei, 1900, pp. 137-79.

Graeser, Andreas, "A propos *huparchein* bei den Stoikern," *Archiv für Begriffsgeschichte*, 15 (1971), 299-305.

—, "Ein unstoischer Beweisgang in Cicero, De finibus 3.27?" *Hermes*, 100 (1972), 492-95.

—, *Plotinus and the Stoics: A Preliminary Study*, Philosophia Antiqua, 22, Leiden, E. J. Brill, 1972.

—, *Zenon von Kition: Positionen und Probleme*, Berlin, Walter de Gruyter, 1975.

—, "Zirkel oder Deduktion? Zur Begründung der stoischen Ethik," *Kant-Studien*, 63 (1972), 213-24.

—, "Zur Funktion der Begriffs 'gut' in der stoischen Ethik," *Zeitschrift für philosophische Forschung, 26* (1972), 417-25.

Graf, Arturo, *Roma nella memoria e nelle immaginazioni del medio evo,* vol. 2, Torino, Ermanno Loescher, 1883.

Graff, Jürgen, *Ciceros Selbstauffassung,* Bibliothek der klassischen Altertumswissenschaft, n.F. 2, Heidelberg, Carl Winter, 1963.

Grant, Mary A. and Fiske, George C., "Cicero's 'Orator' and Horace's 'Ars Poetica'," *Harvard Studies in Classical Philology, 35* (1924), 1-74.

Grant, Michael, *The Ancient Historians,* New York, Charles Scribner's Sons, 1970.

—, *Roman Literature,* Cambridge, The University Press, 1954.

Grant, W. Leonard, "Cicero on the Moral Character of the Orator," *Classical Journal, 38* (1943), 472-78.

Green, Peter, *The Shadow of the Parthenon: Studies in Ancient History and Literature,* London, Maurice Temple Smith Limited, 1972.

Greene, William Chase, *Moira: Fate, Good, and Evil in Greek Thought,* Cambridge, Mass., Harvard University Press, 1944.

Grenade, Pierre, "Le pseudo-épicurisme de Tacite," *Revue des études anciennes, 55* (1953), 36-57.

Griffin, Miriam T., *Seneca: A Philosopher in Politics,* Oxford, Clarendon Press, 1976.

Grilli, Alberto, "La posizione di Aristotele, Epicuro, e Posidonio nei confronti della storia della civiltà," *Istituto Lombardo di scienze e lettere, Rendiconti,* classe di lettere e scienze morali e storiche, *86,* ser. 3:17 (1953), 3-44.

—, *Il problema della vita contemplativa nel mondo greco-romano,* Milano, Fratelli Bocca, 1953.

—, *I proemi del De re publica di Cicerone,* Antichità classica e cristiana, 3, Brescia, Paideia, 1971.

—, "Studi paneziani," *Studi italiani di filologia classica,* n.s. *29* (1957), 31-97.

Grimal, Pierre, "L'Épisode d'Anthée dans la 'Pharsale'," *Latomus, 8* (1949), 55-61.

—, *Essai sur l'Art poétique d'Horace,* Paris, Sedes, 1968.

—, "Nature et limites de l'éclecticisme philosophique chez Sénèque," *Les Études classiques, 38* (1970), 3-17.

—, "Sénèque et la pensée grecque," *Bulletin de l'Association Guillaume Budé,* 4me sér., *3* (1966), 317-30.

—, *Sénèque: Sa vie, son oeuvre, avec un exposé de sa philosophie,* Paris, PUF, 1959.

Gruen, Erich S., *Roman Politics and the Criminal Courts, 149-78 B.C.,* Cambridge, Mass., Harvard University Press, 1968.

Grumach, Ernst, *Physis und Agathon in der alten Stoa,* Problemata: Forschungen zur klassischen Philologie, 6, Berlin, Weidmannsche Buchhandlung, 1932.

Guazzoni Foà, Virginia, *I fondamenti filosofici della teologia ciceroniana,* Pubblicazioni dell'Istituto di filosofia, Facoltà di magistero dell'Università di Genova, 13, Milano, Marzorati, 1970.

—, "Il metodo di Cicerone nell'indagine filosofica," *Rivista di filosofia neo-scolastica, 48* (1956), 293-315.

—, "La terminologia filosofica ciceroniana," *Giornale di metafisica, 13* (1958), 225-42.

Gueuning, Louis, "Horace et la poésie," *Les Études classiques, 4* (1935), 52-73.

Guibal, Maurice-Philbert, *De l'influence de la philosophie sur le droit romain et la jurisprudence de l'époque classique: Essai de synthèse historique,* Université de Montpellier, Faculté de droit, Paris, Recueil Sirey, 1937.

Guillemin, A.-M., "Le satirique Perse," *Les Études classiques, 7* (1938), 161-67.

—, "Sénèque directeur des âmes, I. L'idéal; II. Son activité pratique," *Revue des études latines, 30* (1952), 202-19; *31* (1953), 215-34.

—, *Virgile: Poète, artiste et penseur,* Paris, Albin Michel, 1951.

Guillermit, L., and Vuillemin, J., *Le sens du destin,* Neuchâtel, Éditions de la Baconnière, 1948.

Guite, Harold, "Cicero's Attitude toward the Greeks," *Greece & Rome,* ser. 2:9 (1962), 142-59.

Gummere, Richard Mott, "Seneca the Philosopher in the Middle Ages and the Early Renaissance," *Transactions and Proceedings of the American Philological Association, 41* (1910), xxxviii-xl.

Haarhoff, T. J., "Virgil's Garden of Flowers and His Philosophy of Nature," *Greece & Rome*, ser. 2:5 (1958), 67-82.

—, *Vergil the Universal*, Oxford, Basil Blackwell, 1949.

Hack, Roy Kenneth, "The Doctrine of Literary Forms," *Harvard Studies in Classical Philology, 27* (1916), 1-65.

—, "La sintesi stoica, I: Tonos," *Ricerche religiose, 1* (1925), 505-13.

—, "La sintesi stoica, II: Pneuma," *Ricerche religiose, 2* (1926), 297-325.

—, "La sintesi stoica, III: Dio," *Ricerche religiose, 4* (1928), 481-96; *5* (1929), 20-34.

Hadas, Moses, *A History of Latin Literature*, New York, Columbia University Press, 1952.

Hadot, Ilsetraut, *Seneca und die griechisch-römische Tradition der Seelenenleitung*, Quellen und Studien zur Geschichte der Philosophie, ed. Paul Wilpert, 13, Berlin, Walter de Gruyter & Co., 1969.

—, "Tradition stoïcienne et idées politiques au temps des Gracques," *Revue des études latines, 48* (1970), 133-79.

Hadot, Pierre, *Marius Victorinus: Recherches sur sa vie et ses oeuvres*, Paris, Études Augustiniennes, 1971.

—, "La physique comme exercise spirituel ou pessimisme et optimisme chez Marc Aurèle," *Revue de théologie et de philosophie*, sér. 3:22 (1972), 225-39.

—, "Un clé des Pensées de Marc Aurèle: Les trois *topoi* philosophiques selon Épictète," *Les Études philosophiques* (1978), 65-84.

Hagen, Friedrich von, *Zur Metaphysik des Philosophen L. A Seneca*, Borna-Leipzig, Robert Noske, 1905.

Hahm, David E., "Chrysippus' Solution to the Democritean Dilemma of the Cone," *Isis, 63* (1972), 205-20.

—, *The Origins of Stoic Cosmology*, Columbus, Ohio State University Press, 1977.

Hamelin, O., "Sur la logique des Stoïciens," *L'Année philosophique, 12* (1901), 13-26.

Hampl, Franz, " 'Stoische Staatsethik' und frühes Rom," *Historische Zeitschrift, 184* (1957), 249-71.

Hanslik, Rudolf, "Tacitus 1939-1972," *Lustrum, 16* (1972), 143-304.

Harder, Richard, *Kleine Schriften*, ed. Walter Marg, München, C. H. Beck'sche Verlagsbuchhandlung, 1960.

Harris, Bruce Fairgray, "Cicero as an Academic: A Study of *De Nature Deorum*," *University of Auckland Bulletin, 58*, Classics ser. 2 (1961), 3-37.

Hatinguais, J., "Sens et valeur de la volunté dans l'humanisme de Cicéron," *Bulletin de l'Association Guillaume Budé*, supplément *Lettres d'humanité, 17* (1958), 50-69.

Häussler, Reinhard, *Tacitus und das historische Bewusstsein*, Bibliothek der klassischen Altertumswissenschaften, n.F. 2, Heidelberg, Carl Winter, 1965.

Haverfield, F., "Tacitus during the Late Roman Period and the Middle Ages," *Journal of Roman Studies, 6* (1916), 196-201.

Hay, William H., "Stoic Use of Logic," *Archiv für Geschichte der Philosophie, 51* (1969), 145-57.

Haynes, Richard P., "The Theory of Pleasure of the Old Stoa," *American Journal of Philology, 83* (1962), 412-19.

Heck, Eberhard, *Die Bezeugung von Ciceros Schrift De re publica*, Spudasmata, 4, Hildesheim, Georg Olms Verlagsbuchhandlung, 1966.

Heck, Richard, "Scipio am Scheideweg: Die Punica des Silius Italicus und Ciceros Schrift De re publica," *Wiener Studien*, n.F. *4* (1970), 156-80.

Heibges, Ursula, "Cicero, A Hypocrite in Religion?" *American Journal of Philology, 90* (1969), 304-12.

Heinemann, I., *Poseidonios' metaphysische Schriften*, 2 vols., Breslau, M. & H. Marcus, 1921-28.

Heinze, Max, *Die Lehre vom Logos in der griechischen Philosophie*, Oldenburg, Ferdinand Schmidt, 1872.

Heinze, Richard, *Vergils epische Technik*, Leipzig, B. G. Teubner, 1903.
—, *Vom Geist des Römertums: Ausgewählte Aufsätze*, 3rd ed., ed. Erich Burck, Stuttgart, B. G. Teubner, 1960.
Heldmann, Konrad, "Ciceros Laelius und die Grenzen der Freundschaft: Zur Interdependenz von Literatur und Politik 44/43 v. Chr.," *Hermes, 104* (1976), 72-103.
Henderson, Charles, ed., *Classical, Mediaeval and Renaissance Studies in Honor of Berthold Louis Ullman*, vol. 1, Roma, Storia e Letterature, 1964.
Henry, Margaret Young, "Cicero's Treatment of the Free Will Problem," *Transactions of the American Philological Association, 58* (1927), 32-42.
—, *Relation of Dogmatism and Scepticism in the Philosophical Treatises of Cicero*, Geneva, N.Y., W. F. Humphrey, 1925.
Hentschke, Ada, "Zur historischen und literarischen Bedeutung von Cicero's Schrift 'De legibus'," *Philologus, 115* (1971), 118-30.
Herescu, N. I., ed., *Ovidiana: Recherches sur Ovide*, Paris, Les Belles Lettres, 1958.
Herington, C. J., "Senecan Tragedy," *Arion, 5* (1966), 422-71.
Herrero Llorente, Víctor-José, "Lucano en la literatura hispano-latina," *Emerita, 27* (1960), 19-52.
Herrmann, Léon, *Le Théatre de Sénèque*, Collection d'études anciennes publiée sous le patronage de l'Association Guillaume Budé, Paris, Les Belles Lettres, 1924.
Heynacker, Max, *Ueber die Quellen des Silius Italicus*, Inaugural-Dissertation, Jena, Ilfeld, 1874.
Hicks, R. D., *Stoic and Epicurean*, New York, Charles Scribner's Sons, 1910.
Highet, Gilbert, *The Anatomy of Satire*, Princeton, Princeton University Press, 1962.
—, "Juvenal's Bookcase," *American Journal of Philology, 72* (1951), 369-94.
—, *Juvenal the Satirist: A Study*, Oxford, Clarendon Press, 1954.
—, "The Philosophy of Juvenal," *Transactions and Proceedings of the American Philological Association, 80* (1949), 254-70.
Hijmans, B. L., *Askesis: Notes on Epictetus' Educational System*, Assen, Van Gorcum & Comp., N.V., 1959.
—,"A Note on *Physis* in Epictetus," *Mnemosyne*, ser. 4:*20* (1967), 279-84.
—, "Posidonius' Ethics," *Acta Classica, 2* (1959), 27-42.
Hild, J.-A., "Juvénal dans le moyen âge," *Bulletin de la Faculté des lettres de Poitiers, 8* (1890), 177-89; *9* (1891), 39-54, 106-22, 235-52.
Hirzel, Rudolf, *Agraphos nomos*, Abhandlungen der königl. sächsischen Gesellschaft der Wissenschaft, philologisch-historischen Klasse, *20*:1, Leipzig, B. G. Teubner, 1900.
—, *Untersuchungen zu Ciceros philosophischen Schriften*, 3 vols., Leipzig, S. Hirzel, 1877-83.
Hoffmann, Ernst, *Leben und Tod in der stoischen Philosophie*, Heidelberg, F. H. Kerle Verlag, 1946.
Hohenlohe, Constantin, *Einfluss des Christentums auf das Corpus iuris civilis: Eine rechtshistorische Studie zum Verständnisse der sozialen Frage*, Wien, Hölder-Pichler-Tempsky A. G., 1937.
Holl, Karl, *Die Naturales Quaestiones des Philosophen Seneca*, Jena, Universitäts-Buchdruckerei G. Neuenhahn, 1935.
Holland, Francis, *Seneca*, London, Longmans, Green, and Co., 1920.
Holler, Ernst, *Seneca und die Seelenteilungslehre und Affektspsychologie der Mittelstoa*, Kallmünz, Michael Lassleben, 1934.
Hommel, Hildebrecht, *Ciceros Gebetshymnus an die Philosophie: Tusculanen V, 5*, Sitzungsberichte der Heidelberger Akademie der Wissenschaften, philosophisch-historische Klasse, 3, Heidelberg, Carl Winter, 1968.
—, *Horaz: Der Mensch und das Werk*, Heidelberg, F. H. Kerle Verlag, 1950.
—, "Mikrokosmos," *Rheinisches Museum für Philologie*, n.F. *92* (1943-44), 56-89.
Honig, Richard M., *Humanitas und Rhetorik in spätrömischen Kaisergesetzen: Studien zur Gesinningsgrundlage des Dominats*, Göttinger rechtswissenschaftliche Studien, 30, Göttingen, O. Schwartz & Co., 1960.
Hope, Richard, *The Book of Diogenes Laertius: Its Spirit and Its Method*, New York, Columbia University Press, 1930.

Horowitz, Maryanne Cline, "The Stoic Synthesis of the Idea of Natural Law in Man: Four Themes," *Journal of the History of Ideas, 35* (1974), 3-16.

Hosius, Carl, "Lucan und seine Quellen," *Rheinisches Museum für Philologie, 48* (1893), 380-97.

—, "Lucanus und Seneca," *Neue Jahrbücher für Philologie und Paedagogik, 145* (1892), 337-56.

Hoven, René, *Stoïcisme et stoïciens face au problème de l'au-delà*, Bibliothèque de la Faculté de philosophie et lettres de l'Université de Liège, 197, Paris, Les Belles Lettres, 1971.

How, W. W., "Cicero's Ideal in His *De republica*," *Journal of Roman Studies, 20* (1930), 24-42.

Hubaux, Jean and Leroy, Maxime, *Le Mythe du Phénix dans les littératures grecque et latine*, Bibliothèque de la Faculté de philosophie et lettres de l'Université de Liège, 82, Liège, Faculté de Philosophie et Lettres, 1939.

Huby, Pamela, "The First Discovery of the Freewill Problem," *Philosophy, 42* (1967), 353-62.

Huit, Charles, "Les origines grecques du stoïcisme," *Séances et travaux de l'Académie des sciences morales et politiques*, n.s. *151*:1 (1899), 462-504.

Hultsch, Friedrich, *Poseidonios über die Grösse und Entfernung der Sonne*, Abhandlungen der königlichen Gesellschaft der Wissenschaft zu Göttingen, philologisch-historische Klasse, n.F. *1*:5, Berlin, Weidmannsche Buchhandlung, 1897.

Hunt, H. A. K., *The Humanism of Cicero*, Melbourne, Melbourne University Press, 1954.

—, *A Physical Interpretation of the Universe: The Doctrine of Zeno the Stoic*, Melbourne, Melbourne University Press, 1976.

Hunt, H. K., "The Importance of Zeno's Physics for an Understanding of Stoicism during the Later Roman Republic," *Apeiron, 1* (1967), 5-14.

Hunt, T. J., "The Medieval Tradition of Cicero's Theological Works," *Pegasus:* University of Exeter Classical Society Magazine, 5 (February 1966), 52-57.

Ibscher, Gred, *Der Begriff des Sittlichen in der Pflichtenlehre des Panaitios: Ein Beitrag zur Erkenntnis der mittleren Stoa*, München, R. Oldenbourg, 1934.

Immisch, Otto, *Horazens Epistel über die Dichtkunst, Philologus*, Supplementband *24*:3, Leipzig, Dieterich'sche Verlagsbuchhandlung, 1932.

Ingenkamp, Heinz Gerd, "Zur stoischen Lehre vom Sehen," *Rheinisches Museum für Philologie*, n.F. *114* (1971), 240-46.

Ivánka, Endre von, "Apex mentis: Wanderung und Wandlung eines stoischen Terminus," *Zeitschrift für katholische Theologie, 72* (1950), 129-76.

—, "Die Quelle von Ciceros De natura deorum II, 45-60 (Poseidonios bei Gregor von Nyssa)," *Archivum Philologicum-Eggetemes Philologiai Közlöny, 59*:1-3 (1935), 10-21.

—, "Die stoische Anthopologie in der lateinischen Literatur," *Anzeiger der österreiche Akademie der Wissenschaften*, philosophisch-historische Klasse, *87* (1950), 178-92.

Jackson, B. Darrell, "The Theory of Signs in St. Augustine's *De Doctrina Christiana*," in *Augustine: A Collection of Critical Essays*, ed. R. A. Markus, Garden City, N.Y., Doubleday & Company, Inc., 1972, pp. 92-147.

Jaeger, Werner Wilhelm, *Nemesios von Emesa: Quellenforschungen zum Neuplatonismus und seinen Anfängen bei Poseidonios*, Berlin, Weidmannsche Buchhandlung, 1914.

Jagu, Anand, *Épictète et Platon: Essai sur les relations du Stoïcisme et du Platonisme à propos de la morale des Entretiens*, Paris, J. Vrin, 1946.

—, *Zénon de Cittium: Son Rôle dans l'établissement de la morale stoïcienne*, Paris, J. Vrin, 1946.

Jannacone, Silvia, "Divinazione e culto ufficiale nel pensiero di Cicerone," *Latomus, 14* (1955), 116-19.

Javelet, Robert, "La Réintroduction de la liberté dans les notions d'image et ressemblance, conçus comme cynamisme," *Der Begriff der Repraesentation im Mittelalter: Stellvertretung, Symbol, Zeichen, Bild*, ed. Albert Zimmermann, Miscellanea Mediaevalia: Veröffentlichungen des Thomas-Instituts der Universität zu Köln, 8, Berlin, Walter de Gruyter, 1971, pp. 1-34.

Jędrzyński, Edward, "Horatii philosophia atque conscientia religiosa," *Studia philosophia christianae, 8* (1972), 25-38.

Jefferis, J. D., "The Theology of the *Aeneid*: Its Antecedents and Developments," *Classical Journal, 30* (1934), 28-38.

Jennings, Margaret, "Lucan's Medieval Popularity: The Exemplum Tradition," *Rivista di cultura classica e medioevale, 16* (1974), 215-33.

Johnson, W. R., *Darkness Visible: A Study of Vergil's Aeneid*, Berkeley, University of California Press, 1976.

Jolowicz, H. F., *Historical Introduction to the Study of Roman Law*, Cambridge, The University Press, 1932.

Jones, A. H. M., *The Decline of the Ancient World*, New York, Holt, Rinehart and Winston, Inc., 1966.

Jones, John Walter, *The Law and Legal Theory of the Greeks: An Introduction*, Oxford, Clarendon Press, 1956.

Jones, Roger Miller, "Posidonius and Cicero's *Tusculan Disputations* i. 17-81," *Classical Philology, 18* (1923), 202-28.

—, "Posidonius and the Flight of the Mind through the Universe," *Classical Philology, 21* (1926), 97-113.

Jonkers, E. J., "De l'influence du christianisme sur le législation relative à l'esclavage dans l'antiquité," *Mnemosyne*, ser. 3:*1* (1933-34), 241-80.

Jossa, Giorgio, "L'utilitas rei publicae' nel pensiero di Cicerone," *Studi romani, 12* (1964), 269-88.

Jósefowicz, Maria, "Les Idées politiques dans la morale stoïcienne de Marc-Aurèle," *Eos, 59* (1971), 241-54.

Jungblut, Heinrich, "Cicero und Panätius im zweiten Buch über die Pflichten," *Beilage zum programm des Lessing-Gymnasiums zu Frankfurt a. M. Ostern 1910*, Frankfurt a. M., Enz & Rudolph, 1910.

Kahn, Charles H., "Stoic Logic and Stoic LOGOS," *Archiv für Geschichte der Philosophie, 51* (1969), 158-72.

Kamphuisen, P. W., "L'influence de la philosophie sur la conception du droit naturel chez les jurisconsultes romains," *Revue historique de droit français et étranger*, 4ᵉ sér., *11* (1932), 389-412.

Kassel, Rudolf, *Untersuchungen zur griechischen und römischen Konsolationsliteratur*, Zetemata: Monographien zur klassischen Altertumswissenschaft, 18, München, C. H. Beck, 1958.

Kelber, Wilhelm, *Die Logoslehre von Heraklit bis Origenes*, Stuttgart, Verlag Urachhaus, 1958.

Kelly, J. M., *Roman Litigation*, Oxford, Clarendon Press, 1966.

Kennedy, George, *Quintilian*, New York, Twayne Publishers, Inc., 1969.

Kenney, E. J., "Juvenal: Satirist or Rhetorician?" *Latomus, 22* (1963), 704-20.

Kenter, L. P., *M. Tullius Cicero De Legibus: A Commentary on Book I*, trans. Margie L. Leenheer-Braid, Amsterdam, Adolf M. Hakkert, 1972.

Kerferd, G. B., "The Search for Personal Identity in Stoic Thought," *Bulletin of the John Rylands Library, 55* (1972), 177-96.

Kidd, I. G., "The Relation of Stoic Intermediaries to the *Summum Bonum*, with Reference to Change in the Stoa," *Classical Quarterly, 49* (1955), 181-94.

King, Christine M., "Seneca's *Hercules Oetaeus*: A Stoic Interpretation of the Greek Myth," *Greece & Rome*, ser. 2:*18* (1971), 215-22.

Kleywegt, A. J., *Ciceros Arbeitsweise im zweiten und dritten Buch der Schrift De natura deorum*, Groningen, J. B. Wolters, 1961.

—, "Fate, Free Will, and the Text of Cicero," *Mnemosyne*, ser. 4:*26* (1973), 342-49.

—, "Philosophischer Gehalt und persönliche Stellung in *Tusc.* I 9-81," *Mnemosyne*, ser. 4:*19* (1966), 359-88.

Klingner, Friedrich, "Über die Einleitung der Historien Sallusts," *Hermes, 63* (1928), 165-92.

—, "Über die Recensio der Horaz-Handschriften," *Studien zur griechischen und römischen Literatur*, Zürich, Artemis Verlag, 1964, pp. 455-518.

—, *Virgil: Bucolica, Georgica, Aeneis*, Zürich, Artemis Verlag, 1967.

Klotz, Alfred, "Die Stellung des Silius Italicus unter den Quellen zur Geschichte des zweiten punischen Krieges," *Rheinisches Museum für Philologie, 82* (1933), 1-34.

Kneale, William and Kneale, Martha, *The Development of Logic*, Oxford, Clarendon Press, 1962.

Knight, W. F. Jackson, *Roman Vergil*, rev. ed., Harmondsworth, Penguin Books, 1966.

Knoche, Ulrich, "Cicero: Ein Mittler griechischer Geisteskultur," *Hermes, 87* (1959), 57-74.

—, "Der Gedanke der Freundschaft in Senecas Briefen an Lucilius," *Commentationes in honorem Edwin Linkomies sexagenarii A.D. MCMLIV editae*, Arctos: Acta philologica fennica, n.s. 1, Helsinki, Kustannusosakeyhtiö Otava, 1954, pp. 83-96.

—, *Magnitudo animi: Untersuchungen zur Entstehung und Entwicklung eines römischen Wertgedankens, Philologus*, Supplementband 27:3, Leipzig, Dieterich'sche Verlagsbuchhandlung, 1935.

—, *Roman Satire*, trans. Edwin S. Ramage, Bloomington, Indiana University Press, 1975.

Kohler, Paul, *Epikur und Stoa bei Horaz*, Inaugural-Dissertation, Albert Ludwigs-Universität Freiburg i. Br., Greifswald, Julius Abel, 1911.

Kopp, Achim, *Staatsdenken und politisches Handeln bei Seneca und Lucan*, Inaugural-Dissertation, Heidelberg, 1969.

Kopp, Bernard, "Zur Geschichte der Naturrechtsidee," *Begegnung, 23* (1968), 76-80.

Korfmacher, William Charles, "Stoic Apatheia and Seneca's *De Clementia*," *Transactions of the American Philological Association, 77* (1946), 44-52.

Korzeniewski, Dietmar, ed., *Die römische Satire*, Wege der Forschung, 138, Darmstadt, Wissenschaftliche Buchgesellschaft, 1970.

Krauss, Franklin Brunell, *An Interpretation of the Omens, Portents, and Prodigies Recorded by Livy, Tacitus, and Suetonius*, Philadelphia, 1930.

Krenkel, Werner, "Römische Satire und römische Gesellschaft," *Wissenschaftliche Zeitschrift der Universität Rostock*, gesellschafts- und sprachwissenschaftliche Reihe, *15*:4-5 (1966), 471-77.

Kretschmar, Marianne, *Otium, Studia litterarium, Philosophie und Bios theoretikos im Leben und Denken Ciceros*, Würzburg, Konrad Triltsch, 1938.

Kroll, Wilhelm, "Cicero und die Rhetorik," *Neue Jahrbücher für das klassische Altertum, 11* (1903), 681-89.

—, "Die historische Stellung von Horazens Ars poetica," *Sokrates: Zeitschrift für das Gymnasialwesen*, n.F. 6 (1918), 81-98.

—, "Horaz' Oden und die Philosophie," *Wiener Studien, 37* (1915), 223-38.

Krumme, Ludwig, *Die Kritik der stoischen Theologie in Ciceros Schrift De natura deorum*, Düsseldorf, Dissertations-Verlag G. H. Nolte, 1941.

Kudlien, Fridolf, "Poseidonios und die Ärzteschule der Pneumatiker," *Hermes, 90* (1962), 419-29.

—, "Die stoische Gesundheitsbewertung und ihre Probleme," *Hermes, 102* (1974), 446-56.

Kumaniecki, Kazimierz, "Ciceros Paradoxa stoicorum und die römische Wirklichkeit," *Philologus, 101* (1957), 113-34.

Kunkel, Wolfgang, "Civilis und naturalis possessio: Eine Untersuchung über Terminologie und Struktur der römischen Besitzlehre," *Symbolae friburgenses in honorem Ottonis Lenel*, Leipzig, Bernhard Tauchnitz, 1931, pp. 40-79.

—, *Herkunft und soziale Stellung der römischen Juristen*, 2nd ed., Forschungen zum römischen Recht, 4, Graz, Hermann Böhlaus Nachf., 1967.

—, *An Introduction to Roman Legal and Constitutional History*, 2nd ed., trans. J. M. Kelly, Oxford, Clarendon Press, 1973.

Labowsky, Lotte, *Die Ethik des Panaitios: Untersuchungen zur Geschichte des Decorum bei Cicero und Horaz*, Leipzig, Felix Meiner Verlag, 1934.

Lacroix, Janine, " 'Fatum' et 'Fortuna' dans l'oeuvre de Tacite," *Revue des études latines,* *29* (1951), 247-64.

Ladner, Gerhart B., *The Idea of Reform: Its Impact on Christian Thought and Action in the Age of the Fathers,* Cambridge, Mass., Harvard University Press, 1959.

Laferrière, M. F., "De l'influence du stoïcisme sur la doctrine des jurisconsultes romains," *Compte-Rendu de l'Académie des sciences morales et politiques,* séances de juin et juillet 1859, Paris, 1860, pp. 5-109.

Laffranque, Marie, *Poseidonios d'Apamée: Essai de mise au point,* Faculté des lettres et sciences humaines de l'Université de Paris, Paris, PUF, 1964.

—, "Poseidonios, Eudoxe de Cyzique et la circumnavigation de l'Afrique," *Revue philosophique de la France et de l'étranger, 153* (1963), 199-222.

Lagrange, M.-J., "Marc-Aurèle," *Revue biblique,* n.s. *10* (1913), 243-59, 394-420, 568-87.

Laistner, M. L. W., *The Greater Roman Historians,* Berkeley, University of California Press, 1963.

Lallemont-Maron, Josette, "Architecture et philosophie dans l'oeuvre Virgilienne," *Euphrosyne,* n.s. *5* (1972), 447-55.

Lamacchia, Rosa, "Ciceros Somnium Scipionis und das sechste Buch der Aeneis," *Rheinisches Museum für Philologie,* n.F. *107* (1964), 261-78.

Lana, Italo, *Lucio Anneo Seneca,* Torino, Loescher, 1955.

—, *L. Anneo Seneca e la posizione degli intelletuali romani di fronte al principato,* Torino, G. Giappichelli, 1964.

Landry, Adolphe, "Quelques aperçus concernant la dépopulation dans l'antiquité gréco-romaine," *Revue historique, 177* (1936), 1-33.

Lanfranchi, Fabio, *Il diritto nei retori romani: Contributo alla storia dello sviluppo del diritto romano,* R. Università di Roma, pubblicazioni dell' Instituto di diritto romano e dei diritti dell'oriente mediterraneo e di storia del diritto, 4, Milano, A. Giuffrè, 1938.

La Penna, Antonio, "Il significato dei proemi sallustiani," *Maìa, 11* (1959), 23-43, 89-119.

Lapidge, Michael, "*Archai* and *Stoicheia*: A Problem in Stoic Cosmology," *Phronesis, 18* (1973), 240-78.

—, "A Stoic Metaphor in Late Latin Poetry: The Binding of the Universe," *Latomus, 39* (1980), 817-38.

Last, Hugh, "The Social Policy of Augustus," *Cambridge Ancient History,* ed. S. A. Cook, F. E. Adcock, and M. P. Charlesworth, Cambridge, The University Press, 1934, *10,* 425-64.

Laurenti, Renato; "Il 'filosofo ideale' secondo Epitteto," *Giornale di metafisica, 17* (1962), 501-13.

—, "Musonio e Epitteto," *Sophia, 34* (1966), 317-35.

Lauria, Mario, "Ius gentium," *Festschrift Paul Koschaker,* Weimar, Hermann Bohlaus Nachf., 1939, *1,* 258-65.

Lausberg, Marion, *Untersuchungen zu Senecas Fragmenten,* Untersuchungen zur antiken Literatur und Geschichte, ed. Heinrich Dörrie and Paul Moraux, 7, Berlin, Walter de Gruyter & Co., 1970.

LeBon, Marie-Thérèse, "La 'vera virtus' chez Horace," *Études Horatiennes: Recueil publié in l'honneur du bimillénaire d'Horace,* Travaux de la Faculté de philosophie et lettres de l'Université de Bruxelles, 7, Bruxelles, Édition de la Revue de l'Université de Bruxelles, 1937, pp. 141-46.

LeBonniec, Henri, "Lucain et la religion," *Lucain,* Fondation Hardt: Entretiens sur l'antiquité classique, 15, Vandoeuvres-Genève, 26-31 août 1968, Paris, Librairie Klincksieck, 1970, pp. 161-95.

Le Boulluec, Alain, "L'Allégorie chez les Stoïciens," *Poétique, 23* (1975), 301-21.

Leeman, Anton Daniel, *Gloria: Cicero's Waardering van de Roem en haar Achtergrond in de hellenistische Wijsbegeerte en de romeinse Samenleving,* Rotterdam, M. Wyt & Zonen, 1949.

—, *Orationis Ratio: The Stylistic Theories and Practice of the Roman Orators, Historians and Philosophers,* 2 vols., Amsterdam, Adolf M. Hakkert, 1963.

—, "Posidonius the Dialectician in Seneca's Letters," *Mnemosyne*, ser. 4:7 (1954), 233-40.

—, "Sallusts Prologe und seine Auffassung von der Historiographie," *Mnemosyne*, ser. 4:7 (1954), 323-39; *8* (1955), 38-48.

—, "Seneca's *Phaedra* as a Stoic Tragedy," *Miscellanea Tragica in Honorem J. C. Kamerbeek*, ed. J. M. Bremer, S. L. Radt, and G. J. Ruijgh, Amsterdam, Adolfus Hakkert, 1976, pp. 199-212.

Lehmann, Paul, "Nachrichten und Gerüchte von der Überlieferung der libri sex Ciceronis 'De re publica'," *Studi italiani di filologia classica*, *26-27* (1956), 202-15.

Lefèvre, Eckard, "Quid ratio possit? Senecas Phaedra als stoisches Drama," *Wiener Studien*, n.F. *3* (1969), 131-60.

—, "Schicksal und Selbstverschuldung in Senecas Agamemmon," *Hermes*, *94* (1966), 482-96.

Lepore, Ettore, *Il princeps ciceroniano e gli ideali politici della tarda repubblica*, Istituto italiano per gli studi storici, Napoli, Nella sede dell'Istituto, 1954.

LeHir, Jeanne, "Les fondements psychologiques et religieux de la morale d'Épictète," *Bulletin de l'Association Guillaume Budé*, supplément, *Lettres d'humanité*, *13* (1954), 73-93.

LeMoine, Fanny, *Martianus Capella: A Literary Re-evaluation*, Münchener Beiträge zur Mediävistik und Renaissance-Forschung, 10, München, Arbeo-Gesellschaft, 1972.

Lenaz, Luciano, "Marziano Capella," *Cultura e scuola*, *11* (1972), 50-59.

Lenzen, Hubert, *Senecas Dialog De brevitate vitae*, Klassisch-philologische Studien, ed. Ernst Benz and Christian Jensen, 10, Leipzig, Otto Harrassowitz, 1937.

Leo, Friedrich, *Plautinische Forschungen: Zur Kritik und Geschichte der Komödie*, Berlin, Weidmannsche Buchhandlung, 1895.

Levi, Adolfo, "Sulla psicologia gnoseologica degli Stoici," *Athenaeum*, n.s. *3* (1925), 186-98, 253-64.

Levy, Ernst, "Natural Law in Roman Thought," *Studia et documenta historiae et iuris*, *15* (1949), 1-23.

Liebbrand, Werner, "Stoische Reliquien im geschichtlichen Gang der Psychopathologie," *Confina psychiatrica*, *2* (1959), 1-18.

Liebeschuetz, W., "The Religious Position of Livy's History," *Journal of Roman Studies*, *57* (1967), 45-55.

Lindersky, Jerzy, "The Aedileship of Favonius, Curio the Younger, and Cicero's Election to the Augurate," *Harvard Studies in Classical Philology*, *76* (1972), 181-200.

Lintott, A. W., "Lucan and the History of the Civil War," *Classical Quarterly*, n.s. *21* (1971), 488-505.

Lloyd, A. C., "Activity and Description in Aristotle and the Stoa," Dawes-Hicks Lecture on Philosophy, British Academy, 1970, *Proceedings of the British Academy*, *61* (1971), 3-16.

Lohmann, J., "Über die stoische Sprachphilosophie," *Studium generale*, *21* (1968), 250-57.

Loisel, Gustave, *Marcaureliana: Doctrine néo-stoïcienne de vie religieuse, morale et sociale*, Paris, PUF, 1928.

Lombardi, Gabrio, "Diritto umano e 'ius gentium'," *Studia et documenta historiae et iuris*, *16* (1950), 254-68.

—, *Richerche in tema di "ius gentium"*, Università di Roma, pubblicazioni dell'Istituto di diritto romano, dei diritti dell'oriente mediterraneo e di storia del diritto, 21, Milano, A. Giuffrè, 1946.

—, *Sul concetto di "ius gentium"*, Università di Roma, pubblicazioni dell'Istituto di diritto romano, dei diritti dell'oriente mediterraneo e di storia del diritto, 20, Roma, Istituto di Diritto Romano, 1947.

Long, A. A., "Aristotle's Legacy to Stoic Ethics," University of London, Institute of Classical Studies, *Bulletin*, *15* (1968), 72-85.

—, "Carneades and the Stoic Telos," *Phronesis*, *12* (1967), 59-90.

—, "The Early Stoic Concept of Moral Choice," *Images of Man in Ancient and Medieval Thought: Studia Gerardo Verbeke*, ed. F. Bossier et al., Symbolae: Facultatis Litterarum et Philosophiae Lovaniensis, ser. A, *1*, Leuven, Leuven University Press, 1976, pp. 77-92.

—, *Hellenistic Philosophy: Stoics, Epicureans, Sceptics*, London, Duckworth, 1974.

—, "Heraclitus and Stoicism," *Philosophia*, *5-6* (1975-76), 133-56.

—, "The Logical Basis of Stoic Ethics," *Proceedings of the Aristotelian Society*, ser. 2:*71* (1970-71), 85-104.

—, *Soul and Body in Stoicism*, Berkeley, Center for Hermeneutical Studies, 1980.

—, "The Stoic Concept of Evil," *Philosophical Quarterly*, *18* (1968), 329-43.

—, ed., *Problem in Stoicism*, London, Athlone Press, 1971.

Longrigg, James, "Elementary Physics in the Lyceum and Stoa," *Isis*, *56* (1975), 211-29.

Lotmar, Ph., "Marc Aurels Erlass über die Freilassungsauflage," *Zeitschrift der Savigny-Stiftung für Rechtsgeschichte*, romanistische Abteilung, *33* (1912), 304-82.

Lucas, Joseph, *Les obsessions de Tacite*, Roma aeterna, 8, Leiden, E. J. Brill, 1974.

Luck, Georg, *Der Akademiker Antiochos*, Noctes romanae, 7, Bern, Verlag Paul Haupt, 1953.

—, "Studia divina in vita humana: On Cicero's 'Dream of Scipio' and Its Place in Graeco-Roman Philosophy," *Harvard Theological Review*, *19* (1956), 207-18.

Lueder, Annemarie, *Die philosophische Persönlichkeit des Antiochos von Askalon*, Inaugural-Dissertation, Göttingen, Göttingen, Dieterischen Universitäts-Buchdruckerei, 1940.

Lugarini, Leo, "L'orizzonte linguistico del sapere in Aristotele e la sua trasformazione stoica," *Il Pensiero*, 8 (1963), 327-51.

Lukasiewicz, Jan, "Zur Geschichte der Aussagenlogik," *Erkenntnis*, 5 (1935), 111-31.

Lünenborg, Josef, *Das philosophische Weltbild in Vergils Georgika*, Inaugural-Dissertation, Münster i. W., Bochum-Langendreer, Heinrich Pöppinghaus, 1935.

Luschnat, Otto, "Das Problem des ethischen Fortschritt in der alten Stoa," *Philologus*, *102* (1958), 178-214.

McGann, M. J., *Studies in Horace's First Book of Epistles*, Collection Latomus, 100, Bruxelles, Latomus, 1969.

McGushin, P., "Virgil and the Spirit of Endurance," *American Journal of Philology*, *85* (1964), 225-53.

MacInnes, John, "The Conception of *Fata* in the *Aeneid*," *Classical Review*, *24* (1910), 169-74.

MacMullen, Ramsay, *Enemies of the Roman Order: Treason, Unrest, and Alienation in the Empire*, Cambridge, Mass., Harvard University Press, 1966.

Madden, Edward H., "The Enthymeme: Crossroads of Logic, Rhetoric, and Metaphysics," *Philosophical Review*, *61* (1952), 368-76.

Maguinness, W. S., "The Eclecticism of Horace," *Hermathena*, *52* (1938), 27-46.

—, "Friends and the Philosophy of Friendship in Horace," *Hermathena*, *51* (1938), 29-48.

—, "Seneca and the Poets," *Hermathena*, *88* (1956), 81-98.

Malcovati, Enrica, *Lucano*, 2nd ed., Brescia, La Scuola, 1947.

—, "Lucano e Cicerone," *Athenaeum*, *41*, n.s. *31* (1953), 288-97.

—, "Sulla fortuna di Lucano," *Atene e Roma*, 8 (1963), 27-33.

Mancini, Guido, *L'etica stoica da Zenone a Crisippo*, Problemi d'oggi, 1, Padova, CEDAM, 1940.

Manicardi, Luigi, "Di un antico volgarizzamento inedito delle 'Epistole morali' di Seneca (23.7.05)," *Zeitschrift für romanische Philologie*, *30* (1906), 53-70.

Manitius, M., *Analekten zur Geschichte des Horaz im Mittelalter (bis 1300)*, Göttingen, Dieterich'schen Verlagsbuchhandlung, 1893.

—, *Philologisches aus alten Bibliothekskatalogen (bis 1300) zusammengestellt*, Ergänzungsheft, *Rheinisches Museum für Philologie*, n.F. *47* (1892).

Manning, C. E., "The Consolatory Tradition and Seneca's Attitude to the Emotions," *Greece & Rome*, ser. 2:*21* (1974), 71-81.

—, "Seneca and the Stoics on the Equality of the Sexes," *Mnemosyne*, ser. 4:*26* (1973), 170-77.

Marchesi, Concetto, "La libertà stoica romana in un poeta satirico del I secolo (A. Persio Flacco)," *Rivista d'Italia*, *9*:2 (1906), 303-24.

—, *Seneca*, 2ª ed. riv. e accresciuta, Biblioteca storica principato, 19, Messina, Giuseppe Principato, 1934.

Marco Tullio Cicerone, Scritti commemorativi pubblicati nel bimillenario della morte, Roma, Istituto di studi romani, Centro di Studi Ciceroniani, Firenze, Cartografica, 1961.

Marietta, Don E., "Conscience in Greek Stoicism," *Numen, 17* (1970), 176-87.

Marmorale, Enzo V., *Giovenale*, 2ª ed., Biblioteca di cultura moderna, 474, Bari, Gius. Laterza & Figli, 1950.

—, *Persio*, 2ª ed., Firenze, La Nuova Italia, 1956.

Martha, Constant, *Les Moralistes sous l'empire romain*, 7ᵉ éd., Paris, Hachette, 1900.

Marti, Berthe M., "Cassius Scaeva and Lucan's *Inventio*," *The Classical Tradition: Literary and Historical Studies in Honor of Harry Caplan*, ed. Luitpold Wallach, Ithaca, Cornell University Press, 1966, pp. 239-57.

—, "The Meaning of the *Pharsalia*," *American Journal of Philology, 66* (1945), 352-57.

—, "The Prototypes of Seneca's Tragedies," *Classical Philology, 42* (1947), 1-17.

—, "Seneca's Tragedies: A New Interpretation," *Transactions and Proceedings of the American Philological Association, 76* (1945), 216-45.

—, "La structure de la Pharsale," *Lucain*, Fondation Hardt: Entretiens sur l'antiquité classique, 15, Vandoeuvres-Genève, 26-31 août 1968, Paris, Librairie Klincksieck, 1970, pp. 3-34.

Martin, J. M. K., "Persius—Poet of the Stoics," *Greece & Rome, 8* (1939), 172-82.

Martinazzoli, Folco, *Seneca: Studio sulla morale ellenica nell'esperienza romana*, Biblioteca di cultura, 24, Firenze, La Nuova Italia, 1945.

Martino, Francesco de, "Variazioni postclassiche del concetto romano di *ius gentium*," *Annali della Facoltà di giurisprudenza dell'Università di Bari*, n.s. 7-8 (1947), 107-39.

Martyn, John R. C., ed., *Cicero and Virgil: Studies in Honour of Harold Hunt*, Amsterdam, Adolf M. Hakkert, 1972.

—, trans., *Friedländer's Essays on Juvenal*, Amsterdam, Adolf M. Hakkert, 1969.

Maschi, Carlo Alberto, *La cocezione naturalistica del diritto e degli istituti giuridici romani*, Pubblicazioni della Università cattolica del Sacro Cuore, 2ª ser., 53, Milano, Vita e Pensiero, 1937.

Mates, Benson, *Stoic Logic*, University of California Publications in Philosophy, 26, Berkeley, University of California Press, 1953.

Matthaei, Louise E., "The Fates, the Gods, and the Freedom of Man's Will in the *Aeneid*," *Classical Quarterly, 2* (1917), 11-25.

Mattingly, J. R., "Cosmogony and Stereometry in Posidonian Physics," *Osiris, 3* (1937), 558-83.

—, "Early Stoicism and Its Systematic Form," *The Philosophical Review, 48* (1939), 273-95.

Mattioli, Augusta, "Ricerche sul problema della libertà in Crisippo," *Reale Istituto Lombardo di scienze e lettere, Rendiconti*, classe di lettere e scienze morali e storiche, 73 (1939-40), 161-201.

Mau, Jürgen, "Stoische Logik: Ihre Stellung gegenüber der Aristotelischen Syllogistik und dem modernen Aussagenkalkül," *Hermes, 85* (1957), 147-58.

Mayer-Maly, Th., "Gemeinwohl und Naturrecht bei Cicero," *Völkerrecht und rechtliches Weltbild: Festschrift für Alfred Verdross*, ed. K. Zemanek et al., Wien, Springer-Verlag, 1960, pp. 195-206.

Mazza, Mario, *Storia e ideologia in Tito Livio: Per un'analisi storiografica della Praefatio ai Libri ab urbe condita*, Catania, Bonanno Editore, 1966.

Mazzoli, Giancarlo, "Genesi e valore del motivo escatologico in Seneca: Contributo alla questione posidoniana," *Istituto Lombardo, Accademia di scienze e lettere, Rendiconti*, classe di lettere e scienze morali e storiche, *101*, Milano, 1967, pp. 203-62.

—, *Seneca e la poesia*, Pubblicazioni della Facoltà di lettere e filosofia dell'Università di Pavia, Istituto di letteratura latina, Milano, Casa Editrice Ceschina, 1970.

Melazzo, Lucio, "La teoria del segno linguistico negli Stoici," *Lingua e stile, 10* (1975), 199-230.

Melucci, Pasquale, *Lo stoicismo di Epitteto*, Atti della Accademia Pontaniana, 35, ser. 2, *10*:6, Napoli, Francesco Giannini & Figli, 1905.

Mendell, Clarence W., *Latin Poetry: The Age of Rhetoric and Satire*, Hamden, Conn., Archon Books, 1967.

—, *Our Seneca*, New Haven, Yale University Press, 1941.

—, "Satire as Popular Philosophy," *Classical Philology*, *15* (1920), 138–57.

—, *Tacitus: The Man and His Works*, New Haven, Yale University Press, 1957.

Merchant, Frank Ivan, "Seneca the Philosopher and His Theory of Style," *American Journal of Philology*, *26* (1905), 44–59.

Merlan, Philip, "Epicureanism and Horace," *Journal of the History of Ideas*, *10* (1949), 445–51.

—, *From Platonism to Neoplatonism*, The Hague, Martinus Nijhoff, 1953.

Meyer, Eduard, *Caesars Monarchie und das Principat des Pompejus: Innere Geschichte Roms von 66 bis 44 v. Chr.*, 3rd ed., Stuttgart, J. G. Cotta'sche Buchhandlung Nachfolger, 1922.

Meyer, Hans, *Geschichte der Lehre von den Keimkräften von der Stoa bis zum Ausgang der Patristik nach den Quellen dargestellt*, Bonn, Peter Hansteins Verlagsbuchhandlung, 1914.

Meylan, Louis, "Panétius et la pénétration du stoïcisme à Rome au dernier siècle de la République," *Revue de théologie et de philosophie*, n.s. *17* (1929), 172–201.

Miceli, Riccardo, "La classificazione stoica delle passioni nelle 'Tusculanae' di Cicerone," *Sophia*, *3* (1935), 181–86.

Michel, Alain, "Cicéron et les grands courants de la philosophie antique: Problèmes généraux (1960–1970)," *Lustrum*, *16* (1972), 81–103.

—, "Cicéron et les paradoxes stoïciens," *Acta antiqua Academiae scientarum Hungaricae*, *16* (1968), 223–32.

—, "La causalité historique chez Tacite," *Revue des études anciennes*, *61* (1959), 96–106.

—, "Doxographie et histoire de la philosophie chez Cicéron (Lucullus, 128 sqq.)," *Studien zur Geschichte und Philosophie des Altertums*, ed. J. Harmatta, Amsterdam, Adolf M. Hakkert, 1968, pp. 113–20.

—, *Histoire des doctrines politiques à Rome*, Paris, PUF, 1971.

—, "La philosophie de Cicéron avant 54," *Revue des études anciennes*, *67* (1965), 324–41.

—, "À propos de la *République*: De Cicéron et Tacite à Jean Bodin," *Revue des études latines*, *45* (1967), 419–36.

—, *Rhétorique et philosophie chez Cicéron: Essai sur les fondements philosophiques de l'art de persuader*, Paris, PUF, 1960.

—, "Rhétorique et philosophie dans les *Tusculanes*," *Revue des études latines*, *39* (1961), 158–71.

—, *Tacite et le destin de l'Empire*, Paris, B. Arthaud, 1966.

—, and Verdière, Raoul, eds., *Ciceroniana: Hommages à Kazimierz Kumaniecki*, Leiden, E. J. Brill, 1975.

Michel, Jacques, "Sur les origines du 'jus gentium'," *Revue internationale des droits de l'antiquité*, 3ᵉ sér., *3* (1956), 313–48.

Mignucci, Mario, "Il problema del criterio di verità presso gli stoici antichi," *Posizione e criterio del discorso filosofico*, ed. Carlo Giacon, Bologna, R. Pàtron, 1967, pp. 145–69.

—, *Il significato della logica stoica*, 2ª ed., Bologna, R. Pàtron, 1967.

Modrze, Annelise, "Zur Ethik und Psychologie des Poseidonios," *Philologus*, *87* (1932), 300–31.

Momigliano, Arnaldo, "Note sulla leggenda del cristianesimo di Seneca," *Rivista storica italiana*, *62* (1950), 325–44.

Mommsen, Theodor, *The History of Rome*, new ed., trans. William Purdie Dickson, vols. 4 and 5, London, Macmillan and Co., Limited, 1912–13.

Montgomery, H. C., "The Development of Humanitarianism in Roman Law," *Classical Studies in Honor of William Abbott Oldfather*, Urbana, University of Illinois Press, 1943, pp. 104–21.

Moreau, Joseph, *L'Âme du monde de Platon aux Stoïciens*, Collection d'études anciennes publiée sous le patronage de l'Association Guillaume Budé, Paris, Les Belles Lettres, 1939.

—, *Épictète, ou le secret de la liberté*, Paris, Éditions Seghers, 1964.
Morford, M. P. O., *The Poet Lucan: Studies in Rhetorical Epic*, Oxford, Basil Blackwell, 1967.
—, "The Purpose of Lucan's Ninth Book," *Latomus, 26* (1967), 123–29.
Morris, Brian, "Virgil and the Heroic Ideal," *Proceedings of the Virgil Society, 9* (1969–70), 20–34.
Morris, Kay Don, "A Comparative Study of Marcus Annaeus Lucanus and Seneca the Philosopher," Ohio State University Ph.D. diss., 1959.
Morrow, Glenn R., "Plato and the Law of Nature," *Essays in Political Theory Presented to George H. Sabine*, ed. Milton R. Konvitz and Arthur E. Murphy, Ithaca, Cornell University Press, 1948, pp. 17–44.
Moscarini, Flaviana, *Cicerone e l'etica stoica nel III libro del 'De finibus'*, Pubblicazioni della scuola di filosofia della R. Università di Roma, 2, Roma, Tipografia del Senato, 1930.
Motto, Anna Lydia, *Seneca*, New York, Twayne Publishers, Inc., 1973.
—, "Seneca, Exponent of Humanitarianism," *Classical Journal, 50* (1955), 315–18.
—, "Seneca on Death and Immortality," *Classical Journal, 50* (1955), 187–89.
—, "Seneca on the Perfection of the Soul," *Classical Journal, 51* (1956), 275–78.
—, "Seneca on Theology," *Classical Journal, 50* (1955), 181–82.
—, "Seneca on Women's Liberation," *Classical World, 65* (1972), 155–57.
Muckle, J. T., "The Influence of Cicero in the Formation of Christian Culture," *Transactions of the Royal Society of Canada*, ser. 3, *42*:2 (1948), 107–25.
Mueller, Eduinus, *De Posidonio Manilii auctore*, Inaugural-Dissertation, Leipzig, Bornae, Roberti Noskei, 1901.
Mueller, Ian, "Stoic and Peripatetic Logic," *Archiv für Geschichte der Philosophie, 51* (1969), 173–87.
Mugler, Charles, *Deux, thèmes de la cosmologie grecque: Devenir cyclique et pluralité des mondes*, Études et commentaires, 17, Paris, C. Klincksieck, 1953.
Mühll, Peter von der, "Zwei alte Stoiker: Zuname und Herkunft," *Museum Helveticum, 20* (1963), 1–9.
Murdock, James Raymond, *"Fatum* and *fortuna* in Lucan's *Bellum civile,"* Yale University Ph.D. diss., 1970.
Murphy, James J., *Rhetoric in the Middle Ages: A History of Rhetorical Theory from Saint Augustine to the Renaissance*, Berkeley, University of California Press, 1974.
Murphy, Timothy Maurice, "Early Stoic Teleology," Harvard University Ph.D. diss., 1970.
Murray, Gilbert, *Stoic, Christian and Humanist*, London, C. A. Watts & Co., Ltd. 1940.
Mutschmann, Hermann, "Seneca und Epikur," *Hermes, 50* (1915), 321–56.
Nardo, Dante, "I *Dialogi* di Seneca a Montecassino," *Atti e memorie dell'Accademia Patavina di scienze, lettere ed arti*, classe di scienze morali, lettere ed arti, *86*, parte 3 (1973–74), 207–24.
Nebel, Gerhard, "Der Begriff des *kathêkon* in der alten Stoa," *Hermes, 70* (1935), 439–60.
—, "Zur Ethik des Poseidonios," *Hermes, 74* (1939), 34–57.
Nelson, N. E., "Cicero's *De Officiis* in Christian Thought: 300–1300," *Essays and Studies in English and Comparative Literature*, University of Michigan Publications, Language and Literature, 10, Ann Arbor, University of Michigan Press, 1933, pp. 59–160.
Nettleship, Henry, *Lectures and Essays*, second ser., ed. F. Haverfield, Oxford, Clarendon Press, 1895.
Neuenschwander, Hans Rudolf, *Mark Aurels Beziehung zu Seneca und Poseidonios*, Inaugural-Dissertation, Bern, Bern, Verlag Paul Haupt, 1951.
Nicholas, Barry, *An Introduction to Roman Law*, Clarendon Law Series, ed. H. L. A. Hart, Oxford, Clarendon Press, 1962.
Nietmann, William D., "Seneca on Death: The Courage to Be or Not te Be,"*International Philosophical Quarterly, 6* (1966), 81–89.
Nisbet, R. G. M. and Hubbard, Margaret, *A Commentary on Horace: Odes, Book I*, Oxford, Clarendon Press, 1970.

Nocera, Guglielmo, *Jus naturale nella esperienza giuridica romana*, Università degli studi di Perugia, pubblicazioni dell'Istituto di storia del diritto, Facoltà di giurisprudenza, Milano, A. Giuffrè, 1962.

Nock, Arthur Darby, "Posidonius," *Journal of Roman Studies, 49* (1959), 1-15.

Norden, Eduard, *Die germanische Urgeschichte in Tacitus Germania*, Leipzig, B. G. Teubner, 1920.

North, Helen F., "Canons and Hierarchies of the Cardinal Virtues in Greek and Latin Literature," *The Classical Tradition: Literary and Historical Studies in Honor of Harry Caplan*, ed. Luitpold Wallach, Ithaca, Cornell University Press, 1966, pp. 165-83.

—, *Sophrosyne: Self-Knowledge and Self-Restraint in Greek Literature*, Cornell Studies in Classical Philology, 35, Ithaca, Cornell University Press, 1966.

Nothdurft, Klaus-Dieter, *Studien zum Einfluss Senecas auf die Philosophie und Theologie des zwölften Jahrhunderts*, Studien und Texte zur Geistesgeschichte des Mittelalters, ed. Joseph Koch, 7, Leiden, E. J. Brill, 1963.

Noyen, P., "Marcus Aurelius, the Greatest Practician of Stoicism," *L'Antiquité classique, 24* (1955), 372-83.

Noyes, Alfred, *Horace: A Portrait*, New York, Sheed & Ward, 1947.

Nuchelmans, Gabriel, "Philologia et son mariage avec Mercure jusqu'à la fin du XIIe siècle," *Latomus, 16* (1957), 84-107.

Nutting, H. C., "The Hero of the Pharsalia," *American Journal of Philology, 53* (1932), 41-52.

Nybakken, Oscar Edward, *An Analytical Study of Horace's Ideas*, Iowa Studies in Classical Philology, 5, Scottsdale, Pa., Mennonite Press, 1937.

Occioni, Onorato, *Cajo Silio Italico e il suo poema*, 2^a ed., Firenze, LeMonnier, 1871.

Ogereau, F., *Essai sur le système philosophique des stoïciens*, Paris, Félix Alcan, 1885.

Oltramare, André, *Les origines de la diatribe romain*, Lausanne, Librairie Payot & Cie., 1926.

Opelt, Ilona, "Ciceros Schrift De natura deorum bei den lateinischen Kirchenvätern," *Antike und Abendland, 12* (1966), 141-55.

Oppermann, Hans, ed., *Wege zu Vergil: Drei Jahrzehnte Begegnungen in Dichtung und Wissenschaft*, Wege der Forschung, 19, Darmstadt, Wissenschaftliche Buchgesellschaft, 1963.

Otis, Brooks, *Virgil: A Study in Civilized Poetry*, Oxford, Clarendon Press, 1966.

—, "Virgil and Clio," *Phoenix, 20* (1966), 59-75.

Pacitti, Guerino, "Sul significato ultimo del 'Cato maior' di Cicerone," *Giornale italiano di filologia, 18* (1965), 236-60.

Packer, Mary N. Porter, "The Consistent Epicureanism of the First Book of the Epistles of Horace," *Transactions and Proceedings of the American Philological Association, 72* (1941), xxix-xl.

Palagi, Laura Bocciolini, *Il carteggio apocrifo di Seneca e San Paolo*, Accademia toscana di scienze e lettere "La Colombaria," 46, Firenze, Leo S. Olschki Editore, 1978.

Pallasse, Maurice, *Cicéron et les sources de droits*, Annales de l'Université de Lyon, 3me sér., droit, 8, Paris, Librairie du Recueil Sirey, 1946.

Pantzerhielm Thomas, S., "The Prologues of Sallust," *Symbolae Osloenses, 15-16,* (1936), 140-62.

Paoletti, Lao, "La fortuna di Lucano dal medioevo al romanticismo," *Atene e Roma*, n.s. 7 (1962), 144-57.

Paratore, Ettore, *Biografia e poetica di Persio*, Firenze, LeMonnier, 1968.

—, *Persio e Lucano*, Quaderni della Rivista di Cultura classica e medioevale, 6, Roma, Edizioni dell'Ateneo, 1963.

—, *Sallustio*, Quaderni della Rivista di Cultura classica e medioevale, 12, Roma, Edizioni dell'Ateneo, 1973.

—, "Seneca e Lucano," *Accademia nazionale dei Lincei, Problemi attuali di scienza e di cultura, 363*:88 (1966), 3-23.

—, *Tacito*, Biblioteca storica universitaria, ser. 2:3, Milano, Istituto Editoriale Cisalpino, 1951.

Pascal, Carlo, *Le credenze d'oltretomba nelle opere letterarie dell'antichità classica*, 2 vols., Catania, Francesco Battiato, 1912.

—, *Seneca*, Catania, Concetto Battiato, 1906.

Pasquali, Giorgio, "Cesare, Platone e Posidonio," *Studi italiani di filologia classica*, n.s. *8*, 4 (1930), 297-310.

Pavlovskis, Zoja, "Aristotle, Horace, and the Ironic Man," *Classical Philology, 63* (1968), 22-41.

—, "The Influence of Statius upon Latin Literature before the Tenth Century," Cornell University Ph.D. diss., 1962.

Pepe, Giovanni, "La filosofia religiosa di Epitteto," *Rivista di filosofia neo-scolastica, 8* (1916), 2-20.

Pépin, Jean, *Mythe et allégorie: Les origines grecques et les contestations judéo-chrétiennes*, Paris, Aubier, 1958.

—, *Saint Augustin et la dialectique*, The Saint Augustine Lecture, 1972, Villanova, Villanova University Press, 1976.

Perelli, Luciano, "*Natura* e *ratio* nel II libro del *De re publica* ciceroniano," *Rivista di filologia e di istruzione classica, 100* (1972), 295-311.

Perlich, Dieter, "Otium oder accedere ad rem publicam: Das Problem der politischen Betätigung bei Cicero," *Der altsprachliche Unterricht, 13*:1 (1970), 5-16.

Perret, Jacques, *Virgile*, nouv. éd., Paris, Hatier, 1965.

Perret, Jean Louis, *La transmission du texte de Juvénal d'après une nouvelle collation*, Annales Academiae Scientarum Fennicae, ser. B, 21:1, Helsinki, Suomalaisen Tiedeakatemian Toimituksia, 1927.

Pesce, Domenico, "La morale di Epitteto," *Rivista di filosofia, 30* (1939), 250-64.

Pfeiffer, Rudolf, *History of Classical Scholarship from the Beginnings to the End of the Hellenistic Age*, Oxford, Clarendon Press, 1968.

Pfligersdorffer, Georg, "Lucan als Dichter des geistigen Widerstandes," *Hermes, 87* (1959), 344-77.

—, *Politik und Musse: Zum Proömium und Einleitungsgespräch von Ciceros De re publica*, München, Wilhelm Fink Verlag, 1969.

—, *Studien zu Poseidonios*, Österreichische Akademie der Wissenschaft, philosophisch-historische Klasse, Sitzungsberichte, 232, Abhandlung 5, Wien, Rudolf M. Rohrer, 1959.

Philippson, Robert, "Das 'Erste Naturgemässe'," *Philologus, 87* (1932), 445-66.

—, "Horaz' Verhältnis zur Philosophie," *Festschrift dem König Wilhelms-Gymnasium zu Magdeburg zur Feier seines 25 jährigen Bestehens, Ostern 1911*, Magdeburg, Karl Peters, 1911, pp. 77-110.

—, "Panaetiana," *Rheinisches Museum für Philologie, 78* (1929), 337-60; 79 (1930), 406-10.

—, "Das Sittlichschöne bei Panaitios," *Philologus, 85* (1930) 357-413.

—, "Zur Psychologie der Stoa," *Rheinisches Museum für Philologie*, n.F. *86* (1937), 140-79.

Piacentini, Ugo, *Osservazioni sulla tecnica epica di Lucano*, Deutsche Akademie der Wissenschaften zu Berlin, Schriften der Sektion für Altertumswissenschaft, 39, Berlin, Akademie-Verlag, 1963.

Picard-Parra, Clotilde, "Une utilisation des *Quaestiones naturales* de Sénèque au milieu du XIIe siècle," *Revue du moyen âge latin, 5* (1949), 115-26.

Pichon, René, *Les Sources de Lucain*, Paris, Ernest Leroux, 1912.

Piganiol, André, "Sur la source du *Songe de Scipion*," *Comptes rendus de l'Académie des inscriptions et belles lettres de Paris, 1957*, Paris, C. Klincksieck, 1957, pp. 88-93.

Piot, M., "Hercule chez les poètes du Ier siècle après Jésus-Christ," *Revue des études latines, 43* (1965), 342-58.

Pinborg, Jan, "Das Sprachdenken der Stoa und Augustins Dialektik," *Classica et mediaevalia, 23* (1962), 148-77.

Pire, G., *Stoïcisme et pédagogie de Zénon à Marc-Aurèle, de Sénèque à Montaigne et à J.-J. Rousseau*, Liège, H. Dessain, 1958.

Pittet, Armand, *Vocabulaire philosophique de Sénèque*, Collection des études anciennes publiée sous le patronage de l'Association Guillaume Budé, Paris, Les Belles Lettres, 1937.

Places, Édouard des, "Le platonisme de Panétius," *Mélanges d'archéologie et d'histoire, 68* (1956), 83-94.

Plasberg, Otto, *Cicero in seinen Werken und Briefen,* ed. Wilhelm Ax, Das Erbe der Alten, 11, Leipzig, Dieterich'sche Verlagsbuchhandlung, 1926.

Plinval, Georges de, "Autour du *De legibus,*" *Revue des études latines, 47* (1969), 294-309.

Pohlenz, Max, *Antikes Führertum: Cicero De officiis und das Lebensideal des Panaitios,* Neue Wege zur Antike, 2:3, Leipzig, B. C. Teubner, 1934.

—, "Die Begründung der abendländischen Sprachlehre durch die Stoa," *Kleine Schriften,* ed. Heinrich Dörrie, Hildesheim, Georg Olms Verlagsbuchhandlung, 1965, *1,* 39-86.

—, "Causae civilium armorum," *Kleine Schriften,* ed. Heinrich Dörrie, Hildesheim, Georg Olms Verlagsbuchhandlung, 1965, *2,* 139-48.

—, *Freedom in Greek Life and Thought: The History of an Ideal,* trans. Carl Lofmark, New York, The Humanities Press, 1966.

—, *Gestalten aus Hellas,* München, F. Bruckmann, 1950.

—, *Grundfragen der stoischen Philosophie,* Abhandlungen der Gesellschaft der Wissenschaften zu Göttingen, philologisch-historische Klasse, Folge 3:26, Göttingen, Vandenhoeck & Ruprecht, 1940.

—, "De Posidonii libris *peri pathon,*" *Jahrbücher für classische Philologie,* Supplementband, *24:2* (1898), 535-634.

—, "*To prepon:* Ein Beitrag zur Geschichte des griechischen Geistes," *Nachrichten von der Gesellschaft der Wissenschaften zu Göttingen,* philologisch-historische Klasse, Fachgruppe 1 (Altertumswissenschaft), *16* (1933), 53-92.

—, *Die Stoa: Geschichte einer geistigen Bewegung,* 2nd ed., 2 vols., Göttingen, Vandenhoeck & Ruprecht, 1955-59.

—, "Stoa und Semitismus," *Neue Jahrbücher für Wissenschaft und Jugendbildung, 2* (1926), 257-69.

—, "Tierische und menschliche Intelligenz bei Poseidonios," *Hermes, 76* (1941), 1-13.

—, "Zenon und Chrysipp," *Nachrichten von der Gesellschaft der Wissenschaft zu Göttingen,* philologisch-historische Klasse, Fachgruppe 1, Altertumswissenschaft, n.F. *2:9* (1938), 173-210.

Pöhlmann, Robert von, *Die Weltanschauung des Tacitus,* Sitzungsberichte der königlich Bayerischen Akademie der Wissenschaften, philosophisch-philologische und historische Klasse, 1, München, Königlich Bayerischen Akademie der Wissenschaften, 1910.

Pólay, Elemér, "Zur Geschichte der Rechtswissenschaft im republikanischen Rom," *Gesellschaft und Recht im griechisch-römischen Altertum,* ed. Mihail N. Andreev et al., Deutsche Akademie der Wissenschaft zu Berlin, Schriften der Sektion für Altertumswissenschaft, 52, Berlin, Akademie-Verlag, 1968, pp. 150-92.

Poppelreuter, Petrus Hubertus, *Quae ratio intercedat inter Posidonii Peri pathon pragmateis et Tusculanes disputationes Ciceronis,* Bonn, Caroli Georgi, 1883.

Pöschl, Viktor, *The Art of Vergil: Image and Symbol in the Aeneid,* trans. Gerda Seligson, Ann Arbor, University of Michigan Press, 1962.

—, "Horaz," *L'Influence grecque sur la poésie latine de Catulle à Ovide,* Fondation Hardt: Entretiens sur l'antiquité classique, 2, Genève, Fondation Hardt, 1956, pp. 93-115.

—, *Horazische Lyrik: Interpretationen,* Heidelberg, Carl Winter, 1970.

—, "The Poetic Achievement of Virgil," *Classical Journal, 66* (1961), 290-99.

—, "Poetry and Philosophy in Horace," *The Poetic Tradition: Essays on Greek, Latin, and English Poetry,* ed. Don Cameron Allen and Henry T. Rowell, Percy Graeme Turnbull Memorial Lectures on Poetry, Baltimore, Johns Hopkins Press, 1968, pp. 47-61.

—, *Römischer Staat und griechisches Staatsdenken bei Cicero: Untersuchungen zu Ciceros Schrift De re publica,* Neue deutsche Forschung, 104, Abteilung klassische Philologie, 5, Berlin, Junker und Dünnhaupt, 1936.

—, ed., *Tacitus*, Wege der Forschung, 97, Darmstadt, Wissenschaftliche Buchgesellschaft, 1969.

Pozzi, Lorenzo, "Il nesso di implicazione nella logica stoica," *Atti del convegno di storia della logica*, Parma, 8–10 ottobre 1972, Istituto di filosofia dell'Università di Parma, Collana di "Testi e saggi," 4, Padova, Liviana Editrice, 1974, pp. 177–87.

Pozzo, Gianni Maria, "Il problema morale in Seneca e in Marco Aurelio," *Giornale di metafisica, 12* (1957), 729–33.

Praechter, Karl, *Hierokles der Stoiker*, Leipzig, Dieterich'sche Verlagsbuchhandlung, 1901.

—, "Zu Ariston von Chios," *Hermes, 48* (1913), 477–80.

Pralle, Ludwig, *Die Wiederentdeckung des Tacitus*, Quellen und Abhandlungen zur Geschichte der Abtei und der Diözese Fulda, 17, Fulda, Verlag Parzeller & Co., 1952.

Prantl, Carl, *Geschichte der Logik im Abendlande*, vol. 1, Leipzig, Gustav Fock GMBH, 1927.

Pratt, Norman T., Jr., "The Stoic Base of Senecan Drama," *Transactions and Proceedings of the American Philological Association, 79* (1948), 1–11.

Préchac, F., "Notes sur le texte des Lettres à Lucilius," *Mélanges Paul Thomas*, Bruges, Imprimerie Sainte Catherine, 1930, pp. 574–76.

—, "Pour l'établissement du texte de Sénèque: Glanures médiévales," *Mélanges offerts à A.-M. Desrousseaux par ses amis et ses élèves*, Paris, Hachette, 1937, pp. 357–70.

Prescott, Henry W., *The Development of Virgil's Art*, Chicago, University of Chicago Press, 1927.

Preti, Giulio, "Sulla dottrina del *semeîon* nella logica stoica," *Rivista critica di storia della filosofia, 2* (1956), 5–14.

Pringsheim, Fritz, "Aequitas und bona fides," *Conferenze per il XIV centenario delle Pandette, 15 dicembre 530–15 dicembre 1930*, Pubblicazioni della Università cattolica del Sacro Cuore, 2ª ser., 33, Milano, Vita e Pensiero, 1931, pp. 183–214.

—, "Bonum et aequum," *Zeitschrift der Savigny-Stiftung für Rechtsgeschichte*, romanistische Abteilung, *52* (1932), 78–155.

—, "Jus aequum und jus strictum," *Zeitschrift der Savigny-Stiftung für Rechtsgeschichte*, romanistische Abteilung, *42* (1921), 643–68.

—, *Gesammelte Abhandlungen*, 2 vols., Heidelberg, Carl Winter, 1961.

—, "The Legal Policy and Reforms of Hadrian," *Journal of Roman Studies, 24* (1934), 141–53.

Pucci, Piero, "Politica ed ideologia nel De amicitia," *Maia, 15* (1963), 342–58.

Putnam, Michael C. J., *The Poetry of the Aeneid: Four Studies in Imaginative Unity and Design*, Cambridge, Mass., Harvard University Press, 1965.

Putzner, Gottfried Heinz, *Die ethischen Systeme Platos und der Stoa in ihrem gegenseitigen Verhältnis*, Berlin, Gustave Schade, 1913.

Quatre études sur Lucain, Études de Lettres, sér. 2:8, Lausanne, Faculté de Lettres de l'Université de Lausanne, 1965, pp. 213–58.

Questa, Cesare, *Studi sulle fonti degli Annales di Tacito*, 2nd ed., Roma, Edizioni dell'Ateneo, 1967.

Quinn, Kenneth, *Virgil's Aeneid: A Critical Description*, London, Routledge & Kegan Paul, 1969.

Raabe, Hermann, *Plurima mortis imago: Vergleichende Interpretationen zur Bildersprache Vergils*, Zetemata, 59, München, C. H. Beck'sche Verlagsbuchhandlung, 1974.

Rabe, A., "Das Verhältnis des Horaz zur Philosophie," *Archiv für Geschichte der Philosophie und Soziologie, 39* (1930), 77–91.

Rabbow, Paul, *Antike Schriften über Seelenheilung und Seelenleitung auf ihre Quellen untersucht*, vol. 1, Leipzig, B. G. Teubner, 1914.

Radke, Gerhard, ed., *Cicero: Ein Mensch seiner Zeit*, Berlin, Walter de Gruyter & Co., 1968.

Ramage, Edwin S., Sisgbee, David L., and Fredericks, Sigmund C., eds., *Roman Satirists and Their Satire: The Fine Art of Criticism in Ancient Rome*, Park Ridge, N. J. Noyes Press, 1974.

Rambaud, Michel, "Les prologues de Salluste et la démonstration morale dans son oeuvre," *Revue des études latines, 24* (1946), 115–30.

Rand, Edward Kennard, "The Humanism of Cicero," *Proceedings of the American Philosophical Society, 71* (1932), 207-16.
—, *The Magical Art of Virgil,* Cambridge, Mass., Harvard University Press, 1931.
—, "The Mediaeval Virgil," *Studi medievali,* n.s. *5* (1932), 418-42.
Rauthe, Ranier, *Zur Geschichte des Horaztextes im Altertum,* Inaugural-Dissertation, Albert-Ludwigs-Universität zu Freiburg im Breisgau, Bamberg, Difo-Druck Schmacht, 1971.
Ravaisson, Félix, "Mémoire sur le Stoïcisme," *Memoires de l'Institut impériale de France, Académie des inscriptions et belles-lettres, 21:*1 (1857), 1-94.
Récéjac, E., *De mendacio quid senserit Augustinus,* Paris, E. Leroux, 1897.
Reckford, Kenneth J., "Studies in Persius," *Hermes, 90* (1962), 476-504.
Reesor, Margaret E., "Fate and Possibility in Early Stoic Philosophy," *Phoenix, 19* (1965), 285-97.
—, *The Political Theory of the Old and Middle Stoa,* New York, J. J. Augustin, 1951.
—, "The Stoic Categories," *American Journal of Philology, 78* (1957), 63-82.
—, "The Stoic Concept of Quality," *American Journal of Philology, 75* (1954), 40-58.
Regenbogen, Otto, "Schmerz und Tod in den Tragödien Senecas," *Vorträge der Bibliothek Warburg,* 1927-28, Leipzig, B. G. Teubner, 1930, pp. 167-218.
—, "Seneca als Denker römischer Willenshaltung," *Die Antike, 12* (1936), 107-30.
Reid, J. S., "Tacitus as a Historian," *Journal of Roman Studies, 11* (1921), 191-99.
Reiner, Hans, "Die ethische Weisheit der Stoiker heute," *Gymnasium, 76* (1969), 330-57.
—, "Zum Begriff des Guten (Agathon) in der stoischen Ethik," *Zeitschrift für philosophische Forschung, 28* (1974), 228-35.
Reinhardt, Karl, *Kosmos und Sympathie: Neue Untersuchungen über Poseidonios,* München, C. H. Beck'sche Verlagsbuchhandlung, 1926.
—, *Poseidonios,* München, Oskar Beck, 1921.
—, *Poseidonios über Ursprung und Entartung: Interpretation zweier kulturgeschichtlicher Fragmente,* Orient und Antike, ed. G. Bergsträsser and O. Regenbogen, 6, Heidelberg, Carl Winter, 1928.
—, "Poseidonios von Apameia," *Paulys Realencyclopädie der classischen Altertumswissenschaft,* Stuttgart, Alfred Druckenmüller Verlag, 1953, *43,* cols. 558-826.
Reitzenstein, Richard, "Die Characteristik der Philosophie bei Poseidonios," *Hermes, 65* (1930), 81-91.
—, "Die Idee des Principats bei Cicero und Augustus," *Nachrichten von der königlichen Gesellschaft der Wissenschaften zu Göttingen,* philologisch-historische Klasse, 1917, Berlin, 1918, pp. 399-436.
—, "Tacitus und sein Werk," *Neue Wege zur Antike,* 2nd ed., Leipzig, B. G. Teubner, 1926, *4,* 1-32.
—, "Zu Ciceros De re publica," *Hermes, 59* (1924), 356-62.
Rémy, E., "Dignitas cum otio," *Le Musée Belge, 32* (1928), 113-27.
—, "Sur une application de la morale stoïcienne au ius belli," *Le Musée Belge, 19-24,* (1920), 24-38.
Renan, Ernst, *Marc-Aurèle et la fin du monde antique,* 4me éd., Paris, Michel Lévy Frères, 1882.
Reymond, Arnold, "La logique stoïcienne," *Revue de théologie et de philosophie,* n.s. *17* (1929), 161-71.
Reynolds, L. D., "The Medieval Tradition of Seneca's Dialogues," *Classical Quarterly,* n.s. *18* (1968), 355-73.
—, *The Medieval Tradition of Seneca's Letters,* London, Oxford University Press, 1965.
Rexine, John E., *Religion in Plato and Cicero,* New York, Greenwood Press, 1968.
Riccobono, Salvatore, Jr., "L'idea di *humanitas* come fonte di progresso del diritto," *Studi in onore di Biondo Biondi,* Milano, A. Giuffrè, 1965, *2,* 582-614.
Richards, G. C., *Cicero: A Study,* Westport, Conn., Greenwood Press, 1970.
Richter, Will, *Lucius Annaeus Seneca: Das Problem der Bildung in seiner Philosophie mit einer Beilage, Die Lücken in Senecas Briefen und in de beneficiis I,* Lengerich, Lengericher Handelsdruckerie, 1939.

Ricken, Werner, "Zur Entstehung des Laelius de amicitia," *Gymnasium*, *62* (1955), 360–74.

Rieks, Rudolf, *Homo, Humanus, Humanitas: Zur Humanität in der lateinischen Literatur des ersten nachchristlichen Jahrhunderts*, München, Wilhelm Fink Verlag, 1967.

Riesco, José, "Führt die Philosophie Senecas zur göttlichen Transcendenz?" *Franziskanische Studien*, *49* (1967), 80–109.

Rieth, Otto, *Grundbegriffe der stoischen Ethik: Eine traditionsgeschichtliche Untersuchung*, Problemata, Forschungen zur klassischen Philologie, 9, Berlin, Weidmannsche Buchhandlung, 1933.

Righi, Gaetano, *La filosofia civile e giuridica di Cicerone*, Bologna, Tipografia Militare già delle Scienze, 1930.

Rintelen, Fritz-Joachim von, "Lucius Annaeus Seneca über die 'Einheit des Menschengeschechtes'," *Zeitschrift für philosophische Forschung*, *19* (1965), 563–76.

Riondato, Ezio, *Epitteto: Esperienza e ragione*, Miscellanea erudita, 16, Padova, Antenore, 1965.

Riposati, Benedetto, *Studi sui 'Topica' di Cicerone*, Edizioni dell'Università cattolica del Sacro Cuore, 22, Milano, Vita e Pensiero, 1947.

Rist, J. M., *Stoic Philosophy*, Cambridge, The University Press, 1969.

—, "Zeno and Stoic Consistency," *Phronesis*, *22* (1977), 161–74.

—, ed., *The Stoics*, Berkeley, University of California Press, 1978.

Ritter, Joachim, '*Naturrecht*' *bei Aristoteles: Zum Problem Erneuerung des Naturrechts*, Res publica: Beiträge zum öffentlichen Recht, ed. Ernst Forsthoff, 6, Stuttgart, W. Kohlhammer, 1961.

Roberti, Melchiore, "Cristianesimo e collezioni giustinianee," *Cristianesimo e diritto romano*, Pubblicazioni della Università cattolica del Sacro Cuore, 2ª ser., 43, Milano, Vita e Pensiero, 1935, pp. 1–65.

Robins, R. H., *Ancient and Mediaeval Grammatical Theory in Europe with Particular Reference to Modern Doctrine*, London, G. Bell & Sons Ltd., 1951.

Robiou, Félix, *De l'influence du Stoïcisme a l'époque des Flaviens et des Antonins*, Rennes, J.-M. Vatar, 1852.

Robleda, Olis, "La 'aequitas' en Cicerón," *Humanidades*. *2* (1950), 31–57.

—, "Estudio jurídico sobre el 'Pro Caecina' de Ciceron," *Humanidades*, *1* (1949), 55–81.

—, "Filosofia jurídica de Cicerón," *Studi in onore di Biondo Biondi*, Milano, A. Giuffrè, 1965, 2, 467–82.

Rodier, Georges, *Études de philosophie grecque*, Paris, J. Vrin, 1926.

Rodis-Lewis, Geneviève, *La morale stoïcienne*, Initiations philosophiques, 90, Paris, PUF, 1970.

Rohde, Erwin, *Psyche: The Cult of Souls and Belief in Immortality among the Greeks*, 8th, ed., trans. W. B. Hillis, London, Routledge & Kegan Paul Ltd., 1950.

Rolfe, John C., *Cicero and His Influence*, New York, Longmans, Green and Co., 1928.

Rolland, E., *De l'influence de Sénèque le père et des rhéteurs sur Sénèque le philosophe*, Université de Gand, Recueil de travaux publiés par la Faculté de philosophie et lettres, 32, Gand, E. Van Goethem, 1906.

Romano Domenico, "Motivi politici ed autobiografici nel 'De officiis' di Cicerone," *Annali del Liceo classico "G. Garibaldi" di Palermo*, n.s. *5-6* (1968-69), 21–31.

Rotta, Paolo, "La lettera CXXI de Seneca e la teoria dell'istinto nello Stoicismo," *Raccolta di scritti in onore di Felice Ramorino*, Pubblicazioni della Università cattolica del Sacro Cuore, 4ª ser., scienze filologiche, 7, Milano, Vita e Pensiero, 1927, pp. 130–46.

Round, N. G., "The Mediaeval Reputation of the *Proverbiae Senecae*: A Partial Survey Based on Recorded MSS.," *Proceedings of the Royal Irish Academy*, *72*, C, 5 (1972), 103–51.

Rozelaar, M., "Seneca: A New Approach to His Personality," *Lampas*, *7* (1974), 33–42.

Ruch, Michel, "Le destin dans l'*Énéide*: Essence et réalité," *Vergiliana: Recherches sur Vergile*, ed. Henry Bardon and Raoul Verdière, Roma aeterna, 3, Leiden, E. J. Brill, 1971, 312–21.

—, *Études cicéroniennes*, Paris, Centre de Documentation Universitaire, 1970.
—, "Un exemple du syncrétisme philosophique de Cicéron: *Academica posteriora*, ¶21," *Revue des études latines*, *48* (1970), 205-28.
—, "Horace, Satires I, 3: Études littéraire et philosophique," *Les Études classiques*, *38* (1970), 517-27.
—, *L'Hortensius de Cicéron: Histoire et reconstruction*, Collection d'études anciennes publiée sous le patronage de l'Association Guillaume Budé, Paris, Les Belles Lettres, 1958.
—, *Le préambule dans les oeuvres philosophiques de Cicéron: Essai sur la genèse et l'art du dialogue*, Publications de la Faculté des lettres de l'Université de Strasbourg, 136, Paris, Les Belles Lettres, 1958.
Rubin, Salomon, *Die Ethik Senecas in ihrem Verhältnis zur älteren und mittleren Stoa*, München, C. H. Beck'sche Verlagsbuchhandlung, 1901.
Rudberg, Gunnar, *Forschungen zu Poseidonios*, Skrifter utgifna af kungl. humanistika Vetenskaps-Samfundet i Uppsala, *20*:3, Uppsala, A.-B. Akademiska Bokhandeln, 1918.
Rudd, Niall, *The Satires of Horace: A Study*, Cambridge, The University Press, 1966.
Rutz, Werner, "Amor mortis bei Lucan," *Hermes*, *88* (1960), 462-75.
—, ed., *Lucan*, Wege der Forschung, 235, Darmstadt, Wissenschaftliche Buchgesellschaft, 1970.
Ryle, R. J., "Epictetus," *Proceedings of the Aristotelian Society*, *2*:3 (1894), 123-32.
Saint-Denis, E. de, "La théorie cicéronienne de la participation aux affaires publiques," *Revue de philologie*, *12* (1938), 193-215.
Sainte-Beuve, C.-A., *Étude sur Virgile*, 4me éd., Paris, Calmann Lévy, 1883.
Salomon, Max, *Der Begriff der Gerechtigkeit bei Aristoteles nebst einem Anhang über den Begriff des Tauschgeschäftes*, Leiden, A. W. Sijthoff's Uitgeversmij N.V., 1937.
Samburski, S., "On Some References to Experience in Stoic Physics," *Isis*, *49* (1958), 331-35.
—, *Physics of the Stoics*, New York, Macmillan Company, 1959.
Sandbach, F. H., "*Ennoia* and *Prolepsis* in the Stoic Theory of Knowledge," *Classical Quarterly*, *24* (1930), 44-51.
—, *The Stoics*, London, Chatto & Windus, 1975.
Sandys, John Edwin, *A History of Classical Scholarship from the Sixth Century B.C. to the End of the Middle Ages*, vol. 1, Cambridge, The University Press, 1903.
Sanford, Eva Matthews, "Quotations from Lucan in Mediaeval Latin Authors," *Transactions and Proceedings of the American Philological Association*, *63* (1932), xxxviii-xxxix.
Santa Cruz Teijeiro, José, "El influjo de la retórica en el derecho romano," *Revista de estudios políticos*, *44* (1952), 109-24.
Sauter, Johann, "Die philosophischen Grundlagen des antiken Naturrechts," *Zeitschrift für öffentliches Recht*, *10* (1931), 28-81.
Scarpat, Giuseppi, *Il pensiero religiosa di Seneca e l'ambiente ebraico e cristiano*, Antichità classica e cristiana, 14, Brescia, Paideia, 1977.
Schäfer, Maximilian, "Diogenes als Mittelstoiker," *Philologus*, *91* (1936), 174-96.
—, *Ein frühmittelstoisches System der Ethik bei Cicero: Untersuchung von Ciceros drittem Buche de finibus bonorum et malorum nach Aufbau und Zugehörigkeit auf Grund griechischer Quellen zur stoischen Ethik*, München, Druck der Salesianischen Offizin, 1934.
—, "Des Panaitios *aner archikos* bei Cicero: Ein Interpretationsbeitrag zu Ciceros Schrift De republica," *Gymnasium*, *67* (1960), 500-16.
—, "Panaitios bei Cicero und Gellius," *Gymnasium*, *62* (1955), 334-53.
Schellhase, Kenneth C., *Tacitus in Renaissance Political Thought*, Chicago, University of Chicago Press, 1976.
Schetter, Willy, *Untersuchungen zur epischen Kunst des Statius*, Klassisch-philologische Studien, 20, Wiesbaden, Otto Harrassowitz, 1960.
Schian, Ruth, *Untersuchungen über das 'argumentum e consensu omnium'*, Spudasmata, 28, Hildesheim, Georg Olms Verlag, 1973.
Schieffer, Rudolf, "Silius Italicus in St. Gallen: Ein Hinweis zur Lokalisierung des 'Waltharius'," *Mittellateinisches Jahrbuch*, *10* (1975), 7-19.

Schindler, Alfred, *Wort und Analogie in Augustins Trinitätslehre*, Hermeneutische Untersuchungen zur Theologie, 4, Tübingen, J. C. B. Mohr, 1965.

Schindler, Karl, *Die stoische Lehre von den Seelenteilen und Seelenvermögen inbesondere bei Panaitios und Poseidonios und ihre Verwendung bei Cicero*, München, Salesianischen Offizin, 1934.

Schmekel, A., *Die Philosophie der mittleren Stoa in ihrem geschichtlichen Zusammenhange*, Berlin, Weidmannsche Buchhandlung, 1892.

Schmidt, Peter Lebrecht, *Die Abfassungszeit von Ciceros Schrift über die Gesetze*, Collana di studi ciceroniani, 4, Roma, Centro di Studi Ciceroniani, 1969.

—, *Die Überlieferung von Ciceros Schrift "De legibus" in Mittelalter und Renaissance*, Studia et testimonia antiqua, 10, München, Wilhelm Fink Verlag, 1974.

Schmidt, Rudolphus, *Stoicorum grammatica*, Halle, Apud Eduardum Anton, 1839.

Schmitt, Charles B., *Cicero Scepticus: A Study of the Influence of the Academica in the Renaissance*, International Archives of the History of Ideas, 52, The Hague, Martinus Nijhoff, 1972.

Schneider, Carl, *Juvenal und Seneca*, Inaugural-Dissertation, Würzburg, Würzburg, Werkbund-Druckerei, 1930.

Schnepf, Hermann, "Das Herculesabenteuer in Virgils Aeneis (VIII 184 f.)," *Gymnasium*, 66 (1959), 250-68.

Schönberger, Otto, "Zum Weltbild der drei Epiker nach Lucan," *Helikon*, 5 (1965), 123-45.

Schotes, Hans-Albert, *Stoische Physik, Psychologie und Theologie bei Lucan*, Habelts Dissertationsdrucke, Reihe klassische Philologie, 5, Bonn, Rudolf Habelt Verlag GMBH, 1969.

Schottlaender, Rudolf, "Epikureisches bei Seneca: Ein Ringen um den Sinn von Freude und Freundschaft," *Philologus*, 99 (1955), 133-48.

—, "Persius und Seneca über die Problematik der Freilassungen," *Wissenschaftliche Zeitschrift der Universität Rostock*, gesellschafts- und sprachwissenschaftliche Reihe, 15:4-5 (1966), 533-39.

Schranka, Eduard Maria, *Der Stoiker Epiktet und seine Philosophie*, Frankfurt am Oder, B. Waldmann's Verlag, 1885.

Schubert, Paul, *Die Eschatologie des Poseidonios*, Veröffentlichungen des Forschungsinstituts für vergleichende Religionsgeschichte an der Universität Leipzig, ed. Hans Haas, 2:4, Leipzig, Eduard Pfeiffer, 1927.

Schuetze, Reinoldus, *Juvenalis Ethicus*, Inaugural-Dissertation, Greifswald, Greifswald, Julius Abel, 1905.

Schulte, Hans Kurt, *Orator: Untersuchungen über das ciceronianische Bildungsideal*, Frankfurter Studien zur Religion und Kultur der Antike, 11, Frankfurt am Main, Vittorio Klostermann, 1935.

Schulz, Fritz, *Classical Roman Law*, Oxford, Clarendon Press, 1951.

—, *History of Roman Legal Science*, Oxford, Clarendon Press, 1946.

—, *Principles of Roman Law*, rev. ed., trans. Marguerite Wolff, Oxford, Clarendon Press, 1936.

Schur, Werner, *Sallust als Historiker*, Stuttgart, W. Kohlhammer, 1934.

Schweicher, Gerd, *Schicksal und Glück in den Werken Sallusts und Caesars*, Inaugural-Dissertation, Köln, Köln, Gerd Wasmund, 1963.

Scott, Russell T., *Religion and Philosophy in the Histories of Tacitus*, Papers and Monographs of the American Academy in Rome, 22, Rome, American Academy in Rome, 1968.

Scritti per il XIX centenario della nascita di Persio, Biblioteca della "Rassegna Volterrana," 3, Volterra, Accademia dei Sepolti, 1936.

Sedgwick, Henry Dwight, *Horace: A Biography*, Cambridge, Mass., Harvard University Press, 1947.

Seel, Otto, *Cicero: Wort, Staat, Welt*, Stuttgart, Ernst Klett Verlag, 1953.

Sellar, W. Y., *The Roman Poets of the Augustan Age: Virgil*, 3rd ed., Oxford, Clarendon Press, 1908.

Semple, W. H., "The Poet Persius: Literary and Social Critic," *Bulletin of the John Rylands Library*, 44 (1961), 157-74.

Senn, Félix, "De la distinction du *ius naturale* et du *ius gentium*," *De la justice et du droit*, Paris, Recueil Sirey, 1927, pp. 57-87.

Serafini, Augusto, *Studio sulla satira di Giovenale*, Firenze, LeMonnier, 1957.

Shipley, Frederick W., "The Universality of Horace," *Classical Journal, 31* (1935-36), 135-51.

Showerman, Grant, *Horace and His Influence*, Boston, Marshall Jones Company, 1922.

Siegfried, Walter, "Stoische Haltung, nach Mark Aurel," *Hermeneia: Festschrift Otto Regenbogen zum 60. Geburtstag am 14. Februar 1941 dargebracht von Schülern und Freunden*, Heidelberg, Carl Winter, 1952, pp. 144-63.

Sigsbee, David L., "The *Paradoxa Stoicorum* in Varro's *Menippeans*," *Classical Philology, 71* (1976), 244-48.

Silk, Edmund T., "Notes on Cicero and the Odes of Horace," *Yale Classical Studies, 13* (1952), 147-58.

Simon, Heinrich and Simon, Marie, *Die alte Stoa und ihr Naturbegriff: Ein Beitrag zur Philosophiegeschichte des Hellenismus*, Berlin, Aufbau-Verlag, 1956.

Singh, Raghuveer, "Herakleitos and the Law of Nature," *Journal of the History of Ideas, 24* (1963), 457-72.

Sizoo, A., "Paetus Thrasea et le stoïcisme," *Revue des études latines, 4* (1926), 229-37.

Smalley, Beryl, "Sallust in the Middle Ages,"*Classical Influences on European Culture A.D. 500-1500*, ed. R. R. Bolgar, Cambridge, The University Press, 1971, pp. 165-75.

Smethurst, S. E., "Politics and Morality in Cicero," *Phoenix, 9* (1955), 111-21.

Smiley, Charles Newton, *Horace: His Poetry and Philosophy*, New York, Kings Crown Press, 1945.

—, *Latinitas and Hellinismos: The Influence of the Stoic Theory of Style as Shown in the Writings of Dionysius, Quintilian, Pliny the Younger, Tacitus, Fronto, Aulus Gellius, and Sextus Empiricus*, Bulletin of the University of Wisconsin, 143, Philology and Literature Series, 3:3, Madison, 1906, pp. 205-72.

—, "Seneca and the Stoic Theory of Literary Style," *Classical Studies in Honor of Charles Forster Smith*, University of Wisconsin Studies in Language and Literature, 3, Madison, 1919, pp. 50-61.

—, "Stoicism and Its Influence on Roman Life and Thought," *Classical Journal, 29* (1934), 645-57.

—, "Vergil-His Philosophical Background and His Relation to Christianity," *Classical Journal, 26* (1931), 660-75.

Smit, Anne Marie Marthe, *Contribution à l'étude de la connaissance de l'antiquité au moyen âge*, Leiden, A. W. Sijthoff's Uitgeversmij N.V., 1934.

Smith, R. E., *Cicero the Statesman*, Cambridge, The University Press, 1966.

Snell, Antony, "Lucan," *Greece & Rome, 8* (1939), 83-91.

Solmsen, Friedrich, "Aristotle and Cicero on the Orator's Playing upon the Feelings," *Classical Philology, 33* (1938), 390-404.

—, "The Aristotelian Tradition in Ancient Rhetoric," *American Journal of Philology, 62* (1941), 35-50, 169-98.

—, "Cleanthes or Posidonius? The Basis of Stoic Physics," *Medelingen der koninklijke nederlandse Akademie van Wetenschappen*, afd. Letterkunde, Nieuwe Reeks, 24:9, Amsterdam, N.V. Noord-Hollandsche Uitgevers Maatschappij, 1961, pp. 261-89.

—, "Drei Rekonstruktionen zur antiken Rhetorik und Poetik, III, Horaz ars poet. 391 ff.," *Hermes, 67* (1932), 151-54.

—, "Greek Ideas of the Hereafter in Virgil's Roman Epic," *Proceedings of the American Philosophical Society, 112* (1968), 8-14.

—, "The Vital Heat, the Inborn Pneuma and the Aether," *Journal of Hellenic Studies, 77* (1957), 119-23.

—, "The World of the Dead in Book 6 of the *Aeneid*," *Classical Philology, 67* (1972), 31-41.

Spanneut, Michel, *Permanence du Stoïcisme de Zénon à Malraux*, Gembloux, Éditions J. Duculot, 1973.

—, *Le Stoïcisme des pères de l'Église de Clément de Rome à Clément d'Alexandrie*, 2me éd., Paris, Éditions du Seuil, 1969.

Spargo, John Webster, *Virgil the Necromancer: Studies in Virgilian Legends*, Harvard Studies in Comparative Literature, 10, Cambridge, Mass., Harvard University Press, 1934.

Spitzer, Leo, *Classical and Christian Ideas of World Harmony: Prolegomena to an Interpretation of the Word "Stimmung"*, ed. Anna Granville Hatcher, Baltimore, Johns Hopkins Press, 1963.

Stahl, Gisela, "Die 'Naturales quaestiones' Senecas," *Hermes, 92* (1964), 425-54.

Stahl, William H., "To a Better Understanding of Martianus Capella," *Speculum, 40* (1965), 102-15.

Stanton, G. R., "The Cosmopolitan Ideas of Epictetus and Marcus Aurelius," *Phronesis, 13* (1968), 183-95.

Starr, Chester G., "Horace and Augustus," *American Journal of Philology, 90* (1969), 58-64.

Steele, Robert Benson, "Lucan's *Pharsalia*," *American Journal of Philology, 25* (1924), 301-28.

—, "Seneca the Philosopher," *Sewanee Review, 30* (1922), 79-94.

Steidle, Wolf, *Studien zur Ars poetica des Horaz: Interpretation des auf Dichtkunst und Gedicht bezüglichen Hauptteils (Verse 1-294)*, Hildesheim, Georg Olms Verlagsbuchhandlung, 1967.

Stein, Ludwig, *Die Psychologie der Stoa*, 2 vols., Berliner Studien für classische Philologie und Archaeologie, 2, 7, Berlin, S. Calvary & Co., 1886-88.

Stein, Peter, "The Development of the Notion of *Naturalis Ratio*," *Daube Noster: Essays in Legal History for David Daube*, ed. Alan Watson, Edinburgh, Scottish Academic Press, 1974, pp. 305-16.

Steiner, Hermann, *Theodizee bei Seneca*, Erlangen, E. T. Jacob, 1914.

Steinmetz, Fritz-Arthur, *Die Freundschaftslehre des Panaitios nach einer Analyse von Ciceros 'Laelius De amicitia'*, Palingenesia: Monographien und Texte zur klassischen Altertumswissenschaft, ed. Rudolf Stark, 3, Wiesbaden, Franz Steiner Verlag GMBH, 1967.

Steinmetz, Peter, "Zur Erdbebentheorie des Poseidonios," *Rheinisches Museum für Philologie*, n.F. *105* (1962), 261-63.

Steinwenter, Artur, "Utilitas publica-utilitas singulorum," *Festschrift Paul Koschaker*, Weimar, Hermann Böhlaus Nachf., 1939, *1*, 84-102.

Stella, Luigia Achillea, *Marco Aurelio*, Gli imperatori romani, 11, Roma, Reale Istituto di Studi Romani, 1943.

Stella-Maranca, F., *Seneca giureconsulto*, Lanciano, Fratelli Mancini, 1926.

Stemplinger, Eduard, *Horaz im Urteil der Jahrhunderte*, Das Erbe der Alten, 2:5, Leipzig, Dieterich'sche Verlagsbuchhandlung, 1921.

Stewart, Douglas J., "Sallust and *Fortuna*," *History and Theory*, 7 (1968), 298-317.

Stiglmayr, Josef, "Das Weisheitsideal bei Seneka," *Beiträge zur Philosophia und Paedagogia perennis: Festgabe zum 80. Geburtstag von Otto Willmann*, ed. Wenzel Pohl, Freiburg im Breisgau, Herdersche Verlagsbuchhandlung, 1919, pp. 61-74.

Stock, St. George, *Stoicism*, London, Archibald Constable & Co. Ltd., 1908.

Stockton, David, *Cicero: A Political Biography*, Oxford, Oxford University Press, 1971.

Stough, Charlotte L., *Greek Skepticism: A Study in Epistemology*, Berkeley, University of California Press, 1969.

Strasburger, Hermann, "Poseidonios on Problems of the Roman Empire," *Journal of Roman Studies, 55* (1965), 40-53.

Striller, Franciscus, *De Stoicorum studiis rhetoricis*, Breslauer philologische Abhandlungen, *1*:2, Breslau, Wilhelm Koebner, 1886.

Strohm, Hans, "Theophrast und Poseidonios: Drei Interpretationen zur Meteorologie," *Hermes, 81* (1953), 279-95.

Stroux, Johannes, "Summum ius summa iniuria: Un capitolo concernante la storia della interpretatio iuris," trans. G. Funaioli, *Annali del Seminario giuridico di Palermo, 12* (1929), 639-91.

Stroux, Leonhard, *Vergleich und Metapher in der Lehre des Zenon von Kition*, Berlin, Ernst-Reuter-Gesellschaft, 1965.

Strüber, P. Stanislaus, *Seneca als Psychologe*, Inaugural-Dissertation, Würzburg, Heiligen-stadt, F. W. Cordierschen Buchdruckerei, 1906.

Sullivan, Francis A., "Virgil and the Mystery of Suffering," *American Journal of Philology*, *90* (1969), 161-77.

Sullivan, J. P., ed., *Critical Essays on Roman Literature: Satire*, London, Routledge & Kegan Paul, 1963.

Sullivan, Patrick A., "The Plan of Cicero's Philosophical Corpus," Fordham University Ph.D. diss., 1951.

Süss, Wilhelm, *Cicero: Ein Einführung in seine philosophischen Schriften (mit Ausschluss der staats-philosophischen Werke)*, Akademie der Wissenschaften und der Literatur in Mainz, Abhandlungen der geistes- und sozialwissenschaftlichen Klasse, 1965, 5, Wiesbaden, Franz Steiner Verlag, 1966.

Svoboda, K., "Les idées esthétiques de Sénèque," *Mélanges de philologie, de littérature et d'histoire anciennes offersts à J. Marouzeau par ses collègues et élèves étrangers*, Paris, Les Belles Lettres, 1948, pp. 537-46.

Swoboda, Antonius, *Quaestiones Nigidianae*, Vienna, T. Tempsky, 1890.

Syme, Ronald, *The Roman Revolution*, 2nd ed., Oxford, Oxford University Press, 1960.

—, *Sallust*, Sather Classical Lectures, 33, Berkeley, University of California Press, 1964.

—, *Tacitus*, 2 vols., Oxford, Clarendon Press, 1958.

Tadic-Gilloteaux, Nicole, "Sénèque face au suicide," *L'Antiquité classique, 32* (1963), 541-51.

Talamo, Salvatore, *Il concetto della schiavità da Aristotele ai dottori scolastici*, Roma, Tipografia dell'Unione Cooperativa Editrice, 1908.

Tarn, W. W., *Alexander the Great and the Unity of Mankind*, The Raleigh Lecture on History, *Proceedings of the British Academy, 19*, London, Humphrey Milford, 1933.

Tatakis, Basile N., *Panétius de Rhodes, le fondateur du moyen stoïcisme: Sa vie et son oeuvre*, Paris, J. Vrin, 1931.

Tate, J., "Horace and the Moral Function of Poetry," *Classical Quarterly, 22* (1928), 65-73.

Taylor, Daniel J., *Declinatio: A Study of the Linguistic Theory of Marcus Terentius Varro*, Amsterdam Studies in the Theory and History of Linguistic Science, 3, Studies in the History of Linguistics, 2, Amsterdam, John Benjamins B.V., 1975.

Taylor, Lily Ross, *Party Politics in the Age of Caesar*, Sather Classical Lectures, 22, Berkeley, University of California Press, 1949.

Tescari, Onorato, "Echi di Seneca nel pensiero cristiano e vice versa," *Unitas, 2* (1947), 171-81.

TeSelle, Eugene, *Augustine the Theologian*, New York, Herder and Herder, 1970.

Thamin, Raymond, *Un problème morale dans l'antiquité: Étude sur la casuistique stoïcienne*, Paris, Hachette, 1884.

Theiler, Willy, "Tacitus und die antike Schicksalslehre," *Phyllobolia für Peter von der Mühll zum 60. Geburtstag am 1. August 1945*, Basel, Benno Schwabe & Co. Verlag, 1946, pp. 35-90.

Thévenez, Pierre, "L'interiorité chez Sénèque," *Mélanges offerts à M. Max Niedermann à l'occasion de son soixante-dixième anniversaire*, Université de Neuchâtel, Recueil de travaux publiés par la Faculté des lettres, 22, Neuchâtel, Sécretariat de l'Université, 1944, pp. 189-94.

Thiacourt, C., *Essai sur les traités philosophiques de Cicéron et leurs sources grecques*, Paris, Hachette, 1885.

Thompson, E. A., *The Early Germans*, Oxford, Clarendon Press, 1965.

Thomson, H. J., "Lucan, Statius, and Juvenal in the Early Centuries," *Classical Quarterly, 22* (1928), 24-28.

Tierney, J. J., "The Celtic Ethnography of Posidonius," *Proceedings of the Royal Irish Academy, 60*, Section C, 5 (1960), 189-275.

Tiffou, Étienne, *Essai sur la pensée morale de Salluste à la lumière de ses prologues*, Études et commentaires, 83, Paris, Éditions Klincksieck, 1974.

—, "Salluste et la tradition stoïcienne," *Echoes du monde classique*, *12* (1968), 13-19.

Timothy, H. B., *The Tenets of Stoicism, Assembled and Systematized, from the Works of L. Annaeus Seneca*, Amsterdam, Hakkert, 1973.

Todd, Robert B., "Chrysippus on Infinite Divisibility (Diogenes Laertius VII. 150)," *Apeiron*, 7 (1973), 21-29.

—, "The Stoic Common Notions: A Reexamination and Reinterpretation," *Symbolae Osloenses*, *48* (1973), 47-76.

—, "Synentasis and the Stoic Theory of Perception," *Grazer Beiträge*, *2* (1974), 251-61.

Tomulescu, Constantin Stelian, "Der juristischen Wert des Werkes Ciceros," *Gesellschaft und Recht im griechisch-römischen Altertum*, ed. Mihail N. Andreev et al., Deutsche Akademie der Wissenschaft zu Berlin, Schriften der Sektion für Altertumswissenschaft, 52, Berlin, Akademie-Verlag, 1968, pp. 226-67.

Tracy, H. L., "*Fata Deum* and the Action of the *Aeneid*," *Greece & Rome*, ser. 2:*11* (1964), 188-95.

Traversa, Augusto, *L'Antica e media Stoà dalle opere filosofiche di Cicerone*, Crestomazia latina, 2, Torino, Loescher, 1957.

Tremoli, Paolo, *M. Anneo Lucano: L'ambiente familiare e letterario*, Università degli studi di Trieste, Facoltà di lettere e filosofia, Istituto di filologia classica, 8, Trieste, 1961.

Tria, Giovanni, *Un poema repubblicano ai tempi di Nerone*, Trani, V. Vecchie C., 1891.

Trillitzsch, Winfried, *Seneca im literarischen Urteil der Antike: Darstellung und Sammlung der Zeugnisse*, 2 vols., Amsterdam, Adolf M. Hakkert, 1971.

—, *Senecas Beweisführung*, Deutsche Akademie der Wissenschaft zu Berlin, Schriften der Sektion für Altertumswissenschaft, 37, Berlin, Akademie-Verlag, 1962.

Troeltsch, Ernst, *Gesammelte Schriften*, vol. 4, ed. Hans Baron, Tübingen, J. C. B. Mohr, 1925.

Troplong, M., *De l'influence du christianisme sur le droit civil des Romains*, Paris, Charles Hingray, 1843.

Tsekourakis, Damianos, *Studies in the Terminology of Early Stoic Ethics*, *Hermes* Einzelschriften, 32, Wiesbaden, Franz Steiner Verlag GMBH, 1974.

Tumenas, Justin, *La critique religieuse chez Cicéron*, Grenoble, Société Anonyme de l'Imprimerie Saint-Bruno, 1914.

Turcan, Robert, *Sénèque et les religions orientales*, Collection Latomus, 91, Bruxelles, Latomus, 1967.

Turkowska, Danuta, *L'Hortensius de Cicéron et le Protreptique d'Aristote*, Polska Akademia Nauk, Prace Komisje Filologii Klasycznej, 6, Wrocław, Polskiej Akademii Nauk, 1965.

Uhlfelder, Myra L., " 'Nature' in Roman Linguistic Texts," *Transactions and Proceedings of the American Philological Association*, 97 (1966), 583-95.

Ussani, Vincenzo, "In margine al Comparetti," *Studi medievale*, n.s. 5 (1932), 1-42.

—, "Orazio e la filosofia popolare," *Atene e Roma*, *19* (1916), 1-13.

—, "Per il testo delle tragedie di Seneca," *Atti della Accademia nazionale dei Lincei*, classe di scienze morali, storiche e filologiche, *356*, ser. 8, *8*:7, Roma, Accademia Nazionale dei Lincei, 1959, pp. 489-552.

Valenti, P. Milton, *L'Éthique stoïcienne chez Cicéron*, Paris, Librairie Saint-Paul, 1956.

Vallette, Paul, "Le *De clementia* de Sénèque est-il mutilé ou inachevé?" *Mélanges Paul Thomas*, Bruges, Imprimerie Sainte Catherine, 1930, pp. 687-700.

Vallot, Giampaolo, "La cosmologia stoica nella polemica di Velleio (Cic. *De nat. deor.* I 18-24)," *Atti dell'Istituto veneto di scienze, lettere ed arti*, classe di scienze morali e lettere, *121* (1962-63), 1-15.

Valmaggi, Luigi, "La fortuna di Stazio nella tradizione letteraria latina e bassolatina," *Rivista di filologia e d'istruzione classica*, *21* (1892), 409-62, 481-554.

Van den Broek, R., *The Myth of the Phoenix according to Classical and Early Christian Traditions*, trans. I. Seeger, Études préliminaires aux religions orientales dans l'empire romain, publiées par M. J. Vermaseren, 24, Leiden, E. J. Brill, 1972.

Van Straaten, Modestus, "Notes on Panaetius' Theory of the Constitution of Man,"

Images of Man in Ancient and Medieval Thought: Studia Gerardo Verbeke, ed. F. Bossier et al., Symbolae: Facultatis Litterarum et Philosophiae Lovaniensis, ser. A, *1*, Leuven, Leuven University Press, 1976, pp. 93-109.

—, *Panétius: Sa vie, ses écrits et sa doctrine avec une édition des fragments*, Amsterdam, Uitgeverij H. J. Paris, 1946.

Venini, Paola, *Studi staziani*, Pubblicazioni dell'Istituto di letteratura latina dell'Università di Pavia, Pavia, Tipografia del Libro, 1971.

—, "La vecchiaia nel *De senectute* di Cicerone," *Athenaeum, 38* (1960), 98-117.

Verbeke, Gérard, "Ethische paideia in het latere Stoïcisme en het vroege Christendom," *Tijdschrift voor filosofie, 27* (1965), 3-53.

—, *L'Évolution de la doctrine du pneuma du Stoïcisme à S. Augustin*, Bibliothèque de l'Institut supérieur de philosophie, Université de Louvain; Paris, Desclée de Brouwer, 1945.

—, *Kleanthes van Assos*, Verhandelingen van de koninklijke Vlaamse Academie voor Wetenschappen, Letteren en schone Kunsten van België, Klasse der Letteren, *11*:9, Brussel, Paleis der Academiën, 1949.

—, "Philosophie et séméiologie chez les Stoïciens," *Études philosophiques offerts au Dr. Ibrahim Madkour*, Gebo, 1974, pp. 15-38.

—, "Le stoïcisme, une philosophie sans frontières," *Aufstieg und Niedergang der römischen Welt: Geschichte und Kultur Roms im Spiegel der neueren Forschung*, ed. Hildegard Temporini, Berlin, Walter de Gruyter, 1973, *1*, part 4, 3-42.

—, "Les Stoïciens et le progrès de l'histoire," *Revue philosophique de Louvain, 62* (1964), 5-38.

Vernay, Eugène, *Servius et son école: Contribution à l'histoire des idées juridiques à la fin de la République romaine*, Paris, Arthur Rousseau, 1909.

Vessey, David, *Statius and the Thebaid*, Cambridge, The University Press, 1973.

—, "The Stoics and Nobility: A Philosophical Theme," *Latomus, 32* (1973), 332-44.

Viano, Carlo Augusto, "La dialettica stoica," *Rivista di filosofia, 49* (1958) 179-227.

Villeneuve, François, *Essai sur Perse*, Paris, Hachette, 1918.

Villey, Michel, "Logique d'Aristote et droit romain," *Revue historique de droit français et étranger*, sér. 4:*29* (1951), 309-28.

Virieux-Reymond, Antoinette, *La logique et l'épistémologie des Stoïciens*, Chambéry, Imprimeries Réunies, 1949.

—, "Le 'sunemménon' stoïcien et la notion de loi scientifique," *Studia Philosophica: Jahrbuch der schweitzerischen philosophischen Gesellschaft, 9* (1949), 162-69.

Voelke, André-Jean, *L'Idée de volonté dans le stoïcisme*, Bibliothèque de philosophie contemporaine, Paris, PUF, 1973.

—, "Les origines stoïciennes de la volonté," *Revue de théologie et de philosophie*, sér. 3:*7* (1969), 1-22.

—, "L'unité de l'âme humain dans l'ancien stoïcisme," *Studia Philosophica: Jahrbuch der schweitzerischen philosophischen Gesellschaft, 25* (1965), 154-81.

Voggensperger, René, *Der Begriff des "Ius naturale" im römischen Recht*, Basler studien zur Rechtswissenschaft, 32, Basel, Helbing & Lichtenhahn, 1952.

Voigt, Moritz, *Das jus naturale, aequum et bonum, und jus gentium der Römer*, 4 vols. in 7, Leipzig, Voigt & Günther, 1856-76.

Vollmann, Franz, *Über das Verhältnis der späteren Stoa zur Sklaverei im römischen Reiche*, Stadtamhof, J. & K. Mayr, 1890.

Vonglis, Bernard, "Droit romain et rhétorique," *Tijdschrift voor Rechtsgeschiedenis, 37*:2 (1969), 247-56.

—, *La Lettre et l'ésprit de la loi dans la jurisprudence classique et la rhétorique*, Publications de l'Institut de droit romaine de l'Université de Paris, 24, Paris, Sirey, 1968.

Wageningen, Jacob van, "Manilius," *Paulys Realencyclopädie der classischen Altertumswissenschaft*, new ed., ed. Wilhelm Kroll, Stuttgart, J. B. Metzlersche Verlagsbuchhandlung, 1928, *14*, part 1, cols. 1115-33.

Walker, B., *The Annals of Tacitus: A Study in the Writing of History*, Manchester, Manchester University Press, 1952.

Wallace, Edith Owen, *The Notes on Philosophy in the Commentary of Servius on the Eclogues, the Georgics, and the Aeneid of Vergil*, New York, Columbia University Press, 1938.

Walsh, P. G., *Livy*, Greece & Rome: New Surveys in the Classics, 8, Oxford, Clarendon Press, 1974.

—, "Livy and Stoicism," *American Journal of Philology, 79* (1958), 355-75.

—, *Livy: His Historical Aims and Methods*, Cambridge, The University Press, 1961.

—, "Livy's Preface and the Distortion of History," *American Journal of Philology, 76* (1955), 369-83.

Waltz, René, *Vie de Sénèque*, Paris, Perrin et Cie., 1909.

Wanke, Christiane, *Seneca, Lucan, Corneille: Studien zum Manierismus der römischen Kaiserzeit und der französischen Klassik*, Studia romanica, 6, Heidelberg, Carl Winter, 1964.

Watkiss, L., "The 'Thebaid' of Statius: A Re-appraisal," University of London Ph.D. diss., 1966.

Watson, Alan, *Law in the Making in the Later Roman Republic*, Oxford, Clarendon Press, 1974.

—, *The Law of Persons in the Later Roman Republic*, Oxford, Clarendon Press, 1967.

—, *Roman Private Law around 200 B.C.*, Edinburgh, Edinburgh University Press, 1971.

Watson, Gerald, *The Stoic Theory of Knowledge*, Belfast, The Queen's University, 1966.

Watson, Paul Barron, *Marcus Aurelius Antoninus*, New York, Harper & Brothers, 1884.

Weil, Eric, "Remarques sur le 'matérialisme' des Stoïciens," *L'Aventure de l'ésprit: Mélanges Alexandre Koyré*, Histoire de la pensée, École pratique des hautes études, Sorbonne, 13, Paris, Hermann, 1964, *2*, 556-72.

Wedeck, Harry E., "Seneca's Humanitarianism," *Classical Journal, 50* (1955), 319-20.

Weinreich, Otto, trans. and intro., *Römische Satiren*, Zürich, Artemis-Verlag, 1949.

Weische, Alfons, *Cicero und die neue Akademie*, Orbis antiquus, 18, Münster i. Westf., Verlag Aschendorff, 1961.

Wenger, Leopold, "Naturrecht und römisches Recht," *Wissenschaft und Weltbild, 1* (1948), 148-54.

—, *Die Quellen des römischen Rechts*, Österreiche Akademie der Wissenschaften, Denkschriften der Gesamtakademie, 2, Wien, Adolf Holzhausens NFG, 1953.

—, "Suum cuique in antiken Urkunden," *Aus der Geisteswelt des Mittelalters: Studien und Texte Martin Grabmann zur Vollendung des 60. Lebensjahres von Freunden und Schülern gewidmet*, ed. Albert Lang, Joseph Lechner, and Michael Schmaus, Beiträge zur Geschichte der Philosophie und Theologie des Mittelalters, Supplementband, 3, Münster i. W., Aschendorffschen Verlagsbuchhandlung, 1935, pp. 1415-25.

Wenley, R. M., *Stoicism and Its Influence*, Boston, Marshall Jones Company, 1924.

Wesel, Uwe, *Rhetorische Statuslehre und Gesetzauslegung der römischen Juristen*, Schriftenreihe: Annales Universitas Saraviensis, rechts- und wirtschaftswissenschaftliche Abteilung, 29, Köln, Carl Heymanns Verlag K. G., 1967.

Wessner, Paul, "Lucan, Statius, und Juvenal bei den römischen Grammatikern," *Philologische Wochenschrift, 49* (1929), 296-303, 328-35.

White, Nicholas P., "The Basis of Stoic Ethics," *Harvard Studies in Classical Philology, 83* (1979), 143-78.

—, "Two Notes on Stoic Terminology," *American Journal of Philology, 99* (1978), 111-19.

Whitehorne, J. E. G., "Was Marcus Aurelius a Hypochondriac?" *Latomus, 36* (1977), 413-21.

Wiersma, W., "*Telos* und *Kathêkon* in der alten Stoa," *Mnemosyne*, ser. 3:5 (1937), 219-38.

—, "Die Physik des Stoikers Zenon," *Mnemosyne*, ser. 3:11 (1943), 191-216.

Wiesen, David, "Juvenal's Moral Character, an Introduction," *Latomus, 22* (1963), 440-71.

Wili, Walter, *Horaz und die Augusteische Kultur*, 2nd ed., Basel, Schwabe & Co. Verlag, 1965.

Wilkin, Robert N., "Cicero and the Law of Nature," *Origins of the Natural Law Tradition*, ed. Arthur L. Harding, Dallas, Southern Methodist University Press, 1954, pp. 1-25.

Wilkinson, L. P., *The Georgics of Virgil: A Critical Survey*, Cambridge, The University Press, 1969.

—, *Ovid Recalled*, Cambridge, The University Press, 1955.

—, "Virgil's Theodicy," *Classical Quarterly*, n.s. *13* (1963), 75-84.

Williams, Gordon, *Horace*, Greece & Rome: New Surveys in the Classics, 6, Oxford, Clarendon Press, 1972.

—, *Tradition and Originality in Roman Poetry*, Oxford, Clarendon Press, 1968.

Williams, R. D., *Aeneas and the Roman Hero*, London, Macmillan, 1973.

—, *Virgil*, Greece & Rome: New Surveys in the Classics, 1, Oxford, Clarendon Press, 1967.

Willis, James A., "Martianus Capella and His Early Commentators," University of London Ph.D. diss., 1952.

—, "Martianus Capella und die mittelalterliche Schulbildung," *Das Altertum*, *19* (1973), 215-22.

Wilsing, Niels, *Aufbau und Quellen von Ciceros Schrift 'De re publica'*, Inaugural-Dissertation, Leipzig, Leipzig, Werkgemeinschaft, 1929.

Winterbottom, Michael, "The Manuscript Tradition of Tacitus' *Germania*," *Classical Philology, 70* (1975), 1-7.

—, "Quintilian and the *Vir Bonus*," *Journal of Roman Studies, 54* (1964), 90-97.

Wirszubski, C., "Cicero's *cum dignitate otium:* A Reconsideration," *Journal of Roman Studies, 44* (1954), 1-13.

Wiśniewski, Bohdan, "Sur les origines du *homologoumenos tê phusei zên* des stoïciens," *Classica et mediaevalia, 22* (1961), 106-16.

Witke, Charles, *Latin Satire: The Structure of Persuasion*, Leiden, E. J. Brill, 1970.

Witke, Edward Charles, "Marcus Aurelius and Mandragora," *Classical Philology, 60* (1965), 23-24.

Witt, R. E., "The Plotinian Logos and Its Stoic Basis," *Classical Quarterly, 25* (1931), 103-11.

—, "Plotinus and Posidonius," *Classical Quarterly, 24* (1930), 198-207.

Wolff, Hans Julius, *Roman Law: An Historical Introduction*, Norman, University of Oklahoma Press, 1951.

Wuilleumier, P., "L'Influence du *Cato maior*," *Mélanges de philologie, de littérature et d'histoire anciennes offerts à Alfred Ernout*, Paris, C. Klincksieck, 1940, pp. 383-88.

Xenakis, Jason, *Epictetus: Philosopher-Therapist*, The Hague, Martinus Nijhoff, 1969.

—, "Stoic Suicide Therapy," *Sophia, 40* (1972), 88-99.

Zarker, John W., "The Hercules Theme in the 'Aeneid'," *Vergilius, 18* (1972), 34-48.

Zarrella, P., "La cocezione del 'discepolo' in Epitteto," *Aevum, 40* (1966), 211-29.

Zeller, Eduard, "Beiträge zur Kenntnis des Stoikers Panätius," *Commentationes philologiae in honorem Theodori Mommseni scripserunt amici*, Berlin, Weidmann, 1877, pp. 402-10.

—, *Outlines of the History of Greek Philosophy*, 13th ed., ed. Wilhelm Nestle, trans. L. R. Palmer, New York, Harcourt, Brace and Company, 1931.

—, *The Stoics, Epicureans and Sceptics*, new and rev. ed., trans. Oswald J. Reichel, New York, Russell & Russell, Inc., 1962.

Zetzel, J. E. G., "Cicero and the Scipionic Circle," *Harvard Studies in Classical Philology, 76* (1972), 173-79.

Zieliński, Thadée, *Cicero im Wandel der Jahrhunderte*, 4th ed., Leipzig, B. G. Teubner, 1929.

—, *Horace et la société romain du temps d'Auguste*, Collection de l'Institut français de Varsovie, 5, Paris, les Belles Lettres, 1938.

Zimmerman, Maximilianus, *De Tacito Senecae philosophi imitatore*, Breslauer philologische Abhandlungen, 5:1, Breslau, Wilhelm Koebner, 1889.

Zucchelli, Bruno, "Il destino e la provvidenza in Quintiliano (A proposito del proemio del VI libro dell'*Istituto*)," *Paideia, 29* (1974), 3-17.

Zulueta, F. de, "The Development of Law under the Republic," *Cambridge Ancient History*, ed. S. A. Cook, F. E. Adcock, and M. P. Charlesworth, Cambridge, The University Press, 1932, *9*, 842-81.

INDEX OF NAMES

INDEX OF SUBJECTS

as *psyche*, 27; human *logos* as consubstantial with divine *logos* and as *hegemonikon*, 27–31, 35–37, 42, 43, 45, 46, 51, 56; in Horace, 170–71; in Macrobius, 319–20; in Manilius, 315–16; in Servius, 318; in Vergil, 237; eschatology, 29–31; as signified by myth of Phoenix, 30; by myth of Hercules as apotheosized sage, 30–31, 41; in Cicero, 95, 137, 142, 147, 150, 154; in Lucan, 272; in Silius Italicus, 284, 286, 287, 288, 289; in Vergil, 235–36; treated decoratively in Statius, 279–80; *krasis*, 25; the incorporeals, 25–26; the void, 25–26; time, 25–26; space, 25, 26; *lekta*, 25–26, 53–56; in Augustine, 229–30; in Aulus Gellius, 339; natural law, 31–35, 38, 42; in Cicero, 88–89, 92, 95–104, 110; rejected by jurisconsults, 341–42, 343, 344, 345, 356–71; *logoi spermatikoi*, 31–32; in Macrobius, 320; in Varro, 321; divination as an index of divine providence, 31, 33; in Cicero, 101, 109, 114, 119, 120–22, 153; in Lucan, 356–58; in Persius, 200; in Statius, 276; non-committal treatment in Livy, 300–01; in Tacitus, 306, 307, 308; theodicy, 31–32, 34–35; allegoresis of the pagan gods, 33, 181; in Cicero, 14, 117, 153; fate and contingency, 31–32, 35; in Cicero, 115, 119, 121, 122–26, 153; in Aulus Gellius, 325–26; in Lucan, 254–64; in Servius, 317; in Silius Italicus, 382–83; in Statius, 276–79; in Vergil, 231–36; causation in history, 290–92; rejected in Livy, 299–300; in Sallust, 293–95, 298; in Tacitus, 307–09, 312

ethics, 36–50, 52; in Cicero, 126–52, 153–55; rejected in Livy, 301–02; in Sallust, 293–98; in Tacitus, 310–12; unity and equality of all men, 36–38; in Juvenal, 208–09, 223; rejected by jurisconsults, 341, 365, 367–70, 372–76, 380–82; critique of slavery, 36–37; rejected by jurisconsults, 341, 344–45, 363, 372, 375–80; sexual equality, 36–38; in Vergil, 245; rejected by jurisconsults, 341, 363–64, 372, 380, 382–88; by Juvenal, 207–08, 213–15, 223; by Livy, 302; casuistry, 38, 46; in Cicero, 147–48, 154; the cosmopolis and political theory, 38–39, 40; in Juvenal, 206–07; work, 41; in Cicero, 147–48; in Persius, 198; opposed by Vergil, 228–29; sexual ethics, 39; opposed by Juvenal, 212–15; marriage and the family, 41; in Lucan, 270, 271–72; cannibalism, 39; in Juvenal, 209; doctrine of

the sage, 39–41, 44; in Cicero, 92, 93–94, 108, 127–32, 137, 139, 141, 154–55; in Aulus Gellius, 336–38; in Horace, 168–71, 173, 179–87, 193; in Juvenal, 207; in Livy, 303–04; also criticized by Livy, 302–03; in Lucan, 264–74; in Quintilian, 327–28, 329; in Silius Italicus, 282, 283–89; as rejected or modified by Statius, 279–81; by Tacitus, 310–12; by Vergil, 238–51; vice and virtue, 42, 43–50; in Cicero, 85–87, 130, 134–52, 153, 154; in Aulus Gellius, 336–37; in Horace, 169–71, 172, 193; in Juvenal, 218–22; in Persius, 196–200; in Quintilian, 327–28, 329; idea of justice as rejected by jurisconsults, 341–56, 357–58, 364; the passions, 42, 45–46, 50; in Cicero, 82, 100, 137, 142, 153; in Aulus Gellius, 337–38; in Juvenal, 207; in Macrobius, 319–20; in Vergil, 237; the instincts, 28; in Cicero, 138; in Aulus Gellius, 337; *apatheia*, 42, 44, 50; in Cicero, 130–31, 131–43, 154; in Aulus Gellius, 337, 340; in Horace, 178, 187; *eupatheia*, 42; in Cicero, 134, 143, 154; in Juvenal, 208; the active and contemplative life, 39–40; in Cicero, 77, 90, 120, 144, 146, 154; in Horace, 175; in Persius, 195–98; as criticized by Sallust, 293–98; friendship, 41; in Cicero, 86, 94, 115, 133–35, 155; in Persius, 198; the *adiaphora* or preferables, 44, 46, 48, 49, 50; in Cicero, 86–87, 104, 108, 113, 132–33, 136–52, 154; in Aulus Gellius, 336–38; in Horace, 169–71, 173, 178–79; in Juvenal, 209–12; suicide, 49; in Horace, 171; the sage's personal appearance as an index of virtue, 48; in Juvenal, 207; in Persius, 200–01

epistemology, 51–53; in Cicero, 105–09, 118, 155; in Aulus Gellius, 338; common notions, 52; in Cicero, 83–84; in Horace, 183

logic, 50–56; in Persius, 200; distinction from rhetoric in Varro, 321; propositional logic, 54; hypothetical syllogisms, 53–55; in Augustine, 330; in Aulus Gellius, 339; in Cassiodorus, 333–34; in Cicero, 84–85, 115, 139, 155; in Martianus Capella, 331–32; in Marius Victorinus, 333; negation, in logic, 54; in Martianus Capella, 331; the categories, 55–56

linguistic theory, 53, 56–60; definition of language in Cassiodorus, 333; Diomedes, 326; Aelius Donatus, 326; Aulus Gellius, 338–39; Varro, 321–22;

Studies in the History
of Christian Thought

EDITED BY HEIKO A. OBERMAN